Moreton Morrell Site

£47.50

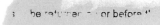

✦ **Third Edition** ✦

SPORT
Marketing

Bernard J. Mullin

Atlanta Spirit, LLC

Atlanta Hawks, Atlanta Thrashers, and Phillips Arena

Stephen Hardy

University of New Hampshire

William A. Sutton

DeVos Sport Business Program,
University of Central Florida

Principal, Bill Sutton & Associates

Human Kinetics

Library of Congress Cataloging-in-Publication Data

Mullin, Bernard James.
    Sport marketing / Bernard J. Mullin, Stephen Hardy, William A. Sutton. -- 3rd ed.
        p. cm.
    Includes bibliographical references and index.
    ISBN-13: 978-0-7360-6052-3 (hard cover)
    ISBN-10: 0-7360-6052-9 (hard cover)
    1. Sports--Marketing. I. Hardy, Stephen, 1948- II. Sutton, William Anthony, 1951- III. Title.
    GV716.M85 2007
    796´.0698--dc22   2006035638

ISBN-10: 0-7360-6052-9
ISBN-13: 978-0-7360-6052-3

Acquisitions Editor: Myles Schrag
Developmental Editors: Renee Thomas Pyrtel and Amanda S. Ewing
Assistant Editor: Jillian Evans
Copyeditor: Patsy Fortney
Proofreader: Anne Rogers
Indexer: Sharon Duffy
Permission Manager: Dalene Reeder
Graphic Designer: Robert Reuther
Graphic Artists: Angela K. Snyder and Denise Lowry
Cover Designer: Keith Blomberg
Photographer (cover): © CarlosBaez.com
Photo Asset Manager: Laura Fitch
Photo Office Assistant: Jason Allen
Art Manager: Kelly Hendren
Illustrators: Tom Roberts and Al Wilborn
Printer: Sheridan Books

Printed in the United States of America   10 9 8 7 6 5 4 3 2 1

Human Kinetics
Web site: www.HumanKinetics.com

United States: Human Kinetics
P.O. Box 5076
Champaign, IL 61825-5076
800-747-4457
e-mail: humank@hkusa.com

Canada: Human Kinetics
475 Devonshire Road Unit 100
Windsor, ON N8Y 2L5
800-465-7301 (in Canada only)
e-mail: orders@hkcanada.com

Europe: Human Kinetics
107 Bradford Road
Stanningley
Leeds LS28 6AT, United Kingdom
+44 (0) 113 255 5665
e-mail: hk@hkeurope.com

Australia: Human Kinetics
57A Price Avenue
Lower Mitcham, South Australia 5062
08 8372 0999
e-mail: liaw@hkaustralia.com

New Zealand: Human Kinetics
Division of Sports Distributors NZ Ltd.
P.O. Box 300 226 Albany
North Shore City
Auckland
0064 9 448 1207
e-mail: info@humankinetics.co.nz

Contents

Foreword

The third edition of *Sport Marketing* accurately depicts the evolution of the sport industry that I experienced as NBA commissioner during the last 20-plus years. Throughout my career at the NBA, I have had the good fortune of working with many of the most talented executives in the industry. As the industry has evolved, so have the leadership and business capabilities at the teams. Now, many of our teams have more than 100 employees who sell tickets and sponsorships; provide great customer service; develop marketing, advertising, and branding strategies; activate platforms for marketing partners and sponsors to drive their businesses; produce TV and radio broadcasts locally; service the media and place proactive messages; develop and produce the shows; and do meaningful work in the community through innovative and socially responsible programs. This text places those activities in a comprehensive framework, showing how the moving parts work together to develop the sport business locally, nationally, and globally.

David J. Stern
Photo courtesy of NBAE

The principal authors have a combination of academic and professional experience that is extraordinary. Their education and experience as university professors provide them with unique perspectives. Their research and analytical skills lead to objectivity and an ability to identify key industry needs. The theoretical framework they have created into which every marketing strategy is set—the marketing planning process—leads to a consistency in all branding, sales, and marketing strategies. Better yet, the authors have practical experience in the field in senior executive capacities covering several segments of the sport industry, which has given them a wealth of knowledge of best practices and the understanding of what actually works and doesn't work. Collectively they have implemented just about all of the best practices firsthand for leagues, sport conferences, and—the most challenging of all situations—start-up teams and turnarounds.

I have observed the work of the authors for a decade as they participated in the way NBA teams conduct their business. Clearly the most significant factors were substantially increasing the sharing of best practices and real data, increasing adoption of direct marketing techniques, and basing team business strategies on the authors' landmark work—the attendance frequency escalator. As a result, most NBA teams today have much more sophisticated database-building and customer relationship management (CRM) capabilities, and they more effectively use direct mail, telemarketing sales, and e-marketing programs to increase trial, improve retention, and drive attendance. These successful teams focus on the stepping-stone approach to fan development: Encourage more people (particularly youth) to play the game, connect players and coaches more favorably with the community, get more fans to watch or listen to broadcasts, progressively encourage those fans to get off the couch or off the computer and sample the NBA game in person, and offer a full menu of full- and partial-season ticket plans designed to move fans up the attendance frequency escalator. The greatest benefit of this approach has been a most significant increase in the lifetime value (LTV) of fans in the respective team markets and ultimately the league itself.

Mixing in their unique intellect and personalities, the authors use their vast academic and practical experience to make this book a must-read for future generations of sport marketers, managers, and perhaps even commissioners.

David J. Stern
Commissioner, National Basketball Association

Preface

There is only one way to describe the massive changes in the sport world since the first edition of *Sport Marketing* came out in 1993: "Holy cow!" as the late Harry Caray always put it. In 1993, most people would have thought that the Internet was a spy ring and a Web page was something in a newsletter of Ducks Unlimited. When our second edition appeared in 2000, the Net was old hat, but it was still the most innovative medium of the age. File sharing was just beginning in 2000. Net nerds would have thought that YouTube was a phrase deriding old media. Hardly. By 2006, YouTube.com had become the hottest site on the Net, where more than a million video clips were viewed each day, many of them sporting events. Marketing executives throughout the sport world got their industry news and data through online services such as Sports Business Daily or SBRnet. More and more trade publications, such as *Street and Smith's Sports Business Journal* or *Athletic Business,* have online versions. In the near future, the move to online information may give new meaning to the old basketball phrase "it's all net!" The cutting edge, however, is wireless technology. We have incorporated many of the latest wireless marketing ideas in this edition, but new products and services are emerging daily.

Some things haven't changed much. The competition for the sport and entertainment dollar is as heavy as ever. Sport marketing is a competitive business involving as much front-office strategy, risk, discipline, and energy as that shown by the players and coaches who figure so prominently in the public's imagination. The third edition of *Sport Marketing* offers abundant examples of the latest issues in the competitive marketplace.

As academics, we have been studying changes in the sport industry for more than 35 years, long before *Forbes* and *Fortune* began to take sports seriously with regular coverage. When we started out as graduate students in the early 1970s, few scholars were willing to accept sport as a serious topic of study. Now leading academics in marketing, management, law, and economics (to name only a few disciplines) are rushing headlong for book contracts on sports. We have both followed and helped to build this growing body of literature. More important, each of us has also worked *inside* the industry, trying to make sense of the ways that fans, players, coaches, the media, equipment companies, and others interact to make the game tick. We have planned, administered, or consulted on literally thousands of events across just about every sport considered mainstream and at just about every level. This book emanates from our own fusion of experience as academics and practitioners. We have written a survey that we hope is as useful for the classroom student as it is for the athletics director of a college or high school or the marketer of a professional franchise.

We have tried to balance theoretical models with case studies from the rinks, fields, courts, slopes, gyms, tracks, and other venues that make up the sport marketplace. If theory is the skeleton that gives structure to thinking, then case studies put meat on the bones. Although our examples are largely from the United States, we hope that much of our thinking will benefit sport marketers in other countries.

The third edition of *Sport Marketing* is much expanded and built on a largely new database, both from academic journals like the *Sport Marketing Quarterly,* from industry serials like the *Sports Business Daily,* and from online sources like SBRnet. Chapters 1 and 2 provide an overview of the sport market and sport marketing as an area of study and as a process. Chapters 3 through 6 consider conceptual tools and steps of preliminary market research and market segmentation, which are critical to overcoming a tendency to equate promotions with marketing. Marketing begins and ends with knowing the consumers' needs and wants; chapters 3 to 6 provide that essential perspective. Chapters 7 through 16 explore the nuts and bolts of marketing plans—the five Ps of sport marketing: product, price, promotion, place, and public relations. We have added a new chapter to this section, "Managing Sport Brands," by Jay Gladden, one of the world's experts on the topic. The last three chapters offer some important elements on control, evaluation, legal issues, and projecting the future.

The world of sport marketing continues to challenge and excite us. We only hope that this edition is as enjoyable to read as it was to write.

Acknowledgments

Our chapter notes acknowledge the sources we have used. In addition, we offer special acknowledgments to a number of people. The first is David Stern, one of the premier sport marketing minds in the world. We thank David for the opportunities to work in the NBA as well as for sharing his insights and providing daily inspiration through his strategic marketing initiatives. We also recognize the contributions and value of the late Bill Veeck, whose writings and innovations continually remind us of the importance of the fans and sport consumer behavior, and also Mike Veeck because he has done the same and forces us to examine our own practices and approaches when we forget about the fans. On the academic side, we are indebted to Philip Kotler for his numerous contributions to the field of marketing, which have influenced our thinking in terms of sport marketing. We are also indebted to Dr. Guy Lewis, who has been instrumental in shaping the academic coursework and program content for many of the undergraduate and graduate programs in sport management. Matt Levine of Source USA, one of the original and leading sport marketing consultants who helped shape the study of sport consumer behavior, has also continued to inspire our thinking. We acknowledge the many academics who contribute to *Sport Marketing Quarterly* and are members of the Sport Marketing Association (SMA), particularly Dr. David Stotlar of the University of Northern Colorado, Dr. Richard Irwin of the University of Memphis, Dr. Dennis Howard of the University of Oregon, Dr. Brenda Pitts of Georgia State University, and Dr. Gregg Bennett of Texas A&M University. The research of our academic brethren and their tireless preparation of the sport marketers of tomorrow provide constant inspiration and motivation to us. We also offer special thanks to our University of Massachusetts connection for their chapter contributions and support: Professors Jay Gladden, Dan Covell, Steve McKelvey, Lisa Pike Masteralexis, and Tim Ashwell (now also a UNH connection).

Many people helped us obtain, organize, and develop materials for the book. Ed Saunders of Nike Bauer; Carrie Jokiel; Dave Perricone of the New Jersey Devils; Joe Bertagna of Hockey East; Abe Madkour and the staff at the *Sports Business Daily* (now an essential resource for anyone trying to make sense of the sport industry); Dave "Hit Dog" Synowka of Robert Morris University; Dick Bresciani and Larry Cancro of the Boston Red Sox; Dot Sheehan, Steve Metcalf, and Marty Scarano of the University of New Hampshire; Charlie Eshbach of the Portland Sea Dogs; Jeff Tagliaferro of the New Hampshire Fisher Cats; Bill Miller and Jill Grennfield of the NHL; Gregg Hanrahan of the United Center; Chris Hardy of the Massachusetts Audubon Society; Jerry Solomon of P.S. Star Games; Dan Migala of the Migala Report; David Stern, Russ Granik, Adam Silver, Scott O'Neil, Aaron Bryan, and Kathy Behrens of the NBA; Vic Gregovits at the Cleveland Indians; Rick Welts, John Walker, Drew Cloud, and Mike Tomon of the Phoenix Suns; Chad Estis of the Cleveland Cavaliers; Jeff Munneke and Bryant Pfeiffer of the Minnesota Timberwolves; John Rooney, a pioneer in sport geography; Eric Woolworth, Michael McCullough, Kim Stone, Andy Montero, and John O'Meara of the Miami Heat; Alex Martins, Chris D'Orso, Matt Biggers, Murray Cohn, Bobby Bridges, Kari Conley, and Shelley Driggers of the Orlando Magic; Lou DePaoli and

David Lee of the Atlanta Spirit; Roger Godin of the Minnesota Wild; Gordon Kaye of the Reading Royals; Dr. Tom Huddleston and Matt DiFebo of the University of Central Florida; Kathy Connors of Octagon; Chris Zamzow of General Motors; Tom Abramson of Vision-works; Buffy Filippell of Teamwork Consulting; Grant McKenzie of Auckland Rugby; Giorgio Gandolfi of Basket de Gigante; and Reggie Williams and Alex Vergara of Disney Sports.

As with any project of this magnitude, we are particularly grateful for the assistance of graduate students Morgan Marr, Praveeta Singh, Jezali Ratliff, and especially Krista Prestigiacomo from the DeVos Sport Business Program at the University of Central Florida, who assisted in researching, editing, developing diagrams and figures, and making sure we stayed on task.

In our capacities as sport administrators and consultants, we have worked with hundreds of dedicated executives, marketers, coaches, salespersons, customer service professionals, public and community relations personnel, and sports information directors who have inspired us with their energy, dedication, and passion. As academics, we thank and salute our students over the years at the University of Washington, Robert Morris University, Ohio State University, the University of Massachusetts, the University of New Hampshire, and the University of Central Florida. These colleagues and students have challenged, stretched, reshaped, and indulged our thinking on all of the topics in this book. We dedicate this book to all of these old and recent colleagues in the hope that we can convey to our readers their wisdom, their enthusiasm, their wonder for learning, and their passion for moving the field forward.

Chapter 1

The Special Nature of Sport Marketing

Objectives

- ✦ To understand the market forces that create the need for enlightened marketing strategies in the sport industry.
- ✦ To understand marketing myopia and other obstacles to successful marketing strategy.
- ✦ To recognize the components of the sport product and of the sport industry.
- ✦ To recognize the factors that make sport marketing a unique enterprise.

The NBA: Sizzle and Steak in the Global Sport Marketplace

In 1992, America's "Dream Team" of NBA stars waltzed their way to a gold medal at the Barcelona Olympics. Opposing players could not attack or defend successfully, but they were happy to fawn over hoops heroes like Magic Johnson, Larry Bird, and Michael Jordan. One player was seen waving at a teammate on the bench to take a picture of him trying to guard Jordan. "Traveling with the Dream Team," said their coach, Chuck Daly, "was like traveling with 12 rock stars. That's all I can compare it to." Following Barcelona, the NBA and its stars would enjoy a decade of global prominence and adulation. It was not just their exquisite skill. It was also the brilliant marketing orchestrated by Commissioner David Stern, who packaged and distributed new NBA products, including "NBA Inside Stuff," "Game of the Week," "NBA Jam," and "NBA Action," to viewers in over 170 countries. Rights fees varied with ability to pay. China got the programming for free, so almost all of China's television households (250 million) watched NBA programs. NBA.com provided language options in English, French, Spanish, and Italian.

Stern's vision took off. By 1997, the NBA was selling nearly $500 million in merchandise outside the United States. Kids from the Dominican Republic to the People's Republic followed their NBA idols: With Michael Jordan leading the charge in his Nike shoes, the NBA became the gold standard for worldwide sport league properties, challenged only by the English Premier League. (1)

The 2004 Athens Olympics saw dreams turn to nightmares for American men's basketball. The team was expected to be another NBA showcase, led this time by Allen Iverson and coach Larry Brown. The Yanks instead suffered embarrassing losses in exhibition matches, played erratically at Athens, and limped home with only a bronze medal. Forward Shawn Marion summed up the new reality of international basketball in 2004: "At least we didn't go home empty handed." Thank God for our women, said many an American pundit. If there was still a "dream team," it was led by Lisa Leslie and her WNBA colleagues, who cruised to gold in 2004 as easily as their 1992 male counterparts had. (2)

Soon everyone was second-guessing the NBA and its product. ESPN basketball analyst Len Elmore blamed the "streetball culture" of individualism—heavily promoted in the NBA—for eroding the team play and defensive skills that were once the core of basketball as a sport. "It was," he said, "the hubris of NBA stardom that doomed our boys." Elmore further wondered if the poor performance would puncture the NBA's worldwide bubble, what he aptly called its "global franchise strategy." Without the "aura of invincibility" that began in Barcelona, "NBA goods might not fly off the shelves as [they] once did, either at home or abroad." Even before the Olympics, NBA Hall of Famer Oscar Robertson had written a scathing op-ed piece in the *New York Times* titled "NBA Markets Style at Expense of Substance." The NBA, he argued, "has made a conscious decision to function as a marketing and entertainment organization, and seems much more concerned with selling sneakers, jerseys, hats, and highlight videos than with the product it puts on the floor."

Had something gone wrong with the NBA and its product? Or, as David Stern argued, had their plans succeeded so well that the rest of the world was not just a potential market, but also a worthy competitor? (3)

Although entrepreneurs have been selling sport for centuries, rational systems of marketing sport are relatively new. In this chapter, we discuss the need to employ modern marketing principles in the sport domain. We examine the sport industry trends of growth and competition that heighten the need for scientific, professional approaches to sport marketing. We consider examples of lingering "marketing myopia" in sport, as well as signs of progress. Next, we consider the components of the sport product and of the sport industry. Finally, we outline the numerous features that in combination make sport marketing a unique area of inquiry and application.

Global Marketing Strategy

Over two decades, David Stern emerged as lord of a far-flung, international empire inappropriately called the National Basketball Association. When Stern became commissioner in 1984 (he had been NBA general counsel since 1978), the NBA was a struggling enterprise, despite stars such as Magic Johnson and Larry Bird. Teams were playing in arenas at less than two-thirds capacity, NBA merchandise sales were only about $15 million, and network television coverage was limited—the finals were shown on tape delay. Worse yet, corporate sponsors were scared off, in large part because of a poor public image resulting from drug scandals and labor strife. As one NBA executive recalled in a 1991 profile of Stern, "If you had 30 minutes with a prospective sponsor, your first 20 minutes were spent trying to convince him that the players weren't all on drugs." (4)

Even before his elevation to the commissionership, Stern had laid the foundation for the NBA to become one of the most successful brand names in sport. He did it by recognizing and using standard tools of marketing. He knew, among other things, that product recognition required a more expansive television package. In turn, the broadcast networks demanded a more stable product with a cleaner image. That meant getting owners and players to agree on several fundamental issues, including revenue sharing, salary caps, and tougher drug testing. As a Spalding executive concluded, "A good marketing guy knows that he has to get the product right before marketing it. That's what Stern did with basketball." (5)

If Stern spent the 1980s getting his product right, he focused the next decade on worldwide product distribution. More than anything, Stern believed in going global. The NBA could create an empire along the lines of British mercantilism—with fine, finished products moving from North America to distant centers of exchange like Moscow, Buenos Aires, Capetown, and Beijing—especially Beijing. Some surveys conducted in 2003 suggested that among China's 1+ billion people, basketball had supplanted soccer in popularity. In the first four years of the new millennium, the Chinese edition of the NBA's *Time and Space* magazine had boomed to a circulation of over 200,000. NBA games were a regular Sunday feature on China Central Television. NBA logos adorned the apparel worn by the coolest kids on China's hoop courts, which now drew the crowds once reserved for Ping-Pong tables.

In fact, basketball had taken solid root in China long before David Stern had set the NBA's marketers loose. In the years after James Naismith drew up the rules of basketball in 1891 at the YMCA Training School in Springfield, Massachusetts, YMCA missionaries hawked the game worldwide as a physical gospel wherever they went. The first Chinese game was held in 1896 at the Tianjin YMCA. Basketball's fluidity, its limited requirements in equipment and facilities, its obvious contributions to fitness, and its special blend of individual skill and team play helped its popularity and provided a safe cover during the ideological cleansing of the Cultural Revolution. If the "team" was king in the 1960s and 1970s, then the individual emerged on the court in the 1990s, just as the People's Republic began its complicated dance with Western capitalism.

When Jeff Coplon traveled throughout China for the *New York Times* in 2003, he found a Chinese basketball culture adjusting to its new open exposure to American and NBA brands. The global and the local were swirling together as Chinese kids started modeling their game after the likes of Allen Iverson, hardly an icon of conformity to authority. But to move ahead in the world of basketball, China would need more than an occasional export like the seven-foot (2.13 m) Yao Ming. It would require quick and spontaneous point guards like 14-year-old Chen Jianhua, who had American scouts and Chinese coaches thinking ahead: an Iverson-like point guard feeding an NBA-seasoned Yao Ming in the 2008 Olympics, to be held in Shanghai? A Pistons' scout summed up the prognosis: "Do they have a shot? Definitely. They're playing at home; I think they can compete with anybody." (6)

As early as 1992, Chuck Daly had cautioned American fans that "there will come a day" when other countries "will be able to compete with us on even terms." To Daly, anyway, the Barcelona Dream Team would then be seen as a "landmark event" in the development of basketball parity. The 2004 Athens Olympics surely marked a big step in that direction. Many

American critics—such as Oscar Robertson—would blame the NBA and its pampered, selfish superstars for America's Olympic decline in men's basketball. But the numbers suggested that the NBA—if not the men's Olympic team—was at the top of its global game. Regular-season NBA attendance was up 1 percent from 2002 to 2003, to an average of 17,056 per game, or 89 percent of collective arena capacity, the fourth-best level in league history. Although ratings on ABC slumped by almost 8 percent, they were up on TNT (16.7 percent) and ESPN (8.3 percent). Better yet, the 2004 NBA finals were broadcasted to 205 countries in 42 languages. The international traffic on NBA.com was well over 40 percent of the total; the league had nine foreign-language Web sites. Yao Ming was only the tallest of the internationals on NBA rosters; the total number had expanded from 65 in 2002-2003 to 84 by the fall of 2004. There was an obvious synergy. For instance, Dirk Nowitzki's success with the Dallas Mavericks translated into five television outlets in Germany. And every new foreign star meant more foreign exposure. By October 2004, the NBA had 212 international television deals.

Of course, the NBA was not without its problems. In November 2004, an on-court scuffle between members of the Pistons and the Pacers spilled over into the stands, producing a televised embarrassment that led the news for several days. Critics found the 2005 NBA finals to be uninspiring, with choking team defenses that limited the displays of virtuosity and scoring that marked the Bird-Johnson-Jordan era. But the brightest star in the finals may have been San Antonio's Manu Ginobili, who is Argentinian. When Ginobili returned home to a hero's welcome, he joined fellow countrymen Andres Nocioni (Chicago Bulls) and Carlos Delfino (Detroit Pistons) as instructors at an NBA development camp for South American players. For David Stern, the math was clear. More international stars were shining in a league whose worldwide reach was still widening. The global marketing strategy was paying off. (7)

Global Competition Works Both Ways

The global economy also boosted prospects for other sport leagues. The National Hockey League and Major League Baseball both attracted top talent from overseas—Europeans to the NHL and Japanese to MLB. But the most pronounced consequences of global games occurred in soccer, the world's number-one game. One and a half billion viewers had watched the 2002 World Cup in the 18 countries monitored by Nielsen Media Research. This included 263 million in China. In the United States, the 85 million English-language viewers were matched by 80 million who watched Spanish-language telecasts on Telefutura and Univision. In soccer's global market, the world's talent moved to European leagues, especially England's Premiership, Italy's Serie A, and Spain's La Liga. If the NBA looked to Europe and China for expansion markets, the Europeans saw America as ripe for the picking. A steady swell of youth soccer players, "soccer moms," and their families had provided a strong base for the United States' successful hosting of World Cups in 1994 (men's) and 1996 (women's). Major League Soccer, hatched after the 1994 World Cup, was averaging crowds over 15,000 by 2004, better than those in Argentine or Dutch leagues. European teams found warm welcomes in their "friendly" tours of the United States. The "Champions World Series," featuring Manchester United, AC Milan, Juventus, and Barcelona, drew over 420,000 for eight games. Rick Parry, a Liverpool executive, recognized the United States as "an important market. All the major clubs are going to have to come here." (8)

There have been a number of consequences of sport's new global market, where branded players and playing styles circulated instantly via satellite networks, followed closely by branded equipment and merchandise. In soccer, the lure of Europe decimated local clubs in Latin America and Africa. Winning titles made a national team more vulnerable, as *The Economist* reported in a 2002 analysis. In 2001, Argentina's under-21 team won the world championship. A year later, two thirds of the team was playing in Europe. "Their fans are fed up: every time they discover a new idol, he is off on the next plane." As the world's best players (and hence the television audience) gravitated to a few European leagues, the old "national" styles of soccer appeared to erode, with a convergence toward a single style. Jorge Valdano, who played for Argentina's 1986 World Cup champions and later served as sporting director of Real Madrid, put it this way to *The Economist*: "Twenty years ago it was easy to say that Latin American football was about technique and talent, and European football was about organization, speed, and fighting spirit. But with television and player transfers, all these trends are coming together." Jose Angel Sanchez went even further, envisioning a football future in which "eventually, you may get just six global brand leaders. People will support a local side, and one of the world's big six. We have to position ourselves for that." In soccer, it was likely that the six global brands would all be European. (9)

Global competition was changing the nature of markets and brands. The NBA was certainly a global brand, like the English Premier League. How quickly would Asia, Africa, Latin America, or Oceania produce a league with similar reach? In the battle for market control, how soon would notions of "national" sport brands yield to those of "continental" brands? Executives of the European Union looked no further than the 2008 Olympics in Beijing. While analyzing medal production at the 2004 Athens Olympics, EU spokesman Reijo Kemppinen noted that EU members combined to win 82 gold medals and 286 total medals, compared to only 35 golds and 103 total medals for the United States. In his words, "The European Union swept the floor at the Olympic Games." Now it was setting its sights on the 2008 Beijing Olympics, where outgoing European Commission president Romano Prodi hoped "to see the EU Member State teams in Beijing carry the flag of the European Union alongside their own national flag as a symbol of our unity." If this new calculus took hold, the Yanks might soon be forced to look to members of the North American Free Trade Agreement (NAFTA) to boost their medal totals. (10)

Weathering Recession and Terrorism

Global competition was shifting the realities of the sport marketplace at the end of the 20th century. So were the booms and busts that marked the millennium's turn. As early as 1998, *Street & Smith's SportsBusiness Journal* asked the headline question: "Is Sports Business Recession-Proof?" The answers were mixed. Most industry insiders said yes (no surprise). But some bankers and economists were less certain. Randy Vataha, an investment banker, worried about the 1990s buildup of luxury seats that would likely be threatened by a recession. As the stock market bubble reached its peak, the ESPN Chilton poll announced that the last half of the 1990s had seen a *decrease* in the percentage of Americans who considered themselves fans of the NFL (–3.06%), the NBA (–11.38%), the NHL (–8.57%), college basketball (–8.45%), and college football (–6.37%); all of this despite general increases in aggregate attendance. Only Major League Baseball had improved its position in the general public's imagination. Was the bubble about to burst? Worse yet, global markets might increase the odds of global recessions. As author Dan Kaplan put it: "Already, overseas turmoil is hurting many sports businesses. Nike Inc. is cutting back on its bevy of endorsers in part because of steep losses overseas. Golf manufacturers have suffered devastating setbacks from a saturated domestic market and foreign recessions." The Japanese economy had lagged, squeezing out its own excesses from the 1980s. Japan's woes oozed into the rest of Asia. Russia and Brazil descended to crisis level as each country struggled with the vagaries of global capital. Would the United States avoid the inevitable? (11)

The answer was soon obvious. The U.S. sport market was not immune to recession. Examples abounded:

✦ Major League Baseball attendance had plummeted after the player's strike of 1994, slowly crawling back by 2000 to prestrike levels. When the economic bubble burst, attendance began another slide (see table 1.1).

✦ Historically low interest rates had rendered housing recession-proof, but they had not protected sport-related construction, which slipped 7.9 percent in the United States between 1999 and 2001. This was in contrast to the 22.3 percent increase in overall construction spending during the same period. (12)

✦ A host of innovative sport dot-coms died in infancy; others were on life support, including Quokka Sports, MVP.com, Fogdog Sports, Total Sports, SeasonTicket.com, and eFANshop.

♦ Table 1.1 Average Major League Baseball Attendance: 1994-2003

Year	Average attendance
1994	31,652
1995	25,260
1996	26,889
1997	28,288
1998	29,285
1999	29,152
2000	30,099
2001	30,012
2002	28,134
2003	28,013

Adapted, by permission, from R. Blum, 2004, "A decade ago, baseball took its last called strike on itself," *Boston Globe* 11 August, D-6.

As two longtime sport business reporters later reflected: "In the sports business world, one of the prevailing memories of that time is of executives from solid, established companies migrating in droves to Internet startups. With the memory comes shock at how ill-conceived the models were for many of those businesses—built on lousy projections of the growth of Internet use and audience habits, or on front-loaded schemes to show quick revenue for an IPO." (13)

♦ ISL Worldwide, a global giant in sport marketing, staggered under the weight of contracts with properties like the Championship Auto Racing Teams, the Association of Tennis Professionals, and the International Tennis Federation. ISL had grown steadily as the marketing arm of the International Amateur Athletic Federation and FIFA, the guardian of the World Cup. In the late 1990s, ISL had grabbed for a share of the North American market, with up-front deals with CART and ATP. As sponsor and media markets dried up, ISL felt its neck in the noose. Soon it was in bankruptcy. (14)

Sponsors began to cut back on their deals. HALO Industries, an Illinois-based corporation, reduced its MLB partnerships in the face of a bankruptcy filing. Christine Noel of HALO spelled the problem out clearly: "In the last 18 months, we've made a strategic decision to pool our money elsewhere. As you can imagine [sport] sponsorship is expensive." Lucent Technologies, a star in the go-go '90s, had its own problems with sports partnerships, as spokesperson Mary Ward warned: "Clearly as we look at streamlining the business and focusing on a very few, very large customers and reducing costs, we'll be looking at all our expenses and [sport sponsorships] would be one of them." (15)

In late 2001, Professor Gil Fried, a well-known sport management scholar, wrote about the new "blood sport" unfolding as the sport boom turned into a bust. Speedway Motorsports, Inc., had announced that it would trim its workforce by 18 percent. The National Professional Soccer League—almost two decades old—had dissolved. Converse was struggling to avoid bankruptcy. AMF, the bowling giant, had already filed for chapter 11 protection. "Will the bloodletting be massive, will everyone go down," Fried asked, "or will only the weakest entities be harmed?" Even ESPN, the bellwether of America's sport passion, saw its daytime ratings decline by 17 percent in the first quarter of 2001 compared to 2002. Worse yet, prime-time ratings were down 25 percent. ESPN's own Charley Steiner put it succinctly: "If sports were a stock, I'd sell it all." (16)

Economic booms and busts were nothing new to old hands in the sport industry, or in any industry. September 11, 2001, was another matter. If terrorists could strike the World Trade Center, what would prevent them from targeting and hitting a major sport venue? It had happened before, as the Palestinian Black September movement demonstrated at the 1972 Munich Olympics. A few years later, novelist Thomas Harris (who created Hannibal Lecter) moved the target to the Super Bowl in a book called *Black Sunday*. Hollywood made it into a feature film. Reality was far more gripping than the movies. In October 2001, Richard Luker, the president of the Leisure Intelligence Group, announced the results of a national poll taken one week after the attack on the World Trade Center. Although a majority of people (56 to 57 percent) believed that playing casual and organized sports was "more important" in "difficult times," and 48 percent believed that watching sports on TV was more important, only 41 percent felt that way about attending sporting events. Would fans stay home? Luker said that he would be "nervous" if he were an owner: "You've got the double whammy of the economy on the cost side and the terrorists on the fear side. If you watch games on TV, it's free and there's no fear." (17)

In fact, things did not turn out quite so badly. As table 1.2 suggests, attendance at professional-league levels did not seem to suffer dramatically from terrorism's trauma.

At the same time, it was not as though the sport marketplace was booming. As table 1.3 shows, the sales of sporting goods—fuel for participation—had been essentially flat since 1998.

Broadcast television ratings continued to slide for some sport properties that had enjoyed the boom years (see tables 1.4 and 1.5). Broadcast ratings for the 2002-2003 NBA playoffs on ABC were the lowest (6.5) since 1971, lower even than the 1981 finals, which had been tape-delayed. Tennis' U.S. Open suffered a similar slide. In fairness, broadcast ratings were slipping for just about everyone on television, as cable systems offered viewers more and more choices.

✦ **Table 1.2** Average Attendance at Selected Pro Leagues

League	2000-2001	2001-2002	2003-2004
NFL	66,078	65,187	66,726
NBA	16,778	16,966	17,059
WNBA	9,072	9,075	9,344
MLS	13,756	14,961	14,898
NHL	16,555	16,759	16,533
AHL	5,473	5,895	5,595

From Kenn Tomasch's Sports Attendance Database. www.kenn.com/sports/index.html.

✦ **Table 1.3** Sales of Sporting Goods (in billions)

1997	1998	1999	2000	2001	2002	2003
$44.4	$45.1	$43.2	$45.7	$45.6	$45.6	$45.8

Adapted, by permission, from N. Aoki, 2004, "Becoming a player," *Boston Globe* 19, October E-1.

✦ **Table 1.4** NBA Selected Ratings on Broadcast Television

Year	Regular season	Finals
1998-1999	4.3	11.3
1999-2000	3.4	11.6
2000-2001	3.0	12.1
2001-2002	3.1	10.2
2002-2003	2.6	6.5

Adapted from A. Bernstein, 2003, "NBA Finals ratings fall to 30-year-low," *Street & Smith's SportsBusiness Journal* June 23-29: 4.

✦ **Table 1.5** CBS: U.S. Open Tennis Ratings—All Men's and Women's Telecasts

Year	Rating	Share
1999	3.5	10
2000	2.8	8
2001	3.0	8
2002	3.0	8
2003	2.0	5
2004	1.8	5

Adapted, by permission, from D. Kaplan, 2004, "CBS draws low ratings for U.S. Open coverage," *Smith & Street's SportsBusiness Journal* September 20-26, pg. 10

The Competitive Marketplace

In March 2002, *Street & Smith's SportsBusiness Journal* ran a special report on "Dollars in Sports." Their research calculated that the sport industry represented about $196.64 billion in expenditures for 2001. An earlier economic study—with a different methodology—pegged the 1995 "gross domestic sport product" at $152 billion, making sport the 11th largest industry in the American economy. Sadly, we have no longitudinal data tracking sport industry growth over time, using generally agreed-upon methods. For now, we can only conclude that the sport industry is growing, but its share of the overall domestic economy may not be growing. And competition for the sport dollar is growing at the pace of a full-court press. (18)

As table 1.6 illustrates, Americans have expanded their consumption of "recreation," of which spectator sports are just a part. In 1970, recreation accounted for 4.3 percent of total

✦ **Table 1.6** Spectator Sports, Amusements, and the Consumption "Pie"

Product or service (in billions)	1970	1980	1985	1990	2001	2002
Total recreation expenditure	93.8	159.7	215	291.8	603.4	633.9
Percent of total personal consumption	4.3	5.3	6.1	7.1	8.6	8.6
Spectator sports admissions	3.7	4.5	4.8	4.8	12.4	13.6
as % of total recreation expenditure	3.9	2.8	2.2	1.6	2.1	2.1
Commercial participant amusements	7.7	15.3	20.0	24.9	79.4	83.7
as % of total recreation expenditure	8.2	9.5	9.3	8.5	13.2	13.2
Video, audio, computer, musical equipment	6.2	12.7	24.7	47.9	115.5	120.8
as % of total recreation expenditure	6.6	7.9	11.4	16.4	19.1	19.1

In 1992 dollars for all except 2001 and 2002, which are in current dollars.

From U.S. Department of Commerce, Statistical abstract of the United States, 1996, Table 401, p. 252, 2004-2005, Table 1229, p. 767.

personal consumption. By 1985, that percentage had jumped to 6.1 percent; by 2001, to 8.6 percent. "Recreation," at least, was getting a bigger piece of the consumption pie. The statistics were not so good, however, for spectator sports, which saw a steady decline as a percentage of total recreation expenditures (from 3.9 percent in 1970 to 1.6 percent in 1990), followed by a slightly higher plateau (2.1 percent in 2001). And where is the recreation dollar going? As table 1.6 suggests, both "commercial participant amusements" (e.g., bowling, skating, and golf) and "video/audio/computer/musical" goods have grown significantly in the last decade as a percentage of all recreation expenditures. One might argue that sports simply can't expand like DVRs or PDAs or iPods. Sports require an infrastructure of fields and stadiums, which are slow to develop. A person won't shell out $800 for hockey equipment if she has no place to play. All this is true; there are some long-standing brakes on the growth of the sport market. But that is not the whole answer. There is great competition for the discretionary dollar, especially inside the sport industry.

Competition is the nature of sport. For well over a century, entrepreneurs and investors have jostled for market space, particularly in professional team sports. Professional baseball's troubles are internal these days, but the game's history is punctuated by a number of wars among rival leagues, the last threat being the Continental League in the early 1960s. Football took center stage in the 1960s with the rivalry between the American and the National Football Leagues. The World Football League and the U.S. Football League followed in the 1970s and 1980s. In 2000, two sport magnates—Dick Ebersol of NBC and Vince McMahon of the World Wrestling Federation—announced a new competitor, the XFL. Like so many of its predecessors, however, the XFL died after its inaugural 2001 season. The most interesting market battle, however, was in women's pro basketball, where the Women's National Basketball Association (WNBA) and the American Basketball League (ABL) offered consumers alternative visions of a "big league," at least until the ABL dissolved in early 1999. The successful Women's World Cup of 1999 spawned the first women's professional soccer league, which opened in 2001 with eight teams. By September 2003, the league had collapsed.

Fear of failure, however, does not rule the world of sport franchises. In 1999, the *Sports-Business Journal* published an analysis of 97 North American sport markets, comparing their aggregate "available personal incomes" to support sport franchises. At that time, Buffalo,

New York, had seven minor league franchises—indoor soccer and lacrosse, roller hockey, arena football, men's and women's baseball, and outdoor soccer—competing for fans along with the Bills, the Sabres, and a half-dozen colleges and universities. The *SportsBusiness Journal* declared Buffalo to be among the "saturated" markets, with a deficit of $7.3 billion of available personal income to support sports. That didn't diminish optimism. As one team administrator had argued a few months before: "I think there's a market for us. It's just a matter of swaying people to spend their entertainment dollar with us." (19)

Openly crass competition has long been a theme in the ranks of college football. The fight for bowl dollars has raised the level, as members of the "Super Six" conferences work to squeeze the life out of their competitors. In 2002, the "big boys" (who grabbed control of NCAA legislation in 1996) enacted a new rule that required all Division IA football programs to average 15,000 in attendance or face relegation to a lower division. This spurred both interesting promotions and creative accounting. Louisiana-Lafayette brought in a petting zoo to attract kids to one game; it upped attendance by 5,000. San Jose State, teetering on the edge of relegation, ran "fiesta-themed" entertainment aimed at area Hispanics. Unfortunately, some of the target consumers felt patronized. Kent State took a different approach: counting all the tailgaters as attendees whether or not they had a ticket or entered the stadium. Because the NCAA rule had not yet defined "attendance," as one Kent State official put it, "we are going to try it until someone tells us to stop." (20)

This was the song at all levels, as one sport competed with all the others for fans and participants. Data suggest that there are always winners and losers. Since 1996, the ESPN Sports Poll has asked a national sample of Americans to indicate the sports of which they considered themselves to be fans. As table 1.7 shows, some sports gained and some lost over the millennium's turn. Of course this did not necessarily translate into similar decreases or increases in attendance. But it did reveal a competitive marketplace.

The Role of Television

Television has helped to build fan bases ever since the 1950s. As much as anything else, the spread of television images has spurred the global markets for certain sport products such as the NBA, Nike, and Michael Jordan. When the worldwide number of television sets per 100,000 people doubled between 1981 and 1997, it seemed that all sport boats could rise with a surge of viewers. In the last decade, however, the focus has changed from broad to narrow markets. The success of sport television—think TBS, ESPN, and Fox—and the excess capacity on broadband cable systems has spawned a host of new specialty sport channels. The late 1990s saw the birth of the Golf and Speed channels, the Outdoor Life Network, and rumors of a tennis channel. The dot-com bust and economic recession did not temper the enthusiasm of channel builders. By late 2002, a raft of new cable networks was all the buzz. These included Blackbelt TV, the Football Network, the Ice Channel, College Sports Television, NBA TV, and the NFL Channel. Could the market sustain this competition? Neil Pilson, one-time president of CBS Sports and a well-known consultant, thought so. "If you reach 300,000 families who are avid figure skating nuts, your efficiencies are quite strong, even though you're not reaching a large total number," he contended. "You're reaching the committed." But even some new network leaders were hedging their bets. Blackbelt's Wesley Hein admitted that "people would say maybe it's not the best timing, starting a network in one of the worst advertising markets in years." (21)

In the aggregate, sports may have grown as a share of the television marketplace, but the bottom line was greater competition

✦ **Table 1.7** ESPN Sports Poll

Auto racing*	+28.6 %
Boxing	–7.3 %
Pro golf	+15.0 %
Pro soccer	–11.6 %
Pro tennis	–4.6 %
College basketball	–15.3 %
Pro football	–5.1%
Pro hockey	–16.0 %
Pro baseball	–6.4 %
Pro basketball	–16.4 %
College football	–7.1 %
Figure skating	–18.9 %

Increase or decrease in percentage of respondents claiming to be fans, between 1996 and 2002.

* Reflects all auto racing, including NASCAR.

ESPN Sports Poll, a service of TNS Sport.

for the fan's attention. This showed up in television ratings, which have long stood as a sign of a league's or even a sport's strength. In the new millennium, a sport property bragged if its ratings stayed flat! Fox Sports and NASCAR did just this in late June of 2003 when they trumpeted a 5.8 rating for their telecasts, the same as the year before. The news was good in comparison to the NCAA men's basketball tournament, whose "March Madness" had slumped 23 percent. If pundits sometimes lamented the demise of the "three-sport athlete," the new networks seemed to threaten the existence of the "three-sport fan." (22)

Struggles at the Grassroots Level

While the "big-time" leagues and networks slugged it out for fans, the competition also raged at the grassroots levels. For the last two decades, the National Sporting Goods Association has tracked participation across a wide range of sporting activities. Recent data on "frequent" (table 1.8) and "youth" (table 1.9) participation suggest patterns of winners and losers. Basketball and golf look flat; soccer may have peaked; skateboarding and snowboarding continue to grow steadily.

Hockey is a good example of a sport with modest growth in casual participation. At the same time, the number of players registered in amateur leagues has been relatively flat: In Canada, it was up only 2.5 percent in 2003-2004 (to a total of 538,000); in the United States, it was up only 0.8 percent (to a total of 446,000). This overall number was buoyed by girls and women. (23)

In America, at least, high school sports felt the most pressure in an increasingly competitive environment. With the general public bombarded with opportunities to consume "big-time" sports on television and the Internet, it was harder to interest fans in high school events. Equipment and apparel companies spent millions supplying big-time college and pro franchises; this meant higher prices for high school programs, just as school districts looked to save money during tough economic times. Florida and Oklahoma administrators trimmed sport schedules 10 to 20 percent. In Utah, high school athletics directors worried that a state senate bill would have even worse effects. Individual districts around the country slashed sports. Some, like California's West Contra Costa Unified School District, relented only after cash infusions from boosters or patrons like the Oakland Athletics. Many more districts tacked on "user fees." In Massachusetts, these fees ranged anywhere from $25 to $850 per sport. Overall high school athletics participation had grown by almost a million in the late 1990s—from 5,776,820 in 1994-1995 to 6,705,223 in 2000-2001. The recession had slowed this growth rate to a total of 6,903,552 in 2003-2004. With competitive pressure from the top and budget pressure from below, the future looked grim. (24)

✦ **Table 1.8** NSGA Total "Frequent" Participants, Age 7+ (in thousands)—National Probability Sample of U.S. Households

	1999	2000	2001	2002	2003
Baseball (50+ days/yr)	4,811	4,694	4,969	4,940	5,600
Basketball (50+ days/yr)	8,881	7,487	8,298	7,784	8,830
Golf (40+ days/yr)	6,434	6,398	5,965	6,043	6,037
Ice hockey (30+ days/yr)	711	788	1,105	988	1,083
Skateboarding (30+ days/yr)	2,960	4,365	4,688	4,499	4,114
Snowboarding (10+ days/yr)	1,633	1,504	1,630	2,034	2,410
Soccer (40+ days/yr)	5,008	5,463	5,712	5,860	4,673
Tennis (30+ days/yr)	2,572	2,402	3,302	3,040	2,259

Data from SBRnet.com.

The sport marketplace certainly appears to be getting more and more competitive. It is a market in which even the most local grassroots team is, in some ways, in competition with professional franchises across the globe. Television and the Internet may create a global community, but it is ruled by competition. There will continue to be organizational winners and losers, launches and funerals. Nothing can ensure success. But sound marketing can surely increase the odds of survival.

Sport Marketing Defined

As the needs and demographic makeup of sport consumers have become more complex, and as competition for the spectator and participant dollar has increased, the demand for professional marketing has also grown. Professional teams, small colleges, high schools, sport clubs, and youth programs have all looked for a better way to attract and maintain consumers. Among other things, they know that they compete for time and money with a host of rivals, including malls, mega-movie complexes, Internet providers, concerts, and museums. Today's marketers clearly need a rational, coherent system that can match sport consumers with sport products. We may call this sport marketing—but what is sport marketing? The term "sports marketing" was coined by *Advertising Age* in 1979 to describe the activities of consumer and industrial product and service marketers who were increasingly using sport as a promotional vehicle. Even a casual television viewer cannot help noticing the use of sport images and personalities to sell beer, cars, and a whole range of other products. (25)

This sense of the term, however, is extremely limited in that it fails to recognize the dominant portion of sport marketing, which is the marketing of sport events and services. This text will recognize two components in sport marketing: the marketing of sport and marketing through sport. A professional team or a soccer club engages in the former; a brewery or an auto dealer employs the latter. Although most of this book addresses the marketing of sport, we also consider (especially in chapter 13) the corporate sponsor, who markets through sport.

Another confusing element is use of the term *sports* (plural) *marketing* rather than *sport* (singular) *marketing*. "Sports" marketing connotes an industry of diverse and uncoordinated segments that have little commonality. Certainly each segment of the sport industry does operate independently and with minimal sharing of managerial practice. However, if standardized management and marketing practice is ever to come to the sport industry, then at some point we need to conceptualize industry segments as a homogeneous entity. In the chapters that follow, we hope first to provide a general theory of sport marketing across all segments, and then to supplement this theory with marketing issues peculiar to separate segments.

Given these notions about the sport industry and marketing, we offer the following definition of sport marketing, adapted from a standard definition of general marketing:

> *Sport marketing consists of all activities designed to meet the needs and wants of sport consumers through exchange processes. Sport marketing has developed two major thrusts: the marketing of sport products and services directly to consumers of sport, and the marketing of other consumer and industrial products or services through the use of sport promotions.*

As we will see, the terms *sport consumers* and *sport consumption* entail many types of involvement with sport, including playing, officiating, watching, listening, reading, and collecting. (26)

♦ Table 1.9 NSGA Statistics of Change in "Youth" (7-17) Participation (1+ times per year, 1993-2003)

Sport	% change 1993-2003
Baseball	–12.3%
Basketball	–5.9%
Golf	13.3%
Ice hockey	9.4%
Skateboarding	60.6%
Snowboarding	242.7%
Soccer	7.9%
Tennis	–32.6%

Adapted, by permission, from National Sporting Goods Association. Available at www.nsga.org/public/pages/index.cfm?pageid=153.

Marketing Myopia in Sport

If sport marketing ideally consists of activities designed to meet the wants and needs of sport consumers, then historically the industry has been guilty of what Theodore Levitt called "marketing myopia," or "a lack of foresight in marketing ventures." (27) We like to call it "the vision thing."

Following are some of the standard symptoms of sport marketing myopia:

✦ A focus on producing and selling goods and services rather than identifying and satisfying the needs and wants of consumers and their markets. Spencer Garrett, part owner and general manager of the successful Pierpont Racquet Club, recognized a problem that plagues many sport teams: "There are industry people who still focus on closing the sale. Membership [we can add "fan"] retention is where the future of the industry lies, so selling has to focus on benefits to the potential member." Selling is a critical component of marketing, but it is not the end-all. (28)

✦ The belief that winning absolves all other sins. Longtime Buffalo Bills owner Ralph Wilson expressed this sentiment recently as he questioned some expenditures. "You go about marketing by winning," he insisted. "That's how you do it. A couple years ago we spent $700,000 on television, advertising the Bills, and we didn't sell five tickets. . . . This is sort of an anomaly, this marketing. Everybody gets carried away with it." Of course, winning does not guarantee a rise in attendance. The New Jersey Devils won Stanley Cups in 1995 and 2000. Neither championship resulted in a serious bounce in attendance, or even in television ratings. (29)

✦ Confusion between promotions and marketing. Promotion—including advertising and special events—is only one part of a marketing mix or strategy. Many fail to see the difference between promotion and marketing. Not long ago, the *NCAA News* ran a feature story titled "Professional Marketing Finds Its Way Into College Basketball." The article hardly described "professional marketing"—only the influx into college arenas of promotional tactics such as NBA-style laser shows, cheerleaders, and halftime shows. Said Jim Harrick, UCLA coach at the time: "In the past, UCLA has had a history of its game being its main attraction. Marketing has become a great asset." Good promotions can certainly be the "sizzle" that sells the "steak," but promotions must be part of an integrated strategy that begins with knowing consumer wants and needs. (30)

✦ Ignorance of competition inside and outside of sport. There are not enough smart teams that recognize competitive trends and use them to advantage. For instance, the Atlanta Hawks had data that showed that their fans were 30 percent more likely than the general population to attend movies four or more times in the last three months. What did they do? They began to use ticket promo ads on the big screen before the movies. Research found that moviegoers have an 80 percent recall the next day, compared with a 15 to 20 percent recall rate from television ads. (31)

✦ A short-sighted focus on quick-return price hikes or investments like sponsorships rather than long-term investments in research and in relationship marketing. This is especially true at the professional levels, where escalating salaries have prompted front offices to focus resources on selling corporate signage, often at the expense of building a large database around small groups, families, and individual ticket buyers. Worse yet, too many teams gouge their fans whenever they sense that demand is greater than supply. In the new millennium, some NFL teams began to charge fans to see preseason practice. In the opposite, enlightened camp was Robert Kraft, owner of the New England Patriots, whose Super Bowl champs have enjoyed a long train of sellouts. Rather than gouge the preseason fans, Kraft understood that they represent future generations of the Patriots Nation. To this end, New England's preseason camp had free admission, free parking, free rosters, and players lingering to sign free autographs. Said well-known *Boston Globe* columnist Dan Shaughnessy, "It's the best sports deal in New England." (32)

Lack of Market Research

When Matt Levine—the "father" of modern sport marketing—broke into the NBA in 1974, the cutting edge of market research belonged to the L.A. Lakers, who collected patron names and addresses on raffle entries available at Forum ticket gates. Levine's boss, Golden State Warriors GM Dick Vertlieb, posed a simple question to Levine: "Isn't there more we could learn than their names and addresses?" (33)

Although lately even the casual sport consumer has completed questionnaires at games, in clubs, or in malls, much of the research is myopic, lacking any "sportsense." For instance, as we discuss in chapter 5, the sport venue requires special considerations of sampling. Simply handing out surveys at the front door will not do the trick. Further, questions on sport "participation" require much more clarity than one normally sees in an average survey. Does playing one round of golf per year—with someone else's clubs—make a person a golfer? Some surveys have suggested this sort of thing. More than a decade after the first edition of this book, the field as a whole still lacks well-designed research that includes both quantitative and qualitative methods (e.g., in-depth interviews). Quick, sloppy surveys will not suffice.

Research failures still exist at all levels. The NFL could not have done serious research when it let Nashville play the 1997 season in Memphis, a long-standing rival city whose residents were not about to support a carpet-bagging franchise. Attendance was an embarrassment. Dallas Cowboys owner Jerry Jones was candid enough to admit the NFL's hubris: "I wish we'd done our homework more. . . . We could have better identified the unique mentality between Memphis and Nashville." Some colleges and universities also operate without research. A recent study of NCAA Division I and II programs suggested that only 32 percent conduct fan surveys at home games. The authors of this book have experienced firsthand some of the frustrations in selling research to executives. Not long ago, we developed a machine-readable fan survey for a big-league team. A few weeks after the surveys were administered, a team employee brought us the completed surveys—dumped and mangled in four Hefty trash bags! Myopia can't get much worse. (34)

The last decade has seen significant developments in database marketing at the "big-time" levels. (See chapter 5 for a close look at what goes on in the NBA.) In the college ranks, Division IA schools like Arizona State and the University of Washington have begun to use sophisticated customer relationship management (CRM) systems, which combine databases with Web sites and e-mails. Consumers register information via Web contests or ticket applications, and marketers send out special promotions to targeted groups with matching interests. Washington's Leslie Wurzinger summed up the CRM approach: "[It] allows us to know who our customers are and what they want. It allows us to tailor our offers according to what they've told us they want, and to do it in a timely manner." But it is not cheap. Arizona State's marketing director Steve Hank estimated that the Sun Devils' CRM system cost about $20,000 to set up and between $25,000 and $30,000 to maintain. Managers at the youth club, high school, and small college levels obviously lack the resources for such sophisticated systems. But, as chapter 5 demonstrates, research can begin with simple Excel files, or even paper files. (35)

Poor Sales Techniques

Although many sport firms have equated sales and promotions with marketing, few have even invested in the sales effort. Historically, sales have been driven by quota and commissions mentalities, with little emphasis on training, tactics, or sales as part of the larger marketing strategy. For instance, why do so many tennis, racquetball, fitness, and health clubs still hire part-time students to work as control desk personnel and double as sales staff? Don't the owners realize that their destiny (and financial stability) is in inexperienced hands? In all but a few clubs, desk personnel are the primary consumer contact (on the phone, at the front desk, and for walk-in prospects). It seems incomprehensible that a business that is subject to high customer turnover, fads, and trends would overlook such a critical marketing function; yet it clearly has done so in the past, in part because of absentee ownership and in part because untrained managers have been hired from the ranks of former participants and coaches. Things are not much better in many minor league franchises, where executives run boiler room sales operations with untrained and highly exploited staff and interns. The philosophy of these executives seems to be: If they can't do it, we'll just fire them and bring in more from the hundreds who have sent in resumes. In all of this, there is no thought to the value of training and incentives, both of which might improve the interaction between the sport organization and its consumers.

The Slowly Growing Sport Marketing Profession

Sport marketing has a long history, dating back to promoters in ancient Greece and Rome. There have been many "golden ages" and growth spurts. David Stern has thousands of predecessors, including the legendary Bill Veeck, one of the most imaginative sport entrepreneurs of the past century and the most creative marketer in the history of baseball (see the photo and sidebar on Veeck on page 16). Boxing had Tex Rickard, who made a name in the first quarter of the 20th century promoting boxing matches with the likes of Jack Johnson and Jack Dempsey. He later ran sports at Madison Square Garden, where the press referred to his young hockey franchise as Tex's "Rangers." In 1928, he was asked by a pundit, "What do you regard as the secret to your success as a promoter—what psychological impulse guides you?" Rickard answered quickly: "It's no secret. By merely reading the newspapers most anybody can tell what the public wants to see." (36)

The field was not much farther along in 1975, when *Sports Illustrated*'s Frank Deford wrote a brilliant profile of Michigan's athletics director, Don Canham—a man widely recognized for leading college athletics into a new age of marketing. Deford focused most of his attention on Canham's frenetic pace and his hustling personality. He was way ahead of his time in the use of direct mail and aggressive advertising (including using airplane banners over Tiger Stadium), and in recognizing the need for commercial sponsorship. More than anything, Canham saw the need to sell the overall experience of big-time college football or basketball. As he said to Deford: "We've got to promote what we have. We've got to ballyhoo the pageantry. . . . We've got to sell the spectacle." To many fellow athletics directors (ADs), Canham's approach threatened the purity of "amateur" sport. Deford recognized this, but he also recognized the key to Canham's success: "There is very little that Don Canham does not take into consideration, and that, indeed, is the first mark of a promoter: concern for the tiniest detail while retaining the broadest vision." We would make only one correction in Deford's description. Canham was more than a promoter. He was a marketer. It is all in the vision thing. (37)

But the presence of celebrity promoters does not make a profession. As late as the 1980s, it was unusual to find a collegiate athletics program that had any staff member whose title contained the word *marketing*. This is slowly changing. By the mid-1990s, data from 291 NCAA Division I and II programs showed that "63% of the administrators in charge of sport marketing were employed full-time in that activity." Further, 20 percent of the positions were designated "sport marketing." (38)

Within the last decade, sport marketers at NCAA Division IA institutions responded to a survey with very high levels of job satisfaction. At the same time, however, they complained that the top administrators at their institutions (e.g., ADs) did not understand the "the role and purpose" of marketing. In fact, athletics directors who responded to the same survey listed "corporate sponsorships" and "game promotions" as their top job priorities. (39)

"Professional" sport marketers also have a way to go before they enjoy salaries commensurate with their skills and responsibilities. In the late 1990s, 421 sport marketing professional across a range of industry segments responded to a survey on compensation and job responsibilities. Although wide variations in compensation make the use of the term *mean salaries* problematic, the numbers (see table 1.10) are sobering, particularly given that the economy was booming, and the executives averaged between 7 and 10 years of experience. With ever-increasing expectations for attendance, sponsor revenues, and booster fund-raising, the pressure was particularly high on marketers in college athletics programs. Yet only 52.4 percent of collegiate respondents in another study indicated that they had attended a professional development program in the previous year, and only 50.8 percent had a budget to support such training. (40)

The authors of this book have interviewed thousands of young people who want to "work in sports" because they "love sports." Like millions of others among the "ESPN Generation," they are deluded by visions of mingling with Derek Jeter, Maria Sharapova, Jack Nicholson, or 50 Cent. Reality is much more of a grind—heavy competition for entry-level jobs (the XFL reportedly had over 50,000 people apply online for 112 positions), low salaries, and long, long hours. Still, those with strong sales skills and an equally strong work ethic have a chance to be discovered by a team or by an executive recruiter such as Buffy Filippell, whose TeamWork Online LLC (www.teamworkonline.com) is highly respected and widely known inside the industry.

Despite lingering myopia, the last 10 years have seen many encouraging signs of "professional" approaches to sport marketing. Among them are the following:

✦ **Table 1.10** Mean Compensation for Sport Marketing Executives

Major league teams	$79,560
League offices	77,500
College/university	44,930
Agencies	103,077
Minor league teams	50,698
Arenas/venues	63,684
Broadcast/media	118,269

Adapted, by permission, from C. Barr, M. McDonald, and W. Sutton, 2000, "Collegiate sport marketers: Job responsibilities and compensation structure," *International Sports Journal* 4(2): 64-77.

✦ More professional sport organizations are employing professional sales staffs that enjoy ongoing training and planning programs. Ron Seaver's National Sports Forum has served the industry for a decade, bringing the top marketing executives together for keynotes, round-tables, and workshops (www.sports-forum.com). Along similar lines, the National Association of Collegiate Directors of Athletics (NACDA) sponsors professional groups such as the National Association of Collegiate Marketing Administrators (NACMA). The International Association of Assembly Managers (IAAM) and the International Health, Racquet & Sports-club Association (IHRSA) offer marketing training programs for their industries. Many other formal organizations and consultants are providing information, training, and professional identity to men and women in the field. See appendix A for an extensive list.

✦ A number of new organizations have been created to develop collective strategies to market segments of the sport industry. For instance, horse racing's track owners, breeders, and events managers recently formed a new trade association, the National Thoroughbred Racing Association. After a sputtering start, the NTRA, with a $34 million budget, now provides a broad vision for marketing a sport that has staggered for a number of years (www.ntra.com). At the grassroots level, organizations such as the Women's Sports Foundation act as clearinghouses for the promotion of events like National Girls and Women in Sports Day. They also offer excellent information on grants, internships, and jobs (www.womens sportsfoundation.org).

✦ A number of journals and magazines, such as *Street & Smith's SportsBusiness Journal, Sports Business Daily, Team Marketing Report, Sport Marketing Quarterly,* the *Migala Report,* and the *International Journal of Sports Marketing and Sponsorship* provide forums for sharing the latest "best practices," research reports, and convention calendars. Industry governance leaders such as the NCAA are providing online resources such as the NCAA Basketball Marketing Resource, which provides "Divisions I, II, and III college basketball marketing directors with a collection of information on the practice of marketing basketball" (www.ncaa.org/bbp/basketball_marketing).

✦ Historians have recently rediscovered the genius of minority marketers like Rube Foster, who built the first stable professional baseball league for African American players in the 1920s. Although the industry still shades heavily to male and white, there has been progress for minorities. A good example is Latino Sports Marketing LLC, a full-service marketing and consulting firm that among other things sponsors an internship program (www.lsmllc.com).

As the field continues to progress, sport marketing will move back to a future that was recognized clearly by old-time "promoters" and "hustlers" such as Tex Rickard, Bill Veeck, and Don Canham.

Bill Veeck: Sport Marketing's Foremost Prophet

Bill Veeck (1914-1986) was bred to sport marketing. His father, William Veeck Sr., was a Chicago sportswriter who switched fields to become president of the Cubs. In the cozy confines of Wrigley Field, young Bill Jr. learned the trade of the baseball magnate, from the bottom up—working with the grounds and concessions crews or with the ticket office, like any good intern today. The short biography on his plaque in the National Baseball Hall of Fame sums up his rich and varied sports life:

BILL VEECK, OWNER OF INDIANS, BROWNS, AND WHITE SOX.

CREATED HEIGHTENED FAN INTEREST AT EVERY STOP WITH INGENIOUS PROMOTIONAL SCHEMES, FAN PARTICIPATION, EXPLODING SCOREBOARD, OUTRAGEOUS DOOR PRIZES, NAMES ON UNIFORMS.

SET M. L. ATTENDANCE RECORD WITH PENNANT-WINNER AT CLEVELAND IN 1948; WON AGAIN WITH "GO-GO" SOX IN 1959.

SIGNED A. L.'S FIRST BLACK PLAYER, LARRY DOBY, IN 1947 AND OLDEST ROOKIE, 42-YEAR-OLD SATCHEL PAIGE IN 1948.

A CHAMPION OF THE LITTLE GUY.

Marketing in today's complex sport marketplace requires Bill Veeck's timeless creativity and customer satisfaction, as well as the latest technology.
Courtesy of Brace Photo

He was a "champion of the little guy" not because he once used a midget as a pinch hitter, but because he believed that everyday fans were baseball's true royalty. His two classic books, *Veeck as in Wreck* and *The Hustler's Handbook,* still hold up as invaluable guidebooks for any would-be sport marketer or executive. He happily considered himself a hustler, but here was his definition: "An advertiser pays for his space. A promoter works out a quid pro quo. A hustler gets a free ride and makes it seem like he's doing you a favor." For high school and small college athletics directors or youth program administrators who need to cut deals on slim budgets, Veeck's hustler should be a prototype.

Bill Veeck also left a legacy of 12 commandments that capture an enduring vision for successful sport marketing:

1. Take your work very seriously. Go for broke and give it your all.

2. Never ever take yourself seriously.

3. Find yourself an alter ego and bond with him for the rest of your professional life.

4. Surround yourself with similarly dedicated soul mates, free spirits of whom you can ask why and why not. And who can ask the same thing of you.

5. In your hiring, be color blind, gender-blind, age and experience-blind. You never work for Bill Veeck. You work with him.

6. If you're a president, owner, or operator, attend every home game and never leave until the last out.

7. Answer all of your mail; you might learn something.

8. Listen and be available to your fans.

9. Enjoy and respect the members of the media, the stimulation and the challenge. The "them against us" mentality should only exist between the two teams on the field.

10. Create an aura in your city. Make people understand that unless they come to the ballpark, they will miss something.

11. If you don't think a promotion is fun, don't do it. Never insult your fans.

12. Don't miss the essence of what is happening at the moment. Let it happen. Cherish the moment and commit it to your memory.

Bill Veeck's 12 commandments offer an effective antidote to marketing myopia. (41)

12 commandments reprinted, by permission, from P. Williams, 2000, *Marketing your dreams: Business and life lessons from Bill Veeck, baseball's marketing genius* (Champaign, IL: Sports Publishing), XIV.

The Uniqueness of Sport Marketing

Overcoming sport marketing myopia requires an appreciation of this special domain of human experience. This book, in fact, rests on a simple premise: that humans view sport as a "special" experience or as having a special place in their lives, and that marketers must approach sport differently than they do used cars, donuts, or tax advice. This is not to say that attitudes or principles do not overlap to some extent. Much of the marketing process is similar, and some of the sharpest industry minds—such as Matt Levine or Dick Lipsey of Sports Business Research Net (SBRnet), the industry's biggest online database—came from a packaged-goods background. Both of these men, however, invested a great deal of time in learning about the special nature of the sport business. Distinct features of the sport domain appear in the product, market, finance, and promotion areas, which we discuss in the following sections. As we hope to convey, sport is different. Although to some extent one can argue that "marketing is marketing," the field is littered with the carcasses of firms (and people) that treated tennis, golf, and basketball as though they were the latest fashion design or tooth whitener.

The Sport Product

A product can be described generally as "any bundle or combination of qualities, processes, and capabilities (goods, services, and/or ideas) that a buyer expects will deliver want satisfaction." A peculiar bundling distinguishes the sport product, including at least the following elements: (42)

+ Playful competition, typically in some game form
+ A separation from "normal" space and time
+ Regulation by special rules
+ Physical prowess and physical training
+ Special facilities and special equipment

Figure 1.1 illustrates the importance that this special bundling has for the sport product. At its core, the sport product offers the consumer some basic benefit such as health, entertainment, sociability, or achievement. Of course, many other products may offer the same core benefit. The sport marketer must understand why a consumer chooses to satisfy a given want or need by purchasing a sport product rather than some other type of product. Why do some people seek achievement in sport while others prefer to raise prize tomatoes? Although research on such a question is sparse, we may assume that the preference relates partially to the generic product components of sport: emphasis on physical activity that is regulated in special game forms. At the same time, the golfers among this "sport" group might scorn tennis, and vice versa. The tennis players may be split into groups that prefer public courts and those that prefer private club membership. One can recognize the complex dynamics behind each level of segmentation (considered in later chapters). The fundamental point, however, is that the sport product is unique.

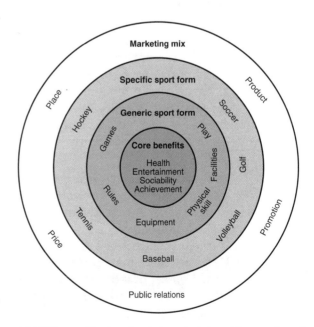

FIGURE 1.1 The bundle of characteristics of the sport product.

Additional elements of the basic sport product—the game or event—make it unusual. Some of these elements reflect the nature of sport as a "service": (43)

◆ *An intangible, ephemeral, experiential, and subjective nature.* Sports are expressions of our humanity; they can't be bottled like tonic water. Even tangible elements like equipment have little meaning outside the game or the event. Few products are open to such a wide array of interpretations by consumers. What each consumer sees in a sport is quite subjective, making it extremely difficult for the sport marketer to ensure a high probability of consumer satisfaction. As baseball executive Peter Bavasi once said: "Marketing baseball isn't the same as selling soap or bread. You're selling a memory, an illusion." Each fan and each active participant creates a different illusion. Each round of golf, each tennis match, each softball game brings a different experience. Equally important, consumers use sport to brand themselves in multiple ways. The same person in Seattle can easily say: I am a Ricky Cravens fan (NASCAR); I am a Storm fan (WNBA); I am a Red Sox fan; I am a Huskies fan. Each of these identities may embrace different aspects of the sport experience—speed and risk in NASCAR, team play in the WNBA, hope and redemption with the Red Sox, and community with the UW Huskies. Thus it is difficult to "sell" the benefits of consuming sport (compared to those of a car) because they are hard to pinpoint or describe. (44)

◆ *Strong personal and emotional identification.* As we will discuss in chapter 4, few products or services elicit passions and commitments like sports. Most readers will remember the first time they were "bitten" by a sports bug—golf, tennis, baseball, hockey, or whatever. The addiction for more is striking. Fan identification with players and teams has spawned its own nomenclature. For example, there's "BIRGing," or "basking in reflected glory," which can be seen in fans' use of the words "we," "us," and "our" when their favorites win, or CORFing ("casting off reflected failure")—as seen when the words "them" or "they" are used to discuss a loss. This strong identification is connected to the general feeling that "I could do that if only I had the chance." In the world of sports it sometimes seems that everyone is a passionate expert. No wonder the success of fantasy games, talk radio, and sport blogs.

◆ *Simultaneous production and consumption.* Sports are perishable commodities. As events, they must be presold, and there are no inventories. Sport consumers are typically also producers; they help create the game or event that they simultaneously consume. Although DVDs, videotapes, or newspaper accounts extend product life in a different form, the original event is fleeting. No marketer can sell a seat for yesterday's game, yesterday's ski-lift ticket, or last night's 10 p.m. time slot on Court Number 1. Day-of-game sales alone are not sufficient, because inclement weather or some other factor may diminish gate sales. Preselling, especially of season-ticket programs or yearly memberships, guarantees a minimum revenue.

◆ *Dependence on social facilitation.* The loneliness of the long-distance runner notwithstanding, sport usually occurs in a public setting. Enjoyment of sport—as player or fan—is almost always a function of interaction with other people. Typically, less than 2 percent of those attending collegiate and professional sport events attend by themselves. Only a few sports, such as running, can be undertaken by a single person. And who watches the Super Bowl alone? Consequently, sport marketers need to recognize the central role of social facilitation.

◆ *Inconsistency and unpredictability.* A baseball game played today will be different from next week's game even if the starting lineups are the same. Numerous factors such as weather, injuries, momentum, rivalries, and crowd response create the logic of "On any given day . . ." Who can predict a no-hitter, or a dog of a game, or the sudden squall on a mountain? Unpredictability is one of the lures of sport, but it makes the marketer's job more complex. New York Mets marketing vice president Michael Aronin, who previously spent 13 years with Clairol, put it this way: "Before, I had control of the product, I could design it the way I wanted it to be. Here the product changes every day and you've got to adapt quickly to the changes." (45)

◆ *Core-product control beyond marketer's hands.* As Aronin suggested, most sport marketers have little control of their core product—the game itself. General managers make trades. Leagues make schedules and game rules. Although there are clear cases of core-product decisions with an eye on marketing (in baseball, one such decision was the designated-hitter rule to create more offense), these decisions are still typically made by coaches and administrators whose agendas are often the game's "purity" or "equalizing offense and defense." For sport team marketers this means selling the "sizzle" as much as the "steak." For Boston Marathon managers, it means selling T-shirts, collector's-item lithographs, and special marathon-label wine. Only one person finishes first, but everyone can have a "winning" memento. (46)

The Sport Market

Following are some special features of the sport market:

◆ *Many sport organizations simultaneously compete and cooperate.* Few sport organizations can exist in isolation. Professional, intercollegiate, and interscholastic sports require other franchises and schools in order to have meaningful competition. The same is true for private and amateur sport clubs.

◆ *Product salience and strong personal identification lead many sport consumers to consider themselves experts.* The "expert mentality" was clearly revealed two decades ago in a famous national survey. Among the respondents, 52 percent said yes when asked, "Do you think you

All of these spectators are golf fans, but each one brings unique experiences to this tournament, and each takes something unique from the tournament. This is the experiential and ephemeral nature of sport consumption.
© AP Photo/Michael S. Green

could play for a professional team if you practiced?"; 74 percent said yes when asked, "Do you think that you could do a better job of officiating than most officials?"; and 51 percent said yes to the question, "Do you think that you could do a better job of coaching than the average coach?" No other business is viewed so simplistically and with such personal identification by its consumers. (47)

✦ *Demand tends to fluctuate widely.* Athletic club members crowd facilities during winter "prime-time" hours and then trade their indoor sports for something else in the summer, when they crowd public tennis courts or golf courses. Each sport form tends to have an annual life cycle, and spectator sport fans are especially prone to quick changes in interest. Season openers bring high hopes and high demand; but midseason slumps, injuries, or weak competition may kill ticket sales.

✦ *Sport has an almost universal appeal and pervades all elements of life.* Although there is clearly a "Western" tradition in most of the world's most popular sports, there is also clearly a wide world of sport. A recent book even claimed to answer the question of "How Soccer Explains the World." What appear to be simple games—soccer, hockey, or basketball—link easily to other facets of our humanity, for better or worse. (48)

✦ *Eating and drinking.* From the Wheaties box to the Bud Light Penguin, sport images are part of the consumption experience. Clearly the "couch potato" is typically watching sports while munching and slurping. Sport brands such as ESPN have moved into the restaurant business to exploit this widespread association.

✦ *Sex.* The sexuality in sport has not only involved men leering at gymnasts and figure skaters. As early as 1975, the Golden State Warriors appealed to female fans with ad campaigns like "We've got five men in shorts who can go all night." Although gender stereotypes and homophobia still abound in the sport world, the marketplace is much more open and complex than ever before. Women soccer players are now embraced as athletes while male soccer players are pursued as sex symbols.

✦ *Religion.* For many people, sports open the gates, not to Sybaris but rather to salvation. According to sport philosopher Michael Novak, sport has many quasi-religious properties, such as ceremonies, asceticism, sacred grounds, and symbols. In some cases, sport seems to transcend religious differences. For example, when the Iranian soccer team qualified for the 1998 World Cup, celebrations in the streets of Tehran joined fundamentalist clerics with liberal university students in ways unimagined in a nation torn within itself over religion, politics, and economics. For that moment, the only ideology that mattered was winning soccer games. Said one engineer, struck by the flow of alcohol (forbidden in Islam), "Not in our wildest dreams would we have thought that people could be acting out this way." In 2001, the hottest ticket in Belfast, Northern Ireland, was at the Odyssey Center, for a new professional hockey team, the Belfast Giants. The team's managing director firmly believed that the Giants' popularity emanated from hockey's lack of any tradition with either Protestants or Catholics in the area. As a city counselor put it: "There's no baggage." Hockey could attract fans of either religious persuasion. (49)

✦ *Politics.* Sports have been an integral part of politics since the ancient Greek tyrants invested their money and names in athletic games (e.g., the Olympics) to secure popularity. In the 1840s and 1850s, boxers sometimes served as "shoulder hitters" who coaxed voters to choose a certain ticket. By the 20th century it was important for any aspiring presidential candidate to show he was a sportsman or an athlete, or at least a fan. Dwight Eisenhower was criticized for his abundant golfing. The Kennedys showcased their touch football games, while hiding JFK's early morning rounds of golf at Hyannisport. Richard Nixon was notorious for (among other things) his love of football. His athletic talents focused on bowling. Bill Clinton and George W. Bush encouraged photo opportunities of their running, because neither had much athletic talent. Perhaps the most interesting intrusion into politics, however, was the use of sports to define target demographics. Bill Clinton famously appealed to soccer moms in 1996. In 2004, George Bush announced that he would win a newly defined voter segment—the "NASCAR dads." He even flew Air Force One to Daytona in early 2004 so he could deliver one of the most famous lines in all of American sports: "Gentlemen, start your engines." Neither "soccer mom" nor "NASCAR dad" represented a clearly defined or empirical segment of voters, but that did not matter. The names resonated with American sporting life, so they stuck. George Bush was not content to ride a NASCAR draft; he also wrapped himself in Olympic rings by running ads during the Athens games that flashed the flags of Iraq and Afghanistan over a voice that said: "At this Olympics there will be two more free nations—and two fewer terrorist nations." If George Bush leveraged NASCAR and the Olympics for votes, Venezuelan president Hugo Chavez resorted to an old "bread and circuses" technique as he geared up for a recall election in the spring of 2004. He added NBA games and other international sport events to the normally drab content on government-run television. During one L.A. Lakers game, the narrator conveyed Chavez's sports and socialism agenda: "It's a free throw for Karl Malone. The Venezuelan revolution [also] makes you free." (50)

In warmer months, many recreational exercisers take to the outdoors, leaving gyms and health clubs to deal with the seasonal decrease in demand for their services.
© Human Kinetics

Sport Finance

The financing of sport encompasses the following special features:

✦ *It is difficult to price the individual sport product unit by traditional job costing.* For example, it is virtually impossible for the sport marketer to allocate fixed and operating costs to the individual ticket or membership. How can one account for the "possible" use of an usher, an instructor, an attendant, or a shower? Further, the marginal cost of providing an additional product unit is typically small. Therefore, pricing the sport product is often based on the marketer's sense of consumer demand—for certain seats, for certain times of day, for certain privileges.

✦ *The price of the sport product itself is invariably quite small in comparison to the total cost paid by the consumer.* As we will see in chapter 10, marketers must recognize the "hidden" costs of sports. The cost of tickets to a ball game may be only one third of a family's total costs, which include travel, parking, hot dogs, drinks, and merchandise—all perhaps controlled by someone other than the team hosting the event.

✦ *Indirect revenues are frequently greater than direct operating revenues.* Because consumers are (and should be) cost sensitive, income from fans or club members is often not enough to cover total expenses, especially debt service to the shiny, high-tech facilities that consumers demand. In pro sports, the strain is magnified by undisciplined owners who have driven player salaries so high. The direct income–expense gap has focused more attention on media and sponsor revenues. The quest for television and signage extends to all levels and segments of the sport industry, in part because the money is there. A good example is the NCAA. Almost 90 percent of the NCAA's total revenues for 2004-2005 ($485.7 million) came from "television and marketing rights fees." And almost all of this amount was from a contract for "March Madness," the men's Division I basketball tournament. By contrast, the NHL has suffered for years without a lucrative national television contract. This, more than anything, accounts for the financial instability that led to the lockout that wiped out the entire 2004-2005 season, an unprecedented event. (51)

Sport Promotion

Promoting sport is not as easy as it seems, despite widespread media attention. Consider the following:

✦ *The widespread media exposure is a double-edged sword*. Unlike a hardware store, sport teams get "free" promotions daily, in the newspapers, on the radio, and on television. Cases in point: In 1997, the *Chicago Sun-Times* and the *Chicago Tribune* published 6,259 articles mentioning Bill Clinton, the elected president and the "leader of the free world." Michael Jordan was mentioned in 4,173 articles. A recent economic impact study by Price/McNabb (North Carolina) estimated that the University of Tennessee at Chattanooga men's basketball team generated $22 million of free media exposure through its 1997 Sweet Sixteen run. At a time of great competition in college admissions, any president or trustee would take notice. On the one hand, this exposure is a blessing, particularly for financially strapped programs at the grassroots level. At the same time, free exposure can lead to laziness, arrogance, and amnesia toward fans. (52)

✦ *Media and sponsors emphasize "celebrities."* Sport marketers—as we will see in chapter 16—work hard to shape their organization's image. This becomes problematic with so much sponsor and media attention focused on a few celebrities, whose expanded egos can lead to wholesale problems both inside and outside the locker room.

A Model of the Sport Industry

Every industry has some discernible shape or form, defined by the ways organizations align. Sport is no different. Theorists refer to these shapes or forms as models. At the same time, any model is a snapshot frozen in time. All industries change their shape. In this final section, we offer a model for understanding the shape of the current industry, as well as a description of the consolidation that is creating important changes in the ways products are produced and distributed to sport consumers.

Several valuable models outline various "segments" of the sport industry. Naturally, any model is to some degree arbitrary. Older models of sport, for instance, stressed a distinct line between professional and amateur organizations. In the last 20 years, however, amateurism has eroded in sport. The Olympics, once the bastion of strict amateurism, are now open to professionals in most sports, depending on the eligibility codes of the various international sport federations. So the old models of the sport industry—cut along "amateur–professional" lines—make little sense these days. In our model of the industry, segments correspond to the organizations' primary marketing functions.

✦ To provide "packaged" events to spectators at the venue or via the mass media.

Professional team sport franchises
Professional tours such as golf and tennis
Arenas, stadiums, coliseums
Racetracks

All of these entities have a common, primary objective: to create an event their target consumers will buy, either live or via the media.

✦ To provide facilities, equipment, and programming to players, who then produce the game form.

College or high school intramurals
Country clubs, resorts, marinas
Commercial facilities (e.g., racquet clubs and bowling alleys)
Corporate, industrial, or military recreation
Camps (e.g., Five-Star Basketball)
Public and nonprofit agencies (e.g., YMCAs, YWCAs, and parks)
Sporting goods companies (Nike, Adidas)
Board game and video game companies (EA, Sega)

Although some of these organizations also host "packaged" events with an eye on spectator ticket sales, their primary objective ends with players playing the sport. When these organizations run events for spectator revenue, they often simply host a governing body that runs the event. This is normal, for instance, when golf clubs host a PGA or LPGA event.

✦ To provide "packaged" games or events for spectators as well as facilities, equipment, and programming for players.
  Intercollegiate athletics
  Interscholastic athletics

College and high school athletics programs continue to walk a tightrope between their "amateur/educational" functions and their bottom-line needs to aggressively generate revenues to pay for their programs.

✦ To provide general administrative support, control, and publicity to other sport organizations and people.
  Regulatory agencies, leagues, or conferences
  Sport media
  Sport sponsors
  Agents
  Management, research, and consulting groups

This segment has seen enormous growth in the last decade. New leagues and governing bodies have grown with the increase in television and sponsor revenues. Likewise, new consulting and research services have jumped into the expanding marketplace.

Consolidation in the Sport Industry

The model just described helps to explain how certain organizations share common missions and objectives, which help to shape the industry as a whole. Like most industries, however, sport is dynamic. For instance, the American economy has seen many cycles of "merger mania" and consolidation. In the late 1800s, cutthroat capitalist competition led to huge monopolies and trusts in steel, railroads, processed foods, and oil. Not to be outdone, some National League baseball owners hatched a plan in 1901 to consolidate ownership into a central trust that would control salaries and redistribute players every season, to ensure better competition. Critics called this structure "syndicate baseball." Although the revolution failed quickly, it stands as a prototype for the centralized ownership structure—now called "single entity"—used in recent leagues such as Major League Soccer and the WNBA. In the last decade, conglomerates have risen across the sport landscape. This has been especially evident in four areas: (1) the team–media connection, (2) sporting goods, (3) skiing, and (4) talent or events agencies.

From Media Teams to Team-Owned Media

One hundred years ago, the big businesses in sport were breweries and trolley companies. Both had something to gain from the connection. Fans drank beer and they needed a way to get to the game. The 1990s saw media/entertainment conglomerates gobbling up sport properties at all points of the distribution chain. The following were the big three rivals:

✦ *Eisner/Disney.* By the late 1990s, Michael Eisner's Disney empire owned the NHL Mighty Ducks, MLB's Anaheim Angels, ABC, ESPN, and a World Sports Center in Orlando, which was the home of the Harlem Globetrotters and the Amateur Athletic Union.

✦ *Murdoch/Fox.* Rupert Murdoch's News Corp. and its Fox Network had already shaken up the American television landscape with *The Simpsons* and *NFL Football* (wrestled from

CBS). When Disney bought ESPN, the dominant sport cable channel, Murdoch countered with his Fox Sportsnet strategy (outlined in chapter 15). Not to be outdone on the team front, Murdoch purchased the L.A. Dodgers in 1997, as a marquee franchise to accompany his minority holdings in other sport teams.

◆ *Turner/Time Warner.* With Ted Turner, it was personal. He just didn't like Rupert Murdoch. Turner was one of the great entrepreneurs in television history. His TBS superstation proved that sports and reruns could make money nationwide, even if the schedule was packed with Turner's Atlanta Braves and Hawks. His CNN succeeded beyond everyone's expectations. When Turner could not buy his way into competition with Disney and Murdoch, he sold to Time Warner, which now had several major sport properties to feature along with Bugs Bunny.

But a funny thing happened to all of this media-driven strategy. The moguls discovered that their media "brands" and media expertise did not ensure successful or profitable sport franchises. And so Disney sold the Angels in 2003 and the Ducks in 2005; Murdoch sold the Dodgers in early 2004. Turner's fortunes took an even wider swing. Time Warner merged with AOL in 2000, creating the biggest gorilla of all the conglomerates. But the gorilla was soon sinking in a swamp of debt. In 2003, AOL-Time Warner sold the NBA's Hawks and the NHL's Thrashers. Turner resigned his position as vice chairman.

None of this, however, dampened enthusiasm for team–media "synergy." There are still plenty of connections. Comcast has ownership interests in the Philadelphia Flyers and Sixers. What appeared to change was the preferred scope and direction of ownership—from national or international media giants owning regional teams to regional teams owning regional media. Two of the most successful franchises in North America—the Yankees and the Red Sox—set the pace with ownership interests in their own cable networks. (53)

Sporting Goods

Mergers are an old story in this business. In the late 1800s, the Spalding Company became the force in the industry by gobbling up rivals. For much of this century, sporting goods were dominated by the "big four": Spalding, MacGregor, Rawlings, and Wilson. Everyone knows today's powerhouses—Reebok, Adidas, and Nike. At the retail level, chains of both full-line (Sports Authority) and specialty (Nevada Bob's) stores have grabbed more and more market share. A 1998 report from the National Sporting Goods Association showed that sales in chains of 10 or more stores had increased from 21 percent of all sales in 1982 to 46 percent in 1992. By the end of the 1990s, sales for these chains exceeded 60 percent of all retail sporting goods sales. According to the National Sporting Goods Association, sales in U.S sporting goods stores (including full-line and specialty stores) increased 25 percent between 1997 and 2002, from $20.04 billion to $25.02 billion. During the same period of low inflation, the population had only grown by 5.6 percent, so these sales figures represented real growth. At the same time, however, the number of stores had decreased by 9.1 percent. Fewer stores were selling more. (54)

The Ski Industry

In 1961, there were about 1,000 American ski resorts, most of them small, family-run enterprises. By 1984-1985, the number had dropped to 727. By 1996, it was 519. By 2004, it was under 500. There is little room for the mom-and-pop ski area; the costs for snowmaking, grooming, ultrafast lifts, and plush restaurants or luxury condos are too steep. "Build it and they will come" has a different meaning in skiing. In 1998, six companies owned 50 of the top 75 resorts. The biggest conglomerates are American Skiing Company (ASC), Vail Resorts, and Intrawest. Said Michael Berry of the National Ski Areas Association: "The small guys, to be very honest with you, are working hard to stay in business." Berry's implied question was, Could they manage to stay in business? (55)

Marketing Players and Events

Except in boxing, agents are a recent phenomenon in the sport world, created by the rise of unions and television. The biggest company is International Management Group (IMG), founded and run by Mark McCormack, who built an empire starting with Arnold Palmer and Jack Nicklaus. Talent from IMG is now everywhere, even at the Vatican (IMG has promoted recent papal tours). Rival firms such as ProServ and Advantage International offered limited competition to IMG—until the late 1990s, when a new conglomerate called the Marquee Group began to shake up the landscape, buying ProServ, ProServ Television, and QBQ Entertainment. In May 1998, another, SFX Entertainment, purchased David Falk's F.A.M.E., home of Michael Jordan. Next, SFX bought the Marquee Group. Then Clear Channel bought SFX. It became difficult for industry insiders to keep track of the shakeouts that occurred during these mergers. Although there might always be a niche for a maverick like Hollywood's Jerry Maguire, a few giant firms appear to be cornering the market for the most lucrative sport talent. (56)

Bigger Is Not Always Better

The sport business, like most of its counterparts, has never been a pure enterprise. Cheats, swindlers, and opportunists have operated openly for centuries. Beer barons have owned franchises solely to sell their suds to thirsty patrons on hot summer days. Radio and television announcers have often been handpicked shills. Although today's executives are more polished, do the more complex connections of these new corporate behemoths create unacceptable conflicts of interest? Some think so. For instance, in April 1998, Chris Berman of ESPN flew out to Anaheim for the Angels' opening-day festivities. Unfortunately, he wasn't on assignment for ESPN's *SportsCenter*. He was a promoter for Disney and Michael Eisner, referring to the conglomerate as "we." One sportswriter correctly referred to Berman as an "on-field carnival barker." (57)

Could the public ever believe that ESPN—so righteous in its attacks on corruption in sport—will be objective in reporting on the Disney empire? And what about the growing conflicts of the agent/marketing/events firms such as IMG? When IMG produces a made-for-television golf, tennis, or skating event, filled with its own stable of athletes (who may or may not receive guaranteed appearance fees), can this be legitimately promoted as a "competition"? Most of the public recognizes that professional wrestling is phony. In the world of conglomerate sports, wrestling may not be alone. NBC sank millions into the XFL, its joint venture with the World Wrestling Federation. But all the media genius and promotional expertise could not rescue a product that was inferior at its core. The players were simply not "prime time," so the XFL could not be positioned as a major league operation. And minor league sports simply don't sell in prime time.

Wrap-Up

Sport is a distinct enterprise. It cannot be marketed like soap or tax advice. A sport marketer is asked to market a product that is unpredictable, inconsistent, and open to subjective interpretation. The marketer must undertake this task in a highly competitive marketplace with a much lower promotional budget than those of similarly sized organizations in other industries. Finally, the sport marketer must do all this with only limited direct control over the product mix. On the bright side, the media are anxious to give wide exposure to the general product, and many opportunities exist to generate revenue through associations with business and industry.

Activities

1. List three reasons for the great need for better sport marketing.
2. Define marketing myopia; give three examples in the sport industry.
3. On the basis of figure 1.1, discuss how two golf players might consume very different products in terms of benefits, sport forms, or marketing mix.
4. Find the names of four sport organizations from a major newspaper to illustrate each segment of the industry identified in this chapter.
5. Discuss the three elements of sport that you believe most contribute to the uniqueness of sport marketing.
6. Identify a sport or a sport organization on the rise and one on the decline. What types of evidence support the notions of either rise or decline? Is the change caused by the "invisible hand" of the market or by the "visible hand" of marketing?

Your Marketing Plan

In the following chapters, you will be asked to develop your own marketing plan, step by step. This activity will allow you to apply the topics that are presented in each chapter. Take advantage of these opportunities, and have fun!

Chapter 2

Strategic Marketing Management

Objectives

◆ To recognize the interacting components of the marketing management process.

◆ To appreciate the core elements of market analysis, product concept, and product position.

◆ To understand the distinctions among the five Ps of sport marketing: product, price, place, promotion, and public relations.

Branding With Music

Sport teams have been "branding" themselves with music for at least a century. At the "Big House" and at Yost Arena, the University of Michigan band rouses all Wolverines with "Hail to the Victors," a song written in 1898, but a song that resonates just as well today:

> Hail! to the victors valiant
> Hail! to the conqu'ring heroes
> Hail! Hail! to Michigan,
> the champions of the West!

And anyone who follows English soccer will (often tearfully) associate an old American show tune— "You'll Never Walk Alone"—with Liverpool FC. In the last two decades, however, America's professional sport teams and leagues have made a calculated decision to wrap their products in more contemporary rock, country, or rap music. This was part of the larger strategy of sport organizations and media conglomerates like Disney and News Corp. Both sides envisioned greater popularity and profits by repositioning sports as "entertainment," especially for a younger generation. As John Vidalin, senior marketing director for the Washington Caps, said in 2003: "It's a music video and video game generation that's coming to our games now. The days of people sitting in the stands and watching just the sport have gone by the wayside. You have to give them more. Lots more." (1)

The National Football League used its biggest television platform—the Super Bowl—to fuse football with "edgy" entertainment in hopes of attracting and keeping a younger, male audience. If the first three decades of the Super Bowl halftime show featured themes such as "Mardi Gras," a "Salute to

Hollywood's 100th Anniversary," and a "Salute to Motown," the millennium's turn saw a shift toward themeless rock, pop, rap, and hip hop, featuring the likes of Aerosmith, U2, Christina Aguilera, and No Doubt. Then the roof (and the cup) came off in the 2004 Super Bowl, when Justin Timberlake ripped off Janet Jackson's bodice, revealing more than the public, or Congress, or the FCC could take.

The NFL cried foul on MTV, who had purchased the rights to produce the halftime show. Janet claimed a wardrobe malfunction. These struck many as lame excuses. Throughout the 1990s, the NFL had moved closer and closer to the world of MTV. As early as 1999, this strategy backfired, when the league had to pull an ad that dubbed rapper Eminem's "My Name Is . . ." over visuals of stars such as Joe Montana and Joe Theisman, creating a "My name is Joe" theme. NFL executives said they did not realize that Eminem's song included references to rape, mutilation, and suicide. The NFL's director of corporate communications unconvincingly suggested that "as these things bubble up through popular culture, they lose their sting. The ad doesn't tie back to the song." Few believed this notion, given that the NFL was taking more chances with its repositioning strategy. The Timberlake–Jackson episode should have been no surprise. MTV had produced the Super Bowl halftime show in 2001, which featured ample amounts of crotch grabbing by NSYNC. As one critic put it: "If the NFL is partnering with MTV, what did it expect to get, Snow White?" The NFL promised to take back full control of its Super Bowl show. Would it also rethink its strategy of repositioning its product as "edgy" entertainment? (2)

Consistent, marketing-minded leadership—complete with a vision and a plan—is a necessity in today's competitive environment. For the high school athletics director, the racquetball club manager, or the commissioner of a professional league, the absence of this type of leadership is a sure ticket to disaster. Of course, having a plan does not ensure success. The NFL's Super Bowl halftime fiasco and the failures of the WUSA or the XFL were failures in deliberate, calculated marketing strategy. The lack of a strategy, however, simply multiplies the odds of failure. In this chapter, we lay out the basic elements required for strategic marketing leadership. We refer to these elements as the marketing management process, a process that combines both strategy (the big picture) and tactics (the details of a plan). Subsequent chapters in this book flesh out the various tactical steps in the marketing management process. This chapter places each step in the broader perspective of strategy.

Sport Strategy Is More Than Locker Room Talk

Despite its stumbling effort on the Super Bowl halftime show, the NFL, like the NBA, remained an industry leader over the last two decades, with clear strategies to develop and position their products in the marketplace of consumer needs. While these leagues face their own challenges to retain prominence and profitability, their success came from carefully developed visions and plans—game plans, to use a sport term. In fact, many successful organizations have borrowed the notion of "game plans" from the successful coaches who have always evaluated their own talent, carefully scouted their opponents, and developed their tactics and playbooks accordingly. In simple terms, that is the essence of strategy, and it is spread from the locker rooms to the front offices of the sport industry.

In its simplest sense, strategy entails setting long-term goals and developing plans to achieve those goals. This requires a continual analysis of the environment and the organization. The challenges of today's marketplace have forced sport executives to think much more strategically, as shown in the following examples from tennis, golf, and ice hockey. (3)

Tennis

In 1960, American tennis had some 5.6 million "participants" (people playing at least once per year). By 1974, tennis was booming with 34 million participants. Then came the "big slump" in the 1980s, as participation dwindled to 13 million in 1985. By 1995, tennis was still only half as popular as it had been 20 years before. The problems in tennis were recognized in 1995 when the Tennis Industry Association, or TIA (a trade association), announced a strategic "Initiative to Grow the Game" from the grassroots level upward. As Brad Patterson, TIA executive director, put it, each tournament, manufacturer, club, association, and pro tour had been marketing itself: "The fact is that nobody was marketing tennis." Tennis, in effect, had lost its position to aerobics, in-line skating, basketball, and other competitors. In the last decade, the United States Tennis Association (USTA) and the TIA have developed a range of programs under such banners as "Play Tennis America" and "Tennis Welcome Center," which included free clinics, free equipment, and organized leagues for all ages. As Patterson reminded his colleagues, "What was missing was that we were not telling people to come out and play tennis." It is difficult to gauge the success of these campaigns. The tennis industry claims that participation is on the rise, while statistics from the Sporting Goods Manufacturers Association and the National Sporting Goods Association (NSGA) suggest flat or declining participation among both casual and frequent players.

In the spectator arena, the USTA recently sought to boost its sagging tournament ratings by creating a "series" with a point system, along the lines of NASCAR. They needed to do something fast. A 2002 ESPN Sports Poll had reported that almost 57 percent of respondents had indicated they were "not at all interested" in the U.S Open—the marquee event. In a 2004 Turnkey Sports Poll, 52.4 percent of sport industry executives felt that getting "recognizable players" was the biggest challenge facing pro tennis. Tennis has a long way to go, but at least it has begun to pursue an integrated strategy. (4)

Golf

In the mid-1990s, golf participation was stagnant. In 1997, the World Golf Foundation (WGF)—a nonprofit entity funded by the PGA, USGA, LPGA, Calloway, Titleist, and others—announced a campaign called "The First Tee," which aimed to develop hundreds of new golf facilities around the country in the next decade. Former President George Bush agreed to serve as honorary chairman of the initiative. The effort stemmed from a simple conclusion that the game of golf was limited only by the availability of facilities. Tiger Woods might excite millions, but millions couldn't take up the game without available, affordable facilities. At the WGF's first GOLF 20/20 conference in November 2000, Chairman Tim Finchem set three major goals for golf to achieve by 2020:

Reach 55 million participants

Reach 1 billion rounds played

Achieve a comparable level of interest in the United States to professional football

By 2002, the number of courses in the United States had increased to 14,725 from 13,528 in 1998. NSGA statistics indicated a rise in the number of one-time players—up to 28.3 million. At the same time, however, the number of frequent players (40+ days per year) had plateaued at 6 million. The number of rounds played had actually decreased in the near term, from 518 million in 2000 to 502 million in 2002. Rounds played continued to slip in 2003, to 495 million. The industry was still struggling to unite around a clear strategy. Many experts felt that too many courses had been built—that the issue was oversupply, not underdemand. While Finchem and the WGF stood firmly behind a grassroots strategy that built the base of novice players, including those in inner cities, Acushnet's chairman, Wally Uihlein, was less sanguine: "GOLF 20/20 is a noble effort, but it's in default and denial of golf's middle-class requisite." Uihlein claimed that Finchem was "a little bit naïve as to our ability to bring in non-middle class components to prop up the numbers." To Rich Luker, who guided the Chilton Sports Poll in the 1990s and now heads the Leisure Intelligence Group, the major problem was not the availability of golf greens; it was the availability of time. Five or more hours for a round of golf is too much in an age of multitasking: "Golf doesn't meet the relevance of a generation for whom option, speed and simplicity are the most important things." Like tennis, golf had a long way to go, but at least it recognized the need for strategy. (5)

Hockey

In the fall of 2004, 32 stakeholders met in St. Paul, Minnesota, for a "Grow Hockey Summit" under the aegis of the International Hockey Industry Association. The IHIA's founding members include major manufacturers such as Itech Sport Products, Nike Bauer Hockey, Sher-Wood Hockey, Hespeler Hockey, and Louisville Hockey, all of whom have an obvious stake in growth. The summit attracted representatives from the NHL, the NHLPA, USA Hockey, Hockey Canada, and the International Ice Hockey Federation. Although the group was helpless to stop a lockout of the world's top hockey league, they did agree on an issue demanding concerted effort: the slow overall participation growth, slacking along at 1 to 2 percent, although much better for females. The summit also recognized the importance of three youth segments: 5- to 8-year-old entry-level players, 10- to 14-year-olds thinking of leaving the sport, and 18- to 34-year-olds entering or reentering. In all cases, the obstacles to growth revolve around cost, time, availability of ice, and perceptions of violence. Attendees circulated a press release in which they committed to developing a strategic plan that included the following:

Increasing accessibility through an emphasis on fun

Partnerships with kids' organizations

Increased skill focus

Renewed focus on ice, in-line, street, and other types of hockey

An international "Grow Hockey Day"

Ties with the retail community, such as a "Welcome to Hockey" kit

Targeted communication to "hockey moms"

Development of "First Goal," a collaboration to include equipment discounts and a mass media campaign

Golf participation is on the decline at the start of the new millennium.

© Human Kinetics

With the NHL in a lockout mode for the 2004-2005 season, hockey was in dire need of a grassroots growth strategy. (6)

Tennis, golf, and hockey leaders began to realize that marketing their sports required broad, integrated efforts—campaigns that would transcend old divisions between amateurs and professionals, between grass roots and elites, and between manufacturers and governing bodies. As the golf, tennis, and hockey industry groups demonstrate, marketing strategy is not a privilege reserved for the "big-time" leagues and teams. It is a necessity for all organizations, all the way down to the grassroots level. In fact, given the financial squeeze at the grassroots level, one might say that marketing strategy is even more essential there. Grassroots leaders cannot defer their marketing efforts simply because they lack a support staff. David Hoch, athletics director at Eastern Technical High School in Baltimore County, Maryland, stated the matter quite clearly: "For many athletic directors, the first stumbling block to starting a marketing program is the work it adds to your already hectic schedule." But, added Hoch, marketing can no longer be viewed as an "extra or frivolous effort. Marketing is just as important as scheduling facilities, evaluating coaches, and the numerous other responsibilities" that any high school AD must address on a daily basis. (7)

Implementing a Sport Marketing Program

The elements of marketing strategy can be conceptualized in models; marketing theorist Philip Kotler has called one model the marketing management process (MMP). We have blended Kotler's model with others (see figure 2.1) to create our version, which we consider both a step-by-step process and a way of thinking. As some of the activities at the end of the chapter suggest, the MMP can be used to develop a marketing plan. But the marketing plan must be integrated into an organization's larger strategic plan, which includes finance, asset management, resource allocation, and personnel management, among other elements. The MMP is the backbone of marketing; it emphasizes interdependencies at all stages. (8)

Although subsequent chapters examine in greater detail the MMP steps (e.g., research, product development, pricing, and promotion), a brief introduction is important here if only to emphasize that decision making is an ongoing, circular process. There is really no off-season in the business world of sport (see the sidebar on strategic opportunism on page 46). As figure 2.1 suggests, a marketing plan aligns tactical details and operations (such as pricing) with broader organizational strategies (such as setting attendance goals). To use a sport metaphor, tactics are the offensive and defensive plays or sets, used for various situations, that collectively make up a strategic game plan for victory. The game plan provides a broad direction to the coach or quarterback, who will pick the specific tactics to be used during the game itself. This chapter introduces that important blend of strategy and tactics.

The strategic steps of the MMP, and their relation to the remaining book chapters, are as follows:

Visualize and position the organization vis-à-vis the market (chapters 3-5, 19)

Develop objectives (chapter 6)

Develop a marketing mix and plan (chapters 7-16)

Integrate the marketing plan into the broader organizational strategy (chapter 17)

Control and evaluate all elements of the marketing plan (chapters 17, 18)

Strategic Step 1: Visualize and Position the Organization Vis-à-Vis the Market

In the following sections, we provide examples of the way core vision and ideology should inform decisions. We also discuss the importance of using a technique known as a SWOT

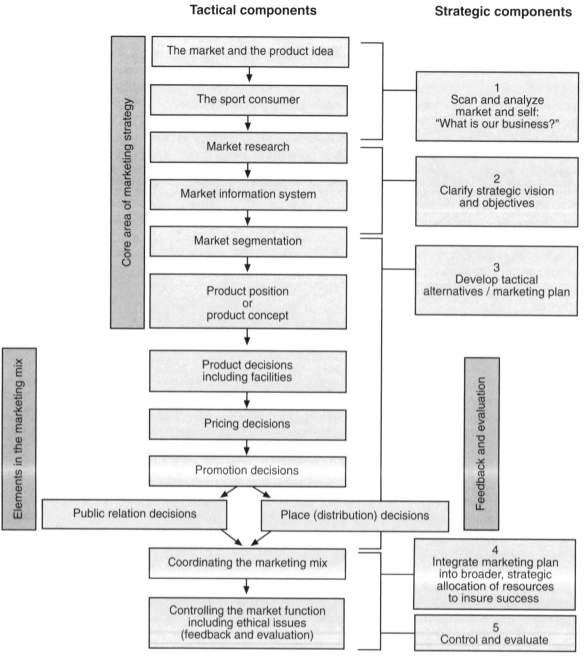

Tactical components

Strategic components

Core area of marketing strategy

- The market and the product idea
- The sport consumer
- Market research
- Market information system
- Market segmentation
- Product position or product concept

Elements in the marketing mix

- Product decisions including facilities
- Pricing decisions
- Promotion decisions
- Public relation decisions
- Place (distribution) decisions
- Coordinating the marketing mix
- Controlling the market function including ethical issues (feedback and evaluation)

Feedback and evaluation

1
Scan and analyze market and self: "What is our business?"

2
Clarify strategic vision and objectives

3
Develop tactical alternatives / marketing plan

4
Integrate marketing plan into broader, strategic allocation of resources to insure success

5
Control and evaluate

FIGURE 2.1 The marketing management process in sport.

Adapted, by permission, from B. Mullin, 2000, Characteristics of sports marketing. In *Successful sport management,* edited by H. Appenzeller and G. Lewis (Durham, NC: Carolina Academic Press).

analysis (strengths, weaknesses, opportunities, threats) that involves the use of marketing information systems, as well as spotting fads and trends (and determining which is which).

Core Vision and Ideology

When we say "visualize" the organization, we borrow from sport psychologists, who teach athletes to "visualize" the process and outcomes of performance. Above all, this means that any strategic plan must operate within the framework of the organization's core vision and ideology, as James C. Collins and Jerry I. Porras argued in *Built to Last: Successful Habits of Visionary Companies,* one of the most successful management books of the last decade. Collins and Porras examined the performance of a set of companies over the last century. What distinguished the firms that seemed "built to last"? In their words:

the fundamental distinguishing characteristic of the most enduring and successful corporations is that they preserve a cherished core ideology while simultaneously stimulating progress and change in everything that is not part of their core ideology. Put another way, they distinguish their timeless core values and enduring core purpose (which should never change) from their operating practices and business strategies (which should be changing in response to a changing world).

To some degree, the NFL has had to ask itself, Does a raunchy halftime display at the Super Bowl represent our core vision as an organization? Such questions have been equally troubling for school and college athletics, whose leaders must balance commercial realities with "educational" core visions. It has not been an easy path. But once again, the fundamental task lies in the effort to develop, recognize, and sustain a core vision, even as the organization changes. (9)

In the last decade, Ohio State University made such an effort under the leadership of athletics director Andy Geiger. OSU Athletics is a mighty big boat to steer—its 36 programs make it one of the nation's broadest and most expensive departments (with a budget over $80 million). Its operating waters are filled with shoals and sharks, as the Maurice Clarett and Jim O'Brien episodes in the early 2000s demonstrated. The program has its problems, to be sure. In early 2005, Andy Geiger announced his retirement because, in his own words, "I find that my work is no longer fun." Despite these problems, Ohio State has been extraordinarily successful both on the field and in the classroom. One reason is the recognition of a core vision, developed during a series of staff meetings based on a shared reading of *Built to Last*.

OSU's core vision rests on six elements, which are spelled out on its Web site and in numerous publications, and which are considered when hiring a coach or developing a marketing plan:

✦ Education and enrichment of the student athlete

✦ Integrity in all aspects of behavior

✦ Innovation in approach and spirit

✦ Excellence throughout the organization

✦ Respect for the individual

✦ A tradition of leadership

As Andy Geiger and his staff knew full well, a core vision can't prevent mistakes or public relations nightmares. But it can steer a big, big boat. (10)

The SWOT Analysis

All strategy begins with an understanding of the environment and your place within it. As executives in tennis, golf, and hockey realized, you must know where you are before you can decide where you want to go or how to get there. Knowing where you are requires a knowledge of consumers and their behavior (see chapters 3 and 4), which in turn requires careful research and the development of a data-based marketing system (DBM; see chapter 5) that supplies timely, accurate, and usable data to decision makers. As we will explain, the elements of the DBM system range from magazine clippings to vast computer databases.

Step 1 often includes what is called a SWOT analysis, a careful analysis of the strengths and weaknesses of the organization as well as the opportunities and threats in the marketplace or beyond. The SWOT analysis relies on the DBM system and reinforces its importance. Marketers must understand their industry and their business, or they are doomed. For a historical case study of the SWOT approach, see the sidebar on "Lucky Les" Harrison on page 35, who was not able to adapt to changes in the marketplace. Later in this chapter, we consider some "megatrends" in the sport industry and offer some tips on culling trends from fads.

Ideally, the SWOT analysis involves a broad range of constituents in the organization. In the last few years, the NBA developed its own internal consulting group (the Team Marketing and Business Operations Group, or TMBO), which, among other things, helped individual franchises develop SWOT analyses. As the NBA's TMBO insisted, narrowly crafted, "top-down" planning, whether farmed out to consultants or not, rarely succeeds because few workers are willing to buy into the effort. Knowing your organization means paying close attention to what Peter Drucker called the "theory of the business," which he defined as assumptions about the environment, the organizational mission, and the core competencies needed to accomplish the mission. Managers must be sure that the "theory" is realistic and widely understood. (11)

Data-Based Marketing Information Systems

Among other things, Les Harrison needed a better data-based marketing information system (DBM). The elements of an effective DBM system can range from a sophisticated, expensive, computerized database to scraps of paper shoved in a coat pocket. In the end, what counts most is the information that infiltrates the decision maker's brain. As we discuss in chapter 5, information can be internal (e.g., a list of season-ticket holders) or external (e.g., regional demographics). Marketers can use readily available secondary data (e.g., compilations in the *Statistical Abstract of the United States*) or develop their own primary research studies (e.g., a fan survey). In the last two decades, the sport industry has seen more large-scale syndicated research, which customers buy from firms such as Scarborough Research or ESPN Sports Poll. In fact, syndicated sport studies began in the 1970s with the work of Dick Lipsey, who now operates the Sports Business Research Network (SBRnet.com), the largest online database in the business. For a list of some standard sources of industry data (magazines and newsletters, hard copy and online sources), see appendix A at the back of this book. The marketer must use all available information to be sure that any plan is realistic. Consumer tastes change, competitors change, technology changes. Any of these changes may require an alteration in the marketing plan. Following are some examples: (12)

✦ Athletic club manager Marla Chavetz built a strong clientele by knowing her consumers. When member surveys showed that a large number of older members had orthopedic problems and that asthma was far more prevalent than anticipated, Chavetz responded with clearer guidelines on dealing with knee and shoulder rehabs as well as working with people who had asthma. Says Chavetz, "The whole point is to identify your clients' needs and to develop programming to meet those needs."

✦ Burton Snowboards increased market share from 30 to 40 percent in the last half of the 1990s by carefully culling the opinions of some 300 professional riders, whose opinions on product design often overruled those of Burton's top designers.

✦ The Florida Panthers, the NFL, and the USTA have employed the Sports Management Research Institute to conduct in-depth fan research, using both traditional methods (focus groups, surveys) and more innovative ones such as "mystery shoppers." As SMRI's CEO Kathy Davis explained: "We put on a hat and pretend we're Joe Fan to experience all the elements. We take pictures, test out toilets. Is there a baby-changing amenity? Is the ATM functioning? Are they friendly when you come into the parking lot?"

Sport Megatrends in the New Millennium

Marketing strategy is not an easy game, especially when the environment is rapidly changing, as it was in the 1950s. Les Harrison is not alone among sport entrepreneurs who lost such a chess match. The last two letters of SWOT refer to a constant scanning of the environment, a search for trends and clues about the future. Of course, there is a big difference between recognizing trends (more of a historical analysis) and forecasting the future. Some trends—such as population growth and demographic shifts—have real predictive power. Consumer tastes are a different matter. Take automobile styles, for instance. In the late 1970s, spikes in the price of gasoline prompted a trend toward smaller, fuel-efficient cars. No one predicted the surge of demand two decades later for tanklike, gas-guzzling sport utility vehicles. Just ask the executives who banked on continued demand for minivans! By 2005, however, big

"Lucky Les" Harrison's Rochester Royals: The Challenge of the Market's Full-Court Press

Basketball—and the NBA—have dominated the imagination of sport marketers in the last decade. Despite the antics of petulant players, the NBA has been a showcase for successful strategies in packaging merchandise, personalities, and athletic skill. An NBA franchise has been the hallmark of a "world-class" city. The glitz of "Showtime," however, has its roots in the dusty armories and small auditoriums of places like Rochester, New York, where the Sacramento Kings were born in 1945—as the Rochester Royals. The Royals' early success and ultimate failure provide enduring lessons in the difficulties of shaping strategy to fit the changing market.*

The Royals' founder was a local star named Lester "Lucky Les" Harrison, who played and managed a number of teams in the loose, semiprofessional associations of the 1920s and 1930s. In 1945, Les and his brother bought a franchise in the National Basketball League, the only real "pro" league of the day. The franchise cost $25,000. The newly christened Rochester Royals played in the NBL's Eastern Division with the Fort Wayne Zollner Pistons (yes, the very same Pistons), the Youngstown Bears, and the Cleveland Allmen Transfers. The team names and locations reflected the small-market, company-team, industrial-league base of the NBL. Still, the NBL had the country's best pro players. It was "the" big league.

The times were changing swiftly, though. In 1946, big arena owners in New York, Boston, Chicago, Detroit, Cleveland, Philadelphia, Pittsburgh, Providence, St. Louis, Toronto, and Washington formed the Basketball Association of America (BAA). Their main purpose was to fill arena dates not taken by their hockey teams in the National Hockey League (NHL) or American Hockey League (AHL). Their first president was Maurice Podoloff, who also ran the AHL. Franchises in the "upstart" league cost only $1,000 to start, but the BAA had high hopes. Although neither side admitted it, another sports war was on, just as there was a war in pro football between the NFL and the AAFC. There would be winners and losers in the struggle between the bigger and smaller markets. Only the shrewd, the ruthless, and the lucky would survive.

The Rochester Royals began with a bang—NBL playoff championships in 1945-1946 and 1946-1947. They consistently sold out Edgerton Park Sports Arena (approximately 4,000 seats). In 1948, they jumped the NBL ship to the BAA, joining three other talent-laden defectors (Minneapolis,

Indianapolis, and Fort Wayne). It seemed to be the right move, because the BAA won the brief league war before reorganizing as the NBA in 1949. Unfortunately, the rise of the NBA and its big-market franchises spelled long-range doom for the Rochester Royals. By 1956-1957, despite an NBA title in 1951 and rising attendance at the 8,000-seat War Memorial (opened in 1955), the Royals were mired in red ink. Their six-year average loss of over $21,000 was the third worst in the league (the league's best annual profit average for 1951-1957 was the Knicks' $89,000, but most teams lost money). In April 1957, Les Harrison packed his team up and moved to Cincinnati, hoping for better profits.

What had gone wrong for a franchise that was the talk of the town in the postwar years? As Hall of Famer Red Holtzman (a Royal player from 1945 to 1953) recalled of those years: "Anyone who was anyone came to our games. It was go to the game and dinner afterward—a Rochester Saturday night ritual." How can one reconcile that memory with Les Harrison's bitter recollection to historian Donald Fisher: "They didn't realize what a good thing they had here. That's all. They didn't realize it."

In fact, the Royals' demise may be seen as a good case study in marketing strategy (or the lack of it). Although the rise of the BAA and its big-market teams might have tilted the playing field, the Royals did not read the strategic environment well. Beyond this—in the clear hindsight of history that Les Harrison did not have—the Royals blundered in some basic areas of sales and promotions. This becomes clearer if we examine their organizational strengths and weaknesses and environmental opportunities and threats.

Organizational Strengths

Les Harrison was a major strength for the Royals. He was a local hoops legend. He knew the town and its culture; he had a good feel for the type of team that would sell in Rochester, even to the extent of signing Italian and Jewish players who could attract their ethnic communities. Further, the Royals were Harrison's sole interest. They were his love affair, not his ego trip. His well-crafted postwar teams had outstanding winning percentages, with playoff championships to boot. Those Royals played to constant sellouts in the Edgerton Park arena. Despite the arena's limited size, the team averaged over 100,000 in annual attendance for league play, an excellent mark for the time.

Environmental Opportunities

The Royals made two major "positioning" decisions during these years. Both appeared to make great sense in light of a changing environment. The first was the jump in 1948 from

---

*This case study (including most of the data and the quotes) is based on Donald Fisher's excellent research in "The Rochester Royals and the Transformation of Professional Basketball, 1945-57," *International Journal of the History of Sport* 10 (April 1993): 20-48. See also Robert W. Peterson, *Cages to Jump Shots: Pro Basketball's Early Days* (New York: Oxford, 1990), 150-166.

(continued)

the NBL to the BAA. Sport history has always worked to the advantage of "big-market" leagues. And most interleague wars end with mergers—think of the NFL-AFL in the 1960s and the WHA-NHL or the NBA-ABA in the 1970s—where a few of the "losing" league's teams merge into the "winning" league. Les Harrison saw the handwriting on the wall in 1948. As Donald Fisher succinctly concluded, "They not only would be bringing new big-city opponents into Rochester, but they were joining a more commercialized business association." The move into the bigger league naturally required a move into a larger arena. Harrison was not alone in promoting the need for a new facility; Rochester boosters of all stripes pushed for it. Big-league teams in a big-league arena were proof of a big-league city. Thus the move in 1955 into the new 8,000-seat War Memorial was a logical step in repositioning the team and the city.

Environmental Threats

The move to the BAA seemed logical in 1948. What was the alternative—to stay in the small-time league? At the same time, the BAA's structure was hazardous for a franchise like the Royals. For one thing, the BAA prohibited its teams from playing an exhibition schedule. Exhibition matches—against anyone who could draw a crowd—had long been a staple of professional basketball and football. But the BAA owners wanted to upgrade the game's image, so exhibitions were out. Only league play was allowed for league teams. This rule especially hurt teams with small arenas who needed to maximize the number of paydays. Worse yet, the BAA rules stipulated that all gate receipts would reside with the home team. This was a killer for the small-arena teams. What good was it to play the Knicks regularly if you couldn't get a piece of their gate, and your gate was already maximized?

Two other threats loomed in the social and cultural environment. They transformed much of American life in the 1950s: suburbanization and television. Both were uppercuts to the chin of clubs like the Royals. The history of pro basketball was tied to urban neighborhoods and ethnic communities. Les Harrison's Royals were but a generation removed from the days when a "pro" game was the opener for a neighborhood dance on the very same floor. The postwar Royals captured attention as the "city's" team only so long as fans lived and pursued their leisure in the "city." But what would happen when the fan base started to move to suburban areas? Some of those nights out at Royals games would be spent building ties to new neighborhoods and communities, at PTA meetings, at Scouts, or the YMCA. Or . . . the family might all sit in front of the new television and

watch Milton Berle. Les Harrison himself recalled that "when TV itself came in, we operated on Tuesday and Saturday nights. Milton Berle put us out of business on Tuesday. And then on Saturday with Sid Caesar and Imogene Coca—they put us out of business."

Organizational Weaknesses

It wasn't just "outside" threats that killed the Royals. In hindsight, they made a major tactical error in their marketing. They killed themselves with sellouts. How can that be? Simple. A team that sells out its arena with season tickets can never hatch a new generation of committed attenders, especially if television becomes an option. The "live" game has special attractions that television cannot match. But fans must be introduced to the live event. If they can't get in the doors, they can never cultivate a taste for "being there."

Bobby Wanzer, Royals player and longtime Rochester resident, sensed this when he talked to historian Donald Fisher four decades later. "In the beginning," Wanzer noted, the Royals "were in demand" with "a lot of season ticket holders." Success had a down side, however, as Wanzer realized: "We couldn't build any new fans because we were sold out. . . . After a while people stopped trying to get tickets." Fan frustrations were aggravated by rumors that the Harrison brothers took advantage of the high demand by scalping their own tickets.

And so, a number of factors piled up on the Royals. The season-ticket sellouts reduced the flow of the fan "escalator" (see the section on p. 42) which might have moved once-a-year fans (e.g., on a birthday) into five-game-a-year fans, and moderate fans into season-ticket holders. The limitations of Edgerton Park Arena, the BAA's restrictive policy on exhibitions, and its lack of revenue sharing all meant that even sellouts could not provide the revenues Rochester needed to compete with teams from New York or Boston.

By 1955, when the team moved into a bigger arena, the roster was no longer filled with young stars, and Harrison's need to pinch pennies made it hard to attract replacements. In 1956, Bill Russell announced that he would sign with the Globetrotters before he would play in a place like Rochester. Harrison made a deal with Boston's owner, Walter Brown. The Royals would pass on drafting Russell (the Celts had the next pick) if Brown would give Harrison his ice show for two weeks a year. Hard-pressed for cash, Harrison had to look at the short term. Two weeks of an ice show was more valuable than Bill Russell. Two years later, the Royals were in Cincinnati.

SUVs were again pinched by increases at the gas pump. Forecasting is an art, not a science. A rigid faith in forecasts has led many an executive, in the words of *American Demographics,* to "plan for a future that never arrives, while a different future passes them by." We have already described two key trends in chapter 1—globalization and consolidation. Here are a few more worth noting. (13)

Women's Sports Continue to Crest In 1970, 1 in 27 girls played on high school teams—less than 4 percent. By 2002, it was 33.5 percent. The reason was simple: Title IX. And the Title IX generation is coming of age, with marketing implications that we will examine throughout the book. To be sure, there have been stumbles at the big-time level, most notably the failure of women's professional soccer—the WUSA. Begun in 2001 on the success of the 1999 World Cup, the WUSA was out of business by late 2003. Analysts blamed the demise on a lack of financial controls, poor media strategy (including the decision to spurn a TV deal with TNT in favor of one with the Pax network), and an overreliance on "soccer moms" as the target audience. As one consultant said, "For Gen-X moms, the whole 'soccer moms' concept is dead." (14)

The failure of the WUSA is a reminder that a strong participant market does not guarantee the success of a professional league. But this does not diminish the growing importance of girls and women to the sport marketplace. Over the last decade, attendance at NCAA women's basketball games has tracked upward sharply at all three divisions, while it has been relatively flat or declining on the men's side. Or, take the case of ice hockey: (15)

- In 1991, USA Hockey had 5,533 registered female players. By 1997, the number was almost 21,000. By 2003 it had reached 48,483. In Canada, female participation had been growing steadily for several decades. But it still rose 10.81 percent between 2002 and 2003, reaching 61,177 players.
- The NHL has estimated that 45 percent of NHL game attendees are female.
- A Fox/TMG poll taken after the Nagano Olympics indicated that over 80 percent of the people who watched the U.S. women's hockey team were either somewhat or very likely to watch a women's hockey game in the near future.
- Equipment manufacturers have begun to make hockey gear designed for girls and women. For instance, Louisville's pants for women have wider hips, a narrower waist, and more pelvic protection than the men's version. CCM's women's "Tack" brand skate is narrower through the heel.

More "Action" at the Grass Roots Women and girls both forged and reflected important links across sport levels—from the grass roots to the elite professionals. Quite often, female athletes seemed to be throwbacks to an earlier age of unspoiled athletes who played for the love of the game and not for the next deal. Sponsors noticed this as they sought to spend their dollars more effectively. The most appealing segment of sports were deemed "extreme" or "action" sports—skateboarding, snowboarding, motocross biking, surfing. In the 1980s, these sports were considered "alternative" and minor. By 2001, they were mainstream and major, and skateboarding had more participants than baseball. Television had the "X-Games" and the "Gravity Games." Tony Hawk had become the new Larry Bird. Experts wondered if the growth would slow or fizzle, but the NFL was not taking any chances. Partnering with the NFLPA, the league channeled some $130 million into the creation of USA Football, whose prime objective was to boost participation in youth and amateur football. (16)

The Digital Revolution Expands In 1999-2000, Internet ticket sales accounted for less than 25 percent of all individual game tickets sold in the NBA. By 2004-2005, this figure had risen to 73 percent. In June 2004, the Turnkey Sports Poll asked 400 senior executives in pro and college sports, "How important is the Internet and Web advertising in your organization's current marketing mix?" Seventy percent answered "somewhat important" or "very important." These executives recognize a trend that has even more implications for grassroots and high

Women's sport continues to grow at all levels.
© Human Kinetics

school sports. People of all ages, especially the young, are seeking basic information on the Internet.

In June 2004, the Pew Research Center released its Biennial News Consumption Survey based on telephone interviews with a national probability sample. Two thirds of Americans (66 percent) indicated that they used the Internet for e-mail and for information, a 12 percent increase from 2000. One of the major shifts in the new millennium has been the steady increase in regular online news consumption—from 23 percent of Americans in 2000 to 25 percent in 2002 to 29 percent in 2004. The trend crosses categories of age, gender, race, ethnicity, and education and appears to be a key driver of Internet use.

The move to Internet news is part of a larger interactive digital trend. Like television and radio decades before, the Internet and the cell phone did not make people less active "couch potatoes." The digital age has simply rechanneled their activities. Fans now expect an interactive Web site that gives them a peek at the sight line they will have when they buy a ticket in a certain section. Drive-time commuters seek a piece of the "juice" by calling up their favorite sport talk radio show. Once at a sport venue, they expect interactive kiosks, and more. In 2006, Sprint Nextel and NASCAR were experimenting with "fourth generation" cell phones that fans could rent at racetracks. These devices would provide video views from cameras attached to race cars; they would also stream live chatter from the drivers and their pit crews, or deliver stats from a NASCAR database. In the future, fans will play the role of television/radio producer/director. And between live events, weblogs (a.k.a. blogs) and podcasts will allow the everyday fan to develop a fan following of his or her own. In short, people are not just consuming the new technology; they are active producers. And the new technology promises new and cheaper avenues to reach these consumers. School, club, and college programs should begin to rethink their heavy reliance on newspaper ads and public service announcements to drive consumer awareness. The emerging markets have been digitized. As *BusinessWeek* summed up the digital revolution as of 2005, when some billion people were online—the Internet has nurtured the "Power of Us." (17)

More Battles Over Ambush Marketing In 1998, a post-Nagano Olympics survey of 512 consumers revealed that 55 percent incorrectly named Pepsi as an official Olympic sponsor. One reason for the confusion was the practice of "ambush marketing," in which a nonsponsor corporation's ads create the image of sponsorship without using any official logos or symbols reserved for a sponsor. At those same Olympics, for instance, Wendy's ran ads with a hockey theme, even though McDonald's was the official sponsor. Events such as road races or marathons, held on open, public venues, face special difficulties. At the 2005 Boston Marathon, one ambush marketing firm hired "guerrillas" to wear sandwich-board signs promoting a nonsponsor. One of them ran onto the course itself and joined a pack of competitors. All for $50 and an arrest by Boston police. Such antics have given rise to a new class of consultants. Before the 2000 Olympics in Sydney, a "top Australian sponsorship expert," Kim Skildum-Reid, offered a series of workshops promising "to teach marketers how to mount and protect themselves from ambush marketing campaigns."

Ambush marketing is a problem with no clear solution in sight. A recent survey found that 88.9 percent of responding sport marketing executives agreed that "ambush marketing can confuse consumers into thinking that a non-sponsor is actually a sponsor." As more sport organizations and athletes push their brands in the marketplace, will this further confuse consumers? If Peyton Manning endorsed Pepsi on television wearing a blue and white uniform (without any Colts image on it), would consumers remember or even care if another cola was the Colts' "official" sponsor? The sorting of multiple sponsorships is an escalating problem, especially in professional team sports where leagues, players, teams, and venues are all looking to push their brands. Short of costly lawsuits, there seem to be few effective antidotes to clever ambush marketing. Jeff Long, the Atlantic 10 Athletic Conference's assistant commissioner for corporate sponsorships, summed up today's reality: "Frankly, as well as it can be done now . . . I'm always surprised there's not more." (18)

Culling the Fads From the Trends

As marketers scan the environment, some trends jump out quite clearly. The rise of aerobics in the 1980s is a good example. Even the casual observer could see this. Nike, on the other hand, was slow to respond to the growing popularity of aerobics and lost that huge market to Reebok. Sport history, however, is also punctuated with lots of fads that lit up the skies for a few years, then fizzled. Examples are the roller skating craze of the 1860s, the bicycle boom of the 1890s, and the miniature golf mania of 1920s. So how can the marketer distinguish between a solid trend and a short-term fad? Consultant Martin Letscher suggested a few simple questions that can help:

- ◆ Does the new development fit with other basic lifestyle trends or changes in the consumer world?
- ◆ How varied, immediate, and important are the benefits associated with the new development?
- ◆ Can the product or service be personalized or modified to meet individual needs?
- ◆ Is it a trend in itself or merely the manifestation of a larger trend?
- ◆ Has the new development been adopted by key consumers who drive change?
- ◆ Is the new development supported by changes in unrelated or surprising areas?

Although these questions are valuable, no system is foolproof. After all, Letscher predicted a long boom for in-line skating, which has declined in popularity over the last five years. Still, Letscher's questions provide an effective framework for analysis. In an industry in which racquetball is hot one year and fly-fishing the next, in which changing tastes in color create wild swings in merchandise from bright pastels to earth tones or teal and black, the marketer must be careful to distinguish fads from trends. (19)

After the SWOT Analysis

After a SWOT analysis, it may be necessary to adjust the organizational strategy and steer a slightly or drastically different course. But an organization must always be careful not to stray from its core vision. As Collins and Porras argued in *Built to Last*, management should (1) develop new alignments to "preserve the core and stimulate progress," and (2) eliminate misalignments—"those that drive the company away from the core ideology and those that impede progress toward the envisioned future." Nike, for instance, expanded its strategy in the 1990s from its original focus on designing and marketing running shoes. Part of the reason was the lesson Nike learned from missing the aerobics market. By the mid-1990s, Nike had expanded into equipment of all sorts, including ice hockey equipment. With its many successful ties to athletes and events, the company even dabbled in the marketing and agent business. Would Nike expand too far from its core vision as a company? (20)

In the late 1990s, Stanford University Athletics decided that corporate signage was moving its programs too far from its educational mission. As then-President Gerhard Casper explained, "Although the financial realities of collegiate sports probably make some corporate sponsorship inevitable, I look forward to a day when this is no longer true. In the meantime, at Stanford we will always make a point of saying that ours are student-athletes, with the emphasis on students." And so Stanford told its sponsors, in effect: "We value your partnerships, but we will limit our exchange to tickets and hospitality. Corporate signs will be removed from our venues." After Athletics Director Ted Leland explained the policy to one alumni group, they gave him a standing ovation. As Leland put it: "You usually don't get a standing ovation for anything but going to the Rose Bowl or disciplining the band." Leland also understood that Stanford's huge endowment enabled it to stay true to a core vision: "If the choice had been either to have advertising or drop sports, we might have come to a different decision." (21)

Like all organizations, Nike and Stanford must constantly assess the realism of their "theory of the business"—what Peter Drucker called the assumptions about (1) the environment, (2) the organizational mission, and (3) the core competencies needed to accomplish the mission. Following are some key triggers for testing these assumptions: (22)

- ✦ When you achieve original goals
- ✦ When something prevents goal attainment
- ✦ When you think you know your consumers well
- ✦ When you don't think you know your consumers well
- ✦ When you sustain rapid growth
- ✦ When growth is unexpectedly slow
- ✦ When you are surprised by success
- ✦ When you are surprised by failure
- ✦ When a competitor enjoys unexpected success or failure
- ✦ When the environment is changing quickly
- ✦ When you haven't seriously questioned your assumptions in two years

Strategic Step 2: Clarify Your Goals and Objectives

The development and reassessment of goals and objectives should emanate from ongoing analysis. Although people sometimes interchange the terms *goals* and *objectives*, goals are typically broad statements, whereas objectives provide more detailed, usually quantified targets. Jim Collins and Jerry Porras found that "visionary companies" typically articulated a few "big, hairy, audacious goals" (BHAGs) that could stimulate progress while preserving a core vision. The Denver Grizzlies Professional Hockey Club, a highly successful member of the International Hockey League in the mid-1990s, included both BHAGs and ordinary goals in its "Community Relations Plan": (23)

1. To create high awareness/visibility for Grizzlies in the community—we want positive publicity for all the programs in which we are involved. (It is not enough for us to do these programs; people have to see pictures, read about us or see our involvement on TV.)
2. To generate goodwill and positive feelings about the Grizzlies in all areas of the community.
3. To develop new programs and support existing programs, which encourage youth participation in ice hockey and street hockey.
4. To identify quality organizations and provide them with Grizzlies tickets to be distributed to 100,000 underprivileged, handicapped or at-risk youths throughout our market areas.

Goals 1 and 2 might be characterized as BHAGs for any sport organization. Positive publicity and goodwill for the whole organization in "all areas of the community"—those are surely big, hairy, and audacious goals. But the Grizzlies' goals also clarified direction in a number of ways. First, they call for publicity that will be measured in media exposure. Specific objectives might be exposure in a certain number of newspaper column inches or features on the evening television news. Second, the goals require goodwill in all areas of the community, measured perhaps by surveys in Denver's various inner-city neighborhoods and suburbs. As the fourth goal suggests, the Grizzlies did not want to be the team of only upscale, professional families. They wanted to be a team for all of Denver. And they set a specific target of distributing 100,000 tickets to particular groups of kids. This was big, hairy, and audacious indeed for a minor league team in a major league market.

Clarifying goals and objectives is what sets the "manager" apart from the "caretaker." It is necessary at all levels. At Technical High School in Baltimore County, Maryland, Athletics Director David Hoch made a clear choice in his marketing objectives. As he put it, the "mission" was not to "boost revenue," but to promote greater awareness. It would have been far easier to raise money via a pizza sale to hard-core families. But that would not expand awareness and loyalty. At Technical High School, "success is measured by how our school's athletic programs are perceived—are we garnering more support?—not in how many dollars are added to the coffers." For Hoch, awareness and knowledge would be the foundation for steadier streams of financial support. (24)

Strategic Step 3: Develop a Marketing Plan

With a mission and objectives in place, the marketer must develop a plan at both the broad (strategic) and specific (tactical) levels. This requires a return to the database to identify the targeted consumer segments (the way the Grizzlies identified inner-city neighborhoods as a specific segment for one of their programs). One of the most important ways for sport marketers to segment consumers is by their position on the escalator of involvement, a concept we examine later in this section. After identifying target segments, the marketer must develop products; prices; distribution systems; promotions; and public relations, media, and sponsorship programs that will ensure the successful attainment of objectives and mission. These functions make up the core of this book—chapters 6 through 16.

Market Segmentation and Determining Key Targets

People are different. That goes without saying. Some sport businesses (e.g., personal training services) treat every consumer as an individual, creating a program tailored to individual needs and capabilities. This is not practical or profitable in all situations. AA Baseball's Portland Sea Dogs, for instance, may tailor ticket plans for corporate sponsors or for special group outings, but they do not have the staff or the resources to approach each person in southern Maine with an individual message. At the same time, the Sea Dogs have more than one message for more than one target market. They recognize market segments consisting of consumers grouped with others with similar characteristics. Marketing theorists have typically considered several bases for segmentation, which we discuss in detail in chapter 6:

+ Demographic information—age, sex, income, education, profession
+ Geomarket information—location of residence, by zip code
+ Psychographic information—lifestyle factors such as activities, interests, and opinions
+ Product usage rate—attendance or activity frequency, or size of donation
+ Product benefits—product attributes or benefits that are most important to the consumer, and consumers' perceptions regarding the major benefits of the product and its competitors

Obviously, any segmentation strategy relies on the DBM system to distinguish marketable clusters. Although marketing theorists differ on definitions, some clusters may be called niches— small groups of consumers who share special, often unfulfilled needs or interests. One might view Rotisserie Baseball (initially at least) as a niche market of statistics-hungry baseball fanatics who relished any chance to argue about player talent and trades, and were willing to spend hours doing so. These days, such sport consumers appear to make up more than a niche.

Marketing databases also create the potential for something closer to individual marketing strategies. This is sometimes called *relationship marketing*. For instance, a database of information on season-ticket holders would allow a marketer to send birthday greetings along with information on special events (such as concerts) or special group deals (for children's birthdays). (25)

Market Development Using the Escalator Concept

User segments are especially important in the sport business because they constitute the sport consumer escalator (see figure 2.2)—perhaps the most important concept in this book. We discuss the escalator from many angles in the chapters that follow, but for now a simple explanation will do. The escalator is a graphic representation of consumer movement to higher levels of involvement in a sport, as a player or a fan. The escalator concept was developed by Bernie Mullin (who adapted baseball executive Bill Giles' simpler "staircase" concept) in a 1978 manuscript that was the basis for this book. The escalator suggests that sport organizations should invest more in nurturing existing consumers than they should in trying to create new ones. Although campaigns to attract new fans are very important, they cannot match for impact a strategy that moves current consumers a few steps up the escalator of involvement and commitment.

The escalator concept has been supported by consumer research among both participants and spectators. In the 1970s, for instance, Dick Lipsey began national, syndicated research on the sporting goods business. These studies, one of which is now the annual National Sporting Goods Association survey, supported some important elements of the sport escalator, including the fact that new participants represented a minor portion of total purchases (from 5 to 12 percent of dollars and from 10 to 20 percent of units sold). It became clear that sport participants moved up an escalator of involvement and that the vast majority of equipment buyers were already playing the sport, and looking for ways to improve. (26)

For team sport marketers, the escalator is crucial, in part because fan surveys indicate clear intentions to move up the escalator. For instance, fans who currently attend three games per year typically indicate their intention to attend five or six games the next year. The key is to create a marketing plan—with an array of elements and tactics—that can satisfy the needs of various consumer clusters and thereby move user groups up the escalator.

At the same time, even a casual fan knows that great numbers of consumers can fall off the escalator at any time. Nike and Reebok suffered serious sales dips in the 1990s, in part because sports had lost their luster as a fashion statement in the youth market. More "earthy" shoes, like the ones Timberland made, became trendy. Similarly, fan defections can become hemorrhages for many reasons beyond a long losing streak. For this reason, as we explain in chapters 6, 11, and 12, the smartest organizations have multiple tactics and plans to reach user segments all along the escalator. The NHL, for instance, had had problems translating the rabid devotion of "local-core" fan groups into anything resembling a strong national consumer base. Television ratings demonstrate clearly that—outside its immediate markets—hockey has not caught on with consumers at the bottom of the escalator. In 2003, the league began running ads in which entertainers like Shania Twain and Jim Belushi explained the finer points of rules, coaching tactics, and playing styles. As an NHL executive put it, "We wanted to have a diverse group of celebrities that would appeal outside of hockey." The NHL needed a much more concerted campaign, all along the escalator, if it hoped to rebound after the lockout of 2004-2005. (27)

Product Development and Positioning

One way to move consumers up the escalator is to design, redesign, and promote products to capture special "space" in target consumers' minds. This is sometimes called "position-

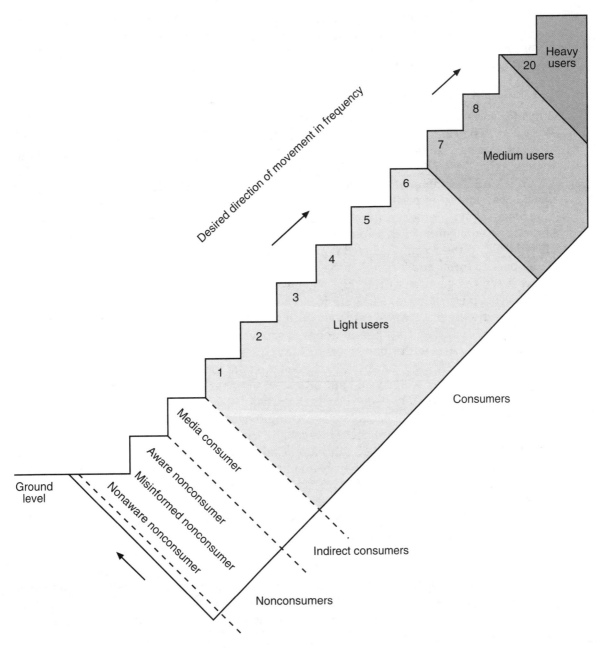

FIGURE 2.2 The frequency escalator for sport attendance and participation.

ing." The concept was promoted in the 1980s by two advertising executives whose book title captured their argument: *Positioning: The Battle for Your Mind*. Their basic mantra was simple: "Positioning is not what you do to a product. Positioning is what you do to the mind of the prospect. That is, you position the product in the mind of the prospect." As we discuss in chapter 7, product positioning is not simply a matter of advertising; it also involves research, development, and design. Some leagues use rule changes to reposition themselves. Baseball redesigned its basic product with the designated hitter, largely to reposition itself as a more exciting and offensive sport in the face of football's smashing popularity in the 1960s. Ice hockey clamped down on the worst of its street-fighting image with tough rules against the "third man in" and against leaving the bench during a fight. (28)

There are many "positions" to occupy in the sport industry. Take the notion of "big-league" sport. It is a fluid marketplace. In the past, many viewed NASCAR as blue-collar entertainment for Southern "Bubbas" and their women. If that was ever true, it surely is no longer: NASCAR has become the hottest growing "big-league" sport for the high-class corporate suits, male or female. One way NASCAR shifted its position was with new, modern megatracks, complete with hundreds of corporate boxes and upscale dining facilities.

By 2004, NASCAR had a 10-month season, with 1,500 races held in 100 venues that ranged over 36 states. One of the most successful was in Loudon, New Hampshire, far from "Bub-baville." As NASCAR's communications director told the *Boston Globe*, the term *NASCAR dads* proved the NASCAR's national impact: "NASCAR dads are everywhere. They're in New England." In fact, the Northeast accounted for a full 20 percent of NASCAR's fan base. The West had 19 percent. More that 13 million spectators watched live NASCAR events in 2003. The association claimed to have 40 million "passionate, hardcore" fans who crossed all demographic lines. (29)

While NASCAR aspired to corporate embrace, Major League Soccer (MLS) Commissioner Doug Logan looked to position his league as an alternative to the corporate-conglomerate glitz of his higher-profile counterparts. Logan articulated his position at the start of the 1998 season: an amalgam of soccer purists, young soccer players (and their moms, no doubt), Hispanics, and the disenfranchised fan (especially the baseball fan) "who reads his news-paper back to front" and is "tired of the players." Emphasizing MLS as an alternative, Logan threw down the gauntlet at the "big" leagues and their emphasis on corporate revenues: "The biggest piece of garbage in American sports is the luxury box, with its couches faced away from the field . . . with everybody eating sushi." Logan's successor, Don Garber, has moved the MLS along a track that emphasizes new soccer-specific stadiums that combine big-league amenities with a grassroots feel for closeness. (30)

Successful athletic clubs have also expanded their product concepts. As one expert argued, a tennis club member will have a hard time justifying her investment if she thinks only in terms of playing time. "If cost-per-play is the driving mechanism for members, they're not going to be satisfied." Members are now "renting space"—with a full range of amenities. On these terms, $20 per person per hour is a good investment. (31)

In a final example, the city of Lancaster, California, repositioned its entire city image by upgrading an athletic facility. This is an old (and very debatable) song at the big-league level—build a big, new stadium and you can get a big-league franchise that will make you a big-league city. Lancaster had another idea: become one of America's major venues for softball tournaments. With a clear vision, Lancaster expanded the city park to include six high-quality diamonds to go with assorted tennis courts, soccer fields, and basketball and volleyball courts. With a new logo and promotional campaign called "Big 6," Lancaster increased its number of softball tournament days from 27 in 1994 to over 75 in 1996. Now expanded to the "Big 8" complex, the Lancaster venue is a regular host for regional and national championships. Regional and national tournaments quite obviously attract revenue—in hotel and restaurant fees and taxes, for instance—from well outside the area. With a careful strategy, Lancaster repositioned itself on both the sport and revenue maps. (32)

The Five Ps in the Sport Marketing Mix

The product is often referred to as one of marketing's "four Ps":

◆ Product (development and positioning)

◆ Price

◆ Place (or product distribution)

◆ Promotion (personal selling, advertising, special events)

Because sport enjoys so much media attention, we treat public relations (usually consid-ered part of promotion) as a separate P.

◆ Public relations

In a service-oriented industry like sport, all the Ps are influenced by how well employees interact with consumers; we could call this "process management." We will see how critical process management is to the running of any promotion. For instance, if stadium personnel

Major league teams and venues are not the only sport products that can be developed and effectively positioned. Cities such as Lancaster, California, have realized they can become a major player in nonprofessional sports such as softball.

© Human Kinetics

are surly to fans looking to exchange "giveaway" T-shirts (often for a different size), those fans—who might well be at their only game of the year—will likely fall off the escalator in the belief that the stadium is a hostile place to bring a family. In a wireless age, it is possible to stay connected to consumers 365/24/7. But that connection must always be positive. Nothing can replace the human touch. Great customer service will always be the major force moving fans up the escalator.

There are many elements and tactics in the mix of any marketing plan. The bulk of this book is dedicated to describing the "best practices" that we have discovered in our three-plus decades in the field. Here are a few suggestions from one of the best practitioners of our time—John Spoelstra, whose work with the Portland Trail Blazers ensured his induction into anyone's sport marketing Hall of Fame.

✦ Bring radio and television production "in house."
✦ Sell at least 80 percent of all tickets before the opening game.
✦ Develop a full menu of season-ticket packages, such as three-game, five-game, weekend.
✦ Don't wait for a superstar. Find other ways to sell your team.
✦ Remember that, on average, 50 percent of revenue comes from ticket sales.

In which of the five Ps would you place each of these pointers? (33)

Integrating the marketing mix is the ongoing challenge for managers, even when they have a clear sense of strategy. Phil Guarascio, who worked at General Motors before taking over the NFL's top marketing position, put it clearly in describing the need to coordinate efforts: "This all has to be orchestrated to work. Fan development, sponsorship activation, and brand management can't be three entities; they have to be one." This is as true for a Pop Warner league as it is for the NFL. (34)

Managing the Plan With "Strategic Opportunism"

Although planning is a crucial feature in any effective organization, managers must be prepared to act—strike or respond—when the situation presents itself, which may not be in keeping with the timetable or outline of a particular plan. As Collins and Porras argued in *Built to Last: Successful Habits of Visionary Companies,* effective companies "distinguish their timeless core values and enduring core purpose (which should never change) from their operating practices and business strategies (which should be changing in response to a changing world)." (220) Sergio Zyman, longtime marketing whiz at Coca-Cola, put it another way in his book, *The End of Marketing As We Know It.* "The reality is that marketing, like science, isn't about knowing all the answers when you start out. It's about experimenting, measuring the results, analyzing them, and then making adjustments based on what you find out. . . . Change my mind, you bet! New info, new tactics. Same strategy. Fixed destination [to sell more]." Zyman knew all about experiments, because he supervised one of the biggest backfires in cola history—the introduction of New Coke in 1985. Within months, the product was pulled and the company reintroduced "Classic" Coca-Cola. A blunder? For sure. But it was a blunder that reinforced the strength of the original Coke brand.

The ability to blend both core continuity and change is one of the hallmarks of effective managers. Daniel Isenberg called this "strategic opportunism": "the ability to remain focused on long-term objectives while staying flexible enough to solve day-to-day problems and recognize new opportunities." Isenberg's research led him to outline certain habits of thinking and acting as the keys to strategic opportunism.

Habits of Thinking

◆ *Collecting ideas.* "In combing the beach or watching for flies, senior managers often collect ideas whose relationship to strategic goals may appear murky at first." These managers create "mental maps" that Isenberg defined as a "rich, multidimensional set of associations among the myriad tasks, people, problems, issues, and goals the manager is dealing with at any one time." One mental map may conceptualize staff responsibilities, especially vis-à-vis a marketing plan. One Division I athletics director we know used his mental map during a chance encounter with an alumnus who was an experienced fund-raiser. Knowing that his current director was about to leave, the athletics director quickly assessed the potential match between the alumnus and the soon-to-be vacant opening. On the spot, he planted the seed for a more formal visit and interview.

◆ *Summarizing.* How can a manager make sense of the daily mountains of data? "The answer is, by climbing up on a hillside every now and then to take a look around, to assess accomplishments, to see how much work is left, even to make sure that draining the swamp is still important." One executive, for instance, would gather notes from the day's or week's meetings and see whether any patterns emerged. Summarizing data in this way can reduce "cognitive burden," "detect new goals," and maintain a sense of direction.

Ways of Acting

◆ *Being planless by design.* Effective managers leave gaps in plans and avoid overly rigid detail in plans, knowing that chance encounters might lead to new ideas and subtle shifts in direction—zigging and zagging.

◆ *Binding to goals.* Even while leaving gaps, effective managers find ways to keep pursuing the most important things. They do this by creating tickler files and to-do lists, and by scheduling priority meetings well ahead of time.

◆ *Piecing the puzzle.* Effective managers understand that ordering the phases and efforts in any plan is not as important as their ultimate integration. They know that sometimes a sequence of "ready-fire-aim" may be appropriate.

"Thinking both strategically and opportunistically is clearly not easy. It requires a tolerance for ambiguity, intellectual intensity, mental hustle, and a vigilant eye for new ideas. It requires, in other words, a tough-minded approach to an inherently messy process, the ability to take action in the midst of uncertainty, to 'sin bravely.'"

Collins and Porras, *Built to Last* (New York: HarperCollins, 1999); Daniel Isenberg, "The Tactics of Strategic Opportunism," *Harvard Business Review* 65 (March-April): 92-97; Sergio Zyman, *The End of Marketing As We Know It* (New York: Harper Business, 1999).

Strategic Step 4: Integrate the Marketing Plan Into a Broader, Strategic Allocation of Resources That Ensure Success

Before, while, and after developing the five Ps—product, place, price, promotion, and public relations—into a plan for action, the marketer must ensure that more senior executives will support the plan. There is nothing worse for a marketer than to develop an imaginative, "can't-miss" plan that fails because it lacks support at a higher level. College athletics staffs face this problem often. Surefire plans for creating a bigger fan base in women's sports linger on the shelf because the limited funds go into promoting the traditional "revenue" sports (usually men's sports) that have historically helped to fund everyone else. Even though shifting money to a promotion of women's sports might result in a greater revenue yield, the risks seem too great. This is almost a self-fulfilling prophesy. Successful marketers make sure they have support as they move along, so Step 4 must be ongoing.

Once adopted, a strategy may require some changes in personnel or in the organizational structure. The historical studies of Harvard's Alfred Chandler demonstrate that successful organizations design and redesign themselves around their strategies, not the other way around. In Chandler's words, "Structure follows strategy." The alert executive has an eye on environmental changes that might require restructuring. Quick changes can be traumatic. In the late 1990s, Coca-Cola walked away from its huge leaguewide sponsorship with the NFL, leaving individual clubs with greater control and autonomy in making sponsor deals in the soft-drink category. Alan Friedman, editor of the influential *Team Marketing Report,* immediately saw the implications. "While NFL clubs have upgraded their front office marketing talent over the last few years, some clubs still don't have executives with full-time sponsorship-development and service responsibility." In the new world of soft-drink sponsorships, restructuring became a priority. (35)

An effective marketing plan will carefully blend all the Ps into a portfolio of activities that move a range of consumer clusters up the escalator. An enlightened school, college, or professional sport program will blend several of the Ps into packages differing in cost and benefits, promoted with different messages, and targeted at different segments or even niches. For a college program, this might mean special plans for students, area families, distant alums, and corporate sponsors. This requires a careful coordination of efforts, with broad support from the athletics director, coaches, players, sport information personnel, facilities managers, and the ticket office. Marketing is not the work of just a few people.

A lack of coordination can dump fans off the escalator like a series of waterfalls. This is what happened to the Kansas City Wizards of MLS in the late 1990s, when average attendance slipped from 12,900 to 8,661 over a single season. The MLS commissioner emphasized, "There are no excuses. Kansas City has a terrific team that plays in a great stadium in a town that prides itself on its sports teams." No excuses except for what one local reporter called "marketing blunders" and gaffes, including unwarranted price hikes and unclear tinkering with the team's name and logo, which muddled any attempts at a brand image and merchandise sales. The Wizards responded to the challenge; by 2004, their attendance averaged 14,816. Marketing blunders crippled the chances of the National Lacrosse League's Washington Power, including a decision to enter the market only 60 days before the first game, coupled with a refusal to buy advertising. The team's owner oozed marketing myopia when he assumed that the area's rabid lacrosse players and fans would automatically show up: "I figured if we put a great product on the field, that product would sell itself." The next year the franchise packed up and moved to Colorado. A missing or mismanaged marketing plan is a sure way to negate a hot market or a great product. (36)

Strategic Step 5: Control and Evaluate the Plan's Implementation

Step Five is another ongoing step. It makes little sense to wait for the end of the season to see if you're in last place!

Marketers (and their bosses) are quick to analyze failures. But analysis, evaluation, and "control" should be everyday events. Sergio Zyman, longtime marketing mogul at Coca-Cola, warned marketers to grab the moment and debrief success as well as failure. "Don't be blinded by your assumptions," he stressed. "Just because you run a promotion and it works doesn't mean that it worked for the reasons that you thought it would." He is correct. Especially in the sport industry—in which marketing plans can unfold on a game-by-game basis—don't wait until the end of the season to debrief. It must be done on an event-by-event basis. (37)

As chapter 17 describes in greater detail, evaluation (or "control") requires not only discussion and "debriefing" sessions, but also rigorous quantitative analysis. Spending marketing dollars on hunches or "feels" is a high-risk game—one that the University of Oregon played in the summer of 2001, when it paid $250,000 (donated by boosters) for a large billboard near Madison Square Garden promoting Joey Harrington for the Heisman Trophy. Was it worth the investment? A Portland *Oregonian* editorial felt so: "From where we sit, that $250,000 is beginning to look like the smartest public-relations money ever spent, dollar for dollar." Harrington finished fourth in the Heisman race, but the Ducks created a buzz and enjoyed many stories in the mass media, including a cover story in *Sports Illustrated* (which also included Oregon State's Ken Simonton). Oregon could have (and may have) quantified the return on investment by calculating the cost of advertising in national outlets such as *Sports Illustrated* or the *New York Times,* and comparing that with the number of "free" promotions they received in the stories. At the same time, they would need to ask whether national media exposure stemmed from a $250,000 billboard or from the Ducks' and Harrington's success on the field. Ultimately the point is not whether one finds the "true" answer; the point is in the pursuit of the answer. (38)

Ultimately, "success" in marketing is determined only through the consumer's eyes. It is a simple equation:

$$\text{Consumer satisfaction} = \text{Product benefits} - \text{Costs}$$

Consumers will provide the answers to the equation. Do they buy the product? Do they use the product? Do they repeat the purchase, or do they try something else? Although marketers must control their own budgets and costs, their more important "control" function is to ensure customer satisfaction. This means monitoring and evaluating indicators of satisfaction, benefits, and cost. We address these in greater detail in chapter 5, but consider here a few examples of possible indicators:

Satisfaction
  Attendance
  Ticket or member renewal rates

Benefits
  Food quality
  Access to and speed of parking

Costs
  Time spent in the parking lot after the game
  Beer spilled on children by a drunken fan
  Embarrassment caused by a surly usher

There are other issues to consider, including ethical principles. At the turn of the 20th century, for instance, white baseball audiences enjoyed the antics of black "mascots," who cavorted between innings like clowns and kneeled near the on-deck circle so their white bosses could rub their wooly heads for good luck. Such were the mores of Jim Crow America. No major league team would consider this acceptable entertainment today, yet some major college and professional teams have resisted change and continue to employ Native American team names and images. In 2004, the NCAA put the squeeze on schools with potentially offensive mascots, requiring a self-study that would be examined by an NCAA committee. This forced some 30 institutions to look more carefully at the impact of "tradition." A year later, the NCAA Executive Committee announced that Native American mascots or images would be banned from all NCAA tournament venues (see figure 2.3). In announcing the decision, the *NCAA News* was emphatic: Event management and marketing would be driven by core principles in the NCAA strategic plan for diversity and inclusion. In fact, any marketing management process (MMP) must consider social responsibility. Beyond the legal issues (see chapter 18), there are ethical dimensions to any marketing plan or decision. Moreover, there are numerous frameworks for ethical decisions—in business, in marketing, in sport, or in any domain of activity. In our experience, however, we haven't found anything better than Laura Nash's simple framework of 12 questions (see below), in her article "Ethics Without the Sermon," to consider when confronting a problem. (39)

FIGURE 2.3 The retirement of the University of Illinois' Chief Illiniwek in 2007 made the university eligible to host postseason NCAA championship events.
© AP Photo/Mark Cowan

1. Have you defined the problem accurately?
2. How would you define the problem if you stood on the other side of the fence?
3. How did this situation occur in the first place?
4. To whom and to what do you give your loyalty?
5. What is your intention?
6. How does this intention compare with probable results?
7. Whom could your decision or action injure?
8. Will you discuss this with affected parties before making the decision?
9. Will your position be valid over the long run?
10. Could you disclose your decision or action without qualm?
11. What is the symbolic potential of your action if understood? If misunderstood?
12. Under what conditions would you make exceptions?

Reprinted, by permission, from L. Nash, 1981, "Ethics without the sermon," *Harvard Business Review* November 79-90.

In the late 1990s, sport ethics seemed focused on Nike's labor practices in the developing countries in Asia. Was Nike exploiting labor with wages clearly unacceptable by American standards? Or, as Nike argued, was the company creating economic opportunities with wages in keeping with local standards? There were more issues, to be sure, and Nike was not alone in trying to justify its management and marketing decisions. The University of Memphis athletics director, R.C. Johnson, once approved a questionable golf outing for the "Tiger Clubs," the major fund-raising entities for the university's athletics. The problem was the golf-outing sponsor, the Horseshoe Casino, which paid Johnson $10,000 to underwrite the "Tiger Clubs/Horseshoe Casino Spring Fling." The sponsor choice upset a number of boosters, and soon the Memphis *Commercial Appeal* picked up the story. The criticism was obvious. At a time when campus gambling had reached epidemic proportions and the NCAA had created antigambling policies, how could U of M justify a booster outing formally sponsored by a casino? R.C. Johnson had lots of explaining to do, and hard decisions to make. Should he dump the event? The sponsor? Hindsight is always easy, but Johnson might well have benefited from asking himself some of Laura Nash's critical questions before he began. (40)

Wrap-Up

Sport organizations clearly face many unique challenges and demands, not all of which they can best meet with frenzied marketing action. Many challenges require considerable thought and a well-planned response. Yet the majority of demands do have comparatively simple solutions once all the data are put together. In the new millennium, sport will continue to be unique, but it will follow one principle experienced without modification in all industries: Those sport organizations most likely to succeed will be the ones that have the best handle on the marketplace. Such a handle comes only with the development, analysis, and integration of every function of marketing. In the following chapters, we consider all of these steps in much greater detail.

Activities

1. Define the five Ps of the sport marketing mix.

2. Find evidence of a sport organization that does an excellent job of recognizing market trends and adjusting its strategy accordingly. How does the organization stay true to a core vision while also repositioning its products?

3. Describe a new product concept that you think would meet unfilled consumer needs in your favorite sport.

4. List the market or consumer segments that most clearly relate to a tennis or golf club near you.

5. From the stories or ads in any newspaper sport section, try to find examples of the five Ps of the marketing mix.

6. Consider the case of the American Basketball League (ABL) versus the WNBA—one of the most interesting contests of sport marketing strategy in the late 1990s, at least until the ABL declared bankruptcy in 1999. Make a table that compares elements of the leagues' strategies. For instance, the leagues made clear choices on "placing" their products. The ABL played during the "traditional" basketball season, whereas the WNBA played during the summer. Their media packages also differed. What about their products, including player talent and rules? How were they different? What about their promotion via ad campaigns? Think of all the ways the leagues differed in the Ps of marketing. Was the WNBA's marketing strategy a key component of its victory over the ABL?

7. Conduct a marketing postmortem on the XFL, which hardly lasted one season, despite the backing of NBC Sports and the WWF. What were the strengths and weaknesses of the XFL's marketing strategy?

8. Look closely at the list of Laura Nash's ethics questions on page 49. Discuss a recent example of an ethical issue in sport marketing and analyze the issue using these questions.

Your Marketing Plan

The first step in this project is to choose (or create) an organization for which you will develop a marketing plan. Your ultimate goal is to prepare a 20- to 30-page plan that helps the organization attain strategic objectives. This plan should become an item in your personal portfolio. Is there an organization that you aspire to work for? Do you have an idea for a sport product that will fill some existing consumer needs or wants?

1. Identify resources for internal and external scanning.
2. Identify the three most important market trends affecting your firm or product.
3. Begin to define your "business" and your product.
4. Develop the draft of your mission statement.
5. Conduct a SWOT analysis (strengths, weaknesses, opportunities, threats).
6. Set some objectives.

Chapter 3

Studies of Sport Consumers

Objectives

- ✦ To recognize the many questions that sport marketers must ask about their consumers.
- ✦ To appreciate the many sources available for analysis.
- ✦ To understand the strengths and weaknesses in many published studies of sport consumers.

Golf Consumers: Are They Just Par for the Course?

Though some data show a drop in the number of rounds played, other data show an increase in golf fandom.

© Human Kinetics

As we saw in chapter 2, the golf industry is struggling to balance the demand to play with the supply of golf courses and equipment. GOLF 20/20's industry report for 2002 showed a continuing decline in the number of rounds played:

Year	Rounds (in millions)
2000	518.4
2001	518.1
2002	502.4

But there was some cause for optimism. Although overall participation was flat, the National Golf Foundation had reported a 38.6 percent increase in the number of junior golfers (ages 5 to 17) between 2001 and 2002. Along similar lines, the ESPN Sports Poll had registered sizable increases between 1996 and 2002 among Americans 12+ years old who considered themselves to be "avid" fans of golf. Male "avid fans" had increased 17.9 percent; females, a substantial 58.5 percent. Over the same time period, the percentage of African Americans who considered themselves "avid fans" jumped a whopping 380 percent. Was golf in trouble, or was the game in a brief participation slump that would rise on a growing fan base? The answer was all in how one viewed the data on golf's consumers. (1)

As we noted in chapter 1, the marketing concept begins and ends with the consumer. The marketer of any commodity—golf, grain, or gasoline—needs to understand who might be interested in buying her product; therefore, the intelligent marketer constantly seeks to answer a series of questions:

- ✦ Who are my consumers—past, present, and future—in terms of both demographics (age, sex, income) and psychographics (attitudes, opinions, lifestyles)?
- ✦ Where do my consumers reside? Where do they work? How do they travel to and from the places where they consume my product?
- ✦ Where, when, and how have my consumers been exposed to my product and its advertising?
- ✦ How and why did they become involved with my product?
- ✦ If they have been committed to my product, why?

This chapter provides an orientation to existing studies on the first general question—namely, who is the sport consumer? Specifically, we will discuss the profiles of sport consumers that have emerged in published studies. Chapter 4 explores the literature on the other questions listed. Chapter 5 outlines the ways that marketers in any sport organization can conduct their own research on consumers. As the case study on NASCAR suggests, there are many reasons for knowing your consumers.

It Pays to Know Your Consumers:
NASCAR Transforms Itself in the 1990s

NASCAR has come a long way from its early days of boot-leggers making a buck on backwoods dirt tracks. In the late 1990s, it transformed itself from marginal to mainstream. The NASCAR fan could no longer be stereotyped as just an old boy in bib overalls chewing Red Man; perhaps the biggest fans were the CEOs of major corporations like General Mills, Kodak, and Anheuser Busch. Or even Thorn Apple Valley, a sausage maker that had committed $15 million for three years to sponsor a car on the Winston Cup (now the Nextel Cup) circuit, NASCAR's marquee series. Corporate executives such as Thorn Apple Valley's Joel Dorfman knew that a NASCAR sponsorship provided exposure like no other sport—to a growing and very loyal audience. In two months of sponsorship, Dorfman saw his products getting shelf space. "We're already getting authorization for our product," he said, "with retailers who weren't interested in us at all before." Seventy Fortune 500 companies saw similar benefits in NASCAR. In 1998 alone, NASCAR banked about $475 million in sponsorships (of the more than $1 billion in auto racing). No other sport came close to this level. (2)

What was behind all of this corporate interest? Simple. A very attractive consumer profile that NASCAR carefully promoted. Some statistics:

✦ From 1991 to 1996, NASCAR attendance (6.1 million for Winston Cup races in 1997) grew 65.5 percent. In the same period, the NBA grew only 16.9 percent; MLB, 5.8 percent; the NHL, 38.1 percent; and the NFL (with little room to grow), only 5.6 percent.

✦ By the late 1990s, NASCAR reported that 38 percent of its fans were female, 65 percent owned homes, 29 percent earned over $50,000 annually, 53 percent were professionals, and best of all, 78 percent used credit cards.

✦ A 1994 study found that 71 percent of NASCAR fans bought NASCAR sponsor products. Compare this to the sponsor brand loyalty of golf fans (47 percent), tennis fans (52 percent), or fans of the so-called big three—the NFL, NBA, and MLB (36 to 38 percent). Even better, 40 percent of NASCAR fans said they would switch brands to a product that became a NASCAR sponsor.

Although other studies suggested that NASCAR fans were not quite this loyal, corporate sponsors were not quibbling. Said Jim Andrews, VP of IEG, Inc., a sponsor research group: "NASCAR has done a very good job of getting the word out—whether it be perception or reality—that their fans are the most brand-loyal fans." In 2004, Nextel's CMO Michael Robichaud claimed that NASCAR fans were also more active Nextel users: "20 percent higher in their average revenue per customer. . . . These are power users in wireless terms." Brian France, NASCAR's CEO, understood the key to corporate partnerships: "We can talk sponsorships all we want, but the core of our business always gets back to the fans." Or, we might conclude, knowing who your fans are.

3M and Western Union are two of many companies that have benefited from NASCAR sponsorship.
© AP Photo/Larry Papke

Types of Sport Consumer Studies

There is no foolproof profile of the "average" player or sport fan, nationwide or worldwide. There are simply too many variables. At the same time, many clubs, equipment companies, teams, and governing bodies (like NASCAR) have conducted enough research to feel comfortable about knowing their consumers. Further, a number of research organizations—increasingly over the last decade—have analyzed America's involvement in sport. Collectively, this research offers a rich database for study. Because the topics and purposes of these studies are so varied, we have chosen to provide an overview of their utility to the sport marketer rather than a synthesis of their contents. Many of the sources we discuss are listed in appendix A for easy reference.

There are many ways to categorize these sport consumer studies. For instance, information can be reported in many formats:

✦ Published newsletters, such as the *NCAA News*, which provides periodic excerpts from its annual participation survey

✦ Internet databases, such as the Sports Business Research Network (SBRnet), which contains archives of multiple studies, including the annual participation report of the National Sporting Goods Association

✦ Public documents such as the annual *Statistical Abstract of the United States*, published by the U.S. Census Bureau, which includes a large section on recreation and leisure

We could group consumer studies in other ways:

✦ By industry segment (sporting goods, high school athletics)
✦ By sport
✦ By consumer demographics (men, women, the elderly)
✦ By consumer activity (spending on equipment, watching on television, participation)

We organize this chapter simply by the frequency and scope of the sport consumer study. We suggest that the research on sport consumers is either "irregular" (hit or miss) or "regular" (annual or periodic) in frequency, and either "narrow" or "broad" in the scope of industry segments or populations it considers. We offer samples of each category in the following sections.

Irregular, Narrow Studies

Irregular, narrow studies are often commissioned by teams, leagues, or sponsors. (3) They are not part of a scheduled research program; often they are one-shot deals. They tend to focus on consumer demographics (e.g., age, income), media or product consumption (e.g., favorite television station or fast food), and sometimes consumer attitudes (e.g., rating of concessions). Although most of them are proprietary and remain unpublished, some are printed and distributed either to inform constituents or to attract sponsors. In the late 1990s, for instance, the NCAA commissioned the Taylor Research and Consulting Group (www.thetaylorgroup.com) to conduct an extensive study of basketball, in terms of "fan intensity and interest, game attendance, television viewership and licensed product ownership," as well as "drivers of, barriers to, and key target segments for improvement in each of the study areas." The results and recommendations helped launch a variety of national and local campaigns to grow the college game for both men and women. The Taylor Group's complete report was distributed to member institutions (and indirectly to the media) as a way to promote the NCAA's stewardship of the game.

Economic impact studies are another common type of irregular study. These are usually linked to the promotion of a facility or an event, in part to justify public support. In 1991, for example, Jewell Productions commissioned both Yale University's School of Organization and Management and National Demographics and Lifestyles, Inc., to analyze the Volvo International Pro Tennis Tournament's fan profile and economic impact on the surrounding community.

Finally, academic journals such as the *Sport Marketing Quarterly* publish occasional studies of specific consumer populations. One recent example provided a look at the demographics, attitudes, and consumption patterns of 475 fans at a World Championship Wrestling event on the campus of Texas A&M University. Studies such as these often provide valuable nuggets of information and rich insights. At the same time, marketers must recognize the limitations of time and place. A study of wrestling fans at a Texas university town venue may not help a wrestling promoter in a Northeast mill town.

Irregular, Broad Studies

Studies of broad, particularly national, populations can require significant investments of time and money. In the sport world, corporations with sport interests have occasionally funded such research. In the late 1970s, for instance, Perrier Waters commissioned the Harris Poll to examine the sport and fitness activities of American adults. It was a logical study for Perrier, which had an eye on the growing interest in healthy living, including the consumption of nonalcoholic beverages. The Harris Poll, which already employed national probability samples, was likewise a logical partner. Among other things, the Perrier Study considered activity levels by age, income, gender, and region. Results suggested that "high actives" (those who spent 360 minutes per week on vigorous activity) tended to be males under 35 who had higher incomes and lived in suburbs in the Midwest or the West. (4)

A few years later, Miller Brewing sponsored a national study of American involvement in and attitudes toward sport. The results contained interesting information on age-group interests. Aging did not mean withdrawal from sport involvement. For example, although the survey indicated that older people (especially those over age 50) attended fewer events, the results also showed very little drop-off in interest in sport as people grow older (see table 3.1). People retain their interest through television, radio, reading, and conversation. The question for the marketer is why this interest does not translate into more active forms of involvement. We will offer some suggestions in the next chapter.

Regular, Narrow Studies

Because they are snapshots of a brief moment in time, even the best irregularly conducted studies are limited in value. They can't help the marketer discover emerging trends in the ever-changing environment. As we discuss in chapter 5, an effective data-based marketing system must include regular, consistent studies of questions that allow for trend analysis.

✦ **Table 3.1** Miller Sport Fan Index by Age Group

Age group	% high to moderate and avid fans
14-17	33
18-24	27
25-34	30
35-49	40
50-64	34
65+	38

Data from Miller Lite Report 1983.

Fortunately, we can learn about large-scale trends in the surveys and reports of organizations such as the NCAA and the National Federation of State High School Associations (NFHS), which publish annual statistics on participation. Although these reports deal with particular populations, they go back several decades and are widely reproduced. Excerpts are often available on the organizations' Web sites (see listings in appendix A).

Table 3.2 offers some statistics culled from the annual NCAA participation survey, which considers the number of athletes on NCAA eligibility rosters. Obviously, this is a very special sample, but given the centrality of collegiate athletics in the American sport market, the data can suggest important trends. Although inclusion on an eligibility roster does not mean that an athlete played in every (or any) game (some might suffer season-ending injuries), we still may assume that each athlete on such a roster has high levels of commitment and involvement. As we look at the data, we note that over a 10-year period, baseball, softball, and soccer have prospered in participation, for both men and women. Even more telling are relative rates of change, especially the explosive growth of women's soccer. Some of this growth resulted from an increase in NCAA membership. The news is not so good for gymnastics, especially for men.

Athletes are not the only "participants" tracked in regular, narrow studies. Several organizations cover trends in corporate sponsorships. One is IEG, Inc., whose *IEG Sponsorship Report* is standard reading at the top industry levels. As we will emphasize in chapter 13, corporate sponsors are a special segment of sport consumers whose objectives include not only entertainment but also exposure. Several companies track sponsor success in gaining exposure and recognition. One is Joyce Julius and Associates, whose *Sponsors Report* is a popular subscription-based publication. Another is Lou Harris & Associates, whose Ad Track poll results are regularly published in *USA Today*. The Ad Track simply conveys consumer responses to major ad campaigns, including those involving athletes. (5)

Regular, Broad Studies

The first regular, broad-based study on sport consumers began during the 1970s. While working for Audits & Surveys, Dick Lipsey (who also began the Sports Market Place and the SBRnet) introduced a syndicated study, using a national probability sample, which measured participation and purchasing habits related to specific types of sport equipment. The study was repeated for 11 years, funded by subscribers such as Nike, Spalding, Reebok, and Rawlings. One important discovery was that new participants accounted for only a small percentage of sporting goods purchases (10 to 20 percent of units; 5 to 12 percent of dollars). The industry, however, had been emphasizing "come-on" equipment targeted to new participants at low cost and low profit. Obviously, the strategy needed adjustment to focus on higher levels of the escalator. Most consumers were looking to move up. (6)

✦ Table 3.2 Participation Changes in Selected NCAA Sports, 1982-2003

Total participants, all divisions

Sport	1982-1983	1992-1993	2002-2003	% change 1982-2003
Baseball	19,220	21,746	27,048	40.7
Softball	8,035	10,356	15,906	97.9
Gymnastics—men	1,569	590	313	-80.0
Gymnastics—women	1,934	1,200	1,366	-29.3
Soccer—men	13,532	14,795	18,835	39.1
Soccer—women	2,743	8,226	19,871	624.0

Data from NCAA, 2004, *1982-2003 NCAA sports sponsorship and participation report* (Indianapolis, NCAA, 2004), 90, 96, 98, 11, 3, 122, 130. Available: www.ncaa.org/library/research/participation_rates/1982-2003ParticipationReport.pdf.

In 1985, the National Sporting Goods Association (NSGA), the trade association for retailers, purchased another Lipsey research project. It is now the annual NSGA Sports Participation study, a widely cited and highly respected trend analysis. The latest 10 years of NSGA data are available at the Sports Business Research Network (www.sbrnet.com), a subscription database; the latest year is available at www.nsga.org.

The NSGA study includes not only participation, but also equipment purchases, for a national sample of people aged seven and older. The NSGA data cover a broader population base than the NCAA or NFHS data, but not always a broader base of sports. For instance, the NSGA does not track gymnastics participation. As table 3.3 indicates, some broad trends run counter to NCAA data. Both baseball and softball had fewer overall participants, and soccer had a much lower growth rate. As we will discuss later, however, the base of NCAA participants is quite different from the sample shown in table 3.3. Playing a sport one time per year does not represent the commitment needed to make a collegiate varsity team.

The NSGA surveys dig deeply into the question, Who plays what? The surveys employ a national probability sample of 10,000 households who complete mail questionnaires; results are broken down by age, gender, income, and residence, among other variables. Consistent methodology yields the most valid trend data. The NSGA has much at stake in tracking trends, especially among youth who might not appear in either NFHS or NCAA data. Over the last decade, for example, the NSGA data showed that traditional sports were not where the action was. As table 3.4 shows, three hotter activities (with explosive growth rates) were snowboarding, mountain biking, and paintball games (which were not even on the charts until 1999).

A number of firms and trade associations do similar research on long-term lifestyle trends with large, national samples, but their reports are often disseminated only to clients (proprietary research) or via very costly reports. Examples include the Sporting Goods Manufacturers Association, American Sports Data, Scarborough Sports Marketing, the Simmons Market Research Bureau, Nielsen Sports Marketing Service, USA Data, and Mediamark Research. Their services, although beyond some budgets, allow marketers to dig below surface trends to segment sport consumers in many ways, as we will discuss in chapter 6. One, more affordable, compendium of such research is By the Numbers, an "annual research guide and fact book" published by

✦ **Table 3.3** NSGA Participation Data for Selected Sports—Americans 7 years and older

Sport	1993	2003	% change
Baseball	16.7	14.6	–12.5
Softball	17.9	11.8	–34.0
Soccer	10.3	11.1	7.7

Numbers represent those who played the sport at least once in the given year (in millions).

Data from SBRnet: Baseball. Available: www.sbrnet.com/Research/Research.cfm?subRID=46; Softball. Available: www.sbrnet.com/Research/Research.cfm?subRID=399; Soccer. Available: www.sbrnet.com/Research.cfm?subRID=399.

✦ **Table 3.4** Some Hot Sports of the 1990s—Americans 7 years and older

Sport	1993	1995	2003	% change 1993-2003
Mountain biking (off road)	4.6	6.7	8.2	78.2
Snowboarding	1.8	2.8	6.3	250
Paintball games	NA	NA	7.4	NA

Numbers represent those who played the sport at least once in the given year (in millions).

Data from NSGA, *Ten year history of selected sports participation.* Available at www.nsga.org/public/pages/index.cfm?pageid=153.

Street & Smith's SportsBusiness Journal. By the Numbers includes excerpts from firms such as Scarborough and Nielsen Media Research, as well as results from some of *SSSBJ*'s own sport industry surveys, such as an annual sponsor survey. (7)

Participation Indexes

National studies can also offer comparisons from one market to another and from any market to the national sample. These comparisons typically appear in the form of an index. An index simply compares the demographic or lifestyle level of a subsample to that of the national sample. An example of indexing may be found in the *Lifestyle Market Analyst,* a standard reference that examines demographics and lifestyles in 210 metropolitan areas of the United States.

Lifestyles are divided into seven categories, one of which is "Sports, Fitness, and Health." Indexing allows the researcher to make some interesting analyses. For instance, a recent edition devoted four pages to tables analyzing American households who golfed regularly. As table 3.5 shows, 27.2 percent of golfing households earn over $100,000 annually. This yields an index of 174, a rate 74 percent higher than the national average. Thus we see that golfing households are 74 percent more likely to earn $100,000 or more, are 52 percent more likely to use a credit card for travel and entertainment, 61 percent more likely to watch sports on TV, and 107 percent more likely to snow ski frequently. This is just a tiny fraction of the analysis offered by such frequent and broad consumer studies.

Reading Sport Consumer Studies

The most important step for the researcher is to recognize the limitations of any study. As we discuss in chapter 5, all market research is limited by time and resources. Researchers make choices about many elements, including the following:

+ *Definitions.* What constitutes a "fan" or a "participant"?

+ *Methodologies.* Interviews? Observations? By phone? By mail? At an event?

+ *Sampling.* A random sample of the whole population? Several random samples grouped or "stratified" by some criterion (e.g., ticket type)?

+ *Specialty indexes.* Many sport market reports develop their own "indexes" of "the best market" or "the best fans." Readers must always be careful to examine and analyze what factors make up the index.

Anyone trying to make sense out of published studies must consider all these questions.

Definitions

Definitions are especially important. For instance, 1997 and 1998 saw many references to a golf "boom" in the wake of Tiger Woods' phenomenal start on the PGA Tour. In some respects

+ **Table 3.5** Sample Profile of Golfing U.S Households

Household characteristics	% of total golfing households	Index
Have income of $100,000 or more	27.2	174
Regularly use credit card for travel and entertainment	20.7	152
Regularly watch sports on TV	59.8	161
Snow ski frequently	18.0	207

Data from SRDS, 2004, *Lifestyle market analyst* (Des Plaines, IL), 810-811.

there was a boom. One industry newsletter—the *IEG Sponsorship Report*—indicated that the corporate world had spent $600 million on golf sponsorships in 1997, which was double the level for 1990. Some data suggested that the boom had started before Tiger Woods. The National Golf Foundation, a trade association, had shown American spending on golf at the $15.1 billion level for 1994, almost double the 1986 level of $7.8 billion. Finally, over 1,300 new courses had opened in the mid-1990s alone. As we have seen, however, the "boom" did not look so strong in another area—participation. The National Golf Foundation estimated that 24.7 million people aged 12 or older had played one round of golf in 1996, which was a decrease from the 1991 level of 24.8 million. Was it a phony boom? Not necessarily, because "one-time play" might not be a good gauge of golf participation. In other words, perhaps fewer people played just one round of golf and more people played multiple rounds. It was all in how one defined *boom*. (8)

Defining Involvement and Commitment

The golf "boom" raises key questions about defining two critical aspects of sport consumption—involvement and commitment. We consider these concepts again in chapter 4, but we cannot emphasize their importance enough. Among other things, they underlie the logic of the escalator (refer back to figure 2.2 on page 43).

As the escalator suggests, even simple awareness is a form of involvement. So is "interest," a frequently measured aspect of sport consumption. Take, for instance, the data in table 3.6, from a survey by Sponsorship Research International that looked at soccer interest among Americans during a period that contemporaries considered a soccer boom-time. These data were culled from 12,000 interviews, with the results segmented by age and gender.

At first glance, table 3.6 seems to contradict notions of a booming American soccer market. Some 80 percent of the sample had either "low" or no interest in soccer, across all categories except the 18- to 24-year-old age group, which we already saw represented in the NCAA data. And even among this "youth" market, so long proclaimed as the future of soccer, almost three quarters were in the low- or no-interest categories.

Did this mean that the soccer boom was a giant fiction? Not at all. Among other things, a suburban-focused sample might have uncovered much higher interest levels. More important, "interest" is only one measure of involvement. What about participation? Perhaps a very high percentage of the interested people moved up the escalator of involvement and became participants. In fact, other contemporary statistics from the Soccer Industry Council and the SGMA suggested that the soccer boom was solid. As table 3.7 shows, participation in soccer was continuing to grow. Total participation grew almost 8 percent from 1995 to 1996, with a 34 percent increase in the adult (18+) category. Obviously, kids were not abandoning the game as they got older.

Defining Participation

Table 3.7 emphasizes another critical aspect of sport consumer studies—defining *participation*. The 18.1 million soccer participants in 1996 were people who played at least once a

✦ **Table 3.6**   Soccer Interest (in %) in the United States, by Age and Gender

	Age				**Gender**	
Interest	**Total**	**18-24**	**25-54**	**55+**	**Male**	**Female**
High	6.8	12.1	5.7	6.4	7.1	6.5
Medium	11.3	15.6	10.6	10.8	12.6	10.1
Low	19.7	21.3	20.3	18.0	23.9	15.9
Not at all	61.4	50.9	63.1	62.7	55.7	66.6

Reprinted, by permission, from "Sports sponsometer: Soccer interest and sponsor awareness," *The Sports Business Daily 1997*, 2(April): 15.

✦ Table 3.7 U.S. Soccer Participation, 1995-1996

Category	1995 in millions	1996 in millions	% increase 1995-1996
Total participants	16.8	18.1	7.7
Male	9.5	10.9	14.7
Female	7.3	7.2	−1.3
Under 18	13.3	13.4	0.7
18 and over	3.5	4.7	34.2
Frequent: 25 or more days per year	7.3	7.7	5.4
Core: 52 or more days per year	3.2	3.2	0.0
Aficionados: Soccer is favorite activity	3.7	4	8.1

Adapted from NCAA, 1997, "U.S. soccer participation, 1995-1996," *NCAA News* 19(May): 2.

year. This is a fairly typical use of the term *participant* (as we saw in earlier NSGA data), but it has obvious limitations. It can be helpful in tracking long-term interest, but it has little to do with marketing the sport. The categories "Frequent," "Core," and "Aficionado" are far more telling because they reflect movement up the escalator. If we look more closely at rates of change at different levels of the escalator, the picture for soccer appears mixed. For instance, the rate of increase of aficionados from 1995 to 1996 was greater (8.1 percent) than that of the overall base of participants (7.7). That was good news; soccer would want to see more consumers at higher levels of interest and commitment. On the other hand, the growth rates for frequent and core participants were slower than that of the overall base. And these data show that overall female participation actually declined, in sharp contrast to the NCAA statistics considering only players on NCAA teams (see table 3.2). (9)

These statistics provide a very limited snapshot—one year's rate of change. Their real importance lies in their more precise approach to defining *participation*. In developing or interpreting research, sport marketers must take great care to remember a key question:

How will I define . . . ?

Casual or careless use of definitions will severely limit the utility of any statistics. Take, for example, one poll commissioned by MLB to examine fan support for league realignment—a very controversial issue. The poll—of 801 "fans" aged 16 or older—supposedly represented the vast population of the baseball nation. When the Associated Press looked more carefully at the sample, however, they discovered that 70 percent of the people in the sample were not aware that MLB was considering realignment. Worse yet, 44 percent had never heard of the expansion Diamondbacks or Devil Rays, and 13 percent had never heard of the Colorado Rockies. Almost half of the sample planned to attend only one game or no games during the season. As the Associated Press concluded, these were "casual fans at best"—hardly the type of "fan" worth making realignment decisions over. (10)

Definitions are not easily developed or agreed on. Take, for example, the notion of "rounds played" in golf. It might seem straightforward enough. But GOLF 20/20 has recognized inconsistency on a number of key constructs, including whether to count complimentary rounds, or whether to count any "start" no matter how many holes are played. In developing its participation survey sent to 15,827 courses, GOLF 20/20 developed its own definition of a "round played": one person who tees off in an authorized start on a golf course, where "authorized" simply means that the start occurred through the proper channels at the facility. It doesn't include people who wander onto the course to play a few holes in the evening, for example. (11)

Definitions matter in all areas of consumption. All too many sport managers still discuss Web site usage in terms of "hits," which is not a useful measure of consumption because it

Did you realize that when purchasing sport or exercise equipment, people are consuming sport? Even members of a gym are sport consumers.
© Bananastock

measures the total number of files accessed and therefore inflates usage. Web marketers have settled on "unique visitors" as a standard measure of Web usage. (12)

Multiple Measures

The most effective research on the sport consumer employs clearly defined, multiple measures of involvement and commitment. As our data have suggested, there are many ways to measure sport consumption. Playing is but one index, and even here one can separate "real" playing from "virtual" playing on a video game. There is also watching at an event or on television, listening on the radio, or reading in the sport section of the newspaper. Moreover, people are consuming sport when they buy equipment—even if they don't use what they buy. After all, how many stationary bicycles now stand idle, with daily use as a clothes hanger? Marketers must consider multiple measures when writing or reading sport consumer research.

Consistent Samples and Methods

Even regularly produced studies occasionally alter the samples or methods of data collection. If this happens, an apparent trend in participation may be a result of changes in record keeping and not in participation at all. For instance, beginning in 1979, the NFHS discontinued collecting participation data from Canadian schools and from junior high schools. This inflated the data collected before 1979. In 1995-1996, the NCAA began including "provisional" members in their participation data, which served to inflate the figures after that date. Along methodological lines, in 1994 the Simmons Market Research Bureau changed its approach to measuring consumer reading habits (for instance, Simmons can tell you what magazines skiers read regularly). This effectively created a fault line in Simmons' data. As one publishing executive put it, "The name is the same, Simmons. Otherwise, you're dealing with a new company." In any of these cases, an unaware researcher would risk grave errors by tracking trends across the fault lines. (13)

Representative Samples

We discuss sampling more thoroughly in chapter 5; its importance cannot be stressed enough. Although the intent is often to represent the broader population, few studies can reach an entire population. Errors in sampling can distort results, regardless of numerical "significance." The classic sampling error occurred in the 1936 U.S. presidential election, when the magazine *Literary Digest* predicted a victory for Alf Landon over Franklin Roosevelt. The prediction rested on the results of a survey of readers. Unfortunately, readers of *Literary Digest* tended to be educated, relatively well-off Republicans; the sample was therefore stacked for Landon. Roosevelt won in a landslide.

Sport consumer studies have had their share of sampling errors. In fact, American Sports Data began its own syndicated national study in 1984 in response to a belief that existing studies were grossly underestimating the size of the sporting goods market. The president of ASD, Harvey Lauer, identified two reasons for sampling errors in existing studies: (1) a focus on participants, when many purchases (especially of running shoes) were by nonparticipants, and (2) an underrepresentation of under-18 youth and young singles. In part, ASD built its study to correct these errors. (14)

Readers must also be careful to consider the statistical effects of sampling. This is particularly true when reading or employing results for decision-making purposes. By their very nature, samples cannot perfectly represent a larger population. There is always some "margin of error" or some "confidence level" or both. The Gallup Poll, for instance, has been asking Americans about their sports interests since the 1930s, which makes it a useful record of changing fan interests. The Gallup Poll is careful to explain the limitations of its samples:

> These results are based on telephone interviews with a randomly selected national sample of 1,024 and 1,011 adults, 18 years and older, conducted March 26-28 and June 8-10, 2001, respectively. For results based on these samples, one can say with 95 percent confidence that the maximum error attributable to sampling and other random effects is plus or minus 3 percentage points. In addition to sampling error, question wording and practical difficulties in conducting surveys can introduce error or bias into the findings of public opinion polls.

If an excerpt in a media story does not describe the statistical limitations of a survey, the reader must infer them. Fortunately, a number of Web sites now offer free and simple tutorials on basic statistics or analyses of polls and surveys. (15)

Analyzing Specialty "Rankings" and Indexes

Every fall, the *U.S. News and World Report* publishes a special issue with lists that rank colleges and universities: the "top 50 national universities," the "top 100 regional liberal arts colleges," and the like. And every fall, colleges and universities complain about their place in the rankings, and especially about the factors used in the rankings. We are assaulted by such rankings all the time—the "most livable city," the "hottest" high-tech region. From time to time, one finds a ranking of the "best sports town" or the "best fans," and nothing creates a controversy like a sport-related ranking. Just think about college football's Bowl Championship Series, and the decisions by ESPN and *USA Today* to disassociate themselves from the ranking. As with all such rankings and indexes, the reader should ask at least two fundamental questions:

What factors are used in the rankings (versus what might have been used)?

How are the factors "weighted" to arrive at a final ranking or index?

In January 2000, for instance, *Street & Smith's SportsBusiness Journal* published a very interesting "fan support index" that ranked fan support in each of the NFL's markets. The index was based on a formula that included both "support" factors worth 60 percent of the score (average attendance, percent of stadium capacity filled during season, attendance fluctuation) and "difficulty" factors worth 40 percent of the score (winning percentage, number of stadium seats per 100,000 residents in metropolitan area, ratio of average ticket cost to every $10,000 of local per capita income, average high temperature for month of December—with domed stadiums assigned a 72 degree temperature). According to this index, Cleveland had the "best" fans and Tennessee had the "worst."

Of course, the rankings might look different if the *SSSBJ* had used different factors. Take the case of attendance. The Arizona Cardinals (ranked next to "worst") would appear to be unfairly penalized by a formula that used both average attendance and percent of capacity. Why? At the time of the survey, the Cardinals played in the mammoth Sun Devil Stadium (with a capacity of 73,014). Sun Devil Stadium was built in 1958 for the Arizona State University team. Although the NFL has some larger stadiums, they were all built with an eye on an NFL team. When the Cardinals designed their new stadium (opened in 2006), it was a slightly cozier facility (63,000 for football), with a retracting roof and all the modern amenities we discuss in chapter 14. All of these factors should drive up the demand for tickets. After all, there are many alternatives to watching football in sunny Arizona. This raises the problem of a further penalty for the Cardinals—a high average December temperature. What if the ranking considered good weather to be a detriment? Why not use a high average September temperature—Phoenix can be boiling in September. Just when fans in Cleveland and Green Bay (ranked number 2) were really thinking football, fans in Phoenix were staying inside their air-conditioned homes, malls, or cars. And so, one can make a case for adding or removing any number of factors, just as one can make a case for reducing the weight of "support" factors to 40 percent and increasing the weight of "difficulty" factors to 60 percent. In this case, the "best" or "worst" fans are a product of an artificial instrument that readers must always challenge. (16)

Wrap-Up

We have offered an introduction to the many sources of information available to the sport marketer. Several sources, such as the Simmons, Harris, Nielsen, and Census Bureau reports, are rather standard fare for any product marketer. Others are specific to the sport industry. Many of the regular, broad studies are syndicated, or available for a price. The marketer may find excerpted information by reading such periodicals as *Marketing News*, *BusinessWeek*, *Advertising Age*, and *Amusement Business*, all of which devote sections to the sport industry. In addition, an increasing number of periodicals deal specifically with sport business issues, including *Team Marketing Report*, *Sport Marketing Quarterly*, *Street & Smith's SportsBusiness Journal*, the *Sports Business Daily (SBD)*, and *Athletic Business*, to name just a few. The *SBD* is especially valuable because it compiles and edits stories from a vast range of sources. It is an essential resource for serious executives and researchers. Finally, there are growing numbers of Internet sources, led by SBRnet. All contain information on recent studies of the sport consumer. (For more sources, see appendix A.)

Although source material is abundant, the marketer must use it judiciously. Most studies are difficult to compare because they use different measures of participation, involvement, social status, and lifestyle. The marketer must also look very carefully at methodologies. Some studies have rather limited samples; others include highly leading questions. For instance, one upstart professional league commissioned a "study" of "fans" in that sport. But even a casual researcher could quickly see that too many questions in the survey led the subjects to make statements unfavorable to the established rival league, which the sponsor of the study was about to sue. Marketers who analyze studies carefully, however, will have a better appreciation and understanding of the consumers of their own sport product. While gathering information on *who* their consumers are likely to be, marketers must also ponder the more difficult question of *why* a person would want to buy or consume their product. This question moves us into the general realm of consumer behavior, a topic we discuss in the next chapter.

Activities

1. What standard questions must a sport marketer ask about consumers?

2. Take an hour in the library, in person or via the Internet, to discover and list all the available sources on consumers of your favorite sport. Try to categorize these sources (e.g., by frequency and scope, by medium of publication).

3. Analyze two of the sources you identified in the previous activity and suggest how you might improve their strength.

4. Provide examples of research that differs according to the scope of the populations or sports analyzed.

Your Marketing Plan

You have picked an organization, considered your "theory of the business" and your mission, conducted a SWOT analysis (strengths, weaknesses, opportunities, threats), and set some objectives. To some extent, you should have already considered your consumers. But after reading this chapter, you might refine some of your thinking. Use some of the data sources described in the chapter (or listed in appendix A) to develop a clearer picture of your consumers. How will you define *involvement, commitment,* or *participation*? Can you identify special segments of consumers?

Chapter 4

Perspectives in Sport Consumer Behavior

Objectives

✦ To recognize the differences among socialization, involvement, and commitment for sport consumers.

✦ To understand the various individual and environmental factors that shape consumer involvement and commitment in sport.

✦ To understand the decision process for sport consumers.

Dreamy Fields

In 1994, an estimated 50,000 people, some from thousands of miles away, visited an Iowa cornfield. Along the way, the pilgrims may have picked up a flyer from the local Chamber of Commerce. The headline read "Is This Heaven? Dyersville, Iowa, Where Dreams Come True." Their destination? Don Lansing's baseball field, featured in the hit movie *Field of Dreams*. Why would 50,000 pilgrims trek to a converted cornfield that was just part of Hollywood's dreamland? Well, we could just as easily ask why thousands buy tennis rackets, golf clubs, bicycles, and fishing rods, and then hardly use them. Or why others pay $2,500 per game for a courtside NBA seat. Or why others train daily like Navy SEALs so they can punish their bodies in grueling "Ironman" triathlons. The answers are as numerous as the people involved. (1)

We have looked in various ways at who the sport consumer is. In this chapter, we examine why people consume sport. To that end, we consider sport consumers within the larger context of general consumer behavior, including various factors that help to explain how people are socialized into sport—how they become involved and committed. Although countless studies, theories, and models attempt to get into the mind of the consumer, we may characterize the factors that influence behavior as either environmental or individual. Environmental factors may include significant others such as family, peers, and coaches; social and cultural norms; social class structure; race and gender relations; climatic and geographic conditions; technology; market behavior of firms in the sport industry; and sport opportunity structure. Individual factors include one's self-concept, stage in the life or family cycle, physical characteristics, learning, perceptions, motivations, and attitudes, as well as the complex process of consumer decision making itself. In this chapter, we consider each of these factors in turn. (2)

As we discuss in chapter 5, sport marketers must look beyond basic demographic research to examine the reasons consumers are (or aren't) aware of, involved in, or committed to their organization or product. Galen Trail, a professor who studies sport consumer behavior, recently lamented to *Street & Smith's SportsBusiness Journal* that "the problem with the sports organizations and their marketers is that when they do market research, they get stuck on the demographics," which Trail claimed explain only 3 to 5 percent of fan attendance. "You can do all the demographic research in the world," he concluded, "and you aren't learning diddly. It's the psychographic research that matters. That's what tells you why people are or aren't going to show up." Demographics are clearly worth more than "diddly," but Galen Trail is correct to say that they are but a small piece of a large puzzle. (3)

Socialization, Involvement, and Commitment

Environmental and individual factors influence how and to what extent people become involved with and committed to sport. Think about your own sport activities, whether as a child, a youth, or an adult. Something or somebody got you interested, somehow, in an activity. Perhaps it was a trip to watch a game, an afternoon playing with a parent or friend, or a television broadcast of an exciting event or championship. A trigger of interest prompted your involvement and perhaps your socialization in a sport.

Sociologists typically consider socialization to be the process by which people assimilate and develop the skills, knowledge, attitudes, and other "equipment" necessary to perform various social roles. This involves two-way interaction between the individual and the environment. Socialization, in turn, demands some kind of involvement, in our case with sport. Involvement takes one of three basic forms: (4)

◆ *Behavioral involvement: the hands-on "doing."* This includes playing at practice or in competition; it also includes the activities of fans at a game (or at home), watching and listening and rooting.

◆ *Cognitive involvement: the acquisition of information and knowledge about a sport.* Players sitting through a chalk talk, and fans at a Boosters Club meeting listening to the coach explain how last week's game plan worked so well, both exemplify cognitive involvement. Magazines, newspapers, game programs, radio, television, and the Internet are key media for cognitive involvement by consumers eager to know more about a sport. In a recent Turnkey Sports Poll, sport industry executives predicted a significant swing over the next five years in where fans "most often" get information—from heavy current reliance on television (39 percent) and radio (31.9 percent) to an overwhelming future focus on the Internet (49.8 percent) and wireless devices (24.5 percent). It is no wonder that newspapers and television stations are duplicating and expanding their best sports features on their Web sites. (5)

◆ *Affective involvement: the attitudes, feelings, and emotions that a consumer has toward an activity.* Pep rallies and pregame locker room talks are standard fare for affective involvement. But so too are the best advertisements. Just think of any Nike ad. Like them or not, these ads stir the emotions about a sport (or about Nike).

Commitment refers to the frequency, duration, and intensity of involvement in a sport, or the willingness to expend money, time, and energy in a pattern of sport involvement. Movement up the escalator normally indicates a deeper commitment. For some sports, like tennis and golf, the ties between involvement and commitment can be dramatic. For instance, a random sample of 468 fans at a Men's Clay Court Tennis Championship displayed the following types and levels of tennis involvement:

◆ 89 percent were tennis players.

◆ 45.7 percent rated their own skills as "intermediate."

◆ 42.1 percent rated their own skills as "advanced intermediate."

◆ 71.8 percent rated tennis as a "favorite" participant sport.

◆ 52.9 percent rated tennis as the "most frequent" sport attended.

◆ 39.6 percent rated tennis as the "most frequent" sport viewed on television.

◆ 75.5 percent owned a racket worth $100 to $199.

◆ 27.8 percent owned a racket worth $200+.

These were highly committed consumers, spending considerable time, money, and energy on the sport of tennis. (6)

The marketer must clearly understand the types of involvement and commitment that consumers represent. The WNBA season-ticket holder who subscribes to fan magazines, attends every game, tracks game statistics, pays for special-content sport Web sites, downloads team information onto her cell phone, plays in a fantasy league, and roots with great emotion is obviously different from the father who brings his child to one game to satisfy a sense of parental duty. The casual spectator who attends a game with a free ticket is distinctly different from the rabid fan watching the same game at home. The act of attendance may or may not reflect or develop a deeper commitment. A similar distinction exists between club members who use many amenities at a facility, and use them often, versus those who don't. The member who swims, plays tennis, regularly attends aerobics classes, and brings children to the club's child care program is far more likely to rejoin than the member who occasionally comes alone to ride a stationary bike.

The committed player, fan, or member thinks more, feels more, and does more. Nurturing the committed consumer is a key goal. So is better research on commitment to sport. As several experts recently asked: "What impact does being a professional football fan have on consumption of football at other levels, or consumption of other spectator sports, or recreational sport involvement?" In the last few years, sport marketing researchers have begun to look much more closely at the nature of consumer involvement, but there is a great deal of work to do on these important topics. (7)

Minnesota Fans Go Wild With Commitment and Identification

The Minnesota Wild—the Gopher State's latest professional hockey incarnation—enjoyed the best of all worlds in May 2003: enlightened owners, a competitive team, a new arena, and America's number-one hockey market. As Michael Farber reported in *Sports Illustrated,* hard-core fans began to queue up in the early morning rain shortly after the Wild had won their second-round series against Vancouver. A block of 4,500 tickets for the Western Conference championship series would go on sale in 12 hours. Kathy Spina and Susan Bakula were among the first hundred in line. "This is a cult," admitted Bakula. Spina, ironically a mental health therapist, invoked an image of Jonestown: "We've drunk the Kool-Aid, symbolically." Soon the Wild marketers wisely opened the doors to the Xcel Energy Center, where the faithful congregated in the lobby, communing with free hot dogs, soft drinks, or their own elixirs. Farber reported that the 4,500 tickets sold out in five minutes. With all season tickets sold in 2003, the Wild had 5,500 people signed up for the "Wild Warming House," the quaint name for the waiting list pool, so evocative of the patient ice fisherman.

But Minnesota fans know their hockey. As Farber reported, 40 percent of season-ticket holders also play the game, not surprising in a state with 188 high school teams that sell out both the girls and the boys tournaments, a history of packing U.S. Olympic teams, and a state university program that wins NCAA championships with a largely home-grown roster. Odds are that Wild fans score highly on the Sport Spectator Identification Scale, an instrument developed by Daniel Wann and Neil Brascombe in the early 1990s. The SSIS asks simple questions such as, "How strongly do your friends see you as a fan of . . . ." Over time, we might expect that more teams will employ instruments such as the SSIS to gauge fan identification across user segments (see chapter 6) and across time. (8)

Environmental and individual factors interact constantly. Although people are influenced by their environment, they are also capable of reshaping the social, physical, and cultural landscape around them. If this were not so, life would be static. Change is part of existence in politics, in art, in music, and in sport. For this reason, the sport marketer must understand the complex dynamics that shape consumers. The model in figure 4.1 depicts the interaction that determines the outcomes of importance to this chapter: socialization, involvement, and commitment in sport. For example, the proprietors of a summer hockey camp must develop the marketing mix that will match the wants and needs of potential consumers. To do so, the proprietors rely on and become a part of this socialization process in sport.

For instance, our hockey camp entrepreneurs must base their marketing mix on their assessment of demand. Do the regional values and norms support hockey to the extent that kids want summer instruction? This may in part relate to climatic conditions; one expects more demand in northern regions. But at the same time, a hockey hotbed like Huntsville, Alabama, may defy climatic trends. A few fanatics may devote much of their lives to promoting a nontraditional sport in a given area and thereby alter local or regional values—and in turn alter consumer attitudes toward the activity. At the same time, potential consumers who have developed a desire to play hockey may lack opportunities to participate because of economic hardship or racial or gender discrimination.

Although marketers adjust or develop the marketing mix for their hockey camp, potential consumers find that a host of individual factors affect their socialization, involvement, and commitment in relation to hockey. Some parents may perceive hockey as a brawling, violent sport that their children should avoid. Some children may be motivated to play hockey because they feel it will "toughen" them. Other children may believe that only big people can play hockey successfully. Such individual and environmental factors will play a part in the decision-making process between parent and child on the question of attending a hockey camp. As figure 4.1 suggests, consumer decision making is the processing of all the knowledge, feelings, and behaviors (both individual and environmental) that results in increased (or decreased) involvement in or commitment to sport. Players and fans alike are constantly making decisions that move them up, down, or off the escalator.

Like all models, figure 4.1 is a picture of a complex process, not a formula that guarantees understanding and correct decisions. This figure should serve to remind the marketer of all the factors to sift through to understand and develop consumer interest, involvement, and commitment.

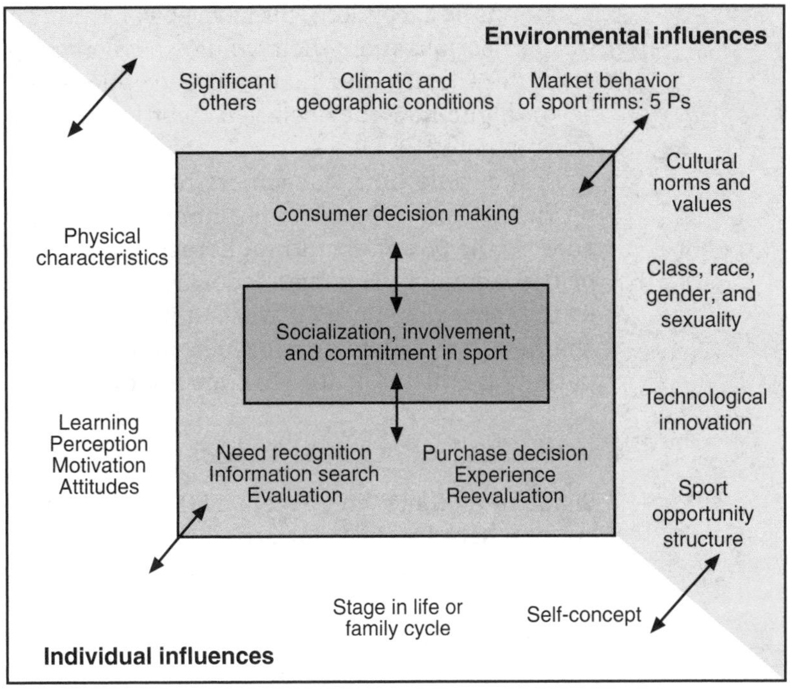

Environmental Factors

Consumers are surrounded by a host of factors that may influence their decisions about sport involvement. As we consider some of the most prominent factors, we stress again the constant interaction between and among them.

Significant Others

FIGURE 4.1 Consumer behavior in sport.

Much of a person's socialization into sport roles occurs through interaction with significant others, who may actively shape patterns of involvement or who may act as role models. Some of the most important are family members, coaches, teachers, and peers. Although these are personal relations, consumers may also have impersonal, distant "reference groups" that are also significant.

Parents play a vital role in introducing children to sport. In the 1980s, a national sample of parents showed the following:

+ About 75 percent almost always or often encouraged their children to participate.

+ About 72 percent encouraged their children to practice their skills away from the game.

+ Only 6 percent encouraged their children to spend less time playing sports.

Sport consumers recognize the importance of family and friends. A recent study of World Championship Wrestling fans showed that only 27.3 percent had found the sport on their own; 22.4 percent had been introduced by parents; 11.1 percent, by grandparents; 19.2 percent, by other family members; and 20.2 percent, by friends. (9)

Peers and friends are very important. In fact, some studies of female athletes have indicated that peers are more significant than family in encouraging participation through adulthood. Studies of health or athletic club members have also demonstrated the importance of the peer network; 61 percent of one national sample said they first became aware of their clubs from friends or colleagues. Further, friends were the single most important factor in getting a person to try the club's offerings; advertising and special promotions had far less impact. These results parallel general consumer behavior. For instance, a study by the *Yankelovich MONITOR* showed the following responses from American consumers:

+ 40 percent said that advice from friends had a strong influence on buying behavior.

+ 57 percent considered advice from a friend or relative a good reason to try a new grocery brand.

+ 60 percent said they seek advice from friends when considering products they know little about.

Sport is no exception: Pals have power. Family and friends may be the most powerful force in sport socialization; their influence colors behavior and attitudes. One study of baseball spectators determined that their perceptions of event quality (e.g., stadium, service) varied according to how they believed their family and friends viewed baseball's popularity and acceptability. (10)

At the same time, consumers have reference groups, heroes, or role models who may be distant and impersonal but nonetheless important. The hit movie *Bend It Like Beckham* showed the power of cultural heroes. For sixth-graders in any middle school, it could also be the seemingly Olympian "cool kids" in the eighth grade. Or for many adolescents, it may be the "cool kids" on MTV, who influence both school and sport fashions. As we explain in chapters 7 and 13, teams, leagues, and corporate sponsors have much at stake in making particular athletes central to consumer reference groups. (11)

Cultural Norms and Values

Significant others tend to convey the beliefs, attitudes, and behaviors that typify their own cultural settings. In a society's broader framework, however, there are many alternative cultures, subcultures, and countercultures that may nurture different lifestyles. This is as true in sport as it is in all areas of living; if not for the dynamics of culture, society would not change over time. A stagnant society would greatly affect sport. Consider, for example, that as late as the 1920s, many U.S. communities outlawed organized sports on Sunday. Can you imagine being arrested for golfing on a Sunday? That is unthinkable today, yet at the turn of the 20th century it happened with some regularity in U.S. cities where cultural groups fought over secularism and the Sabbath. And 40 years ago, who would have predicted that sellouts for the Minnesota high school hockey championship were for the girls? Or that the star hockey team at the 1998 Olympics was a women's team?

America may have some dominant, long-lasting values about sport, including notions of character building, discipline, fitness, and competition—all of which parallel the values of free-enterprise capitalism. These values certainly motivate people to consume sports. At the same time, one can find alternative norms and values. "Slackers" offer new styles of character and discipline in the X Games. Skateboarding and in-line skating appeal to adolescents who value creativity and freedom over adult-directed regimens. Skateboarding will hardly destroy baseball or football. Yet it would be instructive to understand better the values of this and other special sports subcultures. (12)

There are also probable differences in regional values, despite the sweep of television. The Boston Celtics and Boston Bruins, for instance, have been very slow to adopt the glitzy promotions that fill most NBA and NHL arenas—laser shows, strobe lights, smoky and thunderous introductions, cheerleaders, and dancing mascots. These are the very same promotions that have helped build hockey markets in places such as Charleston, South Carolina, and Lafayette Parish, Louisiana. So far, they haven't flown in staid old Boston. But if the Bruins or Celtics want to attract young families, in the age of MTV, how long can they hold out? Says Pat Williams, the Orlando Magic's longtime promotional wizard: "This is a huge, huge dilemma for New England. Is conservative New England capable of handling this all at once? Or do you ease into it?" These have not been easy questions to answer. As sports go global, such cultural issues multiply. Simon Wardle has seen this close up in his work with Octagon's "Passion Drivers" research effort. For instance, he has cautioned sport properties about their efforts to market in China, where fan passion "is much more about participation and active appreciation of skill and technique," as opposed to Europe and North America, where passion is for team brands. (13)

Class, Race, and Gender Relations

Cultural differences often stem from differences in power and influence within a general social structure. Some groups have easier access to rewards and prestige, which may include sport. Americans may believe that sport is an egalitarian and democratic institution; the historical and sociological record indicates something else. The marketer must recognize the difference.

Class

The influence of social class is sometimes subtle. There is little consensus among researchers on exactly what constitutes social class distinctions or how to assess a person's class rank. For some, class is a function of income, education, or occupation. For others, it is a matter of inherited prestige and status, which derive from residence and lifestyle. Numerous scales attempt to describe various strata in the class system. It is clear, though, that differences in class standing relate to differences in lifestyle, including sport involvement.

This complexity is especially acute among many middle-class Americans, to which may be added some people from traditional working-class jobs, such as plumbers and carpenters. Most of these people consider themselves to be middle class, and many of them have household incomes that are similar to those of their white-collar counterparts. However, there are also important differences. "White-collar" middle-class people may spend money on tennis and golf, while their "blue-collar" counterparts may choose to invest in bowling and hunting. In this case, there is a serious difference between purchasing power and purchase behavior. (14)

Table 4.1 offers several simple dimensions by which social class groups have histori- cally diverged in their sport lives. For example, elite sports such as polo, the hunt, and golf, have required great expanses of open space that often are not available to those with lower incomes. Middle-class groups, especially from within the white-collar, managerial segments, have flocked to sports such as football and baseball, where space has been carefully designed and rationalized. Working-class sports such as boxing and dog fighting (still alive, although illegal) grew in confined areas. Basketball's early growth was from patches of playgrounds and small armories to gymnasiums and multipurpose auditoriums—all a long way from the glamour of today's venues.

The reasons certain sports link with certain classes remain somewhat obscure and in need of research. Some activities appeal to the upper ranks because of their esoteric and historically exclusive nature. Golf, polo, and yachting are examples of what Thorstein Veblen called "conspicuous consumption"—clear expressions of wealth and privilege, particularly through membership in exclusive clubs.

At the other end are what some sociologists have called "prole sports," working-class or proletarian activities such as roller derby, motorcycle racing, or demolition derby. Such sports, with their speed, machinery, and danger, may express the peculiar regimentation of the work worlds of this social class.

While both elites and working class folks have focused on expressive uses of their bodies in sport, the middle class has tended to use sport as an instrument for achieving the disciplined life so ingrained in the American corporate lifestyle. Hard work, sacrifice, teamwork, and preci- sion, so closely tied to football and baseball, dominate the ethos of middle-class sport. (15)

✦ **Table 4.1** Some Historical Dimensions of Sport, Class, and Status

Class	Space	Use of body	Ethos
Upper, elite	Usually expansive (golf, polo, hunt)	Expressive	Exclusivity
Middle	Rationally defined (baseball, football)	Instrumental	Discipline, respectability
Working	Limited by circumstance (boxing, dog-fighting)	Expressive	Replicate life conditions of struggle, violence, chance

Data from D. Booth and J. Loy, 1999, "Sport, Status, and Style," *Sport History Review* 30: 1-26.

Of course, life can't be put into boxes. The complexities of history usually confound simple models. Auto racing, especially NASCAR, is a good example. A "prole sport" that started on dirt tracks, it is now produced on highly rationalized, modern tracks for the highest levels of the American elite who sit in glassy boxes above the crowd. Some critics complain that the "big-time" sports are provoking elements of class struggle. Bigger and gaudier skyboxes, expanded areas of expensive club seats, and endless rounds of price hikes seem to indicate to the everyday fan that America's teams have been transformed into private clubs for corporate suits. We return to this issue in chapters 6, 10, and 14. For now, the point is that the marketer must recognize the complexity of the U.S. class structure.

Race

Race relations have a similar impact on patterns of sport involvement. Although it is clear that African Americans are represented in all categories of social class, it is equally clear that they have endured continued racial discrimination resulting in overrepresentation in urban areas and in low-income, low-education categories. In the case of sport participation, even a casual observer can see the dominance of black athletes in basketball, football, and track, as well as their underrepresentation in hockey, golf, and tennis (despite the prominence of Tiger Woods and Venus and Serena Williams). Does this mean that participation is dictated by their genes? Probably not. Contemporary medical and genetic studies have uncovered some differences among population groups (including racial and ethnic minorities) in their proclivity to certain illnesses and their responses to certain drug treatments. At this time, however, there is little credible research on genetic disposition in sports. Rather, African Americans (like Italian or Hispanic Americans) are likelier to excel in the sports that are available through school and recreation programs and appear as viable avenues to status and achievement. As one distinguished geneticist argued, behavioral differences among "racial" groups may have some genetic basis, "but it may also be environmental, the result of diet, or family structure, or schooling, or any number of biological and social factors." (16)

Race is the enduring American conundrum, especially in the sport marketplace. The American public generally embraces the notion that Jackie Robinson opened doors of opportunity, and that the integration of baseball helped spur a revolution in civil rights. And there is no denying Muhammad Ali and Michael Jordan a place in the all-time pantheon of American heroes. On the other hand, economists have provided quantitative evidence of discrimination against black athletes: (17)

- ✦ Two studies on the market for baseball cards suggest that white players are valued more highly than minority players of equal productivity.
- ✦ A study of revenues and racial composition at 42 NCAA Division I basketball programs concluded that "on average, a team replacing a black player with a white player of equal skill gains in excess of $100,000 in annual gate receipts, providing a strong incentive for college basketball programs to discriminate against black recruits."
- ✦ A study of 259 local NBA broadcasts concluded that a team's local ratings went up almost one half of a rating point for every additional 10 minutes of playing time given to a white player.

Recent research has also started to tease out differences between black and white sport consumers. One study of WNBA fans in Atlanta and Columbus, Ohio, found that white spectators were more likely to "make their sport experience an extension of a social outing at a bar or restaurant," and were more likely to buy their tickets in advance. At the same time, southern black spectators were more attracted to promotional giveaways and were more likely to get team information via the radio. There is a great need for more research focused on consumer behavior among racial minorities, in the United States and elsewhere. Although these studies must be read with caution for context, samples, and significance, they suggest clearly that race matters. (18)

Gender and Sexuality

Gender relations cut across both class and race. Historically women have been denied opportunities to participate in most sports, but that has changed considerably in the last three decades, largely because of Title IX. In 1971, only 1 in 27 high school girls played sports. By 1996, the ratio was 1 in 3. The increases in college sports have been equally dramatic. In 1972, U.S. colleges and universities averaged only two women's teams per campus. Thirty years later, that number had quadrupled. It has not been easy. The development of female athletics has been a long struggle involving not only legal challenges to the established, male-dominated structure of competitive athletics in schools and colleges, but also general assaults on cultural values that equate aggressive physical activities with masculinity. Given such conditions, it is not surprising that researchers discovered peer groups to have a greater importance for female athletes than for their male counterparts. (19)

Women also are a major force among spectators, across a host of "big-time" sports. Recent fan surveys have shown that females make up over 40 percent of the fan base in football, indoor soccer, and auto racing. Data from Sponsorship Research International, USA (see table 4.2), show widespread female interest at "medium to strong" levels for the Olympics, the NFL, ice skating, and gymnastics. Nothing has demonstrated the potential for women's sports like the growing interest in women's collegiate basketball, which fueled record-breaking levels of attendance and television ratings from the mid-1990s to the mid-2000s. (20)

Women's sports have clearly come of age, raising some critical questions for marketers. For instance, will women's interests in sport products parallel those of males, or do women, regardless of skill levels, derive different satisfactions from sport involvement? Early studies of sports television viewing—dominated by traditional "male" sports—showed interesting differences between male and female viewers:

+ Men were more emotionally involved in viewing.
+ Men engaged in pregame rituals to "pump up" for the game.
+ Women were more likely to watch sports because others were watching.
+ Women were more likely to work while they watched.

We will look more closely in chapter 6 at research on gender divides in fan interests and behaviors. (21)

Finally, the commercial success of women's spectator sports—whether basketball, figure skating, gymnastics, volleyball, tennis, or golf—raises questions about the sport product. Women's sports appear to offer alternative visions of what sport is or can be. We will return to this in chapter 6. Sport still may be the altar for many male rituals, but females have carved out their own cults, with huge numbers of converts, many of whom are male. (22)

Sexuality has long been a taboo subject, especially in the sport world. In the 19th century, sports were defined as "manly." It was hard enough for straight women to break into this masculine territory, let alone gay, lesbian, bisexual, or transgendered (GLBT) athletes.

+ **Table 4.2** Sports Interest Among a National Sample of 6,000 Females

Sport	Percentage by age reporting an interest of 5 or higher on a 10-point scale		
	18-34	35-54	55+
Olympic Games	69	71	65
NFL	65	53	46
Ice skating	57	62	69
Gymnastics	56	57	57

Adapted, by permission, from "Sports sponsometer: Targeting the female sports audience," *The Sports Business Daily*, 1997, 8(Oct.): 16.

And yet, the tennis world did not crumble when Richard Raskind became Renee Richards. The Olympics were not threatened by Greg Louganis' homosexuality, or by the Gay Games. In the last decade, scholars have begun to examine sexuality and sport, and GLBT activists have pressed more vigorously for opportunities to pursue sports opportunities free of harassment. (23)

Class, ethnicity, race, gender, and sexuality are all part of the swirl of culture. Their effects on consumer behavior are multiple, interrelated, complex, and critically important. As one writer concluded, "Although no one expects every marketer to be an anthropologist, sociologist, or ethnologist, we need to learn how the cultural issues of language, religion, family patterns, gender roles, education, and aspirations affect consumer behavior patterns." This is certainly true in the sport world. (24)

Climatic and Geographic Conditions

Although revolutions in travel and communications have diminished some of the regional variations in sport consumption, there are still some differences based on climate and topography. For instance, Minnesota and Massachusetts still dominate the production of U.S. hockey players. Similarly, the mountainous areas of New England and the West produce far more world-class skiers than other parts of the country. Regional weather patterns have been, concluded GOLF 20/20, "far and away the biggest factor impacting rounds of golf." The dry sun and long coast of California spawned both surfing and skateboarding. Geographer John Rooney recently identified 11 distinct "regions" of sport involvement, from the "Eastern Cradle" to the "Pigskin Cult" of the deep South to the "Pacific Cornucopia" of surfing, skiing, and just about everything else (see figure 4.2). Historians have begun to look at the history of southern approaches to sports, including hunting, auto racing, and baseball. Although regional sport cultures demand much greater analysis, clearly climate and topography have played important roles. (25)

FIGURE 4.2 John F. Rooney Jr.'s American sports regions.
Courtesy of John F. Rooney, Jr.

Technological Innovation

As historian John Betts outlined in a classic essay, technology has had significant effects on the sport marketplace. One hundred fifty years ago, railroads and streetcars expanded and created networks of teams and fans without which there would have been no National League and no national pastime. Around the same time, entrepreneurs in leather goods and paper products recognized the possibilities in focused production of sporting goods. Firms like Spalding, Reach, Wright and Ditson, MacGregor, and Wilson shrewdly drove increased demand with slick packaging, pricing, and promotions—in ways that have been copied ever since. The telegraph, the motion picture, radio, and television each influenced the development of sport consumers. Twenty years ago, marketers viewed television as the most important medium for "mass" marketing. How could we ever go beyond satellite broadcasts? And then along came the Internet. And then WiFi. How will these latest technologies affect sports fans? The big leagues want to know.

One 2002 NFL survey of 1,407 men found that fantasy game players spent about 30 percent more hours per week watching the NFL on TV than the average male (8.4 hours versus 6.6 hours). The NFL planned to increase fantasy content on its Web site. In 10 years, will most fans watch games on two screens—their television and their computer? What about the "third screen"—the cell phone? One survey, by a firm called In-Stat, projected a staggering number—by 2009, 22.3 million Americans would be using a wireless device to watch video. That is a serious market for sport organizations. At the same time, will new technologies like iPods and wireless video increase or reduce present patterns of sport involvement and commitment? (26)

Market Behavior of Sport Firms

The behavior of sport firms has important ramifications for consumer involvement. As subsequent chapters outline in detail, these market activities revolve around product, price, place (distribution), promotion, and public relations—the five Ps of sport marketing. It is clear, for instance, that the vast distribution of sport events via television has had a major effect on enlarging the base of consumers for related products such as novelties and memorabilia. Decisions on how much to televise are part of any team's marketing strategy. Similarly, decisions on club membership fees and promotional campaigns may make or break a consumer's decision to join. New sports typically depend on the marketing behavior of existing suppliers. Snowboarding is a good case in point. In the early 1990s, many ski resorts viewed snowboarding as an intrusive, dangerous, slope-wrecking activity for young, show-off "slackers." Snowboarders were either prohibited, crowded onto limited runs, or forced to pass safety and courtesy tests (which, incidentally, many skiers are also in need of). By the mid-1990s, however, most ski resorts recognized that snowboarding represented the major hope for industry growth. *American Demographics* even predicted that by 2012, snowboarders would outnumber skiers. Market behavior changed dramatically, with resorts developing special areas and events for snowboarders, coupled with aggressive promotions about being snowboarder-friendly. The new market behavior probably hastened the day of the snowboard majority. (27)

The Sport Opportunity Structure

When we consider the array of environmental factors that influence consumer behavior in sport, we can see how complicated the marketer's task really is. This is why segmentation strategies (considered in chapter 6) are so important. They help to categorize consumer groups by some of the important and perceptible environmental (and also individual) factors related to involvement in and commitment to sport. Ultimately, environmental factors combine to create various sport opportunity structures that may vary from social group to social group. The sport marketer may develop a market grid that assesses various locales and groups along the dimensions of involvement and opportunity structure. Figure 4.3 provides a simple grid that the marketer might use for crude sorting. The "country club

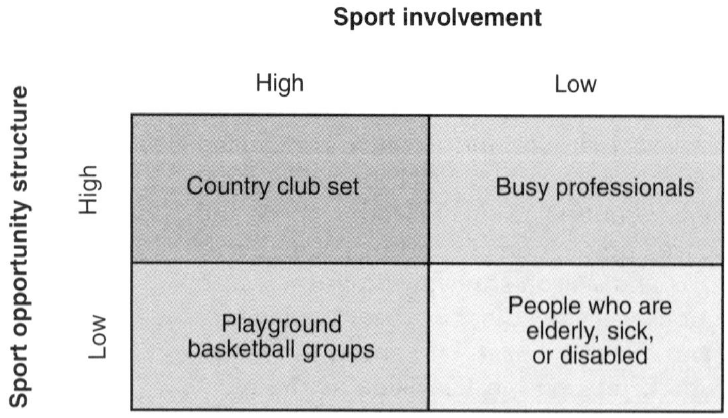

Sport involvement

FIGURE 4.3 The sport involvement–opportunity structure grid.

set" is taking advantage of opportunity and is active. At the other extreme are people who are "elderly, sick, or disabled" who have little opportunity and little involvement. Although all groups deserve attention for different social, ethical, or economic reasons, the marketer is apt to concentrate on the "playground groups" or the "busy professionals." Both groups indicate much about consumer behavior in sport: One group is quite involved despite a lack of opportunity, whereas the other has the economic ability to participate but shows low involvement. In fact, the inner-city "playground" group has been the target of many special promotions. The NHL, Major League Baseball, the NBA, the Ladies Professional Golf Association (LPGA), the PGA, and the United States Tennis Association (USTA) all have programs to boost inner-city interest in their sports. They are praiseworthy, but they also require long-term commitments of resources. Only time will judge commitment and success.

Individual Factors

Environmental factors swirl constantly around the consumer, but individual or internal factors influence the way the consumer interacts and makes sense of that larger world. Among the important factors are self-concept, stage in the life cycle, physical characteristics, the learning process, perception, motivation, and attitudes. We will look at how these may affect involvement in and commitment to sport.

Self-Concept/Self Esteem

Every beginning golfer has felt the sting of self-consciousness after dribbling a 40-yard drive off a crowded first tee. All people hold certain cognitions or beliefs about themselves; these cognitions are not simply the self-view (self-image) but are a rather complex set of interacting perceptions. The most complete theory of self-concept suggests that we have more than self-images (ways we view ourselves); we also have images of how we think others view us (perceived or apparent selves), images of how we would like to be (desired or ideal selves), and images of how we interact with particularly important reference groups (reference-group selves). The proponents of this theory suggest that there is also a fifth image, namely, the real self—what we truly are and never will know, because no mortal ever sees this "true" image. (28)

All of these "selves" make up the self-concept, a fundamental part of motivation into (or out of) sport. For some time, psychologists have known that a positive self-concept spurs greater involvement and commitment. This is why the best coaching manuals stress positive and constructive reinforcement, especially for kids. At the same time, what adult would return for lessons from a golf pro who regularly said, "You stink at golf; don't waste your time with your lousy swing!" One can find traces of the self-concept throughout the industry. For instance, one study of 10,000 youth, aged 10 to 18, revealed three major groups of sport participants, according to similarities in motivation. All had links to self-concept:

+ 40 percent participated "for the image."
+ 35 percent participated "to improve self."
+ 25 percent participated "because of pressure."

Kids are obviously building or protecting their self-image as they make decisions about sport involvement. This goes beyond the playing. In the last two decades more youth (and adults) are wearing "attitude" T-shirts that may well link to the wearer's self-concept. Some are sport-related: "If you can't win, don't play" or "You let up, you lose." (29)

As we discuss in chapter 6, the marketer can segment consumers on the basis of lifestyles and values that relate strongly to the self-concept and associated consumption behaviors. For instance, research indicates that "inner-directed" people—those who seek to fulfill personal needs and self-image—are nearly twice as likely to exercise as "outer-directed" people, who are more concerned with what others think.

Stage in Life or the Family Cycle

The self-concept is a dynamic entity, often changing as a person interacts with the environment. One path of self-development is the life course or the family cycle. With gays and lesbians marrying and raising families, some of our definitions must be broadened, but in all cases, each of us passes through a series of stages that often correspond to transitions in our values, identities, feelings of competence, and attitudes. These transitions, in turn, may have a profound effect on our sport involvement and commitment, even as sport may be an important ingredient in our quest for identity at any stage.

Prominent leisure researcher John Kelly outlined stages of the life course that have particular relevance to our topic (see table 4.3). These stages, of course, vary from person to person, and much more research is needed on their effects. For instance, some data suggest that the "youth" period is especially important in fan development. Recent research by NFL Properties indicated that 43 percent of fans claimed to have become fans of a particular sport by the age of 8. And 60 percent said they had become fans by age 11. This is a staggering number. (30)

Table 4.4, taken from the 2004 *Lifestyle Market Analyst,* offers another glimpse. Using an index that compares each life course segment to a total national average, we can see some clear effects of life stage on golf involvement. Because golf participation is not clearly gauged,

✦ Table 4.3 Effects of Life Stage on Sport Involvement

Stage in life course	Possible effects on sport involvement
Preparation periods	
Youth	Sport activities may be an important part of peer group identity.
Courtship	New relationships and sexual identities either reinforce or conflict with existing patterns of involvement.
Establishment periods	
Singles	Sports and active lifestyles are currently a central part of the "singles" set.
Marriage	Great adjustment is possible with the arrival of children. As children grow, a couple may continue independent involvement, develop integrated family activities, or be controlled by children's activities.
Maturity	With the launching of children, there is more time and independence for new or renewed involvements.
Reintegration periods	
Retirement	More free time and fixed income may force adjustments; spouses may pursue joint or individual activities.
Singles	Death of a spouse may require a shift out of certain group activities.

Data from J.R. Kelly, 1982, *Leisure* (Englewood Cliffs: Prentice Hall), 133-156.

✦ Table 4.4   Golf Involvement by Stage in Family Life Cycle

Stage in family life cycle of household head, by marriage/age/kids in home	% of total U.S. "golfing" households	Index *
Single, 18-34, no kids	8.9	86
Single, 35-44, no kids	5.0	85
Single, 45-64, no kids	7.7	68
Single, 65+, no kids	4.4	52
Married, 18-34, no kids	4.6	139
Married, 35-44, no kids	3.7	123
Married, 45-64, no kids	19.3	126
Married, 65+, no kids	13.2	115
Single, kids of any age	4.7	53
Married, kids under 13	15.9	133
Married, kids age 13-18	12.6	126

*Index:100 equals national "average" rate of participation at each life cycle stage.

Adapted, by permission, from SRDS, 2006, *The Lifestyle Market Analyst 2004*, (Des Plaines, IL), 818.

we can assume a base only of regular golfers, those who golf at least three times per month. Notice the effects. Married golfing households not only make up the overwhelming percentage of "golfers"(total + 69.3 percent); they are also overrepresented in the general population (index greater than 100). There seems to be some link between marital status and golfing.

There has been even less research on how sport may influence the life course. Early, limited research led one scholar to conclude that "age has very little, if anything, to do with sport fan motivation." But more research is needed on both age and the broader life course before we can make confident conclusions. For instance, conventional wisdom long ago created the archetype of the "football widow," abandoned by her fanatic spouse who regularly rendezvoused with his mistress (the team) at the stadium or in front of the television. When ESPN launched 24-hour sports, one wag claimed that the only beneficiaries would be divorce lawyers! Despite such impressions, one research study of 399 adults in Indianapolis and Los Angeles concluded that televised sports played a "generally positive, albeit small role in marital life." (31)

Physical Characteristics

Physical characteristics and abilities, both real and perceived, play a major role in sport consumer behavior. This is logical because the core sport product is a physical activity that often requires strength, endurance, and flexibility. Consequently, body types and demonstrations of physical skill are closely linked to consumer self-concepts and decisions about sport involvement. One need only think of the typical advertisement for an athletic club, which portrays not the normal citizen of the republic but rather a male or female deity of physical culture, glistening in shorts or a cropped top, offering the promise of a similar physique. Such allures appeal to the consumer's ideal self; they are powerful stuff, perhaps as likely to scare off as to attract members.

Worse yet, there is still little programming for people who are physically disabled or even those who are just less capable. Youth sport programs tend to advance those who are already superior at the expense of those who need attention. Prospects are bleaker for people who are elderly; few programs exist. In programs that do exist, potential consumers may be alienated by feelings that they do not have the physical capabilities to enjoy sports. Although the Americans With Disabilities Act has opened doors for both participants and spectators, the thresholds are still hard to cross. In 1998, when a golfer who is physically disabled successfully challenged the PGA Tour rules prohibiting the use of carts, many traditionalists suggested that Armageddon was just around the corner. Sports are still very much the province of people who are able-bodied and not those who are physically challenged.

Learning

Although some physical characteristics are inherited, many are learned. Most people learn to be a competent or skilled athlete despite initial awkwardness. A person also may learn to become a couch potato, content to enjoy the performances of elite athletes in competition on television. Both types of consumers play prominent roles in the sport industry, and who is to say one is "better" or "healthier" than the other? In both cases, however, learning plays a major role in behavior.

A formal definition of learning is "the acquisition of new responses to behavioral cues in the environment, occurring as the result of reinforcement." (32) This definition includes several components common to learning theories. The first encompasses drives or arousal mechanisms that cause a person to act; the desire for esteem is an example. The second includes cues or environmental stimuli that may trigger an individual drive. Advertisements for luxury cars during televised golf tournaments are good examples of cues that attempt to trigger esteem drives. The third component includes reinforcements or outcomes (usually positive rewards) that serve to reduce the drive. The golf fan who purchases a Cadillac may (or may not) learn the connections between lifestyle and esteem.

Several areas of learning theory have special relevance to the sport marketer. For example, cognitive, affective, and behavioral types of involvement correspond to the hierarchy of effects sometimes used to describe consumer purchase behavior. The basic hierarchy suggests that consumers first process information about a product (cognitive involvement) normally through advertising. If additional messages succeed, consumers next develop a new feeling about the product (affective involvement), which may in turn lead them to buy the product (behavioral involvement). This hierarchy is displayed as

Learn → Feel → Do

One way or another, product knowledge is an important variable in consumer behavior. Knowledge links to involvement and commitment in an endless loop. Anyone who has ever been bitten by the "golf bug" understands this. The more you play, the more you want to learn about the game and its nuances. The more you learn, the more you want to play. The same is true for sport fans. One study of minor league hockey fans showed that hockey knowledge—measured by a set of simple questions (e.g., What does *icing* mean?)—accounted for over 12 percent of the variance in games attended. All things being equal, the more fans knew about hockey, the more they attended. On the one hand, this is just common sense. But then consider how

---

Case Study: "Teaching" the X Games

The sport market has never been static. Sports run hot and cold. Some sports, such as gander pulling, die off. And new sports continue to pop up. In the 1980s, stunt bikes, skateboards, in-line skates, and snowboards spawned a host of activities and competitions that became associated with the "slackers" of the so-called Generation X. The profile was a perfect match for ESPN2, which wanted to reach the same children of MTV. Voilà! The X Games were born. In many respects "made for television," the X Games required some consumer learning, especially of the basics—What are the X Games?

ESPN used aggressive teaching tools such as television ads and an Internet site. In 1998, three years into the games, ESPN was still helping consumers learn the basics; for instance, putting a 20-page magazine insert into *Rolling Stone* magazine, a perfect medium for reaching the target audience. The insert included basic information on all the events, which ran from bicycle stunts to sportclimbing, wakeboarding, and street luge. Exquisite visuals were surrounded by text on "the point," or the rules; "the tools," or the equipment; and "the names," or the prominent contestants. The "Guide to the X Games" was an excellent primer. Even a casual reader would feel empowered with the information. (33)

little effort many organizations put into teaching their consumers about their sport the way ESPN has taught the X Games (see the case study on the previous page). (34)

Some researchers suggest that the standard hierarchy "Learn → Feel → Do" may not apply to services, which are intangible and therefore less conducive to initial cognitive messages about product, price, and the like. This is certainly true for many sport products, which often involve intricate physical activities. In sports, consumers may be more responsive to information that triggers their emotions about an overall experience, even if the initial image is limited in its detail. Consumers may be willing to act on such information, try the sport product, and then learn more about it after the trial. In sport, then, the hierarchy may be more like

Feel → Do → Learn

This is certainly the approach of most Nike ads, which look to stir emotions before anything else. It was also the approach of the NBA and its merchandise sponsors when they placed a 12-page insert in the 1997 *Sports Illustrated* NBA preview edition. The pictures—of a diverse set of young men and women in NBA apparel—expressed the fantasies that many fans pursue through "official" merchandise. One woman, clad in a Rockets jacket, looked dreamily across the seats of a trolley car as she considered her playing ability and knowledge. "When Charles Barkley points into the crowd, he's pointing at me" was among the fantasies reported in her caption. She was the mentor; Barkley, the student. (35) The ad was a perfect expression of

Feel → Do → Learn

Some activities, on the other hand, demand a hierarchy of

Do → Feel and Learn

In-line skating, skiing, surfing, and other speed/skill sports may be among such activities. In 1997, Rollerblade, Inc., looked to drive a shakeout in the cluttered market of in-line skating. The prime strategy was a grassroots effort to get more people to try its product. This included giving free lessons in New York City parks and giving thousands of free pairs of Rollerblades to public schools. Rollerblade, Inc., recognized the long history of American sport: There is no better promoter than a national corps of physical education teachers offering millions of kids lessons in Do → Feel and Learn.

In an age of interactivity, the most progressive organizations use exhibits, "fan zones," and Web sites to promote all three elements of the learning hierarchy. We will look more closely at these programs in chapters 7, 11, 14, and 15. The smartest sport marketers understand the centrality of learning to sport consumption. To that end, they even modify their notions of sales, especially with corporate clients. Marketers become teachers, and selling becomes "edu-selling." (36)

Perception

Learning requires the consumer to use perception, which may be defined as the process by which a person scans, gathers, assesses, and interprets information in the environment. Although perception employs the five senses, it involves far more. Perception depends on the characteristics of the person, situation, or thing perceived (stimulus factors) and also the characteristics of the perceiver (individual factors). A roaring crowd may be an exhilarating and uplifting experience for a knowledgeable fan, but a threatening mob to someone else. Our perceptions, then, are something of a filter, influenced by our values, attitudes, needs, and expectations. This filter contributes to selective exposure, selective distortion, and selective retention of the innumerable stimuli that confront us daily. (37)

Consumers and prospective consumers are constantly filtering and interpreting cues about sport products vis-à-vis their self-concepts. Failure to provide congruent and consonant images to consumers will typically reduce involvement. This is why high-priced perfume companies keep their products out of discount stores. The place of purchase enhances the perception of quality.

Like many product and service providers, sport teams have often attempted to develop perceptions among fans that "tickets are going fast," thus elevating a sense of risk over missing something big. Recently, marketing researchers demonstrated that the "scarcity factor" does work.

Sport marketers must be particularly sensitive to a number of perceptual issues, including the following:

✦ *Facility cleanliness.* Long ago, Bill Veeck realized that clean bathrooms were critical to attracting women and families to the ballpark. But men don't love a mess either. "Club dirty" is a prime reason for quitting an athletic club.

✦ *Exposure to violence.* This perception can work both ways, as shown in ice hockey. Some fans love a good brawl; others abhor the goons. The NHL continues to walk a fine line, with Commissioner Gary Bettman trying to distinguish between goonism and a "spontaneous altercation." Can the casual fan—a target market if the NHL wants to grow on television—tell the difference? Worse than television violence is the fear of rowdy, drunken fans. No parent wants to expose children to that form of "entertainment." Some clubs have responded with no-alcohol family zones.

✦ *Risk of injury or embarrassment.* Sport consumers take many risks, to their health and their egos. Studies by Reebok showed that "injury prevention" is second only to "fit and comfort" in consumer decisions about running shoes. Perceptions of high risk turn many people away from active participation. Few people are willing to look like a fool on a ski slope or a treadmill. And how many are turned off by the ads suggesting that only "hardbodies" frequent the athletic club?

✦ *Waste of time, money, effort.* As we will see in chapter 10, consumer costs include far more than the event ticket, the lift ticket, or the greens fee. In an age focused on "quality time," every choice is a risk. As figure 4.4 suggests, consumers create their own perceptual space maps that help them assess choices in terms of effort and risk. (38)

Motivation

Amid a constant swirl of stimuli, can we identify any individual "triggers" of sport involvement? According to motivation theory, environmental stimuli may activate the drive to satisfy an underlying need. Theorists like Abraham Maslow, Henry Murray, and David McClelland have outlined elaborate models explaining how physiological, psychological, and social needs influence human behavior. In the last decade, a number of researchers have focused their efforts on explaining what makes sport consumers tick. At the same time, historians have outlined a number of "long residual" factors that have motivated involvement in sport across vast extents of time and space. The research is extensive and growing, but some motivational factors have emerged rather clearly:

✦ *Achievement and self-esteem.* The notion of winning does matter, for players and fans. In one USTA survey, serious players listed winning as a major reason for playing. Likewise, numerous studies show that fans tend to "bask in reflected glory" when their team wins.

✦ *Craft.* Winning isn't all that counts. For many, developing or enjoying physical skill prompts sport interest. "Learning a new skill" typically ranks high among reasons people list for playing. And the chance to watch a star display great skill brings a crowd to any game.

✦ *Health and fitness.* This is an obvious motive for club membership and equipment purchase. Even golfers can argue that a "good walk spoiled" beats watching television or an afternoon at the office.

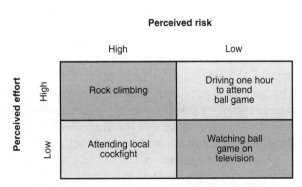

FIGURE 4.4 The risk–effort grid.

Can You Sort Through the Clutter of Slogans?

In our visual, electronic age of slick images and sound bites, advertising campaigns are the primary means of reaching consumers. Most ads try to overcome, even reshape, perceptions in order to reposition their product in the consumer's mind. We look at ads more closely in chapters 11 and 13, but we conclude here with the thought that today's flood of ads creates perceptual clutter for most sport consumers. One NFL Properties survey indicated that only 56 percent of respondents correctly identified a new slogan with the NFL. That was probably a strong level of recognition. So try your luck at matching some recent slogans with the correct organization. Can you sort through the clutter?

1. NHL	A. "I love this game"
2. NTRA	B. "These girls are good"
3. TFN	C. "I live for this"
4. NBA	D. "The coolest game (on earth)"
5. WNBA	E. "I am what I am"
6. LPGA	F. "Who Do You Like Today?"
7. MLB	G. "Enough is never enough"
8. PGA	H. "These guys are good"
9. Reebok	I. "Get in Touch With Your Feminine Side"
10. WTA	J. "This is our game"

Your Score:

9-10	You're ready for *SportsCenter*.
7-8	Not bad, but not quite prime-time material.
5-6	Change your magazine subscriptions.
2-4	You're watching too much Weather Channel.
0-1	It's time to think about another career.

[Answers: 1-D, 2-F, 3-G, 4-A, 5-J, 6-B, 7-C, 8-H, 9-E, 10-I]

✦ *Fun and festival.* Humans have a long history of framing their games with circles of spectators and fun-lovers, who exchange money for sight lines, food, and merchandise. Descriptions of ancient festivals sound much like those of modern events. There was and is more than the contest. What is big-time football without the tailgating? For similar reasons, most new venues contain a concourse, which is the locus of fun and festival—the midway, if you like. Perhaps the most visible symbol of festival is the team mascot, now almost a necessity.

✦ *Eros.* Evidence is clear that many players and fans have erotic motives. There is a certain sexual attraction to sweaty bodies in motion, not all of which are clad in tights or a leotard. In 1975, the Golden State Warriors ran a promotional campaign to attract female fans. The tag line: "We've got five men in shorts who can go all night." Recent pay-per-view promos for Oscar De La Hoya included female voice-overs saying, "You know, Oscar, I could sit around and watch you sweat all night. And that's exactly what I'm gonna do." A recent study of Florida Gator fans showed that they were more aroused at football action shots than at patently erotic photographs. The erotic motive is still somewhat taboo as an academic subject; it demands much more attention.

✦ *Affiliation or community.* "To be with friends or family" is a common reason people give for any sport involvement, as indicated in studies of tennis participation, athletic club membership, and fan motivations. Fan communities have existed for thousands of years, represented in the Roman "factions" of blues, greens, reds, and whites who passionately rooted for their color in the chariot races. Their modern counterparts may wear official merchandise, but the motives are the same. Research has clearly shown that few fans (1 to 3 percent) attend games alone. Being a fan or a participant can become of paramount importance to a person's "social identity," which links to the notion of self-concept we discussed earlier. For some, fan identity was welded in place by adolescence. Dan Mahoney, sport marketing scholar, spent only the first half of his life in New York, but that was enough: "I can live in Louisville for the rest of my life and I'm still going to be seen as a Yankee. It's part of my personality. . . . So following teams to the Northeast helps keep me tied to my overall personality." For others, adopting a new loyalty is part of the move. NBA studies clearly show that transplants

Basking in Red Sox glory!
Courtesy of Alison Kern

readily attach themselves to their new city. Although historical research shows clearly that Americans have always been a people on the move, some wonder about fan identity in an era when players and franchises seem to swirl around like rootless sagebrush.

✦ *Eustress, risk, and gambling.* The emotional ride of rooting is much like that of gambling—an addictive combination of euphoria and stress. It is no wonder that sports and gambling have gone hand in glove as far back as our literary and archeological records will take us.

✦ *Entertainment and escape.* Many fans believe (and report on surveys) that a day at the ballpark or an evening in front of their TV, rooting and cheering, takes their minds off their everyday troubles. Social activists have sometimes attacked this "bread and circuses" aspect of sports, and there may be some contradiction between an escape motive and a "eustress" motive. After all, rooting for the Cubs may be simply trading work troubles for leisure troubles. But who's to tell a fan what is best?

Researchers are beginning to tease out the differences between the motives of fans of men's sports and women's sports, or revenue sports and nonrevenue sports. Although motivations are elusive and difficult to quantify, they will remain essential constructs for understanding consumer behavior in sport. A better understanding of fan motives promises to help marketers develop better communications with their consumer base via promotions, ads, or newsletters. (39)

Attitudes

One of the long-term results of perceptions, learning, and involvement is the growth of attitudes, defined by Kotler as "a person's enduring favorable or unfavorable cognitive evaluations,

For many fans, the teams they support in their youth are the teams they support for the rest of their lives.

© Human Kinetics

emotional feelings, and action tendencies toward some object or idea." People have many attitudes about sport. As we saw earlier, some collective attitudes may become dominant in a given culture. Individual or collective, attitudes often affect sport involvement. Several studies have demonstrated that fans' attitudes toward teams influence their perceptions of enjoyment in watching pro football games. And according to an assessment of the literature on physical activity, an estimated 10 percent of the population may be "intransigent" in their nonexercise behavior. They will probably never become exercisers, and we may assume that they have overwhelmingly negative attitudes about their need or opportunity for exercise. (40)

But positive attitudes toward sport and exercise don't always trigger "positive" behavior. Die-hard fans don't always attend games; hard-core players don't always get to the club to practice. A few years ago, for instance, Prince Manufacturing conducted a national poll on attitudes toward tennis. The survey's main angle and results were summarized in a press release: "More than 7 out of 10 Americans think that playing sports is a good way to meet someone for romance with 8 out of 10 rallying to tennis to make love connections." According to the survey results, sports (at 70 percent) ranked higher on the "love-o-dometer" than bars (41 percent), movies (31 percent), or video dating services (27 percent). Unfortunately for Prince and the tennis industry, the "love-connection" attitude has not translated into involvement. (41)

Marketers naturally try to cultivate positive attitudes toward their products. As we will explore in detail, the marketing mix should be an integrated set of tools that meet consumer needs, thus creating positive attitudes and moving consumers up the involvement escalator. One avenue is the notion of reciprocity (see sidebar on page 87).

Decision Making for Sport Involvement

Given the array of factors this chapter has presented, one can appreciate the difficulty of establishing a standard and rational process by which consumers make decisions about becoming or staying involved with sport products. Nonetheless, such models, even if they are imperfect, can be helpful tools for marketers. We offer one such model, based on a series of steps generally seen as part of consumer decision making (see figure 4.5). As displayed, the consumer's decision to become involved in sport includes several stages: (42)

1. *Need recognition.* Any number of cues, particularly images in the mass media, may trigger the arousal of a need or motive, which may be related to achievement, esteem, affiliation, health, or other sport motives. In short, any of the individual or environmental factors may trigger an arousal of need. Over the last decade, researchers have identified "team identification" as one of the most important factors in determining attendance. In that respect, team identification might be seen as the starting and ending place for each cycle of fan decision making. (43)

Building Positive Attitudes With Reciprocity

In one way or another, we all are both consumers and marketers on a regular basis. Among our families, our friends, our work associates, and our teammates, we give and take information, counsel, humor, and criticism. In the best of conditions, we enjoy sharing relationships. That sharing can be called reciprocity, which can take many forms:

You help me, I'll help you.

You listen to me, I'll listen to you.

You give me a gift, I'll give you one.

Marketers of all types have learned the importance of reciprocity. Todd Crossett's seminal study of the LPGA outlined the basic rules of reciprocity that make or break positive attitudes between players and fans. Players may be "gifted" with skill, but the gift means little without genuine fan appreciation. On the pro golf tour, fans interact with players more intimately than in most other sport venues. Crossett showed how sincere reciprocity builds strong bonds between players and fans. He also conveyed how fragile the bonds can be.

Player accessibility, through autograph sessions and community appearances or service, is a powerful vehicle for reciprocity. Professional team sports have suffered from an erosion of this relationship, with plenty of insincerity and surliness on both sides. With greedy agents and players, it is difficult to nurture reconnections, but marketers should keep trying. College athletics provide better opportunities. More programs should take cues from the University of New Hampshire's national powerhouse women's ice hockey team, which regularly holds postgame autograph sessions to build bonds with its fans. To some degree, every game should be a "fan fest."

There are other forms of reciprocity. The San Diego Padres developed a successful "Compadres" program, which the Padres' Don Johnson says operates on the basis of "golden rule marketing." "Our assumption," said Johnson, "is that if we take care of the fan, the fan will take care of us." Club membership (free to any fan) includes a bar-coded card that fans "swipe" at a kiosk inside the park, thereby accumulating points for every game they attend. The more points they rack up, the more rewards they earn.

Similarly, the AA Baseball Portland Sea Dogs built April and May attendance with their "Adopt a Sea Dog" program, a simple partnership in which 18 local schools adopted a player, who visited the school and gave a motivational talk. In return, the entire school "family"—teachers, students, parents, staff—got a group rate for a game in May. At the game, the school groups participated in various game-day events.

There are many avenues for developing genuine reciprocity, some of which we will explore. At the same time, there are too many examples of ruptured reciprocity, which can spawn a generation of negative attitudes. Gypsy franchises and callous owners may be souring professional sport fans as much as the boorish behavior of player-felons. In a *Los Angeles Times* survey, 59 percent of respondents said that having an NFL team in the area was not important to them. Such attitudes led *U.S. News and World Report* to run a cover story titled "Big League Troubles."

Reciprocity is as easily ruptured as nurtured. But its importance is certain. As Crossett so clearly articulated: "The path to success in sport is paved with gifts."(44)

---

2. *Awareness or information search.* The consumer may have prior awareness of, or may seek information about, products that can satisfy aroused needs. This is a critical stage that marketers must never underestimate. Countless studies of outdoor recreation and sport involvement point to the importance of information about distance to site, time to travel, and beauty of site. Given the consumer's "filter" of perceptions, the marketer cannot make any assumptions about the accuracy of the consumer's perceptions. Worse yet is the possibility that consumers are unaware of the product. One well-known study showed that this was precisely the problem facing the sport/racquet/health club industry: Potential club members were unaware that nearby clubs exist. (45)

3. *Evaluation of choices.* Consumers make product choices at a number of levels. Philip Kotler distinguished these levels as follows:

Product family. Within the health and fitness industry are nutrition products and exercise products.

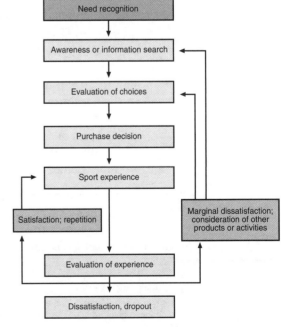

FIGURE 4.5 The decision process for sport involvement.

Product class. Within the exercise family are classes of products such as sports, calisthenics, jogging, and walking.

Product line. Within the sport class are lines of products such as golf, racquet sports, and softball.

Product type. Within the racquet sports line are product types such as tennis, squash, and racquetball.

Product brand. Within the product type of tennis are certain brands of rackets and balls and certain "brands" of facilities and experiences (e.g., the Eagle Tennis Club vs. the town courts).*

4. *Purchase decision.* Numerous questions demand research concerning the sport consumer's purchase decisions. For instance, to what extent are decisions to "purchase" a sport experience (with time, money, effort) planned and calculated or unplanned and impulsive? As one recent review of research reminded marketers, "Studies of sport fans indicate that a majority—especially in baseball, basketball, and hockey—make purchase decisions only a few days before the event." "Walk-up" fans and season-ticket holders obviously require different messages, as we discuss in chapters 11 and 12. (47)

5. *Sport experience.* As Chubb and Chubb suggested, this stage may include a period of anticipation after one has made the decision (thinking about the ski trip a month before it is to occur), a period of preparation (waxing and mounting the skis the night before), travel to the site of the experience, the main experience, and travel from the main experience. (48)

6. *Evaluation of experience.* An effective illustration of evaluation is the consumer satisfaction equation:

$$\text{Satisfaction} = \text{Benefits} - \text{Cost}$$

Satisfaction can relate to social experience, self-concept, skill, or reliability, for example. Benefits relate to characteristics like quantity and duration. Costs can include money, time, ego, effort, and opportunities to do other things. In the end, benefits must outweigh costs. Marketers attempt to maximize satisfaction through the various elements in the marketing mix. But consumers continue to filter the stimuli around them. They can develop positive or negative attitudes for a host of reasons. One of the most important is the consumer's assessment of competence, as a player or a fan. Has the experience enhanced the person's sense of competence and self-worth? Has it strengthened his or her identity as a golfer, a skier, an exerciser, a fan? The answer has a major influence on subsequent behavior. (49)

7. *Postevaluation behavior.* After evaluating, the consumer has three basic choices:

If satisfied, to repeat the experience, and perhaps build a stronger identity or affinity with the activity. Fans of NASCAR reflect high levels of satisfaction, which spills over into brand loyalty to NASCAR sponsors. Satisfied fans typically indicate that they plan to attend more of a team's events in the future—that is, they intend to move up the escalator.

If dissatisfied, to reduce or abandon the activity. Some participants and spectators move down or even off the escalator.

If marginally satisfied or dissatisfied, to reevaluate information and decisions about product choices at various levels (family, class, line, type, and brand).

These loops require much more attention from sport marketers. For instance, although information is increasingly available on youth sport dropouts, we know relatively little about adult dropouts. One of the only studies of adult dropouts involved extensive interviews with NHL Hartford Whaler fans (of course, the Whalers left Hartford in 1997 for Carolina).

---

*The "brand" level of sport products is quite complex. Although consumers consider "brand" differences in sporting goods (Nike vs. Reebok), they are less conscious of brand differences between, say, college hockey and minor league hockey. As we discuss in chapters 8 and 9, branding is a central issue across the sport industry. For now, we can recognize that players and fans sort through loads of information even at the "brand" level. For instance, research has shown that active golfers choose courses on the basis of 17 attributes, including course length and availability of tee times. (46)

The researcher, Craig Hyatt, discovered that most of these abandoned (betrayed?) fans did not follow either the Carolina Hurricanes or the NHL, but they still considered themselves Whaler fans. We can only guess how many sports fans drop off the escalator of present-day involvement and live in the world of memories. What prompts voluntary dropouts? There is much to learn, most of which will require the kind of in-depth interviews that Craig Hyatt conducted. As a recent review of the literature pointed out, we know little about how financial contingencies or other "life-altering events" such as marriage, divorce, or employment change affect sport consumption patterns. (50)

Cool Kids and Early Adopters

In 1997, Malcolm Gladwell wrote a widely read article in the *New Yorker* titled "Annals of Style: The Coolhunt." Gladwell described the work of consumer researchers and marketers like Dee Dee Gordon and Baysie Wightman, who worked for Reebok and Converse in the 1990s. These companies had a great stake in learning more about consumer decision making. They had a central question: If the majority of consumers are influenced by significant others, especially "early adopters," who starts the whole process? Who influences early adopters? The answer seemed to be "cool kids." Gordon and Wightman were experts at finding the "cool kids" in urban neighborhoods, the ones who had an innate knack for knowing and wearing the next big item—in sneakers, in hats, in just about anything. These were the "innovators," who influenced the early adopters. These were the kids who made Hush Puppies and Converse One-Star sneakers the retro, runaway market winners in the 1990s. Cool kids were triggers for what Gladwell called "social epidemics"—in this case, epidemics of buying.

What Dee Dee Gordon and Baysie Wightman knew, however, was that a firm like Reebok should not hunt for cool things; they should hunt for cool kids. In Gladwell's words:

The key to coolhunting, then, is to look for cool people first and cool things later, and not the other way around. Since cool things are always changing, you can't look for them, because the very fact they are cool means you have no idea what to look for. What you would be doing is thinking back on what was cool before and extrapolating, which is about as useful as presuming that because the Dow rose ten points yesterday it will rise another ten points today. Cool people, on the other hand, are a constant.

Gladwell expanded his research into such social epidemics in his best-selling book *The Tipping Point*. Dee Dee Gordon now runs her own successful consulting company, Look-Look, which hunts for cool kids around the world. To succeed in any enterprise that links to fashion, marketers must understand the cool kids. But do cool kids influence established sport products such as the St. Louis Cardinals, the L.A. Lakers, or the Boston Bruins? Does their importance go beyond team merchandise? We would argue that it does. Think of the planning that goes into the game-day promotions for every college basketball team or every minor league baseball team. The target audience is the very audience most influenced by cool kids. Do you want to be ahead of the curve on the next coolest promo? Perhaps a visit with some nearby cool kids would be worth the time. (51)

Wrap-Up

In this chapter, we examined some of the theories that may indicate why people consume sport. Specifically, we considered the literature on sport consumers within the larger context of general consumer behavior. We discussed various factors that help to explain the process whereby people are socialized into involvement in or commitment to sport. We have seen that factors influencing behavior may be either environmental or individual. Environmental factors include significant others; cultural norms and values; class, race, and gender relations; climatic and geographic conditions; the market behavior of sport firms; and society, culture, and the sport opportunity structure. Individual factors include self-concept, one's stage in the life or family cycle, physical characteristics, learning and involvement, perception, motivation, and attitudes.

We have been able to provide only a brief introduction to some of the components in the vastly complex area of consumer behavior. Further research is sorely needed before sport marketers can build effective theories on decision making. In the next chapter, we provide some information on how the marketer should conduct such research.

Activities

1. Define socialization, involvement, and commitment in sport consumer behavior.
2. Describe the most logical indicators of commitment for the following sport consumers: (a) Montreal Canadiens fans, (b) members of a local gymnastics club.
3. Discuss which environmental factors most influenced your involvement in your favorite sport.
4. Why is it likely that the normal "hierarchy of effects" (learn → feel → do) is less applicable with sport consumers than with consumers of detergent?
5. Find a magazine ad for a sport product or team. Analyze how, in your opinion, the ad is trying to influence consumer perceptions of the product.
6. List the steps in the decision-making process for sport consumers. Reconstruct your most recent decision to attend a major sport event. How did your experience compare to the decision-making model?

Your Marketing Plan

Chapters 3, 4, and 5 all concern research on sport consumers. This chapter outlined many of the factors that influence how people become involved in and committed to sport. As you conduct research on the current and possible consumers for your product, event, or organization, pay close attention to the most prominent environmental and individual factors that influence their behavior. This analysis should, in turn, influence your decisions about product development, pricing, promotion, distribution (place), and public relations.

Chapter 5

Data-Based Marketing and the Role of Research in Sport Marketing

Objectives

✦ To appreciate the components and the importance of a data-based marketing information system and the role of customer relationship management (CRM).

✦ To understand the various research methodologies and approaches most commonly used in sport marketing.

✦ To recognize the internal data sources available to sport organizations and the most effective ways to build a database.

If I Could Ask Only One Question . . .

You may wonder what is the most important question to ask in a survey or other forms of market research. (Although the authors have always had our opinion, it was refreshing to find that it has been corroborated by no less than the *Harvard Business Review* [1].) Whether consumers would recommend a particular service or business to their friends is a critical determinant of their feeling about what they have purchased and also their likelihood of purchasing again. In a study of more than 4,000 consumers, Frederick Reichfeld, director emeritus of Bain and Company and also the author of *Loyalty Rules!*, found that, regardless of the industry, the top-ranking question was as follows:

How likely is it that you would recommend [Company X] to a friend or colleague?

Think about it. You can feel strongly enough about your experience to become an advocate or a customer evangelist—or conversely, you can feel strongly enough about it to prevent friends, relatives, and associates from making the same mistake you did. Research shows that, in most industries, there is a strong correlation between a company's growth and the percentage of its customers who are "promoters"—that is, those who say they are extremely likely to recommend the company to a friend or colleague. (2) Compounding this feeling even further is the emotional nature of sport whereby consumers refer to their teams of allegiance in terms of "we" and "our." Furthermore, the power of word-of-mouth promotion in sport should be not only obvious but the "Holy Grail" for sport organizations—a search for fulfillment that never ends.

Chapter 2 introduced the data-based marketing (DBM) information system as an integral part of the marketing process. Chapters 3 and 4 also stressed the need for research to determine who consumers are and why they become involved with or drop out of sport. This chapter provides information about how to establish and maintain an effective DBM system. Specifically, we consider the characteristics of a DBM system and the key questions to ask when gathering data about the general market, individual consumers, and competitors. We also provide an overview of internal and external data sources and primary research techniques, including designs and approaches for sample surveys. Finally, we discuss common problems in sport marketing research as well as applications of the DBM system in the marketing process.

An Integrated Data-Based Approach to Marketing Sport

Basic data for making effective marketing decisions are essential to any organization regardless of its size or scope. Such data are especially crucial to sport organizations because fan and participant trends appear to change so rapidly. Those who market sport products need to gather information systematically and continuously. Rather than taking a reactive approach to communicating with their target markets, which in today's highly competitive entertainment marketplace is often too late to prevent defection by the consumer, sport marketers must take a proactive approach. Using an updated and monitored data-based marketing system to communicate regularly with the consumer is an excellent way to be proactive.

A data-based marketing approach should involve the integration of all data files pertaining to the customer base. It should also integrate those files into one database that provides a 360-degree view of each consumer, detailing every interaction and communication that they have had with the sport organization. This enables the sport organization to effectively target offers and initiate communication based on an understanding of the targeted consumer's history—transactional or otherwise—with the organization.

Data Mining: Predictive Modeling Based on Consumer Behavior Is the Key to Increasing ROI and Lowering Cost of Sale

Data mining can be defined as using powerful search tools to sift through and analyze consumer records. This "mining" is used to determine patterns of consumer behavior that may lead to more efficient marketing activities by targeting consumers with offers that they will be more likely to be interested in and, hopefully, respond to. Data mining helps marketing and sales efforts by predicting which consumers may be more receptive to the offer being presented to the market.

Loyalty cards or advantage-based cards offering discounts on purchases and delivering special offers to "members" are one of the most common methodologies to generate useful consumer purchasing data. When the card is used at the point of purchase (retail or online), details of what the customer is purchasing are recorded and stored, giving the retailer a purchase profile of the customer. Amazon.com, the nation's leading online retailer, monitors its customers' purchases and uses data mining to suggest additional purchases—based on the recorded preferences of other customers who purchased similar items. Amazon.com also provides the purchaser with an opportunity to view recommendations tailored to the customer's purchasing history and also invites the customer to review and update their preferences to ensure accurate targeting and better offers (and hopefully purchases) in the future.

This kind of transactional analysis is commonplace among sport organizations as well. Programs such as Archtics and SmartDM provide data on all types of customer interactions from autograph requests and ticket purchases to fantasy camp inquiries and birthday club memberships. This customer relationship management (CRM) approach is designed to provide the sport organization with a 360-degree view of all the ways that a customer interacts with the organization. This approach does require diligent data mining that involves combining more than one database, inputting and de-duplicating data on a regular basis and maintaining a high degree of data hygiene. The CRM approach takes a committed allocation of resources to maximize the opportunities afforded by such a data collection and management effort. Unfortunately, the sport industry has lagged behind other sales/retail industry segments in terms of their investment and is just now beginning to reap the rewards of "knowing your customer."

Data mining effectively:

+ Profiles customer behavior
+ Predicts future behavior based on past actions
+ Targets prospects more efficiently
+ Generates better lead lists that should lower the cost of sale
+ Improves organizational ROI

Based in part from: C. Cobbs, 2006, "Retailers gather data the same way spies do," *Orlando Sentinel* May 22, pgs A1 and A4.

Characteristics of an Ideal Data-Based Marketing System

A data-based marketing (DBM) system is a comprehensive system that captures essential demographic, psychographic, and product usage information on customers and potential customers for the purpose of enabling direct marketing strategies. Although opinions may vary as to what elements should be included in an ideal DBM system, the following characteristics are generally accepted as important elements for any sport-related organization:

+ It must be centralized; an organization needs to have all of its data located in one system.
+ The various databases need to be fully integrated so that data from multiple sources can be contrasted or merged when appropriate. Duplication of files should be eliminated, and the surviving files should be able to provide a historical/transactional analysis of the consumer's relationship with the sport organization.
+ The marketer (and other users) must be able to retrieve data in the appropriate formats (tables, reports, charts, sales lead lists, etc.) that can be used for decision making, sales and marketing activities, and presentations and proposals.

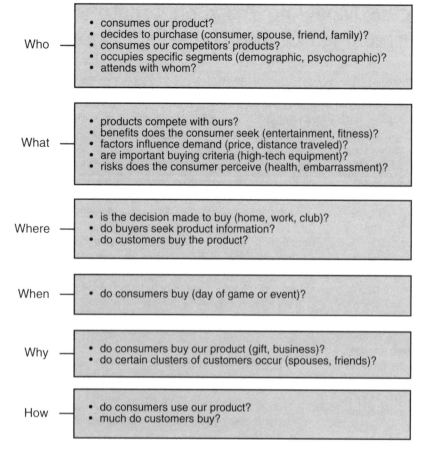

| Who | • consumes our product?
• decides to purchase (consumer, spouse, friend, family)?
• consumes our competitors' products?
• occupies specific segments (demographic, psychographic)?
• attends with whom? |

| What | • products compete with ours?
• benefits does the consumer seek (entertainment, fitness)?
• factors influence demand (price, distance traveled)?
• are important buying criteria (high-tech equipment)?
• risks does the consumer perceive (health, embarrassment)? |

| Where | • is the decision made to buy (home, work, club)?
• do buyers seek product information?
• do customers buy the product? |

| When | • do consumers buy (day of game or event)? |

| Why | • do consumers buy our product (gift, business)?
• do certain clusters of customers occur (spouses, friends)? |

| How | • do consumers use our product?
• much do customers buy? |

FIGURE 5.1   Marketing questions for sport organizations (4).

Only if all three of these conditions are met does a DBM system reach its full potential. Beyond these conditions, however, marketers and managers must agree on how data will be used in decision making. To reach such an agreement, marketers and managers must identify questions such as those outlined in figure 5.1. (3)

Customer Relationship Management (CRM) Systems

According to Forrester Research, businesses were expected to spend more than $3 billion worldwide on new CRM software licenses in 2005. Total spending on CRM—including maintenance, integration, and related hardware and software—was expected to exceed $12 billion. (5)

A CRM system expands on the basic customer demographic, psychographic, and product usage data captured in a DBM system to ideally capture all transactions, inquiries, and interactions between the customer and the organization. For example, a CRM system should capture the number of season tickets a fan has purchased, the seating location, and all of the payment data. Additionally, an effective CRM system should also contain the following fan information (later in this chapter, we demonstrate how this additional data can be used):

+ Key relationships such as the names of family members, administrators, and share partners

+ The number of times they attended games, the names of the opponents, and what seating location and types of extra tickets they purchased

+ Brief notes on all letters, phone calls, and any interactions with fans regarding positive or negative experiences such as parking, concessions, ushers, or fans seated around them

+ The name of the teams they grew up supporting

+ The name of the company where they work and their work contact information

+ Customer surveys

+ E-mail permissions

+ Campaign management touches made to the customer or prospect by the organization (e.g., direct mails, e-mails, wellness calls, etc.)

For maximum effectiveness, DBM and CRM systems have to be fully integrated into the entire e-marketing program of the sport organization. First, the Web site of the team or organization not only has to be a major source of information and interesting and entertaining for the fans or customers of the organization, but it also needs to be a major source of information on ticket sales, plans, and special promotions and act as a springboard to launch sales and transactions.

Data on all fans or customers and prospective customers who visit the organization's Web site need to be captured. Opt-ins and permission to communicate offers to these fans and prospects also need to be obtained. Most sport organizations have very strict data-collection and privacy policies that are essential to protect data and to avoid turning the fan or prospect away from the organization. Spamming existing fans and prospects is not an acceptable practice. If a sport organization experiences a high de-list rate, then it clearly needs to reduce its frequency of e-mails. Without turning fans away, a simple process of registration for all site visitors should be standard practice. Among other metrics to consider are decreasing open rates and click-through rates.

The sport organization's Web site itself needs to be a prominent tool in the direct marketing arsenal. Ticket sales, merchandising, and other product and service information need to be prominently displayed on the home page, "above the fold," with easy, simple, and direct connection for those seeking season, group, and individual game ticket information and merchandise catalogs.

Phoenix Suns' CRM Project

John Walker, senior vice president, Phoenix Suns

There are many and varied definitions of customer relationship management. It's not software, it's not e-marketing, it's not a business process, and it's not an organizational culture. However, it is a combination of all of these. It's about working smarter, pooling resources, maximizing tools, and implementing strategic initiatives around a greater understanding of your customers and their individual needs. Ultimately, it's about generating more revenue. Very simply, CRM is about growing and developing as a business.

Traditional wisdom says that a cultural change within an organization will occur during a CRM implementation. At the heart of this "change" is the internal audit of all business functions (department by department) so that existing processes, and new ones, can be integrated into this company-wide initiative. This is critical because the "360-degree view" of a business's customers can only be achieved if every touch point is identified, systems are put into place to record interactions, and those recorded interactions are reportable by other business units that can be more effective through the use of that information. A by-product of the internal audit will be identifying areas in which daily business processes can be automated and streamlined, thereby making business functions more efficient for employees.

In December 2000, the Phoenix Suns and Arizona Diamondbacks purchased 45 Onyx user licenses and began down the "CRM-initiative" road. The Onyx system was used primarily as a contact management system for the ticket-sales staff, but the database contained many duplicate records. The duplicates were primarily a result of poor integration between multiple ticketing systems and Onyx, the lack of proper database management expertise, and no clear vision for the project. The Suns recognized the high cost of multidatabase support, poor user adoption of existing systems, and the lack of a consolidated customer view. In addition, several other departments within the organization were using manual systems and spreadsheets, all containing discrete "bits" of information about the relationship between the Suns and their customers (sponsors, charitable donors, ticket purchasers, customer service programs, and guest relations programs).

In October 2003, the Phoenix Suns, in partnership with Microsoft Business Solutions, Resolute Solutions Corporation, and SmartDM, embarked on implementing Microsoft CRM into their organization. The properties involved included the NBA's Phoenix Suns, the WNBA's Phoenix Mercury, the AFL's Arizona Rattlers, the America West Arena, and the Dodge Theatre. The objectives of the project were to do the following:

♦ Create *one* consolidated view of the customer in a centralized database, while maintaining organizational security as to what types of information are viewable to each employee

♦ Improve the tracking, forecasting, and accuracy of product sales (measuring the ROI of marketing campaigns)

(continued)

✦ Calculate the revenue contribution, or "share of wallet," of every customer

✦ Provide system tools for ticket sales, customer service, sponsorship sales and service, community relations, and guest relations programs

✦ Increase revenue through cross-selling and up-selling products across multiple organizations and work groups

✦ Achieve the highest user adoption of a CRM solution in professional sports

On June 14, 2004, the Phoenix Suns went live with Microsoft CRM. As of August 1, 2004, over 50 employees had been trained and were using the system on a daily basis. The MSCRM database houses over 270,000 unique records, and a "single view" of each record is available to all employees, based on security. Several ticket sales marketing campaigns have been launched, and status reports are available that measure the overall success (i.e., ROI) of each campaign. As of August 2006, more than $12 million in ticketing revenue has been realized through e-marketing initiatives.

Work flow has been automated between ticket operations and ticket sales, as well as between sponsorship sales

and sponsorship services, and a "queuing" system has been developed for order processing and contract fulfillment. A system for lead assignment has been automated for sales management, and sales funnels are being tracked for each sales rep. An inventory tracking system has been developed for sponsorships and community relations programs (information that was previously tracked on Excel spreadsheets or in hard-copy notebooks) and is available for viewing across the business, based on security. Additionally, the daily data update/hygiene process includes an aggregation of data into one consolidated view within MSCRM, scrubbing against the "National Do Not Call" list, and next-day access to ticketing transactions from five unique ticketing databases.

Although the system is still less than three years old, the Phoenix Suns have established themselves as an industry leader in CRM. The full deployment of Microsoft CRM, including over 80 users, was completed in 2004. The organization is committed to using technology to enhance existing customer relationships, as well as to cultivate and attract new customers.

Building the DBM System

Building an effective database and direct marketing strategy is the first step toward achieving a single, integrated view of customers that can maximize both the customer experience and revenue for the sport marketer. This chapter begins to identify the elements necessary for a solid database and direct marketing strategy, including identifying and using data sources, coding the data, collecting contact information, using customer or fan loyalty programs, updating and cleaning the data, and creating online and offline direct marketing campaigns.

Collecting Information on Stakeholders Who "Touch" the Product

Each year the goal of every sport and entertainment organization should be to obtain and store complete contact information for everyone in the market who has "touched" or is likely to "touch" the product. An example of those who touch the product for a professional team sport include stakeholders who do the following:

✦ Buy or use a ticket

✦ Watch game telecasts

✦ Listen to games on the radio

✦ Buy apparel, videos, and publications

✦ Visit league or team Web sites

✦ Complete an all-star ballot

✦ Coach or play the sport at a youth or adult league level

- ✦ Buy from a league or team partner
- ✦ Play in fantasy leagues
- ✦ Participate in a fan loyalty program
- ✦ Participate in a league or team promotion
- ✦ Enter to win an online sweepstakes
- ✦ Enter to win a contest at a community event

Maximizing the Customer Experience and Maximizing Revenue

Building and using a comprehensive fan database is critical for retaining existing ticket buyers, generating new ticket sales, and increasing the number of games a fan attends. With an effective database, sport organizations can be much more effective in selling to people with an affinity for their product. Segmenting fans by their buying habits, demographics, or interest levels, and tailoring the customized marketing efforts to these specific prospects or customers, provides the ability to more effectively do the following:

- ✦ Up-sell current buyers
- ✦ Increase the number of game tickets purchased and hence improve average attendance frequency
- ✦ Generate new business
- ✦ Increase the rate of renewals for new season-ticket buyers
- ✦ Sell tickets to nonattendees
- ✦ Create cross-selling opportunities (i.e., sell tickets to those who bought merchandise, sell merchandise to those who bought tickets, etc.)
- ✦ Generate a base of referrals
- ✦ Increase customer loyalty
- ✦ Build valuable customer relationships and communications

More sophisticated segmentation is also possible via RFM (RFM means "recency" [use of purchase], "frequency" [use of purchase], "monetary" [how much they spent]) or cluster analysis (Claritas Prism, Axciom Personicx, and so on).

Using E-Mail Marketing Strategies to Drive the Database

Once the database is clean and up-to-date, it can be used to build customized online and offline marketing campaigns, including e-mail marketing, telemarketing, and direct mail. Developing e-mail marketing strategies should be a priority because it offers the most cost-effective way to test and reach customers. The Internet is a cost-effective resource for communicating with potential buyers and collecting their personal or business information and e-mail opt-in permission. Sport organizations must develop a comprehensive strategy designed to maximize the use of—and collection of data on—their Web site, which will serve as a key source for building the database.

Guesstimating the Size of the Database

Sport marketers should evaluate the current size and status of their customer prospect databases. For example, chief marketing officers of NBA teams should perform, at least annually, calculations to determine the size their database should be. First, they need to collect the following data:

A: The total actual in-arena/stadium attendance (turnstile count) for the most recent season

B: The number of games the average fan attended in the most recent season (obtained from focus group surveys or J.D. Power in-arena/stadium survey)

C: The estimated number of different attendees (the total in-arena attendance divided by the average attendance frequency)

D: The projected number of media fans—meaning those watching on TV or listening on the radio, but not attending. (Prior NBA experience reveals that approximately only one in four "media fans" actually attend games, so this calculation would be **C** × 400 percent.)

E: The estimated number of youth and adult sport program participants in the market. (SGMA and NBA data reveal that approximately 10 percent of the total market population within a 75-mile [120-kilometer] radius plays basketball in the United States.) (6)

F: The total traffic annually on the team Web site

G: The total NBA interested and high-potential prospects (**C** + **D** + **E** + **F** − 20 percent for estimated duplication between the data sources)

H: The actual number of individual records currently in the team ticket sales database

I: Shortfall (**G** − **H**)

J: Percent shortfall (**I** ÷ **G**)

Note: This does not include other data sources such as fan mail, e-mail, junior fan clubs, and other broadcast partner or sponsor partner online registration programs conducted by or on behalf of the team outside the arena.

Once these analyses have been performed, the chief marketing officer has an excellent sense of how complete or incomplete the organization's database currently is.

Getting Good Data

You may have heard the phrase "garbage in—garbage out," abbreviated as "GIGO." This concept is especially applicable here because, for the database to be built effectively, the organization must obtain accurate information. The database is only as good as the information in it. Consider Amazon.com. Every purchase from Amazon.com is recorded to create a purchase history for each customer. This allows the company to create a personalized greeting and offer products based on the customer's purchase history. For example, if someone has previously purchased sports nonfiction books on Amazon.com, the Web site immediately welcomes the person by name and suggests recently published sports nonfiction books, thus making the customer's interaction more personal and increasing the probability that the customer will purchase additional products. By recording every instance in which a customer touches a sport organization, the sport marketer can use this information to maximize future exposure and interaction with the team or organization, which also serves as an avenue for customer satisfaction and retention.

Data hygiene is an essential ingredient to effective DBM and CRM systems. Specific issues sport organizations must address are data standardization rules that operate on a "survivor logic." The process for obtaining data must be thought through fully. A team or organization might create a strategy that requires all fans to fill out an application form or a fan profile to purchase tickets. The application should ask for all of the basic contact information (see Step 3, "Collecting Contact Information," on page 100). It is imperative to collect personal information and preferences from each touch point, either online or offline, and to store it in a single database for future marketing and customer relationship purposes. However, all of the information does not have to be collected at the first touch point. Requesting such data at ticket windows on the night of a game would be pretty silly! But professional teams could create a strategy to collect information from customers who interact with teams at other key touch points (via Web site promotions, off-site promotions, player appearances, or prize wheels in the arena that capture not only ticket buyers but also ticket users).

The goal is to use every reasonable source to create a complete view of the customer. This view will allow the sport marketer to learn the fan's habits and buying patterns in order to maximize each fan interaction with the team or sport organization. The more the organization knows about a customer, the more that organization can provide for him or her. The following sections describe a step-by-step guide to building a database.

Step 1: Planning to Centralize the Database

There can only be one centralized database (with Ticketmaster and other ticket vendors still not having fully integrated DBM/CRM systems, this is *not* as simple as it sounds). As the size of the database increases, so will the volume of responses received on direct marketing campaigns. The bigger the database, the easier and more efficient it will be to segment and target lists. Organizations should generate leads or additional information on current buyers from as many sources as possible. Because stakeholders make contact with the organization in so many ways, it is important to track these sources. Following are lists of potential data sources (both team and league) for an NBA team:

Team Data Sources

- ✦ Past and present season-ticket-holder lists
- ✦ Share partners (see Step 3)
- ✦ Current and past additional executives using ticket accounts (see Step 3)
- ✦ Current and past group leader lists
- ✦ Current and past group attendees (see Step 3)
- ✦ Current and past individual game ticket buyers (Ticketmaster lists)
- ✦ Phone calls (sales reps should ask callers for their information as they are talking to them)
- ✦ Box office or walk-up customers (attendants should ask fans for basic contact information when they buy tickets at the box office)
- ✦ Media fans (run promotions or special offers during game broadcasts for fans who watch games on TV or listen to games on the radio, but don't currently buy tickets)
- ✦ Fan clubs and other registration programs
- ✦ Fan mail (contact information from every piece of fan mail should be recorded in the database)
- ✦ E-mail/Internet (get fan information through opt-in permission)
- ✦ Purchased lists (D&B, *Sports Illustrated, ESPN the Magazine,* local subscriber lists, etc.)
- ✦ Corporate sales or sponsor promotions or contests
- ✦ Fan loyalty programs (see Step 3)
- ✦ Guest comment cards
- ✦ Survey cards
- ✦ In-arena promotions (participants should provide information before the contest)
- ✦ Ticket users
- ✦ Requests for schedules, autographs, etc.

League Data Sources

- ✦ Registered users of NBA.com and team Web sites
- ✦ All-star ballots
- ✦ NBA.com sweepstakes entrants

Step 2: Coding the Data

To send targeted offers effectively, marketers must be able to identify the source of the data. Coding is the process of creating fields (category or column information, such as "Lead Source") for types of information and in some cases assigning codes to variables. These "source codes" should map back to the segmentation strategy. Additionally, each transaction with a customer should be coded to reference a specific campaign—outbound or inbound (e.g., wellness calls or a radio advertisement).

In addition to the source of the information, transactional and purchase data should be included to enable marketers to identify buyers from nonbuyers. To create and implement an effective data-based marketing strategy, the entire organization must code the data consistently. This source code is an invaluable piece of information for later deciding the "value" and "return" from each data source. An example was the author's $100,000 mistake at the Pittsburgh Pirates baseball club in the mid-1980s. The Pirates paid an outside fulfillment company $100,000 to have "Homerun Sweepstakes Entrants" data coded. Fans completed an entry blank at Giant Eagle grocery stores to enter the contest with a $100 grocery spree as a prize. Over 1 million entries were cleaned and deduplicated down to 200,000 unique names of fans from western Pennsylvania and eastern Ohio. Direct-mail and telemarketing efforts designed to sell tickets to this database proved to be futile. However, when the customer service department was asked to call a sample group, they discovered that the bulk of the entrants were women over age 35 who lived an average of 50 miles (80 kilometers) or more from Three Rivers Stadium. Because of the distance, this group was unlikely to buy a lot of tickets. So, with properly coded data in hand, the Pirates switched their strategy. The holiday merchandise catalog was mailed to all 200,000 in the database, and over $500,000 of merchandise was sold within eight weeks.

Step 3: Collecting Contact Information

No matter how well developed a database is, it won't be helpful if one doesn't have good, complete data to put in it. Contact information is an essential component of such data. There are five categories of stakeholders from whom it is important to collect as much data as possible: individuals, corporate account holders, shareholders, groups, and members of fan loyalty programs. In this section we provide recommendations on what data to collect as well as strategies for collecting this data effectively.

Individuals For individuals, one should start with a standard data collection form such as the one shown in figure 5.2. These forms can be completed online, returned by mail, or administered over the telephone by a sales representative when completing the sales process.

It's important to gather additional information from individual season-ticket holders, such as the name of their spouse or partner, the number of children they have, and their dates of birth (which will make it easier to target them for camps, clinics, special giveaways, family shows, and so on), favorite type of music, and favorite opposing team. In addition to a standard data collection form, the sport marketer should consider creating a customized version of it for season-ticket holders, asking for this extra information.

Corporate Accounts Corporate season-ticket holders can be powerful revenue generators, and can be reached more effectively if the sport marketer has collected appropriate data. For each contact person within a company account, the following should be collected and stored:

+ Employer name
+ Employer address
+ Work phone number
+ Job title
+ Name of primary account holder's executive assistant, secretary, or administrative assistant

```
First name: _____

Middle name or initial: _____

Last name: _____

Street address: _____

City and state: _____   Zip/postal code: _____

Home phone number: _____

Date of birth (month, day, year): _____

E-mail address: _____


E-mail opt-in permissions:

Please e-mail exclusive [team name] offers and promotions: _____ yes _____ no

Please sign me up for "[name of team e-mail newsletter]," the [team name] free e-mail
news bulletin: _____ yes _____ no

Please e-mail me selected offers and promotions from [team name] partners:
_____ yes _____ no

Please e-mail me exclusive NBA offers and promotions: _____ yes _____ no

My favorite NBA team is _____ (If different from home
market team).

Preferred e-mail format: _____ text _____ HTML
```

FIGURE 5.2 Sample standard data collection form.

+ Names of key decision makers in the company (such as VP marketing, VP sales, VP human resources) who control ticket distribution and allocation to employees, clients, or vendors

This last item is particularly important. All day-of-game e-mails, invitations to team functions, faxes, and so on, should be sent to all of the contacts in the corporate account, unless specifically directed not to do so.

We recommended obtaining the preceding information from the executive assistant of the decision maker on the account. The customer service representative should make contact and build rapport with this person, and when making phone calls to the primary account holder, the customer service representative should seek out or at least acknowledge the executive assistant by name, and offer a reward or incentive for providing the information.

Season-Ticket Shareholders   Season-ticket holders who share tickets are known as shareholders. In addition to collecting the standard data for the primary account holder, one should collect contact information for each person who shares the tickets, and note this information in the primary account holder's file. Each share partner should also have his or her own file cross-referenced with the primary account.

One effective way to obtain this information is to make video board and PA announcements in the arena extolling the benefits to share partners if they register with the team, such as day-of-game e-mails or faxes with special offers for free merchandise and concessions, or team functions with players and coaches. (Note that teams need to make a philosophical decision as to which benefits they are prepared to extend to share partners—such as ticket exchange privileges or the opportunity to make advance purchases of individual game tickets.) The sport marketer should also train customer service representatives and box office staff to record the contact information from all those making payments on a season-ticket account (from checks or credit cards).

Once your data has been collected, use it. It's important to get mail or get opt-in permission to e-mail a group ticket sales brochure and an individual game ticket brochure to each share partner at the beginning of each season, and have a ticket sales representative (TSR) make a follow-up phone call to determine their interest. One should also put the share partner on the list to be called by the customer service representative (CSR) responsible for the primary account, and make at least three contacts per season with share partners as well as the primary account holder. (Note: One should not attempt to sell share partners on purchasing their own season plans unless they raise the issue themselves. To do so will create severe animosity with the primary account holder).

Group Attendees   From group attendees, the sport marketer wants to know their favorite opposing teams to see, the number of games they attend, the average number of attendees in their group, and the activities and interests the group enjoys on a regular basis. Currently, most teams collect substantial contact information only from group leaders. But a couple of strategies can be used to collect data from group attendees as well.

On the game night, a group sales representative (GSR) should meet the group leader at his or her seat and asks whether all agreed-on arrangements and assistance have been received. The GSR should then distribute group attendee satisfaction cards (see figure 5.3). The GSR should visit the group and group leader once more during the game to ensure that they are having a good time. During the late stages of the game, the GSR should collect all of the group attendee satisfaction cards and reward one of the attendees who completed the survey with a gift. The next day the group ticket sales manager should review all of the completed cards for leads on other groups as well as new group leaders. These people should be contacted within two business days of the game. Leads should then be given back to the GSR who generated them as an added incentive to get the cards completed.

Fan Loyalty Programs   The jury appears to still be out on the cost-effectiveness or ROI of fan loyalty programs that hinge their success on raising attendance frequency. The lack of success appears to have been due to the "card-swipe factor," which was a hindrance to usage. Fan loyalty programs were initially designed with several purposes in mind:

Add names to the database

Monitor attendance patterns

Increase ticket utilization via incentivization

Registered respondents are given a "card" to swipe each time they attend a game. Points toward incentives such as merchandise, trips, and so forth are awarded each visit. With modern technology, bar-coded tickets, and higher-value reward programs, particularly from sponsors, it would appear that fan loyalty programs can become cost-effective and much simpler to operate.

As long as fan loyalty programs do exist, they can be used to collect the following information about fans:

{TEAM NAME}

So we can better serve you, please tell us how you enjoyed tonight's event. It will take you a few seconds to complete this card, and you will be eligible to receive {TEAM NAME} prizes! Be sure to include your e-mail address to get free e-mail newsletters from {TEAM NAME}.com so you can keep up with the latest happenings in the NBA and specials in the NBA Store.

The thing I enjoyed most tonight is:

_____

_____

_____

_____

The thing I enjoyed least tonight is:

_____

_____

_____

_____

Please check one:

I definitely will come again _____

I probably will come again _____

I will not come again _____

Your name _____

Home address _____

City _____

Business address _____   {TEAM LOGO}

City_____ State _____ Zip _____

Daytime phone# _____ Evening phone# _____

Fax# _____ E-mail address _____

If I win a prize, you can find me in: Section _____ Row _____ Seat _____

(continued)

FIGURE 5.3 Sample group attendee satisfaction survey card.

{TEAM NAME}

FAVORITE NBA TEAM: FAVORITE WNBA TEAM:

_____   _____

Group leaders receive {TEAM NAME} special benefits. Please review the following list and check any group that you belong to or have an association with:

School/college group	[ ]	Boy Scouts/Girl Scouts, Inc.	[ ]
Neighborhood community	[ ]	Homeowner's association	[ ]
Camp	[ ]	Church/temple/Bible study	[ ]
Charity/community group	[ ]	Fraternity/sorority	[ ]
Support group/club	[ ]	Alumni association	[ ]

The company where either I or my spouse/friend works   [ ]

Service organization (Rotary, Lions, Kiwanis, etc.)   [ ]

Other (Please specify)   [ ]

_____

☐   Yes, I am interested in being a group leader.

☐   No, I am not interested in organizing a group, but please call:

_____

E-mail opt-in permission:

☐   Please e-mail exclusive {TEAM NAME} offers and promotions.

☐   Please sign me up for "{NAME of TEAM e-mail newsletter}," the {TEAM NAME}'s free e-mail news bulletin.

☐   Please e-mail me selected offers and promotions from {TEAM NAME} partners.

☐   Please e-mail me exclusive NBA offers and promotions.

☐   Please e-mail me selected NBA partner offers and promotions.

☐   Please sign me up to receive "Special Delivery," the NBA's free weekly e-mail news bulletin.

_____   _____

(Name)   (Daytime phone #)

Thank you for completing this card. Please have a great time watching the rest of the game, and let us know if there is anything we can do to make your experience more enjoyable.

FIGURE 5.3   *(continued)*

- ✦ Share partner information (Are you a primary account holder of season tickets?)
- ✦ Types of events the fan attends throughout the year (Check what events you would like to attend.)
- ✦ Process through which the fan acquires tickets (How did you acquire your tickets to tonight's events?)
- ✦ When the decision is made to attend events and the influences behind making the decision (When did you buy your tickets?)
- ✦ Media outlets used (favorite radio and TV stations, newspapers)
- ✦ Interests and activities (List your interests.)
- ✦ Children's names and birth dates and permission to enroll them in promotional clubs, etc. (Do you have any children? Would you like to enroll your children in the team's birthday club at no charge?)
- ✦ Restaurant preferences
- ✦ Number of household occupants
- ✦ Number and types of vehicles
- ✦ Associations and groups (Are you a member of a group that you would like to bring to a game?)
- ✦ Opt-ins (Would you like to receive a special newsletter from the team?)

To obtain this information, create a fan loyalty application that serves as a survey. Set up kiosks in-arena where fans can swipe their cards, answer questions about their preferences or habits, and pick up a reward coupon from a team sponsor every time they attend a game. Additional, very substantive or unique awards can then be given at important milestones such as the 10th game attended that season, the "sweet 16th" game attended (a free dessert would be a nice tie-in), the 21st game attended, and so forth.

Best Practices for Growing E-Mail Opt-Ins

Include Valuable and Relevant Content

- ✦ Create a unique value proposition (UVP) that explains the "what's in it for me" to fans and gives them a reason to want to receive e-mail offers and e-newsletters.
- ✦ Give e-mail recipients "first dibs" on anything that has a high demand, such as summer camp sign-up or a player autograph-signing event. For example, run a "First Fifty" contest in which the first 50 recipients who respond to an e-mail receive a special pass to an additional perk at an autograph session, player appearance, meet-and-greet, or other event, such as a unique team or player poster for the player to sign.
- ✦ Use personal notes from players, coaches, GMs, and other highly recognizable personnel from the team that are not posted anywhere else. This can include "behind the scenes" commentary, a player diary, or interviews that incorporate fan questions.
- ✦ Make your e-newsletters interactive and fun by promoting sweepstakes or auctions. Include trivia or funny facts or access to free downloads such as screensavers.

- ✦ Promote benefits on your sign-up and thank-you pages.
- ✦ Up-sell fans with targeted ticket packages (e.g., multiple single game purchasers) with a prompt to sign up for more e-mail offers.

Be Focused

- ✦ The database manager is responsible for database growth and building fan relationships inside the organization, and should be financially rewarded for growing it.
- ✦ The VP of marketing or chief marketing officer (CMO) should set goals and establish a plan to achieve these goals for growing the opt-in database.

Start Collecting Offline

- ✦ Set up sign-up tables with laptop computers at home games or other local community events (or provide paper sign-up sheets on clipboards) where registrants receive an incentive to sign themselves up.
- ✦ Target specific events or groups in attendance with an incentive offer.

(continued)

- ◆ Promote the newsletter on radio and TV drop-ins during broadcasts.

- ◆ Offer a sales incentive at in-arena store checkout tables.

- ◆ Use the phone to obtain e-mail addresses and opt-in permission. Add data collection to existing telemarketing for tickets or make a separate call to request or confirm the fan's e-mail address and ask for permission to send a specific type of e-mail. Be sure to ensure accurate capture by putting solid verification processes in place.

Use the Web Site

- ◆ Prominently promote your e-newsletter with rotating ad banners, one-time pop-ups, or other graphic or text links throughout your Web site.

- ◆ Do not neglect the inside pages of your Web site. Integrate your sign-up information with your content. For example, in a report on a community event, prompt your fans to sign up so they can stay informed about future opportunities to interact with your team.

- ◆ Put opt-ins on all data registration forms and online and offline sweepstakes entries.

- ◆ Activate existing e-mail capabilities, including viral elements.

- ◆ Attach newsletter sign-up links in an auto-response to all inbound e-mail inquiries or in the footer of outbound e-mail.

- ◆ Add a viral element to every e-mail newsletter and offer with a prompt for recipients to forward the e-mail to their friends, colleagues, and family. Be sure to include a link for the secondary audience to sign up themselves.

Explore Third Party Data Sources

- ◆ Integrate data collection programs with related entities or local team sponsors. For example, the managing director of Venue Solutions believes that ticketing data is essential to sport organizations for business planning: "Trends can be identified, ROI on marketing campaigns can be analyzed and new programmes can be developed. By cross-referencing across multiple information sources, this adds value across all business departments." (7)

- ◆ Add ticket purchasing data (e.g., Ticketmaster) to the overall database.

- ◆ Rent or purchase a list from a reputable list broker, such as Full House Sports Marketing, InfoUSA, or Yesmail.

Best Practices in Managing Data Flow

If it hasn't become clear by this point in the chapter, let us spell it out for you: In developing a sound database marketing strategy, it is essential to implement a clear procedure by which data is collected, processed, and used. Each organization should adopt the following five steps of data flow:

1. Collect data from a wide variety of sources, including ticket buyers, ticket users, group attendees, newsletter subscribers, media fans, contest entrants, sport participants, and purchased lists.

2. Process the data, including merging, purging, cleaning, and deduplicating.

3. Centralize the data in a single repository.

4. Use the data for online and offline marketing activity, e-mail promotions, telemarketing, customer service, and direct mail promotions, as well as at various customer touch points.

5. Learn from the results by carefully tracking campaign effectiveness and customer interactions. In other words, continually test different offers to small samples of the database, analyze the response rates, and *learn* from discovering what strategies are working and get the highest response.

Role of Market Research

As sport franchises and leagues try to maintain and build their sponsorship and fan rosters, the quest for top-notch research becomes critical. But before making a plunge into research activities, these sport organizations must first determine what it is they wish to accomplish. (8) Once the focus has been established, the organization can determine the questions they want answered and the best methodologies to use to answer those questions.

These are standard questions that appear in various forms in most types of market research. They may serve as useful prompts in helping the marketer determine the answer to the all-important question: What do you hope to discover in your market research? The resulting information can be categorized into three main sets: general market data (aggregate analysis), data on individual consumers, and data on competitors.

General Market Data

First, the marketer needs to define the extent of the market area. A concept used in the retail industry is that of the "critical trading radius." The critical trading radius was initially conceived as a system of concentric circles of mileage, with the facility location as the center and 5-, 7-, and 10-mile (8-, 11-, and 16-kilometer) radii as milestones. Because of the variance in traffic congestion and in some cases the absence of a direct route, the concept has been redefined as a series of radii based on customer traveling time to the sport facility rather than straight mileage.

The size of the critical trading area varies with the segment of the sport industry. A commercial fitness facility has a 20-minute driving-time radius within which 80 to 85 percent of the members and potential members reside or work; a retail sporting goods store in an urban or suburban area has a similar trading area. In rural areas, the radius naturally expands. The trading radius also increases as the degree of competition decreases. For a professional sport team, an intercollegiate athletic event, or an event at a coliseum, stadium, or arena, up to 80 percent of the market resides within a one-hour driving- or traveling-time radius (longer for weekend events). For a small ski resort near a densely populated area, the radius will be an hour or less. For a large, popular ski resort or a sport or entertainment destination resort such as Hilton Head Island in South Carolina or Disney World in Orlando, Florida, the trading area is unlimited and virtually global. The concept of traveling time rather than straight mileage reflects more accurately the decision criteria for a consumer and consequently predicts potential demand more precisely.

The critical data to be kept on hand concerning the nature and extent of the market area are as follows:

✦ *Size of the market.* The size of the market is the total number of people living or working within the critical trading area. This indicates whether the market is big enough to support the sport product.

✦ *The demographics of people residing or working in the critical trading radius.* Specifically, demographics entail a breakdown by age, gender, income, ethnicity, or other variables relevant to the profile of target consumers. From these data, the marketer is able to predict the total market potential. When industry averages are available, marketers can predict quite accurately the total demand for a particular product. For example, for many years the bowling industry has had the demand standard of one bowling alley for every 10,000 people. At the same time, studies such as those described in chapter 3 (e.g., Simmons Annual Survey) can indicate whether an area's income, age, or gender composition matches national profiles for bowling.

✦ *The purchase behaviors and consumption patterns of those residing and/or working within the market.* Data on the spending patterns of consumers help the marketer determine potential market demand. Marketers have found demographics extremely useful in determining the profile of potential consumers, yet demographics have their limitations. For example, a 35-year-old, college-educated, white professional male who lives in Iowa is simply not the same "animal" to a marketer as the similarly profiled person who lives in New York City. The major difference is lifestyle characteristics, which are called psychographics and are usually captured through studies of attitudes, interests, and opinions. Psychographic studies tend to be expensive, and they are difficult to undertake. Soliciting psychographic data requires a great deal of effort, and respondents are not always forthcoming in offering opinions and attitudes. Consequently, many marketing decisions are made in the absence of such research. When no hard demographic data are available, or when the data bear no relationship to the product being marketed, it is essential that the marketer perform at least a "quick-and-dirty" pulse check of consumer attitudes about key product attributes. An example of this process might be a verbal sampling of opinions of participants in a road race about certain aspects of the race's total organization, registration process, marketing, course layout, and goody bag. Or for a more comprehensive study, the marketer might ask people to complete surveys on their attitudes concerning several brands or models of running shoes. First the marketer can ask respondents to identify product attributes such as price, tread design, color, and weight that are critical in their choices of shoes. Next they can rate each shoe on each attribute identified. From these data the marketer can develop a strong idea of product attributes that influence and help determine product choice. The marketer can also "guesstimate" the strengths and weaknesses of the product according to consumer perception and, similarly, develop some general ideas about the competition's strengths and weaknesses.

◆ *The level of spectatorship or participation in a sport broken down by demographic categories.* This identifies the profile of the target consumer of any given sport. The marketer designs all promotional strategies and advertising media choices to reach a target market segment. For example, to create awareness about the WNBA, the league used the Lifetime Network (a cable station that attracts a high percentage of female viewers) to televise a portion of its games, hoping to attract the female market.

◆ *Data on future trends.* No organization can exist without considering the future. The ability to project future trends may be even more critical in sport than in other industries. Sport continues to operate in a highly volatile marketplace: Fads are coming and going; labor agreements are constantly being modified; sponsorship agreements, entertainment expenses, and charitable contributions relating to sport are under government review; and the growth and impact of technology offer both solutions and problems. With sport trends apparently running in seven-year cycles, no aspect of the industry can be taken for granted or viewed as insulated from change.

Perhaps the most vivid illustration of such change is the fitness club industry. The majority of facilities in this industry segment started in the eastern United States in the 1960s as indoor tennis clubs. New trends developed in California and spread east as clubs added bars and lounges, weight rooms (free weights and later Nautilus-type equipment), racquetball courts, aerobic dance studios, cardiovascular fitness centers, pools, saunas, pro shops, and day care centers. The more sophisticated clubs have now moved into injury rehabilitation, stress management, diet and nutrition classes, cardiovascular screening, family fitness programs, and complete child care and programming. Few other industries have experienced such marked changes so quickly, yet it is clear that evolutions in this segment of the sport industry still have some way to go! Although other sport industry segments have not altered their concepts quite as drastically, changes in the marketplace for their products have been equally volatile. (9)

There is an old saying that all of marketing boils down to how well you know the market. There can be little doubt that knowledge of the market is critical to marketing success, even if other important factors affect success. Obviously, the impact of the Internet greatly alters market size and the market definition of size and proximity. This will be addressed specifically later in this chapter.

Data on Individual Consumers

Ideally, marketers have the names, addresses, and phone numbers (ideally, cell, business, and home phone numbers as well as fax numbers and e-mail addresses) of all of their consumers so that they can communicate with them directly. In the case of private clubs, season-ticket holders, subscriber services, and the like, these data are part of a registration purchase, and the records form a consumer file for each account. A large portion of these data can also become part of the organizational database and can be imported or exported as the need arises. Comprehensive databases can be easily updated and monitored as a regular business practice.

Although it is a common and accepted practice to gather information at the time of purchase or registration, people often miss numerous opportunities to add to the database. For example, professional sport franchises that qualify for postseason play often return unfilled ticket applications containing the names and addresses of potential ticket purchasers who should be added to the database. At golf events, it is common for major corporate sponsors to offer prize drawings as an incentive to capture the names of potential consumers. Although the sponsor capitalizes on this opportunity, in many cases event managers fail to secure the information from the sponsors to use in their own marketing efforts for the following year. Retail establishments that ask for the zip code of consumers making purchases should also be capturing their contact information, including names, addresses, and e-mail.

The data on existing customers that are most critical to marketing decision making are as follows:

- Names, addresses, e-mail addresses, and phone numbers of consumers—to be used for communication, correspondence, and direct mailings and telemarketing.

- Frequency of purchase or attendance, use of product type and quantity of product purchases, and dates of purchasing or attendance—to be used for tracking usage frequency, targeting low-frequency users, and upgrading existing customers from lower-priced products or options to higher-priced products or options.

- Method of payment, location where product was purchased, and lead time—to be used to determine price, distribution outlets, promotional effectiveness, and lead time in promoting events and ticket distribution.

- Media used and source of awareness (i.e., the media source that generated the customer)—to be used to determine promotional effectiveness, advertising reach and effectiveness, targeting of appropriate consumers, and appropriate media outlets.

- The pattern of consumption—to determine, for example, whether the consumer consumes alone or with family or friends, or what the consumer does before, during, or after consuming the sport. This information is extremely valuable in strategic market planning, particularly in answering the following questions: What promotional items or offers should be considered? Is a particular event day more likely to attract families, couples, business groups, or children? What types of concessions are most popular? What type of music should be played during the event? Should the marketer promote more to the father, mother, single female, or child?

In short, the marketer's goal in establishing an integrated database is threefold: to be able to identify consumers by name, to be able to communicate with them on a regular basis through a variety of media, and to be able to discern the variances in consumer buying and usage patterns by creating segments of the total user universe.

There are many ways to integrate an effective DBM system into current operational practices and procedures. Archtics, a Ticketmaster product commonly used by professional sport organizations, is a relatively inexpensive, easy-to-use program that provides a format for creating a variety of database files that the organization can use effectively for a variety of tasks.

Data on Competitors

An effective marketing organization should have up-to-date information on competitors, including price lists, product lines, promotional strategies, and possibly a description of services as well as comparisons among all similar organizations. A competitor can generally be defined as an organization offering similar products or services whose critical trading radius overlaps more than 25 percent of the marketer's own trading radius. Usually this means that the competitor's facility or retail outlet will be located within a 30-minute traveling time of the marketer's own facility.

In the fitness club industry, it is common to have all new employees visit competing facilities as part of their orientation. During this visit, they critique the competitor for strengths and weaknesses. This practice is also common in a variety of other sport venues and operations. For example, salespeople from one retail outlet visit a competitor's store and ask questions, observe customer interactions, critique product placement and other logistical issues, and so on. Professional sport franchises often conduct similar research in cities with multiple franchises, a practice that is effective because the various franchises often serve the same customers. Another way to obtain this type of information is to hire "mystery shoppers" who visit the operations of competitors and report on their experience.

Similar to data on competitors, sport organizations—particularly those that are part of professional sport leagues—should have marketing information classified as best practices from other member teams. Because teams within a professional league such as the National Basketball Association (NBA) do not compete against each other off the court (in a business sense), they should regularly share best practices—strategies and techniques that have been proven to be effective in one market and have the potential to be adapted or modified and used in other markets. The NBA's Team Marketing and Business Operations (TMBO) Department collects, regularly distributes, and schedules meetings to share best practices collected from NBA teams in the entire league.

Data Sources for an Effective Data-Based Marketing System

Once the marketer understands the important questions to ask in creating an integrated data-based marketing system, she must grapple with data sources to answer them. The two major sources of data are internal sources (within the organization) and external sources (outside the organization). This chapter addresses methods by which these data can be generated, stored, retrieved, and used to maximum effect at minimum cost. Figure 5.4 illustrates the sources and processes at work in an effective DBM system.

As the model suggests, information emanates from the marketplace of consumers and nonconsumers through either internal or external sources, which the organization must effectively manage. Given the potentially vast array of information sources, marketers must integrate the material in ways that enable effective strategic planning and decision making. Such planning and decision making result in the overall product that enters the marketplace for consumer and nonconsumer reaction. The feedback loop is essential for measuring the effect of a marketing decision on the general population. It is also important for measuring how the population perceives a marketing decision. Let's turn to the two basic types of sources: internal and external.

Internal Data Sources

Often, most of the data needed for principal decisions in marketing are gathered in the normal day-to-day operation of the business. Most organizations have opportunities to use internal sources of data for much of their marketing information. Unfortunately, organizations often overlook and underuse these sources. A brief review will suggest the potential benefits of using internal data sources.

◆ *Sales records.* Every "charge" or "check" sale identifies the customer's name and possibly his or her address—information that should be recorded before payments and checks are processed. If possible, the sales staff should record a code number that describes the

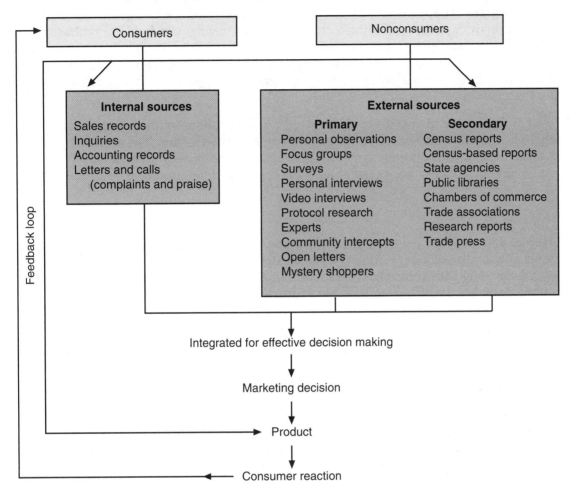

Population as a whole

Consumers	Nonconsumers

Internal sources
Sales records
Inquiries
Accounting records
Letters and calls
    (complaints and praise)

External sources

Primary
Personal observations
Focus groups
Surveys
Personal interviews
Video interviews
Protocol research
Experts
Community intercepts
Open letters
Mystery shoppers

Secondary
Census reports
Census-based reports
State agencies
Public libraries
Chambers of commerce
Trade associations
Research reports
Trade press

Feedback loop

Integrated for effective decision making

Marketing decision

Product

Consumer reaction

FIGURE 5.4 A basic design for a data-based marketing system.

sale; this will be most useful later. This information can be used to extend special offers to previous customers before announcement of sales to the general public, as well as in other marketing efforts designed to make the customer feel special. We discuss this aspect in greater detail in chapter 12. Additional names can be generated from lists of participants in contests, drawings, program registrations, catalog lists, and the like.

✦ *Inquiries.* Requests for play-off tickets contain names and addresses. Even telephone inquiries are a good source of potential customers. The marketer may offer incentives such as free or discounted items to induce people to inquire about the product (and thus provide their names). Addresses on fan mail requesting autographs should also be added to a marketer's database. In addition, requests for catalogs and any other consumer- or organization-initiated information should be integrated into the master database.

✦ *Accounting records.* Accounting records contain names that should be placed on mailing lists for direct promotional mailings. Season-ticket holders, corporate sponsors, and companies supplying the organization with goods and services may feel obligated to buy tickets, merchandise, memberships, and so on.

✦ *Letters and phone calls of complaint or praise.* Positive and negative letters and phone calls merit attention and follow-up. The name of the writer or caller should be recorded in the database, and a list of complaints and compliments should be compiled and monitored over time.

◆ *Web site registrations.* Visitors to team or organizational Web sites are an excellent source because they are demonstrating an interest in the team or organization. Web site visitors should be given the opportunity to "opt in"—that is, grant their permission to be contacted by the team or organization; without this permission, regulations forbid organizations to contact them directly. According to Seth Godin, author of *Permission Marketing*, four rules help marketers understand permission: (1) Permission is nontransferable; (2) permission is selfish; (3) permission is a process, not a moment; and (4) permission can be canceled at any time. (10)

All of these types of data (from sales records, inquiries, accounting records, letters, etc.), when integrated, form the internal data system. As with all data, files and lists must be checked against each other to avoid duplication and inaccuracies. Remember, the cost of not having such data is much greater than the cost of maintaining the data.

External Data Sources

External data sources, those originating outside the organization, may be categorized as either primary or secondary. Primary sources are studies or surveys that the organization initiates directly with consumers, competitors, or other organizations. Secondary sources contain data that are already published or compiled.

Primary Data Sources

Unless the marketer is in an industry that has sophisticated market research programs performed by trade organizations, he will invariably need some specific market segment information. In the majority of cases, this will come from primary market research—that is, research that the organization has originated (from either internal or external sources). The standard methods of primary market data collection are personal observation and surveys, including questionnaires and interviews. Before discussing each of these methods, we should first examine the rationale for conducting primary market research. There are a number of excellent reasons for conducting surveys, most of which relate to gathering knowledge to improve marketing performance. Marketers conduct surveys to do the following:

◆ Communicate with the target market
◆ Assess one's position in the market
◆ Establish a demographic profile of the audience
◆ Initiate data-based marketing efforts
◆ Benchmark and evaluate operational elements
◆ Gather information essential for sponsorship renewal and/or solicitation of new sponsors, or for determining the reaction to new concepts, products, or services

Communicating With the Target Market   A survey provides a vehicle for two-way communication between the team and its supporters. The team asks questions, and the supporter responds. For this reason, it is essential in any survey to provide the fan with a general question, such as, If you could give any message to the team president/ownership, what would that message be? This type of question provides an "open door" for fans to communicate whatever they believe is important to the team management. Input from the fan might be in the form of a suggestion, a complaint, or even praise. The most important thing to remember in conducting a survey is to ask the questions that are important to you—and if the goal is really to create a two-way dialogue, you must show the same courtesy to the fan.

Assessing One's Position in the Market A team can use a survey to get an idea of how respondents view it in relation to other entertainment options available to them. Do they enjoy attending your basketball game more than they enjoy attending a soccer game, and if so, why? This type of research will provide insight into the importance and effectiveness of entertainment and promotions—and possibly concessions—as well as the overall experience of attending.

Establishing a Demographic Profile of the Audience Successful marketers must know not only their target market, but also the actual market they are attracting. If, for example, the team is approaching a sponsor who wants access to young men between the ages of 18 and 24, the team should be able to verify that this audience is in fact attending the games. Survey research can provide this documentation. The following categories are commonly used to generate a demographic profile:

- Age
- Marital status
- Gender
- Household income
- Educational background
- Postal code
- Size and composition of household

This information is essential not only in the preparation of sponsorship proposals, but also for the purpose of selecting the proper radio station to use for advertising or the correct postal codes for direct-mail efforts.

Initiating Data-Based Marketing Efforts Registration forms such as those commonly used for ticket purchasing can easily be modified to function as a survey as well. Because these information forms contain names and addresses, they can be used to initiate or expand data-based marketing efforts. For example, a season-ticket holder registration form, which normally contains information relating to the purchaser such as name, address, and number and location of tickets can also ask for the names of spouses and children, their birth dates, preferred radio station, and the like. The database of information from this "minisurvey" can then be used in future marketing campaigns for tickets to other sports, summer sport camps, children's clinics, and so on. These data can also be provided to sponsors for their marketing purposes. Figures 5.5 and 5.6 show sample surveys for Maloof Sports and Entertainment and the Miami Heat, respectively.

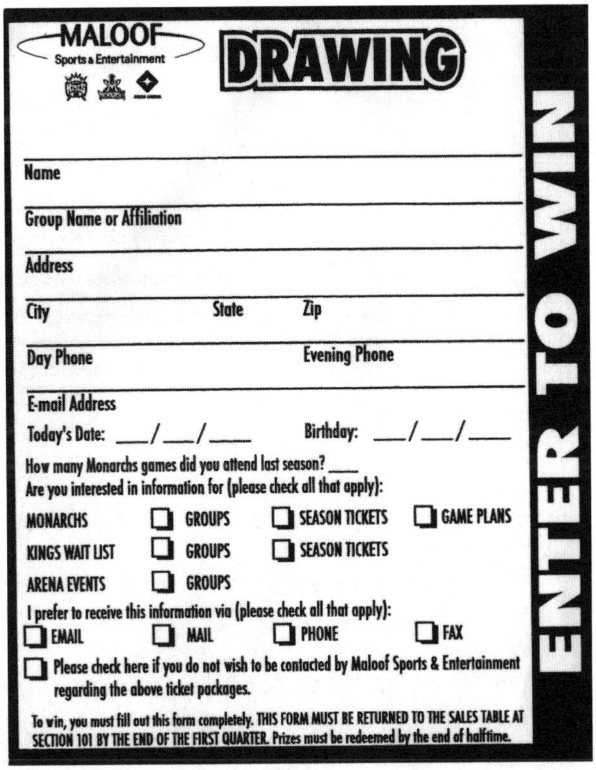
MALOOF Sports & Entertainment

DRAWING

ENTER TO WIN

Name

Group Name or Affiliation

Address

City State Zip

Day Phone Evening Phone

E-mail Address

Today's Date: __/__/__ Birthday: __/__/__

How many Monarchs games did you attend last season? __

Are you interested in information for (please check all that apply):

MONARCHS ☐ GROUPS ☐ SEASON TICKETS ☐ GAME PLANS

KINGS WAIT LIST ☐ GROUPS ☐ SEASON TICKETS

ARENA EVENTS ☐ GROUPS

I prefer to receive this information via (please check all that apply):

☐ EMAIL ☐ MAIL ☐ PHONE ☐ FAX

☐ Please check here if you do not wish to be contacted by Maloof Sports & Entertainment regarding the above ticket packages.

To win, you must fill out this form completely. THIS FORM MUST BE RETURNED TO THE SALES TABLE AT SECTION 101 BY THE END OF THE FIRST QUARTER. Prizes must be redeemed by the end of halftime.

FIGURE 5.5 Maloof Sports and Entertainment sample survey.
Courtesy of Maloof Sports & Entertainment.

Benchmarking and Evaluating Operational Elements In services marketing, customer satisfaction is a crucial element. Sport provides a service: entertainment. Because the marketer does not control the on-field product and cannot guarantee the performance and result of the product, the sport team must provide quality product extensions. Product extensions are

MIAMI HEAT

SUMMER HEAT

First Name _____ Last Name _____
Address _____
City _____ State _____ Zip _____
Daytime Phone _____
E-mail Address _____
Date _____ Location _____
Representative _____

Please sign me up to receive the following Free e-mail topics from the Miami HEAT:

❏ HEAT Mail - the HEAT's e-newsletter
❏ Miami HEAT events and promotions
❏ AmericanAirlines Arena events and promotions
❏ Miami HEAT and AmericanAirlines Arena partner offers

On average, how many HEAT games do you attend in a season?

❏ 0
❏ 1-3
❏ 4 +

I am most likely to go to a game with...

❏ Business Associates/Clients
❏ Family
❏ Friends

I am interested in the following:

❏ Season tickets   ❏ Single Game Tickets
❏ Partial plan tickets   ❏ Group tickets to a family show
❏ Group tickets   ❏ Other sporting events

I would like to refer the following person:

First Name _____ Last Name _____
Phone Number _____

What would encourage you to attend a Miami HEAT game?

_____
_____
_____
_____

FIGURE 5.6 Miami Heat sample survey.
Courtesy of Miami Heat.

elements relating to the fan's entertainment experience such as concessions, parking, music, halftime entertainment, clean rest rooms, ushers, merchandise for sale, and tailgating areas. It is essential for marketers to evaluate these product extensions to ensure that they incorporate everything possible to ensure fan satisfaction. Once the initial survey has established the ratings or "benchmark," the marketer can evaluate these same elements the next year against the benchmark to determine whether, in the mind of the ticket purchaser, the situation has improved.

Gathering Information for Sponsorship Activities   Although surveys are generally designed to enable the organization to be responsive, they can also play a valuable role in helping the organization become proactive. Such a proactive role could entail evaluating ticket holders as a group in relation to the products or services offered by current or potential sponsors. When Wood Selig, the director of athletics at Western Kentucky University, was working for the University of Virginia, he had this to say about the use of surveys:

> In our surveys, we ask a core of questions to be utilized for our current sponsors and to help in future sales efforts. These questions include items such as favorite fast food restaurant, number of nights spent in a hotel last month, etc. We can then use this information to demonstrate to a McDonald's that they are the preferred fast food restaurant among our respondents and therefore they are reaching their target market. If say the results show that Pizza Hut, a current sponsor, is not faring well, then we can work with Pizza Hut to create some opportunities to help improve their status. We also try to be future focused in our surveys as they relate to sponsors. If perhaps we are looking to add a car dealer, we could ask our respondents via the survey if they are planning to purchase or lease a new vehicle in the next 12 months. We can then use the results to help a car dealer justify why they should become involved with the University of Virginia Athletic program and how they can benefit from that association. (12)

A number of firms specialize in generating sponsorship-related data. These firms provide general trend data, or for a fee they will conduct research specifically for a particular organization or event. Turnkey Sports & Entertainment is an example of such a firm.

Secondary Data Sources

We cited some of the standard secondary data sources in the sport industry in chapter 3 when we discussed the sport consumer. But many other sources are worth investigating, including the following: (13)

Turnkey Sports & Entertainment

Turnkey Sports & Entertainment is one of the industry's most recognized and trusted names. Turnkey provides its clients comprehensive solutions in three core areas:

- ✦ **Turnkey Intelligence** helps properties and sponsors develop key audience and marketplace insights quickly and cost-effectively. Turnkey's Intelligence products are, by far, the largest collectors of custom fan data in the industry. In addition, relationships with Acxiom-Direct and Greenfield Online provide clients with a broad range of powerful market intelligence tools including direct marketing and consumer panel solutions.
- ✦ **Turnkey Search** helps properties and sponsors identify and recruit the very best management talent that matches the chemistry of the organization. Turnkey's differentiator is its specialization in live events, sports, sports media, and entertainment.
- ✦ **Turnkey Finance** delivers knowledgeable, experienced, and objective financial advisory services to clients for valuations, appraisals, fairness opinions, and feasibility studies.

Turnkey Sports & Entertainment owns the Turnkey Sports Poll, the industry's continuing survey of senior-level executives and owners which probes the hottest issues inside sports. The results of the poll appear weekly in *Street & Smith's SportsBusiness Journal*.

Learn why more than 100 clients across the industry trust Turnkey by visiting www.TurnkeySE.com.

Courtesy of Len Perna and Turnkey Sports & Entertainment

◆ *Census reports.* Census reports are a basic source of statistical information that is primarily demographic (e.g., income, age, marital status, education, size of household). Census reports are published by both federal and state agencies and are available from any Department of Commerce office.

◆ *Census-based demographic reports.* Two valuable sources that regularly extrapolate information from census data are the *Rand McNally Commercial Atlas and Marketing Guide* (Skokie, IL: Rand McNally) and a publication of National Demographics and Lifestyles, *Lifestyle Market Analyst* (Wilmette, IL: Standard Rate and Data Service). Both provide general demographic information on most metropolitan areas—data that the marketer can use as the basis for comparisons.

◆ *State agencies.* Agencies such as state departments of recreation often have state and local data on sport consumption as well as an inventory of state facilities and programs.

◆ *Public libraries.* Libraries can provide historical information on businesses and organizations in the community.

◆ *Chambers of commerce.* Chambers of commerce usually employ research directors or contract externally for research relating to the local business environment. This service may be free to chamber members and may be available to nonmembers for a fee.

◆ *Trade associations.* Trade associations exist to help businesses in a given field, and often provide extremely useful information on that industry to their membership. Whether an association will release information to nonmembers depends on the industry. The sporting goods industry has a variety of trade associations that vary in their pursuit of data and their willingness to share data. The best reference for addresses and phone numbers of sport organizations, including trade organizations, is *Sport Marketplace,* published annually by Franklin-Covey.

◆ *Professional (syndicated) research services.* These companies are in the business of providing information: A.C. Nielsen, Simmons Market Research Bureau, American Sports Data, Inc., Joyce Julius and Associates, Team Marketing Report, Audience Analysts, and Performance Research. Research services have their own regular surveys and reports that are available for sale. Special and customized projects can be more expensive.

◆ *Trade and scholarly press.* Trade and scholarly publications can be important not only because their advertising space is designed to target a market segment, but also because they reveal collective experience as well as competitor information. These publications also reveal trends in other areas. Examples of trade publications are *Street & Smith's SportsBusiness Journal, Sporting Goods Directory, Sporting Goods Dealer, Team Marketing Report, Amusement Business,* and *Marketing News.* A large group of publications address professional sports. Each commissioner's office provides some information to individual clubs. Information on collegiate athletics comes from *NCAA News, Athletic Administration, Athletic Management,* and *Athletic Business.* Two research journals, the *Journal of Sport Management* and *Sport Marketing Quarterly,* contain excellent material and resources. (See appendix A for a list of appropriate Web sites.)

Types of Primary Market Research Used in Sport

Because of its nature and variety, the sport product lends itself to a number of research methodologies for the organization to consider and ultimately select. Examining these methods provides insight into their aims and benefits.

Personal Observation

Many managers perform unstructured research of their own; informal talks with friends, employees, and customers are usually the rule. Although these "surveys" are unstructured, they do have some value. For years, Hall of Famer and baseball owner, the late Bill Veeck, maintained that the only way to understand the real desires of baseball fans was to mingle with them in the stadium and watch how they interacted not only with the game on the field, but also with the activities and people around them. Veeck's success with promotions stemmed in large part from his personal knowledge of fan behavior. Such grassroots involvement by executives has been linked to some of the Japanese breakthroughs in international marketing.

The observational method allows people in the market to act "naturally"—that is, of course, if the observer remains undiscovered, as Bill Veeck obviously could not. But the kind of information observers can obtain is limited; although they can observe behavior, they cannot find out income and home address, for example. For these and other reasons, marketers tend to rely on direct questioning of consumers. (14)

Focus Groups

Research using focus groups is highly individualized, not mass-oriented like research using paper surveys. A focus group usually consists of 10 to 12 participants chosen because of one or more common characteristics; for example, they may be season-ticket holders, males between the ages of 18 and 24, or former players. A moderator, usually someone from outside the organization but familiar with the sport product, serves as a facilitator. A focus group usually lasts between one and a half and two hours and concentrates on two or three predetermined issues. Focus groups are often used in conjunction with survey research. Sometimes they are conducted before a survey is administered to help develop the survey instrument. They can also be used subsequently to a survey for the purpose of testing the findings or assessing response to proposed changes or new programs.

Asking the Right Questions

In some cases it's not what you know, but what you don't know. Several years ago, the LPGA hired Bill Sutton to assess consumer reactions to a proposed new merchandise line by conducting focus groups on-site at LPGA Tour events. Bill was excited about the opportunity to assess, firsthand, the consumers' reaction to the products he had to show them. He randomly selected 10 participants from among the crowd attending the tournament and arranged to meet them later that afternoon at the entrance to a room in the clubhouse where the focus group would meet.

He greeted people as they entered, provided each person with a name tag, and offered refreshments. He watched as the participants milled around the room and touched and admired the merchandise. This, at least so it seemed, would be a rather easy task with a clear-cut resolution. Fifteen minutes later Bill realized how wrong he was.

After people had assumed their places at the table, Bill identified himself and explained what they would be doing that afternoon. He then asked people to introduce themselves and explain their level of interest and involvement in the sport of golf. He was interrupted by Stan, a man in his early sixties who wanted to know whether he could ask a question before the session began. Bill replied, "Sure, Stan, what would you like to ask?" Stan asked the simplest—yet the most central—question. A researcher in most cases assumes that a participant understands the topic to be discussed. But Stan said, "I'm not sure what the LPGA is—can you tell me what it is?" Before Bill could answer, seven other participants indicated that they did not understand what the LPGA was and would really like to know.

Realizing the importance of the question, Bill began to answer, knowing that the group would never talk about merchandise that afternoon. The results? In short, the merchandise program was delayed several years, and another initiative was designed and developed: the LPGA Fan Village, a fan reception and interactive area, located at selected LPGA events (and later sold as a sponsorship to Target) to help the LPGA communicate its mission and purpose to fans attending its events. The hope was that a better understanding might increase the level of fan involvement and also the number of fans of the LPGA. In two short years, this project has been an enormous success, and the Fan Village, now sponsored by Target, includes an area devoted to the new LPGA merchandise line.

Surveys and Questionnaires

There are several situations in which a sport marketer would want to conduct a structured market survey:

- ◆ When considering the launch of a new product or service or a major revision of an existing product or service.
- ◆ When dealing with a highly volatile (changeable-elastic) market.
- ◆ When considering a revision of a pricing structure across stadium or arena seats; considering revamping price differentials between various products or seating areas; or changing the product line, item, or mix (of particular note in today's marketplace, this refers to priority-seating programs, personal seat licenses, club seat programs, and so on).

The major instrument of structured research is invariably a formal survey instrument known as a questionnaire. The following sections present guidelines on conducting questionnaires and surveys.

On-Site Surveys

On-site surveys or audience audits are highly effective for determining the attitudes and feelings of people actually attending games. One can distribute the survey as people enter the game or when they are in their seats. Several factors affect the response rate: (1) whether people have a pen or pencil; (2) whether they bother to return the surveys; and (3) whether they receive a small token in exchange for their time. Experience shows that the most effective method is to distribute the surveys to people in their seats before the game or at halftime, give them a logoed pen as a gift for their time, and remain in the stands to collect the surveys. This generally provides a completed-survey return of over 80 percent. See appendix B for an example of an on-site survey.

In conducting on-site surveys, the surveyor must consider and address several aspects in order to guarantee accuracy and protect against bias. One of these is frequency. Surveys must be conducted often enough to ensure against biases such as day of the week, opponent or attraction, starting time, presence of a promotion, or (in the case of team sports) "halos" caused by circumstances such as a winning streak. It is also important that the complexity of the survey fit the situation. Because of the likelihood that respondents may become distracted as a result of their surroundings, survey content should be simple.

Mail Surveys

Organizations most commonly use mail surveys to survey a consumer group that has been identified through records or other types of lists. Obviously, having correct addresses for the target market is key to a successful mail survey. For this reason, the most common targets for mail surveys are health club members, season-ticket holders who own one or more tickets and have completed an application that the team has on record, and registrants from past events or purchasers of past goods or services. Other targets might include a particular postal code (for a mass mailing) or people who have purchased their tickets with credit cards, thereby providing the information needed for the mailing.

Because with mail surveys the obligation is with the addressee to complete and return the survey, response rates are significantly lower than with other forms of research. Depending on the size of the population receiving the mail survey, a response rate of 20 percent or greater is acknowledged as acceptable. One key point to remember in using a mail survey is that because the respondent is "out of touch" with the source of the survey, the instrument should be simple and should not contain questions that could be interpreted more than one way. For example, a question such as, When is your preferred starting time for Pittsburgh

Pirate games? assumes that there is little or no difference between weekdays and weekends. Past research and practices have shown that there are significant differences. Thus the question would need to be divided into two parts—weekdays and weekends—or asked as two distinct questions to ensure that the reader understands the intent. See appendix B for an example of a mail survey.

Telephone Surveys

Similar to mail surveys, telephone surveys are more efficient if one can identify an appropriate target group. Although random-dialing programs are available, telephone surveys are most effective when the intent is to contact a specific group.

Telephone surveys are highly applicable across the general population if they are used to measure awareness, particularly relating to publicity or advertising. For example, if the team is announcing a ticket campaign or offering sport clinics for youth, and has been advertising and publicizing this information, a telephone survey can confirm whether this knowledge is reaching the market and which channels are most effective.

Telephone surveys are cost-effective and can be performed from one central location, or at subsites throughout the country if the interest is in a national sample. Because of people's work habits and family obligations, most surveying is done in the evening or on weekends. The practices of telephone solicitation and telemarketing are negatively affecting the success of telephone surveys because of the increasing numbers of uninitiated calls coming to households throughout the United States and Canada. People are using unlisted phone numbers and caller ID systems in part to limit access to members of the household. The National Do Not Call List is a registry that allows consumer the opportunity to "opt out" of telemarketing lists and solicitations conducted by companies or their marketing agents.

Computerized Surveys

Computerization has given us the opportunity to improve the survey process. Through computerization the surveyor can create an interactive, self-directed survey methodology. Computerization also eliminates data-entry costs and the lag time between gathering and analyzing the data. Del Wilber & Associates was one of the first firms to advocate this technology, naming their version Rapid Audience Profile System (RAPS). A major advantage of computerization is the ability to create "branches" within the questionnaire that are triggered on the basis of a response to a previous question. For example, an automotive company sponsoring an event may wish to know the likelihood of car-purchasing behavior among its audience. Thus a question might be, Do you plan on leasing or purchasing a new vehicle within the next six months? Respondents who answer no continue down the main path of the questionnaire; those who answer yes can be directed to a branch of the questionnaire that might include one or more questions specifically related to this anticipated purchase. Sample branch questions might be, Which automobile manufacturers are you considering? Will this be a purchase or lease? What is the manufacturer of your current vehicle? This branching ability provides a significant advantage over traditional paper surveys.

Another major advantage of this technology-based approach to market research is the turnaround time. Traditional research methods include time for data entry—a process in which the data gathered during the research are coded and entered into a computer program for analysis (usually SPSS or similar programs that allow analysis and segmentation of the information according to how the organization wishes to view it). Computer-based programs such as RAPS and TEAM (Team & Event Assessment Model, developed at the University of Massachusetts) eliminate the data-entry step and enable the researcher to review the results within minutes of completing the data collection. This can be particularly important because it permits the event or organization to make timely changes or improvements in areas identified by the respondents. The main disadvantages of this method are the following:

+ Limitation of possible sample size because of the number of computers available
+ Reading speed and comprehension level, which will influence the time necessary to complete the survey
+ Computer failure, power outages, or related concerns

One of the most significant improvements to the computer-based surveys has been portability. It is now relatively common to use handheld devices such as PDAs to collect data on site. PDAs allow the interviewer to move freely throughout a venue and conduct surveys dealing with certain aspects of an experience immediately after it happens rather than using a terminal-based interview station located at the exit area.

Personal Interviews Another popular and commonly used survey approach is the personal interview. People are generally willing to be questioned, and they are often flattered to be asked their opinion and to participate in a survey. Interviewing offers several advantages:

+ The interviewer can provide clarification if the respondent does not understand what is being asked.
+ The interviewer can probe to find out more detailed information.
+ It is easy to record comments and observations.

The greatest danger in personal interviewing is that the interviewer may deliberately or inadvertently "lead" the respondent to answer the question in a certain way. Leading usually occurs because of facial expressions, changes in intonation, nods of approval, and the like.

Video Interviews Video interviews are usually four to six minutes in length and are often recorded at the game or event. The purpose of a video interview is to provide not only the response to the question, but also the facial expressions, animation, and emotion associated with the response. (15) Video interviews are a form of qualitative research in that they not only elicit answers to questions but also offer an opportunity to find out why the respondent provided a particular answer. Video interviews are most effective when used in concert with a written survey. A method related to video interviewing is an ethnographic approach that involves videotaping consumer behavior at sporting events to provide a permanent record of learned behaviors that don't necessarily emerge during the survey process (16), either because the question doesn't provoke the emotional response or because the question isn't asked at all. In the sport setting, use of video can have significant value for observing community relations activities, interaction with mascots, retail operations, concessions areas, and so forth.

Community Intercepts One of the most effective yet least utilized forms of research is the community intercept. Researchers use community intercepts to identify any barriers that people perceive to exist (correctly or incorrectly) so that the team can address them through its marketing efforts. Simply stated, in addition to asking why people are attending (on-site surveys), community intercepts allow one to ask why people aren't attending. The community intercept can also be used to document media patterns, gain reaction to new concepts, and compare the subject of the survey (e.g., a team, health club, venue) to its area competition. (17) See appendix B for an example of a community intercept.

Community intercepts are usually conducted as interviews but can, depending on the venue and type of audience, be administered as a pass-out survey similar to the on-site survey described earlier. In sport, community intercepts usually occur at places (other than at the actual event or game addressed in the research) where people socialize or pursue leisure activities. Such locations could include, among others, sports bars, fitness centers, and theaters and movie complexes. The community intercept elicits perceptions and misperceptions that exist about the sport organization in the community as a whole—the community including people who may have attended a game as well as those who may not have. Both viewpoints are essential to assessing the status of marketing initiatives and future planning. If attendance is to increase, current attendees must attend more frequently; but in addition, a percentage of those who have not previously attended must also attend.

Protocol Research   One of the emerging methods of consumer research involves a type of interview process known as "protocol research." This entails getting the consumer to answer certain questions while she is in the process of decision making. Although protocol research has been validated as a method of understanding the general approaches to decision making (it is the foundation of cybernetics), consumer and marketing researchers have not used it extensively. As John O'Shaughnessey notes in his book, *Why People Buy*, organizations should find ways to have the consumers think aloud at various times: (a) before they buy (anticipatory account); (b) during their purchase (contemporaneous account); and (c) after they have bought (retrospective account).

When enough of these protocols have been recorded, certain patterns may emerge. (18) For example, protocol research may indicate that people may not consider corporate sponsorships before they purchase, or that teens tend to purchase athletic footwear in malls where they have at least three purchasing options to consider.

Panel of Experts   The panel of experts survey method is not used as much as it should be. It is comparatively simple to put together a group of experts in any industry. One of the most successful methods employing experts is called the "delphi method." With this method, experts individually rank certain questions concerning the issue; the group then sees the collective (averaged) findings, and some discussion follows. The experts then vote again, and the process is repeated until there is a general consensus on a particular issue. Experts are often used to predict trends in sales of sporting goods equipment, to judge the effectiveness of certain promotions, and to gauge trends in club memberships, to name but a few areas. The overall effect, in most cases, is a quite accurate prediction. (19)

In sport, consumer panels are more common than expert panels. In this research process, consumers are selected for the panel because of their history or experience in purchasing the products or services of interest. These panels are selected from a database that is either purchased from an outside source or derived from the records of the entity initiating the research. The individuals are then contacted regarding their willingness to serve over a specific period of time, often two to three years. Thus consumer panels usually serve in longitudinal studies performed to measure behavior patterns and trends over time. This is a particularly valuable approach as new products and concepts enter the marketplace or as new ad campaigns promote these products and services.

Respondents on such panels usually receive compensation or some type of benefit and may also receive the products under consideration for trial use and feedback. The Sports Illustrated Readers Poll and subscribers to *Golf Magazine* are examples where respondents not only share opinion but also test products and provide feedback. Consumer panels are usually very successful, in part because the participants feel special in having access to information and products before the general public does, and in part because use of these panels is cost efficient for the manufacturer or supplier. (20)

Internet and Web Site Surveys

A newer methodology that is becoming popular in terms of adaptation and utilization is the Internet or Web site survey. The ease of designing a Web page complete with a survey instrument, the almost overnight results, and the absence of cost and staff time are very attractive factors. The number of Internet users has been growing rapidly; according to a 2007 study, an estimated 69.4 percent of people in the United States and Canada reported that they have access to the Internet. This figure shows a 114.7 percent growth in Internet use since 2000. (21) Age also plays a key role in determining who is online. A recent study showed that while a whopping 87 percent of teenagers (ages 12-17) are online, only 26 percent of 70- to 75-year-olds access the Internet. (22)

This creates a sample bias because this group may not be representative of the group the cyber-researcher is interested in.

Convenience and cost are two of the benefits most evident in Web-based surveys. Web-based surveys can be custom designed or created through inexpensive programs such as Survey Monkey, which can help design questions. Web-based surveys offer a number of benefits:

- ✦ They can be completed within a given time parameter at the discretion of the respondent.
- ✦ They are inexpensive—no paper, printing, postage, data entry, or interviewing costs are involved.
- ✦ Large amounts of data can be collected simultaneously and within a short time.
- ✦ Data are collected in a usable format and have already been entered.
- ✦ The Web site can be used to provide information or show images and concepts that the respondent can review and evaluate.

Open Letters

One of the simplest and most economical ways to learn about the consumers of your product or service could be to simply invite them to write to you. Researchers who ask people to write are opening the door for communication—hence the term "open letter." (23) Letters of this type might indicate what is on the mind of the consumer, possibly complaints, praise, or suggestions for improvement. Open letters are valuable because they provide the words and convey the feelings of the consumer, but because they might not arrive in sufficient quantity, they should be used as an addition to other forms of research that are both more quantifiable and more reliable in terms of sample size. The open-letter format may also be adapted to fax, 1-800 phone messages, e-mail, and so on.

Mystery Shoppers

According to noted sport marketer Jon Spoelstra, the most valuable information emerges via personal experience and observation. (24) Although it is incumbent on management to occasionally "survey" the premises, interacting with patrons and noting consumer behaviors and operational weaknesses, surveying and observing may not be enough for a comprehensive assessment of all event operations. Likewise, the visual presence of management is sure to inspire even the unfriendliest of employees, thereby adversely affecting any opportunity for capturing the "true" service encounter between the event patron and staff. Enter the mystery shopper, a.k.a. secret shopper. In the technique known as the mystery shopper, a person who works for an organization is hired to observe employees and operations in the same organization or that of a competitor and to compile a report. This approach is becoming more popular in sport settings because of the high levels of interaction with customers.

Mystery shoppers look and act like ordinary customers, and their job is to evaluate the service and attention the ordinary customer receives. Mystery shopping has been used for many years in marketing research to evaluate customer satisfaction and employee performance and satisfaction, as well as for other purposes requiring a dispassionate and unobtrusive data collector. (25) In the sport setting, an approach based on personal observation would require mystery shoppers to visit the workout floor, bleacher seats, concession stands, ticket outlets, pro shops, or wherever they might gather information about consumers, products, and the distribution system that brings them together. (26) The mystery shopper audit can generate valuable feedback on such details as employee knowledge and performance, facility cleanliness, waiting time, concessions quality, and security. (27)

Integration of Primary Data Sources

To be truly effective and to develop a valid, inclusive, and comprehensive organizational "picture" through research, managers are now finding it best to integrate several of the methodologies discussed in this chapter instead of relying on just one approach. Integrating qualitative practices (e.g., focus groups) with quantitative practices (e.g., a mail survey) is more likely to provide the manager with not only statistics but also the rationale behind respondents' answers.

One might think of a benchmark market research study as one that employs a number of the methods described in this chapter. An example of such a study is an analysis sponsored by the United States Tennis Association and the Tennis Industry Council. Called "Why People Play," the study addressed some key questions for an industry that has seen declining participation rates and interest in general. These were the questions that the marketers centered their research on:

+ Who plays tennis? How often? Why?
+ Why do players quit and why do many return or rejoin?
+ What are the perceptions of players, ex-players, and nonplayers?
+ What are the barriers to participation?
+ What can the industry do about these barriers and perceptions?

In addressing these questions, the research team conducted a three-phase study. Phase 1 involved a series of personal interviews with groups of "tennis experts," including manufacturers, retailers, members of trade and professional associations, publishers, club owners, and corporate sponsors. The interviews helped the researchers develop initial hypotheses and identify factors related to the questions at hand. Phase 2 consisted of 11 focus-group discussions throughout the country, involving mixtures of players, ex-players, and nonplayers. These discussions allowed the researchers to refine the earlier hypotheses and gain a sense of relevant factors, especially those involving attitudes, behaviors, and motivations. Phase 3 was a telephone survey, based on a refinement of Phases 1 and 2 and conducted with a random stratified national sample of 1,200 people that included 600 players, 300 ex-players, and 300 nonplayers.

Although, of course, no study is perfect, this study had a methodologically balanced design (28) and is an excellent example of an organization mindfully using several of the tools in the market research toolbox.

Common Problems in Sport Marketing Research

The researcher must be aware of a number of common problems in marketing research that are not necessarily unique to the sport industry but are relevant nevertheless. Close attention to these areas is necessary to ensure the effectiveness of the DBM system. These are some questions that researchers commonly face:

- How many people should I survey to be accurate?
- How dependable are my findings?
- Where should demographic questions be placed in a survey?
- How can I be assured of a random population for the survey?

Marketers address these questions with appropriate sampling and questionnaire design techniques.

Sampling

Typically, one cannot collect data from all fans, all club members, or all users. The purpose of sampling is to allow researchers to make generalizations about a population based on a scientifically selected subset of that population. A sample, therefore, is intended to become a microcosm of a larger universe. (29) For this reason, researchers must always be concerned with the representativeness of the sample. They must ask and answer the following questions:

- *What is the structure of the population to be surveyed?* If the population is a homogeneous group, then a simple random-sample survey (see table 5.1) can be used. If the population is not homogeneous (i.e., it is segmented), then a random stratified sample survey is required (the proportion of each segment in the total population is represented in the sample population). A good example is the on-site survey where fans are segmented by the type of seat (general admission, reserved, etc.) that they purchased. Therefore, the research team ensured that the sample in the study approximated the overall attendance segmentation by seat type.
- *How can randomness be en-sured?* This is a particular problem with on-site surveys and audience audits. If a researcher gives a questionnaire to every person passing through the gate, she might not get the stratified sample that she intended. It may be necessary to make assumptions that people in aisle seats have a certain randomness; or distributing surveys in concession areas may ensure a higher degree of randomness.

- *How reliable should the results be?* Before marketers say "100 percent," they must realize that reliability involves a cost–accuracy trade-off. A marketer who just wants a general idea should survey friends, customers, and fellow suppliers to get a feel for the market. If predictive reliability is required, then it is necessary to use a sufficiently large, random sample. Such a survey must use a well-planned questionnaire administered by trained researchers. The larger the sample, the more predictive the results. For example, to state the results with a 95 percent level of confidence (meaning that in 95 cases out of 100 this is expected) may require a sample size of at

+ Table 5.1 Minimum Sample Sizes for Small Populations

Population size (N)	Sample size with a 5% margin of error and 95% confidence level	Sample size with a 5% margin of error and 99% confidence level
500	218	250
1,000	278	399
1,500	306	460
2,000	323	498
3,000	341	544
5,000	357	586
10,000	370	622
20,000	377	642
50,000	382	655
100,000	383	659

Adapted, by permission, from L.M. Rea and R.A. Parker, 1997, *Designing and conducting research: A comprehensive guide* (San Francisco, CA: Jossey-Bass, Inc.), 121. By permission of John Wiley & Sons, Inc.

least 400, but to state the results with a 99 percent level of confidence (in 99 cases out of 100 this is expected) may require a sample size of almost 800. However, as sample size increases, so do the survey, interviewer, and processing costs. (30) This is the trade-off in market research.

Designing the Questionnaire

These are important points to remember in designing the questionnaire itself: (31).

+ The questionnaire should contain only questions for which the marketer really needs answers.

+ The marketer should have a feel for the kind of answer he expects to get and should also know what he will do with each answer (how he will interpret each response).

+ Simple, objective, precoded questions (with responses provided or scales) are easier to interpret and analyze than are open-ended questions.

+ Demographic questions (age, income, etc.) should come at the end of the questionnaire. In an interview process, these same questions might be printed on a card for the respondent to fill in so that it is not necessary to ask the questions aloud.

+ Similar and related questions should be grouped together on the basis of topic areas. Such questions should be in a logical sequence and should flow from general to specific.

+ When the questionnaire uses precoded or semantic differentials (i.e., asks subjects to choose between opposite positions, such as good–bad, enjoyable–not enjoyable), it should not present a large number of these questions in sequence, because some respondents may become bored with the questions and begin answering them without reading or thinking about them.

+ The marketer should use semantic differentiation with care when asking attitudinal questions. (Many respondents will not have thought in terms of these topics and questions and hence may be forced into erroneous responses.) In many cases, and time permitting, there is value in following up these questions with the question, Why? This not only provides the rationale for the response but also ensures that the respondent has understood and thought about the question.

+ The questions should be free of ambiguities.

+ Each question should have a distinct purpose. Often, though, it takes more than one question to generate the data needed to make a decision. Questions may be interrelated and may be initiated from the responses of previous questions.

+ Because a survey is a form of communication, it is often a good practice to offer the respondent a final open-ended response to the organization directing the research. This ensures that the communication process is two-way and that the researcher is not missing any issues of substance. This question might be stated as follows: Are there any issues that were not covered in the survey that you would like to address and discuss? If so, please list and explain your feelings regarding these issues.

Analyzing Survey Data

Undoubtedly the greatest advantage in using precoded (forced-choice) responses is that the data are easy to input into a data-entry/analysis program. The ideal (and most commonly used) computer program for data entry and analysis is SPSS/PC+, a sophisticated and multifaceted program with a thorough tutorial on the use of the package as well as on certain basic statistical procedures. The system is menu-driven, featuring context-sensitive help screens. Cross-tabulations (analysis of responses through examining the response by variable segmentation, such as female season-ticket holders, youth aged 14 to 18) are produced efficiently and quickly. Add-on packages to produce graphic interpretations and presentations are also available. Overall, SPSS/PC+ is a comprehensive system capable of performing for both the professional statistician and the less experienced researcher. (32).

Wrap-Up

The data-based marketing system links the market and the marketer and is therefore the lifeline of marketing. Perhaps the factors most critical to marketing success are the marketer's ability to (1) collect accurate and timely information about consumers and potential consumers and (2) use this data to create marketing plans specifically targeted to meet the needs of specific consumer groups (known as target market segments). Marketing-mix decisions must be based on accurate and comprehensive data on the market, the competition, the way the market views the product, the pricing structure, and the promotional messages transmitted about the product. Simply stated, anything short of a complete DBM system leaves the door open for competition to erode the organization's product position and stature and to eat into its market share.

The marketer can select from a wide variety of options for collecting the data needed to generate the appropriate information. There is no one way of collecting data that is best for all organizations. The organization needs to determine its marketing priorities and the information it needs to proceed with market planning. It then needs to determine the most efficient method to accurately gather the data on its consumers, potential consumers, and competition.

The data generated in the data-based marketing system show the marketer that not all consumers think the same way or have the same needs or wants that they expect the product to fulfill. The recognition that consumers have different aspirations, needs, or wants, and the grouping together of consumers based on certain characteristics common to a group, constitute what is called *market segmentation*. The process of dividing consumers into several target market segments is essential to any marketing strategy development. We turn to that process in the next chapter.

Activities

1. What is the goal of an effective data-based marketing system?
2. What is the essential difference between qualitative and quantitative research?
3. Design an effective 20-item questionnaire focusing on attendance and enjoyment issues as they relate to attending collegiate women's basketball games.
4. Identify a minimum of five secondary data sources that could provide information about trends relating to youth sport.
5. Visit a local health or fitness center. Determine the types of organizational records that the center has available. Ask how these records are used in terms of marketing efforts. Do they effectively generate a consumer profile? If not, what other types of information need to be solicited to generate an effective consumer profile?

Your Marketing Plan

In examining the organization that you previously selected as the focus for your marketing plan, identify the areas on which you will need additional data (from both primary and secondary sources) before setting realistic objectives and determining strategies and tactics. What are the most effective ways to secure such information? What part will research play as you assess the effectiveness of your marketing plan?

Chapter 6

Market Segmentation

Objectives

✦ To appreciate the central role of segmentation in the marketing process.

✦ To recognize the standard bases of market segmentation in sport.

Women Learn to "Putt for Dough"

In the late 1990s, surveys by the National Golf Foundation suggested that 5.7 million women made up 22 percent of the American golf market. Their average age was 42, their average household income was $66,000, and their average annual golf spending was $649. There was one more, critical statistic: 40 percent of all women golfers held managerial, professional, or administrative positions. This was a large group of people (over 2 million) for whom golf might have great business as well as leisure value. After all, male executives had long fostered the ethos of making deals on the fairways. Jane Blalock, a top LPGA touring pro, had known this before she retired from competition in 1986. Her sport could provide great executive development among women, if they only got a little help. Blalock recognized the need for partnerships to power her vision. Hence, the Jane Blalock Company began promoting and running LPGA Golf Clinics for Women. For over 15 years, at 14 to 15 sites per year, the clinics have trained thousands of women who pay ($275 in 2004) to learn the craft, the etiquette, and the networking power of golf from touring and teaching professionals. Corporate partners like Fidelity, Pepsi, American Airlines, and Hallmark (to name a few) have joined the effort. Blalock neatly summarized her vision: "Women miss out on a lot of quality time with clients when they can't go out on the course at the sales meeting. We want to break down the barriers and intimidation many women feel about the game." (1)

Jane Blalock had researched the market. She recognized the links among sport, lifestyle, and a

Jane Blalock, leading the way in women's golf.
Courtesy of the Jane Blalock Company

clearly defined group of people. The LPGA clinics were designed to satisfy some unmet needs of that group. In short, Blalock had employed a segmentation strategy.

The ability to segment a market is made possible by the kind of market research we discussed in chapter 5. In this chapter, we explain segmentation, its centrality to the marketing process, and its feasibility. Next, we look at the common bases for segmenting the sport market: state of being (demographics), state of mind (psychographics), product benefits, and product usage.

What Is Market Segmentation?

Market segmentation is a key concept in this text because it creates the bridge between managerial analysis and managerial action. It provides a conceptual framework on which a sport marketer builds promotional strategies.

In simple terms, market segmentation is the process of dividing a large, heterogeneous market into more homogeneous groups of people, who have similar wants, needs, or demographic profiles, to whom a product may be targeted. The Jane Blalock Company, for instance, does not target its clinics to all golfers, or even all female golfers. Instead, the focus is the female executive golfer. Such segmentation is basic to most successful marketing efforts throughout the world. Even within the massive global marketing strategies of corporate giants such as McDonald's and Coca-Cola, marketers recognize that consumers in Germany are different from consumers in Japan. If technology has made the world smaller, it has not homogenized the world's cultures. Neither has television created a "mass mentality" within a nation of television viewers such as the United States. To the contrary, the scores of channels now available on any cable television system reflect the fragmentation of the marketplace. (2)

The sport marketplace is just as segmented. As chapters 3 and 4 indicate, there is no single profile of the sport consumer. The consumer profile varies by sport, by place of residence, by life situation, and by a host of other factors. One thing is clear, however: Segmentation rules. Sport television provides clear evidence. Twenty years ago, the "broadcast" networks dominated sport television. Sport junkies (a very important segment of men) had little choice in their viewing. Then came HBO and ESPN, cable networks that began to widen the choices. ESPN especially wagered its program schedule (and its corporate life) on the sport junkies to whom the old networks had appealed a few times per week. In recent years, "narrowcasting" has spawned even more clearly defined segment strategies, such as the Golf Channel, where the patrons at Jane Blalock's clinics can continue their education at all hours of the day.

Given the competitiveness of the sport market and the intangible nature of most sport products, market segmentation is both logical and necessary. A product is nothing more than a "bundle of benefits." The deeply committed fan may want special privileges that come with a season ticket (newsletter, special functions with the team), whereas the infrequent fan may need a telephone or Internet ticket-ordering system that reduces anxieties and hassles over ticket purchase. The young executive who uses a racquetball club on a frequent basis may require a club that provides laundry service. Another member may prefer fewer amenities for lower fees. Segmentation, then, is designed to maximize consumer satisfaction; yet it is also a marketing tactic to maximize market response. Thus segmentation should not be carried to the point beyond which it no longer provides meaningful returns. The Seattle Storm might wish to maximize attendance by individualizing ticket packages to suit the desires of every fan, but that would not be feasible. The Storm's marketing staff identify and target segments they can reach.

Identifiability, Accessibility, Responsiveness

Several issues are important in choosing whether to segment a market—the identifiability, accessibility, and responsiveness of potential segments. (3)

First, a marketer must ask, Can the segment be identified or measured in terms of its size and purchasing power? The marketer may make this determination using the kind of research discussed in chapter 5. At the same time, some segments may be difficult or prohibitively expensive to identify. For instance, professional baseball clubs did not spend time in the last decade trying to determine the size or strength of the market for a Beanie Baby or bobblehead doll promotion. The raging success in other markets was enough for them to go with a gut instinct that the items were hot everywhere, at least for the moment. A golf course developer, however, would want to research a local or regional market before making a $15 million investment.

Second, the marketer must ask, Can the marketer access the segment? Is it possible to gain access to these groups of consumers individually without upsetting marketing efforts aimed at other segments? Our Beanie Baby and bobblehead promoters had no problem with this. A few weeks of promotional ads brought out more than enough Beanie Baby collectors. Things are not so easy, however, for a state high school association trying to promote its championship games, especially in "minor" sports. The time between play-off rounds is often short, upsets happen with regularity, and fan bases are segmented by community identity. It is not feasible for most state associations to prepare special contingency plans for each team that might advance. Hence, campaigns tend to be broad-based promotions of high school sports.

Finally, the marketer must ask, Will the segment be responsive? Two questions need to be answered here. The first is whether the product will match the wants of the chosen segment. The second concerns the significance of the segment. Is it worthwhile (given segment size and response) to break down product characteristics and promotional efforts sufficiently to reach a segment?

The marketer must address all of these factors in deciding whether (and to what extent) to pursue segmentation.

Segment or Niche?

You may sometimes hear the term *niche strategy*; it is not quite the same as segmentation. Marketing theorists distinguish segments from niches largely on the basis of size and competition. Segments are large but also prone to competition. Consider, for instance, adult, male football fans. Colleges and pro leagues compete for this audience, at live gates, on television, and with merchandise. A niche may be smaller (perhaps even Jane Blalock's golfers), but typically, larger firms ignore a niche. In sport marketing, niches have also been distinguished from segments on the basis of sport specificity. Niches arise from the sport market; segments are imposed on the sport market. For example, the Sled Dogs Company developed its product in the early 1990s—a miniski and boot combination—with an eye on a part of the existing in-line skater population. Specifically, it targeted skaters (most of whom are young) who had no winter activity. "Sled Dogs" were simply a way to skate on snow. The niche started in a group within sport: in-line skaters who had no winter counterpart. Unfortunately for the Sled Dogs Company, much of this niche market has since adopted snowboarding, in part because ski resorts recognized the same market potential and began embracing snowboard "shredders." (4)

In the early 1980s, most skiers would have considered snowboarding a small (and annoying) niche. Jake Burton thought otherwise. He saw a niche that could grow. The Burton Company has memorialized its history in the company's poetic vision statement, which captures the early mentality of an alienated niche market:

> We stand sideways.
>
> We sleep on floors in cramped resort hotel rooms.
>
> We get up early and go to sleep late.
>
> We've been mocked.
>
> We've been turned away from resorts that won't have us.
>
> We are relentless.
>
> We dream it, we make it, we break it, we fix it.
>
> We create.
>
> We destroy.
>
> We wreck ourselves day in and day out and yet we stomp that one trick or find that one line that keeps us coming back.
>
> We progress.
>
> Burton Snowboards is a rider driven company solely dedicated to creating the best snowboarding equipment on the planet.

Of course, the history of many popular sports is a progression from niche to mainstream markets. And who is to say what the next wave will be? The 2004 feature film *Dodgeball* spurred a spike of adult interest in the game. Bill DePue, vice president of the National Amateur Dodgeball Association, told *Athletic Business* magazine that "Our web site got 2,000 hits a month before [media coverage of the movie]. . . . Since then, we've had days in which we get 4,000 hits." As we discuss in chapter 15, niche marketers have used the Internet aggressively. (5)

"Niches" or "segments"? Much of the distinction is semantic, especially within the sport industry, where many firms exist in a single-sport domain. In both cases, however, the key questions of identification, accessibility, and responsiveness remain.

Four Bases of Segmentation

Market segments are formed on the basis of differentials in consumer wants and desires; that is, segments derive from consumer satisfaction. Four bases are commonly used for segmentation, each of which rests on an assumption that homogeneity in one variable may relate to homogeneity in wants and desires. Following are the four common bases:

+ Consumers' state of being (demographics)
+ Consumers' state of mind (psychographics)
+ Product benefits
+ Product usage

Typically, marketers employ cross sections of segments—middle-income, Hispanic families in a baseball team's metropolitan market, or affluent and "active" older people who live within 20 minutes of a particular athletic club. We will discuss integrated or "nested" approaches to segmentation at the end of this chapter. The following sections, then, must be understood to represent very fluid categories.

State-of-Being Segmentation

State-of-being segmentation includes the following dimensions, which are generally easier to measure than state-of-mind or product benefits:

Geography

Age

Income

Education

Gender

Sexual orientation

Race/ethnicity

Each of these dimensions is discussed in the following sections.

A consumer's age puts her in one market segment, but so do other factors, such as her income level and proximity to facilities.

© Photodisc/Getty Images

Geography

There are several clear principles of geographic segmentation in sport:

+ *First, proximity rules.* A simple survey of participants will typically support the long-recognized relationship between proximity and activity or involvement. Basically, the closer a person lives to a sport facility, the more likely she is to become involved with activities there.

+ *Know your clusters.* Good internal marketing data from ticket applications, membership inquiries, and similar sources often reveal geodemographic "clusters" of consumers who are especially important. Abundant software is available to help with mapping. All the marketer needs are consumer zip codes to couple with other data, such as types of purchases (season tickets? full membership?), frequency of participation, and income. Mapping allows the marketer to see whether certain suburbs or neighborhoods are especially prone to a certain product. Those areas can be targeted for special campaigns, especially direct mail and telemarketing. Claritas is one of the best-known companies for this kind of analysis, especially its Prizm system. (6)

✦ *Value your outer rims.* Some consumer clusters may come from considerable distances. These represent "outer-rim" markets that can repay extraordinary attention in terms of advertising, promotions, radio, or television networking. The recognition of outer rims in sport date at least as far back as baseball's early radio broadcasts. Midwest major league teams such as the St. Louis Cardinals developed fan bases at great distances, nurtured largely by radio. Outer-rim markets are logical targets for group sales and special events. But in football, with relatively few home games (mostly on Sunday afternoons), outer rims mean season tickets. When the Rams and the Raiders deserted, Los Angeles was left without an NFL team, so the San Diego Chargers spent several hundred thousand dollars on an ad campaign in the L.A. area. In effect, it became a potential "outer-rim" market for the Chargers. First, the Chargers had to seek an exemption from the NFL rule that prohibits marketing outside a franchise's 75-mile (120-kilometer) radius. That was no problem. Second, and more difficult, the Chargers had to cultivate a potential market of fans up to 160 miles (256 kilometers) away (for those in the north of Los Angeles County).

✦ The Chargers are not alone in their campaign for outer rims. The Seattle Seahawks have long maintained an outer rim of Alaskan fans, over 1,000 miles (1,600 kilometers) from the Kingdome. The Miami Dolphins have looked to develop a wider rim of markets, both to the north and to the west, possibly through partnerships with media outlets and corporate sponsors in places such as Naples, Vero Beach, and Port St. Lucie. State universities have cultivated outer rims by scheduling some "home" games at venues in other parts of their home state. (7)

✦ Some outer rims are also what might be called "borderlands," in that they rub against the territory of a competing organization. A good example is the central swath of Connecticut, which is the borderland between the Yankee Empire and Red Sox Nation. A 2003 survey showed a clear line of demarcation running through Hartford and Middlesex counties. It is important turf because it contains the highest per capita income in the country and represents a gold mine in cable revenues. The Red Sox have been aggressive in courting this borderland. At one Hartford rally, owner Tom Werner announced that "we want to welcome all those Connecticut Yankees who don't want to be in King George's court," a reference to Yankee owner George Steinbrenner. Some of the jousting has been in good fun, but it has been a marketing competition as hot as that on the field. (8)

Age

The old notion of the "generation gap" contains obvious truth—the young have different tastes and lifestyles from their parents, who in turn diverged from their own parents. Marketers talk about "cohorts" rather than generations (e.g., the Depression cohort, the baby boomer cohort). Musical tastes, sexual mores, approaches to debt or savings, and fashion sense are but a few of the cohort touchstones. In some cases, we may include sporting tastes. For instance, an ESPN Sports Poll survey of fan interest in the USTA's U.S. Open tennis championship suggested significant differences between those under and over 25 years of age. In particular, tennis had serious work to do with the teenage market (see table 6.1). Tennis was not alone. In the fall of 2004, the NFL grappled with a 21 percent decline in viewership among 12- to 17-year-old boys. Sport organizations have learned that kids in this demographic can be most effectively found on the Internet, where they download music and movies, shop, and participate in virtual communities such as MySpace.com (54 million registered users as of 2006). A recent survey found that 46.7 percent of males aged 14-19 used the Internet to find information about sport. (9)

Youth have been a target of sport promotions for over a century, often with the idea of building character through baseball, or basketball, or just about any sport. In the early 20th century, the "sports curriculum" swept gymnastics and calisthenics to the background of the burgeoning physical education programs in U.S. public schools. After World War II, organized youth leagues exploded in the suburbs, first in baseball and then across a broad range of sports. Starting ages drifted downward, so that today, under-8 travel teams are the norm. But registration does not ensure commitment. In fact, American youth appear less and less committed to mainstream modes of fitness, exercise, and sport, at least as measured in national surveys. Young people may not be interested in their parents' sports. The industry has responded in two ways:

✦ Table 6.1 Tennis Shows Its Age

Overall		By age group						
U.S fans	12-17	18-24	25-34	35-44	45-54	55-64	65+
25.4	16.6	20.5	26.2	25.8	30.7	21.9	31.2

Percentage of respondents to an ESPN Sports Poll of 1,351 fans who were either "somewhat" or "very" interested in "last year's" USTA U.S. Open

Data from Street & Smith's SportsBusiness Journal, August 26-September 1, pg. 22, 2002.

✦ *Get 'em to the action to do →feel →learn.* Baseball in particular has recognized the need for special efforts to get kids on the escalator. The logic of nurturing fans at a young age was accentuated in MLB because of the long strike in 1994-1995, which dropped many longtime fans off the escalator. In luring kids back, teams started letting kids run the bases between innings of some games. They let kids sing the national anthem or throw out the first pitch. They dropped ticket prices for kids 14 and under. The National Hockey League needed similar aggressive strategies as it sought to repair damage from the lockout that cancelled the 2004-2005 season. (10)

✦ *Repackage the product for youth.* A number of bowling alleys have created late-night, weekend slots devoted to the youth of either Generation Y or X. Using tag lines like "Extreme Bowling" or "Rock 'n' Bowl," proprietors transformed their premises with night-glow balls, strobe lights, and heavy-metal music. Bowling was not alone. *Sports Illustrated* launched *SI for Kids.* Its circulation has reached 1 million. In 2003, the New York Jets launched the Generation Jets—a culturally diverse and hip set of young cartoon characters who all happen to be Jets fans. The Generation Jets have their own television show and form the core link for other Jets

Case Study: The Ethics of "NASCAR for Kids"?

In the late 1990s, NASCAR (like most sport organizations) aggressively targeted the family and youth markets. Said NASCAR's director of communications worldwide, John Griffin: "We're going after youth as a whole. We want to continue in our direction of becoming more of a white-collar sport, where it's mom, dad and the kids sitting around the TV and rooting for their favorite driver on Sunday. We're going after urban youth as much as any other youth." The youth campaign has included NASCAR toys, games, theme parks, cafés, a cartoon show, even a NASCAR Barbie doll. This was all logical, but NASCAR had to make one major alteration in these youth and family products. It had to cut out the tobacco references that were so prominent in the wider NASCAR image. The NASCAR Barbie might have a Pennzoil patch, but no Winston. But one had to wonder: What would kids compete for with their toys and their imagination, if not

the Winston Cup? And when Mommy and Daddy took the kids to the live event, how could they prevent the clear link between the NASCAR and the Winston brands? Winston has since dropped its NASCAR sponsorship, but until 2007 NASCAR still had the Busch Cup. One might argue that NASCAR was no more responsible for protecting kids from alcohol images than the NFL or any number of universities. That is correct. But if sports claim to stand for healthy lifestyles, they must be especially vigilant in the way they pursue kids. They must continually ask several of Laura Nash's 12 ethics questions:

What is your intention?

How does your intention compare with probable results?

What is the symbolic potential of your action if understood? If misunderstood? (11)

initiatives such as youth football camps and school–community outreach programs. It was a brilliant twist on traditional "kids clubs" that exist at collegiate, minor, and major league levels. Rather than offer membership in some amorphous "club," the Jets created characters—with names like Blitz, ASKA, and XL—who would become the kids' friends. (12)

Sport marketers will always have an eye on youth campaigns. As the case study on NASCAR suggests, however, these often raise special ethical issues.

The senior or "maturity" market is another target for special marketing plans. As the baby boomers and GenXers grow older, they bring their vast cohort into another life or family stage. In the next quarter century, the over-50 market will grow far faster than the under-50 market. Increasingly, baby boomers will move from their "family" stages to empty-nest and single stages. More research is needed on the sporting attitudes, lifestyles, and subsegments of this maturing market, but the implications are obvious for sport marketers from the major leagues to the local athletic club. There are, however, some simple questions for any marketer to ask about plans proposed for any "graying" segment:

GenX, GenY, and GenZ?

Although it is not easy or always logical to create clear generational cohorts that represent distinct lifestyles and outlooks, some demographers and marketers revel in developing and using catchy terms to describe just such phenomena. "Baby boomers" (people born between 1946 and 1964) have been analyzed for decades. GenX and GenY are two of the most recent groups of interest. GenXers were born roughly between 1965 and 1981 (years vary in the literature), whereas GenYers were born after 1981. GenXers were described as independent, cynical, and slackers. They were the original snowboard and skateboard "shredders," the children of grunge music, the target of the X Games. Of course, they are now at a different level in their life cycle, so parenting, PTA meetings, and coaching soccer are more central to their lives. There are even subgroups of GenX, such as the "yoga mamas" who are more affluent and spend lavishly on their kids and on their own fitness as mothers. Yoga mamas have boosted sales of $200 designer diaper bags and $800 strollers that they can push while jogging.

The youngest yoga mamas may also belong to GenY—a cohort also called the millennials and the baby boom echo generation. They are about 78 million strong in America—three times larger than their predecessor—and they represent some 16 percent of the population. But they have great buying power. In contrast to GenXers, they are described as traditional in their values, optimistic, tolerant, and committed to diversity. Like their predecessors, only more so, they are media-savvy multitaskers who demand interactivity. As one expert advised marketers, "Today's youth expect interactivity within their various interests. Passive entertainment is rapidly being replaced by active participation across virtually all types of media." Marketers have scrambled to reach GenX, GenY, yoga mamas, and many other special consumer segments. Soon enough, they will be looking at a GenZ. (13)

Some GenX women have grown up to be "yoga mamas," with the financial means and the will to spend money and time on their own fitness.
© Getty Images

Does the program speak to aging's possibilities, as opposed to its limitations?

Does the program have motivated leadership?

Is the program user-friendly? (14)

Education and Income

Education is certainly related to income. Like their counterparts in golf, members of the tennis industry target more affluent, highly educated consumers (although not exclusively). The data suggest that this segment is more inclined toward involvement and commitment to tennis. For instance, a recent survey by Scarborough Research indicted that 70 percent of "loyal" professional tennis fans had at least some college education. Thirty-two percent enjoyed at least $75,000 in household income. Similar Scarborough research indicated that almost 44 percent of Boston Red Sox fans enjoyed over $75,000 in household income. With Fenway's ticket prices the highest in baseball, they need it. (15)

Geodemographic clustering matches income with residence and, presumably, lifestyle. Although a certain income is no guarantee of a particular lifestyle, it is frequently a central index. National Football League football can demand high television-rights fees because it delivers males with relatively high disposable incomes. Golf does not draw as many, but its income profile is even better. That's why luxury car companies advertise during golf telecasts. Some sports are even more closely tied to high incomes. Take polo. The U.S. Polo Association (USPA) claims to have some 280 clubs and 3,700 members, and it would like to grow even faster than its recent rate of 1 to 3 percent per year. But when novice-level group lessons cost $100 per person, more advanced instruction runs at double that cost, and polo ponies run from $50,000 to $70,000, we expect that polo will stay linked to the wealthiest demographics. In fact, polo is so valuable that in the late 1990s, the Polo Ralph Lauren Company sued the USPA's magazine, insisting that it drop the name "Polo." The Lauren Company, which had obtained a trademark for the term *polo*, complained that *Polo* magazine was now overstepping its bounds, focusing "not on equestrian sports but on sophisticated fashions and elegant lifestyles." We might ask, Was there ever a difference in the world of polo? (16)

Gender

As sport marketers have recognized the importance of a "female" market, they have discovered two distinct facets to segmentation strategies. First, women and girls are a special group of consumers with special needs and wants. Second, women's and girls' sports are a special type of product, with benefits distinct from those in men's and boys' sports. The first is appropriately considered demographic segmentation. The second is really benefits segmentation, considered later in the chapter.

Sport firms have recognized women as a special segment for over a century. For the most part, however, marketing strategies focused on rather glib visions of the "fair sex"—very white, relatively affluent, and limited in capabilities. Bicycle companies made V-shaped women's frames to avoid criticism that cycling forced women into unladylike positions. Golf and tennis firms made smaller clubs and rackets for women. Baseball teams promoted "ladies' days" to elevate the image of their crowds. This was segmentation, but it was a far cry from Jane Blalock's intent. The women's sport market is no longer an afterthought to the "real" market for men. Title IX and Billie Jean King ushered in a new era that is now coming of age. The female fan base for the dominant men's sports is nearing equity— by one account, some 43 percent for the NFL, 46 percent for MLB, and 46 percent for the NBA. (17)

The words of one NFL executive capture the widespread desire to win with women: "Women are of critical importance to us. They control the TV dial on Sunday afternoons and decide what sport their kids will get involved in. We have to make these gatekeepers comfortable." One national survey found that male respondents who were "avid" or "somewhat avid" sports fans and whose wives were also avid fans attended 57 percent more games than did avid male fans whose wives were not. The NFL has been ahead of the game in cultivating these female gatekeepers, launching a series of seminars in 1997 in 10 cities. The tag line was "Football 101." For a nominal fee, women could hear presentations on equipment, rules, and tactics. In Pittsburgh, the class also toured the locker room and practiced plays on the field. Some students viewed football in the same way that Jane Blalock views golf. Susan Gray, a shipping clerk from Irving, Texas, said she came to the Cowboys' clinic because she no longer wanted to get left out of football talk at the office: "It might be nice to know the difference between a running back and a wide receiver." Other women were not amused, including Jeanne Clark, a former national board member of the National Organization for Women. In Clark's view, "Football 101 sounded like long-ago stories in teen girl magazines, warning the football novices that a little inside knowledge of quarterbacks and linebackers was necessary if you wanted to catch that handsome football hero." Concluded Clark, "They're making a lot of gender assumptions that are unwarranted." (18)

The female sport consumer market will only grow stronger, with more professional leagues, more specialized equipment, more magazines, and television networks that recognize special interests, wants, and needs. More firms, such as the Women's Sports Foundation and Moving Comfort (running wear), are run by and for women. Regardless of a marketer's gender, however, there is little return on a patronizing message or a one-shot, low-budget program. As Donna Lopiano, executive director of the Women's Sports Foundation, concluded: "Selling to women is different from selling to men." One recent survey at four Midwest university basketball games found that women were far more concerned about venue cleanliness, rest room experience, quality of sound system, and overall staff service. Men were far more concerned about parking. One might say that Bill Veeck knew this long ago from casual fan interaction, and that social science has just supported his insights. (19)

At the same time, sport marketers must avoid lumping women into an amorphous category. Some critics argue that such gender myopia doomed the WUSA, the women's professional soccer circuit that started in the euphoria of the 1999 Women's World Cup and was out of business by 2003. James Chung, a marketing consultant who studied WUSA consumers, claimed that the league lumped too many women into the category of "soccer moms." As Chung put it: "For Gen-X moms, the whole 'soccer mom' concept is essentially dead. They don't view themselves the same way as Baby Boomer moms. But that's what the WUSA tried to sell, and the strategy fell on deaf ears." (20)

The Gay and Lesbian Market

Historically taboo markets in the sport world, gays and lesbians continue to struggle for recognition, opportunity, and understanding. The last few years, however, have seen clear progress. A 2005 national survey commissioned by NBC and the USA Network reported that although 61 percent of respondents agreed that homosexuality "should not be accepted" as a way of life, 86 percent agreed that "it is okay for male athletes to participate in sports even if they are openly gay."

In 2001, the Minnesota Twins ran a promotion called "Out in the Stands" sponsored by *Lavender* Magazine, the area's major GLBT (gay, lesbian, bisexual, transgendered) publication. A Twins VP stated emphatically that they were "open and accessible to any fan." Perhaps the Twins were responding to an incident the year before, when two lesbians were ejected from Dodger Stadium for allegedly kissing in the stands. The Dodgers had to apologize profusely and promise to better train their stadium attendants. L.A.'s WNBA franchise, the Sparks, was much more aggressive in courting GLBT fans, kicking off L.A.'s Gay Pride week in 2001 by partnering with Girl Bar—a 12,000-member lesbian club. Such targeted marketing campaigns (as opposed to mass media campaigns) are probably more effective ways to reach GLBT groups. At the same time, marketers must be prepared to stand their ground if there is public backlash from conservative groups. Corporate sponsors have watched the success of the Gay Games, where they have enjoyed high (33 percent) recall rates among attendees. These high levels of commitment, coupled with high income and education profiles, led *American Demographics* to label the gay and lesbian market "an untapped goldmine." (21)

Race and Ethnicity

American history has been heavily influenced by enduring struggles between natives and immigrants, and among races and ethnic groups. The nation's motto—*e pluribus unum* ("out of many, one")—captures part of this ethos. Opinions still diverge on whether the motto represents an achievement or a goal. Battles over bilingual education reflect opposition on the emphasis: the "unum" or the "pluribus." And minority groups increasingly challenge the right of white, European immigrants to control the definitions of the American "unum." America is less a melting pot than a mosaic.

Cultural diversity is both the American strength and the American conundrum. In some ways, the sport world has provided the most vivid theater for this struggle. Jack Johnson, Joe DiMaggio, Eddie Gottlieb, Althea Gibson, and Roberto Clemente are just a few names that represent millions of athletes, promoters, and fans for whom sport has been a touchstone of racial and ethnic pride and tension. Although the dominant leagues, teams, and clubs have gradually opened their doors to qualified athletes of any color, they have been slower to pursue minority fans. That is changing, however, in response to the obvious. Americans of African, Asian, and Hispanic descent represent a third of the population. In some markets, they are a majority. By some estimates they will be a national majority by 2020. They represent important consumer bases that demand diligent respect, not benign neglect.

African Americans have been historically underrepresented as targeted consumers in professional and collegiate sports. Some numbers bear this out. For instance, ESPN Sports Poll data in 2002 indicated that only 18.3 percent of NBA "fans" were African American, despite the overwhelming dominance of black players. At the same time, another poll reported that nearly 50 percent of African American respondents were "somewhat" or "very" interested in the U.S. Open tennis championship—more than double the level of white respondents. We may guess that the Williams sisters had something to do with this. But was the tennis industry also more engaged with African American consumers? As we discussed in chapter 5, we must be careful in using secondary data, especially in teasing out the meaning of "fans." At the same time, the numbers cry out for more analysis. (22)

In what areas does this consumer fit? Is the sport industry marketing to him as well as they could?
© Human Kinetics

The Hispanic market has been pursued more aggressively than other ethnic markets, perhaps because it is the fastest-growing minority segment, projected to represent one quarter of all Americans by 2050. Latino nights are common in baseball venues; so are grassroots events such as the MLS's four-on-four Futbolito tournaments; so are Spanish radio and television broadcasts. As one expert put it: "If you really want to get at this growing market, you need to do this all the time: do marketing in Spanish, have ticket sellers who speak Spanish, sell foods that Latinos like." (23)

Sport marketers are beginning to recognize several important principles for success in reaching minority segments: (24)

✦ *Use minority firms, individuals, and icons.* In 1998, the St. Louis Cardinals engaged FPM/Fuse, a minority-owned ad agency (now Fuse Advertising: www.fuseadvertising.com), to create a campaign aimed at attracting more black fans to Busch Stadium. With good reason. Although the St. Louis metropolitan area was 17.4 percent black, and although the Cardinals had enjoyed Hall of Fame careers from a host of African Americans including Bob Gibson and Ozzie Smith, black attendance had lagged behind—making up between 1 and 3 percent of all fans for over a decade. The FPM/Fuse $100,000 campaign used bus, billboard, and radio ads featuring black players such as outfielder Brian Jordan, who said, "God gave me the ability. My parents gave me the opportunity. Everything else I earned." Clifford Franklin, FPM/Fuse partner, expressed the gist of the campaign message as "hard work, dedication, and focus." Major League Baseball has expanded such efforts with its "Baseball's Diverse Business Partners Program."(25)

◆ *Recognize diversity and change within minority groups.* Major League Soccer franchises have been very active in addressing their Hispanic fan base. For good reason: Hispanics accounted for 23 percent of all Major League Soccer fans in the late 1990s. But the rapidly evolving Hispanic population will require changes in strategy. Said consultant Dean Bonham: "The Hispanic market is lower- to middle-income right now, but can be described as a soccer-educated demographic with dispensable income that's growing at a very rapid rate." The NBA's Miami office is the center of the league's efforts to reach Hispanic fans. But the staff includes a diverse "Hispanic" background, including Cuba, Panama, Brazil, Uruguay, Costa Rica, Argentina, Puerto Rico, and Peru. The lesson is simple: There is no single "Hispanic" market. (26)

◆ *Recognize minority consumer loyalty.* In the summer of 1998, Street & Smith Publishers announced a new annual football "preview" magazine: *Street & Smith's Black College Football.* The prospectus ad for this joint effort with the Historically Black Collegiate Coalition noted some of the superstars who had played at HBCUs (historically black colleges and universities), including Jerry Rice and Walter Payton. But it also emphasized that "black college sporting events are attended by more African Americans than any other type of sporting event in the country." (27)

State-of-Mind Segmentation

State-of-mind segmentation assumes that consumers may be divided by personality traits; by lifestyle characteristics such as attitudes, interests, and opinions; and by preferences and perceptions. The most noteworthy approach to state-of-mind segmentation was developed by the Stanford Research Institute (SRI). Called the Values and Lifestyle (VALS) typology, it assumes that attitudes, opinions, desires, needs, and other psychological dimensions collectively govern daily behavior. VALS identifies eight segments of the adult population, based on resources and primary motivations (ideals, achievement, and self-expression). The segments are as follows:

Innovators

Thinkers

Achievers

Experiencers

Believers

Strivers

Makers

Survivors

VALS is used extensively in proprietary research. For instance, telecommunications companies have used VALS to identify components that will be attractive to "early adopters." We are not aware, however, of recent studies of sport consumers using VALS as a base. The possibilities of state-of-mind segmentation, however, are intriguing. For instance, Discovery Communications, which runs the Learning Channel and the Discovery Channel, uncovered eight segments among its viewers. The "Machos," who composed 12 percent of viewers, were 76 percent male, largely blue-collar, average in income, and oriented toward "action" programming, including sports and war. In contrast, the 15 percent of viewers who were "Scholars" were 54 percent female, urbane, upscale, and favored programming in archaeology, history, and anthropology. Discovery Communications can use the knowledge to create and promote programming for the various segments. We might project similar segments among ice hockey fans—"Rumblers" who revel in aggressive hitting and fighting and "Aesthetes" who focus on skill, craft, and grace. (28)

Recent research in sport consumer behavior has opened up other prospects for state-of-mind segmentation, particularly in terms of fan loyalty and identification. Galen Trail and his research team have, for instance, developed the "point of attachment" index that measures fan identification with product elements such as team, coach, players, and university. Along similar lines, Dan Mahoney, Bob Madrigal, and Dennis Howard developed the "psychological commitment to team" (PCT) scale that measures fan loyalty to a particular team. Sport organizations—at any level—with a substantial fan database could administer such instruments to discern possible state-of-mind segments based on levels of identification or loyalty. In other words, marketing research can now provide empirical substance to old notions such as "hard-core" or "marginal" fans. Marketers could then develop different marketing plans for each segment, which may now be identifiable, accessible, and responsive. (29)

There is much at stake. Major League Soccer, for instance, has grappled with the problems of appealing to both hard-core soccer fans and the casual fans (think youth soccer families) who always seem to represent the future. This has led MLS to make wild swings in rules. For instance, in the 1990s, MLS rules required that a clock show the official time and that shootouts would ensure a winner. These rules were intended to please casual fans whose frame of sports reference was the NFL. But these rules flew in the face of world soccer tradition, where the referee kept the official time and where a tie was honorable and even exciting. In 1999, MLS commissioner Don Garber announced a change of direction—no shootout and no official clock. The MLS, it appeared, was ready to stick with a "hard-core" base that it hoped was growing as Americans learned more about the "pure" game of world football. (30)

Product Benefits Segmentation

Benefits segmentation is closely related to state-of-mind segmentation. After all, the sport product is a bundle of benefits. If those benefits don't exist in the consumer's mind, then they don't exist at all. Sport marketers have adopted benefits segmentation in many ways. The most easily illustrated applications are in the sporting goods industry. Take athletic shoes. The competitive runner who logs over 60 miles (96 kilometers) per week seeks the product benefits of support, shock reduction, and long wear; the intermediate tennis player seeks sound grip and comfort; and the casual sneaker purchaser is just looking for a light and fashionable shoe to use as regular footwear. Each purchaser is looking for totally different benefits and will be best served by totally different shoes.

The motivational factors discussed in chapter 4 provide insights into the benefits sought by sport consumers. Affiliation, achievement, status, health, and fitness, in various forms and configurations, are certainly related to benefits that consumers perceive from sport consumption. Team marketers, for instance, know that season-ticket holders expect exclusive benefits such as access to inside information (often via newsletters) or special events (autograph sessions). Special groups, on the other hand, look for scoreboard recognition, on-site liaisons, discounts, and team promotional materials to drum up interest. The most successful sport organizations understand the importance of identifying the core benefits that define their products in their consumers' minds. For example, in the late 1990s, the NFL defined its "six core equities" (with sample symbols) as follows:

+ *Action/power:* hitting, circus catches, the NFL shield
+ *History/tradition:* leaves, NFL legends, tailgating

- ✦ *Thrill/release:* fans/players laughing, screaming
- ✦ *Teamwork/competition:* the "steel curtain" defense of the Pittsburgh Steelers Super Bowl champions
- ✦ *Authenticity:* the pigskin, muddy field, blood
- ✦ *Unifying force:* groups of fans, teams

These "core equities" may be viewed as core benefits, to be cultivated in live events, broadcasts, videos, programs, and merchandise. (31)

The steady rise of high-performance, commercialized women's team sports (e.g., college and pro basketball, international soccer, and ice hockey) appears to be a case in alternative benefits more than demographics. To be sure, fan research does suggest that women's team sports attract a wider age range than their male counterparts. And the generally lower prices are more attractive to families. But the strong male base—30 percent in-arena and 50 percent television for the WNBA—belies notions that women's sports are a "chick thing." As an NCAA survey revealed, fans of women's basketball, regardless of gender, enjoy a game that in their minds is distinctly different (e.g., "below the rim"), played by athletes who are more articulate, more accessible, and yes, more like role models than the men. Women's sports are evolving rapidly; time will test the margins of these product differences. The WNBA, for instance, suffered a 4.5 percent decline in average attendance during the 2005 season—enough to spur league president Donna Orender to promise harder work at branding and positioning: "Everyone has a sense of what the WNBA is, but we have to refine it." The league would do well to focus on benefits segmentation. (32)

Unfortunately, sport managers are often out of touch with the "benefits" segments in their fan base. In this state of ignorance, they can hardly hope to fashion a strategy that does not alienate one group or another. One recent investigation of an NHL franchise and its fans, for instance, found that the team envisioned a strategy that would appeal to both "tradition" (classic merchandise for the hard-core fan) and "dynamism" (rock music for the casual, especially young, fan). Unfortunately, the team strategy belied an ignorance or avoidance of other key segments revealed in the fan research. In particular, the franchise was neglecting "social" fans who needed special group rates and better fan rituals (like signature songs or cheers) to encourage their attendance. Marketing researchers have found ways to identify segments of benefits in sport consumers' minds. Managers must start to use that research. We look closer at such strategies in chapter 7, when we consider product positioning. (33)

Product Usage Segmentation

We know that product usage segmentation is also quite significant and that it interacts with consumers' state of mind. Here, marketers have concentrated on the "heavy half," or heavy users of the product. In many markets, the so-called 80-20 rule applies, according to which 80 percent of market consumption comes from only 20 percent of the consumers. Sensitivity to factors of the marketing mix has been shown to vary significantly with product use. In sport, we have long been cognizant of the various usage patterns (e.g., the season-ticket holder versus the individual-game ticket purchaser). This is true across most sports, for players and fans alike. Research on the women's 1990s golf market, for example, showed that "occasional" golfers (one to seven rounds per year) made up over 50 percent of all the golfers but accounted for only 12 percent of the total rounds played. Meanwhile, "avid" golfers (25+ rounds per year) accounted for 64 percent of the total rounds played. Along similar lines (see table 6.2), the "light" fan segment of one MLB club made up an estimated 43 percent of 1990 total attendees (different people attending), but only 19 percent of total tickets sold. "Heavy" fans accounted for only 14.4 percent of the attendees, but almost 30 percent of tickets sold. In the NBA, suite, club, and season-ticket holders account for just over 60 percent of all tickets sold, but over 80 percent of team ticket revenue. Whether the sport is basketball, golf, tennis, or weightlifting, the "heavy-half" rule seems to apply. (34)

Table 6.2 also illustrates how a baseball club shifted from a reliance on light users in 1976 to a distribution more weighted toward heavy and medium users. In effect, this club had moved fans up the escalator of involvement. Although heavy users may return greater immediate dividends, the sport marketer must aim to satisfy the needs of each group as much as possible to ensure a steady stream of light, medium, and heavy users, because the light user of today may be the medium user of tomorrow and the heavy user of next year. Chapters 11 and 12 address the need for special promotions for different user groups. For instance, special groups may fit into the category of light users, but they have special needs and interests. Many have particular interests in some charitable cause, or seating in a special area, or special recognition on the scoreboard. The smartest marketers offer a full menu of group benefits.

✦ **Table 6.2** User Segments and Estimated Attendance Impact on a Major League Baseball Club—1976, 1990

Segment	Number of games	Year	Percentage of people	Estimated percentage of attendance
Heavy	11+	1976	4.2	20.4
		1990	14.4	29.6
Medium	3-10	1976	29.4	45.5
		1990	42.7	51.1
Light	1-2	1976	66.4	34.1
		1990	42.9	19.3

Several summary points about usage segmentation demand emphasis:

✦ Not all consumers consume at the same rate.

✦ The levels of consumption (e.g., heavy, medium, and light) vary from sport to sport, so the relative importance of usage rates (in terms of total attendance or participation) differs from sport to sport.

✦ The levels of consumption are likely to vary from age group to age group. Thus, sport spectatorship and consumption show a life cycle pattern. It is also likely that—for any given set of consumers—levels of consumption vary by other variables (state of being, state of mind, benefits).

✦ It is essential that the sport marketer maintain opportunities for consumers to consume at many usage levels. That is, the marketer should not depend too heavily on season-ticket sales and thus exclude the occasional user. This mistake cost the Rochester Royals dearly, as we read in chapter 2. This latter problem is well known to the Boston Bruins, who were sold out for many years primarily through season-ticket sales. Once Bobby Orr left and fan interest declined, there were no light users and few medium users to replace the "defecting" season-ticket holders.

✦ An increase in sales volume is much more likely to be generated by an increased frequency or higher consumption rate of existing users than it is from an increase in first-time users.

Sport organizations should also conceptualize (and segment) use in terms of breadth of activities. In this case, the notion of a heavy user should include the number of different activities as well as the frequency of participation. Marketers could develop a grid to visualize segmentation along the dimensions of breadth and frequency. Internal marketing data, as discussed in chapter 5, can be placed within the grid. Figure 6.1 provides a sample grid for a hypothetical Bruins fan base. Only three cells are filled in here, but the concept of such a grid is the important point. Specific group names are not crucial, but as seen in tables 6.3 and 6.4, they are sometimes used for shorthand. For instance, "captains" are clearly committed in breadth and frequency; they are the hard-core fans. On the opposite end, "cubs" represent the bottom of the involved-fan base. They are highly prone to falling off the escalator and may well turn their attention to another sport before they actually attend a game. Such a frequency/breadth grid with all the cells filled in would provide the basis for promotional

Frequency / Breadth	High frequency (>10 times/month)	Medium frequency (5-9 times/month)	Low frequency (1-4 times/month)
High breadth (>3 activities)	"Captains": read game stories daily; attend five games/month; buy programs; watch all away games on TV		
Medium breadth (2-3 activities)		"Growlers": Share miniplan; wear Bruins hat; watch weekly telecast	
Low breadth (1 activity)			"Cubs": Watch big game on TV

FIGURE 6.1 Sample frequency/breadth grid for Bruins fans.

campaigns. Indeed, a strategy that aims for breadth of activities may provide the club with a buffer to prevent members from becoming bored and burned out and thus from defecting.

Tables 6.3 and 6.4 present similar user groupings developed by the National Thoroughbred Racing Association and the Professional Golfers' Association of America. The point is that users can be conceptualized along the lines of frequency and breadth, to create targets for separate marketing plans.

✦ Table 6.3 User Segments Identified by the PGAA

Name	% of golfers	Average household income	Rounds per year	Amount spent per year	Sex
Dilettantes	27	64.2 k	16	1.1 k	M
Tank tops	17	36.7	13	570	M
Pull carts	15	32.2	32	1.4 k	M
Public pundits	13	50.6	52	2 k	M
Junior league	13	57.8	24	1.6 k	W
Country clubber	9	77.3	69	4.4 k	M
Swingin' seniors	6	31.3	42	1.6 k	W

Data from *American Demographics* 1995.

✦ Table 6.4 National Thoroughbred Racing Association User Groups

Name	Frequency and breadth	Number
Core	Handicappers who know sport and bet 5+ times per year	3 million
Light	Love social aspects more than sport; bet 5 times or less per year	28 million
Socialites	Mostly female who love track atmosphere, do not bet	9 million
TV fans	Mostly female, do not attend track, do not bet	33 million

Data from L. Mullen, 1999, "Demographics survey surprises NTRA," *Street & Smith's SportsBusiness Journal*, November 8-14, pg. 7.

Integrated Segmentation Strategies and Tactics

As noted earlier, our divisions of segmentation—state of being, state of mind, benefits, and usage—are simply organizational conveniences. Sport marketers must recognize that successful marketing plans will typically require the integration of these divisions. For instance, the PGAA user groupings outlined in table 6.3 link rounds played (usage) with household income (state of being). And, as most teams with an extensive database know, certain geographic areas may have a higher rate of "avid" fans than other areas, related to proximity, or income, or some other demographic or lifestyle variable.

Today's myriad cable networks often represent particular clusters of demographic and psychographic consumer segments. This has encouraged new integrated advertising strategies. For instance, when the TNT network looked to promote Steven Spielberg's spring 2005 miniseries *Into the West,* it developed an integrated strategy that recognized a division of the target audience into six separate segments—history lovers, family saga watchers, action seekers, truth seekers, western lovers, and generation "why"—each of which represented a slightly different combination of age, gender, and television viewing habits. TNT's research also demonstrated that each of the segments was prone to particular media habits, so rather than run the same advertisement across a number of different media outlets, TNT developed separate ads for each target audience. Ads that focused on the Battle of Wounded Knee or the gold rush were placed on the History Channel and on a wrapper cover of *National Geographic*. Ads that accentuated the multigenerational drama of several families were placed on the finale of *Desperate Housewives* and in *People* magazine. (35)

The Miami Heat are even more sophisticated. With financial support from the NBA, the Heat developed a database with some 700,000 entries containing data on age, income, zip code, lifestyle and consumption patterns, and Web site activity, among other variables. The Heat uses e-mail campaigns to reach targeted clusters in the database. For instance, when 150 season-ticket blocks were shifted from group to individual sales, the Heat quickly identified a cluster of names that fit a particular profile of income, residence, and past purchase behavior. Targeted e-mail campaigns have thus replaced cold calls and print and broadcast advertisements with a dramatic increase in return. During the 2004-2005 season, the Heat received almost 11 dollars in revenue for every dollar spent on the database research and staff. (36)

Although TNT's and the Heat's efforts are obviously more expensive than most sport organizations can afford, the principle may be applied at any budget level: the development of a consumer database (see chapter 5) that contains demographic, psychographic, lifestyle, and product usage data. Data analysis may identify consumer clusters or segments that are accessible and responsive to marketing plans. Sport marketing researchers have already developed survey instruments that measure lifestyle characteristics related to game attendance in professional ice hockey and basketball. These could be adapted for use in other sports. Identified clusters of fans could then be sent special ads or promotional offers via e-mail or direct mail. (37)

Wrap-Up

Segmentation is truly central to the notion of knowing one's consumers, because segmentation recognizes that consumers vary along a number of dimensions that the marketer may use to form the basis of specialized strategies. Therefore, the marketing information system should be keyed in to the notion of segmentation, and research should examine the possible bases for meaningful segmentation of the marketplace. Whether segmentation makes the most sense in terms of psychographics, demographics, usage, benefits, or some combination will depend on the marketer's knowledge of and feel for the market. Indeed it makes sense to pursue a relational approach to segmentation. That is, consumer segments distinguished by "benefits sought" should be evaluated for any internal homogeneity on the basis of demographics, psychographics, or usage. Discoveries of such relationships will provide fruitful insight for improved communication with such target segments. In any case, however, the decision maker must recognize that people can and must be distinguished from one another. Whether the business is pro basketball, high school lacrosse, or public parks and recreation programs, it is hard to consider any plan a marketing plan if it doesn't incorporate some aspect of segmentation.

Activities

1. Define segmentation. Describe the differences among segment identification, segment access, and segment responsiveness. Think of examples in the sport world of segments that might be identifiable but not accessible or responsive.

2. What are the basic components of state-of-being segmentation? Give examples of the state-of-being segments most important to your local college women's basketball team.

3. Define state-of-mind segmentation. Try to find an ad for a sport product or team that appeals to a state-of-mind segment.

4. Explain why the heavy-user segment is so important to sport marketers. Use table 6.2 to explain.

5. How would you relate the notion of benefits segmentation to the discussion of motivation in chapter 4? List and compare the benefits of attending an MLB game and playing golf at the nearest public golf course.

Your Marketing Plan

Can you define the core benefits of your product(s)? Will any of these benefits link to consumer segments defined by demographics, psychographics, or product usage? You should begin to clarify, at the least, the product usage segments in your consumer base. Try to fill in a frequency/breadth grid for your consumer base. Use figure 6.1 as a guide.

Chapter 7

The Sport Product

Objectives

✦ To recognize the elements of the sport product that contribute to its uniqueness in the wider marketplace of goods and services.

✦ To learn the process involved in product development as well as its relation to the concept of the product life cycle.

✦ To understand product positioning, product image, and product branding, and their roles in successful sport marketing.

"If You Can Play Soccer Indoors, Why Not Football?"

"It's the best two hours and 10 minutes of football you'll ever see," claimed Jack Youngblood, former NFL star (with the L.A. Rams). Was this the West Coast Offense run to perfection by Steve Young and the 49ers? Not quite. Jack Youngblood was the president of the Orlando Predators, who were decidedly not an NFL franchise. Their game was played indoors, with eight players per team; no punting; narrow, extended goal posts surrounded by netting to keep errant kicks and passes in play; full pads; and—best of all—hockey boards to bounce opponents into. It was Arena Football, the new AFL, the brainchild of Jim Foster, who had conceived the product in 1981 after watching indoor soccer. "I turned to my friend," recalled Foster, "and said, 'If you can play soccer indoors, why not football?'" It took boundless energy, his life savings, and six years of experiments before Foster saw the AFL's birth in 1987 as a four-team league with a deal for ESPN coverage. Foster's product concept had several key dimensions:

Football's basic form adapted to arenas

League controls on franchise costs (i.e., salaries) to keep ticket prices attractive to football fans who could not afford the NFL

A spring/summer season that would tap both the interminable cravings of football fanatics and the arenas' desire to book dates when their anchor tenants (hockey and basketball) were off-season

Foster's formula worked. The 1987 season saw an average attendance of 12,600. Television ratings were quite respectable. And the next two decades proved that the new product was much more than a fad. Although average attendance slipped in the 1990s, it recrossed the 12,000 mark in 2004. The AFL also attracted deep-pocket investors. In May 1998, the NFL owners approved a change in policy that would allow ownership of an AFL franchise. Tom Benson of the New Orleans Saints immediately bought a franchise. Several years later, Jerry Jones bought the Dallas Desperados. Then John Elway joined Pat Bowlen and Stan Kroenke to buy the Colorado Crush. NBC cut a deal to carry 70 regular-season games and four play-off games in 2003. This all drove franchise values to unheard-of heights. In 1999, the Associated Press reported that "AFL teams that once went for $500,000 now have a price tag of close to $5 million." By 2003, the league was asking $12 million for a new franchise. And for those investors (and fans) not living near AFL franchises, there was AFL2. (1)

As discussed previously, sport products are bundles of benefits. Jim Foster is one of many entrepreneurs who has designed a new sport product that offers benefits to satisfy consumer wants and needs. In this chapter on the sport product, we begin to delve into the marketing mix, or the five Ps of sport marketing—product, price, promotion, place, and public relations. First, we review the elements that make the sport product unique. These include the event, the ticket, the organization, the facility, and equipment and apparel, to name a few. Next, we discuss the intricacies of developing products, including the concepts of line, item, and mix; procedures for launching new products; and the product life cycle. Finally, we examine positioning and branding, the most critical parts of contemporary product development.

What Is the Sport Product?

The sport product is a complex package of the tangible and the intangible. When you hear the word *golf*, you think of little dimpled balls and oversized "metal" woods that are, in different ways, standardized. They are tangible elements of the golf product. But the "golf experience" is hardly standardized: It can be total frustration for the occasional duffer and total infatuation for the addict. It is no different in any other sport, because all sports depend on human performance. As we discussed in chapter 1, this makes the marketer's job challenging in several respects. (2)

✦ *The sport product is inconsistent from consumption to consumption.* Today's friendly racquetball game is totally different from last week's game against the same opponent, even though all the elements—time, court, skill, equipment—appear unchanged. As Fox Sports president David Hill concluded, "If there's one great thing about sports, it's that it's unscripted. And the guy in the white hat doesn't always get to kiss the horse. Sports is the last frontier of reality in television." Part of the inconsistency stems from the sensual and emotional nature of involvement. Every game, every event is a unique mix of touch, smell, taste, sight, and sound. For the fan or for the participant, it is the uncertainty and the spontaneity of the sport product that make it attractive. As Rick Jones of the GEM Group put it, the consumer, not the marketer, is "in control" of the final experience. (3)

✦ *The "core" game or performance is just one element of a larger ensemble.* Players or fans rarely consume the game, event, or contest in isolation. The sport "experience" includes the atmosphere of the venue, the equipment, the apparel, the music, the concessions, and the pre- and postgame festival. All of these elements extend the sport product beyond the contest itself, for players and fans alike. In some cases, the contest is almost secondary. Satellite television and the Internet, with their instantaneous, worldwide reach, have prompted an increase in sport events that exist less for their intrinsic value and more for their ability to deliver product extensions. One industry executive expressed the widespread belief that more events would "be created purely to sell specific brands and products such as shoes and apparel. Events will be the integrated marketing sales engine of the future." A casual look at the Olympics, the Super Bowl, or the Extreme Games suggests that this future has been slowly arriving for some time. (4)

✦ *The marketer typically has little control over the core product and consequently must focus efforts on product extensions.* In the new millennium, Real Madrid of Spain's La Liga fashioned a strategy that leveraged the core product (soccer games) to generate product extensions. The team broke world "transfer" (purchase-price) records in buying the contracts of star players like Luis Figo, Zinedine Zidane, and David Beckham. Although Real Madrid expected to win games with its all-star cast, the team was even more confident that it would expand its global sales of merchandise and sponsorships. And even though the stars and the team stumbled—failing to win a major trophy in 2004—a study by the Harvard Business School certified the success of this strategy. By 2004, ancillary revenue was expected to double from its 2001 mark. Marketers cannot control the contest, especially the winning and the losing. But it is worth repeating Don Canham's decades-old wisdom: "We do not market that Michigan football is Number 1, because next year we may not be! Instead we market a fall weekend in Ann Arbor." In sport marketing, winning can never be the only thing! (5)

The Sport Product: Its Core and Extensions

As figure 7.1 suggests, the sport product is both an integrated ensemble and a bunch of components with lives of their own. At the core is the "event experience," composed of four components:

Game form (rules/techniques)

Players

Equipment and apparel

Venue

Whether we consider a friendly game of three-on-three on a hot asphalt court or a Memphis Grizzlies game in the lush surroundings of the FedEx Center, we will find the common features of game, players, equipment, and venue. Everything else builds on these components. Take the game of golf. Even though the duffer has a different experience from the scratch golfer, the particular nature of rules/techniques, equipment, and venue joins the two players and distinguishes golf from tennis. Moreover, it is the "playing out"

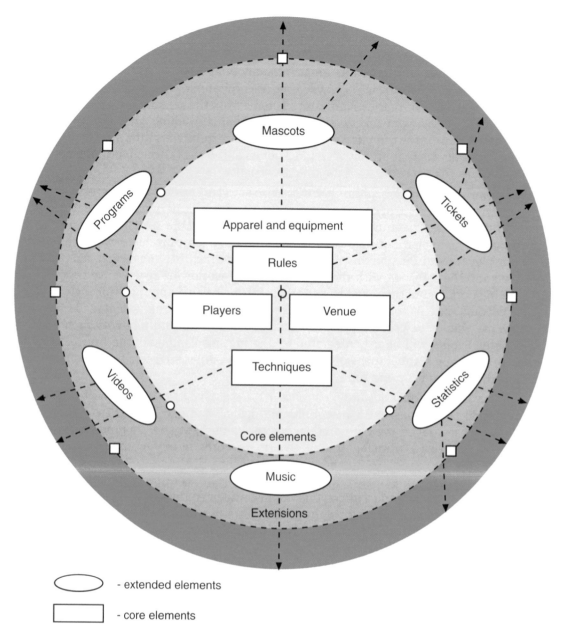

- extended elements

- core elements

FIGURE 7.1 Core elements of the sport product and a sample of extensions.

of rules/techniques, equipment, and venue that makes sport products distinct from all other products.

As figure 7.1 also suggests, the event experience may include an abundance of supplements. These are the things that move us from the playground to the FedEx Center: coaches, tickets, luxury boxes, programs, video, music, memorabilia, and mascots. A supplement is simply a product component that enhances the value (and often the price) of an event experience. At the same time, any product component—from the player to the mascot—can also become a product extension, with a life (and sales) beyond an event or even a season of events.

For example, uniform designs and colors have been part of the sport event for centuries. Fans in the ancient Roman stadiums cheered for chariot drivers of particular stable colors—red, white, green, blue. Many of today's teams are known by their colors. Say "the Crimson" around Boston and most fans will think of Harvard. Say "Crimson Tide" south of the Mason-Dixon line and any football fan will think of Bear Bryant and Alabama. In the last two decades, uniform design became part of broader strategies that extended the event into everyday apparel. Every major league team expanded its properties division to oversee the careful development and sale of merchandise, including "official" team jerseys. Among other things, this meant that two basic uniforms—home and away—were no longer enough. Teams developed "secondary" home and away uniforms. Some were retro and some were avant-garde, but they shared a logic. If big-league players showcased new uniforms at the live event, plenty of people would buy replicas at their local department stores.

As another example, the San Diego Chicken became a major sport figure in the late 1970s. The comic mascot livened up the sport crowd at any venue willing to book him. Pro and college teams took note and created their own mascots as elements that transferred an event into "showtime." In 1994, Dave Raymond, the longtime alter ego of the Philadelphia Phillies' "Phanatic," decided to go out on his own. He created a mascot-for-hire called "Sport," who could assume any team's identity and guarantee a crowd-pleasing performance. But Sport was not limited to sports; he was happy to extend his special "event" experience to conventions, trade shows, and hospitals.

Perhaps the cheesehead headwear more than the sweatshirt identifies this man as a Green Bay Packers fan.
© AP Photo/Eric Gay

Fan groups and their behaviors—so much a part of the live experience—can become commodities of their own. The Green Bay Packers "Cheeseheads" spawned a hot piece of novelty headwear. As the sidebar on fan behavior on page 152 suggests, however, marketers have some responsibility for maintaining fan civility.

In the following sections, we discuss many elements that make up the complex sport product. The list is not exhaustive. (6)

No marketer can guarantee fair play and friendly crowds. On the other hand, marketers may demand a measure of fair play in the mix of any promotion. Marketers may also work with the event staff to improve crowd decorum. There can be a fine line between nurturing entertainment and degrading fair play. Should ushers prevent fans from waving papers and towels to unnerve a player at the foul line? This may depend on the level of competition.

There are always questions to ask. Should a college marketer pursue a deal with an auto body shop that wants to sponsor the "toughest collision" at each home hockey game? This sounds innocent enough, but what if it prompts fans to cheer loudest at each hit, no matter how vicious or illegal? And what if the sponsor runs newspaper and television promos that juxtapose pictures of tough hockey hits and auto wrecks? What is the message to fans? What is the message to families who have lost children in "tough collisions"? We go back to three of Laura Nash's questions in "Ethics Without the Sermon":

What is your intention?

How does this intention compare with probable results?

What is the symbolic potential of your action if understood? If misunderstood?

Ethics require both principles and common sense. So does marketing and maintaining sport products with enduring value. (7)

Fan Behavior: A Key Product Component

Sport events are very much a matter of winners and losers. There is no getting around this. The simplicity of recognizing a win or a loss is the factor that makes events and athletes such rallying points for passionate interest. On the other hand, any game requires some boundaries of behavior. Players are subject to rules that proscribe abusive taunting or profanity. What about fans? They are an essential part of any event. Fans move the core sport product into the realm of spectacle; they expand the drama. But they can also poison the atmosphere and promote violence. There is nothing new in this. Fan riots occurred in the ancient world. Gangs of hooligans stormed fields of play with some regularity in the 19th century. Still, the news is filled with stories suggesting that fan behavior is getting worse.

In December 1997, a mob of Alabama high school football fans attacked two officials. Just prior to the melee, the game's announcer had berated the officials over the public address system, taunting them and complaining that they "needed to go back to school." In February 1998, spectators cheered as a New York high school hockey player was hauled off in handcuffs for assaulting a referee. When profanity and taunting reached intolerable levels in 2004, the University of Maryland established a special student committee to prepare a code of conduct for fans at the Comcast Center. Some critics argued that restraints on student behavior would violate First Amendment rights, but State Attorney General John Anderson supported the university's efforts to maintain a civil environment at its sports events.

Even with legal cover, however, there is no easy way to control a student section of fans, especially if several hundred chant a profanity in unison. It is one thing to eject an isolated drunk. It is another to attempt a mass ejection of an entire section. The most successful initiatives have seen partnerships between administrators and students. As Lehigh University's athletics director Joe Sterrett put it, the best way to get student support of a fan behavior policy "is to involve them in creating the plan." Lehigh administrators identified a core group of student fans who established imaginative but positive chants and songs as alternatives to profanity-laced taunts. Among other guidelines in creating a set of "House Rules," the Lehigh group considered a fundamental question: Would you be embarrassed to have your parents or little brother or sister sitting next to you? Lehigh students now promote the "House Rules" at fall orientations, on arena video displays, and via in-game announcements. (8)

The Game Form

As we noted in chapter 1, sport always contains some kind of game form that includes rules and techniques. Each sport has its own special features that may make it especially attractive to certain consumers. For instance, basketball has speed, agility, physical contact, power, and grace. If James Naismith—who invented the game in 1891—could see the San Antonio Spurs play today, however, he would be surprised at the radical changes in his product. Senda Berenson, who quickly adapted Naismith's game for women, would be even more surprised at a WNBA game. Of course, game forms change all the time. Players invent new moves (see sidebar on page 153), and rules committees tinker with this or that as they work to balance offense and defense. Three classic basketball examples are the 24-second shot clock, the three-point line, and the goaltending rule.

One might argue that changes in rules and techniques are comparable to design changes in any consumer product; sort of like making a tastier, low-fat potato chip or a faster computer chip: Changes are made to satisfy consumer wants and needs. To some extent this is true. The American college football rules committee first allowed forward passing in 1906 with a clear eye on public opinion about the deadly nature of the "mass" game. Likewise, American League owners approved baseball's designated hitter in 1973 in an effort to jack interest and attendance; National League owners, with higher average attendance and more new ballparks, felt no such urgency. As the NHL and the NHLPA attempted to rebound from the lockout of 2004-2005, one of the prominent initiatives was a set of rules changes geared to increasing scoring and skilled play.

On the other hand, most changes in rules and techniques revolve around attempts to gain or balance competitive advantage. The everyday consumer is a secondary interest. A clear example is the change in Indiana high school basketball. In 1996, the Indiana High School Athletic Association (IHSAA) ended the long-standing "single-class" approach to its annual championship. For two years at least, there would be no Davids slaying Goliaths as the movie *Hoosiers* so poignantly depicted. There would be four classes of competition, which supporters claimed would mean fairer competition and more trophies. Unfortunately, the fans didn't quite see it that way. Tournament attendance in 1998 was down 6 percent for girls and 21 percent for boys. Television ratings were down, and overall revenue dipped to its lowest level in 18 years. The IHSAA appointed a citizen's advisory council to develop a survey that would examine whether the change should be permanent. The IHSAA's problem underscored the lesson that sports can't market themselves. (9)

Star Power

The most memorable event experiences build drama from the playing surface outward. Players and coaches are the keys, as all successful promoters learned from the likes of Tex Rickard and Christy Walsh. These architects of American sport's "golden age" in the 1920s recognized the need to accentuate the struggles of hero against villain or mind against muscle. Their strategy was simple—star power. Babe Ruth, Jack Dempsey, Knute Rockne, Bobby Jones, Helen Wills—these are the names we remember and associate with that fabulous era.

In some respects, things have not changed much; the drama of sport still requires star power. On the other hand, today's players and coaches are extended beyond the event far more than their predecessors were. Players still provide most of the script in sport. They can make or break teams and leagues. The great Pelé is a good example. Before he signed with the New York Cosmos of the North American Soccer League, the team averaged 5,000 fans per game at Randall Island. With Pelé, the team moved to Giant Stadium and drew over 50,000 on a regular basis. American soccer's newest phenom is young Freddy Adu, who signed a $2 million, four-year contract with Major League Soccer in 2004—purportedly the league's biggest contract ever. No matter that Adu was only 14 years old. Nike had already signed him to a two-year, $1 million deal. And even if Adu was far from a major "impact" player on the field, he was credited with boosting league-wide attendance over 4 percent. In some cases, his presence doubled attendance at rival venues. Pundits called it the Freddy Factor or the Freddy Effect. (10)

Real star power means a presence that transcends the actual playing. Venus and Serena Williams are good examples. Along with several other young, flashy players, they made the Women's Tennis Association (WTA) Tour a very hot product. Sports writer Mike Lupica

Can "Moves" Be Patented?

Skill, craft, and "moves" have always been a central attraction to the sport consumer. Kids model the actions of more established players—a sibling, a local school hero, or a professional star. Movies extended the audience for the special skills of elite athletes. Fans in Walla Walla could see Babe Ruth's swing, Helen Wills' volleys, and Joe Louis' jabs. Television multiplied the images and the modeling. It became easier for athletes to see and learn the latest "moves" and innovations. Dick Fosbury's "flop" quickly changed the face of high jumping. Icky Woods' "Icky shuffle" set off a national storm of end-zone celebrations. Jimmy Connors and Chris Evert changed the game of tennis with their patented two-fisted backhand strokes.

Fans and broadcasters have long discussed the "patented" moves of this or that player. Now patent attorneys

at the New York firm of Pennie & Edmonds have suggested that "patented" moves can really be patented. Why shouldn't Kareem Abdul-Jabbar have protected his "Sky Hook," asks F. Scott Kieff: "What we find remarkable is that this is viewed as remarkable." In their view, Dick Fosbury should have received royalties from those who copied his revolutionary move. Coaches who dream up distinctly new tactics (the "West Coast Offense" perhaps?) would get some income from copycats, a notorious breed in football. But is any sport move, technique, or team play ever really original? Would sports patents lead to a cadre of new patent protectors who would monitor games around the country, ensuring that no one took a free ride with a hook shot, a two-fisted backhand, or a postscore celebration? We will examine some of these issues in chapter 18. (11)

captured Venus Williams' attraction: "From the beaded braids on her head to the way she carries herself on the court [she] makes you come into the stadium instead of walking the other way. If she is on television, she jumps out of your set." Jennie Finch has similar attributes, which are helping to sell the National Pro Fastpitch softball league. Although Finch's salary is capped at $10,000, her celebrity earns her almost $500,000 in annual endorsements—a stunning endorsement/salary ratio of 50 to 1. Star talent, or its absence, can make or break entire leagues. Just as Joe Namath may have saved the American Football League in the mid-1960s, the absence of household names has been, in the words of one racing writer, the "malady that plagues" both the Indy Racing League (IRL) and the Championship Auto Racing Teams (CART). For some time, they have slumped into the shadows of their star-studded cousin NASCAR. Sponsors are keys to broad product extension. As we discuss in depth in chapter 13, drivers and athletes help nonsport sponsors reach the sport audience of educated, affluent, energetic men, women, and families. But it is a two-way street. Legions of NASCAR fans know which driver endorses Pepsi or Gillette. At the same time, every sponsor ad that uses a NASCAR image also promotes NASCAR as a sport. (12)

Something called the "Q-Score" attempts to measure the American public's embrace of celebrity figures. As Terry Lefton explained, "hundreds of millions of advertising decisions are predicated" on the annual Q-Score reports, one of which is specific to sports. Marketing Evaluations/TvQ annually surveys several thousand 12- to 64-year-olds in a national probability sample. Respondents rate over 400 sport figures along scales such as "never seen or heard of" or "one of my favorites." The 2005 scores demonstrated that star power does not end with a playing career. Michael Jordan still ruled, with a 49 score. Tiger Woods ranked second with a 40, along with Joe Montana and Nolan Ryan. Mia Hamm was the top-ranked woman, scoring a 33. (13)

Star power is not exclusive to players. Many coaches, like Mike Krzyzewski, are considered stars as well.
© AP Photo/Gerry Broome

Coaches and owners can also be stars, and fundamental parts of a product. For instance, John Madden ranked sixth in the 2005 Q rating. When many people think of the NFL, they think of John Madden. Bill Parcells had similar stature. When he left New England for the New York Jets, Parcells' presence alone helped boost ad sales 20 percent for televised Jets games. He generated similar enthusiasm when he went to Dallas. Then there are the owners. Just think of George Steinbrenner and the New York Yankees. For three decades the names and the images have gone hand in hand. Of course, this linkage can also be problematic. When American Malcolm Glazer grabbed control of Manchester United—arguably the world's leading sport brand—his image generated widespread hostility among the team's fans. Among other things, Glazer (who also owned the NFL's Tampa franchise) required heavy borrowing ($490 million) to buy the club at a $1.47 billion price. Fans worried that ticket prices would escalate and that all televised games would move to pay-per-view so that Glazer could wring out the estimated $55 million per year interest payments on the loan. Glazer's son Joel insisted that "we are long-term sports investors and avid Manchester United fans." But the fans were not so sure. Time will tell whether the Glazer name and image will be a boon or a drag on the mighty franchise. (14)

As the Glazer case suggests, star power can be dangerous, especially at the professional level, where franchises and leagues have a difficult time controlling the actions of players. Stars can often haunt them. And images can turn quickly from gold to tarnished brass. Take the case of Mark McGwire. In the 1998 MLB season, McGwire (along with Sammy Sosa) changed the nature of every game he played in, boosting attendance, television ratings, and general interest. It was a special boon for rival hosts, who stood to double or triple average attendance. As he approached the Babe Ruth and Roger Maris records, McGwire appeared on television interviews wearing a cap from the Abbey Seal Restaurant in Orange County, California. Immediately, the restaurant's owners said they were "inundated with calls from coast to coast and overseas"; anything with McGwire's identity was an extension of the home run record chase, a hot commodity. In early 2005, however, his image was quite different. Along with Sosa and other baseball players, he had appeared in front of a Congressional committee investigating steroid abuse in sports. McGwire's testimony—filled with evasion—fueled public concerns that the recent assaults on baseball's batting records were the result of chemicals and not of hard work. Between 2004 and 2005, McGwire's Q-score dropped from 33 to 20. (15)

Although neither agents nor teams can control all elements of players' or coaches' performances or behavior, the last decade has seen greater efforts to enhance their interpersonal skills and their product value. One example was the Corel WTA Tour and the United States Tennis Association, which promoted a media skills training program for players in the late 1990s. The NCAA Champs/Life Skills program for Division I athletes is an even more comprehensive example. This mandatory educational program covers not only communication skills but also such issues as substance abuse, eating disorders, and stress management. Some firms have begun to offer services to college prospects, helping them create promotional packages to better sell their skills to recruiters. The National Scouting Report, for example, offered packages ranging in cost from $895 to $2,495, for which high school prospects received a range of benefits including DVDs, Web sites, promotional e-mails, and fancy resumes. Whether the products were worth the price remains to be seen. (16)

Equipment and Apparel

As noted earlier, equipment is part of the "core" product for any sport consumer. No sport is played today without equipment, and much of it is increasingly "high tech" (see sidebar on page 161). The latest attempt to assess the total revenues of the American sport industry found the sales of sporting goods and licensed merchandise to comprise 18.6 percent of the $194.64 billion total. But equipment and merchandise take on a life beyond the core-event experience. A glove, a stick, or a hat is a tangible connection to a game or a match—for players and fans alike. And as we discussed in chapter 4, sport merchandise is a critical part of the learning process in any sport. Sport-related T-shirts, jackets, and ball caps became a badge of personal identity in the 1980s and 1990s, as any parent or teacher knows well. (For more detail on merchandising, see chapters 8, 9, and 14.) Merchandise even resurrected dead franchises. When Snoop Doggy Dogg wore a Springfield Indians hockey jersey in his hit 1995 video *Gin and Juice*, sales jumped 500 percent, vaulting the Indians to third place in American Hockey League merchandise sales. It didn't matter that the Indians franchise had died in 1994 or that the jersey design was over a decade old. Retro was in. (16)

Equipment innovations have continually pressed the boundaries of sport performance. Pole vaulting moved through distinct chapters as poles evolved from bamboo to metal to fiberglass. The plastic helmet and the face mask revolutionized blocking and tackling in football. Inventors and manufacturers continually seek the new product that will sweep the market. Some innovations are controversial, such as "square-grooving" or "spring-like effects" in golf clubs—innovations that have pitted manufacturers against the USGA, sometimes into litigation. Governing bodies typically react to innovations that appear to affect the integrity of playing skill, safety, or competitive fairness. In the late 1990s, for example, the International Ski Federation (FIS) banned the racing suits worn by Picabo Street and others because their technology was unavailable to competitors. The NCAA recently adjusted the specifications for aluminum baseball bats when technological advances produced batted balls with dangerously high velocities. We can expect more high-tech products on the horizon, ready to create more profits for manufacturers and more tension for rule makers. (17)

Memories

One thing is clear in sports: History captivates and motivates consumers. Arguments about the best player of all time, interest in "retro" sweaters or hats, and the proliferation of halls of fame at every level in every sport—all testify to the power of the past. In the spring of 2005, five cities bid aggressively to host the NASCAR Hall of Fame. Unlike an Olympics or Super Bowl, the NASCAR Hall would generate tourist income every year for its host city. Some historical artifacts have reached staggering values. In December 2004, Sotheby's auction house sold a baseball bat for $1.28 million. Of course, it was not your everyday bat. It was the 3-foot-long, 46-ounce gargantuan stick that Babe Ruth swung to hit the first home run in Yankee Stadium, the "House that Ruth Built." Sport memorabilia has a long history, and collectors have sought investments for well over a century. Counterfeiters have followed closely behind, so the major leagues have hired "authenticators" such as Deloitte and Touche, who attend events such as the World Series to slap artifacts with special holograms and numbers that are used to register the authenticity of a ball, bat, hat, glove, base, or even an empty champagne bottle. Since 2001, MLB's program has authenticated over 650,000 items. The stakes are high. Mark McGwire's 70th homer ball fetched $3 million. The Red Sox lineup card from Game 4 of the 2004 World Series drew $165,000 at auction. Red Sox first baseman Doug Mientkiewicz held on to the "final out" ball, which he referred to as his "retirement fund." It would be a sizable fund. Dan Shaughnessy of the *Boston Globe* referred to the ball as the "Hope Diamond of New England sports." One local expert estimated its immediate value as "a million dollars. Who knows." (18)

The memories that swirl around historical data and artifacts are a key component to consumer commitment, a phenomenon recognized by the smartest sport organizations. Following are some examples of marketing memories:

✦ In the spring of 2004, the NHL developed a series of television promotions called "Bring the Cup Home" promoting the history and tradition of the Stanley Cup. When the league returned from its lockout, it quickly used memories to "bring the fans home."

✦ The National Thoroughbred Racing Association jumped on the success of the 2003 feature film *Seabiscuit*. The popular film's compelling story about the Depression-era victories of an underdog horse and jockey spurred more media interest in racing, which in turn spiked attendance over 10 percent at tracks around the country.

✦ With grassroots, "street cred" promotion by fashion leaders such as Reuben Harley, demand for Mitchell & Ness "retro" uniforms took off in the new millennium. In February 2002, the price of a Wes Unseld 1978 Washington Bullets model shirt reached $430. As Harley explained to *Sports Illustrated*, "This isn't a fad. These uniforms are the history of sports. Styles come and go, but you can't change the '79 Magic Johnson jersey."

✦ The Schottenstein Center at Ohio State University has a concourse that includes a number of interactive kiosks telling the story of Buckeye athletic history.

✦ Penn State Athletics contracted with sport historian Ronald Smith to develop a card game called "Penn State Memento." Players had to match pairs of cards that contained images of Nittany Lion sports trivia. The game box includes a blurb from Joe Paterno: "This game is a superb way to keep your memories of Penn State alive and well."

Some fans might prefer a few more victories in the here and now, but memories are a compelling sport product, and they are not just for big-time sport programs. A high school or a sport club can nurture its own history with something as simple as a mural prepared by a class or by players and their families. (19)

Novelties and Fantasies

Sport toys and novelties go back over a century, but they were never as clearly tied to integrated marketing strategies as they are today. In 1997, the NBA along with Mattel, and the

NFL along with Hasbro, entered into major deals for toy lines. The NBA had a Barbie Doll line, with the WNBA slated to follow. The NFL launched a "Pro Action Athlete" collectible line; NASCAR had driver figurines. When Hasbro let its exclusive deals lapse in 2001, the McFarlane Company moved into the market with figurines so real their photos were often confused with those of real players. The NASCAR teams saw another market in recycling old tires, which fans happily bought for $5 to 10 each. Said one consumer about his purchase: "I'm going to keep it on my floor at home, next to my bed. You know, so that I can see it first thing in the morning when I wake up." (20)

Major league and minor league teams have continually searched for hot collectibles to drive promotions and fan loyalty. Beanie Babies were hot in the 1990s. In 2001, the Chicago Cubs partnered with Topps to create a set of 10 trading cards of current or former Cubs to be given away at different points in the season. By 2004, many clubs had linked with local newspapers to sell collectible pins and coins. (21)

Fantasy leagues are growing. Fans want to pretend they are general managers; they want extra passion when they watch games. What better adrenaline boost than to follow a set of players you have drafted to your team—even if in reality they all play on different teams. Fan research conducted in 2004 by Ipsos determined that 6.4 percent of the U.S. population played fantasy sports. That translated into 14 million adults. The leading sport was NFL football with 3.7 percent of the population. The highest-playing demographic was males, aged 18 to 39; 15.8 percent of them played fantasy sports. *Sports Illustrated* even calculated the 2004 Gross Rotisserie Product (GRP) by adding estimates of league entry fees (averaging $95), licensing deals, Web services, fantasy publications, and tip/expert services. The total—$1.65 billion! (22)

Then there are the fan fests, fantasy camps, and cruises, which have developed for two simple reasons. The first is the meteoric rise in price of tickets, concessions, and parking at big-league events. The standard event in any sport gets less and less accessible to the majority of potential consumers. If fewer people can afford to get on the consumer escalator, how can they sample the sport product "up close and personal"? At the same time, even the most committed consumers want to learn, feel, and do more. Fan fests, fantasy camps, and cruises were the answer, with free or low-cost fests at the entry level and high-cost cruises or camps for consumers willing to pay for closer contact with past or present-day players. The intent behind all these products was clearly expressed when the LPGA announced the new LPGA Fan Village in 1997. The 2,400-square-foot (730-square-meter) multimedia entertainment and information center—sponsored by Target Stores—would travel with the tour. At the village, fans could enjoy the following:

Fan–player photo opportunities

Rules and technique seminars

Health and fitness forums

Club-fitting and hitting areas

Pictorial time line of LPGA highlights

Video and computer displays

As former LPGA Commissioner Jim Ritts concluded, the Fan Village was a "fun and entertaining way to satisfy our fans' appetite to get closer to the realness of our players and to learn more about our organization." The NFL, NHL, NBA, NCAA, and MLB have the same objectives at their fan fests. Individual franchises have jumped on the concept. Colleges and universities have also developed their own fan fests. Notre Dame was among them. In 2004, 52 campers paid $4,290 each to practice in real Notre Dame equipment under the tutelage of present and past Fighting Irish coaches, then play in a final flag football game in Notre Dame Stadium. The Chicago Bulls took it one step further, offering fans the chance to be a floor sweeper during a game. The price tag? $1,200. For $1,500, a fan could play reporter and file a story on the club's Web site. (23)

The Venue

All sports have a venue, a field, or a facility as part of the product package. We look more closely at the sport "place" in chapter 14, but it is clear that teams and franchises are closely aligned with their venues, which are the cauldrons of powerful memory and community. Historian Bruce Kuklick captured this well in his monograph on Philadelphia's historic Shibe Park, longtime home of the city's major league teams: "Meaning and the items that bear it are fragile. The meanings accrue over time in their visible embodiments, artifacts like Shibe Park. Memories do not exist in the mind's isolation but are connected to objects and stored in them." A fan's identity, particularly in a large city, often resides in the stories or the recollections that link people and events with a place. A place like Shibe Park offered special rituals that made Irish or Italians into "Philadelphians." The same may be true for any venue. Small towns everywhere have sport venues ripe with tradition and collective memory. The fear of losing this kind of distinct identity agitated critics of the "cookie-cutter" stadiums that sprang up in the 1970s. The newer "retro" parks like Camden Yards seem to represent a swing back to Kuklick's sense of a distinct community place—a modernized version of Wrigley Field or Fenway Park. At the same time, in the new ballparks, fans are more segregated than ever according to their ability to pay for high-priced loges, club seats, and skyboxes. (24)

Many of today's venues have such broad appeal that they provide significant revenue streams outside of game days. When the new owners of the Boston Red Sox looked to reverse the "Curse of the Bambino," they had to find revenue to compete with the Yankees. But ticket prices were already the highest in baseball. And there were limits to expansion—a few hundred seats atop the Green Monster and a new section in right field. But

Safeco Field offers more than just a venue for watching a baseball game. Fans can enjoy the Bullpen Market in center field, Lookout Landing on the upper deck, Outside Corner Picnic Patio directly above the Home Plate, and the Children's Hospital Playfield.
© AP Photo/File

there were plenty of open dates on Fenway Park's calendar—some 284 of them. So the Red Sox began to advertise for parties, weddings, and business meetings inside Fenway's friendly confines. Rentals were not cheap. It might cost anywhere from $1,000 to $100,000, depending on numbers, location, and quality of food. Nonetheless, "rentals" went up from 20 bookings in all of 2003 to 92 by mid-October 2004, when the Sox began their play-off run. In baseball-mad New England (a.k.a. Red Sox Nation), everybody wanted to get to Fenway, including delegates to the Democratic National Convention, who took batting practice one afternoon. The Red Sox were not alone in this approach to product extension. Seattleites could enjoy dinner for two at home plate in Safeco Field. Giants fans could rent space in AT&T Park for their own fantasies. (25)

Venues can sometimes be a drag on the total product package. In the contentious world of professional sport, owners sometimes insult their venues worse than they impugn their players at arbitration. The New York Islanders took this to the extreme in September 1998. Embroiled in a battle with the Spectacor Management Group, which managed the Nassau Coliseum, the Islanders greeted their season-ticket holders with a letter that included a warning about the safety of the coliseum's sound system. The Islanders claimed that Spectacor would not let them inspect the hoists thoroughly. Would the massive speakers fall on top of unwitting fans? A final promise to protect fans and players from "any conditions we believe to be unsafe" was hardly reassuring. (26)

Personnel and Process

If the core sport product is a performance or an event, then successful marketing depends on the people who process the product. A.J. Magrath argued persuasively that personnel and process are additional Ps in the marketing mix. Any fan who has gone to numerous "giveaways" at sport events knows the frustration of receiving the wrong size or of being told, "Sorry, we're all out . . . we didn't expect so many fans today." The actions of a surly attendant or the hopelessness of a botched promotion can never be replaced or repaired. The consumer cannot return or exchange the experience. In the consumer's eyes, personnel and process are inextricably linked to the product. (27)

Charles L. Martin's research on customer relations in bowling centers led him to coin a telling phrase: *All sports are "contact" sports.* The consumer simply cannot access the product without contacting personnel in the sport organization. An intrinsically fine core product may be destroyed by lackluster personnel or process performance. Martin found that both highly and lightly involved bowlers rated "courteous personnel" among the most important attributes of a bowling center. Bernie Mullin recognized this in his work with the Pittsburgh Pirates and the Colorado Rockies. His inspiration was the "guest-centered" philosophy of Disneyland and Disney World. Martin, Mullin, and the Disney enterprises offer some simple tips to any sport organization:

+ Emphasize common courtesy, especially sincere "thank-yous," even when making change.
+ Make "extratransactional" encounters with customers, beyond what they normally expect. This shows extra concern for their satisfaction.
+ Be proactive. Offer assistance before being asked. Work to solve problems immediately. Treat consumers as though they were guests in your home.
+ Increase complaints. Encourage consumers to speak their minds. In the language of Disney, "Ask the guests what they want . . . then give it to them." Only then will the organization know how to satisfy the consumer.
+ Develop a theme and a consistent ethos of service that cascade through the venue—in signage, color, cleanliness, personnel appearance, and a tenacious belief that all consumers have "special needs."
+ Incorporate personnel procedures and training into company policy.

Little things do matter. Roving concierges who can supply binoculars, cell phones, or even reservations for a postgame dinner will become more common in the next decade. The various processes involving sport personnel—ticket-taking, front desk management, locker room attending, concessions operations, skills instruction, and field maintenance—are essential features of the product. They cannot be overlooked or taken for granted. As we noted in chapter 4, the "golden rule" may be expressed in a word: *reciprocity*. (28)

The Ticket and Other Print Materials

Few people realize the full value of a ticket to an event. The obvious uses are to provide a receipt, to guide people to their seats, and to communicate the terms and conditions of purchase. Statements of limited liability are standard these days. But these mundane applications are just the tip of the iceberg in terms of marketing potential. The ticket can clearly be used both as a promotional tool and as a source of revenue. Many collegiate and minor league baseball teams use the ticket as an advertising medium for sponsors. Other organizations have been quick to use it for a promotional tie-in—having drawings of ticket numbers for prizes, for example, or printing redeemable coupons (often for fast food) on the back of the ticket. Tickets often carry prestige (not to mention scalping value) that turn them into souvenirs. World Cup and Super Bowl tickets include an embedded hologram that makes counterfeiting much more difficult.

The value of ticket access is reflected in the rise of personal seat licenses—one-time payments for the right to buy season tickets in a particular seat. Personal seat licenses have become a standard way to fund new stadiums. At the same time, turning seats into quasi-private property can backfire. In 1995, the Denver Broncos announced that season-ticket accounts could be transferred only to family members. They changed their minds in 1997 after being hit with a $35 million class action suit. (29)

Other print materials can extend the product. Programs are one example. Besides including player, coach, or game profiles and statistics, rules, and records, programs can include lucky numbers used for special prize drawings. And like tickets, programs can be tailored for big events, with added features that make them collectibles. Teams, clubs, and leagues can also publish magazines and newsletters. Few sport organizations in North America match the reach of Manchester United, whose magazine can be purchased at newsstands all over Britain; NASCAR, with its magazine *Inside NASCAR*, may be one of them. Many groups have high-quality serials that circulate to members and season-ticket holders. The *NCAA News*, a tabloid weekly, is available at a nominal price to the general public. (30)

Electronic Products

The *NCAA News* began in the 1960s; by the 1990s, standard print circulation was no longer enough to ensure connecting with key target segments. The *NCAA News* went online at the association's Web site: www.ncaa.org. We will examine Internet marketing along with radio and television more closely in chapter 15. Collegiate events and heroes—and all sport products—gained popularity via innovations in communications that started in the 1840s, when New York newspapers began printing telegraph dispatches of bare-knuckle prizefights. Motion pictures, radio, television, and the Internet each brought new opportunities (and problems). At this point we simply emphasize Internet sport as part of a larger development in electronic and digital products. Following are some examples:

✦ In the late 1990s, MLB Properties and Donruss introduced a series of CD-ROM player cards for $21.99 apiece. The New England Patriots opened a Web site—www.patriots.tripod.com—that allowed fans to pull down and trade "virtual collectibles," such as team marks and pictures, in license-protected bundles that could be traded but not altered. Some could be limited editions that might rise in "value" with a player's performance. Such products give a whole new meaning to the notion of "trading" cards. (31)

✦ Although music and sport have been linked for over a century (football fight songs, "Take Me Out to the Ball Game"), recent years have seen more aggressive connections. NASCAR formalized its marriage to Nashville with CD compilations, such as "NASCAR: Runnin' Wide Open," that featured songs by Billy Ray Cyrus, Rick Trevino, and even Kyle Petty. Alphabet City Music Productions began creating in-venue music videos tailored to rally fans of client franchises. Alphabet's special-edition Chicago Bulls CD sold over 300,000 copies. (32)

✦ Sport properties also moved their stories to DVD. Within a month of winning the World Series, the Boston Red Sox and MLB Productions had a DVD on the market, with advanced sales of 300,000. (33)

✦ Hollywood continued its affair with baseball and other sports. In 2004, the Farrelly brothers filmed in Fenway Park using real players and crowds as props for *Fever Pitch,* the story of an obsessed Red Sox fan (lots of candidates for that role). CBS, which was fined by the FCC for its 2004 Super Bowl disaster, displayed its repentance with a prime-time show called *The Clubhouse,* in which a batboy learned life's lessons. (34)

✦ The highest-profile sport products enjoy extension in video games. ESPN and the NFL combined with Sega to create ESPN NFL 2K5, which sold two million copies (at $20 each) between July and September 2004. This put some heat on the industry frontrunner, Electronic Arts Inc.'s Madden NFL, which had gained worldwide domination for a decade. Consumer loyalty, however, allowed Madden NFL to charge $50 and still move four million units. (35)

Wherever there is new technology, there is also a new sport product. Although marketers must not trade taste for technology (see sidebar, this page), there is no question that technology is helping to drive the sport market.

The Organization

Ultimately, all of the product elements can add value to the individual team, club, league, or association. That is the ultimate objective of a careful marketing strategy. Players, equipment, venues, merchandise, books, movies, and Web sites can all combine in the consumer's mind as representations of a particular organization. This is why all major leagues have divisions called "Properties" or "Enterprises." Integrated product strategies yield values through synergy, meaning that the whole is more than just the sum of the parts. This is why professional franchise values continue to escalate despite salary pressures and fan antagonisms. Sometimes

Are There Penalties for Bad Taste?

High technology is now an expectation of fans in college and professional sport venues. Laser lights, high-energy music clips, instant replays on the big screen—for a $50 ticket, we expect no less. But high-tech packaging does not always prove that the medium is the message. Some messages are so outrageous that we wonder, What could they have been thinking? Here are two examples:

✦ In November 1997, the San Jose Sharks crossed the line with their music playlist. In two separate games against teams with African American players, the events crew played the pop song "Dirty White Boy" after a black player was sent to the penalty box. The public uproar forced Sharks VP Malcolm Bordelon to admit: "Mistakes. Embarrassing mistakes."

✦ 1998 ads for the new NFL video game called NFL Xtreme promised that "after the coin toss, anything goes. . . . It's a helmet-popping, trash-talking, late-hitting free-for-all." *Sports Illustrated* correctly asked, "How can the league come down on cheap-shot artists and hotheads while also endorsing this video?" One NFL executive responded that it was, after all, only a "fantasy game" that was "consistent with how to get the attention of the upper-teen and early-20s market."

"Entertainment" is a clear objective underlying any sport product. But Laura Nash reminds us of at least one other obligation with her question, "Whom could your decision or action injure?" (36)

we gasp at franchise selling prices—$530 million for the NFL expansion Cleveland Browns or $1.5 billion for Manchester United. But if we begin to add up all the values associated with the core- and extended-product elements, these selling prices make more sense.

The same perspective is needed with recreation and athletic clubs. Spencer Garrett, general manager of the Pierpont Racquet Club of Ventura, California, argued two decades ago that club owners had to form a partnership in the minds of their members. As Garrett insisted, most members would have a hard time justifying their investment on a simple cost-per-play basis. They must recognize that each visit is a rental of the whole club and all of its amenities: a hard match on a quality court, a hot sauna, a friendly exchange in a clean locker room, a snack in the lounge, a tip on racquet maintenance in the pro shop. Thus the member pays for a whole ensemble of activities characterized in a word—*club*. (37)

Key Issues in Sport Product Strategy

As we discussed in chapter 2, strategy is essential. Here we discuss the major issues of sport product strategy: differentiation, product development, product position, brands, and product and brand cycles.

Differentiation

Spencer Garrett articulated a central, ongoing struggle for all managers and marketers—ensuring that their product is conceived, packaged, and positioned in a way that resonates in the minds of their consumers. If consumers don't recognize the club, the team, the player, the event, or the equipment as meeting their needs, then marketing becomes a one-way drive to oblivion. Like all successful coaches who must tinker with their lineups and their strategies, marketers must continuously revise, delete, and add elements to their comprehensive product. Unlike coaches, however, marketers must consider their consumers and their competitors simultaneously. Whether the product is new, established, or old, the challenge is ever-present—make the product distinctive and attractive in your consumers' minds.

As an example, take Nike's image battles. The Nike "Swoosh" is as recognizable today as Mickey Mouse or McDonald's golden arches. Despite ups and downs in sales and profits, Nike looms as a dominant force in the wide world of sport. As Nike's Phil Knight is the first to recognize, however, getting to the top and staying there require constant reinvention and reconfiguration. In the early 1980s, for instance, Nike was temporarily toppled from preeminence by Reebok, which captured the fast-swelling aerobics market. As Knight recalled later, "We made an aerobics shoe that was functionally superior to Reebok's, but we missed the styling. Reebok's shoe was sleek and attractive, while ours was sturdy and clunky." Nike survived and then thrived by repackaging and reconfiguring its products to include style as well as performance. Moreover, Nike began to use aggressive television ads to focus consumer attention on this shift. In Knight's words, "Our advertising tried to link consumers to the Nike brand through the emotions of sports and fitness. We show competition, determination, achievement, fun, and even the spiritual rewards of participating in these activities." Nike ads have succeeded because of these emotions. But in the 1990s, Nike's foreign manufacturing and labor practices stirred equally strong emotions, forcing Knight to admit that Nike had "become synonymous with slave wages, forced overtime and arbitrary abuse." This was a distinction that Nike could do without, so the company had to continue repositioning itself in the public's imagination. (38)

The competition between the ABL and WNBA is another example of differentiation. In 1997, women's professional basketball provided sport fans with two new products—the ABL and the WNBA. The league "war" revisited product battles that had dotted the sport landscape back as far as the 1880s when the American Association challenged the National League's choke-hold on big-time baseball. Issues included the following:

- *Markets and venues.* The ABL played in midsized markets and venues, such as Columbus (Ohio) and Richmond (Virginia). The WNBA played in the big-market venues of the "parent" franchises—New York, Los Angeles, Cleveland, Phoenix.
- *Star appeal.* Both leagues pushed for star talent. The WNBA had the best-known players (Lisa Leslie, Rebecca Lobo, and Sheryl Swoopes), but the ABL grabbed eight of the 1996 Olympic team members.
- *Television.* What counted most here was NBA leverage; the WNBA enjoyed secure television packages with NBC and ESPN, whereas the ABL got limited exposure on BET and regional sport channels.
- *Season of play.* The ABL played in the "traditional" period (October to February), whereas the WNBA played a summer schedule.

The WNBA and the ABL pressed their product distinctions to the public in 1997. Gary Cavelli, the ABL's founder, hammered away at the WNBA for relegating women to secondary status with a summer season that was little more than a filler for NBA arenas. But the public didn't seem to care. If the ABL was to survive, it would not be on the basis of its playing season. The choices were clear, for players and fans. It was almost David against Goliath, except that David was offering higher average salaries than Goliath. And that was the rub. Without the clout of big markets and big media, the ABL strained to stay afloat with a higher payroll than its rival had. In early 1999, the ABL declared bankruptcy; however, the brief league war will be remembered for providing one of the starkest product contrasts in sport history. (39)

As the ABL case suggests, marketers must constantly evaluate and reevaluate their products, especially as they exist in consumers' minds. Philip Kotler defined differentiation as "the act of designing a set of meaningful differences to distinguish the company's offering from competitors' offerings." Sport products can be differentiated on the basis of any or all of the elements we have discussed. Many people, for instance, see women's basketball as more of a "team" game, requiring more precision passing, and men's basketball as more of a one-on-one, above-the-rim, slam-dunk game.

Marketers must use their knowledge and imagination to recognize the ways their products may be distinct in the consumer's mind. As a simple exercise, take a standard LPGA event compared to a standard NFL event. How are they different? Table 7.1 offers some possibilities. The nature of the game, the way fans are framed around players, their proximity to players, and their chances of interaction with players all help to distinguish pro football from tour golf. Any and all of these could be helpful in developing surveys and promotions that might clarify important distinctions for other sport products. Marketers are limited only by their imagination. (40)

✦ **Table 7.1** Sport Product Differentiation: The LPGA and the NFL

Element	LPGA	NFL
Game form	High skill, slow pace	High skill, high pace
Framing of fans around players	Clustered around course; fans can move with players	Uniframe, determined by venue seating; little or no movement by fans
Proximity to action	Very close	Distant
Chances of exchange with players	High	Low

Product Development

Marketers must continuously develop the product. This may include deleting, revising, or adding any one or more of the elements that make up the comprehensive bundle of benefits. Product development includes two standard steps:

- ✦ Generation of ideas
- ✦ Screening and implementation of ideas, which includes refinement of the product concept, market and business analysis, development of the actual product, market testing, and commercialization

An excellent example of a brilliant development strategy was the introduction by hockey's San Jose Sharks of their colors and marks in the early 1990s, largely under the leadership of Matt Levine, long regarded as the "father of modern sport marketing." A small task force developed a list of key criteria to be used in name selection. These criteria included clarity, regional links, brevity, and graphic potential. With the name "Sharks" in the forefront of their minds, the team held a name sweepstakes to generate even more ideas, as well as interest. More than 2,300 different names came in, with the name "Sharks" running second to "Blades," which was never seriously considered because of its gang implications.

With a name and an image under design, the next step was colors. Here the Sharks used a number of steps, including "bypass" interviews with 800 season-ticket depositors who rated various color schemes, and consultations with expert designers such as L.L. Bean. The final product was a raging success—teal and black colors that accentuated a cartoon-like "Sharkie" who was crunching a hockey stick. In 1992, after one year of public distribution, sales of San Jose Sharks merchandise had reached $125 million. By the end of 1994, the Sharks were the number-one seller of NHL merchandise. In the ever-changing market of popular taste, however, Sharks merchandise sales drifted downward, so that by 1997, they ranked 21st in the NHL. Other teams had jumped on the Sharks' innovations and had redesigned their uniforms. By the late 1990s, the Sharks were back at the drawing boards. (41)

Product innovations often walk a fine line between success and failure. In the end, of course, it is consumers who determine the results. Theories of innovation suggest that consumers grapple with five perceptual issues as they decide whether to adopt a product innovation: (1) relative advantage of the new product over old preferences, (2) complexity or difficulty in adoption and use, (3) compatibility with consumer values, (4) divisibility into smaller trial portions, and (5) communicability of benefits. Researchers studying a small sample of Cleveland Cavalier fans (who had attended at least one game) in the Akron-Canton area found that all five issues came into play when the Cavs moved from the Richfield Coliseum near Akron to the new Gund Arena in downtown Cleveland:

- ✦ *Relative advantage.* The greater travel distance often outweighed the benefits of the beautiful new arena.
- ✦ *Complexity.* Issues of distance, time, parking, and safety might be too daunting.
- ✦ *Compatibility.* Of the women sampled, 91 percent said they rarely or never visited downtown Cleveland.
- ✦ *Divisibility.* Some fans could not link higher ticket prices to the benefits of a new facility.
- ✦ *Communicability.* Aggressive ad campaigns did not register with some fans; one respondent was not even aware of the new arena.

The Cavs did address these issues in the promotional campaign associated with their move, and the success of the Gund Arena (now Quicken Loans Arena) supports the Cavs' move to downtown Cleveland. The research results listed, however, reinforce the virtues of careful planning for all product innovations. (42)

Product Position

The elements in any sport product should contribute to a coherent image; product development should not be pursued haphazardly. Further, the sport organization must get this image across to the consumer. When all elements of the product provide the same message, the image is clear and distinct. A major factor influencing the reception of this image is consumer perception. As the Cleveland Cavs study suggests, consumer perceptions may be selective and inconsistent. Just think of the prospects if the sport organization is also inconsistent in the images it sends out!

The bottom line is the product's position in the minds of the target consumers. Marketing campaigns often focus on "positioning" or "repositioning" the product in consumers' minds. Positioning strategy, however, is especially tough in the sport industry, where media images are so public and where they are often beyond the control of team and league marketers. Ice hockey provides a good example: What is pro hockey's core—skill or violence? As professional hockey expanded beyond Canada and the American "Rust Belt," the game has continually wrestled with its sense of self. For at least a century, hockey has tried to balance speed and skill with violent hitting and tight checking. What has made pro hockey different from any other sport, however, is its longtime embrace of bare-knuckle fighting. No other professional team sport allows fighting with such relative impunity (a five-minute penalty). Hockey is also the fastest sport of all, in which quick moves and elusiveness still allow smaller players such as Wayne Gretzky and Paul Kariya to excel. Hockey, however, has found it hard to balance the images of bloody mayhem and graceful playmaking. In the 1990s, for instance, the NHL ran a $1.7 million national television ad campaign, tagged "Share the Glory": It highlighted, in the words of one NHL team executive, "what the game really is—speed, finesse, grace, and style—as opposed to the perception that we're the World Wrestling Federation of the sports world." But not all pro franchises shared this sense of the game, especially minor league teams in southern markets. The Winston-Salem Ice Hawks filled their sales campaign with radio spots promising "the return of workingman's hockey . . . I'm talking about body-crashing, puck-screaming, helmet-cracking, gloves-dropping American hockey." The struggling New York Islanders decided that skill and grace wouldn't sell. Their sales campaign used "Fighting Without Ear Biting" as a tag line. Fans at all levels of the escalator were left to reconcile the images. (43)

The battle for positioning occurs at all levels, in all sports. Horse racing and bowling have mounted multimillion-dollar campaigns to reposition their products as hip and hot, especially in the minds of younger consumers. The National Thoroughbred Racing Association's campaign was entitled "Go Baby Go" and emphasized the racetrack's unique combination of yelling, screaming, and (maybe) making money that might prove that "you haven't let this politically-correct, calorie-counting climate we're living in turn you into a cream puff." (44)

When Mannie Jackson purchased the Harlem Globetrotters from the International Broadcasting Company in 1993, the legendary franchise was a ghost of its glorious past. Attendance and profits had decreased drastically in only six years. Jackson brought the Trotters back to prominence and profitability by repositioning them away from the "clown" image they had acquired. While retaining their humor, the Trotters took on more legitimate competition, ran clinics for kids, and made speaking appearances wherever they played. This, in turn, made them much more attractive to corporate sponsorships, which further increased their position in the public eye. (45)

Along similar lines, NCAA Division I programs, especially in urban markets, must develop strategies to distinguish their programs from the rising number of pro teams in basketball, hockey, baseball, and lacrosse. Starting in 2003, the NCAA began a series of television ads that focused on the stories of student athletes who balance academics and athletics. It was the least the NCAA could do to counter the "commercial" image that resonated when it signed a $6 billion rights deal for "March Madness." (46)

If high school sports are to remain solvent, their administrators must emulate Novi, Michigan, athletics director John Fundukian, whose annual "Athletics Highlights" bulletin focuses attention on the distinct contributions of high school athletics to the local community. Among other things, Fundukian has emphasized statistics showing the relation between participation and academic performance. (47)

Sergio Zyman, longtime marketing whiz of Coca-Cola, described positioning as a matter of managing the five images of any organization or product. Here are the five images, using the Boston Celtics as a point of analysis:

1. *Trademark imagery.* The Celtics' leprechaun is a well-known mark, needing little management.

2. *Product imagery.* This has been a major problem for over a decade. The team has not been very good, especially when compared to its illustrious past. Worse yet, at one point in the late 1990s the owner even referred to the team as "stinky."

3. *Associative imagery.* The Celtics lack a well-known association with a cause such as the Jimmy Fund, a campaign against childhood cancer to which the Red Sox have been closely linked for over 50 years.

4. *User imagery.* Celtics patrons are now broadly painted as "corporate suits," not die-hard basketball fans.

5. *Usage imagery.* Unlike the most recent, raucous glory days of Larry Bird, Robert Parrish, and Kevin McHale in the old Boston Garden, current usage imagery seems to be boring nights among the "suits" at the overpriced and cavernous TD Banknorth Garden. (48)

Clearly, the Celtics have a great deal of work to do on four of the five images. In fact, most teams and leagues have focused on trademark imagery (*marks* being the general term for images and names associated with a product). For instance, the NCAA has become more aggressive about protecting the use of the word-mark "Final Four," which is trademarked for use only with the NCAA Division I men's basketball tournament. Other NCAA championships must now develop their own marks. Ice hockey embraced the term "Frozen Four," which has worked well. The Division I men's and women's soccer championship committees developed a "Name the Game" promotion with Nabisco. Fans who entered the top three names received trips, shopping sprees, and soccer balls. The contest, however, failed to uncover a name that resonated with the public. See chapter 8 for a more detailed examination of redesigning marks. (49)

The Product-Space Map

Positioning strategies can benefit from the use of perceptual space maps, which are formed by asking consumers to rank certain product attributes. The critical attributes vary from

Sport Products and "Stickiness"

As we discussed in chapter 2, sport properties have increasingly linked their products to hip-hop and rock music. The NFL's Super Bowl marriage with MTV is just one example. Malcolm Gladwell, author of the best-selling book *The Tipping Point,* might call this an attempt to increase the Super Bowl's (and the NFL's) "stickiness" with 12- to 18-year-olds. The NFL hoped to glue the images of athletic skill, grittiness, and high-collision competition with the high-energy show of Janet Jackson, Justin Timberlake, and their background of dancers. In other words, make pro football "cooler" by linking it to pop music. The search for "stickiness" is crucial to any positioning strategy. If we are assaulted by thousands of messages and commands each day, the challenge is how to make a message "stick" in the mind of a consumer. What Gladwell's "Law of Stickiness" suggests is that problems with stickiness are often not problems in the overall message or plan or product. They are often little things that can be changed "by tinkering, on the margin, with the presentation of [the] idea." For instance, one experiment with university students found that a brochure on health issues was not enough to prompt students to visit the health center for an inoculation. But one small change boosted the success rate from 3 to 28 percent: adding a map and a schedule. As we discuss in chapter 10, any team ticket brochure has lots of room to change, delete, or add the information that will push a ticket campaign over the tipping point. The same is true for any element of the sport product. In Malcolm Gladwell's words, "There is a simple way to package information (or a product) that, under the right circumstances, can make it irresistible." (50)

product to product and from sport to sport, but the following example illustrates the principle (see figure 7.2). Suppose the University of Durham wanted to conceptualize the position of its very successful women's ice hockey team in the minds of local (25-mile, or 40-kilometer, radius) consumers, including students at the university. The U of D women's team draws only 900 to 1,200 fans per game, at low prices, whereas the less successful men's hockey team sells out every game, at four times the price. Many factors drive the attendance levels, but the athletics marketers want to get a better sense of where women's hockey fits in the minds of current and potential fans.

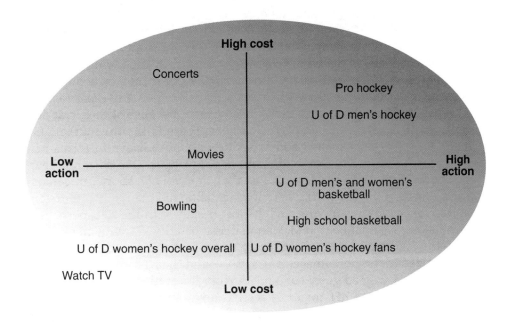

FIGURE 7.2   Product-space map of U of D women's ice hockey.

To do this, they would develop a survey (such as those described in chapter 5) to administer at athletic events on campus and at local malls. On the survey, they might ask consumers to indicate their levels of attendance at or involvement in a number of activities, including U of D events. They also might ask consumers to indicate their perception of the cost (time and money) and the excitement or action levels in the same activities. The levels are rated on a 10-point scale. Using the results, the marketers could construct a product-space map that suggests the relative positions of these activities along the dimensions of cost and excitement or action.

The results might look like those in figure 7.2. Note that U of D women's ice hockey had a position in the minds of "overall" area consumers that reflected low cost but also low action. Respondents saw the games as more exciting than watching television, but much less exciting than high school basketball. But suppose the marketers also noticed that the U of D women's hockey position had a more favorable position among consumers who indicated a high interest in or involvement with women's hockey (women's hockey "fans"). For these people, U of D women's hockey was low cost and high action. This would be even more significant if consumers with high interest or involvement in other activities (say, bowling) didn't have the same sense of increased "action" in their sport. It would indicate that U of D women's hockey had real upside potential for a shift in image and position. Women's hockey might simply need more aggressive promotion of its excitement and action.

Product-space maps can also be useful in conceptualizing market segments. The U of D research might include demographic information that reveals different market segments for women's hockey. For instance, U of D students will likely perceive women's hockey as a low-cost product because their ID cards get them into all games for free. Older people outside a five-mile (eight-kilometer) radius, however, may mistakenly believe that U of D women's hockey costs as much as U of D men's hockey. Here is a segment worth addressing, because research shows that women's athletics generally attract a wider age range of fans than men's athletics do. (51)

Category Positioning

Sergio Zyman had many interesting episodes in his career with Coca-Cola. One of the most instructive was the "born to die" campaign of Tab Clear, a product few people remember. In the 1980s, Coke had spent millions developing Diet Coke, so why would they introduce Tab Clear, which seemed to be just another diet drink? In appearance, Tab Clear was a competitor to Crystal Pepsi. But Crystal Pepsi was not a diet drink; it was intended to compete with Seven Up and Sprite. As Zyman explained, Tab Clear was an attempt to reposition a category: "Our goal was to kill the whole clear cola category by muddying it up." And this is exactly what happened. "Consumers could never figure out if they were supposed to buy clear colas because of what they tasted like—as a matter of fact, Tab Clear tasted nothing like Crystal Pepsi—or because of what they looked like, or because of their calorie content. So, very shortly, both Crystal Pepsi and Tab Clear disappeared from the market." (52)

Sport marketers talk a great deal about positioning, but always in terms of discrete products—this team or that price of equipment or that league. One does not hear discussion of repositioning whole categories, such as a whole level of a sport. But consider Vince McMahon and the short life of the XFL. Perhaps McMahon did not really intend to compete against the NFL for the long haul. Although he lost money with the XFL, perhaps he knew it would fail all along. Could it be that McMahon developed the XFL with an eye on category repositioning—in this case the whole category of professional football? Vince McMahon may have recognized that media images of the WWF and the NFL were converging—lots of hooligan bad boys; a few good guys; soap opera story lines; high-tech, glitzy productions; and gratuitous sexuality. The XFL might be seen as an attempt to pull pro football's image even closer to that of professional wrestling. That would be bad for the NFL and good for the WWF. In short, the XFL may have been an attempt to reposition the category.

Brands and Branding

Over the years, coaches, writers, and fans have discussed certain "brands" of play—the Notre Dame brand of football, the Soviet brand of hockey, the Brazilian brand of soccer. In recent years, the concept of "branding" has swept the sport industry. Branding is both a means and an end to product differentiation. Brands can be created or retained in the names, marks, designs, or images of any one or more of the product elements described in this chapter. Nike successfully built its overall brand (the "Swoosh") as well as special product brands (Air Jordan). Phil Knight explained how the ad firm of Wieden & Kennedy helped to build the special image of the Nike brand that was so hot in the late 1980s and early 1990s: "They spend countless hours trying to figure out what the product is, what the message is, what the theme is, what the athletes are all about, what emotion is involved. They try to extract something that's meaningful, an honest message that is true to who we are." (53)

Over the last decade, the king of sport branding has been ESPN, whose parent corporation, Disney, pushed the ESPN brand as a major weapon in its marketplace showdown with Fox and Time Warner. ESPN brand products have included the following:

- ✦ ESPN flagship network with its SportsCenter core
- ✦ ESPN2, ESPN News, and ESPNU
- ✦ ESPN Radio
- ✦ ESPN Sports Zone Web site
- ✦ ESPN Espy Awards show
- ✦ ESPN *The Magazine*

- ✦ ESPN CDs and video games
- ✦ ESPN Zone restaurants

ESPN, like Nike, was very conscious about building brand equity, a crucial concept for sport marketers. On its face, brand equity is a relatively simple concept: the added value, or equity, that a certain product has by virtue of its brand name. Coca-Cola, Disney, and ESPN are good examples. Put their name or image on a product and it is worth more than a generic product of similar quality. Why? Because Coke, Disney, and ESPN have spent a great deal of time and money building brand equity.

Several components of brand equity have special interest to sport marketers, especially in events where the "product" is an intangible perception or memory:

Name recognition or awareness

Strong mental or emotional associations

Perceived brand quality

Strong customer loyalty

The successful men's and women's hockey teams at the University of New Hampshire are branded together on these combined pocket schedules.

Courtesy of the University of New Hampshire Athletic Department

Marketers can build brand equity through any of the various product elements. Even the strongest organizations have analyzed their brand equity. In 2005, for instance, the National Football League hired a specialty firm to study its brand presence and strength. One of the outcomes was a "brand book" with rules to govern the use of NFL images in any sponsors' ads. Such strategies will be discussed in detail in chapter 8. (54)

Product and Brand Cycles

Product and brand strategies must consider various stages in the life of any product, product element, or brand. Some theorists have referred to these stages as the product life cycle, with several standard stages:

Introduction

Growth

Maturity

Decline

Other theorists have attacked the notion of a standard life cycle as an unsupported concept that, in the worst scenarios, could become a self-fulfilling prophecy whereby managers would reduce support for a product because it had reached its "decline" stage. Sport products vary in the actual shape of their developmental and life cycles. The following are speculations about sport product life cycles:

- ✦ Game forms that enjoy any kind of maturity seem to be resistant to decline. Baseball's popularity hit a low in the 1960s and early 1970s, rebounded in the 1980s, and then had to rebound from the strike of 1994. But MLB is in solid shape. On the other hand, many people wondered if the NHL would stagger from the lockout in 2004-2005. NASCAR had a long, flat maturity. The last few years have seen a huge spike of "rejuvenation." Both Arena Football and the WNBA have moved beyond the introduction stage. What will their growth curves look like?
- ✦ Teams and franchises have much more volatile and unpredictable cycles than those of their overall sports. Team and franchise cycles are more subject to owner or management whims, economic downturns, and labor issues.

+ Equipment cycles appear more technology-driven than apparel cycles.
+ Apparel cycles blend the more stable trends in game forms with the wide fluctuations of fashion.

The concepts of product or brand life and competitive cycles deserve much greater attention from researchers. There may well be discernible trends of importance to practicing marketers. (55)

Wrap-Up

In this chapter, we have begun our investigation of the marketing mix, or the five Ps of sport marketing—product, price, promotion, place, and public relations. We reviewed the features that make the sport product unique and outlined its various components. These include the game or event and its stars, equipment and apparel, novelties and fantasies, the venue, personnel and process, the ticket, electronic and digital products, and finally the organization itself. We also discussed the intricacies of product development, including developing new products, positioning, branding, and the product life cycle. As much as possible, products must be shaped to meet the needs and wants of the consumers targeted in prior research.

Activities

1. Investigate the Web site of your favorite sport organization. List the various product components (as discussed in this chapter) that you find on the Web site.

2. Fans are a key part of the core sport product. Develop a set of policies and plans for ensuring that your organization's fans or consumers will be a source of positive energy and not vulgar profanity or complaints. Explain how you will train and use stadium or arena staff, coaches, and players in this effort. You may want to consider employing ideas from the sidebar on reciprocity in chapter 4.

3. Try your hand at a new product image, mark, or logo for the merchandise of your favorite sport organization. What are the key elements of this image that you think will make it attractive to consumers? How will you protect your product's value? Use ideas from readings (note page numbers).

4. Prepare an outline that shows at least three dimensions on which brand image differs between Nike, the World Wrestling Federation, and the WNBA.

Your Marketing Plan

1. Briefly outline a new digital, virtual, or interactive product for your organization (perhaps to be placed on your Web site).

2. Create a product-space map, like the one in figure 7.2, that indicates where your product can be positioned in a competitive marketplace.

Chapter 8

Managing Sport Brands

Jay Gladden, PhD

University of Massachusetts at Amherst

Objectives

✦ Discuss the full scope and importance of brand management and branding in the sport setting.

✦ Demonstrate an understanding of how brand equity is developed in a variety of sport settings.

✦ Identify and discuss the sources of brand associations for teams, athletes, agencies, and other sport entities.

And the World's Strongest Team Brand Is . . .

Not the Los Angeles Lakers, the Dallas Cowboys, or even the New York Yankees. Think globally! Think soccer, or "football," as it is called throughout the rest of the world. Manchester United of the English Premier League is arguably the world's strongest sport team brand. In 2002, "Man U" reported a profit of $50.4 million. (1) This was driven by the fact that Man U's average attendance was 67,160, they received $90 million in revenues from media deals, and Nike signed a 10-year sponsorship contract with Man U worth $473 million—or an average of $47.3 million per year! (2)

As a testament to their popularity, starting in 2003, Man U took part in the "ChampionsWorld Tour," in which teams from around the world play a series of exhibition or "friendly" matches in North America. In 2003, average attendance for ChampionsWorld Tour events featuring Man U was 52,821—in 2004, the average attendance was 39,811. (3) By comparison, the average attendance for Major League Soccer (MLS) in 2004 was 15,559. (4) In a country like the United States where soccer is arguably seen as the "fifth major sport" behind football, basketball, baseball, and hockey, these attendance numbers are a testament to the popularity of Man U as a professional sport brand. By comparison, if the New York Yankees played a series of games in Europe, would they draw 40,000 to 50,000 fans? Not likely.

Since the mid-1990s *branding* has become a very popular term in the spectator sport industry. Almost every day, it seems, you can read about a different sport organization embarking on some new "branding" initiatives. The fact that such initiatives are occurring is a very good sign for the sport industry. Chapter 1 of this book described the sport marketing myopia that has often pervaded the sport industry. This myopia was characterized by a short-term focus on revenue generation rather than a long-term focus on developing loyal customers. Sport organizations that look at themselves as "brands" to be managed are taking an important step away from such myopic tendencies. As you will soon see, branding is vitally important to the long-term health and success of a sport organization.

This chapter begins by answering the question, What is branding? In doing so, it provides an understanding of branding and brand management with a particular focus on the spectator sport setting. Following the introduction and definitions of concepts, a more in-depth discussion on the development of brand equity is provided. Central to this discussion is a focus on how brand associations are formed by organizations involved with sport, including teams, sponsors, athletes and sport management and marketing agencies. Throughout this chapter, examples from the sport setting are provided so that you can see how these concepts are at work in the sport setting.

So what is branding? Branding starts with a brand, which includes the name, logo, and symbols associated with the sport organization. (5) For example, the Nike brand name and the Nike "Swoosh" are both very important components of the Nike brand. Similarly, both the nickname "Liberty" and the logo that includes a version of the Statue of Liberty are both important components of the WNBA's New York Liberty "brand." Ultimately, the brand name and marks associated with a sport organization provide a point of differentiation from the other sport products that exist in the marketplace. These names and marks are important facets of branding as evidenced by the fact that more than half of the teams in the NBA, NFL, NHL, and MLB have modified their uniforms (and sometimes their logos) since 1995. (6)

However, it would be myopic to think of branding as simply the management and manipulation of an organization's marks. The brand name, logos, marks, and colors of a sport organization serve as a starting point in the brand management process. They serve to trigger other feelings and attitudes toward the sport organization. When a Boston Red Sox fan hears the team's name mentioned, a wide variety of thoughts may come to mind, including the Red Sox 2004 World Series victory (its first in 86 years!), the fabled "Green Monster" outfield wall at their home field Fenway Park, or great players who have worn a Red Sox uniform such as Ted Williams and Carlton Fisk. The brand is, as author Daryl Travis suggested, "like a badge that lends you a certain identity." (7) Thus, a key point about branding is that it goes much deeper than the names, symbols, and marks of an organization. Branding really is about what a customer thinks and feels when she sees the marks of a particular brand.

As it relates to the sport setting, what a consumer thinks and feels toward a sport-related brand is developed based on experiences that consumers have when consuming sport (for example, attending a game, watching a game on television, or watching highlights of a game on ESPN.com). The benefits provided by consuming sport are much more experiential than tangible. You cannot touch or taste an actual baseball game, whereas you can taste the toothpaste you put into your mouth. Additionally, what makes the experience of consuming sport so unique is the emotion tied to sport. Sport has the ability to trigger emotions that are arguably not like other leisure or entertainment products available. Can you think of an experience that triggers your emotions (good or bad) like watching your favorite team play its rival in a game that has play-off implications?

Being experiential and emotional actually lends sport organizations some advantage here. As author Marc Gobé stated:

What other product can produce the thrill and excitement of sport?
© Human Kinetics

> In this hypercompetitive marketplace where goods and services alone are no longer enough to attract a new market or event to maintain existing markets or clients, I believe that it is the *emotional* aspect of products and their distribution systems that will be the key difference between consumers' ultimate choice and the price that they will pay. By emotional I mean how a brand engages consumers on the level of the senses and emotions; how a brand comes to life for people and forges a deeper, lasting connection. (8)

Think about your favorite team for a minute. Beyond its name and marks, how long does it take you to come up with a memory that has some emotion attached to it? Spectator sport is quite unique in the variety of emotions that are generated and in the level of emotional involvement that consumers have with their favorite sport team or athlete brands. This emotional involvement can also be favorably transferred to sponsors of sport. How else can you explain the fact that many NASCAR fans will buy only the products of the corporations that sponsor their favorite drivers? Logic goes out the window when brands are able to create such emotional connections.

This, then, is one of the key goals of branding—to create such a strong impression in the consumers' minds that when they see or hear something that includes a brand's name or see its logo, marks, or colors, they experience intense positive feelings. As Declan Bolger, chief marketing officer for the Portland Trail Blazers, put it: "People make decisions based on emotion, and reinforce them with logic." (9) If a sport brand triggers positive emotions, it will be easier for the sport marketer to engage fans and consumers in the products of that sport brand.

Importance of Brand Equity

When a sport organization is able to achieve a strong image in the consumer's mind, it realizes brand equity. According to David Aaker, a leading expert on branding, brand equity is "a set of assets and liabilities linked to a brand, its name and symbol, that add to or subtract from the value provided by a product or service to a firm and/or that firm's customers." (10) Strong positive emotional connections formed between the fan and a team are an example of the assets to which Aaker refers. The New York Yankees' 26 World Series wins have helped create a number of strong emotional connections with the Yankees brand that can be seen as assets. However, the sport marketer must also be wary of creating negative feelings toward the sport organization. For example, during the late 1990s and early 2000s, the NBA's Portland Trail Blazers experienced several incidents in which players were arrested for running afoul of the law. This repeated criminal behavior created some negative impressions in consumers' minds that could be viewed as liabilities linked to the brand.

Benefits of Brand Equity

When a team such as Manchester United (mentioned at the beginning of this chapter) is able to generate a wealth of assets linked to its brand, the team is thought to have high brand equity. This is the ultimate goal for the sport franchise manager because there are a number of benefits to having high levels of brand equity. Perhaps most important, the loyalty to the team brand increases when brand equity levels are high. Which team has higher brand equity—Major League Baseball's Chicago Cubs or Kansas City Royals? Even though the Cubs have not won a World Series in around 100 years, they regularly sell out games at their home field, Wrigley Field. In contrast, the Kansas City Royals struggle to fill half of their stadium, Kaufman Stadium, for most games. Although neither team has had great success recently, the Cubs arguably have a stronger brand because of unique brand assets such as Wrigley Field, which exists in a nice Chicago neighborhood about one mile (1.6 kilometers) from Lake Michigan. Achieving high levels of brand loyalty allows the sport marketer to realize increases in revenue through ticket and merchandise sales. Brand loyalty also typically results in a larger viewing audience for events, which in turn allows the sport organization to realize higher broadcast fees for the rights to televise their games or events and attract more sponsors looking for widespread television exposure in a sponsorship.

The case of the Cubs also underscores the fact that winning is *not* the only important factor in the creation of brand loyalty. In fact, research has documented that factors other than winning are more predictive of brand loyalty for North American professional sport teams. (11) Again referring back to chapter 1, do you remember how a "winning is everything" mentality was an example of sport marketing myopia? Researchers have actually documented that winning is *not* everything and that other factors contribute to the realization of ticket sales, corporate sponsorship sales, and other positive revenue outcomes. (12) In fact, there are a variety of ways in which sport marketers can create equity for their brands, many of which are discussed later in this chapter. The important point here is that brand equity creates brand loyalty. As chapters 12 and 13 point out, relationship marketing is central to the development of loyal customers. Similarly, building relationships with the customers of a sport organization can also help enhance the brand.

Less Drastic Revenue Declines When the Team Loses

Because strong brands have high levels of loyalty, they are better able to withstand downturns in fortunes on the field. Although winning is not the only creator of brand equity, there is no question that teams reap short-term benefits when they win. However, how many teams are able to compete for championships year in and year out? If you said "not many," you are right. Very few teams can attain high levels of success over prolonged periods of time. The myopic sport marketer sees the organization's fortunes tied to the performance of the team on the field. The sport marketer who adopts a longer-term view, however, focuses on other things that can be done to enhance brand equity so that when the team loses, fortunes do not drastically decline.

Again, take the Chicago Cubs as an example. Here is a team that has not won a World Series in almost 100 years, yet still draws large crowds for its home games. The Cubs made the play-offs in 2003 and attracted 2,962,630 fans to Wrigley Field. However, just three years earlier, coming off a season in which they lost 95 games, the Cubs lost 97 games, but still drew 2,734,511 fans. (13) So yes, performance may affect attendance, but when a team has high brand equity and high brand loyalty, the dropoffs are much less extreme. Figure 8.1 depicts the revenues over time of two teams that experience cycles of winning and losing, one with high brand equity and the other with low brand equity. Where brand equity is high (Team A), revenue declines are less drastic over time as the team's fortunes change. Meanwhile, where brand equity is lower, much more drastic revenue changes are seen as the team wins and loses (Team B).

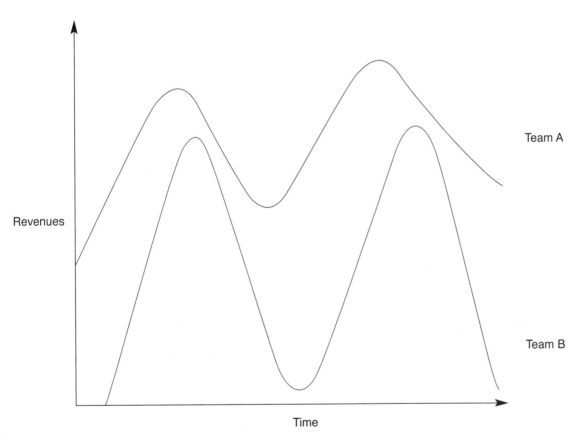

FIGURE 8.1 Revenue fortunes for teams with high and low brand equity.

Ability to Charge Price Premiums

Another potential benefit of high brand equity is the ability to charge price premiums. (14) In the sport setting, in which it is often challenging to have revenues exceed expenses, this benefit can be particularly important. Team Marketing Report annually publishes a report called the *Fan Cost Index,* which highlights both the average ticket price for a professional sporting event and the average cost of attending for a family of four. Table 8.1 documents the five teams with the highest ticket prices in Major League Baseball, the National Hockey League, the National Football League, and the National Hockey League. Although some teams regularly made the play-offs prior to 2004, such as the New England Patriots, Los Angeles

✦ Table 8.1 Teams With the Highest Ticket Prices in the Major Professional Sport Leagues for Teams Playing in 2004

NFL	Average price	NBA	Average price	NHL	Average price	MLB	Average price
New England Patriots	$75.33	Los Angeles Lakers	$75.40	Detroit Red Wings	$57.11	Boston Red Sox	$40.77
Washington Redskins	$68.12	New York Knicks	$64.10	Philadelphia Flyers	$57.06	Chicago Cubs	$28.45
Kansas City Chiefs	$67.26	Sacramento Kings	$63.20	Toronto Maple Leafs	$56.90	Philadelphia Phillies	$26.08
New York Giants	$66.67	Houston Rockets	$59.05	New Jersey Devils	$54.67	New York Yankees	$24.86
New York Jets	$66.39	Boston Celtics	$57.02	Boston Bruins	$54.10	Seattle Mariners	$24.01

Data from www.teammarketing.com/fci.cfm. September 24, 2004.

Lakers, Detroit Red Wings, and New York Yankees, quite a few teams, such as the Washington Redskins, Boston Celtics, and Philadelphia Phillies, had not been a part of the play-offs for quite a while prior to 2004.

Although the team with the highest average ticket price in each league had experienced significant success prior to 2004, several important indicators also support the notion that teams with high brand equity are able to charge price premiums. For example, the average Red Sox ticket is more than $12 more expensive than the average Cubs ticket (the second-highest average ticket price). Both teams play in similar stadiums, have high levels of brand equity, and experienced significant success in 2003 (both losing in the League Championship Series). Yet the Red Sox were able to charge $12 more per ticket. This is a testament to the strength of the Boston Red Sox brand throughout New England. In looking at that list, we are not surprised to see teams such as the Celtics, Maple Leafs, and Giants on the list given their long histories within their respective leagues.

More Corporate Interest

As noted in chapter 13, corporate sponsorship is an ever-increasing presence in sport today. Although corporations clearly see the benefits in this marketing method, another reason for the increased presence may be sport organizations' efforts to regularly seek new revenue streams. However, more events than ever are looking for sponsorships, and sponsors are getting more discerning about which events they sponsor. One factor that sponsors may consider is the strength of the sport organization's brand. For example, NASCAR sponsors realize that both the governing body (NASCAR) and a number of the individual drivers (Jeff Gordon, Jimmie Johnson, Dale Earnhardt Jr.) have high levels of brand equity. One of the contributing factors to this high brand equity is the emotional connection and commitment that the fans have toward the race teams. As a result, sponsors are attracted to NASCAR teams because they know these brands hold powerful places in the minds of consumers.

Sport organizations with high brand equity take advantage of the fact that many corporations might be interested in becoming a sponsor by increasing the price of the sponsorship package. Think for a minute . . . what sport event or organization can charge the most for a sponsorship? If you said the Olympic Games and NASCAR, you are correct. Taking the Olympic Games as an example, the International Olympic Committee (which oversees the Olympic Movement and has the responsibility for selling Olympics sponsorships) is able to charge approximately $60 million to be a sponsor of the Olympics for a four-year period! Similarly, in 2003 NASCAR signed a 10-year, $750 million deal with Nextel to become the title sponsor of the NASCAR Championship. (15) Obviously, NASCAR's high levels of brand equity have helped contribute to the willingness of Nextel to pay such a huge rights fee.

Licensing and Merchandising Opportunities

Sport organizations with strong brands are also better able to develop brand extensions, or to use "a brand name established in one product class to enter another product class." (16) For sport organizations, this means using the organization's name to launch new products to enhance revenue streams. Some sport organizations have taken advantage of their brand strength to sell team-logoed merchandise in a team-owned merchandise store, open restaurants bearing the organization's name, and create television programming and even channels bearing the organization's name. For example, the Pittsburgh Pirates have "Pirates Clubhouse Stores" from which they sell Pirates logoed merchandise. At the league level, the National Basketball Association has opened not only a merchandise store (the NBA Store), but also a restaurant (NBA City). Adopting a little different perspective, the NBA has also used its brand to extend into professional women's basketball (with the WNBA), and into minor league basketball (with the National Basketball Development League). At perhaps an even grander level, the National Football League and the National Basketball League both have created cable television stations (the NFL Network and NBA.com TV, respectively).

How Brand Equity Is Developed

Now that we have established the important benefits of brand equity (and their relationship to long-term revenue generation!), you are probably thinking, OK, how is brand equity developed? That is a good question. According to brand researcher Kevin Keller, there are essentially two key components to developing brand equity: (1) the creation of awareness about the brand and (2) the creation of a brand image. (17) For example, think about your favorite professional athlete for a minute. First, and most obviously, you are aware that the athlete exists. This is brand awareness. The second step is a little more challenging. What adjectives come to mind when you think of that athlete? Or, why is that athlete your favorite? Your answer probably has something to do with the way the person plays the sport or his or her personality both in and out of competition, right? The combination of these elements is what we call the brand image.

Brand Awareness

As brand researcher David Aaker put it, "an unknown brand usually has little chance." (18) If a potential consumer is not aware that a minor league hockey franchise exists 20 miles (32 kilometers) from her home, then the minor league hockey franchise has no brand awareness. For this reason, brand awareness is often seen as the starting point in developing brand equity. The easiest way to define brand awareness is to refer to it as *the ability of a consumer to name the brand's existence when its product category is mentioned.* For example, if we were to ask a resident of Charlotte, North Carolina, to name all of the professional sport franchises in the area, and he did not name minor league baseball's Charlotte Knights, then the Knights would not have brand awareness.

The two most important components to building brand equity are brand awareness and brand image; brand image cannot be developed, however, without brand awareness. Developing brand awareness is typically not an issue for major league sport franchises such as NBA, NFL, NHL, MLB, and MLS teams. However, it does become more challenging for events, facilities, and minor league sport franchises. Additionally, a primary challenge for a sport agent representing a new athlete is to create brand awareness for her client. Similarly, you may be familiar with "Heisman Hype," in which colleges and universities undertake publicity campaigns to promote their star athletes for college football's most outstanding player award. In 2002, the University of Oregon purchased advertising space in New York's Times Square to promote its Heisman candidate, Joey Harrington. This is a great example of an effort to develop brand awareness.

The development of brand awareness is also very important for corporations sponsoring events. Sponsors pay to be associated with athletes, teams, events, and leagues (often called "sport properties"). Part of their expectation is likely to be that fans of those sport properties will feel better about the corporate sponsor because they are supporting the property. Such a transfer of goodwill cannot happen if the consumer is not aware of a corporation's sponsorship efforts. If you have even the most remote interest in professional race car driving, you are probably aware that Nextel is the sponsor of the overall points championship. However, are you aware of the other NASCAR sponsors? What about the individual team sponsors? How many of Dale Earnhardt Jr's sponsors can you name? For this reason, sponsorship evaluation usually involved measuring the level of awareness of the sponsorship.

Brand Image

Although the concept of brand awareness is fairly easy to grasp, understanding brand image is more difficult. This is because brand image is the cumulative impact of all the associations with a particular brand. (19) Take out a piece of paper and think about your favorite team. Now, time yourself. Spend one minute writing down all of the words and phrases that come to mind when you think of that team.

The words and phrases that you have written down are called brand associations, because they represent the thoughts that the mention of a brand name triggers. If you were thinking of the New York Yankees, you may have been thinking such things as "world champions," because of the many World Series the Yankees have won. Or, you may have been thinking about Monument Park, the area in the outfield of Yankee Stadium where statues of Yankee greats stand. In both of these cases, these are unique, strong, and favorable thoughts. This is the goal in developing a brand image—to develop unique, strong, and favorable brand associations. Marketers of sport may have an advantage when it comes to creating unique associations. Where else is the product so packed with drama because of an unknown outcome? Where else is there such high emotional involvement between the consumer (the fan) and the product (the game or event)?

The key is making sure that these brand associations are both strong and favorable. This is not necessarily the easiest task given the fact that the outcome of the event is unknown. And, as noted earlier in the text, you cannot control when a team performs well, or when an athlete gets hurt. In an ideal world, we would be able to know when the team we were marketing was going to succeed. That way, we would know that fans would have strong and favorable associations with winning. However, the team's ability to win in the current or upcoming year is undetermined. Thus, although winning most certainly can create a strong, unique, and favorable brand association, sport marketers should focus their energies on nurturing this association in advance of a team's actual performance.

These young fans have already developed loyalty to a brand image.
© Getty Images

One aspect of winning can serve as a valuable brand association—past success. After Michael Jordan retired from the Chicago Bulls in 1998, the Bulls immediately entered a rebuilding era. However, to date, they have been successful in playing before capacity crowds despite the fact that their record has not been very good. This may be due to their marketing efforts, which have reminded fans of the six NBA world championships that the Bulls won in the 1990s and suggested that now is the time to get tickets before they become good again. Thus, a *tradition* of past success can be a very important brand association. Given the traditions of competing for national championships at schools such as Duke University (men's basketball), the University of Michigan (football), and the University of Connecticut (women's and men's basketball), fans of these schools have strong associations with the past accomplishments of their teams.

Beyond success and tradition, a variety of other sources of brand association exist in sport. A sampling of these will now be discussed.

Sources of Brand Association With Teams

The success of the team is one source of brand association, but other aspects of the team and its marketing, promotion, and publicity efforts can develop strong brand associations. These include, but are not limited to, the following:

- ◆ Logo, marks, nickname, and mascot
- ◆ Owner(s)
- ◆ Players
- ◆ Head coaches
- ◆ Rivalries
- ◆ Entertainment package surrounding the game or event
- ◆ Stadium or arena in which a team plays

Although branding is more than just managing the organization's logo, the logo, marks, nickname, and mascot can all create strong, unique, and favorable brand associations. Take the team colors as an example. Los Angeles Lakers fans would probably mention the purple and yellow uniform colors, Oakland Raider fans often refer to their team as the "silver and black," and University of Michigan fans have strong associations with the "maize and blue." When creating or changing a logo, teams should take great care to consider the ways brand associations can be developed. For example, should the nickname represent a unique feature about the location of the team, as is the case with the Phoenix Suns (referring to the perpetual sunny, warm weather in Phoenix) or the Pittsburgh Steelers (hearkening back to Pittsburgh's history as a steel town)? Or, should the logo contain colors that are fashionable and attractive (such as the San Jose Sharks using teal in the early 1990s when that color was popular)? Or, should the nickname be easily translatable into a mascot that can create strong brand associations in the minds of kids (as is the case with Benny the Bull, the mascot of the Chicago Bulls)? All of these things need to be considered when changing the logo or nickname.

Very often the owner(s) of the sport franchise are the most visible team personnel aside from the head coach and the players on the team. Through their actions, owners can generate positive brand associations. For example, when Ted Leonsis purchased the Washington Capitals (of the NHL), when Howard Schultz purchased the Seattle Supersonics (of the NBA), and when John Henry and Tom Werner purchased the Boston Red Sox (of MLB), they all publicly stated initiatives geared toward pleasing their fans or making their fans prouder of the team. In a similar vein, Mark Cuban receives and responds to e-mails from fans of the Dallas Mavericks (of the NBA) on a daily basis. By doing this, he creates the impression that he cares about the fans' opinions, thus creating a favorable brand association. What about George Steinbrenner, the owner of MLB's New York Yankees? Although baseball fans who do not like the Yankees tend to have negative associations with Mr. Steinbrenner, Yankee fans tend to have very favorable associations with him because he is committed to winning championships and does everything in his power to do so.

A more obvious source of brand associations for teams is the players themselves. However, a variety of associations can be developed in association with the players. For example, associations could be formed based on how a player actually performs. Michael Jordan was perceived to walk on air, particularly in his early years with the NBA's Chicago Bulls. Shaquille O'Neal of the NBA's Miami Heat is a supremely gifted center who just happens to be seven feet (213 centimeters) tall and weigh more than 300 pounds (136 kilograms)—thus, his size factors into the associations. Associations can also be formed around a player off the court. For example, not only is Tim Duncan's (of the NBA's San Antonio Spurs) on-court play a source of positive associations, but his off-the-court behavior is as well. Duncan was named the 2004 "Outstanding Young San Antonian" by the Rotary Club of San Antonio, largely because of his efforts in raising money for breast cancer research and supporting educational and athletic programs for youth. (20) In doing this, fans of the Spurs have another reason to form strong associations with Tim Duncan. Not only is he a great player, but he may also be perceived as a "good guy" or as charitable for these endeavors off the court.

Similarly, the head coach of a team can serve as a significant source of brand associations. If you are a football fan, think about the brand associations that coach Bill Parcells of the Dallas Cowboys generates: very successful coach, strict disciplinarian, very direct and honest with the media. Similar to players, the potential for associations with coaches goes beyond their actual performance on the field. Given the fact that high-profile college athletes play for their teams only for a maximum of four years, head coaches can be an even more important source of brand associations on college campuses. For example, Tom Brennan, the University of Vermont men's basketball coach, is a popular figure in Vermont, not only because of his team's success on the court, but also because he cohosts a humorous morning show on the radio. Similarly, Joe Paterno provides a very strong association with Penn State football. As Guido D'Elia, Penn State's director of brand communications, put it: "The bell ringer for the [Penn State] brand is a 77-year-old man who believes in doing things the right way win, lose, or draw. That is respected around the nation and that is typical at PSU." (21) What about Pat Summitt? The women's basketball coach at Tennessee is such a popular figure in Tennessee and women's basketball circles that she has her own Web site: www.coachsummitt.com.

A word of caution must be offered with respect to players and coaches as sources of brand associations. Player mobility at the professional team sport level is as great as ever, with few players being a member of the same team for their entire careers. Further, many high-profile collegiate athletes now stay at their universities for only one or two years before turning professional. This means that a team should not singularly focus its brand-building efforts on one player, particularly when that player's contract is nearing an end. Professional and collegiate coaches are also quite mobile these days. Thus, although they can be tremendous sources of associations, their departure can cause a significant loss of brand associations that ultimately hurts the team's brand. One way to counteract such departures is to understand if and how the player or coach played a role in building the team brand and then sign players and coaches who either have the potential to build similar associations, or have the potential to build their own unique and favorable associations. Does this mean that owners and athletics directors should consider the marketing implication of their coaching decisions? Based on the preceding discussion of how they create brand associations, the answer is yes.

The opponents of a particular team can create strong brand associations for the team. For example, the Boston Red Sox–New York Yankees rivalry serves as a very strong brand association for both MLB teams. Such rivalries and the great games that are played between teams (such as the historic 2004 American League Championship Series in which the Red Sox won after being down three games to none) create long-lasting memories that motivate sport fans to follow teams. At the college level, rivalries exist at all levels and serve to create strong associations among not just sport fans, but all alumni. Although they play at the Division III level (the lowest level of college competition in U.S. intercollegiate athletics), the Amherst (Massachusetts) versus Williams (Massachusetts) and DePauw (Indiana) versus Wabash (Indiana) football games are so popular that they are typically televised by regional sport providers. Thus, strong brand associations can be reinforced not only by attending one of these games, but also by watching them on television all over the country.

As noted in chapter 11, the effective use of promotional elements can greatly enhance the experience people have at games. This enhancement of the entertainment package through promotional tactics such as giveaways and on-court, on-ice, or on-field promotions during time-outs and intermissions can serve to create strong brand associations. Earlier it was mentioned that the NBA's Chicago Bulls have been able to maintain very large crowds despite not having a successful team since 1998. Although their nurturing of brand associations tied to past success might be part of the reason for this, another reason could be the fact that Bulls games are highly entertaining despite the fact that the team often loses. In college athletics, several unique factors can create strong brand associations tied to teams. For example, at the University of Mississippi, "the Grove" serves as a popular tailgating area both before and after games. At Ohio State University, fans are often in the Ohio Stadium 30 to 45 minutes in advance of the game so that they can see the nationally renowned marching band enter the stadium and execute its pregame routine. Finally, where college athletic events attract large and loud student sections (such as at Duke University men's basketball games), this can also serve as a source of brand associations. In fact, when asked what would enhance their enjoyment of college athletic events, season-ticket holders (who are not students) often mention larger and louder student sections.

Another way that the entertainment experience can be enhanced is through a focus on the service elements that a consumer experiences when attending a game. Think about all of the experiences that you have when attending a game—these could theoretically form a brand association. Some facilities offer unique cuisine items at their concession stands, whereas others have unique features built into the stadiums, such as a cigar bar at the Wachovia Center in Philadelphia or a swimming pool at Chase Field in Phoenix.

Marching bands also help develop brand associations.

© Human Kinetics

Now more than ever, the stadium or arena can serve as a source of brand associations. Strong brand associations are typically formed around two types of arenas these days: (1) those with long histories and traditions and (2) new facilities that are built with many features to enhance the customer experience. Facilities such as Wimbledon (tennis), the Daytona International Speedway (auto racing), Yankee Stadium (MLB), Fenway Park (MLB), Lambeau Field (NFL), Old Trafford (English Premier League), and Notre Dame Stadium (college football) all have long histories of hosting significant sporting events. Because of the tradition associated with these venues, consumers may form strong brand associations. With the stadium construction boom that started in the early 1990s, though, there has been an increased focus on building facilities that not only generate more revenue but also have unique features that form strong brand associations. This is particularly true when considering baseball stadiums. Since 1992, stadiums such as Camden Yards (Baltimore), Jacobs Field (Cleveland), Coors Field (Denver), and Safeco Field (Seattle) have all incorporated features that are reminiscent of baseball a long time ago. Because there is no standardized size for a baseball stadium, the unique feature can be tied to the dimension of the park, such as the hill in center field at Minute Maid Park in Houston. Or, the actual location of the park can create a unique association. At both AT&T Park in San Francisco and PNC Park in Pittsburgh, home runs can land in bodies of water.

Brand Associations Based on the Benefits of Consumption

Beyond the features and aspects of the sport product, brand associations can also be developed based on the consumer needs that are satisfied or the benefits that consumption provides. For example, nostalgic (remembering and perhaps glorifying a past experience) memories can serve as a source of brand associations. Whether it be recollections of following a team with a family member or friend or remembering the elation felt when a team won a championship, nostalgic memories can serve as a strong source of association. For these reasons, a hidden benefit for teams that own or partially control their own cable networks (often called regional sport networks, or RSNs) is the ability to generate programming that will foster these nostalgic memories of team accomplishments. For example, New England Sports Network (NESN) is owned by the Boston Red Sox and distributed through cable networks for free to most of New England. That affords the Red Sox a unique opportunity to create programming (particularly in the winter months) that reminds people of the march to the 2004 World Series title.

Social benefits can also serve as a source for brand associations. A parent could form a strong association tied to a minor league baseball team because it provides a platform for the parent to do something fun with his or her children. Think about your college's or university's athletics programs. You may have some associations tied to attending games with a large group of friends.

If a person feels identification with a team, this can serve as a source of brand associations as well. Identification with a team entails several things, mostly tied to what it means to be a fan of a particular team. In the case of the Boston Red Sox, being a Red Sox fan means that you are a member of "Red Sox Nation." In essence, *Red Sox Nation* is a term that creates a sense of belonging to a group or even special "club." Up until the 2004 World Series, membership in this club meant being a part of a group that often suffered when the team failed to win a big game. However, with the 2004 World Series championship, the Red Sox Nation celebrated as a group. For example, 3.2 million people turned out for a parade in Boston to celebrate the World Series title. Just as identification can form with a team, so too can it form with a particular geographic location. In this sense, identification with a city can be exhibited by someone following a sport team. For example, someone from Chicago living in another part of the country could demonstrate to people that he is from Chicago by wearing a Chicago Cubs hat. Further, when the Cubs finally win the World Series, people will see it as a positive reflection on *their* city.

Brand Associations in Other Realms of Sport

Beyond team sport, brand management is important throughout the sport realm. For example, the development of brand associations is also important to the following segments of the industry:

✦ Sponsors
✦ Athletes
✦ Agencies
✦ Health clubs

How sponsors create brand associations   One motivation for companies to sponsor sporting events or programs is to either enhance or reinforce the brand associations with their company. This motivation is based on the belief that image attributes of the entity being sponsored can be transferred to the sponsor. A sponsor such as Gatorade or PowerAde might seek to align itself with the best college basketball or football teams to reinforce the perception that their sport drink is of high quality and used by the best athletes. Similarly, Nike, Reebok, Adidas, and others often fight for the footwear and apparel rights associated with the professional sport leagues, college athletics programs, and athletes. This is probably at least partially due to the desire to be associated with the best.

Beyond perceptions of quality, other brand associations might be transferred to the sponsor. Several classic examples include the Air Jordan basketball shoe and the Mountain Dew sponsorship of action sports. Coinciding with their launch of the Air Jordan basketball shoe (containing Nike's then-revolutionary air-pocket technology), Nike ran an advertisement featuring a young Jordan running and jumping to the background noise of a jet engine. (22) This ad provided the nexus for Nike to create the perception that the Air Jordan helped people jump higher. Whereas Nike used an athlete endorsement to create a brand association, Mountain Dew used a new sporting genre to completely redefine its image. Dating back to 1960, Mountain Dew was perceived to be a drink of people in rural areas (mostly the southern United States). In 1992, Mountain Dew launched a new campaign under the tag line "Do the Dew" that featured people taking part in risk-taking activities such as skydiving. They followed this up by becoming one of the first sponsors to get involved with the emerging action sports captured by events such as the X Games and the Dew Action Sports Tour (note the title sponsor). By undertaking these actions, Mountain Dew completely redefined itself as cool, edgy, and exciting. (23)

The Air Jordan and Mountain Dew cases demonstrate how the image of a sport entity can help create strong, unique, and favorable associations for the sport brand. They also raise a practical point for all sponsorship decision makers: The image of the sport entity you are thinking about sponsoring should have the potential to either reinforce or positively alter your brand associations as a sponsor. (24) Think about how the "Priceless" advertising campaign has used

Are people who snowboard more likely to drink Mountain Dew? That's the idea Mountain Dew hopes to convey by its sponsorship of "extreme" sports.
© Photodisc

MasterCard's different sport sponsorships (such as with Major League Baseball and the World Cup of soccer) to create associations of emotion and savoring the moment tied to the MasterCard brand. In contrast, also consider the potential for negative associations that occur when an athlete runs afoul of the law, or a college athletics program is found to have violated NCAA rules. Might this create a negative association with a sponsor by virtue of its involvement with that particular sport entity? Perhaps! Within 24 hours of the announcement that American cyclist Floyd Landis had tested positive for elevated levels of testosterone while winning the 2006 Tour de France, hearing-improvement company Phonak (the sponsor of Landis and his race team) quickly disassociated itself with Landis. Clearly, Phonak wanted to send a clear signal that it did not want to be associated with someone who does not obey the rules.

As discussed in chapter 13, successful sponsorships require a strong relationship between the buyer and the seller of the sponsorship program. For this to happen, both must receive benefits. In some cases, the sponsorship seller may receive image benefits above and beyond the cash and in-kind contributions they might receive from the sponsor. For example, take the case of the WNBA. Upon formation, their ability to secure very visible name brands such as Spalding probably also helped lend credibility to the league. On a smaller scale, think about an event in your local area, such as a road race or grassroots soccer tournament. These events probably tried to secure brand-name sponsors as a means of generating credibility for their event, particularly in their first years of existence.

Because some of these associations with corporations may be formed based on the experience that users have when consuming the brand, a new form of branding through sponsorship has emerged—branded entertainment. In the "Branded Entertainment" sidebar on page 185, author Joe Smith describes this new trend. As Smith notes, the sport industry is often considered one aspect of the larger entertainment industry when these opportunities are undertaken. Smith offers a few examples of sport-related branded entertainment activities. Can you think of others? Have you ever attended a fan festival affiliated with a pro or college team that has interactive games for people to participate in? For example, Boston College turns one of its campus recreation centers into a Fan Zone on football game days. If you walk into the Fan Zone on a football Saturday, you will see kids in line waiting to participate in different football-related activities, such as throwing a football with accuracy. This is an example of a team's branded entertainment effort. Take another example, the Richard Petty Driving Experience, in which people pay to drive a NASCAR car on a race track. This "experience" is sponsored by a variety of companies, including Good Year and DuPont. (25) As existing NASCAR sponsors, it could be argued that DuPont and Good Year are just trying to add a branded entertainment element to their involvement with auto racing.

How athletes create brand associations   As noted in the previous section, one of the associations with Michael Jordan was that he could walk on air. Other associations might have been "clutch player," "prolific scorer," and "champion" based on his style of play and his achievements. Because professional athletes can make money from corporate endorsements, having strong, unique, and favorable associations is very important for an athlete. In fact, player agents should view the players they represent as brands and attempt to develop strong brand associations with their clients.

The Jordan example illustrates the two ways athletes can generate brand associations for themselves. First, they can generate associations based on their performance in athletic competition. These associations are derived from their accomplishments, from their style of play, and from any signature moves that they create. Terrell Owens, wide receiver for the NFL's Philadelphia Eagles, will long be remembered for removing a Sharpie (note the branded sponsorship opportunity) pen from the goal post padding and signing the football he just received for a touchdown in a game. A second way that athletes can generate associations is through their actions off the court. For example, former WNBA player Rebecca Lobo undertook significant efforts to raise money for charities, earning her recognition by *USA Weekend* as one of its Most Caring Athletes in 1998. (26) In each case (Owens and Lobo), the associations serve to create an image that may or may not be appealing to sponsors.

Branded Entertainment

Joe Smith, graduate student, University of Massachusetts Sport Management Program

Bernd Schmitt opened his book *Experiential Marketing* with the following declaration: "We are in the middle of a revolution. A revolution that will render the principles and models of traditional marketing obsolete. A revolution that will change the face of marketing forever." (27) This statement, although made in 1999, remains true in today's business world for a number of reasons. Consumer behavior trends have ended the days of mass marketing and caused businesses to focus on customization and personalization. For example, the evolution of basic network television to digital cable has given viewers the ability to watch specialized channels such as the Home Shopping Network, the Game Show Network, or five different ESPN channels. The technological advances in television also allow consumers to skip commercials using digital video recorders, such as TiVo.

The latest change in consumer behavior has caused marketers to explore a new advertising medium, branded entertainment. This approach is designed to reach the consumer in a unique way that not only promotes the brand, but also provides an element of entertainment. According to Schmitt: "What they want is products, communications, and marketing campaigns that dazzle their senses, touch their hearts, and stimulate their minds." (28) *Advertising Age* coined the term "Madison + Vine" to describe this segment because of the combination of the marketing methods of Madison Avenue with the entertainment content of Hollywood and Vine. In a way, this practice is an augmentation of the product placement techniques utilized throughout television's Golden Age in the 1950s. (29)

Branded entertainment campaigns typically involve the contribution of four key players: the company building the brand, a specialized marketing agency, an entertainment sector, and a marketing medium.

✦ *Brand.* In traditional product placement marketing, a product is simply viewed on camera, and at best may be used in some way by one of the program's characters. In branded entertainment, the brand has a more interactive role. In some cases, the brand is the main character in the program, and the plot falls in line with the brand's message. In addition, companies generally enjoy a higher level of creative input with branded entertainment. For example, the 2003 Chrysler Million Dollar Film Festival was created specifically to generate awareness of the new 2004 Crossfire and 2003 Pacifica. The competition began with the submission of a short film. The 25 films selected appeared on the Chrysler Web site, where visitors had the opportunity to vote. Ten filmmakers were then selected for the semifinals where they each developed and produced a 10-minute short film that featured a Chrysler Pacifica or Chrysler Crossfire. Five finalists were invited to spend the summer at Universal Studios creating a complete feature-

film production package. The winner was then crowned at a two-day event in Toronto, Canada, and received a $1 million production-and-distribution deal. (30) The unique benefit of this campaign was that Chrysler gained the rights to 10 short films that starred one of its new car releases.

> *Suggestion for success:* As in this example, it is important that a visible parallel exists between the brand's perceived image and the entertainment medium.

✦ *Agency.* The responsibility of the marketing agency in helping create branded entertainment is to find an entertainment sector that provides a good fit with the brand and facilitate that relationship through an appropriate marketing medium. A number of companies are beginning to offer branded entertainment services. The majority of these are specialized divisions of entertainment companies, traditional advertising firms, and corporate consulting agencies. For example, Hypnotic provided the agency capabilities for the film festival case previously mentioned. The agency also developed and produced four short films for Reebok. The campaign, aimed at driving online traffic, was launched with an advertisement on CBS during Super Bowl XXXVII. Reebok noticed a substantial return with 800,000 online registrations in five months and over 15 million short film downloads. (31)

> *Suggestion for success:* In the new competitive world of advertising, it is essential that the agency ensures both a demographic and personality fit with the entertainment.

✦ *Entertainment.* The entertainment sector most commonly associated with branded entertainment is film, but campaigns are becoming apparent in sitcoms, music, fashion, gaming, and sport. For example, Jaguar partnered with Grammy-award-winning artist Sting to promote its product through a television commercial. Sting's song "Desert Rose" plays throughout the commercial. The advertisement debuted March 20, 2000, and aired in various markets worldwide. According to iMedia Connection, the partnership benefited both parties, as Sting enjoyed a hit single and Jaguar lowered the median age of its buyers by 10 years. (32)

> *Suggestion for success:* The entertainer must not sacrifice his or her content for the brand.

✦ *Medium.* A number of marketing mediums are available for these campaigns, but the most popular are television, the Internet, and video game consoles. Chrysler used a number of marketing mediums, as the films were viewed online, in movie theaters, and at car dealerships nationwide. The rapid growth in technology has allowed the Internet to enjoy a number of benefits. First, the Internet is extremely

(continued)

Managing Sport Brands ✦ 185

targeted because consumers are able to surf Web sites tailored to their unique interests. Second, the Internet enjoys the benefit of being extremely viral with the ease of sending e-mails and instant messages. For example, Burger King launched its Subservient Chicken Web site on April 7, 2004, which gave visitors the ability to ask a chicken to perform various tasks by typing words or phrases into a command box. Twenty million hits were recorded on the Subservient Chicken website within the first week of its launch. (33)

> *Suggestion for success:* The use of multiple mediums will allow the brand to generate awareness through multiple outlets.

Throughout the development of branded entertainment, companies have combined the sport and entertainment sectors under the same umbrella. Many of these campaigns are used primarily in the film, television, fashion, and music sectors. It is important to understand the benefit of sport with branded entertainment, because it can be used on multiple levels. First, brands can use sport as an entertainment medium to generate awareness. For example, companies may ride the popularity of sport video games or fantasy sports to promote their products. Second, a sport team can use other entertainment mediums to increase its perceived image. The San Francisco 49ers, for example, implemented this technique with their latest partnership with Airborne Entertainment, Inc. Fans will now have the opportunity to download 49er ringtones and wallpapers directly to their mobile phones. (34) Branded entertainment has become the latest trend in this business world revolution because of the unique approach it offers to reaching consumers.

How agencies create brand associations   Sport marketing and management agencies are typically not visible entities to the average consumer, although they are very visible behind the scenes of events—to the athletes they represent, the sponsors they are helping to activate sponsorships, or the event management crew responsible for the logistics of the event. So, how do these agencies (at which some of you will invariably be employed) generate brand associations? The easiest answer is through the clients they represent. David Falk made a name for himself as a player agent at least partially through his representation of Michael Jordan. Another answer is through the people who work for the agencies. For example, prior to his passing, Mark McCormack, founder of IMG and a sport marketing industry leader, was a strong association linked to IMG. Sport marketing agencies also generate brand associations through the way they deliver their services. For example, Velocity separates itself from other sport marketing agencies that provide corporate consultation (helping sponsors identify and leverage sponsorships) by focusing exclusively on corporate consultation and not on other areas of business such as athlete representation.

How health clubs create brand associations   Do you work out? Do you use health club services such as cardiovascular and weight equipment? If so, you are a member of the market targeted by health clubs. Some of you may be fortunate enough to have facilities on your campus that are free of charge. If so, what brand associations exist in your mind with respect to those facilities? Are they too crowded at peak times? Do they offer enough hours? Embedded in these two questions are potential associations for health clubs. Those of you who are not satisfied with your facilities on campus may have looked at health clubs in your town. If so, don't you hold brand associations with each of them? One might be big and spacious, but perhaps a little more expensive. Another might be smaller but less expensive. These perceptions represent potential associations. What about the staff at the different health clubs? Are they friendly? Are they helpful? As is the case with professional sport teams, brand associations can be formed on the basis of the service provided by the front-line personnel.

Wrap-Up

Regardless of the sport setting, hopefully you now recognize that branding entails much more than managing logos and marks. Sport organizations that successfully manage their brands create both awareness and a strong image for their products. Organizations that are successful in this endeavor will receive a variety of benefits, including increased fan or consumer loyalty and increased revenue.

Activities

1. Manchester United, Real Madrid, and Chelsea are three of the strongest professional soccer ("football" outside the US) brands. Visit their Web sites: www.manutd.com; www.realmadrid.com; and www.chelseafc.com and identify how the Web sites are used to create, reinforce, and nurture strong, favorable, and unique brand associations.

2. Think for a minute: what are the brand associations with your school's athletic program? A useful way to do this is to ask some friends what comes to mind when they think of your school's athletic teams. It may also be useful to focus in on one team in particular. Once you have your list prepared, identify which of these are strong, unique, and favorable. Are there negative associations that need to be overcome?

3. Based on your assessment of the strong positive and negative associations with your school's athletic program, develop three strategies to either nurture these brand associations or to overcome the negative brand associations.

4. Let's say that Major League Baseball has decided to put an expansion franchise in Portland, Oregon. What would be a good nickname for that team? Why would that be a good nickname? (Hint: the answer needs to have something to do with brand associations.)

Your Marketing Plan

1. Analyze the name and logo of your product. Does it trigger positive memories in consumers? If not, should it be changed?

2. Identify the various associations that are created by your product. Are they positive or are they negative? Are they unique? Develop strategies to reinforce and nurture the positive associations and brainstorm what must be done to manage the negative associations.

Chapter 9

Licensed and Branded Merchandise

Dan Covell

Western New England College

Objectives

✦ To understand the structure of the licensor–
  licensee relationship.

✦ To recognize the various segments of the
  licensed and branded merchandise industry.

✦ To realize the importance of licensed and
  branded merchandise for revenue generation,
  the development of organizational brand equity,
  and the enhancement of fan identification.

✦ To identify the impact of changing styles and
  trends and of manufacturer and organizational
  competition on the licensed and branded merchandise industry.

Throwbacks

The throwback craze, a fashion trend popularizing the old uniforms and styles from teams, leagues, and years gone by, has been a smash hit in the apparel business. Howard Smith, Major League Baseball's senior VP for merchandising, stated, "We haven't witnessed a trend this far-reaching in our business in a long time." (1) Companies such as Stall & Dean of Brockton, Massachusetts, and family-owned Mitchell & Ness (M&N) of Philadelphia specialize in creating pricey, authentic replica, licensed versions of old Major League Baseball (MLB), National Basketball Association (NBA), National Football League (NFL), National Hockey League (NHL), and American Basketball Association (ABA) uniforms and warm-ups from various defunct pro and amateur teams. These firms have barely been able to keep up with demand, much of which has been prompted by high-profile hip-hop performers and professional athletes.

The sartorial efforts of these famous consumers reintroduced to the world the Houston Astros' red, yellow, and orange rainbow; the #25 Jose Cruz version worn in 1975 runs $400 (which, noted *Sports Illustrated*'s Steve Rushin, "makes Joseph's amazing technicolor dreamcoat look sober in comparison"). The powder blue look worn by Bob McAdoo's now-defunct Buffalo Braves in 1975 runs $260; Dave (Tiger) Williams' #22 orange, yellow, and black, 1983 flying-V Vancouver Canucks sweater costs $300; and the simple maroon #33 Washington Redskins jersey worn in the 1940s by QB "Slingin'" Sammy Baugh earned the octogenarian Texan a five-figure royalty check in 2002. (2)

Peter Capolino, president of M&N, got into the retro business in 1985 when he found 12,000 yards (about 11,000 meters) of wool flannel in a warehouse and used it to make vintage Brooklyn Dodgers and New York (baseball) Giants jerseys for wistful, aging baby boomers. In 1997, Mike DiGenova, M&N's senior developer for basketball, was inspired to produce a 1978 Wes Unseld Washington Bullets throwback after attending a retro night in Washington during the NBA's 50th anniversary season. DiGenova worked from old photos and other sources to match jersey fabrics, stitching, colors, and lettering, but because few manufacturers still had the machinery necessary to make the jerseys, production was delayed three years, and eventually outsourced to a factory in Iowa. The detail in the replication—custom-dyed stripes knit into fabric, tackle-twill numerals—means that each jersey was essentially handmade. In 1999, M&N secured a license to reproduce all NBA jerseys worn between 1946 and 1997, and now has exclusive licensing agreements with the big four pro leagues to manufacture authentic jerseys that have been out of use for more than five years. The urban market styles also demanded that the items be sized beginning at XL and running up to XXXXXL, meaning that jerseys came down to the knees of even the largest of wearers. As a result, the extensive amount of material needed for such items drove up item prices. (3)

In his book, *The Tipping Point: How Little Things Can Make a Big Difference*, author Malcolm Gladwell argued that fashion trends, along with more general social changes, emerge because of three characteristics: contagiousness, stickiness, and the rapidity of change due to one big moment (see our discussion of stickiness in chapter 7). This is supported by research by Higgins and Martin, who discovered a diffusion-by-innovation process in which organizations target influential people in the communications process. (4)

The explosion of the throwback trend exemplified each of Gladwell's phenomena. Contagiousness, the first characteristic, develops because of the efforts of a handful of exceptional people. For M&N, this meant the efforts of Capolino and DiGenova, who worked to recreate the vintage replica uniforms, and of Reuben "Big Rube" Harley, the company's director of urban marketing, himself a throwback aficionado. In 2001,

Sammy Baugh in the *original* #33 Washington Redskins jersey.
© Associated Press

Harley finagled his way into a party thrown by rapper and clothing designer Sean Combs (a.k.a. Puffy, Puff Daddy, P-Diddy, Diddy), and got instructions from the rapper to build him a wardrobe a piece at a time. The cultural influence that Combs and other rappers exhibit over urban youth (and in turn, suburban and international youth) would mean that if the rappers wore it, the kids would want to buy it. Harley was what Gladwell called a "connector": an individual, self-confident, sociable, and energetic person who knows many people and can link them. Harley was also what Gladwell identified as a "maven": someone who loves a product or idea and wants to share the information with others. Finally, Harley was a "salesman," able to convince others of the merits of an idea or product.

The second characteristic of trends is the "stickiness factor," which relates to how people identify and remember information. Companies struggle to get their concepts and products to "stick" in the minds of consumers through advertising and positioning by crafting a message that conveys the essence of their product or service. In the case of throwbacks, the stickiness was the newness of the looks (usually more colorful and graphically bolder than contemporary garb) and a connection to history, and the basic fan identification factor that drives the licensed and branded product market (outlined later). The uniforms could appeal to younger customers because the looks were unique. They could also appeal to older fans who could remember when the stars of their youth actually wore the togs in game competition. The mavens, connectors, and salesmen (and saleswomen) then translate this message from the innovators to mainstream customers.

The last factor to tip a trend is the "one big moment." It came for throwbacks in 2001 when Combs debuted 11 M&N jerseys as he cohosted the American Music Awards on ABC. Harley said NBA star Shaquille O'Neal called the next day, wanting every piece Combs wore. Said Capolino: "The hip-hop artists have fights and they get mad at me if I give someone a throwback first. . . . Millions of kids saw their music videos, and I don't have a sleepy company anymore." M&N sales topped $40 million in 2003, and total throwback sales, including hats, jackets, and related clothing, are expected to top $750 million by the end of 2003. Recent NBA sales grew from $2 to $3 billion, thanks largely to the retro craze, and the big four pro leagues have been sponsoring numerous "retro" and "vintage" nights, games, and events to feature the old-school looks. Throwbacks were now another in a long line of apparel and footwear trends that tipped, such as Hush Puppies and Airwalk sneakers, as cataloged by Gladwell. Bill Simmons of *ESPN Magazine* summarized the popularity of the trend this way: "These days, because of free agency and impatient front offices, not only do stars bounce around, but teams switch uniform styles as often as Christina Aguilera changes her hair. . . . That's the thing about throwbacks: you never have to worry. Pete Maravich isn't getting traded from the '77 Jazz. Nolan Ryan isn't getting traded from the '80 Astros. Not only are you exercising a form of personal expression—this player was cool, this uniform looks cool—but you aren't blowing $200 on a potential lemon." (5)

What Are Licensing and Branding?

Licensed products are those items of clothing or products bearing the name or logo of a popular collegiate or professional sport team. Branded merchandise includes products bearing the name of the manufacturer, the most significant of which is apparel. These two types of products comprise a substantial portion of the apparel sales industry. Sales of these items produce revenues in the billions of dollars worldwide, and are the third-highest source of domestic revenue for major sport properties. (6) The following statistics provide a larger sense of the revenues associated with these segments:

✦ In fiscal year 2004, licensed product sales for both the NFL and MLB reached $3 billion; for colleges and universities, $2.6 billion; for the NBA, $2.5 billion; and for the NHL, $1.5 billion. The NFL is the world's seventh-largest brand in terms of licensing, behind Disney, Warner Brothers, and four others.

✦ Sales from apparel specifically designed for women comprises 15 percent of MLB totals, 10 percent of NBA totals, and 5 percent of NFL totals. Greg Grauel, vice president of apparel for Reebok, said: "When you realize that women make up over 40 percent of the viewership and attendance at games, not to focus on merchandising to them would just be ridiculous."

✦ The colleges and universities that sell the most licensed products and apparel generate about $7 million a year in sales, about 6 percent of which involves the sale of replica jerseys.

✦ Since its creation in 1990, Electronic Arts (EA) Sports' "Madden NFL Football" video/computer game has earned over $1 billion in sales, making it one of the most successful video games ever produced. Consumers spent $9.7 billion on computer games in 2003; 30 percent of that went to EA, the core of which is sports games.

✦ After ESPN ran an ad featuring Watersmeet Township School (a high school located on the Upper Peninsula of Michigan; enrollment 77) and its offbeat team nickname, the Nimrods (a term that first appeared in the Book of Genesis, meaning "mighty hunter," but has a decidedly dorkier contemporary connotation), the school earned $80,000 in two months from gear sales, and established sales agreements with retailers Lids, Eastbay, and Champs Sports. (However, Lower Merion [Ardmore, Pennsylvania] High School scuttled a similar deal with Nike, who sought to produce replica jerseys, jackets, and headwear using the name of former player Kobe Bryant, after the NBA star was hit with criminal and civil suit rape allegations. The agreement could have netted the school $100,000 over a five-year period.)

✦ Sean John Clothing, the branded apparel line launched by rapper Sean Combs in 1999, earned $300 million in retail sales at 2,000 stores in 2003.

✦ A recent report on the direct economic impact of fantasy sports in the United States estimated that $1.65 billion was spent in 2004, including $1.44 billion on league entry fees. The study also estimated that $300 million of work hours were used by players toward their fantasy teams. (7)

But what does licensing and branding mean, specifically? Baseball historian Warren Goldstein noted that many early baseball teams (such as the Cincinnati Red Stockings in 1869) got their names from their distinctive game apparel, and that these uniforms created a sense of apartness, defining who was a player and who was not. In the late 1940s, the NFL's then-Los Angeles Rams brought a more refined stylistic approach to this apartness when running back Fred Gehrke, an art major in college, painted his drab brown leather helmet blue, then painted gold ram horns on each side. Author Michael MacCambridge called Gehrke's efforts "a masterpiece of pop art. As a utilitarian move, it was equally successful, making the team and its players instantly recognizable." Popular sport illustrator LeRoy Neiman (whose career got a boost by doing paintings and drawing of '60s QB idol Joe Namath) said of the design: "It is the most effective pop art symbol in all of sports. It captures the very essence of the helmet—to ram someone." A few years later, Dallas Cowboys general manager Tex Schramm had grown dissatisfied with the team's all-white uniforms and worked privately with uniform supplier Rawlings to create a unique color, one never seen before on a uniform, that would be at once shiny, blue, and distinctive. The created hue, called metallic blue, could look gray, silver, or light blue, depending on the lighting. Once Schramm saw the pants, he contacted helmet manufacturer Riddell to match the color for their helmets. MacCambridge described this look, which debuted in 1964, as calling to mind "nothing so much as the shimmering spacesuits of the Mercury 7 astronauts." (8)

Today, these distinctions are illustrated convincingly at the University of Oregon, where head football coach Mike Bellotti allowed his players to choose the Ducks' current bright yellow jersey color scheme (designed by Nike under the auspices of Oregon alum and athletic benefactor Phil Knight; Nike's creative director for apparel said, "We're always presenting [Oregon] with innovation and ideas. They say yes to some and no to others") over the protests and negative reviews of many fans and alumni. Nike calls the color "lightning yellow," but critical wags called it "jaundiced," "urine," or "banana peel." Said Bellotti, "My wife hated it, but my players loved it. I guess you know who won that one." (9)

Davis commented that clothing styles are a transmitted code that can impart meanings of identity, gender, status, and sexuality. Licensed and branded apparel communicates on each of these levels, and is based on the premise that fans will purchase goods to draw them closer to their beloved organizations and athletes. Writer Bill Simmons described the early days of buying player-specific licensed products this way: "Fans bought them because they wanted to dress like players on the team. Not only were we supporting our guys, but the player we chose became an expression of sorts." In the gang-torn sections of Los Angeles in the 1980s, it meant that residents could wear the black-and-silver apparel of the then-hometown Raiders, favored for the colors and also because they were sported by rappers such as Ice Cube, Easy-E, and Ice-T (presaging the catalysts of the contemporary throwback boom), and steer clear of the violence associated with wearing red (the color of the "Bloods" gang) or blue (the color claimed by the "Cripps" crew). (10)

When writer Mark Bowden walked around Philadelphia's Lincoln Financial Field recently, he observed what he called "a summary history" of the NFL's Eagles in the licensed jerseys worn by the fans in attendance. "Many of the old-timers," wrote Bowden, "still wear the team's traditional kelly green . . . marking that old era you'll find jerseys bearing the numbers of retired heroes such as Harold Carmichael (17), Bill Bergey (66), Ron Jaworski (7), Reggie White (92), and a multitude of others. . . . Now a metallic teal (the franchise's new color [it's officially called "jade" by the club]) predominates among the masses, [and] just about every starting player on the current Eagles roster is represented [in the stands], from the obvious ones—quarterback Donovan McNabb (5) . . . to receivers, defensive backs, kickers, linebackers and even linemen."

These days, as a result of licensing and branding, when you and your significant other decide to tie the knot, one (or both) of you can walk down the aisle in a $1,800 full-length crinoline and satin wedding dress emblazoned with the logo of the New York Yankees, complete with pinstripes and matching wristbands, and a matching $350 tuxedo. Requests for the ensembles have been pouring in from across the country, and Manhattan's Greenwich Village designer Linda Bekye has plans for Los Angeles Lakers and New Jersey (soon to be Brooklyn) Nets versions as well. No word on whether George Steinbrenner, Yogi Berra, or John Sterling are available to give the reception toast.

After the reception, you can pick up a pack of ego-enhancing Jumbo Condoms for the honeymoon, manufactured by Global Protection Corporation, whose owner, Davin Wedel, named the product after the trademarked elephant mascot "Jumbo" of Tufts University, his alma mater. Once you two settle down, you can purchase $30 replica NBA jerseys and $55 varsity jackets, and maybe a warm-up suit for your dog (manufactured by Sporty K-9 NYC—it is estimated that 66 percent of dog owners buy a holiday gift for their pet, and 40 percent bring them home a souvenir from their vacations). You can then go to the NFL's Web site to buy a $15 NFL team-licensed 25-foot tape measure from Innovative Concepts to help you figure out whether your couch will fit through the stairwell into your new apartment. And in your final days, it means that you can spend $2,000 for a licensed fiberglass casket bearing the logo of your alma mater or other favorite school. The models are estimated to last about a thousand years after burial.

We buy licensed and branded products in large part because we want them rather than need them, and we choose them because we want the world to know that we identify with a team, activity, player, or sport organization. (11)

A History of Licensed Products

In 1924, sports writer Francis Wallace observed in the shops along Fifth Avenue in Manhattan displays and neckties in the colors of what he termed the aristocracy of the gridiron: Army (black and gold), Harvard (crimson), Notre Dame (navy, green, and gold), Princeton (black and orange), and Yale (blue). In 1947, University of Oregon athletics director Leo Harris and Walt Disney agreed to allow the school to use Disney's Donald Duck image for the university's mascot. Although these were some early steps toward the development of licensable properties, the University of California at Los Angeles is generally credited with being the first school to enter into a licensing agreement in 1973 with a manufacturer when its school bookstore granted a license to a watch manufacturer. The NCAA formed its properties division to license championship merchandise in 1975, but it does not administer licensing programs for member schools. Significant revenue growth began in the late 1980s, when the University of Notre Dame, which began its licensing program in 1983, experienced a growth rate of 375 percent from 1988 to 1989. Collegiate licensed product sales totaled $100 million in the early 1980s. In 1995, sales reached $2.5 billion. The peak for licensed sales for major college and pro licensed products was 1996, with sales of $13.8 billion. That figure had slipped to $11.8 billion by 2001. (12)

Industry Structure

The licensing industry can be broken down into several facets. As we have already discussed, there's licensed merchandise, professional league licensing, and collegiate licensing. The industry also includes players association licensing, licensing programs of other sport organizations, international licensing, and licensing in professional individual and tour sports. And of course, there's branded merchandise. The following sections will explore these facets in detail.

Licensed Merchandise

The manufacturers of licensed products—the licensees—include well-known sport apparel and footwear companies such as Nike, Reebok, and Russell Athletic, prominent video and computer game manufacturers 989 and Electronic Arts (EA), and hard-goods manufacturers such as ArtCarved (jewelry), Mead (stationery), and Pinnacle (trading cards and memorabilia). Licensees pay teams and leagues—the licensors—for the right to manufacture products bearing team and school names, nicknames, colors, and logos. Sport organizations transfer the right to use their names, marks, and logos to other companies so that these companies may use them in producing products for sale.

If these names and logos are registered with the U.S. Patent and Trademark Office, they are referred to as trademarks. A trademark is defined under the Federal Trademark Act of 1946, commonly referred to as the Lanham Act, as "any word, name, symbol, or device or combination thereof adopted and used by a manufacturer or merchant to identify his goods and distinguish them from those manufactured or sold by others." The law defines trademark infringement as the reproduction, counterfeiting, copying, or imitation in commerce of a registered mark, and bars companies that do not pay for the right to use these trademarks from manufacturing products bearing those marks. The act was amended in 1996 to protect famous marks from dilution by similar marks. (13)

To be claimed as property, these names and logos must be registered with the U.S. Patent and Trademark Office (PTO) in Arlington, Virginia. Only the owner of a mark may apply for federal registration. The application must include a drawing of the mark, a written description of the mark, the identification of the goods and services for which the registration is sought, and the basis for filing. Once this process is completed, these names and logos become trademarks of the organization. After creating affiliated marks and logos, sport organizations should conduct a trademark search to determine whether a conflicting mark exists. To make such a determination, the PTO determines whether a likelihood of confusion exists (whether consumers would be likely to associate the good or services of one party with those of another as a result of the use of the marks).

To be conflicting, the marks need not be identical, just substantially similar. Certain specified Patent and Trademark Depository Libraries throughout the United States perform trademark searches for a small fee. The term of a federal trademark is 10 years, with 10-year renewal terms. Between the fifth and sixth year after the date of initial registration, the registrant must file an affidavit setting forth certain information to keep the registration alive. If no affidavit is filed, the registration is canceled. (14)

Licensing enables schools and teams to generate brand recognition and interest and to increase revenues with very little financial risk. The licensees assume the risk by manufacturing the product, then pay a fee to the licensor, called a royalty, for the use of specific trademarks on specific products. Royalty fees generally range from 4 percent (for toys and games) to 20 percent (for trading cards and video games) and are based on gross sales at wholesale costs. Apparel royalties range from 11 percent for on-field items to 15 percent for player-identified items. (15) Wholesale costs are those paid by the retailer, not the price paid by consumers. Certain agreements also call for licensees to spend a minimum amount on the promotion of products, require a minimum annual royalty payment regardless of sales, or both. Licensees use the established images and popularity of sport teams to boost their sales.

In some cases, however, the clear determination of ownership is not so simple. When the NFL sought recently to allow third-party companies to sell its library of photographic and video images of players and game highlights, 75 of the several hundred photographers who created much of the archive argued that they owned the copyrights to the images, and were demanding that the images be returned if their monetary and ownership demands were not met. The archive has been built primarily by photographers who shoot games "on spec," which means that they pay for their own equipment, transportation, and the sending of the film to the league. In return, they receive back the images the league does not want, and hold copyrights to the images the league retains. The league then sells these for commercial, journalistic, and internal league uses, with the proceeds divided evenly between the league and the photographers. However, if no deal is reached and the photographers receive all their images back, they cannot sell them without league permission. Annual sales of archived images are approximately $1 million. (16)

So what happens when an organization believes its logos and trademarks have been infringed on? In the case of Western Kentucky University (WKU), located in Bowling Green, Kentucky, you sue; specifically, the Italian television company Mediaset, in court in Milan, Italy, for $250 million. WKU claimed the company copied its mascot, Big Red, in creating the mascot Gabibbo (who had a chart-topping CD in 1990 in Italy) for its satirical comedy show "Striscia la Notizia" (translated literally as "Stripping the News"). WKU created Big Red in 1979, but did not trademark it until 1991; Mediaset trademarked Gabibbo a year earlier than WKU trademarked Big Red. The best evidence in favor of WKU is an interview given by the show's creator, Antonio Ricci, to an Italian magazine in 1991; in the interview he claimed that he had based Gabibbo directly on Big Red. Ricci later recanted, claiming he was joking and that he had never seen Big Red. (17)

The financial implications of protecting a sport organization's trademark are significant, as was seen recently when Georgia Tech spent $800,000 to win a $600,000 settlement in a copyright infringement case with the Salt Lake City Buzz, a minor league baseball team. Tech claimed that the team infringed on its Yellow Jacket mascot, "Buzz." At risk was about $300,000 in annual licensing revenues that Tech used to pay for scholarships and other athletic expenses. Said a Tech spokesperson, "The issue all along was not just financial. Licensing is a little more than selling t-shirts. It's brand awareness. Buzz . . . is one of Georgia Tech's biggest symbols." As a part of the settlement, the Salt Lake City team opted to adopt the nickname "Stingers." Other schools are not so concerned. At California State University at Long Beach, the school's baseball team uses "Dirtbags" as an unofficial nickname to supplement the school's official "49ers" moniker. The name was coined in 1989 when the team had to practice on an all-dirt field, but then qualified for that year's College World Series, the school's first-ever appearance. The name has become popular with fans, and the school can earn as much as $50,000 from sales of related products. Although the school has copyrighted the script wordmark used, it has not trademarked the nickname. In 2004, when the Washington Redskins' offensive line coach nicknamed his charges "dirtbags," recalling the "Hogs" of the team's glory days of the 1980s, Long Beach wasn't worried. Director of Marketing Tim Dickson said, "as long as [the Redskins] don't use the exact same logo, it's not a big deal. The name itself is not going to be a problem for us. It is pretty funny though." (18)

Organizational image issues must also be considered in trademark infringement cases. At the 2002 U.S. Open, held at the venerable Black Course at Bethpage State Park on New York's Long Island, the United States Golf Association (USGA) sought to stop off-site vendors from selling unlicensed logo merchandise. According to USGA personnel, the efforts (supported by New York State Police) were as much about the quality of illegal merchandise as protecting against lost income. USGA lead attorney Romaney Berson noted that the organization's concern "is that someone buys something with our logo on it, they tend to assume we're responsible for it. The lettering on the shirt runs, the cap falls apart, whatever it may be, they're going to blame us. It makes us look bad." (19)

Professional League Licensing

The licensing programs in professional sport leagues are administered by a for-profit branch of the league, generally referred to as a properties division. Properties divisions approve licensees, police trademark infringement, and distribute licensing revenues equally among league franchises. Properties divisions usually handle marketing and sponsorship efforts as well. However, recent developments in the NFL have begun to challenge the degree to which all such league revenues will be equally distributed. Although an estimated two thirds of the league's nearly $5 billion in annual revenue is shared equally among the 32 franchises, some franchises—primarily those in smaller markets—are arguing that an even larger percentage should be shared, whereas others—namely owners such as Jerry Jones of the Dallas Cowboys and Daniel Snyder of the Washington Redskins—are seeking to control more of the distribution of licensed goods. Currently, teams control only their team stores and catalogs, whereas the league controls all other deals to sell goods and pools the proceeds. (20)

The NFL was the first professional league to develop a properties component in 1963, under the leadership of then-Commissioner Alvin "Pete" Rozelle. When Rozelle was the general manager of the then-Los Angeles Rams in the late 1950s, he enlisted the company that licensed products for film star Roy Rogers to set up a Rams Store near the team's offices on Beverly Boulevard, and sold everything from T-shirts (costing $1.25) to earrings and highball glasses. The most popular item? A bobblehead doll, which sold for a dollar. A few years later, New York City's Saks Fifth Avenue featured a "Giants Locker Room" holiday window display, which included a full range of Giants souvenirs and a child-sized Giants uniform. The first license the NFL granted was to Sport Specialties. David Warsaw, the founder of the company, had worked with Chicago Bears owner George Halas in the 1930s in selling Bears merchandise and had later developed licensing agreements with the Los Angeles Dodgers and Rams. (21)

By the late 1970s, each NFL team's licensing share was believed to be nearly half a million dollars annually. According to author Michael MacCambridge, NFL Properties was a vehicle "to expand the presence and profile of the league . . . it became a kind of extended lifestyle choice. Pro football wasn't just for Sundays anymore . . . those who chose to identify with a particular team could now pay for the privilege, with handsome hats, T-shirts, and other souvenirs." MacCambridge credits the mid-'60s efforts of NFL Properties and the consistent quality of league-licensed merchandise (along with the powerful visual productions of NFL Films), as a significant contributor to helping "tip" the league to its present level of unsurpassed popularity. It was not only the revenue the merchandise produced, but also the "sophisticated aura" that was created around the league that was unrivaled by other sport properties. (22)

MLB followed with the creation of its properties division in 1966, although many teams that had strong local sales were reluctant to give up their licensing rights to the league. Indeed, some teams were loath to share their marks with licensees because of their perceptions that such actions would cheapen the product. George Weiss, general manager of the New York Yankees, recoiled at the notion of licensing agreements, saying, "Do you think I want every kid in this city walking around with a Yankees cap?" NHL Enterprises began formal league-governed licensing in 1969, and NBA Properties initiated activities in 1982. (23)

The following outlines the key partners of MLB's on-field apparel licenses, with each agreement signed for five years; they are worth more than $500 million combined:

✦ Majestic Athletic: Exclusive MLB Authentic Collection supplier of on-field game uniforms, batting practice jerseys, outerwear, T-shirts, fleece, and turtlenecks to all 30 MLB clubs as well as the domestic and international retail markets.

✦ New Era: Exclusive MLB Authentic Collection supplier of headwear to all 30 clubs as well as the domestic and international retail markets. New Era also maintains its rights as the exclusive supplier of MLB Authentic Collection celebratory headwear for the winners of the League Championship Series and the World Series.

✦ Nike: Exclusive MLB Collection supplier of performance apparel and casual wear to all 30 clubs as well as the domestic and international markets.

✦ Twins Enterprises: Exclusive supplier of nonauthentic headwear to the domestic mass market. Twins also maintains rights to produce MLB Authentic Collection celebratory headwear for division winners and wild-card teams. (24)

League licensing works in areas beyond clothing and apparel as well. Gatorade and the NFL reached a sponsorship deal in 2004 worth an unprecedented $500 million over eight years, under which Gatorade (owned by Pepsi) will supply the league with $1.2 million in product and $16 million in marketing commitments. This landmark agreement would not have been possible without the existence of the NFL Properties Collective Trust, a pact between league franchises that allows sponsors such as Gatorade to use the marks and logos of all teams, as well as secures product placement on team sidelines during games. There is no way Gatorade would spend this amount of money without the ability to use the marks and logos of all 32 teams in communicating the sponsorship to consumers. (25)

Players Association Licensing

Players unions also administer licensing programs. The Major League Baseball Players Association (MLBPA) was the first to enter into such an agreement in the late 1960s when then-Executive Director Marvin Miller entered into a two-year, $120,000 pact with Coca-Cola to permit the beverage manufacturer to put players' likenesses on bottle caps. Such royalties helped fund the emerging union's organizing activities. Miller also negotiated a comprehensive agreement with trading card manufacturer Topps Company in 1968. Topps was permitted to continue manufacturing trading cards bearing player likenesses for double the player's previous yearly fees (from $125 to $250), and it paid the union 8 percent on annual sales up to $4 million and 10 percent on all subsequent sales. In the first year, the contract earned the MLBPA $320,000.

Players associations also work to enforce trademarks, an action apparent most notably in the lucrative and growing fantasy league gaming market. Recently, SportsLine signed an agreement with Players, Inc., the licensing subsidiary of the National Football League Players Association (NFLPA), guaranteeing the association at least $1 million in royalties through 2009. The company made $15.9 million from the site's fantasy portion in 2002, a 34 percent increase over 2003, with the site's NFL-partnered league attracting 1.3 million paid users. Fantasy licenses are estimated to begin with an upfront fee of $25,000, with 7.5 percent of revenues to be paid as royalties. Active policing of the market ensures that members are compensated for the use of names and likenesses. According to Greg Ambrosius, the president of the Fantasy Sports Trade Association, "It used to be thought of as [something for] just geeks and hard-core fans. But this isn't just a small closet hobby anymore. This [expletive] is a big, big industry, and it's all due to the Internet." The business is so big that mainstream retailers such as home electronics chain Best Buy are beginning their own branded fantasy football, in part because research has shown that people who play (93 percent of whom are white males with household incomes of close to $90,000) also bought high-definition TVs. (26)

However, some players, notably baseball's infamous Barry Bonds and retired hoopster/pitchman Michael Jordan, elect to separate themselves from union agreements and operate their own licensing programs. It is common for elite players to also garner a premium in union deals if their names and likenesses are used in packaging and commercials, but now Bonds must negotiate his own deals with companies such as trading card manufacturers (except Topps, which has always dealt with players individually). It is believed that Bonds chose this path to capitalize on an impending assault on Henry Aaron's all-time home run total of 755 (depending on the outcome of steroid use investigations), but even Jordan participated in the union-negotiated agreements with trading card companies and jersey manufacturers. (27)

Collegiate Licensing

Many NCAA Division IA schools, either through a department in the athletic department or through an office that handles all institutional licensing, administer their own licensing programs much in the manner of professional league properties divisions. They deal directly with licensees, and retain all profits derived from fees and royalties. The benefit of self-maintenance is that schools can retain a greater portion of sales revenues. The remainder of Division IA schools, such as the smaller pro leagues and many IAA schools, enlist the services of independent licensing companies to manage their programs. The Collegiate Licensing Company (CLC), formed in 1981, acts on behalf of nearly 200 colleges, universities, bowls and conferences, the Heisman Trophy, and the NCAA as their independent licensing company. Client colleges pay a portion of the royalties (usually 50 percent) to CLC for their efforts. (28) The benefit of enlisting a licensing company is the fact that these companies usually have a higher degree of expertise in dealing with a vast variety of licensees, and a greater facility in creating new and innovative design concepts.

Apparel manufacturers also use athletics department sponsorships as a tool in leveraging licensed product sales. For example, Nike expends millions in cash and apparel annually to outfit teams at the University of Michigan (for as much as $28 million over seven years), the University of North Carolina, Ohio State University, and the University of Texas, while Adidas has similar deals with UCLA, the University of Notre Dame, and the University of Tennessee. Together, these two industry giants have agreements of varying sizes and scope with 200 schools. These deals not only contribute to the brand visibility of these companies (even though NCAA rules restrict manufacturer logos on uniforms to an area of 2.5 square inches [6.25 square centimeters]), but also serve to prime sales of licensed products and to procure future endorsement deals with athletes from these schools. At the University of Texas, that means that all coaches and athletes (except swimmers and divers, who wear Speedo suits) are outfitted head to toe in Nike apparel and footwear in practices, competitions, and official appearances. So important is this blanket coverage for Nike that publications and sport information staffers monitor photos and media interviews to ensure that competing manufacturers' apparel doesn't slip into departmental publications. Nike keeps vigil as well, as reported by Chris Plonsky, Texas' director of women's athletics. "If TV coverage shows one of our athletes stepping off a team bus with a cap that's not Nike's," she said, "they'll call it to our attention." (29)

Given the right product and sales environment, smaller manufacturers can also profit in the collegiate apparel business. Sports Belle (SB), a Knoxville, Tennessee, company founded and owned by Jesse Lee, is one such firm. SB was formed in 1974 to make uniforms for girls and boys high school teams, but has struggled to match the resources of Adidas, Nike, and Reebok in the collegiate market. SB has a longtime agreement to make uniforms for the men's basketball team at Saint Joseph's University of Philadelphia. The school's undefeated 2003-2004 regular season, reaching the regional finals in that year's NCAA Division I men's basketball tournament, led by the play of Naismith Award–winner guard Jameer Nelson, brought welcomed exposure for SB. Lee has seen schools such as the University of Tennessee drop his company for more lucrative agreements with Adidas and others. Lee doesn't pay coaches and schools to wear his product ("We sell uniforms, and my money has to come from there," he said), but 8 of the 64 teams in the 2004 NCAA Division I women's basketball tournament wear SB togs. Lee first saw the Saint Joe's Hawks play in the finals of the 1996 National Invitation Tournament in New York, and was appalled at the team's uniforms. "I told my sales rep: 'Get that coach. Let's sit down and talk. That school and our company go together.'" Lee provides the school with a unique look, as observed by Hawks head coach Phil Martelli, who said after watching a tournament game between the University of Wisconsin and the University of Pittsburgh (two Adidas schools): "They both had the exact same uniform. I was sitting there thinking, 'Shouldn't a uniform be like a kind of expression about your uniqueness?'" Lee hopes so, but is still worried that, unique or not, the Hawks will drop SB if one of the big dogs drops a load of cash in the collective lap of Martelli and Saint Joe's. (30)

Licensing Programs of Other Sport Organizations

Many sport organizations, including the United States Olympic Committee (USOC) and the Ladies Professional Golf Association (LPGA), act as licensors to develop revenues and increase organizational awareness. In the case of the USOC, Section 110 of the Amateur Sports Act of 1978 grants the organization the right to prohibit the unauthorized use of the word *Olympic* for trade purposes. The USOC Licensing Program returns 82.7 percent of proceeds from sales of Olympic merchandise back to athletes through the funding of training programs and athlete grants and services. (31)

A recent example of the strength of such an agreement was during the 2002 Salt Lake City Winter Games, when Canadian apparel maker Roots sold nearly $50 million of U.S. Olympic Team licensed merchandise. Roots, which opened its first store in Canada in 1973 and now has over 140 there with another 80 in Asia, provided apparel for the Canadian and British teams as well. The company was initially seen as a last resort for the USOC, which had offered the rights to manufacture team apparel to Adidas, Nike, and Reebok, each of which declined. Roots secured the agreement for less than $1 million in up-front cash and a minimum royalty requirement. Roots sought the deal to gain entrée into the U.S. market, and provided at no charge for U.S. athletes parade outfits, warm-ups, casual wear, and "podium jackets" to be worn for medal ceremonies. One product in particular, the U.S team beret, became wildly popular with consumers. The Olympic Superstore in Salt Lake City sold 2,000 of the $19.95 items in five minutes; the U.S. TV shopping network QVC sold 10,000 in three minutes. The original run of 50,000 units sold out quickly, and production was upped to 250,000. Initially, many U.S. retailers had been loath to stock Olympic products because of poor sales histories, but the distinctive look created by Roots and the USOC, using light and dark blues, lowercase fonts, and snowflake designs, and a surge in patriotism following the terrorist attacks of September 11, 2001, stoked unprecedented demand. (32)

Following the Salt Lake City success, Roots has become the official team outfitter (except for medal ceremonies clothing, provided by Adidas) for the USOC through the 2008 Beijing Summer Games (along with official supplier status for the 2004 Summer Olympic teams from Barbados, Canada, and Great Britain). The company planned for a sales repeat with a "unisex poorboy" hat (retailing for $34.95) for the 2004 Athens Games, but changes in international politics dictated a different design approach for Roots in outfitting the U.S. team. One U.S. track coach admitted that "it would be good if we low-keyed it" when going around Athens during the 2004 Summer Games, in reference to a backlash against the United States following the second Gulf War and the toppling of Iraqi leader Saddam Hussein. A USA Gymnastics staffer said of team apparel: "We have encouraged our athletes to be careful about wearing USA-branded apparel when they are out and about as a safety precaution." But Roots did not change its design approaches, stating that the looks would be designed in a "tasteful, proud, American way." (33)

Other sporting goods product manufacturers also use licensing to prompt sales of their products. A recent study found that 25 percent more Americans participated annually in bowling (91 million in all, making it the nation's most popular competitive sport) than voted in the 1998 Congressional elections. Although overall bowling participation is high, the number of league bowlers has dropped significantly in recent years. Why has league bowling declined? In *Bowling Alone*, his study of changes in American community involvement, Robert D. Putnam noted that this is a reflection of a general trend in American life: People are less likely to be involved in public life, and to join civic and community groups, churches, and political parties. This also includes involvement in traditional team and sport organizations. (34)

Brunswick, the maker of bowling balls, ball bags, and related bowling equipment and apparel, uses licensing agreements to keep people interested in purchasing equipment. Through agreements with NASCAR and NASCAR drivers, the NFL, college athletics departments, Disney, Warner Bros., and the estate of Elvis Presley, they promote sales of their "Viz-a-Ball." Bowlers can purchase the $140 balls with 360-degree graphics depicting five of their favorite drivers (including Tony Stewart and the Earnhardts Senior and Junior); 10 NFL teams (including the Green Bay Packers, Tampa Bay Buccaneers, and San Francisco 49ers); 10 schools (including the University of Florida, the University of Nebraska, and Penn State University); and cartoon characters such as Winnie the Pooh, Betty Boop, and SpongeBob Squarepants. Brunswick uses the cartoon balls to target young consumers, hoping that they will in turn become lifetime bowlers and purchasers of Brunswick bowling products.

International Licensing

What's the world's most popular sport team? Most Americans would probably choose the New York Yankees, the Dallas Cowboys, or the Los Angeles Lakers. Most non-Americans would say it is the British soccer team Manchester United (a.k.a. Man U). The club was founded in 1878 as the Newton Heath Lancashire and Yorkshire Railway Company Cricket and Football Club for the purpose of providing recreational opportunities for working-class men in the city of Manchester in Lancashire in northwest England. In the summer of 2001, thousands of people turned up in the early morning at the airport in Bangkok, Thailand, to welcome the team, and later that week, 65,000 screaming devotees jammed the city's national stadium (as another 15,000 disappointed souls unable to get in watched on a giant video screen outside) to witness the exploits of these nonnative luminaries as they defeated the Thai national team 6 to 0 in an exhibition game. The scene was played out across Asia that summer, including in Singapore (where an exhibition drew 44,000) and Malaysia (with a match crowd of 100,000). In recent years the club has toured Korea, Japan, Australia, and South America, and had U.S. tours in 2003 and 2004. Man U has boasted some of the world's best and most marketable stars, such as David Beckham, and has even tapped into America to sign goalkeeper Tim Howard, a native of North Brunswick, New Jersey. (35)

So how can Manchester United, a soccer team from a fading industrial city in England, be the world's most popular team, and not the Yankees, the most successful American professional sport franchise, located in the world's best-known city? First of all, soccer is the world's most popular sport, and as pointed out by Man U CEO Peter Kenyon, "Most American sports are only played on the shores of the U.S. The U.S. has got some very strong franchises, but in order for a franchise to be international, the sport has to be international." In sport organizations seeking to expand their markets across national boundaries, or for those sport organizations that focus on international sports and international competitions, the fact that sport is a product native to all markets and cultures is a definite advantage. However, although certain sports such as basketball and soccer (the game people outside the United States know as "football") enjoy international popularity, each culture also favors and identifies with different sports. In England and India, it might be cricket. In Indonesia, badminton. In Japan, sumo. The U.S. market is saturated with sport, but Americans tend to think of baseball as the "national pastime," and American football draws huge levels of spectator interest. But although baseball has strong followings in Japan, Korea, and the Caribbean, our brand of football draws little notice outside the United States. (36)

Certainly Man U has become a global brand in part because of its degree of current on-field success in the world's most popular sport, winning the "treble" (the English Premier League championship, the English FA Cup, and the UEFA Cup [the European Club championship]) in 1999, something no English team had ever done. And United has a tradition of international success (they were the first English club to play in European competitions) and resiliency, such as when eight star members of the exceptionally gifted 1952 team were killed in a plane crash in Munich, only to have manager Sir Matt Busby rebuild the team to prominence in a few short years. After the resurrection, many staunch supporters of other football clubs adopted the Red Devils as their second-favorite side, which has eroded somewhat given the recent success of the club. Like the Yankees, Cowboys, and Lakers in the United States, Man U is now a team many fans love to hate. (37)

Man U has leveraged its popularity to generate significant revenues. Sponsorships account for 6 percent of all club revenues, and include a $439 million deal with Nike that runs through 2015, and a $45.1 million deal with telecommunications company Vodafone that expired in 2004. Television counts for 26 percent of revenues ($45 million in 2000), including income from the team's own network, MUTV, a cable subscription channel devoted to the club. Gate receipts totaled $55 million in 2000 (32 percent of all revenues), even though a season ticket for games at Old Trafford (capacity 67,500) costs the equivalent of $630. By comparison, the top season ticket at Yankee Stadium costs over $5,000, nearly nine times that of Man U's, whose ticket prices are in the middle range of Premier League clubs. In 2001, the club turned a profit of $24 million on revenues of $182 million. The estimated value of the club is now $1.5 billion. By comparison, the Yankees, Cowboys, and Lakers, the gold-standard troika of American team sports in the 1990s, were worth only $1 billion *combined*. (38)

Man U has reached this level of success in part because it has developed an organizational understanding that Man U is a brand, and much of that brand identity has come from attention to licensed product sales. In the early 1990s, Edward Freedman came to Man U from EPL rival Tottenham, where he had been head of merchandising. His background with soccer and retailing led him to determine that the club needed to get distribution throughout the United Kingdom for Man U products, and that much of the quality of its existing products were substandard. Said Freedman of Man U's management at the time: "They did not understand what a brand was, they had never realized they *had* a brand, that Manchester United *was* a brand" [authors' emphasis]. Freedman's licensing and retailing experiences focused on improving customer satisfaction, improving the club's own retail shops (to include huge new stores in Dublin, Kuala Lumpur, Cape Town, and Singapore), creating merchandising relationships with other UK retailers, and broadening the product line to include a magazine and videos, air fresheners, and jigsaw puzzles. He also created agreements with banks to use the Red Devil mascot to promote youth savings accounts. Freedman used licensing and retailing to reach what he called "a large number of untapped Manchester United supporters." (39)

Licensing in Professional Individual and Tour Sports

Individual professional sports, through their agents and advisers, usually handle licensing agreements on their own. Although this makes licensing money more difficult to attain for lesser-known athletes, as with commercial endorsements, the potential exists for highly recognizable athletes to earn significant licensing revenue over which they have more control than do most athletes in professional team sports. Nowhere is this truer than for well-known drivers in NASCAR, where the top drivers earn more in licensing than from their racing salaries or winnings. Before the death of legendary driver Dale Earnhardt Sr. on the last lap of the 2001 Daytona 500, sales of Earnhardt's licensed products (including the most popular product apparel, die-cast cars, and trading cards) reportedly accounted for 40 percent of NASCAR licensing sales, totaling $50 million. However, following his death, the sale of Earnhardt licensed products, including a new line of memorial products, continued to boom, reaching $60 million in 2001. In addition, over 14,000 other Earnhardt collectibles were for sale on the online auction site eBay (nearly 10,000 more than Michael Jordan items), including a $7,000 limited-edition

59-inch (150-centimeter)-tall Snap-On tool box and a $120,000 1996 Chevrolet Camaro Z-28 SS (one of three made). Retail sales for all NASCAR products in 2003 were reported to reach $2 billion. One company, Action Performance (AP), a publicly held company located in Phoenix with sales of $400 million in 2003, owns a 1-million-square-foot (305,000-square-meter) manufacturing facility in China with more than 6,000 employees, churning out 18 million die-cast cars a year. Sixty percent of AP's sales come from die-cast cars, which AP sells from 32 trailers at each of the 36 Nextel Cup Series races, along with online and catalog sales. (40)

Licensing means money for extreme and action sport athletes as well. Skateboarding icon Tony Hawk earns $1.5 million annually for licensing agreements with companies that produce video games, action figures, equipment, and apparel. Total sales for Hawk-branded products—including clothing, skateboards, his Boom Boom HuckJam events, and Activision video games—grossed $300 million in retail sales in 2003. Hawk's long-term deal with game maker Activision, signed in 2002, included a $20 million advance, a royalty agreement of $1.50 per game, and use of a private jet (only the John Madden franchise sells more games). In addition, BMX biker Dave Mirra earns $1 million from similar deals. (41)

Branded Merchandise

Unlike the many licensed products described earlier, plenty of other lines of clothing eschew the use of team marks and use their own brand names, marks, and logos to sell merchandise. The sale of branded merchandise, those products bearing the name of the clothing manufacturer, is a substantial part of the apparel sales industry. It is estimated that retail sales of clothing for teens, the main target for branded products sellers, is 14 percent of the $175 billion clothing market. To observe this, walk into the nearest Abercrombie and Fitch, Aeropostale, American Eagle Outfitters, or Timberland store. These retailers derive a substantial portion of their sales from athletically themed yet nonlicensed clothing. At Abercrombie and Fitch (A&F), you will find dim lighting, pulsing dance-rock music, and large black-and-white posters of scantily clad and extremely attractive Anglo-Saxon youths. You will also find tables, shelves, and racks of T-shirts, rugby shirts, pants, and sweats, mostly altered with rips and tears to seem preworn, and emblazoned with any number of A&F logos. Many of these designs seek to connect with a specific sport or activity ("A&F Football" or "Weekend Warrior"), a nickname of a fictitious athletic team ("Abercrombie Bears"), or some make-believe summer camp, fishing or hunting guide service, or ski resort. A&F, like these other retailers, along with hip-hop apparel companies such as Akademics, Ecko, Rocawear, and South Pole, and companies such as fashion brand Puma, seek to develop their own brands and identities in relation to sport and culture in general rather than pay for the right to gain direct affiliation benefits through the use of those of existing specific sport organizations. Other retailers such as Pacific Sunwear (which began as a single surf shop in Newport Beach, California, in 1980 and now has annual sales of $846 million) and Quicksilver (which has 800 stores nationally, with overall company revenues of $975 million in 2003) build their sales on products based on use in surfing and water sports. (42)

In addition, many apparel and footwear companies such as Adidas, Hummel, Puma, and Reebok, which are active in the selling of licensed products, also develop their own brand logos and marks to sell apparel and merchandise, allowing them to derive greater profits. Hummel and Puma in particular have sought to develop their companies as athletic fashion brands. Hummel, a privately held soccer equipment and fashion company (founded in 1923, it claims to be the world's oldest soccer equipment company) based in Aarhus, Denmark, had sales of $140 million in 2003. The company (which has no connection to the German figurine manufacturer of the same name—your grandmother probably has some of them) did well in licensing with European team soccer jerseys in the 1970s and 1980s, mainly on the strength of new distinctive design elements such as its military-style chevron design on jerseys sleeves. But now that Nike and Adidas dominate soccer equipment and licensing, Hummel has been forced to re-create the company through fashion initiatives, reviving the retro-polyester styles that made the company hot in the 1970s, distributing products in boutiques in Europe, Asia, Los Angeles, and New York. The new designs got publicity when worn by pop icon Jennifer Lopez. In 2004, Hummel introduced a line of high-end soccer cleats, including a hand-sewn kangaroo leather pair priced at $400, nearly twice the price of the nearest competitor. Hummel has also gotten back into licensing through a recent deal with English Premier League team Aston Villa, but there is a fashion angle here as well. Hummel's Brian Kukon hopes that high-end apparel such as leather jackets will be worn by Aston Villa fans Ozzy Osbourne and British royal Prince William. "They are an asset for the club," said the former Adidas executive, "just like Jack Nicholson [is for the Los Angeles Lakers]." Hummel is taking a similar path to that of German apparel and footwear maker Puma, which has reemerged in the apparel and footwear market through the sale of limited-edition shoes and apparel to boutique shoppers, then used this cachet to sell plainer, lower-priced models though national chains and some licensing. Said one industry expert: "The cool, expensive stuff props up the Puma brand, and the cheap stuff makes the money." (43)

Since Puma has taken this approach, which was a change from its traditional running and soccer lines that lost the company money every year from 1986 to 1994 (when it had $250 million in debt), its sales have grown 30 percent each year since 1997. In 2004, Puma had a cash surplus of 174 million euros and is now the world's fifth-largest maker of athletic shoes (4.5 percent of the $17 billion athletic footwear market worldwide), with share prices tripling to 168.71 euros. Puma's CEO Jochen Zeitz said that before he joined the company, it had been run by "people who thought Germany was the center of the universe and that everything made for the German market could be exported to the world. No one thought about the consumer." Puma's brand manager Antonio Bertone rationalized this new fashion approach: "The only thing that reliably stimulates someone to buy is aesthetics. The way a (product) looks." Zeitz concurred, noting: "The majority of shoes get sold to the casual consumer, so you can't appeal from a performance point of view. You have to appeal to coolness as well." (44)

Even venerable boxing equipment manufacturer Everlast, founded in the Bronx in 1910 and supplier to legendary pugilists such as Jack Dempsey, Joe Louis, and Muhammad Ali, has made the jump into licensing. Even though the company still makes 90 percent of the world's boxing gloves, sales for all its boxing gear accounts for only 5 percent of all its sales (approximately $600 million in 2004). The rest comes from footwear, fitness equipment, licensed clothing lines, cosmetics, jewelry, nutrition bars, and fragrances. (45)

In addition, some celebrities who have been used by athletic apparel companies to promote their products are now jumping into the market. In the last several years, music performers such as Sean Combs (Sean John), Jay-Z (Rocawear), Eminem (Shady), 50 Cent (G-Unit), Jennifer Lopez (Sweetface Fashions, along with the perfumes "Glow" and "Live" and a "JLo" retail store in Moscow), and Eve (Fetish) have all created branded fashion clothing and product lines. Although some have done well (Sean John and Rocawear), others such as Shady and G-Unit have proven to be less than stellar sellers. However, industry experts say these lines sell as well as many established fashion lines, and the lines that do best are those with which the celebrity is intimately involved and those that have a clearly defined fashion image. Crystal Williams, a 19-year-old student at Bronx (New York) Regional High School (the main target demographic for these companies), said that although a celebrity name doesn't necessarily mean she will buy a product, "it's quality and pricing . . . a lot of celebrity clothes are reasonably priced." Fellow shopper Keith Sean added, "If I were a celebrity, I'd definitely do [my own line]." (46)

Current Issues and Trends in Licensing and Branding

It should be clear by this point in the chapter that trends are important in licensing and branding. The following sections will discuss some of the key issues and trends of licensing and branding such as brand identity; electronics and technology; conduct among licensees, licensors, and manufacturers; and product innovation.

Brand Identity

As described earlier, licensed products communicate messages relating to identity, gender, status, and sexuality; fans purchase goods to draw them closer to their beloved organizations and athletes. Langehough took this notion further, stating that such items not only reflect personal identity, "they can also serve to transform it," and cited the work of French philosopher Jean Baudrillard, who observed that "sign value"—the amount of status attributed by consumers to products and brands—serves less to meet consumer needs and more as a measure of meaning, prestige, and social standing in consumer society. In investigating the importance of athletics on American college campuses, Toma noted that school mascots and logos "represent an array of symbols distinctive to the institution in ways that evoke pride and success . . . these symbols connect people with institutions by evoking, symbolizing and epitomizing them," and cited the work of Anderson and Stone in noting that logos provide institutional stakeholders with concrete representations of who and for what the institution stands. (47)

Sport logos, wrote Steven Skov Holt, "go after the eyeballs; they race, animate, and graphically collide with one another at breakneck speed, and their aggressiveness in seeking attention is matched only by their precise placement on the body, equipment, or playing surface." They are part of a corporate approach to sport product imagery "where the exterior of many products is transformed into a carefully composed marketing collage." But to do this effectively, sport organizations must craft images and marks that communicate not only clear visual and design elements, but also the exact concrete symbolic and sign value the organization wants to be perceived as possessing. (48)

To achieve this end, many sport organizations have sought to establish valued perceptions through the redesign of their uniforms, marks, and logos. A trend was established in the mid-1990s after the success of the logos and colors introduced by expansion teams such as the San Jose Sharks and the Anaheim Mighty Ducks. Other franchises jumped on the redesign

You can tell from their matching clothing that these fans all support the same team.
Courtesy of the Miami Heat

bandwagon, as seen in the 32-month period from January 1995 through August 1997 when 25 teams introduced redesigned logos, uniforms, or both. However, these actions were seen as efforts mainly aimed at pumping up related licensed product sales rather than intentional efforts to rebrand the clubs. Recently, the NFL's Atlanta Falcons and Seattle Seahawks discovered in focus group research that their fans thought their logos did not represent the speed, focus, and intimidating characteristics of either the respective fowl or the teams. The Seahawks opted to streamline their aviary mark, replaced kelly green with steel blue, and added a fluorescent green to their color scheme. Staff in Atlanta altered the flying falcon side silhouette logo that had been in place since the franchise's inception in 1966, adding dark red and silver and tilting the mark forward to create a sense of movement. Said Dick Sullivan, the club's vice president of marketing: "We kept hearing from fans that they wanted to keep the identity but wanted more color, excitement, and fierceness." (49)

There are risks with rebranding efforts, however, as indicated by one industry expert who noted: "The danger in making a change is whether you're sacrificing the historical identity of the club just to be trendy." The Toronto MLB franchise chose the nickname "Blue Jays" from 4,000 fan suggestions in a name-the-team contest before joining the American League in 1976. Although only one entry cited the name, the team, then owned by Labatt, Canada's largest brewer, chose the entry because it had the word *blue* in the name, and, according to one official, "Um, Blue is our biggest selling pilsner beer" [author's emphasis]. It was hoped that the name would prompt fans to derive a strong connection between Labatt's product and the club; the club also hoped that the name eventually would be abbreviated by fans and sports writers to "Blues," bringing the identification to its alcoholic beverage even closer. The team incorporated a red maple leaf—the national symbol of Canada—in its design scheme, but the leaf was swept out of the team's new designs in 2004. The team has used the maple leaf to align itself with the nation at large, much in the way the cross-town NHL franchise has done for decades, and to position itself against the Quebec-based and Francophone-focused Montreal Expos, which had begun play several years earlier. The bagging of the leaf upset some Canadians, but a Jays VP said of the decision, "We wanted the brand to stand more on its own. People know we're a Canadian club. We want to appeal to our fans from Western New York . . . we no longer want to be thought of as exclusively Canadian." (50)

Although this was less of an issue for the Falcons and Seahawks (relatively young franchises with few past seasons of glory), some teams have returned to their visual pasts in their rebranding efforts, or have redesigned in an effort to find a design family that works. Before the 2001-2002 season, the NBA's Detroit Pistons scrapped their teal, black, red, and gold mix and dual-exhaust, auto-horse logo introduced five years before in favor of the red, white, and blue ensemble worn by the two-time champion "Bad Boys" teams of the late 1980s (to promote the new look and to combat perceptions that it was introduced solely to squeeze money from fans, the Pistons offered discounts at retail stores on new merchandise to any fan who brought in apparel with the old designs). The Seattle SuperSonics also did the same, whereas the Cleveland Cavaliers and Houston Rockets redesigned looks in line with discontinued color schemes. The Phoenix Coyotes chose to rebrand in 2003, just a few years after the team's move from Winnipeg. After the team had gone through an ownership change and an impending move to a new arena, the club used outside research and design firms to get input on new marks. Team executives also sat in on sessions with fans. The team chose the marks and colors most liked by fans, reconfiguring its coyote logo to denote aggression and speed, and opting for a red and sand color scheme. The team's public relations staff used the release of the new marks in September 2003 to reconnect with media during a time important to priming ticket sales for the upcoming season. They released the new looks early on the team's Web site to acculturate fans toward using the site as an information conduit. (51)

Because league teams share all licensing revenues equally, the new approach to focus on the branding impact of marks, uniforms, and logos is a more compelling reason to redesign than to increase product sales, but many of the new marks, logos, and uniforms have received mixed reviews. The Falcons' new look has been called cluttered. Said a design professor at the

University of Georgia: "Whatever appeal the old logo had came from its geometric abstraction of the natural form. The new one retains the awkward wing-down pose, but forfeits the formal quality that makes it okay. It just looks goofy." However, products bearing the name and number of QB Mike Vick sold well in 2003, even though he missed most of the year because of an injury. Team success is usually the best indicator for high-selling merchandise, as noted by San Diego Padres reliever Trevor Hoffman, who said of his team's new look introduced in 2004 in conjunction with the opening of Petco Park, the team's new home grounds: "Ultimately, it's the way we play on the field that's going to make any uniform look good." (52)

Electronics and Technology

Although much of the licensed market relies on apparel sales, a growing portion of sales are coming from electronic and technology products. The top-selling U.S. video and DVD of all time? The NFL Films production chronicling the 2001-2002 championship run of the New England Patriots. Not just of *sport* videos and DVDs—of all videos and DVDs, period. Number two? The 2003-2004 version of the Pats' Super Season. As noted earlier, EA Sports dominates the sport games market. Company founder Trip Hawkins saw the market as "a predictable business that had a strong following," and the company realized, according to

Cross-Licensing—Cowboy Up!

It was late August 2003, and the Boston Red Sox seemed to be in the throes of yet another late-season swoon. The team had just lost two out of three games to the Oakland Athletics, and had fallen further behind the New York Yankees in the American League East divisional race, with the denizens of the hated "Evil Empire" due in town in a few days for a pivotal three-game series. In the locker room after the game, media members were going through their routine of interviewing players about the outcome. When they questioned first baseman/outfielder Kevin Millar about the club's prospects, he took umbrage at the cloud of doom portended by fans and media alike. Millar had already achieved local cult status because of his animated and outspoken personality (a contrast to the often dour, petulant, and/or reserved public demeanors of Sox stars Manny Ramirez, Nomar Garciaparra, and Pedro Martinez.) After some college buddies sent the club a video of him lip-synching to Bruce Springsteen's "Born in the USA," the team then showed the video on the Fenway Park scoreboard screens late in games, dubbing it "Rally Karaoke Guy," a takeoff on the "Rally Monkey" video phenomenon used by the Anaheim Angels in their World Series–winning run in 2002. Millar, a Los Angeles native who attended college in Texas, challenged the citizenry of Red Sox Nation to "cowboy up," a phrase meaning to get tough and buckle down. The term was unfamiliar to those who spoke the elongated vowel sounds ("cah" is something you drive; "bah" is where you go to watch the game and quaff if Fenway "Pahk" is sold out) native to regional patois. *Wicked,* as an all-purpose adjective that usually stands in place of the word *very,* they knew, but "cowboy up"? The closest cowboys ever got to Fenway was when the Dallas NFL franchise played the Patriots down Route 1 in Foxborough.

But soon after Millar's call to arms, the phrase caught on with fans. As the team regrouped to win the AL wild card and came from 0-2 down to win the Divisional Series playoff against the A's, fans began wearing Western garb to games and the phrase appeared on a banner on the state house a few blocks away from Fenway's storied Green Monster and on electronic highway signs around the region. Fenway area street vendors—many of whom make a living on selling an array of unlicensed "Yankees suck" goods—began selling products bearing the phrase.

The phones started to ring off the hook (and the Web site hits totaled in the thousands) in the Wyoming offices of Harry Talermo, the president of Wyoming West Design, which owns the trademark on Millar's locker room utterance (get it?). The company focuses on licensing and selling products such as silver belt buckles and pickup truck mud flaps, but now they were wondering what was going on in Boston. Soon thereafter, in time for the Sox' postseason run, Talermo signed licensing deals with the club and other manufacturers for caps, T-shirts, blankets, and teddy bears, and flew to Boston to work with local police to crack down on the counterfeiters. However, after the comeback series win against the A's pumped up sales further, a stupefying Game 7 American League Championship Series loss to the Evils, due in large part to the well-documented eighth-inning brain lock of soon-to-be-former Sox manager Grady Little, meant that the "cowboy up" caps, T-shirts, and sweatshirts going for $30 to $50 were soon on sale at deep discounts. But Talermo, a former tennis pro from Finland, remained upbeat: "We never thought it would spread to baseball, but it did. Maybe it can go pretty much anywhere it wants to go." (53)

one industry expert, that the advent of each new season brought the chance to update games with personnel changes and new statistics, creating a "phenomenon of selling again, again, and again." The value of these deals to manufacturers and licensors is undeniable. In 2004, EA Sports, which owns 90 percent of the football game market, entered into a four-year deal with Players, Inc., worth $1 billion. The company earned revenues of $2.3 billion in 2003, and also has agreements with MLB, the NBA, the NHL, and NASCAR. (54)

Advances in technology have been seen most dramatically in sport video and computer games, in which graphical advances have moved games from the video Stone Age of Pong and Atari to the point where NASCAR drivers such as Dale Earnhardt Jr. use new games to train for actual driving. NASCAR believes so strongly in EA Sports that it has an exclusive agreement with the company for licensed sport games. The advances have also been a boon to licensors, allowing EA Sports to create FIFA Soccer 2004, complete with 10,000 specific international stars from 350 specific teams and 16 leagues around the world.

But now video games are not just solo endeavors. Console and game manufacturers see online gaming (along with downloadable game upgrades) as the real future of the industry, with 1.2 million users playing online as of 2004. Microsoft's Xbox Live generates $50 million a year from its 150 online games, which includes $50 annual subscription fees and a $70 starter kit that includes a headset that allows players to talk as they play online. Ninety percent of EA Sports new releases in 2004 included online features. One reviewer of Microsoft's Xbox game system noted that the manufacturer recently updated the system's capability to support online fantasy leagues through the addition XSNSports, a Web-based service that allows live game players to set up leagues with groups of friends and track the season's progress. The innovation allows players to store and maintain their statistics over the course of a season of gaming. Microsoft then released NFL Fever 2004, the first game to support the new service. To use the service, a player logs on to a support Web site and creates a league, then sends e-mail invitations to potential participants. The participants then log in and enter information to join the league. Once the players are set, the league creator organizes a schedule and the players face off on Xbox Live as normal, using a specific username and password to track their team's progress, such as league standings, scores, stats, and trade proposals. Players can also participate in Microsoft-organized tournaments, and the game's graphics create virtual gridders who blink, sweat, and get dirty, and coaches who stalk the sidelines between plays emoting tips and tirades. In addition, targeted advertising and product placement in online games could also generate significant revenue for companies through virtual stadium signage in sport games, which could be customized based on the demographics of the online players. (55)

Technological advances in the communications industries have also led to advances in licensing. The XSNSports system just described enables NFL Fever 2004 players on Xbox Live to receive all gaming information on their cell phones, and a recent effort by cellular phone and service company Cingular encourages new and existing customers to order officially licensed (through CLC) college fight song ringtones. Customers create a text message with their phones, enter the word *ring* followed by the specific ringtone code for their favorite school, send the text message, and then save the ringtone in the phone's profile. The downloading of the ringtone could be done for little as 99 cents.

Licensee, Licensor, and Manufacturer Conduct

Licensed and branded footwear and apparel manufacturers have had a significant impact in the world of high school and intercollegiate athletics. Both Nike and Adidas, for example, have jumped headlong into sponsorship and equipment provision agreements with summer all-star basketball camps and high school and Amateur Athletic Union (AAU) basketball traveling all-star teams in hopes of finding the next LeBron James. These companies engage in these activities to establish connections early with high-profile young players so that these prospects will later be more likely to attend colleges and universities with whom these companies have sponsorship agreements. Ultimately, the hope is that if these young athletes continue to perform at high levels, they might eventually be seen wearing Nike or Adidas shoes in the NBA. As part of the no-holds-barred efforts to snap up potential future stars such as DerMarr Johnson, Lamar Odom, and Tracy McGrady, however, these companies have established connections with prep school coaches and people of questionable reputation like street agents. (56)

From a business standpoint, this early action on the part of Nike and Adidas is understandable. Locking up the next LeBron could mean millions, maybe billions, in future sales. Unfortunately, this results in the future of these young athletes being placed in the hands of schools and individuals who are more interested in furthering their own interests than they are of furthering those of the athletes. Codes of conduct or codes of ethics help clarify and outline the guidelines for behavior in various organizations. Implementing such codes in organizations in the licensed and branded apparel and footwear industry, however, is not always simple and straightforward.

Colleges and universities are not exempt from claims of athlete exploitation. In 2004, the University of Connecticut (UConn) licensed and sold jerseys (for $49.99) and hats (costing $26.99) bearing the numbers of star basketball players Ben Gordon, Emeka Okafor, and Diana Taurasi at the campus bookstore, online, and through retail outlets such as Bob's Stores. NCAA regulations passed in 1992 bar schools from using player names and likenesses to sell products, and also bans student-athletes from promoting commercial ventures, but the UConn bookstore Web site touted one of the "favorite player hats" as honoring "the team player who wears the #3 UConn jersey for women's basketball," i.e., Taurasi. Critics of these practices, such as NCAA President Myles Brand and former UCLA football player Ramogi Huma (the head of the Collegiate Athletes Coalition, a California-based organization he founded to advocate for better living conditions for student-athletes), argued that UConn and other schools are acting unethically and contradictory to the spirit of the NCAA rules in licensing and selling these products. Said Brand: "My concerns are over the potential inconsistency between our making certain requirements on student-athletes about endorsements, namely they cannot make any, and the schools themselves then using what would be endorsement material for revenue." Huma said athletes such as Gordon, Okafor, and Taurasi should share in the proceeds from the sales of the apparel. "The reason [the products] are being sold . . . is that these are famous players," Huma claimed. "If a player gets a cut of the sale of his or her jersey, that does not mean the player is a professional." (57)

Although licensors have quality control over the images on licensed products, they do not control all operations of the licensees. Licensees are independent businesses, and as such conduct their business as they see fit. But licensors have come under criticism for this as well: Recently the NBA was forced by public pressure to pull from its Fifth Avenue store in Manhattan $60 sweatshirts imported from Myanmar (formerly Burma). The National Labor Committee (NLC), an antisweatshop organization, accused the league of violating a federal law against selling products from Myanmar. The director of NLC said the country is "one of the most vicious dictatorships in the world," where workers are paid as little as seven cents an hour. Hip-hop star Sean Combs' line of apparel, Sean John, has also been accused of using sweatshop labor in Honduras, with workers making 90 cents an hour. (58)

Because of these poor standards and practices, it is not uncommon for licensors to be seen as responsible for them as well. Colleges and universities are especially susceptible to this sort of scrutiny, given the heightened sensitivities of educational communities and institutional educational missions, which are further enhanced by the religious affiliations at some schools. When the University of Wisconsin made public its licensing agreement with Reebok, certain personnel at the university questioned Reebok's business practices and labor relations with Southeast Asian manufacturers, claiming that Reebok shoe assemblers in Indonesia received only $2.45 per day. A petition circulated by professors stated, "If the University of Wisconsin advertises a firm like Reebok, it accepts the conditions under which Reebok profits." The university's agreement with Reebok also contained a clause stating that university employees would not disparage Reebok, but after considerable campus outcry, the clause was omitted from the contract. (59)

In response to this sort of criticism, many schools have published a code of conduct for all licensees. Notre Dame, affiliated with the Congregatio a Sancta Cruce (CSC) order of the Catholic church and particularly susceptible to such criticisms given its combined status as a religious institution and a perennial football power, has composed a code that states that the school is "committed to conducting its business affairs in a socially responsible manner consistent with its religious and educational mission." Consequently, Notre Dame stipulates that all licensees must meet the university's stated standards for legal and environmental compliance, ethical principles, and employment practices. Codes of conduct such as Notre Dame's establish norms that reinforce individual and organizational ethical behavior. (60)

A final ethical issue faced by sport organizations involves the depiction of their logos, marks, nicknames, and mascots and the context in which they are viewed. This issue has been raised specifically by those who are offended by the way schools and professional teams portray Native American mascots. Schools such as Florida State University, the University of Illinois, and the University of North Dakota (a few of the over 4,000 schools and colleges that use Native American nicknames and mascots), and professional clubs such as the Atlanta Braves, the Chicago Blackhawks, the Cleveland Indians, and the Washington Redskins have come under fire for perpetuating negative stereotypical images of violent and primitive Native Americans. Although many schools and colleges such as Dartmouth College (originally founded in the early 1700s to teach Christianity to Native Americans), Stanford University (whose football team was dubbed "the Indians" because former football coach Glenn "Pop" Warner had come from the Carlisle Indian School in Pennsylvania, where he had coached Native American football and Olympic standout Jim Thorpe), and the University of Tennessee at Chattanooga dropped Native American nicknames and mascots as early as three decades ago, other organizations have responded to these accusations from organizations such as the National Coalition Against Racism in Sports and Media and the National Congress of American Indians by claiming that their depictions are meant to honor Native Americans and their heritage. The Cleveland Indians state that the club's nickname is connected to former player Louis Sockalexis, a Penobscot tribe member from Old Town, Maine. The University of Illinois uses a befeathered "Chief Illiniwek" on licensed products and to lead the school band onto the field at home football games. (61)

Many schools and colleges have agreed with the claims that their logos, marks, and mascots are racist and should be changed and have acted to do so, but professional teams have fought the notion, some in court. In 2003, the Washington Redskins won a suit filed by activists who sought to prove the trademark name was disparaging to Native Americans. U.S. District Judge Colleen Kollar-Kotelly threw out the 1999 decision by the U.S. Patent and Trademark Office board to cancel six of the team's trademarks, citing not her opinion on the racist nature of the marks (to many Native Americans, the epithet "redskin" is as offensive as the "N word" is to African Americans), but rather that the board had relied on "partial, dated and irrelevant evidence submitted by the activists." The decision was the final step in a legal battle that began in 1992, and protected the approximately $5 million earned annually by the club in licensing sales. Team owner Snyder has consistently stated that he would not change the team's name. It is interesting to note that George Preston Marshall, the longtime owner of the team, was an avowed racist. The Redskins were the self-professed "Team of the South" and played "Dixie" at its games into the 1960s, and were the last NFL team to field an all-white roster. Marshall defended his stance by vowing, "We'll start signing Negroes when the Harlem Globetrotters start signing whites," but was forced to alter his segregationist stance when federal funds were used to construct D.C. (later RFK) Stadium, effectively outlawing discriminatory hiring practices by any tenant. (62)

Product Innovation

The licensed and branded product market relies on innovations of all sorts, and products can come in all forms. Consider the most venerated licensed product, the trading card. Millions of American youths grew up collecting the cards that bore the likenesses and statistics of their favorite baseball and other sport stars. Two such youths, Fred Harris and Brendan Boyd, later wrote that late March—the time they could buy baseball cards at their local convenience store—marked the time that the "long agony of winter was almost over. . . . Oh, they were beautiful and reassuring to behold, brand new and glistening crisply in their packages. Packed into cardboard cartons of 24 and 120, stuck behind glassed partitions and stacked on counters. An indication that the world was still in order, a promise of pleasant days and easeful nights . . . our surviving of another school year seemed possible." (63)

Topps, which began in 1890 as the American Leaf Tobacco Company—an importer of tobacco for independent cigar manufacturers—soon became the dominant force in the market. The company switched to making chewing gum during the Great Depression of the 1930s, then in 1951 started to use sport trading cards, specifically baseball cards, to sell bubble gum. Card collecting was popular as early as the late 19th century, and companies included sets of Civil War generals and Native American chiefs inserted in cigar packs. The most valuable card of all time, a Honus Wagner card issued by the Sweet Caporal Company in 1910, was discontinued after Wagner, a nonsmoker whose likeness was used without his permission, objected. Other companies such as Goudy Gum and Bowman had specialized in cards, and had most of the market sewed up through deals with star players. As noted earlier, the company entered the market by signing contracts with legitimate minor league prospects, first with as little as $1, later increased $5. Topps negotiated a comprehensive agreement with the MLBPA in 1968 in which the company was permitted to continue manufacturing trading cards bearing player likenesses for double the player's previous yearly fees (from $125 to $250, now up to $500), and paid the union 8 percent on annual sales up to $4 million and 10 percent on all subsequent sales. Company personnel would do all the photography and write all the copy for the backs. (64)

Topps dominated the baseball card market until 1981, when a federal court antitrust decision broke their stranglehold, leading to an explosion of competition. By the late 1980s, new card varieties developed a speculative market, with consumers flooding the market with cash seeking to buy cards as investments. The market bubble grew until 1991, when sport card sales topped $1.2 billion, then burst, settling to annual sales of $300 million by 2004. In response, card makers have struggled to regain market share with new products and sets, such as cards with pieces of bats or game-worn uniforms affixed to them. In 2003, four separate card companies released 87 separate sets of cards. In addition to these new sets is a $500 five-card pack of basketball cards released by the Upper Deck Company in 2004, which eclipsed the previous industry-high price of $150. Included in some will be the actual NBA logo off game-worn jerseys of Michael Jordan and Carmelo Anthony. Each pack will contain at least one rookie autographed patch card and other autographed patch cards featuring the likes of Kevin Garnett, Kobe Bryant, Bill Russell, and Julius Erving. But industry experts who believed some cards in the set could be resold for as much as $20,000 were wrong—one card featuring swatches from Bryant and James sold on eBay for $62,100. (65)

Another recent product innovation was the release by Fleer Trading Cards of 15,000 sets of "America's Jews in America's Game," the brainchild of Brooklyn native Martin Abramowitz. The set includes a card for all 142 Jewish major leaguers from 1871 through 2003, including Hall of Famers Hank Greenberg and Sandy Koufax, as well as lesser lights such as Mike "Superjew" Epstein and Moe "The Rabbi of Swat" Solomon. The set is available only to those who make a $100 contribution to the American Jewish Historical Society (AJHS), which spent $25,000 to underwrite the project. MLB, the MLBPA and the National Baseball Hall of Fame and Museum have supported the project as well. Interest in the sets has been high, says Abramowitz (who works for the Combined Jewish Philanthropies of Boston), who initiated the series because he wanted a complete set of all Jewish players for himself, and there were no cards for 40 Jewish players. He tracked down all the player photographs himself. "Five years ago, I was sitting at the kitchen table with my son . . . lamenting that I'll probably never have a complete collection (of Jewish players). He said off-handedly, 'So make your own cards.' I feel a sense of obligation to complete the record of American Jewish ballplayers and to do justice to their memory." The popularity of the set led to a two-day celebration of Jewish players at the National Baseball Hall of Fame and Museum in August 2004, with several of the featured players attending. (66)

So what's next? Stall & Dean is hoping it might be roller derby jerseys. The company introduced a line for women modeled on jerseys worn by women's teams from the 1950s, 1960s, and 1970s, such as the New York Bombers and Reilly's Renegades. Said the manager of a retail store in Brooklyn, where the jerseys sell for $120: "I've only got three left. A lot of the girls like the tight fit." This is supported by the sales of mainstream women's licensed products, toward which industry experts are looking with increasing interest. According to Susan Rothman of NFL Properties, the priorities for female customers are: "No unisex. No oversized guys' T-shirts. Women want color, more form-fitting styles, and smaller graphics." (67)

Stay tuned to see whether roller derby duds make it big, but M&N's Harley remains the undaunted pied piper of vintage looks, stating "This isn't a fad, because it can't be. These

Epilogue: Throwbacks Continued

By the end of 2003, the throwback trend was in full force. Manufacturers involved in licensing, such as Majestic, had jumped on the trend, turning out cheaper items without player names or numbers for as little as $45. Russell Athletic introduced a line of college football throwbacks featuring grid stars of yore, including Marcus Allen (University of Southern California), Dick Butkus (Illinois), John Elway (Stanford), Bo Jackson (Auburn University), Deion Sanders (Florida State) and Jesse Sapolu (the University of Hawaii), in large part because, as noted earlier, current NCAA amateurism rules forbid schools from licensing or selling jerseys bearing the names of current collegiate players. The hottest seller of the vintage bunch? The #12 black-and-gold Purdue University jersey worn by now-ABC commentator Bob Griese, who quarterbacked the Boilermakers to the Rose Bowl in the mid-1960s. Said a Detroit-area retailer who has sold many throwbacks, Griese's included, the market is "almost entirely urban." The impact of rappers and hip-hop culture on moving the licensed and branded product market has not gone unnoticed by the industry giants either. Because 80 percent of Reebok's sporting apparel isn't used in sporting activities at all, but rather worn for fashion, the company recently signed Jay-Z, 50 Cent, Mary J. Blige, and producer/performer Pharrell Williams to endorsement deals. Leagues and retailers were beginning to contract directly with hip-hop stars to sell product as well, as MLB Properties and Finish Line did for Snoop Dogg's 2004 Projekt Revolution summer tour (which also featured Linkin Park and Korn). The deal called for Snoop to wear MLB Authentics hats and jerseys in the 20 MLB markets on the tour. Finish Line used Snoop in back-to-school in-store promotions, and MLB also created for the tour a 53-foot (16-meter) "Access to the Show" trailer, replete with batting and pitching cages and a selection of merchandise. (68)

But every trend has an end, even though rapper Fabolous implored his connections at M&N on his album *Street Dreams*: "Rube, tell Pete to keep 'em coming." The cooling for throwbacks began when Jay-Z released his *Black Album* in 2003. According to Dave Schneider, manager of Jimmy's, a chain of family-owned urban clothing and footwear stores in southern Connecticut, the day after the disk was released, his customers, mostly young African American males, came in and were looking for something new. "Jay-Z rapped on one song ["What more can I say"], 'I don't wear jerseys . . . give me a crisp pair of jeans and a button-up,'" recalled Schneider, "and the kids came in asking for oxford-cloth, button-down dress shirts. Our sales of throwbacks dropped 50 percent." (However, Jay-Z couldn't leave the licensed world entirely, as he rapped on "Encore": "When I come back like Jordan wearing the 45," a reference to the jersey number Michael Jordan wore on the resumption of his career after retirement the first time.) A few weeks later, Jay-Z appeared on the cover of *ESPN Magazine* with Denver Nuggets forward Carmelo Anthony, sporting the look about which he rapped. (69)

Were the throwback glory days ending, just as they were for mesh trucker hats and the Hilton sisters? Some disagreed, and were creating niche throwback products to continue the trend. Claude Johnson, who worked as a licensor for the NBA during the 50th anniversary year, was moved to create apparel based on the uniforms of black basketball teams of the 1920s and 1930s such as the Smart Set Athletic Club of Brooklyn and the Washington 12th Streeters. The "Black Fives" line has caught on in more urbane rather than urban settings (noted Princeton University professor Cornel West is a customer) as a result of a look that Johnson called "clean and preppy . . . Not everyone likes big, loud letters and numbers." Companies such as Headmaster, Inc., of California were also pushing collegiate niche looks in early 2004, signing 100 current and former players from the Big Four leagues to exclusive deals, including Lou Gehrig (Columbia University), Jerry Rice (Mississippi Valley State), and Isiah Thomas (Indiana University). The company expected to make $15 million in 2004 not by tapping the urban market, but rather by scaling back the sizes and prices of products to reach "mainstream-demographic consumers." This niche approach may extend the throwback trend further. (70)

uniforms are the history of sports. They're just like the players wore them, down to the fabric and the stitching and lettering. Styles come and go, but you can't change the 1979 Magic Johnson jersey. It has its place in time." (71) Only time will tell whether Harley is correct, but as writer Bill Simmons opined in defense of wearing licensed product: "As Seinfeld once joked, we're rooting for laundry, anyway. So why not wear the laundry?" (72)

Wrap-Up

The licensed and branded products and apparel industry continues to generate significant revenues. Teams and leagues earn a certain percentage of sales, called royalties, on items bearing their logos. Leagues and players associations administer licensing programs on the professional level. Colleges may administer their own licensing programs or may enlist the services of organizations such as the CLC. People are needed to work in many areas in both the sporting goods and licensed products industries. These areas cut across many other segments of the sport industry, including professional sport, intercollegiate athletics, recreational sport, and the health and fitness industry. Wherever there is a need for the right clothing or product to announce that a person is connected to a sport property or activity, the licensed and branded product industry is there to fill the need.

Activities

1. What advantages does licensing provide to sport entities? To licensees?
2. Describe the steps involved in the licensing process. What are the components of licensing agreements?
3. If you were a collegiate athletics director, would you opt for an independent licensing program, or would you enlist the services of a licensing company? Why?
4. Describe the difference between a licensed product and a branded product. What recent trends have affected the sales for each?
5. What are some of the reasons sport entities choose to redesign logos and color schemes? What are the risks involved in these decisions?

Chapter 10

Pricing Strategies

Objectives

- ✦ To understand core issues of price versus cost, price and value, and the setting of pricing objectives.
- ✦ To understand the main pricing practices used in the sport industry.
- ✦ To recognize the special factors that influence any pricing strategy.

Prices Send Gallery Gods to the Penalty Box

When Bobby Orr led Boston's "Big, Bad Bruins" to the Stanley Cup in 1970, the celebration may have been loudest in Boston Garden's upper balcony, the home of the famous "Gallery Gods." As vocal as they were knowledgeable, the Gallery Gods represented the everyday, working-class fan. Orr's winning goal was payback for 29 years of loyal, Cup-less rooting, often for cellar-dwelling teams.

Unfortunately, loyalty became an endangered ethos when professional sport entered the age of free agents and corporate suits. Higher payrolls for players and administrators meant only one thing—higher ticket prices—especially in pro hockey, which lacked a strong national television package. By 1998, Bruins ticket prices in the new FleetCenter were the highest in the National Hockey League. The cheapest price for "upper-bowl" seats was $24 per seat when purchased as part of a season-ticket package. The same seat on a single-game basis cost $29. In the "lower bowl," where the elevation didn't induce nosebleeds, the seats were $60 per game.

The higher prices meant fewer Gallery Gods such as Roger Naples, a 77-year-old Bruin die-hard. The 780 remaining faithful had to pool their money into 300 season tickets. In effect, escalating prices had shoved some of the most committed Bruin fans *down* the escalator of involvement. Higher prices and some mediocre teams also drove attendance levels well below capacity, to about 15,000 per game in the 17,565-seat FleetCenter (now the TD Banknorth Garden). The season-ticket base dropped 30 percent, from about 16,000 in 1995-1996 to around 10,500 in 1997-1998.

The Bruins responded with several pricing strategies. First, they announced a dramatic $9.50 (39.5 percent) decrease in prices for 7,500 upper-bowl seats. Not all prices went down, however. Five thousand lower-bowl seats went up by $5 (8.3 percent). The "Robin Hood" strategy sat well with Roger Naples, who offered a common reaction: "Hey, they're the rich people. Take it from them. . . . Lemme tell ya, it was the best move they ever made. . . . I think you'll see a lot of the Gods come back and buy seats again." Matt Brennan, Bruins director of ticket operations, corroborated Naples' common sense. "Generally speaking," said Brennan, "it's gone over very well. One of the nice things is, some of the people who dropped their season tickets . . . they're coming back."

The Bruins were on to something. In the next two years, almost half of the NHL's teams jumped on the price-cutting wagon, often repeating the Bruins "Robin Hood" strategy. NHL fans had become increasingly price sensitive, and franchises had to be much more creative in their strategies. The lockout of 2004-2005 only made matters more precarious. When the players and owners settled, the Bruins were among the first teams to announce across-the-board price cuts, as well as the return of some $10 seats, last seen almost two decades before in the old Garden. In the words of Bruins executive Charlie Jacobs, "The key up front is to let people know we are back and to thank people for their support."

Price is one of the five Ps in sport marketing. Decisions to raise or lower prices have both short- and long-term effects on consumer involvement and commitment. Fans such as Roger Naples understand (often better than team marketers) some fundamental principles in pricing sports. For one thing, although price drives consumer perceptions of product value, consumers also have limits on total costs. When the Bruins cut prices, Roger Naples figured that the average guy could now go to three or four games per year instead of one, maybe even taking "a couple of kids." The frivolous fan, he added, might even splurge on a "$2.50 hot dog or a $4.75 beer." That is where Roger Naples drew the line. "Not me," he swore. "At those prices, I have my beer after the game." (1)

Marketers must be very clear on the objectives of their pricing strategy. The Bruins made a clear statement with their 1998 "Robin Hood" strategy. They were also responding to supply and demand. In this chapter, we consider the notion of market demand. We also outline traditional pricing strategies such as break-even, cost-plus, and their variants. Finally, we consider special factors in sport pricing such as penetration and skimming, lead time, user-segmentation pricing, time- and place-segmentation pricing, and the role of pricing in public relations and promotions.

The Basics of Pricing

Marketers must recognize the vast range of product elements that require pricing. In the sport world, these include the following:

✦ Hard or soft goods (equipment or apparel)

✦ Tickets

✦ Memberships

✦ Concessions (food, novelties)

✦ Information (magazine, cable subscriptions)

✦ Access for corporate entities (entitlement space, signage, banner ads)

✦ Image ("Swoosh"/photo)

These elements are priced according to a range of variables, including location (seat or parking), time (athlete's or court), quality, and quantity.

Price is a critical element in the marketing mix for a number of reasons. First, prices can be readily changed. Second, in certain market conditions (specifically, where demand is elastic), price is one of the most effective tools. Third, price is highly visible; hence, changes are easily communicated, resulting in possible changes in consumer perceptions. Finally, price is never far from the consumer's mind.

Core Issues

The core issues in any pricing situation are cost, value, and objectives. Remember our central equation:

$$\text{Satisfaction} = \text{Benefit} - \text{Cost}$$

Cost is the most visible and often most compelling part of the equation. In a recent survey, female golfers listed the following factors (by percentage) as "important" in decisions about purchasing equipment:

Price (76 percent)

Value (54 percent)

Brand reputation (29 percent)

Selection variety (27 percent)

Service (17 percent)

This is probably not far from the results one would get from Roger Naples and the other Gallery Gods as they consider ticket purchases. Price, as we said, is never far from the consumer's mind. (2)

Cost Versus Price: Developing a Cost Index

As Roger Naples recognized, the price of a ticket does not represent the real "cost" of attendance, which would include travel, parking, and concessions (that is, if Roger buys a hot dog and a beer at the game). The difference between a marketer's sense of "price" and a consumer's sense of "cost" holds true in most forms of sport involvement. For instance, the real "cost" of golfing includes at least the purchase or rental of clubs, bag, and shoes; the purchase of balls, tees, and glove; cart rental (pull or ride); greens fees; travel to and from the course; and postgolf refreshment at the "19th hole." Note also that golfers might pay a range of prices for these elements according to certain values such as tee time availability, course difficulty, and aesthetic appeal.

Skiers face even greater total costs for their experience. For instance, in the 1990s the Michigan Ski Industries Association estimated that the average adult skier spent $114.60 per day, in the following proportions (by percent):

- Retail (26 percent)
- Entertainment (10 percent)
- Lodging (18 percent)
- Transportation (9 percent)
- Tickets (17 percent)
- Ski rental (4 percent)
- Food (14 percent)
- Lessons (2 percent)

The obvious point is that marketers must appreciate total "cost" from the consumer's perspective, which often includes elements priced by three or four different providers. (3)

In the team sport industry, this approach to cost was first championed by *Team Marketing Report*, a leading industry newsletter. Since 1991, *Team Marketing Report* has tracked the "fan cost index" (FCI) for every team in MLB, the NBA, the NFL, and the NHL. The FCI includes the following price elements for a family of four:

- Four "average-price" tickets
- Two small draft beers
- Four small soft drinks
- Four hot dogs
- Parking for one car
- Two game programs
- Two adult-size caps

In 2003-2004, for example, the NHL average FCI was $253.65, up 2.8 percent from the prior year. The New York Rangers ranked 12th in average ticket price ($44.58) but were 8th in total FCI (in part because of high parking costs). The Red Wings had cheap parking, but their high ticket average ($57.11) took them to the top of the FCI rankings. The NHL average ticket price was $43.57. The lowest FCI belonged to the Carolina Hurricanes ($193.06). (4)

The fan cost index—now widely distributed via other publications such as *USA Today*—has been an invaluable service to fans and marketers alike, even if some teams have objected to the formula. One year, for instance, the Boston Red Sox distributed a one-page press release claiming that their FCI (the Red Sox ranked second in MLB) did not factor in stadium size, availability of parking, cost of living, or special discounts. According to the Red Sox, if you took only the price of the best 33,871 seats (Fenway Park's capacity at the time) in each MLB stadium, the Red Sox would look much better. *Team Marketing Report* editor Sean Brenner responded that this argument entirely missed the point of the FCI, which is meant to be a relative measure. Fans will make up their own minds about the cost of living and the number of seats. After all, Fenway Park's coziness and limited seating can also increase demand for tickets. And Fenway's lack of team-controlled or public parking leaves many fans in the hands of greedy owners of nearby gas stations, retail stores, and hotels that cram extra cars into their lots at prices that rose to $1,000 during the Red Sox run to a World Series championship. Although the Red Sox cannot control those parking costs, they are reality in the life of Red Sox Nation. There is an ultimate logic to the FCI—ticket prices alone do not tell an accurate story. (5)

Value and Price

A higher price—or higher total cost—is not a categorical evil to consumers. Consumers often perceive a higher price to indicate higher quality; conversely, lower prices often suggest lower quality. This seems especially true with hard goods such as sport equipment. But the relationship is extensive. In 1996, for example, *CBS/Fox Sports Marketing* reported on consumer research into the optimum pricing of sport videos. The ideal price point was $14.98. Consumers were hesitant to pay more. On the other hand, consumers felt that lower prices reflected lower quality. (6)

Numerous teams and leagues have learned the hard way about the price–value relationship. The XFL failed for many reasons, but price/value was one of them. For the XFL, the NFL was an obvious basis of comparison. The XFL marketers clearly wanted to avoid a price so low as to suggest an inferior product, yet the XFL's fan demographics, facilities, and low product recognition precluded prices near the NFL range. They found themselves in a Catch-22. Low prices suggested low quality, which reinforced low prices, which . . . ad infinitum.

As collegiate women's programs have grown in stature, they have correctly begun to charge admission to events that had been free. Fans have discovered quickly that women's sports are worth the ticket price. These perceptions are critical to the marketing effort. Women's programs have become more aggressive about equating their prices (and total fan costs) to particular values, such as accessible and articulate athletes who enjoy higher graduation rates than their male counterparts. To many fans, this is a value worth paying for.

Consumer perceptions somehow link price (and total cost) with value. Marketers must recognize this and attempt to explain the connection. Product values may include these elements:

- ✦ Quality (including a sense of rivalry, competitiveness, and star power)
- ✦ Convenience (including proximity to venue and parking)
- ✦ Aesthetics
- ✦ Cleanliness, comfort, security
- ✦ Availability (of tee times, of good seats)
- ✦ Durability

These are just a few of the elements of value. Like total cost, value lives in the mind of the consumer. The marketer's job is to understand consumer perceptions of cost and value and to price accordingly.

Pricing Objectives

Although sport marketers must consider consumer perceptions of cost and value, they must also consider their organization's objectives when setting product prices. Depending on the nature of the organization (private versus public, profit versus nonprofit), the marketer may be influenced by some of the following objectives:

- ✦ Efficient use of resources (personnel, space)
- ✦ Fairness (consumers' ability to pay)
- ✦ Maximum participation opportunities
- ✦ Positive user attitudes or image
- ✦ Maximum product exposure and distribution
- ✦ Profits
- ✦ Survival

The push and pull of various objectives can lead to interesting pricing schemes. In the fall of 1997, for example, club seats for the NHL's Washington Caps and the NBA's Washington Wizards had a ticket face value of $48. This seemed like odd arithmetic, given that club seats were sold only on a season basis at $3,500 apiece, and if divided by 41 games, a single game should have cost $85.37—not $48. The *Washington Post* quickly discovered the most probable objective behind the pricing. If the new MCI Center—home to the Caps and the Wizards—

hoped to market the club seats to corporations and lobbyists, the face value of the ticket could not exceed the U.S. Senate's $49.99 limit on gifts to senators or their staffers! (7)

Standard Approaches to Pricing

There are several standard approaches to pricing that operate to varying degrees in the sport industry. In most cases, a common set of factors comes into play. These factors include the following: (8)

- Production costs, including salaries and facilities.
- Market conditions—namely, the supply and demand for a product that will, to some extent, define the market price. This relates to population density, average income, the consumer's sense of product value, the levels of product brand equity, and the availability of alternatives.
- Competitors' prices—not just of similar products, but also of any other products competing for the same consumer dollar (e.g., movies or a few drinks in a bar might well compete with an evening at a baseball game).
- Organizational objectives, including profit and distribution targets.
- Product or event frequency—MLB tickets cost less than NFL tickets in large part because MLB teams play 81 home games whereas NFL teams play 10.
- Brand strength—that is, team record, sales, advertising image.

Break-Even Analysis

There are two main elements of cost: fixed costs (FC) and variable costs (VC). Fixed costs, often referred to as overhead, consist of fundamentals such as stadium rental, taxes, and office equipment. Variable costs vary with output and include costs such as wages, material costs, and the cost of food and drinks at concessions. An example of a break-even analysis for the production and sale of soccer balls unfolds as follows given that FC + VC (per unit quantity produced) equals total cost (TC). (9)

XYZ Soccer Ball Manufacturers have the following cost:

$$FC = \$100,000$$

$$VC = \$11.50 \text{ per ball}$$

$$TC = FC + VC \text{ (per unit quantity produced)}$$

As figure 10.1 indicates, the slope of total costs parallels that of variable costs, but always at a higher point that reflects the fixed costs of $100,000. So at a production level of 4,000 balls (units),

$$TC = 100,000 + (11.50 \times 4,000)$$

$$= 100,000 + 46,000$$

$$= \$146,000$$

as indicated in figure 10.2. The price to break even at sales of 4,000 would be

$$146,000 = \$36.50$$

Although most firms will not price their product at just a break-even level, the analysis is instructive in several key areas.

First, as shown in figure 10.3, fixed cost per ball decreases as output increases (i.e., overhead allocated to each ball decreases as more balls are produced). A second key concept in a break-even analysis is that of contribution (toward paying off fixed costs). The contribution margin equals the selling price (SP) in excess of variable costs per unit:

$$Contribution = SP - VC$$

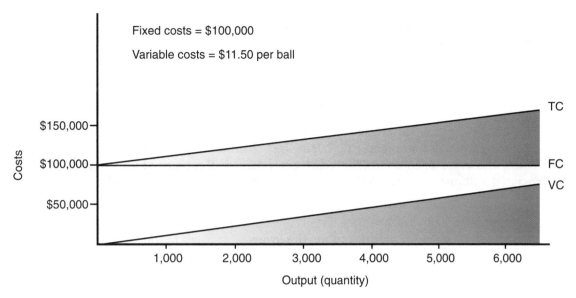

Fixed costs = $100,000

Variable costs = $11.50 per ball

FIGURE 10.1 Cost versus output for XYZ soccer balls.

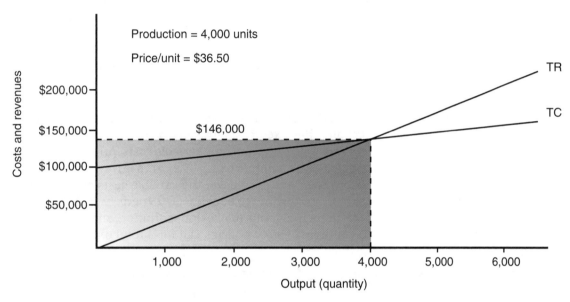

Production = 4,000 units

Price/unit = $36.50

$146,000

FIGURE 10.2 Break-even analysis for XYZ soccer balls.

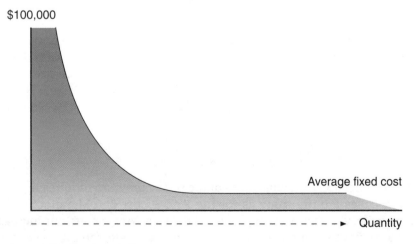

$100,000

Average fixed cost

Quantity

FIGURE 10.3 Average fixed cost per ball.

From our previous example for XYZ Soccer Ball Manufacturers, we can determine the contribution for each ball sold as follows:

$$SP = \$36.50$$
$$VC = \$11.50$$
$$\text{Contribution} = \$25.00$$

This analysis tells us how much each ball is contributing toward paying off the overhead of operating the ball manufacturing business. Contribution also provides an easy way to calculate the break-even point. The break-even point is the point at which all fixed costs associated with producing a product are covered through sales of the product.

$$\text{Break-even point} = \frac{FC}{\text{Contribution}}$$

$$FC = 100{,}000$$

$$\text{Break-even point} = \frac{\$100{,}000}{25} = 4{,}000 \text{ units}$$

The importance of break-even analysis to sport marketers lies in the implications it has for off-peak pricing in court clubs, health clubs, hockey rinks, and the like. During off-peak hours, when courts would remain idle at full price, a manager should charge anything above variable cost. Pricing slow periods in this manner allows the manager to soak up overhead costs through the receipt of additional revenues that otherwise would not have been received. The business could not remain in operation for the long run if all time periods were priced in this manner, but any contribution to overhead is good policy as long as people do not begin to switch from more costly peak hours.

Publicly sponsored sport programs often price their services using a variant of break-even pricing. In this case, on the philosophy that fixed costs (especially fields and facilities) are paid for by taxpayers, programmers will try to recapture only variable costs. An example is the Smallville Recreation Department's two-week summer camp. The camp is run on Smallville's existing fields and facilities. Therefore, the price must cover the variable costs of counselors, lifeguards, and other program leaders, plus any fringe benefits (at 25 percent of wages), and the supplies and materials used to run the programs (balls, transportation, snacks, shirts).

If the camp accommodates 80 youth and safety policies call for a total of six personnel, the variable costs might look like this:

(a) 6 leaders at \$7 per hour × 6 hours per day × 10 days = \$2,520

(b) Fringe benefits = 25 percent of (a) = \$630

(c) Supplies = \$1,600

Total variable costs = \$4,750

With 80 campers, the price would be \$4,750 ÷ 80 = \$59+ per camper.

If the Smallville Recreation Department budget is in a squeeze, the programmers may be forced to recapture some of their overhead costs as they price the camp. This would contribute to the costs of overall administration, facilities, and maintenance. In this case, the department may decide to recapture for overhead 10 percent of variable costs. Continuing our scenario, total costs would be increased by 10 percent, or by \$475. Therefore, the price per camper would be

$$\frac{\$4{,}750}{80} + \frac{\$475}{80} = \$5{,}225 = \$65 \text{ per camper}$$

Although the philosophy and objectives of the public program require slight adjustments, the pricing principles are the same as for the XYZ Soccer Ball Manufacturers. (10) In the soccer ball example, variable costs are represented as having a constant increase as output increases. As a result of economies and diseconomies of scale, the actual situation does not conform to this simplistic model, but rather looks more like the model in figure 10.4.

Economies of scale often accrue from such things as bulk-rate discounts on materials or higher attendance levels that result in more efficient use of stadium personnel. Diseconomies of scale can occur when an organization becomes so large that communication breaks down or personnel become overloaded. This results in a less efficient, more costly operation.

In figure 10.4, the profit maximization point exists at the point where the largest gap occurs between total revenue (TR) and total cost (TC). Table 10.1 continues the XYZ Soccer Ball Manufacturers example.

The additional cost of producing one unit is defined as the marginal cost (MC), which in this example is $10. Similarly, the change in revenue (marginal revenue, MR) can be calculated. Not surprisingly, the change in revenue at any level of sales will be exactly equal to the selling price. Therefore,

MC = VC per unit for the last unit produced

MR = selling price (SP) of last unit sold

Marginal revenue tells us how much additional (extra) revenue we receive from the last unit sold. Marginal cost tells us how much additional (extra) cost we have incurred by producing that last unit sold.

Given that fixed costs, by definition, do not change with output, variable-cost changes (marginal cost) are the only cost changes we experience when we change production output levels (up to existing capacity levels). Hence,

MR – MC = change in profits, or

MR – MC = marginal profit (MP)

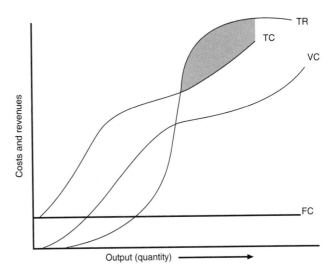

FIGURE 10.4 Realistic break-even analysis. TR = total revenue; TC = total cost; VC = variable cost; FC = fixed costs.

✦ Table 10.1 Fixed Costs and Variable Costs According to the Number of Units Produced

Soccer ball units produced	FC ($)	VC ($ per ball)
0-10,000	100,000	10
10,001-19,999	100,000	8

9,000 produced: TC = $100,000 + $90,000 = $190,000
9,001 produced: TC = $100,000 + $90,010 = $190,010

It should be obvious, then, that at any sales level the marginal revenue (selling price) less the marginal cost (variable cost) will be the contribution. As we pay off overhead, we approach the break-even point. Hence, we contribute to the break-even point and to profits and reduce the amount of loss. Once all overheads are covered, we break even (at this point, contribution equals overheads).

Beyond the break-even point, each unit sold contributes (adds) to profit. If the straight-line break-even analysis were true, we would add to profit ad infinitum. Of course, it is not true. Instead, we find that to sell more of a product, we usually have to drop the price. Hence, marginal revenue decreases. In figure 10.5, the plotted line, called the marginal revenue curve, is sloping downward. This is actually the demand curve for the product. Similarly, the marginal cost curve drops to show economies of scale, but eventually rises to show diseconomies of scale. Hence, the marginal cost curve is U-shaped.

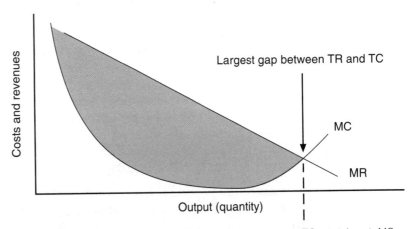

FIGURE 10.5 Profit maximization point. TR = total revenue; TC = total cost; MC = marginal cost; MR = marginal revenue.

As long as marginal revenue is greater than marginal cost, the producer is adding to profit. As soon as marginal cost is greater than marginal revenue, the producer detracts from profit. Thus, as figure 10.5 shows, the point of maximum profit (profit maximization) is the point at which marginal cost equals marginal revenue, because all possible additions to profit have been made. (11)

Cost-Plus Pricing

The cost-plus method of pricing is also common in the sport industry. This method uses the following simple formula: Costs plus a desired profit equal price. For this system to be effective, accurate information on both fixed and variable costs must be available.

To illustrate this method, we can use an example involving the concessions operation of an intercollegiate athletics program. Suppose the director decides to run her overall concessions pricing on a cost plus 40 percent basis. She might begin with hot dogs, a fast-selling item, and mark them up by 100 percent. Thus, hot dogs will sell for twice their cost. Markups may vary for other products—cola at 400 percent, programs at 200 percent, novelties at 10 percent, and so on—so that the total return is 40 percent.

Athletic clubs may use a form of cost-plus pricing to determine member fees. In this case the manager carefully estimates the total fixed and operating costs to support the desired number of members. For example, Club X projects 900 members, and its management estimates total costs for one year to be $500,000. To maintain a profit margin of $100,000, which requires an overall revenue target of $600,000, the club will have to charge as follows:

$$\$600,000 = \$666 \text{ per member}$$

This fee, of course, represents an average. Tennis members may pay more than fitness-only members; individuals will pay less than families; pay-as-you-go members may pay more or less than members who pay monthly dues, depending on their club usage. Thus, management will have pricing flexibility as long as membership fees average out to $666.

Break-even analysis, cost-plus analysis, and their variations are valuable tools for the sport marketer. At the least, they can provide some baselines against which to develop pricing strategies. Further, the same concepts may be helpful in pricing sponsorships. A sponsor might be asked to pay for the total cost of an event, the variable costs, or the break-even cost difference between revenues and expenses. (12)

Capitation Pricing

Capitation pricing—or offering a price "per head" or per person—is a concept that some fitness clubs have borrowed from the health care providers they target for group rates. Capitation pricing is typically used on a group basis. A good example is the one-year contract signed in the 1990s between Albuquerque's New Mexico Sports and Wellness Centers and the 150-employee New Mexico Heart Institute. The contract gave all the institute employees a "membership" at a total cost that equaled the price of 33 individual memberships. This bulk rate meant a capitation of $10 per employee, which created a high perceived value for the New Mexico Heart Institute. At the same time, the New Mexico Sports and Wellness Centers estimated that only 22 percent (or 33) of the 150 employees would actually use their facilities. Although the actual number of regular users turned out to be 40, the capitation represented only a modest "group" discount that, in turn, created a bulk-revenue stream. Capitation may be a useful approach for any sport organization seeking to maximize use of a seatless facility—a museum or a hall of fame, for example. (13)

What the Market Will Bear

The most common approach to pricing sport products is to take "what the market will bear." This approach is largely based on experience and comparisons. The Boston Bruins and other NHL teams learned from their repricing experiences as they worked to win fans back after the Great Lockout of 2004-2005. The "market" approach to pricing can result in radical adjustments,

Permanent Seat Licenses (PSLs): A Recent "Deep Well" for Sport Managers

Ever since baseball became an avowedly capitalist enterprise, with the founding of the National League in 1876, sport managers have looked to discover "deep wells" of revenue, including the following:

◆ Tickets

◆ Concessions

◆ Stadium signage

◆ Radio and television rights

◆ Expansion franchise fees

◆ Public subsidies for stadiums

A casual look at history suggests that managers and owners have pumped each well as dry as possible—with higher prices and fees—then have continued to search for new ones. In 1968, the Dallas Cowboys discovered a deep well (an appropriate metaphor) as they developed a financing package for their new stadium. They floated bonded seat options, priced between $300 and $1,000, that gave the bondholder first rights to buy Cowboy season tickets. This appears to be the first time that a team required fans to pay a fee for the "right" to buy a ticket. College football programs grabbed the idea in the 1980s with "priority seating" plans. Under this arrangement, season tickets in the most desirable sections of the stadium (often between the 40-yard lines), were available only to "friends" or boosters who donated money to the athletics department.

In the 1990s, the frenzy to attract or retain NFL franchises spawned a related "deep well" called the "permanent" or "personal" seat license—the PSL. Like its Texas Stadium forebear, the PSL was an instrument of stadium financing. The NFL's Carolina Panthers, using a strategy developed by Max Muhleman for the Charlotte Hornets of the NBA, built their new $247.7 million Charlotte stadium with $90 million from PSLs. They promoted PSLs as necessary to build a stadium that would attract an NFL franchise. With a range of PSL prices ($600 to $5,400) and an effective publicity campaign, the Panthers succeeded in tapping a well without alienating their market of fans. Others have not been so successful. The Oakland Raiders attempted to sell "personal seat licenses" that had a 10-year life, after which the Raiders would sell them again. This plan resulted in low sales (only 60 percent sold in the first four years) and heavy criticism for the Raiders, who already suffered from a "greedy" image.

PSLs (whether "permanent" or "personal") have become a fixture in stadium and arena deals. Offering a new price challenge to team owners and managers, they clearly present a new "cost" to the fan. Some analysts fear that owners will become reckless in forcing this new "well tap" down the throats of ticket holders in old stadiums. The *Wall Street Journal* described an "uproar" over PSLs that would lead to "angry fans and empty seats." (14)

---

especially when one is pricing new products or when a team suffers a losing streak. For example, after signing Tiger Woods to a lucrative contract, Nike hoped that a "Nike Tiger Woods" line of golf shoes would replicate the success of Air Jordan basketball shoes—high demand and high prices. They were wrong. The market did not support the new shoes, which bore a price tag of $225. Soon, Nike introduced a second line of Tiger Woods shoes, with a new price of $160. *Golfweek* magazine claimed that the price reduction was a "direct response to retailer and consumer outrage."

As another example, take the Seattle Seahawks in the 1980s. They had 55,000 season-ticket holders, and the waiting list was 30,000. Heady times for any franchise—except that the high proportion of season tickets meant that few people could begin at the low end of the escalator. Worse yet, the high demand provided no incentives, and shortsighted marketing saw only a gravy train or a "deep well" (see the sidebar on permanent seat licenses on this page). By the mid-1990s, poor field performance and arrogant ownership pushed season-ticket sales down to 37,000. To fill the empty seats, the Seahawks began to offer more $10 seats. Pricing based on what the market will bear represents the dominant approach among sport teams—from high school to the pros. (15)

Special Pricing Factors

There are several additional factors to consider in pricing, regardless of which approach one employs. These include market demand, lead time, user segmentation, discounting, "smoothing," and the actions of competitors.

Market Demand

In pricing strategies, economic market conditions play an essential role, whether one is pricing equipment, club memberships, or tickets (something ticket scalpers know better than anyone, as shown in the sidebar on page 225). The concept underlying economics and price setting is elasticity of demand. Note the following formula:

$$\text{Elasticity of demand} = \frac{\text{Percentage change in quantity demanded}}{\text{Percentage change in price}}$$

This concept is a measure of how sensitive a market is to price change. An inelastic demand occurs when a given percentage change in price results in a smaller percentage change in quantity. An elastic demand exists when a given percentage change in price results in a larger percentage change in quantity. Unitary demand exists when a given percentage change in price results in an equal percentage change in quantity. Figure 10.6 details this concept graphically. (16)

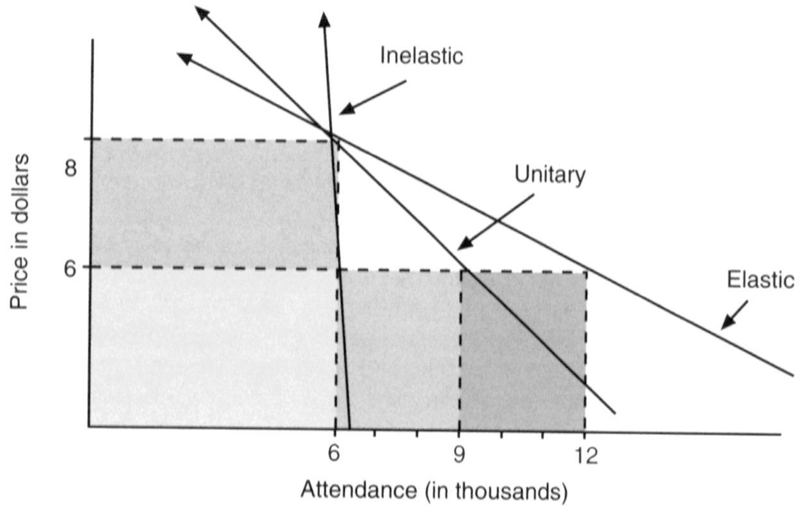

With the inelastic curve, as we can see, a price increase of $2, or 33 percent, leads to a decrease in quantity demanded of only 3.2 percent (from 6,200 to 6,000 attendees). It is obvious that a manager here can increase prices and revenues at the same time. In fact, that is one way of looking at inelastic demand. Changes in revenue will parallel changes in price, in either direction. The opposite would be true with an elastic curve. Here the same 33 percent price increase would result in a reduction of attendees from 12,000 to 6,000—a 50 percent decrease. With unitary demand, the price rise would be equaled by the percentage reduction in attendance, 33 percent, resulting in no change in revenues.

In the sport industry, we are faced with a constantly changing demand curve that includes elastic, inelastic, and unitary components. Figure 10.7 illustrates how this curve might look.

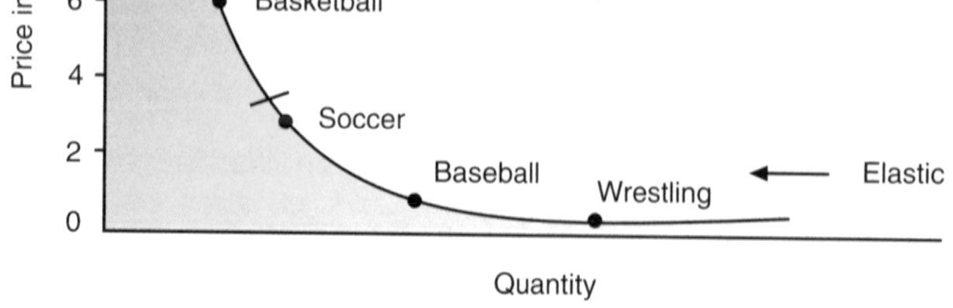

Soccer and baseball have relatively elastic demands; football and boxing have relatively inelastic demands; and hockey and basketball approach unitary demand. Managers at either end of the curve can manipulate price, although for different reasons. For those sport organizations in the middle of the curve, price change has a unitary effect on demand so that the other Ps of marketing become more important for increasing revenue. The accuracy of figure 10.7 awaits more careful attention and testing, by analysis of historical cases, experiments, or consumer surveys. (17)

FIGURE 10.6   Elasticity of demand.

FIGURE 10.7   The demand curve for the spectator sport industry.

A clear grasp of consumer demand can help marketers make critical decisions regarding pricing strategy. A good example is the choice between penetration and skim pricing. *Penetration pricing* is pricing in the lower range of expected prices, in the belief that an elastic market exists and that the lower price will increase the quantity purchased. *Skim pricing* is pricing high in the expected range of prices, in the belief that demand is price inelastic. In this case, the higher price charged will generate more revenue. Goods may also be priced above the skim price. These are overpriced luxury or prestige products. Goods priced below the penetration price are classified as salvage or bargain priced and can be perceived as cheap. Sometimes a good is overproduced and then must be dumped at such bargain prices.

Because *price* is synonymous with *value*, managers do not like to lower prices or let fans in free because this may cheapen the product's image. In place of lowering price, most sport marketers will use nonprice promotions such as bat nights, cap days, or jacket nights, or entertainment events such as postgame fireworks, to attract additional consumers. These promotions lower in the consumer's mind the perceived cost of an event while not cheapening the product image by reducing the ticket price.

The pricing of product extensions (souvenirs, concessions, parking) is also very important in the sport industry because of their large impact on profitability. Very often, visible extensions such as hot dogs and beer will be discounted. The discounts are aimed at increasing the volume of these products so that overall profitability is increased. It is also believed that sales of other items will increase in this situation.

Scalping: The Last Bastion of Capitalism

Ticket brokers and scalpers may be the purest practitioners of market pricing. "Ticket guys" (as scalpers call themselves) have enjoyed a wider market as sport events have grown in status. In September 2004, for a regular-season game against the Yankees, one online ticket broker offered dugout-level tickets to Fenway Park—normally $250 to $300—for $925 each. The same firm offered private suite tickets (with a face value of $70) for $825 each. Streetwise teenagers were not gouging as much, probably because the Red Sox were aggressive in helping uphold the state's antiscalping law, which limited markups to $2 plus "service charges." But the temptations are great. A $500 face value Super Bowl ticket can sell through a broker for $2,500 to $3,500—months ahead of the game. If the match-up is a hot one, street sales might bring $50,000. As one "broker" puts it, face value is "a meaningless term." No wonder Vikings coach Mike Tice scalped his tickets. Unfortunately for Tice, he was caught and fined $100,000 by the NFL.

Of course, in an enterprise as speculative as trying to guess the value of next year's orange crop, there are no surefire winners. When a team starts losing, ticket values can drop faster than television ratings. Take the Washington Redskins. With a decade of play-off appearances from 1982 to 1992, the Redskins built a huge demand for seats—as of 1998, they still had 40,000 people on a waiting list for season tickets. But a move to a new stadium with 25,000 more seats, coupled with several dismal years on the field, left ticket brokers and scalpers watching their investments drip onto the sidewalks in front of Jack Kent Cooke Stadium. A "club"-level seat for the November 1998 game against the Philadelphia Eagles had a face value of $125. It was selling on game day for $60. Hot tickets can turn cold in one day. Scalpers who made a killing before Game 3 of the Yankees–Red Sox American League series in 2004 were lucky to sell Game 4 tickets for any profit. With the Red Sox down three games to none, there was little frenzy for tickets.

There is actually a governing body of ticket speculators, the National Association of Ticket Brokers, established in 1994 (www.natb.org), that claims to have 200 members. Whether working as a broker out of an office or as a scalper hawking on the streets, such "ticket guys" buy and sell blocks of tickets with a hopeful eye on higher demand at the right time. The laws on ticket speculation and scalping vary from state to state, so some "ticket guys" must keep one eye on the police while the other eye is on the ever-shifting market of supply and demand. Season-ticket holders who sell to speculators must also be wary. More franchises are monitoring eBay and walking the streets outside their venues. When they identify (sometimes through purchase) season tickets dumped on the market, they will penalize the season-ticket holder, sometimes with revocation of their valuable asset.

And the latest trend is for teams to enter the "secondary market," in essence becoming the intermediaries between buyers and sellers, and cutting the scalpers out of the process. In these cases, teams typically run the secondary market in partnership with brokers such as Ticketmaster, StubHub, Tickets.com, or RazorGator, to name a few. This trend has dressed the old scalping process up with snappy Web sites and team approval. Time will tell whether it puts the scalpers out of business. (18)

Lead Time

In pricing sports, another important factor to consider is the lead time required for purchase. The average amount of time between ticket purchase and the date of the event typically decreases as the price for the event decreases. This means that an event such as an MLB game sees much higher day-of-game sales and impulse buying because ticket prices per game in MLB are lower than, for instance, those for an NBA basketball game. Day-of-game advertising obviously targets these last-minute-decision consumers, who typically view ease of access (to tickets and to venue) as a large part of the "cost" mix. Before the Internet, toll-free numbers and credit card purchase options proved very effective in reaching late or impulse buyers. As we also discuss in chapter 15, direct sales via Web sites has helped to reduce the lead-time effect as well. Electronic database management has proven to be the most effective way to reach late decision makers with messages that effectively convey cost and value.

User Segmentation

The concept of user segmentation is a valuable one in sport pricing. Based on his extensive experience in spectator sports, Matt Levine argued some years ago that corporate season-ticket holders, group-ticket purchasers, and individual or limited-game-purchase patrons each have different reactions to price increases. Corporate season-ticket holders, said Levine, "are not significantly influenced by orderly and reasoned price increases as long as preferential seating is assured." Group purchasers typically have preset price ranges in mind before pursuing tickets. As Levine cautioned, "Be in that range or be out of the group business." Individual or limited-game-purchase patrons are the most susceptible to defection because of price increases. (19)

As Levine noted, groups are a special user segment, and they are quite hotly pursued by sport marketers today. Encouraging groups is a particularly effective way of attracting new consumers. Typically, marketers will reduce ticket prices according to the size of the group. Thus, a small college football program might offer group discounts in the $10 ticket section as follows:

Single ticket at $10

25-50 tickets at $8

51-100 tickets at $6

100+ tickets at $5

Although group discounts are sound policy, it is not wise to offer such discounts in the most expensive ticket zone. Patrons who pay the top prices expect a degree of exclusivity.

College athletics programs typically employ a basic user-segmentation pricing strategy in their reduced prices for student tickets. Here, the successful programs trade off potential revenue for fervent and boisterous student support. Recent data on Division IA football suggests little change in a long-standing practice. Typically, from 10 to 20 percent of stadium seats are allotted to students at a discount or for nothing, representing a significant loss in potential gate receipts. In a similar fashion, public recreation agencies will often segment users, and user fees, on the basis of ability to pay. Thus senior, low-income, or nonprofit groups will pay less than higher-income or commercial groups. Typically, children enjoy lower charges at recreation facilities, which is a standard practice in need of closer thought. In fact, children often cost more to service in terms of supervision and damages. (20)

Athletic clubs have become more sensitive to user segments in their pricing strategies. This has led to "unbundling," or breaking a full-time, full-service membership into packages of restricted access, such as Monday-Wednesday-Friday only. This may be the best vehicle for attracting older people, families, and "deconditioned" defectors who do not want to invest high monthly full-service dues for facilities they may not get around to using. In this case, clubs may have to trade off secure cash flow for market expansion. (21)

Sport teams unbundled their season tickets in the 1980s with miniplans that targeted user segments between the single-game consumer and the season-ticket holder. In today's professional sports market, rarely does one find a drastic and bare choice between the full-season and the single-game ticket. Except in pro football, wide-ranging menus are the order of the day. This is especially true in baseball: Baseball fans can typically purchase plans for a full season, a half season, a set of midweek nights, or a set of weekends, or they can buy the increasingly popular "flex book" of coupons redeemable for any combination of available tickets. The miniplan is a recognition of the sport consumer escalator, on which marketers hope to move people up in small increments of involvement and commitment. In a recent season, for instance, the San Francisco Giants expected to sell about 15,000 "six packs"—six games for the price of five, with the bonus game a clash with the Dodgers. The Giants built their miniplan on research showing that about one third of their fans came from outside the metropolitan Bay Area. Said Giants Vice President of Communications Bob Rose: "This stretches out people who usually do two or three games a year." (22)

To Discount or Not to Discount

Discount pricing is a topic with no simple answers in the sport industry. Some people believe that aggressive discounting is an important tool for attracting and keeping casual fans, special groups, and even some users higher up the escalator. Others believe that discounting can cheapen overall product value, especially in the eyes of consumers paying full price. What to do? The best answer may be, It depends. For instance, two marketing professors examined price and promotion data from six MLB teams during the 1999 season. The teams were the Reds, Red Sox, Royals, Cubs, Tigers, and Mets. In a very sophisticated analysis, the researchers found important links between the type of promotion—price discount (PD), giveaway (something of monetary value), or special feature (something of intrinsic value)—and two "timing factors" (weekend games and games against rivals). Only two teams in the sample used price discounts—the Reds and the Royals. Although price discounts were not as effective in increasing attendance as either giveaways or special features, they did link statistically to average increased attendance of some 5,000 fans, with even better results during the week against a nonrival. As the authors concluded, "In general, it appears that, given the positive impact of PDs for the Reds and Royals, PDs may currently be underutilized." (23)

Time and Place "Smoothing" or Variable Pricing

Athletic club managers have sometimes unbundled their prices by time, typically "prime" versus "nonprime." In this case the proposition is simple. Any revenues generated by renting courts when they would otherwise be empty act as a contribution to overhead costs even if the additional revenues do not fully cover costs. Prime-time hours are most often booked up. Nonprime hours have slack usage. By charging different prices during the two periods, managers hope to equalize demand during peak and nonpeak hours. The pricing scheme must indicate to the consumer that there are real savings for using nonprime hours. In management terms, this is called "smoothing" demand. One must be careful, of course, that any smoothing strategy does not siphon too much demand from the higher-priced, prime-time or prime-place service.

Historically, the most obvious use of smoothing has been in price variation by seat location in stadiums and arenas. Proximity, line of sight, and demand are usually the key factors in "scaling the house." Some prime locations are obvious, such as courtside in any NBA venue. At Madison Square Garden, for instance, 2004-2005 Knicks season tickets ranged over 10 different price points—from $10 to $330 per game, depending on location. Ticket scales reveal the influence of demand in facilities that house more than one anchor (or principal) tenant. For instance, in the mid-1990s, the same upper-bowl seat in the FleetCenter cost $10 for a Boston Celtics game and $29 for a Bruins game. A few poor seasons without Larry Bird, coupled with the move to a bigger facility, and the Celtics' streak of 664 sellouts was quickly over. Demand was still high for the choice seats; it was nonexistent for those in the top rim. Vice President for Marketing Stuart Layne summed up the pricing strategy: "What we are trying to do now is price by demand." (24)

Another example of price/place smoothing is seen in signage deals. In the world of sports, not all signs are equal. Field-side or courtside signage, especially on the "TV side" of a venue, sells for more money because it generates more exposures of the buyer's name. The Colorado Avalanche, for example, began selling three categories of dasher board signage—$50,000, $110,000, and $135,000—based on their determination of the visibility to fans watching at home or in the venue. (25)

In the last few years, more professional teams have been pricing by opponent and by day of the week. The practice has been called "variable pricing," an odd term given that teams have for a long time priced seats variably by location. And collegiate football programs have often charged more for "special" dates such as homecoming. In 2001, the University of Michigan began adding a $5 premium to tickets for the Ohio State football game. In this case, the term *variable* probably reflects the media's and the public's mixed response to these new dimensions of variable pricing in professional sports. The Colorado Rockies are recognized as Major League Baseball's pioneer in variable pricing. In 1998, the Rockies began adding a premium to games on weekends and/or against key rivals such as the Dodgers or the Giants. The Mets created a color-coded system that reflected time of the year, day of the week, and opponent, although the premiums only affected individual game tickets—season-ticket holders were spared. Some fans groused. "It's gouging," one Cleveland fan told the *New York Times*. Most others recognized that variable pricing was here to stay. The only question would be how teams would tweak the variables of place, time, and opponent. One Boston Bruins executive even promised variable pricing by the hour. Tickets to a weak opponent might go down as the game approached, or a hot ticket might go up, if there were any left. Will sports ticket prices become as variable (and possibly as confusing) as airline ticket prices? Time will tell. (26)

Responding to Competitors

Shifts in market demand for a firm's products are often the result of a competitor's actions. This is a constant part of life in the retail world, as any sporting goods dealer knows, especially when it comes to price cutting. A few years ago, Foot Locker began slashing prices of Nike, Adidas, and Timberland shoes—in some cases over 30 percent—in an obvious response to sluggish back-to-school sales. Not only did this put pressure on other retailers to cut their prices, but it also diminished the perceived value of all name-brand shoes. Alan Cohen, chief executive officer of Finish Line stores, was not happy: "For a primary retailer to denigrate these brands is a travesty and a tragedy." Of course, Cohen didn't have to follow suit and slash his prices, but he obviously felt the squeeze. (27)

Foot Locker and Finish Line operate in several markets at once. They must respond to local conditions, yet their products are produced and promoted by international corporations; and their competitors include mail-order and Internet retailers who know no boundaries, have less overhead, and can offer the same products at a lower margin. The conditions are different for teams and franchises whose products are distinct in their market (e.g., Nebraska Cornhusker football) and whose "competitors" exist at a more generic level (e.g., televised sports of any kind). Athletic club owners have yet another set of conditions: They typically face strong local competitors with similar products and services (e.g., the local YMCA or the town recreation league).

In all of these cases, however, marketers must identify who their competitors really are, monitor competitor activities (including pricing) that affect market demand, and prepare alternative tactics to meet competitor actions. Typically, the tactics involve price, quality, or some combination of the two—that is, raising or lowering price, raising or lowering the actual or the perceived quality of the product, or both. Although there is no magic formula for reading the market and responding to competitors' pricing, it is obvious that planning will beat simple reacting. (28)

Pricing Ice in Eskimo Country

Carrie Jokiel Lindow, operations manager, O'Malley Ice Arena, Anchorage, Alaska; captain, women's ice hockey team, University of New Hampshire, 1999-2000

From October through April, Alaska's average temperature is 24 °F. With ice all around, how do Alaskan hockey rinks get some 8,300 registered players to come inside to skate, on average, four hours per week? There are many ways, but careful pricing is at the top of the list.

In the Anchorage area, there are nine arenas. These rinks have helped develop dozens of Division I NCAA players, as well as several NHL stalwarts, including Scotty Gomez, two-time Stanley Cup champion with the New Jersey Devils, and Ty Conklin, University of New Hampshire All-American and current goaltender for the Columbus Blue Jackets. Of the nine rinks, seven are subsidized by the Municipality of Anchorage, one is run by the University of Alaska at Anchorage, and another, the O'Malley Ice Arena, is privately owned. O'Malley is a state-of-the-art facility with the largest indoor running track in the state, an elite training facility, pro shop, and upstairs restaurant/pub offering views of both rinks. A multisport atmosphere is apparent when people walk in the door, promising more than just a couple of sheets of ice. Private ownership of the O'Malley Ice Arena allows for more managerial freedom, but because there is no subsidy, all costs are borne by the customer. This demands creative marketing and sales.

The ice prices differ between the O'Malley Ice Arena and the city rinks. City rinks sell their ice for around $250 per hour. Premium ice (for "adult" leagues) at the O'Malley Ice Arena goes for $305 per hour. Over 60 teams call the O'Malley Ice Arena their home, and over 150 youth teams practice there seven days a week. So with the premium price difference, how do we keep customers coming in the door?

Our fundamental pricing strategy recognizes variations in ability to pay and attractiveness of time. We price accordingly (see table 10.2).

We also offer skating sessions for those who don't necessarily want to commit to a league. We have coined the term "Pond Hockey" for a session of ice that lasts for an hour up to an hour and a half. There are different age groups, and kids or adults come in and pay $10 per session to play with whomever shows up. Similarly, we offer Noon Hockey every weekday for $8 per hour.

Finally, we know that Alaskans love their two and a half months of summer. Everyone wants time off to go fishing and to be outside enjoying the sunshine. This can create a big problem for an ice arena, so we try to be as accommodating as possible. We maintain our summer operations by holding clinics, camps, special events, summer tournaments, and spring leagues. We have also seen a big rise in personal trainers who rent an hour of ice for private lessons. We reduce our summer prices to $250 per hour at night, and all daytime prices are negotiable.

Including parents, all of the adult and youth players, as well other spectators, the O'Malley Ice Arena was host to approximately 350,000 visitors last year. That is half of our state population and a number that is guaranteed to grow over time. Careful pricing has a lot to do with our success.

✦ **Table 10.2** O'Malley Ice Arena Pricing

Time/age	Price/hour	Reason
6:00 a.m.	$215	Sells well with youth teams in the winter because it is cheaper, before school for the players and before work for the coaches.
7:15 a.m.	$200	This ice time is a little cheaper because it is more of a rush to get older kids to school, but the younger kids don't start school until 9:00 a.m., so it is still attractive.
Youth	$295	This is the regular youth price for ice after the day ice period.
High school	$265	During the high school season teams practice at 3:00 p.m. We are able to negotiate a higher price due to demand.
Adult	$305	This is the price for adult league teams, co-ed league teams, and women's league teams.
Day 8:00 a.m.-2:00 p.m.	Negotiable	There is low demand for ice at this time. We usually hold freestyle sessions for figure skaters or hold Noon Hockey and Pond Hockey.
After 10:00 p.m.	Negotiable	Also a lower demand. A twilight league has been set up at lower prices for times after 10:00 p.m.

Writing About Price and Value

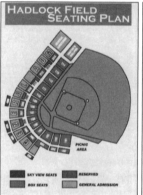

Brochures are a key element in marketing sport products—from tickets to merchandise and memberships. Brochures are especially critical to teams and clubs. Most brochures fold up to mailing size, and they come in all colors and layouts. The most effective ones, however, contain key elements that link price with value. We see these elements clearly in the pocket brochures of the highly successful Portland Sea Dogs and New Hampshire Fisher Cats (AA baseball). The following elements in the brochures link price with value:

+ A clear image of the venue, its ticket locations, and directions to the venue.

+ A clear table of discounts, if they are part of the plan. Both brochures are aimed at individuals and groups rather than potential season-ticket holders, but notice the tables emphasizing the discounts for groups, children, and seniors.

Ticket brochures must clarify price, cost, and benefits as successfully as the Portland Sea Dogs' brochure.
Courtesy of Portland Sea Dogs

+ A focus on value-added. Notice the paragraphs on amenities such as the Portland Room, the picnic package, or the "Grand Slam" package. Although pocket brochures have limited space, larger group brochures often have calendars that indicate the promotions for each game.

+ A calendar, if lead time is an issue.

For some teams the key added value will be a new or renovated stadium. In all cases, however, the brochure must be careful not to promise what it can't deliver. For this reason, many franchises avoid pictures of managers, coaches, or players. After all, they may be fired or traded during the season or even before the season starts. This scenario haunted the Seattle Mariners in the early 1980s, when they made new manager Maury Wills the poster boy for media guides and pocket schedules. A Hall of Fame player, Wills seemed to be a surefire symbol of quality for the young franchise. Unfortunately, the symbolism backfired when the Mariners sacked Wills early in the next season. Whether marketing tickets or memberships, the key is to communicate value as well as cost. (29)

Remember the Escalator: Pricing, Public Relations, and Promotions

Longtime sport consumers, like Roger Naples and his colleagues among the Gallery Gods, have seen players and owners come and go. One thing they can count on, however, is higher ticket prices and higher total costs. Some wonder whether fans have reached their limit. In May 2000, *Sports Illustrated* ran a feature article entitled "Hey Fans: Sit on It!" which depicted a Fat Cat owner smoking a stogy. The article compared the decade's rise in the Consumer Price Index (20 percent) with the rise in the average ticket price for the NHL, NBA, NFL, and MLB (80 percent). Although player salaries had increased at an even higher rate, economists maintained that salaries did not drive ticket prices. Fans seemed to agree. A Harris poll commissioned by *Sports Illustrated* indicated that 85 percent of fans believed owners were more interested in their own bottom lines than they were in "making it possible for Joe Fan to attend games." Owners, it seemed, cared far more for the corporate crowd than they did for Gallery Gods like Roger Naples. (30)

Everywhere sport consumers turned, there seemed to be an arrogant executive wrenching up their costs. Following are some examples from the last decade:

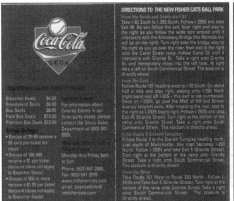
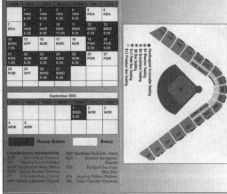

Ticket brochures must clarify directions, schedule, and discounts as successfully as the New Hampshire Fisher Cats' brochure.
Courtesy of New Hampshire Fisher Cats

✦ The PGA of America announced that golf fans would have to pay a nonrefundable $5 fee to enter a lottery for 1999 Ryder Cup tickets. Organizational officials claimed that the "entry fee" was needed to cover telemarketing and ticket-processing costs, although this sounded lame in light of ticket demand. Within a week, 30,000 people had applied for the 10,000 (of 30,000 total) tickets available to the public. The *Boston Globe*'s "Consumer Beat" columnists accused the PGA of running an "illegal lottery." (31)

✦ After what their own president called a "disappointing" and "least successful season," the Anaheim Mighty Ducks raised ticket prices for the fifth straight year. Worse yet, President Tony Tavares bluntly announced that he "made no apologies" for the increases. *Orange County Register* columnist Randy Youngman didn't see it the same way. He found Tavares' attitude "nonchalant and unapologetic" and "particularly galling." In a nutshell, it was "typical Disney arrogance." (32)

✦ After agreeing to pay the NFL $600 million per year for the rights to Thursday and Sunday night games, ESPN announced plans to hike its fees to cable operators by 20 percent. Cable executives expected similar hikes over the eight-year length of ESPN's deal with the NFL. In the end, who would pay? The local consumer, through higher monthly cable fees. (33)

An arrogant tone in announcing price hikes is a sure way to push consumers off the escalator. Even hikes for reasonable cause can backfire. In 2004, the Madison, Wisconsin, school district raised ticket prices 50 percent (from $4 to $6 for adults, from $2 to $3 for students) in an effort to close a $10 million budget deficit. They hoped to generate an additional $112,000 in revenue. Instead, attendance at football games fell drastically, requiring the district to reverse itself in midseason and revert to the lower prices. For public schools and colleges, price hikes can trigger political backlash. When the New Jersey State Interscholastic

Athletic Association jacked prices for postseason tournament tickets, State Assemblyman John Burzichelli introduced a bill to control such "outrageous and unconscionable" actions. (34)

Fortunately, there are models for imaginative pricing campaigns. One run by the Pittsburgh Penguins in May of 1987 is a good example of mixed success. The Penguins, who had missed the NHL play-offs for five consecutive years, announced an average season-ticket price increase of roughly 15 percent. To reduce public indignation, the club added a special "Playoff or Payoff" provision for all fans who purchased their tickets by July 1 of that year. Under the plan, these fans would receive a $1 per game ticket refund if the Penguins did not make the play-offs. The Pens wanted to demonstrate special value to their loyal fans. Although the policy assuaged some of the negative feelings among fans, and although it may have helped sales, the Penguins failed to make the 1988 play-offs. The payoff was considerable. (35)

Although few sport organizations can be expected to go to these extremes, most try to add a message about value to any communications on price. This is especially true for sporting goods retailers, who must price their products higher than the department stores and discounters. As one executive explained, the best policy is to emphasize quality, value, range, and expertise to the 70 percent of consumers who are concerned about these things in addition to price. To these consumers, "Price is important but not the key element. They are most interested in value." The same is probably true for most fans. (36)

At times, especially in new venues, sport franchises misjudge the desirability of seat locations or even of overall demand. A weak team performance can exacerbate the problems. If a price reduction is necessary, one might as well be up front about it. The Carolina Hurricanes of the NHL took this route when they slashed most single-game tickets by $10 after a dismal performance on and off the ice in 1997-1998. Hurricane owner Peter Karmanos announced the price reductions by saying, "We admit that we priced the tickets too high. We are begging for forgiveness and putting our money where our mouth is." (37)

Wrap-Up

As we have noted, the majority of sport pricing decisions are based on what the market will bear; prices are set in relation to what the organization believes the consumer is willing to pay for the product. It may seem that, to some extent, sport managers have a captive market. If you are not prepared to pay the price to see Denver Broncos NFL football, then you will not see it live. However, the Broncos and similar clubs do not compete for the entertainment dollar only with other NFL teams. There are several substitutes for NFL football in the Denver area. Among them are college hockey, professional baseball, movies, restaurants, and other forms of entertainment. All of these activities compete for the consumer entertainment dollar.

Sports are truly a complex product. In making pricing decisions, the sport organization must consider the cost and availability of substitute products. The sport manager must try to determine how much this sport really competes with other forms of entertainment, as well as how people view it in comparison to the other forms. Good demographic information on sport consumers can tell a great deal about a product's competition. Similarly, surveys can tell a great deal about how much the public values the product and how elastic or inelastic demand may be. On the basis of demand, competitors' actions, and other factors, the organization can create a pricing strategy that meets its objectives. Although the marketer can take many approaches to pricing, there is no substitute for knowing the market.

Activities

1. Explain the differences among the following pricing strategies: break-even, cost-plus, capitation, time and place smoothing, skim, and penetration. Find examples of each in a sport setting.

2. Explain the difference between a marketer's view of "price" and a consumer's view of "cost." Using the concepts in this chapter, develop a set of at least six ingredients for a "Consumer Cost Index" that could be used to compare costs in the sport industry segment of your marketing plan. Be sure to consider "hidden" costs that typically influence consumer decisions. Include a brief justification for each ingredient and a projected *average* cost for each category.

3. Consumers associate price with value. Assume you are the new marketing director of a franchise with a history of selling discount tickets. The new owners have mandated no more ticket discounting. Create a strategy to overcome negative consumer responses to this new policy.

4. Find a recent example of a sport organization that encountered very negative publicity for a pricing move. What would you have done differently?

5. Define market demand. Try to find a sport example that demonstrates how price can reveal elasticity or inelasticity of demand.

Your Marketing Plan

1. Carefully articulate the objectives that will control the pricing strategies for your organization. Then map out pricing strategies for your primary products—be they events, memberships, or hard or soft goods. Consider how you will approach the various segments of your consumers, as well as how you will respond to competitors or to uncertain demand.

2. Examine a few ticket, product, or price brochures in the sport industry segment of your marketing plan. List the main strength and the main weakness of each brochure, using the notions of layout, "value," and price segmentation discussed in the text. Using your critique, begin to outline a brochure that details prices and values for the products in your marketing plan.

Chapter 11

Promotions

Objectives

◆ To recognize the complexity of promotion with respect to the various forms it can assume as part of the marketing mix.

◆ To identify integral elements of promotion and the various approaches used in advertising.

◆ To understand promotion in a historical context and consider how that context has evolved as a result of the importance of media and sponsorship relationships.

◆ To recognize the key characteristics of effective promotional programs and campaigns aimed at expanding existing consumer bases and at increasing the frequency of consumption.

Beanie Babies Are Dead—Long Live Bobbleheads (We Hope!)

Rally Drummer for 30 Years

Cleveland Indians turn fans into bobbleheads: Longtime Cleveland Indian fan John Adams was commemorated as a bobblehead to celebrate his loyal commitment to the team. John's first game with the drum was August 24, 1973, and he has since then missed only 28 games due to work.

Courtesy of Tom Fagan

In the second edition of this text, we were extolling the virtues of Beanie Babies, which are now passé (but could reemerge in some mutated future promotional campaign). Bobbleheads have dominated the stadiums and arenas (and retail shops and mail promotions) of the United States and Canada for the past five years. (In 2005, the graduating class at the DeVos Sport Business Management program had a bobblehead created for each of the faculty members).

Bobbleheads have been used to commemorate both active and retired players, their accomplishments, their physical attributes, or their batting or fielding prowess. There have also been bobbleheads to commemorate mascots, dancers, broadcast personalities, and even fans (the Minnesota Timberwolves created a bobblehead of one of their most visible fans as a giveaway premium).

To say that bobbleheads are highly sought after is an understatement. In 2001, Ichiro mania was at its height—Ichiro Suzuki was playing in his first season with the Seattle Mariners (he had been a major star in Japan) and was the leading vote-getter for that season's All-Star Game (and has since been a perennial All-Star). For their game on Saturday, July 28, of that year, the Mariners planned to give away 20,000 Ichiro bobbleheads. Unfortunately, more than 45,000 tickets had been sold. Thus, the Mariners had to undertake precautions and institute rules for the giveaway. The bobbleheads were locked in a warehouse and protected by guards until they were delivered to Safeco Field and distributed Saturday morning beginning at 10 a.m.

The rules designed by the Mariners included the following:

Fans could begin lining up at midnight on Friday.

Bobbleheads were given to the first 20,000 fans—one per person—and if one person had multiple tickets, that person had to get back in line for each bobblehead.

Cutting in line resulted in being removed from the line and placed at the end of it.

Uniformed Seattle police officers and Mariners security staff were present overnight.

Any collectors soliciting bobblehead dolls inside the stadium or on stadium property were removed from the property. (1)

Oh yes—Ichiro bobbleheads were selling for $35+ on eBay and other Internet sites within 12 hours after the ball game!

This chapter focuses primarily on advertising and the premise of promotion. Publicity in sport, and its inherent elements of public relations, media relations, and community relations, is addressed in depth in chapter 15. The sales process, including personal selling, is examined in detail in chapter 12. In this chapter, after discussing how these basic activities apply to promotion, we consider their potential for moving consumers up the escalator of increasing involvement. (2)

The Catchall P: Promotion

Promotion, another of the Ps in sport marketing, is a catchall category for any one of numerous activities designed to stimulate consumer interest in, awareness of, and purchase of the product. Basically, promotion involves the vehicles through which the marketer conveys information about product, place, and price. More important, promotion is a critical mechanism for positioning a product and its image in the mind of the consumer. Promotion concentrates on "selling" the product; without sales, a company will not be in operation very long. Although selling does not equal marketing, it is a vital component.

The marketing term *promotion* includes the following forms of marketing activity:

+ *Advertising*: any paid, nonpersonal (not directed to individuals), clearly sponsored message conveyed through the media
+ *Personal selling*: any face-to-face presentation in which the seller has an opportunity to persuade the consumer
+ *Publicity*: any form of exposure in the media not paid for by the beneficiary or within the beneficiary's control or influence
+ *Sales promotion*: a wide variety of activities including displays, trade shows, sampling, coupons, premium items, exhibitions, and performances

To be successful, promotional efforts should follow the AIDA approach. That is, such efforts should include the following steps:

A: Increase awareness

I: Attract interest

D: Arouse desire

A: Initiate action

When we think of the term *promotion,* we are drawn to the Veeck family—the late Bill and his son Mike. We refer to the Veecks throughout this text, but one of our favorite images of the term *promotion* was coined by Mike Veeck at the National Basketball Association Game Presentation Workshop in 2003. (3) When asked what the word *promotions* meant to him, Mike responded by suggesting that to be effective in promotions, people may have to change the culture of their organizations. Mike began writing the letters on a white board and this is what he produced:

P = people, publicity, price, planning, and passion

R = relevant, reward, risk, research, and reaction

O = opportunity, originality, and organization

M = motivation, momentum, money, and media

O = outrageous

T = TRY

I = innovate, initiate, incite, idea, and imagination

O = overdeliver

N = Never say NO

S = smile, shake-it-up, service

To get a grasp on what the P in promotion means, think about the concepts in this list and consider them throughout this chapter.

Advertising

As with all promotion, the core of advertising is effective communication. That is, advertising is a communication process and is subject to the same problems as any other communication process. A major problem in advertising is perceptual distortion, which occurs when the receiver of a message interprets it differently from the way the sender intended. This phenomenon can cause misunderstanding of advertising messages, which may prevent marketers from reaching advertising goals. Thus, in terms of advertising and other promotional activities, the sport marketer must operate under the axiom that perception is reality. In other words, the sport marketer must attempt to ensure that the message is targeted and that it is clearly specific so that the receiver comprehends it. If this doesn't happen, the sport marketer will have to work to address the misperception and correct it—because for the consumer, this misperception has become fact.

Multipurpose athletic and fitness clubs have recognized the need to communicate to a target market that may want the same things—better appearance, conditioning, and health—but with varying degrees of intensity. Thus the advertising message must not be limited to beautiful bodies sweating to "feel the burn." Such messages suggest too much agony and single-minded purpose for whole segments of the market who fall into the categories of "deconditioned" and "dropout." For some, the perception might be that they are not in condition to join a fitness club or that more pain than enjoyment is involved. The fitness industry has worked diligently to create advertising campaigns that present images combining fitness, sociability, achievement, fun, and togetherness (family orientation). Perceptual distortion cannot be completely eliminated, but through attention to message construction, the marketer can reduce the amount of distortion. (4)

What Should Advertising Accomplish?

According to Batra, Myers, and Aaker, an advertising message can have a variety of effects on the receiver or intended audience. (5) An advertising message can create awareness, communicate information about attributes and benefits, develop or change an image or personality, associate a brand with feelings and emotions, create norm groups, and precipitate behavior. Sport shares many of these same advertising goals. News releases and press conferences, very common in sport, are used to create awareness about new developments such as personnel moves, product innovations, upcoming promotional events, or special events and activities.

On the following page is an actual press release from the NBA and Nokia. The release has multiple purposes, including the following:

- To explain the relationship between the NBA and Nokia
- To discuss the rationale for the relationship
- To identify what will happen as a result of this partnership
- To define the roles of each party
- To detail the potential significance of the partnership
- To provide contact information for follow-up by interested parties

Although a press release is considered publicity rather than advertising, it is apparent that the promotional information and the way it can be presented can often blur the lines between advertising and other forms of promotion—paid or unpaid.

Assessing advertising effectiveness entails a number of key considerations:

- *Wasted circulation.* One problem in advertising is wasted circulation, which occurs when advertising reaches consumers not within the target market of the organization. This happens to some degree in almost all campaigns—but how can the marketer keep it to a minimum? As stated earlier, a good starting point is the delineation of the target market; an organization

NBA AND NOKIA EXPAND PARTNERSHIP INTO CHINA

NBA and Nokia to Provide First-Ever North American Sports League Video Content to Mobile Phones in China

BEIJING, May 23, 2005—The National Basketball Association and Nokia have reached a multi-year agreement to expand their U.S. relationship into Greater China, marking the first time video content of a North American- based sports league will be made available on mobile phones in the region.

As the Official Mobile Phone of the NBA in Greater China, Nokia will enable their mobile users to access embedded NBA video highlights of the 2004-05 NBA season and 2005 All-Star Game. Beginning the second half of this year, Nokia is expected to offer NBA team logos and NBA Java games in its mobile phones, allowing the youth segment to enjoy the exciting and entertaining content anytime and anywhere.

This summer, Nokia will participate in China's first-ever NBA Jam Van, an NBA touring fan event featuring various basketball activities and NBA-themed attractions. Nokia will further showcase their new products to the league's fans in the region through nationally televised NBA games and programming on Central Chinese Television (CCTV), 16 regional broadcasters in China, Hong Kong and Taiwan and on NBA TV in Hong Kong. They will also partner with NBA.com/China, in which the top ten plays of the week will be highlighted through the Nokia "Courtside Countdown." Additionally, Nokia will conduct a gift with purchase promotion across China throughout the summer.

Nokia will support Basketball without Borders, the international basketball and community relations outreach program for young people that promotes healthy living, friendship and education. The first-ever Basketball without Borders Asia will take place July 14-17 at the Beijing Olympic Training Facility in Beijing, China.

"The youth is the future and represents the market trends. Expanding the partner relationship with the NBA is the core part of Nokia's youth marketing strategy," said Colin Giles, Nokia Senior Vice President, Customer & Market Operation, Great China Area. "As a symbol of energy, passion and dreams, the NBA is very popular among young consumers in China. Nokia also wins more young consumers' attention by continuously launching fashion products with cutting-edge technology. The cooperation between Nokia and the NBA will help Nokia position itself in the youth segment and strengthen our brand image of innovation, leadership and fashion."

"Nokia's position as an industry leader in China, combined with our relevance among young, tech-savvy basketball fans across the region, makes for a perfect opportunity to unite our global brands," said Heidi Ueberroth, NBA Executive Vice President, Global Media Properties and Marketing Partnerships.

"Nokia's selection of the NBA to help grow its business in its largest market in the world demonstrates our connection with a passionate, youthful fan base in China and will help us meet the growing demand of these fans to connect with the game," said Mark Fischer, Managing Director, NBA China.

In May 2004, the NBA and Nokia agreed on a multi-year alliance making Nokia the Official Mobile Phone of the NBA and WNBA in the United States. The deal marked the first time fans in the U.S. were able to receive daily video content from a major sports league on their wireless phones.

An estimated 300 million people play basketball throughout the region. In recent surveys, 75% of Chinese males ages 15-24 said they were NBA fans, more than 40% stated that basketball is their favorite sport to play and four of their top five athletes are NBA players. This past regular season, NBA games were broadcast on 15 television networks and watched by more than 30 million viewers per week. NBA.com/China, launched in 2002, averages more than 3 million page-views per day. NBA merchandise is available in more than 20,000 retail locations throughout the region.

Nokia total sales and exports in China for 2004 are greater than 6.9 billion USD, including net sales of 3.6 billion USD, (which represented a 44% increase over 2003) and exports of 3.3 billion USD (56% higher than 2003). Local purchases in China reached 3.1 billion USD (25.6 billion RMB) and Nokia's accumulated investment in China by 2004 is 2.18 billion USD (18 billion RMB). Nokia-initiated Xingwang (International) Industrial Park has introduced investment of 10 billion RMB.

ABOUT NOKIA

Nokia is a world leader in mobile communications, driving the growth and sustainability of the broader mobility industry. Nokia connects people to each other and the information that matters to them with easy-to-use and innovative products like mobile phones, devices and solutions for imaging, games, media and businesses. Nokia provides equipment, solutions and services for network operators and corporations.

ABOUT NBA

Since its founding in 1946, the NBA has truly become a global phenomenon that transcends national boundaries. With 30 teams in the United States and Canada, NBA games and related programming are broadcast to 214 countries in

(continued)

43 languages via 157 telecasters; they are one of the largest suppliers of sports television and Internet programming in the world. NBA.com, with more than half of all visits to the site coming from fans outside the United States, has nine language-specific international destinations for fans around the world. The NBA is a recognized leader in global sports marketing with 13 offices around the world. From June to November 2004, the NBA conducted 36 events with 30 partners on six continents. The league opened the 2004-05 season with 81 international players from 35 different countries and territories.

CONTACTS:

Issued by NBA Asia, Limited, and Nokia (China) Investment Co., Ltd.
For more information, please contact:

Nokia
Cai Yun

NBA
Cheong Sau Ching
E-mail: scheong@nba.com
Marcus Chu
E-mail: mchu@nba.com
Eric Schuster (N.Y.)
E-mail: eschuster@nba.com

must know whom it is trying to reach. If an organization has good geographic, demographic, and psychographic information on its target markets, then it can choose media placements that will maximize exposure to the target market and minimize wasted effort.

✦ *Cost per exposure.* Another issue related to media selection is cost per exposure, which is merely the measure of cost required to reach one consumer through the various media under consideration. Using cost per exposure data along with target market profiles, an organization can reach the greatest number of people within its target market at the lowest cost.

✦ *Determining the creative approach.* After all media and cost decisions have been made, the creative part of advertising begins. One starting point for developing an effective creative strategy is called the knock-knock scenario. The scenario begins with a knock-knock on the door. The door opens. The person behind the door frowns. The salesperson says, "You should buy this product because it makes your life easier [better, more fun, more exciting, etc.]." The person opens the door and says, "Come on in and show me." And the salesperson is on his or her way to making a sale. (6) Some marketing questions and issues must be addressed via the creative component. What is the goal of the ad? What is its message?

✦ *Measurement.* Assuming that a creative campaign is under way, how will the organization measure its effectiveness? Organizations spend a great deal of money on advertising, but much less on finding out how well advertising works, mainly because of the difficulties inherent in measuring the effectiveness of ads. A traditional method of evaluating ads is to measure sales response in the period following an advertising campaign that has been aimed at immediate sales, but this method has several limitations. The first is the problem of the time lag. How long does it take for an ad to be effective? Are current sales the result of yesterday's ads, last week's ads, or the ads placed six months ago? No one can answer these questions. Another problem is that all advertising may not be aimed at immediate sales; some advertising may have an effect over a longer time period. How can an organization take this into account? These two limitations must be addressed if one is to use sales results to measure advertising effectiveness.

There are other ways to evaluate the effectiveness of advertising. One is to offer a discount if the consumer brings in the ad (in sport this is usually a clipped print ad, but it can also be a soft-drink can from a sponsor involved in the promotion); a simple count of the ads redeemed provides some measure of the effect of the campaign. Other methods include recall and recognition tests, as used by Stotler and Johnson in a study of stadium advertising, (7) and scannable cards that document attendance, purchases, and other transactions appropriate to the sport venue.

Ultimately, running a successful ad campaign relies on two basic elements: knowing the product and knowing the consumers. Ads are simply a means of communicating information about the product or service to the consumer.

Advertising Agencies

One issue facing sport marketers is that of determining when to do the work themselves, or "in-house," and when to employ an advertising agency. All advertisers, by definition, use some form of media to accomplish organizational objectives. (8) Depending on the size and type of the organization wishing to use an advertising campaign, it may be necessary to employ an advertising agency to help in developing the ad and in working directly with media outlets to disseminate the message. The advertising agency is usually involved in making the creative decisions (decisions about how the message is conveyed) and the media decisions (about which form[s] of media to use). In many cases, the advertising agency not only designs the campaign, but also selects the media and purchases the media time (electronic) and space (print). To ensure that the advertising message is targeted to the proper market segments, and through the channels with the highest potential for impact, the advertising agency may also employ a research firm to conduct consumer research or may purchase existing research reports. Experts suggest that an organization take the following seven steps before employing an advertising agency:

1. Have a comprehensive marketing plan in place, or ensure that the advertising agency will help you create a comprehensive marketing plan—not just a media plan.
2. Make sure the agency is interested in your organization's success—not just in winning awards, but in increasing sales and revenue.
3. Choose an agency that has comprehensive marketing skills; advertising is only one element of marketing. Sales promotion and public relations are essential as well.
4. Determine the target market and how to reach it efficiently. Mass advertising may be desirable at some point, but a targeted approach is the essential first step.
5. Find out who will be handling your account. What are their experiences? Relationships? Style?
6. Make sure that all written copy is customer centered.
7. Select an agency that views itself as a partner in your business. The agency personnel should feel as though their stake is in your success, not in the popularity of the advertising. (9)

The Advertising Communication Process

Figure 11.1 shows the Batra, Myers, and Aaker model of the advertising communication system. Advertising communication always involves a perception process and four of the elements shown in the model: the source, a message, a communication channel, and a receiver (note that the receiver can also become a source by talking to friends or associates—this is referred to as word-of-mouth communication). (10)

+ *Source*—Can be defined as the originator of the message. There are a number of types of "sources" in the context of advertising, especially in the area of sport. For example, the NBA is a source of advertising in disseminating its message—"I love this game." The Cleveland Cavs, an NBA team, can also be a source for their own advertising message—"Ya gotta be there." As another example, Nike might disseminate a brand message that can also be associated with Foot Locker, a retailer of the Nike brand.

+ *Message*—Can be defined as both the content and the execution of the message. In practice, it is the actuality of what the receiver of the message has perceived.

+ *Channel*—Refers to one or more kinds of media, such as the Internet, radio, television, newspapers, magazines, billboards (fixed and movable), point-of-purchase displays, signage,

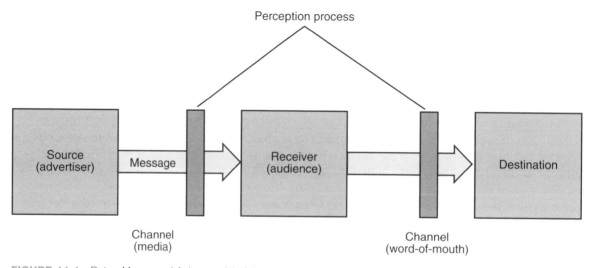

Perception process

Source (advertiser) → Message → Receiver (audience) → Destination

Channel (media)

Channel (word-of-mouth)

FIGURE 11.1 Batra, Myers, and Aaker model of the advertising communication system.

Advertising Management, Fifth Edition, by Batra, Myers, and Aaker. Copyright 1996. Reprinted by permission of Prentice-Hall, Inc., Upper Saddle River, NJ.

logo placement (on scoreboards and other sport-related properties such as dasher boards, in-ice, racing cars, uniforms, message boards, premium items, and game programs), virtual signage, and special events. DVD T-shirts ("DVtees") and the New Era/Yankee cap image are excellent examples of the new type of channels being used by today's sport and entertainment marketers.

◆ *Receiver*—Commonly refers to the target market. This is the intended audience for the message. The receivers (or audience), as in the case of any target market, usually share certain demographic or psychographic characteristics. In the context of sport marketing, these characteristics may include type of tickets owned, zip code, past purchasing history, children living in the household, past or current sport interest or affiliation, and demographic segmentation such as age or income.

◆ *Destination*—In many cases the message doesn't end with the receiver because the receiver may continue to disseminate the message via word of mouth or personal

Innovative images cut through the clutter and not only gain consumer attention but media interests as well.

Courtesy of Tom Abramson, Vision Works

contact, thus becoming a source. This is especially true in the case of sport, which because of its emphasis and place within society elicits significantly more interest and coverage (media) than most other topics. Proprietary research conducted for MLB's FanFest and for the Pittsburgh Pirates indicates that a significant portion (over 20 percent) of fans attending a promotional event, or a game with a promotional event, found out about the event from a family member or friend. (11)

Advertising Media for Sport

We have examined the advertising message model and what advertising hopes to accomplish. A sport organization must decide which form or forms of media to use in an advertising campaign. In the following section, we examine the various advertising mediums most commonly used in sport. Some are common to all forms of advertising, whereas some are best suited to sport or unique to sport; each has its own set of advantages and disadvantages.

Signage

Signage includes printed messages or logos identifying a sponsor or event on any of the following types of materials: banners, street-pole attachments, billboards (fixed or movable), scoreboards, electronic message boards including LED displays, posters, and dasher boards or rink boards. It also includes impressions such as in-ice or on-field messages, rotational courtside messages, on-field or on-court logos, and virtual signage (superimposed on blank stadium walls and playing surfaces but visible on television). (12) The definition of signage has also been expanded to include logo placement opportunities, which are most commonly found on racing cars (of all types); racing boats; driver uniforms; professional golfers' caps and shirts; and professional tennis players' caps, headbands, and rackets. In some cases, the name of the sponsor is also the name of the team, as in English football (soccer) or Italian basketball (i.e., Benetton Basket, the 1997 Italian League Champions).

Although signage conveys a message, it is not a spoken, scripted, or consistent message. The message that signage conveys is more accurately described as an impression: The message is received and acted on based on the awareness and feelings of the receiver with regard to the sender. Because of the high amount of clutter (number of advertising messages and impressions) in American society, many messages or impressions are not received because the intended audience has built up an immunity—that is, has become so accustomed to advertising messages that they do not stand out. As sport marketers have become more and more reliant on advertising revenue from sponsors wishing to communicate to their audiences, they have had to search for new ideas and creative concepts and placements for these messages. Several studies have shown that creative placement results in higher recognition and reception of the message. Stotler and Johnson concluded in a 1989 study that advertising messages that were part of the game—for example, placed on or in front of the scorer's table—were more effective than other placements. (13) Pope and Voges found that automobile manufacturers looking to increase product awareness were effective in achieving the objective using on-site displays and vehicle and equipment signage. (14)

Exposure to corporate names and logos at sport venues can increase product awareness and may subsequently lead to loyal product consumption by spectators. (15) This potential for consumption of sponsor products and services plays a key role in the level of creativity and ingenuity we find in sport advertising (see figure 11.2). In February 2006 at the NBA All-Star Game in Houston, Toyota was able to leverage its unique position of becoming the first NBA partner to also hold naming rights to the all-star venue—Houston's Toyota Center. Toyota was able to use February's all-star week in Houston as a launching pad for a variety of activities including the rollout of a national sweepstakes, the introduction of new car lines, and a sponsorship of the all-star practice sessions. This was in addition to the Tundra

FIGURE 11.2 The Toyota Tundra zone.
Courtesy of Houston Rockets

Zone that features a permanent vehicle display in the Toyota Center, not only a venue for the All-Star Game, but also the home of the NBA Houston Rockets. (16)

Signage is often one element of an integrated sponsorship purchase. It may be the most important element of the sponsorship for some companies and just a "value-added component" for others (i.e., not the core benefit but a benefit of secondary value or importance). For example, Shell Oil entered into a sponsorship agreement with baseball's St. Louis Cardinals that focused on teaching fans to keep score. The Shell Oil logo was displayed throughout the season on the Cardinals' matrix scoreboard along with instructions on how to score each play. Given that the Cardinals average over 20,000 fans per game for 81 games and that a baseball game contains a minimum of 27 plays, the Shell logo is guaranteed to generate an absolute minimum of 43,740,000 impressions per season. Because Shell has the second-most identifiable logo in the world, according to Shell marketer Harry Dunn, logo recognition is not the key element of this sponsorship. Driving traffic to Shell stations is the primary objective, so Shell also distributed 500,000 scorecards through its local stations. The signage created awareness and recognition and generated traffic and sales at the local stations. (17)

Signage is one medium that can be enhanced and expanded via the new technologies and media at our disposal. In its simplest application, virtual signage creates an image unseen by fans at the game but crystal clear to television audiences. With added bells and whistles, virtual signage allows for constant updating of images and placement of logos where an actual sign might distract participants, such as the middle of a tennis court. Most important, it allows advertisers to target their message to a particular geographic audience. While viewers in the United States may see an ad for Coors, Canadian audiences can be looking at a sign for Molson. This technology has already been used for the international broadcast of the Super Bowl, with Coca-Cola as a lead sponsor. With the exception of showing messages on the wall behind home plate during MLB telecasts, and providing the virtual first down marker for collegiate and professional football games, virtual signage has not gained much traction in the United States. This could be in part due to the popularity of LED signage, which, if used properly, can bring a sponsor's message to life, but is most likely related to the inability to construct effective guidelines for virtual signage and to prevent it being used by ambush marketers to alter the ads during a telecast. Imagine the impact of changing the advertising content at the Super Bowl if one competitor could take advantage over another by changing how a sign appears to home viewers.

We have seen limited virtual signage in baseball telecasts mostly on the blank wall behind the batter. Most of these virtual ads are team-controlled and promote ticket purchasing opportunities through the home team. However, given the limited opportunities to capture the interest and attention of the viewer, can Augusta's fairways, the NBA's center court, the NFL end zones, Fenway's "Green Monster," and the NHL's goal areas be far behind?

LED Signage: Bringing Your Message to Life

Chris Heck, vice president of team marketing and business operations, National Basketball Association

In layman's terms, LED signage presents moving, changing, dynamic graphic images that the sport arena or stadium uses as a continuous display for general and specific advertising or visual entertainment for the audience. LED signage is a powerful vehicle for market visibility and sponsor recall. Creating a "wow" factor is what facility managers, corporate spokespersons, and game presentation directors should aspire to when communicating with their customers. LED signage provides displays that depict sharp images, brilliant color, and larger-than-life pictures that are essential to capture the attention of sport fans and concertgoers who are exposed to thousands of messages every day. LED signage can be combined with sound to provide a multidimensional forum that brings the message to life for its audience.

LED signage has numerous advantages over static and rotational signage, namely the following:

- ✦ Higher resolution and clarity
- ✦ Movement
- ✦ Animation
- ✦ Sound
- ✦ Portability—can be updated by simply programming: no hard production costs or delays
- ✦ Flexibility—variety of sizes and shapes
- ✦ Real-time alterations
- ✦ Life cycle—can be updated electronically as frequently as needed
- ✦ Increased inventory—no space needed to store

Perhaps the greatest advantage of LED signage is that it permits the venue, organization, or team to sell advertising based on time and not space. Thus, every purchaser's message has a prime location and can be given as much exposure as the purchaser desires.

LED technology can be used to send messages not only on scoreboards, but also in traditional signage areas.
Courtesy of NBA Entertainment

✦ Table 11.1 Top Athlete Endorsement Earnings

Athlete	Sport	Endorsements (in millions)
Tiger Woods	Golf	$70
LeBron James	Basketball	$35
Andre Agassi	Tennis	$24.5
Maria Sharapova	Tennis	$20
Shaquille O'Neal	Basketball	$14
Michelle Wie	Golf	$10
Serena Williams	Tennis	$8
Annika Sorenstam	Golf	$6

Data on male athletes from www.sportsillustrated.cnn.com/2004.writers/pete_mcentegart/05/14/money.list/index.html.

Data on female athletes from www.abcnews.go.com/Sports/print?id=2403872; www.cbsnews.com/stories/2005/10/05/national/printable917086.shtml; www.findarticles.com/p/articles/mi_m1365/is_9_34/ai_114702189/print.

Endorsements

Brooks and Harris incorporated the work of McCracken and of Friedman and Friedman in defining a celebrity athlete endorser as a well-known celebrity athlete who uses his or her fame to help a company sell or enhance the image of the company, products, or brands (see table 11.1). (18) According to McCracken, a celebrity athlete can assume one product endorsement style or a combination of several styles. These are (1) the explicit mode (I endorse this product), (2) the implicit mode (I use this product), (3) the imperative mode (you should use this product), and (4) the co-present mode (in which the athlete merely appears in some setting with the product). (19)

According to Burt Sugar, the first recorded instance of a modern athlete's leasing his name (to endorse a sport product) occurred on September 1, 1905, when Honus Wagner (later enshrined as one of the first four members of the Baseball Hall of Fame) of the Pittsburgh Pirates gave the J.F. Hillerich & Son Company permission to use his name on its Louisville Slugger bats for a consideration of $75. Other athletes, such as Ty Cobb and Babe Ruth, soon began to endorse products for payment. (20) The earliest endorsements involved sport-related products, and some of the most effective endorsements today are of sport-related products (e.g., Michael Jordan for Nike). (21)

The growing popularity of pro football, basketball, baseball, golf, tennis, and motor sports has led to the proliferation of the sport celebrity. Brand identity has become one of the primary reasons that advertisers so closely link their products with sport; fans seem to identify as closely with the sponsor as with the sport itself. Michael Jordan popularized Nike's Air Jordan shoe. After leading his team to a Super Bowl victory, quarterback Joe Montana responded to a commentator's question about what he was going to do next by exclaiming, "I'm going to Disney World." And NASCAR joined with Kellogg's to promote the Winston Cup auto racing series on the backs of 20 million cereal boxes. (22)

The selection of endorsers should always be predicated on the product/service and its target market. However, the 2004 SportsQ scores suggest that for all the notoriety and dollars attracted by whoever is anointed as *the next big thing* in any sport, retired athletes are generally held in higher regard among the public. Of the top ten scorers, seven were retired athletes (rank in parentheses) including: Michael Jordan (1), Cal Ripken Jr. (3), Nolan Ryan (4), Willie Mays (4), Wayne Gretzky (6), Joe Montana (6), and Julius Erving (9). The active athletes were: Tiger Woods (2), Jerry Rice (8) and Jackie Joyner-Kersee (10). (23)

The trustworthiness and influence of Michael Jordan are evidenced by his total endorsement value. One example of Jordan's endorsements is his multimillion-dollar contract with Rayovac (batteries). According to *Sports Marketing Letter*, Rayovac believes that using Jordan could reduce to nearly zero the time it will take to educate consumers—especially single-use battery purchasers—on the advantages of its new product. Rayovac's product is the only rechargeable alkaline on the market. As opposed to one long-life use for a regular disposable alkaline, the Rayovac product gives as many as 11 long-life uses. So why do they need Jordan?

Jordan, the company believes, will grab instant attention and instant recognition for the battery. Also, the imagery is a tight fit. Expect to see advertising themed on Jordan and the product as "the best of their kind," "the greatest ever," and the like. And who is a better choice to endorse a renewable battery than a superstar whose basketball career has proven to be renewable? (24)

But who are the next generation of endorsers? Obviously LeBron James and his $90 million endorsement deal with Nike (25) merits serious consideration. 2006 NBA Final MVP Dwyane Wade, Olympian Shaun White, NY Yankee superstar Derek Jeter, and soon-to-be Hall of Famer (if he ever retires) Roger Clemens would stand out on the sports side. But with hip hop and rap gaining mainstream appeal, there's growing acceptance of performers (such as 50 Cent and Snoop Dogg) crossing over to acting and commercial endorsements. Look for this trend to continue; as marketers increasingly search for an edge to create product buzz, Snoop Dogg and other controversial celebrities remain just the ticket. That's why AOL, which lost 2.2 million subscribers in 2003, used Snoop in its ad for software. According to brand marketing chief Len Short, "Snoop had the kind of attitude and surprise we wanted." (26)

"Since the days of Babe Ruth and Joe DiMaggio, people have known that athletes pulled in attention in some fashion." (27) If it's attitude and surprise you are looking for, look no further than professional athletes. In the last decade there have been numerous incidents leading to adverse publicity and courtroom appearances involving professional athletes. In the minds of many, including corporate America, these incidents have become all too common on the sport pages and front pages of newspapers as well as fertile material for television, radio and Internet programming, such as ESPN's Outside the Lines, and many other outlets. Spousal abuse, sexual misconduct, drug usage, assault, and even murder have been paired with athletes such as Latrell Sprewell, Rae Caruth, Mark McGwire, Kobe Bryant, Barry Bonds, Maurice Clarett, and most recently 2006 Tour de France winner Floyd Landis. While attorneys representing the corporation endorsed by the athlete push hard for contract language and morals clauses that allow a company to end the deal at the first whiff of a scandal, player representatives try to set a high bar for termination—namely that the athlete be convicted of a crime. (28)

The case of Kobe Bryant is an interesting one. His McDonald's agreement was not renewed, and his new Nike contract—complete with a signature shoe that was to be released in 2004—was paid but he was not utilized as an endorser, and the shoe never made it to market. However, as predicted by Mike Levine, COO of Van Wagner Sports Group—"if acquitted in a trial, and he's acquitted in a convincing fashion, it's not impossible that he could reemerge as a leader in the endorsement environment." (29)

A successful parody of the "problem or selfish athlete" was created by Budweiser, who gave us fictional superstar "Leon"—who, while poking fun at some of the stereotypes of today's athletes, had plenty of time to sell beer and make a "live" appearance at the World Series. (30) On another note, "Leon" could be an indicator of what might happen in the future when a "character" that has been created and can be controlled is brought to life in a scripted reality commercial. Although it is live television, there is no real-time or reality consideration because the character has been provided with the dialogue and has been inserted into our lives via an event happening in real time, in this case the World Series, which happened to be broadcast from Busch Stadium. (31)

Using the popularity of entertainers—particularly rappers with dark pasts—to sell mainstream products is particularly interesting. With hip hop ruling the world of popular music these days, it is interesting to see Snoop Dogg portrayed as a mainstream personality by DaimlerChrysler in ads with Lee Iacocca and 50 Cent hawking cross-trainers for Reebok. As consultant Mel Poole pointed out, wouldn't it be interesting if soccer moms who buy minivans and shoes ever wake up to the lifestyles and view of women that these two artists promote through their music? The potential backlash against Reebok and DaimlerChrysler could be unprecedented. (32)

One way to lessen the risk in using celebrity athletes as endorsers is to tie their compensation into product sales by offering them stock options. Dan Marino has an equity share in LaRussa Italian foods; Michael Jordan and Cal Ripken have an equity relationship with Oakley sunglasses; and Tiger Woods received stock for his involvement in the Official All-Star Café. (33)

Retired athletes are another safe alternative to using current athletes. According to former head of talent marketing for SFX Steve Rosner, "What guys do after hours is very much an issue. So it's a little bit safer to go with someone who is 40 years old and credible." (34) Not only are they safer, but their credibility and relevance has been nurtured because "all of them grew up in front of us, blossoming at a time when the emergence of ESPN and the investments of a few sneaker companies changed the way consumers view athletes." (35)

Is using retired athletes a defendable and profitable strategy? If you have your doubts, table 11.2 depicts the 2004 top 10 athletes in terms of their SportsQ scores. Note that only two are still active performers.

In a less traditional approach, some clever marketers have hit on another solution to control the behavior, and hence the image, of their endorsers—make sure they're dead. Advances in video technology and computer imaging have permitted companies such as Dirt Devil, Mercedes-Benz, and Coors to "resurrect" such cinema and television stars as Fred Astaire, Ed Sullivan, and John Wayne. Why use dead celebrities? There are several reasons. First, "Dead celebrities allow advertisers to tap into feelings of nostalgia about times spent gathered around the television watching classic shows—an emotion that reverberates with baby boomers in particular." Second, with dead celebrities—who can no longer get arrested or offend consumers—advertisers know what they are getting. Latching on to celebrities such as Dennis Rodman can prove embarrassing to advertisers. "With dead celebrities, their qualities are known," said Tom Cordner, creative director of Team One Advertising. "They can't get you in trouble. They're a safe bet." (36)

Sport marketers have embraced this tactic as well. ESPN's flattering movie of Ty Cobb was heavily used to promote the 1998 baseball season. Jackie Robinson appeared on Wheaties boxes and commemorative Coca-Cola bottles; he was thanked by famous current athletes in a Nike commercial, and Robinson's estate was projected to earn millions of dollars in endorsement fees—all after he had been dead for 25 years. (37) Given the reception and success of this type of advertising, will we soon see Babe Ruth pitching hot dogs or endorsing beer, or perhaps Babe Didrikson promoting the attributes of golf equipment? Stay tuned.

Print Media

Print media is the inclusive term used to refer to newspapers, magazines, brochures, posters, programs, point-of-purchase displays, and direct mail. Among all forms of print media, newspapers have several clear-cut advantages. They are timely because they are published daily. Day-of-game, membership-promotion, or special sales advertising can be placed in a newspaper with only short advance notice. Compared to electronic media such as television, newspaper advertising is lower in cost. Sport and business sections seem to be the preferred spots for ad placements geared to attracting sport consumers, although the lifestyle-type sections and weekend special sections

✦ Table 11.2 2004 SportsQ Scores Top 10

Ranking	Athlete	SportsQ score
1	Michael Jordan	49
2	Tiger Woods	44
3	Cal Ripken Jr.	42
4	Nolan Ryan	41
4	Willie Mays	41
6	Wayne Gretzky	39
6	Joe Montana	39
8	Jerry Rice	38
9	Julius Erving	36
10	Jackie Joyner-Kersee	35

Reprinted, by permission, from T. Lefton, 2004, "Old pros rule SportsQ scores, starting with Jordan," *Street & Smith's SportsBusiness Journal* May 10-16, pg. 11.

are also excellent placement areas. (38) Magazines have the advantages of very high print quality and color reproduction. However, they are usually published weekly or monthly, and they can be rather expensive. These types of print advertising are declining in terms of the percentage of the advertising budget—with more money being spent on Web site advertising and e-marketing.

Posters offer the organization a degree of control, because the organization can determine where and when to distribute them. They can also be self-financing: The organization can sell advertising space on the posters to pay for the printing and materials. High school and collegiate athletics programs often use posters listing schedules and upcoming promotions and special events to promote their various athletic teams. One limitation of posters is that they are limited to an immediate area of exposure impact dependent on attraction and traffic flow.

Game or event programs can pay for themselves and can even generate a profit, in many cases, through the sale of advertising space. The program itself, with its photographs, stories, and statistics, promotes the organization or event and serves as an excellent public relations tool. Host Communications, based in Lexington, Kentucky, is one of the industry leaders in the game/event program marketplace.

Posters and programs may also be part of a point-of-purchase (POP) promotion—a promotional activity that takes place at the moment of purchase. Retailers have relied for years on POP promotions. For example, a sporting goods store may offer an instant rebate through a couponing program at the store to encourage the purchase of a specific brand of athletic footwear during the customer's visit. Using POPs is often referred to as reminder advertising. Reminder advertising works in several ways. It can enhance the top-of-mind awareness of the brand, thus increasing the probability that the consumer includes the brand on the shopping list or purchases it as an impulse item. Additionally, it can enforce the key elements of the national advertising campaign at the point of purchase. (39)

Pocket schedules have been a key print element for sport teams for many years. The primary function of a pocket schedule is to convey team schedule information—game times, opponents, and dates—in an inexpensive yet convenient format. The pocket schedule is also used to list all of the promotional events and giveaway days in the upcoming season as well as to provide contact information and ticket purchasing instructions (see examples of pocket schedules in chapter 10). The pocket schedule also serves as a revenue generator because it usually contains the logo of a sponsor who assumes the printing and production costs for the schedule. Finally, the pocket schedule can be used to promote an image or theme that can be related to the team or a player. The 2004 Denver Broncos—having lost a number of significant and recognizable players through trades, retirements, and free agency—opted to use their 2004 pocket schedule to convey to fans that they still possessed a number of marquee and pro bowl caliber players. Four different Bronco players were featured on various cover versions of the pocket schedule, and the fifth version showed a fan with a painted face and Bronco jersey cheering. According to James Merilatt, publications manager for the Broncos, "We wanted to do something that keeps the image of the Broncos in the front of our fans' minds. By utilizing a sponsor-related promotional piece that we were already producing, we were able to accomplish this without incurring additional expense." (40)

Direct-mail advertising is used widely in the sport industry. Its major advantage is that it reaches only the people the organization wants to reach, which minimizes spending on circulating a message to people who have little interest in the contents. Organizations often promote season tickets, partial ticket plans, and single-game tickets through direct mail. One common approach in selling tickets is to cultivate leads from credit card purchases and to develop a direct-mail piece, such as a ticket-plan brochure, to mail to cardholders. This results in a highly targeted direct-mail campaign because the target audience has already demonstrated a familiarity with and interest in the product. (41)

When designing any print materials, the sport marketer should consider the following guidelines:

+ The headline must flag down the target reader and pull him or her into the text about the product, offering a reward for reading on.

+ Because most people reading print ads never read beyond the headline, it is also crucial that the headline and the visual component complement each other so well, and "tell the story" so clearly, that someone who looks only at the headline and the visual can "get the message" without having to read a word of the body copy.

+ The body copy should be detailed and specific, should support the headline, and should be readable and interesting. (42)

Research has shown that people recall information better when it is presented both pictorially and verbally (43); for this reason, sport marketers should use carefully designed images to convey their message. Advertisements describing upcoming promotional items, or brochures describing facility renovations, should contain photographs and artists' renderings whenever possible.

Broadcast (Electronic) Media

In this section, we consider radio, television, scoreboards, and public address systems. Chapter 15 deals with the creation and management of broadcast networks for event distribution. All are critical media for reaching today's consumer. Scoreboards (which can also be classified as signage for external advertisers) and public address systems represent internal advertising mediums; they cost virtually nothing and offer effective reach to a target market that through its presence in the venue has demonstrated an interest in and ability to purchase the product. Scoreboards and public address systems can perform a variety of functions. They can be used to sell announcements or provide message space for local businesses; to announce future games, other venue events, special events, or promotional activities; and to recognize groups in attendance in order to encourage them to attend again. (44)

Radio

Radio provides an audio message that can be powerful, and radio can be relatively inexpensive. Major League Baseball teams offer 30-second advertising spots for season-long ad campaigns that run for as little as $200 per spot (in Kansas City) to as much as $1,700 per spot (in Los Angeles). (45)

Good copy read by an announcer with a following, backed up by the appropriate "action," noise, or music, can take us to the game or club. Radio plays to the imagination and lets us hear what we wish while letting our minds create a "picture" that may be based on past memories, hopeful expectations, or perhaps just wishful thinking. Because each radio station (and format type) has its own audience, sport organizations can choose a particular format on the basis of its compatibility with their own target market.

In an ethnically diverse country such as the United States, radio also permits sport organizations to offer broadcasts and advertising opportunities in languages other than English. This enables some organizations, particularly those located in south Florida, the Southwest, California, and New York, to reach out to their fans. The trend to broadcast in Spanish could become more mainstream over the next 10 years as the Hispanic population continues to grow. This fact has not been lost on the San Diego Padres, a team located less than 25 miles (40 kilometers) from Mexico, within a metropolitan area that is home to more than 600,000 Hispanics. Spanish-language broadcasts also provide additional sponsorship and advertising opportunities, according to Don Johnson, the Padres' vice president of marketing: "Because many of our sponsors also have Hispanic marketing departments, they have additional advertising budgets. Miller Brewing Co. is the U.S. domestic beer sponsor for the Padres, while Tecate is the Hispanic domestic beer sponsor. Some of the sponsors we've signed would not be here if it wasn't for the Hispanic broadcasts. It's really opened the door for a lot of new opportunities." (46)

Some sport organizations, particularly minor professional leagues and some college programs, may be too small or too limited in geographic appeal to attract radio advertisers. In such cases, it can be advisable to sell advertising space on a league- or conference-wide basis. For example, the University of Oregon, Oregon State University, Washington State University, and the University of Washington formed a partnership to offer advertising opportunities at all four schools when they learned from the Northwest Ford dealers that an all-inclusive package better fit the dealers' needs and their advertising budget. This combined approach lets the Northwest Ford dealers share the advertising costs and also reap the benefits of a much broader geographic market than they could afford as individual firms. (47)

One of the fears of sport marketers is that sport radio and game broadcasts skew to an older audience. Because this perception would also limit the universe of potential radio advertisers, it merits attention and a search for a possible solution. The Philadelphia Phillies have discovered a unique way to attack this perception and hopefully increase younger listenership. According to John Brazer, manager of promotions for the Phillies, "We found out that mostly adults listened to our games on the radio and when we looked at our programming, we found that most of the features were targeted at adults with almost nothing for children." Thus the Phillies will try to make their broadcasts more kid-friendly through features such as a roving reporter who will report live from remote parts of the stadium, such as the bull pen and dugout. The features will run during the first three innings of the games so that kids can hear them before they go to sleep. (48) In the long run, the hope is to create a new generation of listeners who will continue as adults, enhancing the radio-rights and advertising revenue potential.

Television

Although radio has its benefits as compared to television, most notably cost, nothing compares to television in advertising reach and the ability to convey to a mass audience the attributes of an advertiser's product or service. Television has grown in a relatively short time from the three national networks and the Public Broadcast System to four major networks—and arguably 20 or more national networks, plus hundreds of other highly segmented channels (e.g., SpeedWeek and RSN's such as Fox Regional Sports Networks) located throughout the country, in view of their availability to mass audiences through cable or satellite broadcasts.

Television reaches the largest number of people, and it conveys sight and sound. The consumer can watch Barry Bonds hit a mammoth home run or see the fans do the "wave"—and can hear the crack of the bat or the roar of the crowd. Although television coverage—particularly of events such as the Olympics and the Super Bowl—can be expensive, advertisers have found this medium to be a critical element of their marketing mix.

Just as a story can be told in several ways, audio and visual elements can be combined to produce several types of television commercials. Television commercials can incorporate the following types of structures:

+ *Story line*—Telling a story. The message has a beginning, middle, and end.
+ *Problem-solution*—Presenting the viewer with a problem to be solved and the sponsor's product as the solution to that problem.
+ *Chronology*—Delivering the message through a series of related scenes. Facts and events are presented sequentially as they occurred.
+ *Special effects*—Achieving memorability through the use of some striking device, such as an unusual musical sound or pictorial technique.

- *Testimonial*—Advertising by word of mouth. A well-known figure—or an unknown man in the street—vouches for the value of the product.
- *Satire*—Using sophisticated wit to point out human foibles. This form is generally produced in an exaggerated style, perhaps as parody.
- *Spokesperson*—Using an on-camera announcer who attempts to sell via personal, intimate selling, or perhaps via the hard sell.
- *Demonstration*—Using some sort of physical apparatus to demonstrate the product's effectiveness.
- *Suspense*—Telling a story, as with the story-line approach, but incorporating a high level of drama into the buildup of curiosity and suspense until the ending.
- *Slice-of-life*—Beginning with a person needing to make a decision or in a situation requiring a solution. This approach then shows how the solution has worked.
- *Analogy*—Instead of presenting a direct message about the product, conveying the message through comparison with something else.
- *Fantasy*—Using caricatures or special effects to create fantasy surrounding the product and product use.
- *Personality*—Relying on an actor or actress rather than an announcer to deliver the message. The actor plays a character who talks about the product, reacts to its use, or demonstrates its use or enjoyment. (49)

The NBA's Seattle Supersonics combined the fantasy, story-line, and personality approaches using members of the team instead of actors to win five Clio awards for their advertising campaign "Coming to Your Home." This campaign featured video of Sonics players and coach George Karl showing up unannounced in unlikely places throughout the community. "Coming to Your Home" sent the message that the Sonics were televising 56 games on free or cable television, moving away from the pay-TV package they'd offered in previous years. At the same time, the campaign provided a link between the Sonics players and the community. The ads were shot using video instead of film to achieve the feel of a home movie, emphasizing the intimacy and spontaneity of the moment. (50)

The use of sport and its celebrities or stars to advertise other products via television has become part of our everyday lives. The success of the Miller Lite campaign (see the case study on page 254) and the popularity of a Coke commercial starring future NFL Hall of Famer "Mean" Joe Greene—a commercial so loved it became a movie (51)—testify to how effective these types of commercials can be. USA Today's "Ad Track" (see table 11.4) lists the most effective sport-themed television advertising campaigns since 1995.

In the late 1990s, television advertising began to move away from the widespread use of athletes and began embracing the "everyday athlete" and "weekend warrior" types. Reebok and Nike slashed their athlete endorser budgets in favor of showing everyday people in their athletic pursuits. One company, Lamkin Corp. of San Diego, a manufacturer of leather golf club grips, went so far as to parody Nike's famous "I am Tiger Woods" ad with its own "I am in the woods" campaign—an attempt to relate more to the average golfer and suggest a cure for a problem. The ad shows a series of hapless duffers whacking ball after ball into thick shrubbery and moaning, "I'm in the woods." The advertised cure, naturally, was a new leather Lamkin grip. (52) New Nike and Reebok commercials depicted everyday people running, playing basketball, or in-line skating. The advertising message? Our products are for everyone, not just elite athletes.

Not all sport-related commercials are effective, and some can alienate viewers—the exact opposite of the commercial's purpose. Take the case of Nike in the 1996 Summer Olympics. With ads costing up to $700,000 for a 30-second prime-time spot, Nike elected to show a commercial that included a scene of a runner throwing up. Although Nike's intent was to display the gritty realism of sport competition, the ad generated hundreds of letters from consumers outraged by the spot. (53)

✦ Table 11.3 Effective Sport-Themed Television Advertising Campaigns

Advertiser/year	Athletes	Percentage of public perceiving the ad to be effective
McDonald's/1995	Michael Jordan, Larry Bird, Charles Barkley	47
Taco Bell/1995	Shaquille O'Neal, Hakeem Olajuwon	42
Nike/1997	Tiger Woods	40
Nike/1996	Anfernee Hardaway, Michael Jordan	39
Nike/1995	Drew Bledsoe, Marshall Faulk	34
McDonald's/1995	Dan Marino, Emmitt Smith, Drew Bledsoe, Barry Sanders	32
Nike/1998	Gary Payton, Kevin Garnett, Jason Kidd	29
Sprite/1995	Grant Hill	29
Visa/1996	Hakeem Olajuwon	27
Mountain Dew/1998	Michael Johnson	26
Reebok/1996	Emmitt Smith	23
Right Guard/1997	Scottie Pippen, Charles Barkley	23
American Express/1997-1998	Tiger Woods	22

Based on M. Wells, 1998, "Ads featuring athletes: They shoot, they score," *USA Today* 13: 5B.

Billboards, Blimps, and Buses

Outdoor ads placed on billboards, on movable trailers, or on buses can provide a highly visible message, depending on the location and the duration of placement. Price varies according to location, number, and length, but this excellent form of advertisement can be relatively inexpensive compared to television. Fixed billboards can remain in place over a long period of time, providing repeated exposure and thus reinforcement of the message. Fixed billboard locations can also be used for "teaser campaigns" that start out by posing a question and subsequently present the answer a little at a time.

Billboards mounted on trailers and driven throughout the marketplace have become commonplace at large special events such as all-star games and Olympic festivals.

The purpose of a movable billboard is twofold. The basic purpose is to draw attention to the event and the message of the advertiser. A second purpose is to expose more people to the message than would ordinarily be the case because a billboard moves throughout a city, on highways, and within other high-traffic locations.

Other effective promotional devices are bus cards, placards on the exterior of buses, and "take-one" boxes, sometimes containing team schedules or ticket applications, that are placed in buses, trains, or taxi cabs. Some teams, such as the Phoenix Suns and the Pittsburgh Pirates, have actually used entire buses to display promotional messages.

Movable billboards have proven to be a successful promo vehicle.
Courtesy of William A. Sutton

Case Study: The Miller Lite Campaign

Beer companies have relied on sport as an ingredient in their marketing brew since time immemorial, and almost always successfully. In 1973-1974, Miller decided to test a series of commercials with "virgin" spokespersons because the feeling was that an actor would come across as just another actor endorsing a product, possibly lessening the commercial's believability. Subscribing to both the governmental and voluntary codes holding that active athletes could not endorse alcoholic beverages (because doing so would imply that alcohol increases their physical prowess), Miller opted for ex-athletes and characters who exuded machismo. After successful testing and a warm response in terms of sales, the commercials went national in 1975, with the theme "Everything you always wanted in a beer. And less."

McCann-Erikson, Miller's agency, assembled 34 characters—the highest use-of-athlete quotient in the history of sport advertising. They included former NFL stars Dick Butkus, Bubba Smith, Nick Buoniconti, and Deacon Jones;

former NBA star Wilt Chamberlain; former NHL stars Jacques Plante and Boom-Boom Geoffrion (who discussed the attributes of the beer in French); and original New York Met "Marvelous" Marv Throneberry.

The commercials not only worked artistically, they worked commercially. In a marketplace in which a six-pack of beer was suddenly cheaper than Coke, Miller Lite took the almost nonexistent category of light beer up to 2.5 million barrels in its first year of national distribution. By 1976, sales had doubled to 5 million barrels; and in 1977, by the best estimates available, it had more than doubled again to 12.5 million barrels, or between 8 and 10 percent of the beer market.

With the commercial, called by some a Madison Avenue production and by others a stroke of genius, Miller Lite had created the low-calorie market much as Xerox had created the photocopier market. And the success story behind the success story of Miller Lite has been its effective use of sport and sport stars. (54, 55)

The Pirates have turned public transportation into advertising opportunities.
Courtesy of William A. Sutton. Reprinted, by permission, of the Pittsburgh Pirates.

Blimps and small planes trailing advertising banners are also very popular forms of outdoor advertising. Companies such as Budweiser, Fuji, and Goodyear have highly visible blimps that travel to major sporting events. The Goodyear blimp, probably the most famous of these ships, provides aerial views that are integrated into the television coverage in ABC's *Monday Night Football*.

Promotional Concepts and Practices

The remainder of this chapter deals with promotional concepts and practices in the sport industry. As previously noted, we will examine sales strategies and techniques in chapter 12; but the concepts and practices discussed in this section do have sales implications and applications. To explain how promotional concepts and practices have evolved in the United States, we will begin by examining the birth and development of promotional activities in sport.

Some of the greatest promoters in American history were involved in the promotion of sport and entertainment activities. P.T. Barnum, Albert Spalding, C.C. Pyle, Tex Rickard, Abe Saperstein, Rube Foster, J.W. Wilkinson, Ned Irish, Bill Veeck, Charlie Finley, Evel Knievel, Don King, Mike Veeck, Madonna, Howard Stern, and even Dennis Rodman are just a few of the innovative minds that sought to promote their products (or themselves) in most imaginative ways. See the following promotions timeline for some perspective on the development of promotion.

✦ Promotions Timeline: 1850s to 2000s

Decade	Activity
1850s	First intercollegiate athletic event—crew—between Harvard and Yale, held in New Hampshire and sponsored by a railroad to promote its line and a new vacation route to prospective fans.
1880s	Albert G. Spalding publishes the *Spalding Baseball Guide*, an instructional piece that in reality was an attempt to create and expand the marketing for his products by teaching people how to use them. Spalding becomes the "official baseball" of the National League, and promotion of the ball as "official" through the Spalding catalog and through retailers begins.
	Chris Von der Ahe, St. Louis magnate, leads the creation of the American Association, a rival to the National League. The AA promotes cheaper tickets (25 cents compared to 50 cents in NL) and beer. NL owners scoff at the "Beer Ball League" and at Von der Ahe's use of special promotions and entertainment features.
1900s	First recorded instance of an athlete lending his name—Honus Wagner—to endorse a product, Louisville Slugger (bats), for payment ($75).
	The Doubleday legend (that Doubleday invented baseball) is created to position baseball as a uniquely American game.
	Ty Cobb and Honus Wagner promote Coca-Cola as "The Great National Drink of the Great National Game."
	Bull Durham (smoking tobacco) begins buying outfield signage and offering a prize to any player who hits the sign with a batted ball during the course of a game. This led to an increase in stadium signage and the use of this medium to promote products.
1910s	Tex Rickard creates "spectacle" in boxing through promoting the purse (displays of the prize money) to the public, creating public interest and free media coverage prior to the actual event.
	First sport award given for the purpose of product publicity; Chalmers Motor Car Co. donates a car to the MLB batting champion.
1920s	The role of the sport agent as a promoter begins to emerge as Christy Walsh represents Babe Ruth in his non-Yankee contracts.
	Red Grange and C.C. (Cash & Carry) Pyle team up to use a superstar to promote the new NFL and give it credibility.
	William Veeck Sr., wanting to introduce baseball to a new segment of fans (and children), begins broadcasting Chicago Cubs games on the radio.
1930s	The Kansas City Monarchs of the Negro Leagues develop a portable lighting system to enable them not only to play their games at night but also to "barnstorm" and take their game to various cities throughout the United States; the concept was so successful that for six years the Monarchs elected not to join the Negro National League, preferring to barnstorm.
	Night baseball is introduced in the major leagues in Cincinnati.
	Ned Irish promotes college double-headers at the Madison Square Garden, ushering in a golden age of New York City basketball that ends in the gambling scandals of the 1950s.

(continued)

✦ Promotions Timeline: 1850s to 2000s *(continued)*

Decade	Activity
1940s	The tobacco industry becomes more involved in the game of baseball—Chesterfield cigarette signs become a functioning part of the scoreboard in baseball parks with the "h" being lit to signify a hit and the "e" being lit to signify an error. First nationally televised World Series.
1950s	Bill Veeck introduces "Bat Day"—the first of many giveaway days featuring premium items, very commonplace today. The debut of *Sports Illustrated.*
1960s	International Management Group founded by Mark McCormack, initially as a vehicle to represent Arnold Palmer; IMG is now the largest sport marketing agency in the world. Signing and marketing of Joe Namath by the New York Jets and the American Football League (AFL)—once again the credibility of an interest in a superstar promotes an entire league. First Super Bowl between the NFL and the AFL; success of this venture coupled with the Sports Broadcasting Act led to the merger and growth of what is arguably America's *real* national pastime.
1970s	*Ball Four,* by then-New York Yankee Jim Bouton, is published; the first book that portrayed athletes as real people with real problems and behaviors. Miller Lite embarks on a national advertising campaign using past sport figures (34 of them); the largest quotient in the history of sport advertising. ESPN begins broadcasting as the first 24-hour-per-day sport television network.
1980s	The commercial success of the 1984 Los Angeles Olympics organized by Peter Ueberroth proves that corporate sponsorship can make the Olympic Games a profitable enterprise. The first collegiate bowl game sells its naming rights—the USF&G Sugar Bowl. The arrival and marketing of Michael "Air" Jordan—perhaps along with Muhammad Ali the most recognizable sport personality in the world.
1990s	The emergence of women's professional team sports—basketball (American Basketball League and WNBA) along with fast-pitch softball and soccer. The World League of American Football (now NFL-Europe) premieres to capitalize on European interest in American sports as well as to provide opportunities for satellite television and merchandising sales. Direct TV and Primestar home satellite television services are offered along with packages such as the NFL Sunday Ticket, which permits viewers not only to follow their favorite team regardless of where they live but to follow every team. MLB, NBA, NHL, Major League Soccer, WNBA, and NCAA soon follow suit. Fox becomes the fourth national network, using its purchase of NFL television rights and broadcasting schedule to promote its programming, Fox Sports Net; a syndication of regional sport networks soon follows. Grassroots marketing through the creation of interactive fan festivals, aimed at fans in markets hosting all-star games and the Super Bowls, begins. MLB's FanFest, NBA Jam Session, NHL FANtasy, and the NCAA Hoop City are initiated to entertain fans in host cities while at the same time providing a platform for their sponsors to interface with the public.
2000s	Reintroduction of bobbleheads—the dolls fill stadiums and arenas across the country and in fast-food restaurants as toys for kids. Authentic memorabilia become premium giveaway items, although replicas are still present. Promotions take on a new twist with a publication such as a comic book with the Dallas Mavericks. Comic book promotions position athletes as superheroes. HDTV is introduced on ABC, NBC, and ESPN; NFL Kickoff Live free concerts generate excitement for the upcoming season as well as paying tribute to the many Americans serving in the U.S. military. Steroids and other performance-enhancing drugs cast doubt on authenticity of records and also athletes as desirable endorsers. NBA plays 2007 All-Star game in Las Vegas, making the league the first major team sport to play in Las Vegas. Retro merchandise is reintroduced, such as the NBA Hardwood Classics Line, invigorating the merchandising and retail segments. NBA TV premieres the first exclusively dedicated one-sport network, followed in 2005 by the NFL Network. LED signage replaces traditional static signage, allowing sponsors to become more animated in messaging. Cell phones add portability to sports information and broadcasting. Fantasy leagues become popular. Military Days are a consistent theme day at games nationwide. Reality TV penetrates sports in the form of ESPN, i.e., "So You Want to Be an Announcer."

Data from G.E. White, 1996, *Creating the national pastime: Baseball transforms itself 1903-1953* (Princeton, NJ: Princeton University Press); B. Sugar, 1978, *Hit the sign and win a free suit of clothes from Harry Finklestein* (Chicago: Contemporary Books), 327-329.

The Hallmark Event

A "hallmark event," as Ritchie defined it, is a major one-time event (or recurring events) of limited duration, developed primarily to enhance the awareness, appeal, and profitability of a tourism destination in the short term, the long term, or both. Such events rely for their success on uniqueness, status, or timely significance to create interest and attract attention. (56)

Hallmark events promote not only the destination, but also the activity as well as the organizations associated with or responsible for the event. Successful hallmark event staging also serves to promote the destination as attractive or the group as qualified or suitable for hosting other similar hallmark-type events. (57) For example, in the late 1990s, the city of San Antonio, Texas, hosted such hallmark events as the NBA All-Star Weekend (All-Star Game and Jam Session), the NCAA Final Four, and the Builders Square Alamo Bowl (an annual event). Because of its success with these events, San Antonio was also selected to host the NCAA women's Final Four in 2002 and the men's Final Four in 2004; the city is also under consideration to host the Pan-American Games.

Many leagues, teams, and other sport-related organizations create hallmark or special events to promote their sport or activity to interested publics. They do this with the aim of strengthening or expanding existing relationships or initiating and cultivating new relationships and growing the overall base of support. Each of the three major sport leagues has such an event. The NBA has the NBA Jam Session in February in conjunction with its All-Star Game; the NHL offers the NHL FANtasy in conjunction with its All-Star Game in January; MLB offers MLB FanFest at its All-Star Game in July. Finally, the NFL offers the NFL Experience during Super Bowl week in January. The NCAA offers Hoop City at its annual men's and women's Final Four championships, and major Division I collegiate conferences, such as the Southeastern Conference, have similar promotional events during their conference championships. These events serve as effective promotional vehicles by doing the following:

+ Promoting the host organization to the general public
+ Promoting the sponsors of the event (and their products)
+ Promoting the sport in general
+ Promoting the event itself as a revenue-generating opportunity
+ Attracting significant media interest and coverage
+ Promoting the destination as a site for tourism and future hallmark events

Internet Sites, Web Pages, Blogs, and More

As technology has evolved, particularly in relation to the media, so has the opportunity for fans to identify with teams and players. (58) Technological developments have also given fans who don't live near their teams more opportunity to maintain or increase their affiliation. Internet sites, Web pages, chat rooms, and blogs meet these needs and at the same time serve as promotional vehicles. The Internet, and specifically an organization's Web site, can be used to promote the organization by providing information that was not as readily available in the past. This information can include any or all of the following elements:

+ Organizational history
+ Schedule of events, games, activities
+ Biographical information on players or performers
+ Links to related Web sites or pages (in the case of a league, links to sites of all member teams) (59)
+ Ticket-purchasing options (60)
+ Merchandise sales opportunities (cyberstores)

- Chat rooms and the e-mail addresses of players, broadcasters, management, or front office personnel to facilitate communication
- Statistics
- Fan pages
- Newspapers or other publications
- Video or audio clips of game action or highlights
- Special pages devoted to dance teams, mascots, or other organizational features
- Surveys and other means to provide feedback

Dan Migala, publisher of *The Migala Report* and a regular contributor to *Street & Smith's SportsBusiness Journal,* offered the following thoughts on six essential elements for any Web site: (61)

1. *"What's New" section.* Because a Web site thrives on newness, this section helps users immediately discover new information and ultimately increases the likelihood that they will visit the site more frequently.

2. *Search engine or site map.* A simple search engine allows users to type in a keyword to find information on things such as schedules or parking quickly and easily.

3. *Feedback mechanism.* Consumers want to be heard. Organizations such as the Buffalo Bills offer a customized menu that allows users to direct their feedback to a specific department—ticket sales, community relations, and so on. An automated response, which lets users know that their message has been received, is an excellent feature. Most important, however, is the fact that the most successful sites read all of the feedback they receive and respond to it.

4. *Phone numbers.* Organizations should make sure not only that they list appropriate phone numbers—group sales, store, ticket hotline—on their sites, but also that they make them visible and easy to find because users are still likely to pick up the phone with a question.

5. *Privacy policy.* If a site asks visitors to volunteer information about who they are (and most Web sites do), it has become de rigueur to draft and display a privacy policy.

6. *Simple traffic reports.* The most successful commercial Web sites generate revenue from a variety of sources such as advertising. To generate advertising revenue consistently, a site must conduct and showcase research that allows prospective advertisers to both qualify and quantify an online ad buy (e.g., track page requests, unique visitors, time on-site, or orders).

Reprinted, by permission, from D. Migala, 2004, "If your web site doesn't have these features, you're losing business," *Street & Smith's SportsBusiness Journal,* 7(25): 35. © Dan Migala.

In addition to Migala's suggestions, we offer the following suggestions, which are particularly of value to teams and venues involved in ticket sales:

- A "virtual view" offered by Ballena or a similar product that permits a potential buyer to select a seat location, click on that location, and access the view of the playing surface from that particular seating location. It may even permit analyzing comparative seat locations and views.
- A link for purchasing tickets, renewing tickets, or providing direct access to sales personnel

Short for "Web log," a blog is a narrative that offers a point of view and invites a response. Blogs can be developed by anyone with a Web address, and organizations can use them not only to share a point of view but to disseminate information, solicit a reaction, or attempt to create an image or alter a perception by posing as someone outside the organization. Depending on the topic or the lack of information about a subject combined with a need to know, blogs can take on a life of their own and can become a valued channel of information. For example, during the NHL hockey lockout and the cancellation of the 2004-2005 season, Pelle Eklund (a fictional name) created the Hockey Rumors Blog, which can be found at www.hockeyrumors.blogspot.com. The author was getting information on the labor talks from a well-placed "insider" at the NHL and sharing the information. Because little information was available, this blog was generating as many as 200,000 page impressions per day (a Google measurement term used for advertising purposes). Although it was acknowledged to be just rumor, it became a credible source for hockey fans seeking information—so much so that "Eklund" is attempting to turn the spot into a professional enterprise of some sort. (62)

Sales Promotions

Sales promotions, which can take the form of price-oriented or non-price-oriented tactics, are an essential part of any sport organization's marketing strategy. In general, nonprice promotions include special events, giveaway items, and other tangible incentives, whereas price-oriented promotions involve discounting or other price-related manipulations. Although research suggests that many fans are attracted to price discounts, price promotions may be dangerous if they cheapen the image of the product. Organizations normally use price promotions only when they are facing an elastic demand schedule. Giveaways of the basic product should be avoided because they may indicate to the consumer that the product is not worth anything and because they can infuriate customers who have already purchased the product.

Whenever possible, the best customers—those who have purchased season tickets—must be protected and not "cannibalized" by the promotion. Season-ticket holders should receive something comparable to the discount or item included in the promotion. Teams should proactively address their season-ticket holders prior to the season either in a letter, an e-mail, a fan forum, or at all three. The message needs to state that the team will be involved in special promotions and discounting during the upcoming season. A rationale, such as trying to increase the fan base or to make sure that every fan, regardless of household income or size, has an opportunity to attend a game, should be conveyed to the season-ticket holders. The season-ticket holders should then be given a specific amount of franchise dollars (scrip) or coupons to use at concession stands during the course of the year to offset the impact of the planned promotional activities. Not only does this minimize the number of potential complaints, but it also creates a reservoir of goodwill among the season-ticket holders who can now be ambassadors and spread the word regarding how the team has treated them.

Concepts and ideas such as two-for-one nights, adding value to a package, half-price nights, and family nights can be effective promotions to increase ticket sales. For example, baseball's Class AA Tennessee Smokies have cut a juicy deal for their fans. Fans purchasing tickets in advance are offered the Texas Roadhouse Tuesday Family Rib Night package. For $39, purchasers receive four tickets, four hats, two adult rib dinners, and two children's rib dinners—a $130 value. "Tuesday has generally been a slow day for us but we are now averaging between 200 and 250 packages sold and it isn't even our peak season yet," said John Zietz, director of sales for the Smokies. (63)

When relying on sponsors to help underwrite the cost of a sales promotion or to provide a revenue stream, the organization must realize that the promotion needs to work for everyone: the fan, the organization, and the sponsor. For example, the Class A (baseball) Piedmont Boll Weevils, located in North Carolina, recently teamed with Dr. Pepper on a ticket-redemption program that could result in the redemption of as many as 1 million tickets at no cost to the fan. Dr. Pepper was seeking to promote its lesser-known soft-drink brand, Sun Drop. Dr. Pepper entered into an agreement with the Boll Weevils to provide up to 1 million logoed soft-drink cans that could each be redeemed for one free admission to one of six preselected Boll Weevil games during the 1998 season. The Boll Weevils received a cash payment of $5,000 and the exposure of the soft-drink cans. Sun Drop received the affiliation with the Boll Weevils and access to their target market of teenagers, and the fans received free admission to one or more games in exchange for purchasing the product—a promotional win-win-win situation. (64)

Unfortunately, it's easy to get carried away in the spirit of promoting. Markdowns, contests, sponsorships, sweepstakes, holiday sales, special events, open houses, and the like are often initiated with little thought of the desired long-term outcome. This is especially true in sport. When one examines the long list of promotions that baseball teams might offer during the course of the season (see the following rankings of top promotions and giveaways), it becomes readily apparent that sales promotions should be designed with the concept of reverse planning in mind. By reverse planning, we mean that you need to determine what it is you want to accomplish in the long run and then strategically plan initiatives and activities that will help achieve this specified goal.

Price promotions involve some type of discount, rebate, or other financial incentive in relation to the product or service purchased. According to Donald Ziccardi,

> Sales promotion strategies have become the quick fix for companies desperate for customers, fanatically assembled to adjust for economic swings, fashion trends, calendar shifts, and the weather, without taking into account the overall marketing plan. However, there are long-term effects on the company's image and on customers. For one, sales promotion activities can overshadow the advertising efforts instead of reinforcing them. Second, customers have been conditioned to shop only when there is a promotion. A price break, or a storewide sale, could trigger a big sales gain, but then the company could suffer a huge falloff the very next day. (65)

In sport, one negative effect is that attendance is traditionally down for the event immediately following a promotion. If a promotion does nothing more than induce people to attend one game instead of another, then it is not effective. This pattern indicates that fans are "cherry picking"—attending games only when there is a promotion. When cherry picking occurs, the value of a sales promotion is minimal unless the promotional item is sponsored by someone other than the sport organization.

As previously mentioned, nonprice promotions include giveaway items or premiums, fireworks nights, autograph days, and so on. The late Bill Veeck, owner of the Cleveland Indians, St. Louis Browns, and Chicago White Sox, was the master of the nonprice promotion. Veeck, the inventor of bat day, recognized the importance of attracting new fans by implementing special theme days such as ladies' days and A-student days. Veeck used fireworks, had roving entertainers, gave away orchids and other premiums, and practiced a promotional philosophy that said "Every day was Mardi Gras and every fan was king." (66) Veeck recognized the need to market something other than the core product, realizing that you cannot always field a winning team but you must provide entertainment every day. Thus, he pioneered nonprice promotions in sport to help placate fans whose team might not be winning, to keep them interested in coming out to the park.

A problem with giveaway days is that, depending on the premium item, they may hinder souvenir or concession sales. The marketer must attempt to measure how

✦ Promotions

Top promotions at MLB games this season, ranked by total dates

Rank	Promotion	No. of dates	No. of teams
1	Fireworks	142	19
2	Run the bases	112	15
3	Concessions discount	93	13
4	Autographs	56	10
5	Concert	50	10
6	Family day	45	8
7	Charity event	43	9
8	College night	40	8
9	Fan appreciation day	39	22
10	Cultural celebration	37	11
11	Senior citizen specials	36	3
12	Kids day	35	11
13	Business day specials	33	7
14	Celebrity appearance	26	2
15	Ladies night	24	7
16	Win a trip	22	2
17	Youth league day	21	8
18	Win a car	19	2
19	Educational day	16	7
20	Play catch	14	3
21	Mascot day	12	8
22	Photo day	11	11
22	Team history tribute	11	7

Top sponsor presence among companies involved with promotions at five or more MLB games this season

Rank	Company/brand	No. of dates	No. of teams
1	Pepsi	78	7
2	Great Clips	43	5
3	McDonald's	20	4
4	Anheuser-Busch	19	4
5	Coca-Cola	16	5
6	Ball Park Franks	11	2
7	Dodge	10	2
8	Bank of America	8	3
9	AT&T	6	3

Reprinted, by permission, from P. Williams, 2006, "Clubs change face of freebies," *Street & Smith's SportsBusiness Journal*, June-July 26, pg. 1.

much sales these giveaways create versus how much they eliminate. Thus, to avoid an adverse effect on souvenir sales, a cap day should involve a cap that does not resemble those sold at the stadium. For example, the cap for the Pittsburgh Pirates' 2006 Cap Day could be a replica of the 1979 Pirate cap, or perhaps a replica of a Pittsburgh Crawford's cap from the Negro Leagues, which are not sold at the merchandise stands. However, in relation to the promotion, uniform replica jerseys from either of those eras could be sold, hoping to capitalize on the promotion. The same consideration applies to giving away or discounting food items. For instance, a promotional staple in minor league baseball is 10-cent hot dog night. This promotion is usually underwritten by a sponsor, in most cases jointly by the stadium concessions company and its hot dog supplier. Although the club loses out on the sale of hot dogs, the higher attendance, coupled with parking fees and soda and beer sales, more than makes up for the loss.

A concessions-related promotion held in the 1970s has gone into the annals as one of the most ill-conceived promotional events in the history of sport—namely, Ten-Cent Beer Night at Cleveland's Municipal Stadium on June 4, 1974. The result of that particular promotion? As one might have expected, drunken, unruly fans stormed the field during the game, which was ultimately forfeited to the visiting Texas Rangers. (67) Safer alternatives such as Dollar Dog (hot dogs) have become part of our promotional content. However, you will still find the beer-related Thirsty Thursdays promotion in minor league sports.

Timing is another key element in the planning of promotions for sport organizations. The concept of timing includes day of the week, opponent, starting time, time of the season,

✦ Giveaways

Top items being given out at MLB games this season, ranked by total dates

Rank	Giveaway	No. of dates	No. of teams
1	Cap	73	26
2	Bobblehead	69	22
3	T-shirt	59	19
4	Baseball card	58	20
5	Magnetic schedule	47	29
6	Poster	30	13
7	Figurine	26	14
8	Autographed item	24	2
9	Calendar	20	15
9	Lapel pin	20	11
11	Tote bag	19	13
12	Hot Wheels/Matchbox/die-cast car	16	5
12	Build-a-bear (or similar product)	16	10
14	Baseball glove	11	11
14	Game-worn shirt	11	10
16	Lanyard	10	10

Top sponsor presence among companies involved with giveaways at 10 or more MLB games this season

Rank	Company/brand	No. of dates	No. of teams
1	Pepsi	25	9
2	Topps	23	8
3	Coca-Cola	17	5
4	Miller Brewing	15	4
5	Upper Deck	13	12
5	Verizon Wireless	13	8
7	Anheuser-Busch	12	7
8	Chevrolet	11	7
8	McDonald's	11	5
10	AT&T	10	5
10	DHL	10	9

Reprinted, by permission, from P. Williams, 2006, "Clubs change face of freebies," *Street & Smith's SportsBusiness Journal*, June-July 26, pg. 1.

and time between scheduled promotions. The sport marketer must determine whether it is better to schedule a promotion against a better draw or a weaker draw. A better draw is an opponent that the consumer perceives as an attractive or effectively performing team, or an opponent with a "superstar" who attracts significant media attention and hype. In 1998, when Mark McGwire and Sammy Sosa were in hot pursuit of Roger Maris' record of 61 home runs in a season, they attracted significant interest on the road, even though their teams were not performing up to expectations. Promotions scheduled on nights when they were playing might attract an even larger crowd than normal. Perhaps a team is scheduled to host the Atlanta Braves over a weekend; scheduling the promotional activity on a weekend usually results in higher-than-average attendance. Teams such as Notre Dame (football), the Dallas Cowboys, the Chicago Bulls (when Michael Jordan was playing), the New York Yankees, and the University of North Carolina (basketball) would constitute examples of good draws. For an illustration of scheduling promotional activities, see the case study on page 263.

✦ **Table 11.4** 1998 Major League Baseball's Most Effective Promotions

Ranked in Terms of Percentage Attendance Increase

Rank	Promotion	% increase	Number of fans
1	Beanie Baby	37.4	9,175
2	Beach towel	26.4	7,779
3	Umbrella	20.1	5,330
4	Coupon	20.0	5,249
5	Baseball cap	19.9	5,370
6	Fireworks	19.1	3,998
7	Hat (not baseball cap)	17.3	4,822
8	Bat	15.0	4,177
9	Heritage/Family Days	14.9	3,116
10	Beanbag toy	14.4	4,453
11	Schedule magnet	13.8	1,079
12	Shirt	13.3	3,774
13	Helmet	13.1	3,573
14	Fan appreciation	12.1	3,535
15	Camera day	11.3	1,847
16	Photo	11.1	1,985
17	$1 concessions	9.2	1,572
18	Businesspeople	8.9	1,987
19	Growth chart	8.6	490
20	Backpack	8.0	2,468

Note: Increase is calculated by comparing all teams' average attendance with attendance on all promotional dates.

Reprinted from M. Sedlak and W. Suggs, 1998, "The list: most effective major league baseball promotions," *Street & Smith's SportsBusiness Journal*, 1(25): 35.

Table 11.4 depicts some of the most successful promotional activities used throughout MLB during the 1998 season. Table 11.5 shows other innovative MLB promotions.

Promotional Components

The proper way to use sales promotion is to design and conduct balanced and creative sales promotional activities. An effective promotional campaign consists of the right type of activities conducted at the appropriate time, appealing to the target market. (68) In this section, we briefly describe and give examples of some program activities.

The Theme

In developing the theme or creative component of a promotion, one needs to ask and answer a number of questions before developing an effective creative strategy. Table 11.7 lists the questions to ask and indicates the reasons for asking them. Although this may seem like a function of advertising rather than promotions, it is an issue that promotional planning should address each year.

✦ **Table 11.5** Other Innovative MLB Promotions

Date	Team	Promotion	Distribution
5/9/04	Atlanta Braves	Mother's Day flower giveaway	1st 10,000 moms
6/20/04	Atlanta Braves	Father's Day necktie giveaway	1st 10,000 dads
5/29/04	Chicago White Sox	Dog Day	Tickets available
8/28/04	Cleveland Indians	50th Anniversary 1954 commemorative baseball	1st 20,000 fans
8/29/04	Cleveland Indians	Scout Day—Indians patch	Youngsters 14 and under
9/6/94	Seattle Mariners	Cloverdale Meats Mariners Back to School Lunch Box Day	
6/25/04	Seattle Mariners	Belated Father's Day Cloverdale Mariners grill set	1st 5,000 men
9/1/04-9/5/04	International Week	9/1—Italian; 9/2—Polish; 9/3—Irish; 9/4—Hispanic; 9/5—Negro League Celebration	
6/20/04	San Francisco Giants	Emerald Nuts Father's Day BBQ set	
6/24/04	San Francisco Giants v. LA Dodgers	Spend the Night on the Field; Game @ 4:05	Tickets available
8/21/04	San Francisco Giants	8th Annual Dog Days of Summer	Tickets available
8/29/04	Montreal Expos	Expos Backpack	10,000 fans
5/8/04	Oakland A's	Plaid reversible bucket hat (Burberry knockoff)	7,500 women
6/20/04	Philadelphia Phillies	Bull's BBQ Apron	Males 15 & older
5/9/04	Anaheim Angels	Mother's Day frame	Females 18 & older
8/13/04	Anaheim Angels	Back-to-school binder	18 & under
5/2/03	Philadelphia Phillies	Mother's Day pink cap	Females 15 & older

Courtesy of Morgan Marr

Scheduling Promotions: The Case of University of Central Florida (UCF) Football, the 2006 Season

Sport marketing professionals in the collegiate ranks are often faced with a dilemma regarding promotional activities for sporting events. On one hand, the coach would like to have every game promoted; on the other hand, sponsors want to be linked to an event promotion that will generate the greatest number of impressions and attract the most media coverage. The promotional game planning matrix depicted below can serve as an aid for the sport marketer when determining which games might need promotional assistance to achieve respectable attendance while also identifying other games that might sell out with a promotional boost.

The promotional game-planning matrix takes two primary factors into consideration. The left column of the matrix presents the first factor: *Game Date/Time*. This is the day and time during the week when the event is scheduled to take place. The top row of the matrix illustrates the second factor—*Opponent*. These factors are classified as favorable or unfavorable based upon the following conditions:

✦ *Game Date/Time*. Favorable days are identified as those days and game starting times with the best chance to attract the potential spectator. Over time, weekends have proven to be the best time to attract fans to attend sporting events. In the case of collegiate sport, the development of television networks, and most recently Regional Sport Networks (RSNs)—and their insatiable need for programming—has widened the traditional window of collegiate football scheduling from Saturday to encompass almost every day of the week with the exception of Sunday (dominated by the NFL) and Monday (again the NFL with ESPN's Monday Night Football). Unfavorable days are those days with the least chance to attract potential spectators—in this case Tuesdays would be the least attractive day followed by Wednesdays and Thursdays. Fridays present an interesting case because while they are an excellent day to attract spectators, Friday is typically the night reserved for high school football and the competition could harm both groups. On the other hand a great opponent on a Friday night might prove to be very successful for the collegiate sport marketer.

✦ *Opponents*. Identifying an opponent as favorable or unfavorable is not necessarily based on the opponent's win-loss record. A favorable opponent could be a school with a storied tradition in one sport, say football, that is therefore perceived to be a "name" (e.g., Notre Dame). Another factor is name recognition. For example, Marshall, which dominated Division I-AA and then the MAC Conference prior to moving into Conference USA, would not be considered a favorable opponent despite the success of its program and the fact the NFL players such as Oakland's Randy Moss have played there. However, a University of Southern Florida (USF) team that went to a bowl game, is located less than a two hour drive away and travels well, and is considered a rival, would be an excellent opponent regardless of their record.

Now that we have defined our classification of days and opponents, we can develop our matrix. Favorable days and opponents will be designated with an **"F"** while unfavorable days and opponents will be designated with a **"U."** Consider the 2006 UCF schedule shown in table 11.6.

For evaluating favorable versus unfavorable days, this particular football model is ideal. The Southern Mississippi game on Tuesday, September 26th is obviously unfavorable and would be rated as a **"U."** As discussed previously, the Friday night game could go either way, but it is scheduled to be televised on ESPN, which, given the comparatively short history of UCF football, might make it a more attractive event. The University of Alabama-Birmingham (UAB) game on November 25th—the Saturday following Thanksgiving—could be a less favorable date depending on team performance up to that point.

When evaluating favorable versus unfavorable opponents, it is often helpful to weigh the pros and cons of the opponent by analyzing the positive and negative impact of the conditions previously discussed. Thus opponents with more positives than negatives would receive a positive rating. For example, Rice would receive a **"U"** rating based upon the following criteria:

✦ Rice is perennially a poor performing team in terms of win-loss record

✦ Rice is a small private school with few fans and alums living within a 90-mile radius of Orlando

✦ Rice is not a team that has been on television in Orlando

✦ **Table 11.6** 2006 UCF Schedule

Date	Day of the week	Opponent
September 2	Saturday	Villanova
September 16	Saturday	University of Southern Florida (USF)
September 26	Tuesday	University of Southern Mississippi (USM)
October 13	Friday	Pitt
October 21	Saturday	Rice
November 4	Saturday	East Carolina
November 25	Saturday	University of Alabama-Birmingham (UAB)

(continued)

Scheduling Promotions: The Case of University of Central Florida (UCF) Football, the 2006 Season *(continued)*

- Rice fans are not known for traveling far distances to support their teams
- Rice is not perceived to be a "rival"

On the other hand, Pitt would receive an **"F"** rating based on the following criteria:

- Pitt is a member of the Big East Conference—highly recognizable in Orlando
- Pitt recruits well in Florida so there will be a number of Florida natives on their squad
- Pitt's former coach Dave Wanstadt is a highly recognizable name, having been the coach of the Miami Dolphins
- An ESPN appearance will be perceived to be a sanction that this is perceived to be a big game by the media and the casual fans
- October is a big tourism month in Orlando
- Pitt has a history of television appearances and plays name/recognizable opponents

After the Game Date/Time and the Opponents have been classified as favorable or unfavorable, the dates and opponents are entered into the appropriate box in the matrix. Games labeled FF—favorable day with a favorable opponent—may need little promotional assistance, but if following the peak on peak theory (promote the games with the best chance of selling out—favorable opponent and favorable game date), it may be wise to secure resources and allocate promotional assets to try maximize the opportunity to sell out the game. Likewise, UU games will need the most assistance—but a case could also be made to ignore these games and concentrate on the games in which at least one element is favorable. So for the UCF schedule in this case, the games would rate out as follows (also see figure 11.3):

- Villanova: UF (Although Villanova is not a favorable opponent, it is the home opener following UCF's most successful season in history.)
- USF: FF (UCF's self-perceived biggest rival—a member of the Big East and defeated UCF last season.)
- USM: UU (Lackluster match-up on a Tuesday night.)
- Rice/East Carolina and UAB: FU (All Saturday games with less than star-quality opponents.)

		Opponent	
		Favorable	Unfavorable
Day	Favorable	FF (USF)	FU (Rice,East Carolina,and UAB)
	Unfavorable	UF (Villanova)	UU (USM)

FIGURE 11.3 The promotional game-planning matrix.

Most marketing themes that are effective are short, simple, and easily understood. Coca-Cola's "Always the Real Thing" is a very simple message: All other products are not the real thing but instead are imitations and are inferior to the real thing. The aim of Nike's former theme, "Just Do It," as well as of the current theme, "I Can," is to fit almost any situation and almost any target market: With these shoes, you can do whatever activity you wish, or perhaps none at all. "Just Do It" and "I Can" do not suggest the value of any sport or athlete over another. These messages emphasize participation, without implying serious competition or belittling low-key recreational activity.

✦ Table 11.7 Questions to Be Answered When Formulating a Creative Component

Question	Rationale
What does this customer want?	Identify the target market; understand what they think and why; know what they value; have documentation of their purchasing habits.
Does our product fit the consumer?	Does the consumer understand the product? How does the perception of the consumer differ from the reality of the product?
How will the competition affect our objectives?	Know and understand the competition, how it operates, and its objectives. Whom does the consumer consider as a competitor?
What is the competitive consumer benefit?	What is the statement of benefit the consumer expects from a brand? From an organization? The benefit to the consumer must be clearly stated.
How will marketing communication make the benefit believable to the consumer?	There must be persuasive communication that gently, subtly, and credibly convinces the consumer that the product and its benefits are worthwhile and superior to those of other similar products in the marketplace.
What should be the personality of the brand?	The personality must give the brand a life and soul with which the consumer can easily identify. It should differentiate the brand from the competition.
How will the consumer define the product?	How is the message positioned in the mind of the consumer? Is it best because it was first? Is it more contemporary? Longer lasting? Fun?
What are the main communication and action objectives?	What action should the consumer take as a result of the message? Do we expect the consumer to call for information? To go directly to a retailer?
What contact points (mediums) should be used to reach the consumer?	What is the best communication strategy to reach the target market? Direct mail? Television? Telemarketing? Open house?

Adapted from exhibit 5-2 in D.E. Schultz, S.I. Tannenbaum, and A. Allison, 1996, *Essentials of Advertising Strategy*, 3rd ed. (Lincolnwood, IL: NTC Business Books).

Whenever possible, the theme should capitalize on unique aspects of the product or the marketplace. When moving from Winnipeg to Phoenix, the NHL Jets changed their name to the Coyotes—an image more in tune with the desert environs surrounding Phoenix. The name and location change provided the Phoenix franchise with a marketing theme capitalizing on the new home—"Experience the coolest game in the desert." (69)

When selecting a theme or a name, the marketer should try to ensure that the theme cannot be turned against the organization. Prior to their emergence as a baseball power in the mid-1990s, the Cleveland Indians were a woeful collection of poor performers with little interest and identification outside of their own market. The marketing department in the early 1990s hit on the theme "The Tribe—This is your team." When team performance was even worse than expected, the theme was turned into a joke: The Tribe—This is your team—who else would want them?

Product Sampling

An effective method for getting new products off the ground is to distribute samples to the public. The beauty of sampling is the lack of risk to the customer. When there is no charge, people will try almost anything. Gatorade is a company that has long emphasized sampling. Gatorade maintains a presence at thousands of sport venues throughout the United States and Canada where it uses sampling to test consumer reaction to new flavors, to introduce products, and to explain why Gatorade is important. Gatorade maintains a high presence at events such as marathons, triathlons, and volleyball tournaments and in other settings where the potential consumer is active and building a thirst.

Reebok is another company that uses sampling. Reebok has taken to the streets with a van and trailer setup to encourage consumers to try on their latest model of DMX athletic shoes.

At these Reebok locations there are no salespeople—just "shoe techs" who explain the shoe and provide demonstration models for the consumer to try on. This more nontraditional type of sampling is also becoming prevalent in larger sporting goods stores, which may use court surfaces or running tracks to enable the customer to really sample the product.

As in most sampling situations, use of discount coupons or sales in conjunction with the sampling opportunity can prove highly effective.

The Open House

The open house is similar to the free trial offered in sampling, but is geared toward attracting people to a facility such as a fitness club or YMCA to encourage them to join activity-based sport programs. Promotional activities similar to the open house can also be used to interest consumers in purchasing products such as ticket plans for spectator games or events.

Fitness clubs realize that to be interested in a membership, prospective purchasers need to "experience" the club before determining whether or not it is right for them. This experience often takes the form of a free visit or trial membership (usually one week) and comes complete with an orientation and personal consultation. Often a YMCA or fitness club will schedule a one-day or a one-week open house that enables prospective members to sample not only the facilities and equipment but also the programming—aerobics, child care, sport leagues, and so forth.

On the spectator-sport side, the Orlando Magic held an open house in March 2003 to give fans a behind-the-scenes look at what happens during the course of a basketball game. The day's activities included guided tours of the locker rooms; an opportunity to meet current players and the mascot; participate in a clinic conducted by the dance team; autographs; shooting baskets on the court; and an opportunity to see what seats were available for the upcoming season and to personally select seats.

Coupons

Coupons are a popular and accepted promotional strategy, but they must be appropriate to the image and style of the organization. In some cases, people may perceive couponing as a move that cheapens the organization's image and reflects desperation to get sales—particularly if the organization has no history of offering coupons. Fitness clubs offering two memberships for the price of one, or free memberships for payment of a maintenance fee, are sometimes perceived to be in this situation.

All coupons are in some form of print (even Internet coupons usually must be downloaded and printed before they can be presented). In sport, the most popular types of coupons appear in newspapers or in booklets sold as discount coupon booklets (typically referred to as an "Entertainment Book") that are available in most large American cities and feature two-for-one dining and entertainment offers. One of the most popular coupon ads used by spectator sport organizations targets the family and features the approach "all this for one low price." These coupons, usually found in a newspaper, can be clipped and presented at the box office. They present an offer—usually a price promotion—that may include four game tickets, four hot dogs, four soft drinks, popcorn, and usually parking or a game program for a price between $39 and $79, depending on the level of the organization.

In many cases, the coupon is for certain games only, and the organization may have selected the games by opponent or by day of the week. This type of offer is usually extended for opponents described as weaker draws and for less attractive game days (usually Monday through Thursday), although some teams may elect to offer this type of promotion on Friday evening or Saturday afternoon.

Bundling

Bundling is the practice of offering additional amenities or benefits if the consumer purchases the product or service in a package. In some cases, the product is discounted so that the bundling actually results in a cash savings. Consumers may, for example, be able to purchase a three-year fitness club membership at a discounted rate along with free personal training sessions or classes. A professional sport team may elect to discount the cost per game in a ticket plan or may "bundle in" parking privileges, free statistics sheets, a lounge area for certain levels of ticket holders, and so forth. The NBA's Cleveland Cavs offer their club-seat holders such benefits as 15 general admission tickets to a game during the season at no extra cost, membership benefits at two area golf clubs, a special lounge area to use before and after the game and at halftime, and waitperson service in their seat locations. (70)

Contests and Sweepstakes

Contests and sweepstakes add glamour, glitz, excitement, and fun to the promotional mix. Although most sport patrons don't expect to win, it is often an interesting promotional strategy to offer fans the possibility of winning or of watching someone else compete in a contest. In the mid-1990s, Coca-Cola and the NFL offered a promotional contest, "Monsters of the Gridiron," that included a grand prize but also featured numerous opportunities to win product from Coca-Cola or merchandise from the NFL. Designed to spur the sale of Coca-Cola while providing an association with the NFL and featuring the "personalities" of some NFL players, this contest was popular and successful. In late September and October (to tie in to Halloween), purchasers of Coca-Cola found a 900 number on the inside of the bottle cap; when they called the number, they received a message from one of the "NFL Monsters" that would also inform them if they were a winner.

On the level of the local team, contests such as cash scrambles are used to entertain and to promote a sponsor. In cash scrambles, the participants grab as much cash as they can in a limited amount of time while providing entertainment for the fans in the stands.

Premiums and Redemptions

Organizations use premiums and redemptions to attract new consumers and also to encourage greater frequency on the part of existing consumers. A premium item can sometimes be combined with a special event to achieve better results. One of the most popular annual promotions for the Pittsburgh Pirates is their beach promotional weekend. Each season the Pittsburgh Pirates give away a beach towel as a premium item on a Thursday evening game. This is followed up on Friday and Saturday with related activities including coupons to an area water park and a beach party outside the stadium (complete with music, 240 tons of sand, and virtual surfing); in 2004 they attracted a crowd of 32,304 fans on a Thursday night—which was nearly double the Pirates' average of 17,354 for weeknights. (71) This philosophy would seem to be a popular concept. According to Steve Violetta, executive vice president of the San Diego Padres, "giveaways are fine, but you want to try and build them into something more." (72)

At MLB's FanFest, held annually in conjunction with the all-star game, title sponsor Pinnacle Brands, a trading card manufacturer, combines premiums and redemptions. When visiting the Pinnacle booth, consumers get one free package of trading cards and learn that if they purchase four more packages (sold by merchants on-site), they can redeem the five wrappers and receive a free collectible, a limited-edition trading card not available anywhere else.

To increase consumer attendance at baseball games, the Oakland Athletics pioneered a thematic promotion called "Year of the Uniform" that involved premium items. The promotion encouraged consumers to attend multiple (six) Oakland A games by providing a different clothing-item premium (sponsored by Adidas) to members of the target market (those under age 14) at each designated game. One game featured a cap, another a jersey, another wristbands, and so on. This was a promotion geared to a target market and designed to increase frequency of attendance (a move related to the concept of the frequency escalator described later in this chapter). This promotion, introduced in the early 1980s, is still successful for a number of teams. Using the theme "Dress Your Kid From Head to Toe," the Pittsburgh Pirates had eight kid-targeted giveaway dates during the 1999 season. (73)

Astute marketers will use premium items that expand their product distribution beyond the game or event and create impressions year-round if possible. Current NCAA director of marketing, licensing, and promotions, Dennis Cryder, who at one time worked for the Kansas City Royals, was very deliberate in considering the types of promotional premiums he would distribute when he was with the Royals. He selected premiums with a high "residual distribution," such as ski caps and school notebooks; this meant that the image and message—not to mention the number of impressions—of Royals baseball would resurface regularly throughout the year. (74)

Street Promotion

Street trends—or "tracking what is cool"—is a hot topic as mainstream businesses, both click and mortar-and-brick, are trying to crack the tastes, preferences, and styles of the elusive youth culture. It is important to listen to the progressive street culture—the collective thinkers and influencers that are behind youth's latest infatuation with digital pets, wash-in glitters and mascara hair colors, electronic music that can't be found on any radio station, and the list goes on and on. Why? "Because more than $36 billion in expendable income is dictated by those fads and trends." (75)

A number of footwear companies, most notably Nike, Reebok, and Adidas, have taken to the streets to showcase and promote their products by putting them in the hands of perceived leaders who can influence sales and set trends. "Taking to the streets" includes the Reebok van, the Nike Hummer, and other visible signs of the companies' presence, but also much more. It involves interaction through activities, but mainly just through conversation—getting to know people and what they're about so that the companies can design appropriate products and communicate with consumers effectively.

Because apparel trends begin in big cities, understanding the urban youth market as well as targeting it effectively is the secret to fortune in the athletic footwear business. Reebok employs Khari Streeter and DeMane Davis to keep in touch with the target market by hanging out with young people and their friends in the entertainment industry. Streeter and Davis have served as creative directors for a Reebok television ad starring Allen Iverson, and according to Streeter, they "bring Reebok a legitimate point of view" from the streets. (76)

Generation X, the baby boomer "echo," the "dot-com generation," and Generation Y are all categories for segments of today's youth that marketers find attractive but in some cases difficult to reach. The values of these groups sometimes reflect the values of the late 1960s and early 1970s. For example, some of these segments have referred to a new technology used by Reebok as "techorganic—combining breathable natural fabrics with protective synthetics; and fashion fabrics that mix synthetics with all-natural fibers." (77)

Consider the rationale of Lea, a 23-year-old design assistant living in New York City, for her purchase of a pair of Adidas shoes: "I bought these Adidas shoes because they're totally vegan [do not contain any animal or animal by-products]—I know Adidas didn't even think about it, maybe don't even care. But they have no leather on them—all synthetic. And they look good too." (78) Is this what Adidas had in mind when planning the marketing strategy for the shoes?

An aim of street promotions is to reach not only vegans, but also hip-hoppers and other pop segments. Contact with the street could provide a marketer with the knowledge that among some groups the word *extreme* isn't cool: It's a word used by "ordinaries" to describe activities outside their range of interests. How can marketers avoid mistakes resulting from a lack of knowledge about their potential consumers? It's important to get the help of members of the target segments in designing promotional strategies. Specialty agencies such as Sputnik can help traditional companies reach target markets that are difficult to contact.

The Ultimate Goal: Moving Consumers Up the Escalator

The ultimate goal of promotion in sport is to increase awareness and interest and subsequently consumption of the products or services. When launching a new sport product, such as the NHL's latest additions, the Nashville Predators or the Columbus Blue Jackets, the marketer has little choice but to attract first-time (new) consumers. It is understandable that in such a situation sport marketers will expend the majority of their efforts on mass media advertising to attract a broad market base. However, once the product is off and rolling, many forget to change their approach and become locked into the "new-consumer" mentality. Yet the data show that the more mature a sport organization is, the lower the impact of new consumers is on its total attendance or participation figures. This is the case not just in terms of new consumers as a percentage of existing consumers, but also in terms of attendance frequencies of new consumers versus "old" consumers. The impact of new consumers is often minimal and short lived. For example, competition for a championship often attracts a number of "new fans," but in reality it is the increased attendance of old consumers, or "core attendees," that dictates the long-term financial viability of the franchise. The "new-consumer" myopia is perhaps acceptable for sport industry segments in which total demand is low, such as professional soccer, or for some professional baseball markets, such as Montreal. However, it is in these very sports that high supply of the product (a baseball franchise could have an inventory of 4,050,000 [81 games × 50,000 seats] during the course of a season) creates considerable room for increased attendance frequency on the part of existing customers.

This myopia is not limited to spectator sport; in fact, it is endemic to most segments of the sport industry. Perhaps the only explanation for this widespread ignorance within sport marketing is the limited amount of market research conducted by sport organizations in general, and the low priority given to research in the budgeting process and the strategic plan. Any research data on attendance or participation frequency of sport consumers will reveal that the 80-20 rule (i.e., 80 percent of all goods consumed in a particular category are consumed by 20 percent of all persons consuming the product) does not apply to all sport segments. The impact of the so-called heavy, medium, and light users will vary greatly from sport to sport.

The intelligent approach to sport promotion is to bring consumers progressively up a gradient of involvement and commitment. Bill Giles of the Philadelphia Phillies called this the "staircase approach" (see figure 11.4); the marketer attempts to move the fan up the stairs so that a light user becomes a medium user and potentially a heavy user. (79)

The Staircase Versus the Escalator

Although the staircase is similar in concept to the escalator and provides an excellent foundation, it has limitations. First, it assumes that each step in the process entails a distinct and perhaps difficult movement. Second, it implies that all light users are on the same step. Observation of attendance frequency distribution shows that neither assumption is true. Sport consumers are distributed in terms of their attendance or participation frequency across

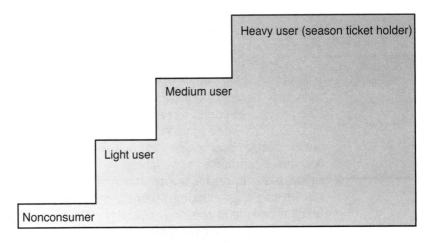

FIGURE 11.4 The staircase approach to sport marketing.

a continuum that runs from 1 through N, where N is the maximum number of events, games, or contests that consumers can attend (or of days on which they can consume the product). The N in professional sport varies greatly; for example, the NFL has 8 home dates; the NBA, 40; and MLB, 81. The N for other sport industry segments also varies greatly, from the approximately 240 days that a Vermont ski resort could be open to the 360 days that a typical YMCA/YWCA or fitness center could be open. In fact, the frequency distribution is better represented by an escalator, which has many steps that all appear to run into one another. The step between a heavy-light user and a light-medium user is just one extra game attended or one more visit to a ski slope.

Before the consumer gets into the ranks of existing consumers, she passes through several stages. Bill Giles used the generic term *non-consumer* but there are several forms of nonconsumption. Research suggests that as many as 50 percent of all people who consider themselves sport fans have never attended a game. (80) We can therefore construct three levels of the consumer hierarchy:

+ The nonaware nonconsumer is unaware of the existence of the sport product and consequently does not attend.

+ The aware nonconsumer is aware of the sport product but does not choose to attend. Presumably the product does not offer the benefits this person is looking for, or this person has no need for this type of product.

+ The media consumer is aware of the sport product and does not consume directly (by purchasing it from the organization) but does consume indirectly through the media. This type of consumption is not limited to spectator sports but is also seen in participant sports that receive media exposure.

Recent research using community intercept methodology (81), which involves interviewing the general population about their attitudes and perceptions with regard to their local sport teams (professional and collegiate), has enabled us to expand the nonconsumer category to include another level: (82)

+ The misinformed nonconsumer is aware of the product and wishes to consume directly but does not do so because of misinformation or misperception. The misinformation usually relates to the cost of attending, the availability of tickets, or safety concerns. Often the source of the misinformation is word of mouth from friends or relatives. The misinformed consumer usually consumes the product indirectly through the media.

Figure 11.5 shows the escalator with these lower levels of consumers. The promotional effort and expense required to move consumers up the escalator are usually considerably less than those required to move nonconsumers onto the escalator to begin direct consumption. But more important, response is likely to be considerably greater from existing consumers than from an unaware or disinterested public, unless the existing customers are already satiated.

The frequency escalator depicted in figure 11.6 illustrates the attendance levels of consumers. As consumers move up the escalator, total attendance and organizational profitability increase. The goal is not only to attract new consumers so that they get on the escalator, but also to get consumers already on the escalator to move up by increasing their attendance. Figure 11.6 makes it apparent that attendance would increase greatly and financial fortunes would change drastically if each of the consumers attending one game per season would increase attendance to two games per season.

Further support for the approach of targeting existing consumers comes from the well-known fact that existing satisfied customers are an organization's best salespeople. For most segments of the sport industry, 70 percent of all consumers are referred by word of mouth from existing customers. Marketers have a high stake in keeping current consumers active and satisfied. Indeed, promotional efforts should focus initially on moving existing customers up the escalator.

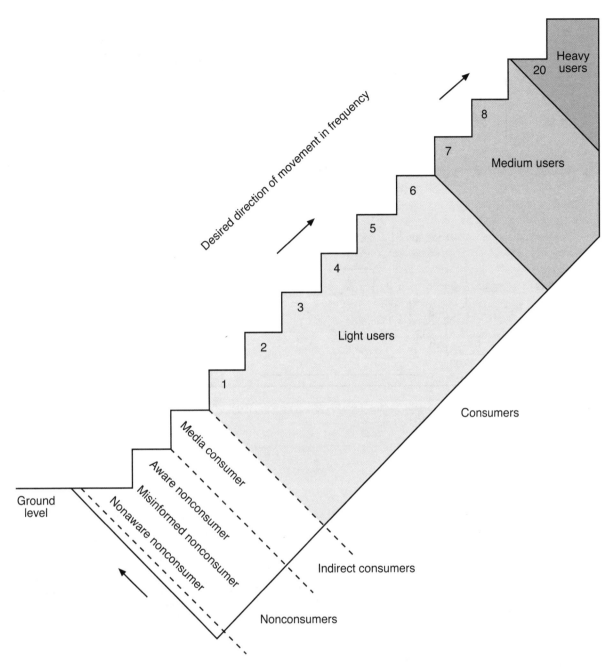

Heavy
users
20

8

7

Medium users

6

Desired direction of movement in frequency

5

4

3

2

Light users

1

Consumers

Media consumer

Aware nonconsumer

Misinformed nonconsumer

Nonaware nonconsumer

Ground
level

Indirect consumers

Nonconsumers

FIGURE 11.5 The goal of all sales efforts is to get consumers on the escalator by trying the product. The next goal is to move them up the escalator by increasing their frequency of purchase.

The Promotional Planning Model

Obviously, marketers of new products or new organizations, or those moving into new markets, face a different situation. Beyond this, the most sophisticated campaigns target both existing and potential consumers, concentrating more heavily on current users. Figure 11.7, showing the promotional progression planning model, is a framework for such a campaign.

To be effective, promotions must be arranged and directed. Promotions such as giveaways, all-inclusive one-price nights, and discounts, as well as events such as fireworks, concerts, and other forms of entertainment, have an audience—but it is a limited audience. Promotional strategies must be developed with the entire range of attenders in mind: first-time attenders, parents bringing children, price-conscious attenders, partial plan holders, miniplan holders, season-ticket holders (personal and corporate), and attenders not participating in any plan or

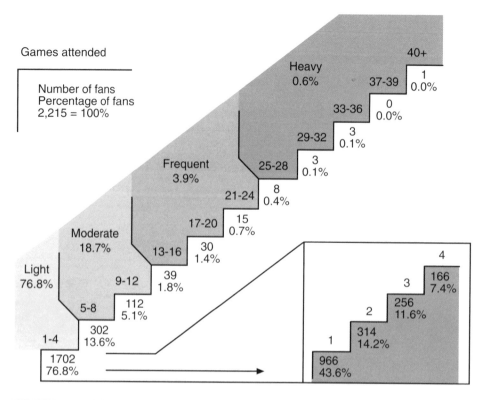

Games attended

Number of fans
Percentage of fans
2,215 = 100%

Heavy
0.6%

40+
1
0.0%

37-39

33-36
0
0.0%

29-32
3
0.1%

Frequent
3.9%

25-28
3
0.1%

21-24
8
0.4%

17-20
15
0.7%

Moderate
18.7%

13-16
30
1.4%

Light
76.8%

9-12
39
1.8%

5-8
112
5.1%

1-4
302
13.6%

1702
76.8%

4
166
7.4%

3
256
11.6%

2
314
14.2%

1
966
43.6%

FIGURE 11.6 A frequency escalator showing fan attendance analysis for a play-off-qualifying NBA team. All figures are rounded.

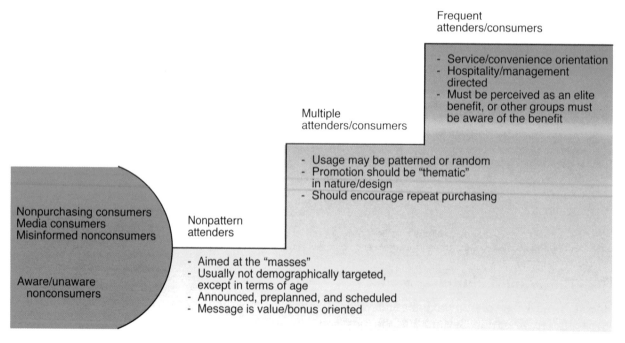

Frequent
attenders/consumers

- Service/convenience orientation
- Hospitality/management directed
- Must be perceived as an elite benefit, or other groups must be aware of the benefit

Multiple
attenders/consumers

- Usage may be patterned or random
- Promotion should be "thematic" in nature/design
- Should encourage repeat purchasing

Nonpurchasing consumers
Media consumers
Misinformed nonconsumers

Aware/unaware
nonconsumers

Nonpattern
attenders

- Aimed at the "masses"
- Usually not demographically targeted, except in terms of age
- Announced, preplanned, and scheduled
- Message is value/bonus oriented

FIGURE 11.7 Promotional progression planning model.

package. The importance of addressing all stages of the escalator is brought home by the situation of the Orlando Magic. The Magic, a team that offered only full-season tickets—thus having all heavy users—has faced some challenges in terms of ticket sales after the free-agency movement of Shaquille O'Neal, injuries to star player Anfernee "Penny" Hardaway, and poor performance on the court. A team that once enjoyed near or full sellouts for all of its games has found itself without any medium-level users to move up the escalator. The team thus faces the task—difficult at best—of almost instantly convincing media consumers to become heavy users.

Level 1: Nonpattern Attenders/Light Users

The consumers on the first level may be classified as having no established attendance pattern (first-timers, people with free tickets, spontaneous attenders, bargain hunters, giveaway collectors such as those who come for Beanie Babies, and so on). These people are motivated to attend by a variety of factors including the opponent; the weather; the day of the week; giveaways, special events, and discounts; team performance; and the opportunity for social interaction with friends, coworkers, or relatives. Interest in the sport, distance from the stadium, and financial resources may or may not be factors.

These nonpattern attenders, who for the most part are light users, would appear to be the easiest of all consumers to move up the escalator. Given that light users attend or participate at the lowest frequency level (many attend only one or two games or participate in activities one to four times per year), they obviously have the greatest room for improvement in frequency. The experiences of organizations that have applied increased-frequency programs show that this is in fact true for most light users, although some consumers, regardless of the offers or efforts involved, cannot be moved. Activities that succeed in increasing the frequency of light users are also effective in attracting nonconsumers for trial involvement.

Level 2: Multiple Attenders/Medium Users

Multiple attenders can be categorized as those consumers attending between 10 and 30 percent of a team's home games or participating in an activity between 10 and 30 percent of the available dates. Multiple attenders may or may not be purchasers of partial plans or miniplans. There are several reasons for nonplan ownership. Some consumers may be unaware that such plans exist; others have time commitments or work schedules that would not easily accommodate a plan with set dates. Still others, because of availability of seats at the ballpark or the number of golf courses in the area, for example, perceive no advantage to having such a plan—availability outstrips demand.

Plans offered to these consumers to increase (and stabilize) their frequencies should use a menu approach to attract interest and break down reasons for not purchasing. This means offering several options at different price points and with different benefits.

Level 3: Frequent Attenders/Heavy Users

Frequent attenders include half-season-plan holders, full-season-ticket holders, club-seat purchasers, and luxury-suite holders. In terms of participation, this group would include the membership at a golf, tennis, or fitness facility and the season-pass holders at a ski resort, for example. Promotional strategies aimed at this level must include all of the benefits and opportunities offered to light and medium users, but must also include one or more elements perceived as attractive and elite (not available to consumers at lower levels). Such strategies usually emphasize customer service, hospitality, comfort, convenience, location, priority, increased communication, interaction, and special discounts on related product extensions. This approach not only convinces medium users to become heavy users, but also retains heavy users and decreases reasons for defection (decreasing involvement at one level and dropping to another level, or dropping off the escalator entirely). The benefits of being a heavy user need to be promoted to both light and medium users so that they understand the value of moving up the escalator—and hopefully to convey the fact that they are missing out on something of value.

Defectors—Descending the Escalator

Regardless of the product or service offered, there will be consumers who have overpurchased or overcommitted to an opportunity. These consumers then seek to downgrade their involvement or commitment or to terminate it. Organizations must give careful attention to developing programs to attract consumers to the various levels without "cannibalizing" consumers from higher levels.

In the following chapter on sales, we offer specific programs to attract consumers to each of these levels; we discuss how to retain and move them up the escalator and how to prevent them from defecting.

Putting It All Together: An Integrated Promotional Model

In attempting to articulate the aggregate value of fully integrated promotional campaigns, it is obvious that while ticket sales and revenue are a major component of most promotional campaigns, there are several marketing platforms involved that can "boost" the value and impact of a promotional campaign.

- ◆ As a marketing platform:

  To establish a foundation and a brand for future applications

  To create an environment that will build equity/value each year

  To develop a "blueprint" to emulate for future platforms and campaigns

  To create a market "buzz" to initiate on and off the "sports pages" through grassroots and guerilla marketing activities and extensions

- ◆ As a revenue platform:

  To develop a sales platform for increased ticket, sponsorship, and broadcast sales volume

  To build attendance, which in turn affects and increases ancillary venue-related revenue streams such as parking, concessions, and merchandise

- ◆ As an entertainment platform:

  To create a memorable experience that brings fans back

  To deliver new broadcast and Internet opportunities and features

  To strengthen the emotional connection between the sport product and the fans or purchasers

For those reasons, it might be advantageous to consider promotional campaigns as the hub of wheel with the spokes of the wheel representing the various departmental units if the sport organization that can enhance and build upon the promotional concept as well as capitalize on the opportunity through a variety of platforms (see figure 11.8).

Starting at the center of the wheel—the promotional concept—this is the focal point and should have goals and objectives as well as primary and secondary strategies and, whenever possible, a "hook" to draw in the attended audience. For the 2006 NBA Finals, the Miami Heat created a promotional concept for the playoffs that carried into the Finals named "White Hot" (see photo on the cover of the textbook). "White Hot" referred to the way the team was playing, the game atmosphere—all seats were covered in white—the dance team wore white outfits, the team wore their white uniforms, and the team launched a line of "White Hot" merchandise.

Examining each "spoke" of the wheel will provide some insight into the successful planning of an integrated promotional model.

Wrap-Up

Promotion is a commonly used term in sport marketing. For most, promotion includes advertising, personal selling, publicity, and sales promotion. At the core of promotion is communication—the attempt by an organization or entity to reach its audience. To be effective, the promotional activity must cut through the clutter of the marketplace, inform and persuade the targeted recipient of the message, and hopefully initiate some type of action on the part of the recipient. Advertising through a variety of traditional mediums and new media, and

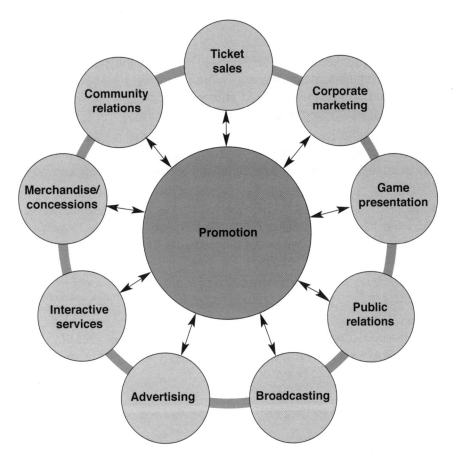

FIGURE 11.8 Promotional wheel.
Created by Hersh, Mullin, and Sutton.

also via personal selling through endorsements, is evolving and changing as a result of technological innovations and the ineffectiveness of past practices. This evolution will continue, and new techniques and practices such as use of the Internet and street marketing will be judged on their effectiveness to deliver the appropriate demographic.

Promotional activities are a valuable strategy to attract new consumers as well as to increase the frequency (participating, purchasing, attending) of current consumers. In determining how to implement such activities, the reverse planning process—knowing what you want to achieve through the promotion—is an essential organizational approach.

Promotional activities, which can take the form of price-oriented efforts such as discounting and packaging, or nonprice efforts such as giveaways and special events, are an essential part of attracting consumers and increasing their frequency or volume. The theory of the consumer escalator suggests that promotions should be a coherent package in which the aim is to ensure a balance among light, medium, and heavy users.

Because the repeat user is the lifeblood of the sport organization, investing extensive time and money in an effort to attract one-time patrons is a questionable strategy. Even if a sponsor underwrites the cost of a giveaway, the marketer must consider the resources (staff, time, advertising) spent on attracting consumers who may be nothing more than "cherry pickers." Obviously, any strategy should include attempts to attract nonusers—but should not neglect any groups currently on the escalator, who typically provide the bulk of all product consumption. Ultimately, each organization must determine the ideal balance in its promotional strategy. Tactics will include some combination of advertising, personal selling, public relations, and sales promotions. However, successful strategies will recognize the tendency for many consumers to move up an escalator of consumption. Although large numbers may jump off at any point, into the vast recesses of defection, a sound strategy will maintain a steady flow of patrons moving upward.

Activities

1. Interview 15 to 20 students at your institution to determine the most effective way of reaching them (i.e., communicating a message). After identifying the best methods, determine how your athletics department should attempt to communicate with students (both on and off campus) with regard to attending athletic events.

2. Using the same audience as in Activity 1, determine whether price or nonprice promotional activities would be more effective in attracting college students to athletic events (note that this point may be moot on your campus if students are admitted free to all athletic events).

3. When watching television over the next two weeks, keep an advertising journal and classify each advertisement that you see according to the list of structures for television commercials on page 251. Which commercial type was the most prevalent? Which commercial ad type was the most effective? Why?

4. Identify five athletes whom you believe could become effective endorsers. Select a product for each and explain why that person would be an effective endorser for that product.

5. Using a product or service of your choosing, conduct some research activities in order to profile the consumer group and construct a frequency escalator for that product or service. Develop a series of strategies to change light consumers to medium consumers, and medium consumers to heavy consumers.

Your Marketing Plan

One of the greatest challenges in marketing is communicating your message to your intended audience. How will advertising and promotional activities help you disseminate your message to your intended target market? How will you use these same activities to initiate action on the part of your intended target market? How will you change these approaches after six months? After two years?

Chapter 12

Sales

Objectives

- ✦ To define what sales is and its role in marketing.
- ✦ To provide an overview of the various sales methodologies used in sport.
- ✦ To illustrate, through the use of examples, some successful real-life sales applications.
- ✦ To show the importance and impact of retention and service activities as they relate to the sales process.

Influencing the Heart, Followed Closely by the Mind and the Wallet

Two of the biggest influences on consumer behavior today are arguably Oprah Winfrey and the Walt Disney Company. Oprah made history in 2005 by giving away a brand new Pontiac to each member of her preselected audience and building the show around a trip to the Pontiac plant. The result: Pontiac is 22% ahead of projection in sales for the vehicle. But to paraphrase a song title, nobody does it better than the Walt Disney Company.

Disney executive Andy Mooney changed the future of the consumer product division with a very simple idea: package some of Disney's most popular female characters under a single brand and market them to a built-in audience of millions of little girls. Thus, the Disney Princess line was born. The Disney Princess line—so named because of little girls' age old fascination with princesses—is based on six princesses who were featured in Disney films (see table). Each of these princesses possesses a characteristic or trait appealing to girls. Based on that premise, the Disney Princess line has grown from $200 million in its inaugural year of 2000 to more than $2 billion today—an increase of more than 900%.

In the Walt Disney World (Orlando, FL) theme park, Disney offers breakfast with the princesses, numerous meet-and-greets, an all-princess dance performance with six daily shows, and, most recently, a tea party with Ariel. As of 2006, the Disney Princess is the third-largest consumer-products line, trailing only Winnie the Pooh and Mickey Mouse. The line has grown from dolls, costumes, and toys to software, toiletries, and bedsheets. Disney seems to have adopted the mantra of the great showman P.T. Barnum, who said, "Children have ever been our best customers," and we might add that the path to parents is through the hearts, minds, and imaginations of their children. (1)

Princess	1st movie appearance	Movie	Trait
Snow White	1937	Snow White	Kindness
Cinderella	1950	Cinderella	Beauty, grace
Aurora	1959	Sleeping Beauty	Loyalty
Ariel	1989	The Little Mermaid	Curiosity
Belle	1991	Beauty and the Beast	Beauty, intelligence
Jasmine	1992	Aladdin	Sense of adventure

Sales is the "lifeblood" of any sport organization. Whether it be of tickets, media rights, sponsorships, signage, advertising, luxury suites, or any of the sport products, sales accounts for the majority, if not all, of the revenue.

According to Ron Seaver, founder of the National Sports Forum, "Nothing happens until somebody sells something." (2) Unfortunately, the word *sales* or the term *salesperson* usually conjures up images of "hucksters"—people using guile and persuasion to talk customers into buying products they might not want at prices they sometimes can't afford. In this chapter, we attempt to change this perception by exploring the various sales methodologies the sport industry uses; distinguish between product-oriented and customer-oriented sales; and examine the concept of "aftermarketing," or what should happen after the sale to ensure that the purchase is a win–win situation for both the seller (the sport organization) and the purchaser (the sport consumer). This emphasis on relationship marketing (building long-term relationships that grow) and lifetime value (the true measure of a consumer's value to the organization over time) will illustrate the value of the sales process to a sport organization and the professionalism of the sales approaches used in this industry.

As we have discussed earlier in this book, sport marketing differs from other types of marketing in a variety of ways. One difference is the presence of emotion. This is also the case for the sales aspect of sport marketing. In sport, the sales process may involve an emotional element that may be, but usually is not, an element of the majority of sales taking place throughout the world every day. This emotional element can be either an aid or a hindrance, usually depending on the public perception of the sport product at that time. In 2005, the Chicago White Sox won the World Series and still struggled for market share with the rival hometown Chicago Cubs. Neither team had won a World Series since the White Sox had done so in 1917—yet the Cubs, who fell far below expectations, still drew a respectable attendance of 2,342,834, whereas the White Sox recorded a final attendance record of 3,099,993 during the 2005 season. (3) Why? Because the Cubs—historically described as "lovable losers"—play in Wrigley Field. The emotional ties manifested in "pride in place," combined with the tourist attraction of Wrigley Field and the opportunity to sit in the fabled bleachers, makes a poor on-field product much more attractive to the consumer.

This chapter addresses the types of sales strategies and tactics most commonly employed in the sport industry. We illustrate these strategies and tactics through examples and insight from expert practitioners from a number of organizations, primarily within the context of tickets or sponsorship.

Figure 12.1 depicts a critical relationship among the media, sponsors, and fans. This relationship is essentially symbiotic, because the three elements feed off each other to create the types of conditions that attract additional fans.

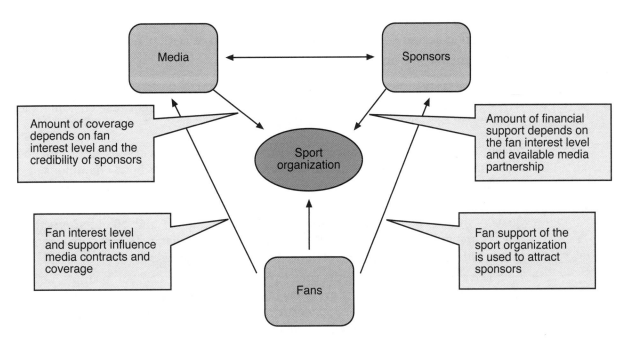

FIGURE 12.1 Relationship among media, sponsors, and fans.

The *media* provides coverage according to the interest fans have in the sport. The media is also influenced by the credibility the sport or organization has with its sponsors. *Sponsors* provide financial support for the sport or organization based on fan support. The more fans there are, the more interactions occur among sponsors, product, and fans (the target market). *Fans* and their support of the sport organization are used to attract sponsors. Their level of interest and support influences media contracts and coverage.

Hall of Famer Yogi Berra once said, "Nobody goes there anymore; it's too crowded." (4) In his inimitable style, Yogi captured the goal of any event marketer, to create a crowd—because a crowd attracts a crowd. The game or the venue must become the place to be. The crowd is important because it provides credibility to people in the media, who then deem the event worthy of coverage and attention. Media coverage and interest function to create value for the sponsors, who rationalize their costs on a cost-per-exposure basis. The larger the crowd is, the more exposure and value the sponsors receive. In the words of many sport marketers, the goal is to put "meat in the seats." This is accomplished through sales.

Sales Defined

Sales is the revenue-producing element of the marketing process. In the strictest sense of the word, selling is the process of moving goods and services from the hands of those who produce them into the hands of those who will benefit most from their use. (5) It usually involves the application of persuasive skills and may be supported by print, audio, or video messages designed to promote the product or its brand as essential, the best, or desirable. In some cases, the salesperson might be able to give the consumer the opportunity to sample or experience the service or product.

In this chapter, we define and explain sales by referring to the thoughts and ideologies of a famed sport marketer, the late Mark McCormack, founder and chairman of IMG (International Management Group)—arguably the world's leading sport marketing and athlete-management organization. As McCormack explained, selling consists of

the process of identifying customers,

getting through to them,

increasing their awareness and interest in your product or service, and

persuading them to act on that interest. (6)

One can also explain sales as customer performance: When a customer purchases a product, he performs the act of buying. (7) In sport, four main factors cause customers to perform or to fail to perform:

+ *Quality.* How well is the product or service performing? The win–loss record for the 2005 Chicago White Sox, the drawing power of the 2006 Super Bowl champions, the Pittsburgh Steelers, at home and on the road, and the "star power" of the Miami Heat are all excellent illustrations.

+ *Quantity.* In what quantity is the product sold—for example, 1 unit, 10 units? A person might purchase a miniplan for the WNBA Minnesota Lynx that includes 5 games rather than a full-season ticket, which includes more than 15 games.

+ *Time.* Does the consumer have the time to consume the product? For example, family obligations, work schedule, and everyday life might dictate that she does not. To make the purchase of a golf membership worthwhile, for example, the person usually must average 45 or more rounds of golf per year.

+ *Cost.* Cost relates not only to the overall cost, but also to such aspects as payment options and value received for the purchase price. Many fitness clubs position the cost of membership as cost per day: Isn't your health worth 74 cents a day?

Getting the customer to purchase, and retaining that customer, will dictate how successful a salesperson or a sport organization really is and how viable the future of the person or the organization will be.

What Makes a Good Salesperson?

Are salespersons born or made? The debate has raged for centuries. In the opinion of experts, the naturally born salesperson is a myth; salespeople are made, not born. (8) People usually learn the skills needed to be successful by developing good listening skills, being comfortable speaking to strangers, and having an aggressive attitude in the context of wanting to succeed. These traits are generally learned and developed through experience and modeling; over time, they form another critical element in a successful salesperson: confidence. These are the qualities Mark McCormack looked for in salespeople in his sport marketing agency:

+ Belief in the product
+ Belief in yourself
+ Seeing a lot of people (sales-call volume)
+ Timing
+ Listening to the customer (but realizing that what the customer wants is not necessarily what she is telling you)
+ A sense of humor
+ Knocking on old doors
+ Asking everyone to buy
+ Following up after the sale with the same aggressiveness you demonstrated before the sale
+ Common sense (9)

What Is a Good Sales-Oriented Organizational Structure?

The organizational structure and style of the organization form a key element in determining the overall success and impact of the sales department's efforts. Organizational structure and style include the following:

+ *The reporting structure* (whom you report to—your immediate supervisor) in an organization.

+ *The relationships between departments that are integral in the sales process.* For example, in structuring any organization involved in the sale of tickets, the relationship between the box office manager and the ticket-sales department is critical because of possible offers and incentives and the subsequent redemption of those offers. Figure 12.2 illustrates the model NBA team organizational chart for ticket sales and service departments.

+ *The organizational style or philosophy* with regard to producing support materials (e.g., brochures, direct-mail pieces, advertising) used in the sales process.

+ *The sales developmental process within the department.* Most sales departments begin their salespeople in entry-level-type sales positions. In sport, this often involves starting them in telemarketing (discussed later in this chapter) and letting them progress according to performance. The typical sales-development progression begins with telemarketing and leads to group sales, then to season-ticket sales, and finally to corporate sales, which often involves sponsorships and other high-priced products such as luxury suites. According to sport sales consultant Jack Mielke, organizations should establish separate and distinct departments for ticket and sponsorship sales and divide ticket sales into season, group, corporate, and telemarketing. (10) Obviously, this depends on the size and scope of the organization, but it is a good practice—similar to the approach used in professional fund-raising—to produce specialists who become experts in that particular area.

+ *Determining the composition of the sales force and compensation mix for the sales staff.* In this process, one determines the number of full-time sales staff, the number of part-time sales staff (if any), the use of outside sales services (usually a telemarketing agency), and the way sales personnel will be compensated. Compensation is usually a combination of salary and commission (a percentage of the sales generated). Commission percentages vary according to the salary/commission ratio and the product being sold, and according to whether the sale is a new sale or a renewal.

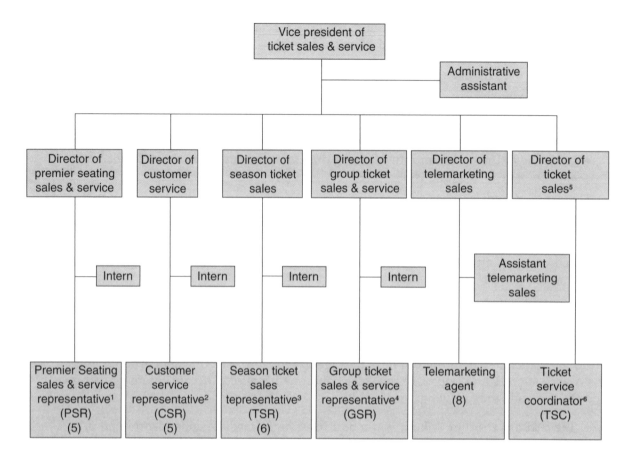

Notes:
1. One premier seating sales & service representative (PSR) per each 500 premier seats.
2. One customer service representative (CSR) per each 750 season-ticket accounts.
3. One season ticket sales representative (TSR) per each $500,000 of new season-ticket sales revenue to be generated.
4. One group ticket sales & service representative (GSR) per each $500,000 of group business (new and renewed).
5. Director of ticket sales may also be the director of box office operations in many teams' structures.
6. Ticket service coordinators (TSC) are responsible for building season-ticket and group accounts, processing payments, printing tickets and delivering tickets. The number of TSCs depends on the degree of support provided by arena box office personnel.

FIGURE 12.2 NBA organizational chart.

Vic Gregovits, senior vice president of sales and marketing for the Cleveland Indians, began his career in sales and has worked in a sales capacity for almost 20 years with teams such as the Cleveland Cavs, Philadelphia Eagles, and Pittsburgh Pirates; he is now in his second tour of duty with the Cleveland Indians. According to Gregovits, managing a sales team is an ongoing process that involves daily attention to the activities at hand. Gregovits discusses his approach in the "Developing and Managing a Sales Department" sidebar on page 283.

Because of multiple franchise ownership or involvement in a variety of enterprises by ownership, some sales staffs are multitask oriented. The NBA/WNBA relationship is one of the most common examples of multitask sales staff. Joe Clark, vice president of ticket sales and services for the San Antonio Spurs, who also own the SBC Center, the WNBA Silver Stars, and the minor league hockey entity Rampage, offers some insight regarding managing such an enterprise in the case study on page 284.

Developing and Managing a Sales Department

Vic Gregovits, senior vice president, sales and marketing, Cleveland Indians

When developing and managing a sales staff, you must continually evaluate the structure of the staffing and also the individual members of the staff. As part of my evaluation process, I ask the following questions:

- ✦ Has the sales staff been properly trained?
- ✦ Does the sales staff have the resources it needs to accomplish the established goals?
- ✦ What are the strengths and weaknesses of the sales team or its individual members?
- ✦ How can the various personalities and styles of the individual members be used to complement each other and benefit the team as a whole?
- ✦ Is an effective incentive structure (e.g., commissions and bonuses) in place that will motivate salespeople to achieve their individual goals and the team goals, thus rewarding them financially?

An examination of each of these questions will provide some insight into the management and evaluative process that I employ.

Has the sales staff been properly trained?

A manager must ensure that the sales staff are intimately knowledgeable about the product they are selling. Knowledge and confidence go hand in hand. If salespeople know all aspects of the product, they will feel confident that they can fully present the product to the customer and answer any questions the customer may have.

Another very important part of training is role-playing. We use role-playing for familiarizing the sales staff with possible scenarios that they may encounter and for rehearsing their presentations. It is important that the sales personnel have an opportunity to play both roles, that of the salesperson and that of the consumer; this ensures that they understand the process from both sides. After the role-playing, I recommend holding a group discussion to share the perceptions of the sales team about the activities.

Does the sales staff have the resources it needs to accomplish the established goals?

When a salesperson makes a sales call, he or she must have all the tools necessary to make this presentation impressive, memorable, and effective. It is my responsibility to make sure that the sales personnel have the appropriate literature (brochures, order forms, diagrams, and so forth) to support the product they are selling. However, as with my earlier point, the salesperson must have detailed knowledge about the product. One way to effectively evaluate whether the sales staff have the tools and training they need is to periodically accompany them on sales calls.

What are the strengths and weaknesses of the sales team or its individual members?

When you are trying to identify the strengths and weaknesses of a salesperson, you need to analyze his or her techniques. You can accomplish this, as I have already said, by going on sales calls with each team member or, in telemarketing situations, listening to team members' phone solicitations to verify that they are asking the right questions. Going over sales reports is another way to review performance. By reviewing the sales reports, the manager can assess whether the salesperson is stronger at selling one type of product over another, "up-selling" or upgrading consumers to higher product levels, renewing current customers, and so on. By determining which type of package a salesperson sells most often, you can identify his or her strengths and weaknesses. Someone who concentrates on upgrading or renewing packages may have a strength in customer relations and up-selling while possibly exhibiting a weakness in "cold calling" or initiating new sales. Someone who concentrates on new sales may have a weakness in postsales account service. It is important to have a good mix of personalities and styles to balance the sales staff.

How can the various personalities and styles of the individual members be used to complement one another and benefit the team as a whole?

Once you have determined the strengths and weaknesses of your staff, you should structure your department to maximize individual strengths. This may mean allocating certain people to concentrate on selling the products they know best. This will make the entire staff very efficient. However, it is important that you also help these individuals overcome their weaknesses. You do not want to stereotype people with regard to their sales skills. As a manager, you must continue to help each person grow and broaden his or her skills. Individual goals should refer to both the strengths and the weaknesses of the salesperson.

Is an effective incentive structure (e.g., commissions and bonuses) in place that will motivate salespeople to achieve their individual goals and the team goals, thus rewarding them financially?

The incentive structure should be developed with three things in mind: team goals, individual sales staff goals, and a fair commission structure. The team goals specify the budgetary numbers that the team as a unit needs to achieve. The individual sales goals add up to the team goals. The object is to

(continued)

motivate the individuals to achieve their own targets, which in turn achieves the team goal. Two things, commissions and competition, should provide the motivation. The commission structure motivates by functioning as an immediate reward for the sale. The competition acts as an incentive, through recognition and peer pressure, to sell more. Monthly sales contests with monetary rewards create not only competition and peer recognition, but also additional compensation and gratification. It is also a good idea to have a trophy or some visible token (special parking space, opportunity to travel with the team, and so on) for the winner to display. Besides serving as a constant reminder for the winner of last month's performance, this is a source of motivation to the other competitors and a reminder of what they are capable of achieving.

The underlying factor in all of these areas is fairness. Fairness is critical in managing a sales force. Be accessible to all your team members, and be encouraging and empathetic to their needs and desires. Goals are achieved by a team, and effective management of that team ensures a realistic chance of achieving or exceeding expectations and goals.

Managing a Multitask Sales Staff

Joe Clark, vice president of ticket sales and services for the San Antonio Spurs

We all know that salespeople are the lifeblood of an organization!

So how do we capitalize on and maximize the effective use of a salesperson's time so that the company, customer, and salesperson all stand to benefit? One way would be to equip the sales team with multiple products to sell. In San Antonio, at Spurs Sports & Entertainment, we have challenged both ourselves as a management team as well as our 23-person sales force to be creative and innovative in their approach to ticket sales. By offering three professional sport franchises for the sales force to sell, as well as tickets for family shows and concerts for the AT&T Center, we have managed to create a sales team that is challenged to think outside the box in their daily sales efforts.

To market effectively to the various demographics that will be targeted, it is critical to first understand who your audience is and what the best methods of communicating with your customers are in order to gain their signature on the dotted line. One way of determining this is through the use of various prism clusters to more efficiently target your marketing and sales initiatives. Having three distinctly different products to sell (NBA, AHL, and WNBA) requires that salespeople ask the right questions of their audience during the sales process. By better understanding the profile of their prospects, they will be able to work through the sales process more effectively and generate more sales for all franchises they are selling. In addition, salespeople will be better equipped to cross-sell the other franchises to the customers, as well as gain referrals by knowing the make-up of the prospect. Teaching your sales staff to recognize that each customer is uniquely different and that we must market to them differently is vital to being successful in selling tickets for multiple franchises.

Selling multiple franchises can also be very challenging both from a salesperson's perspective and from the manager's perspective. To be successful, both sides must be very disciplined, focused, organized, and above all else be excellent planners:

+ *Discipline* is required to know what products you are tasked with selling for each franchise and the timing of when to sell these products. Discipline in this way allows both sales people and managers to know what the end goal is for each franchise. A salesperson must understand that he will be asked to generate revenue for all franchises and not just the most popular one. With this basic understanding a salesperson and manager will be able to keep the creative ideas flowing between each other to aid in generating ticket sales for all franchises.

+ *Focus* on the sales goals is another area that both a salesperson and manager must maintain. Being focused will create accountability for both the manager as well as the salesperson. Without proper focus, sales targets could be in danger of falling through and target results will not be achieved. Set daily, weekly, and monthly goals for each franchise.

+ *Organization and planning* are crucial components of being successful when selling multiple franchises. Having to balance ticket sales programs between multiple franchises, particularly when the seasons overlap, can be a real challenge for any sales executive or sales manager. Ticket offers, inventory, and pricing will vary significantly from franchise to franchise. It starts with the manager, who must be clear and concise in communicating the offers to the sales team. Then the sales executive must take personal accountability and grasp the numerous offers by taking the initiative and role-playing how to take the offer to market. Many times there could be six to seven events in a week, and just as in the airline industry, an empty seat is a lost opportunity. So planning ahead to maximize each game from a group sales perspective as well as from an individual ticket sales perspective is very important.

A final component that must be considered when managing multiple franchises is creating a fun atmosphere for the sales team to thrive in. This culture begins and ends with the manager and his or her creativity, sincerity, and passion for filling seats. The goal should be to create an atmosphere in which the sales team can succeed in reaching the goals of the franchise in a fun and positive manner:

◆ Daily/weekly sales contests—One of the most effective ways of doing this are having dedicated sales contest days/weeks for the sales team by offering higher commissions and letting the sales team determine the commission rate based on creative methods. Examples that have been used include bowling for dollars, shooting free-throws or hockey pucks, dice-rolling contests, and even having a donut hole-eating contest to determine commission rates. Other sales-effective contests include using sales brackets similar to March Madness as well as receiving entries (hockey pucks) based on hitting certain levels of revenue generated into a drawing for an all-expense paid vacation to Atlanta. All of these sales contests bring focus and attention to the products that you are selling, but all of these concepts require one thing, which is for the managing team to always be thinking ahead and planning out new opportunities to meet the financial objectives of each franchise.

◆ Players and coaches of the franchise should be engaged to participate in making the sales calls. Split up your sales team into two teams and have players be the team captains and conduct a call night in which the sales team is focused on a franchise's non-renewed accounts or prospects. Enjoy pizza, award prizes, and ask the players to share their stories on the phones with the prospects you are contacting.

◆ One of the best ways to implement your strategic plan is to get input from your sales team. Have them come up with the plan. Of course, you may have your ideas and thoughts on what the plan should look like, but it is how you get to the plan that is important. Involve your sales team in the process and be sure to take the role of a facilitator by leading your sales team to the goal line through the use of effective open-ended questions. Once you have consensus from the sales team, you will have more sales success than simply developing the entire plan yourself and rolling it out to the team. Not only does this concept create an active, engaged, and involved sales group, but they will also have more buy-in and hence accountability to perform.

◆ Compensation—Award bonus dollars to the sales members that meet and exceed their sales quotas for the franchises. Consider a bonus opportunity for the entire sales team should all of your franchises achieve their targeted sales goals.

Finally, there are many challenges that one faces with managing a multitask sales staff and much is learned through trial and error. Having said that, the challenges are certainly worth the effort when you see a sales team that truly works together as a team to achieve success for the company (franchise), their customer, and of course, themselves.

What Is a Good Sales-Oriented Structure?

Figure 12.3 depicts a possible organizational structure for a marketing department in a professional sport franchise—and specifically, how the ticket-sales department could be structured. As we have previously mentioned, the relationship between ticket sales and the box office is essential, but so are other relationships such as that between

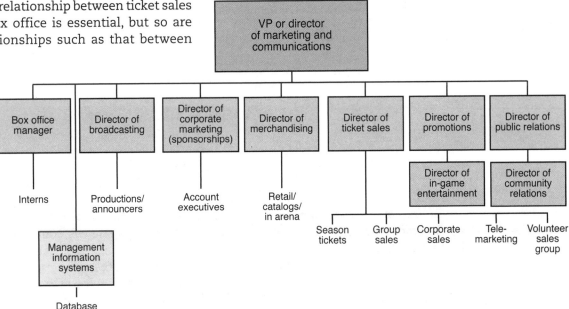

FIGURE 12.3 How ticket sales fit into sport marketing.

data-based marketing personnel and ticket sales. This relation is critical because of the practice of data-based marketing (discussed later in this chapter), which would be asked to provide segments of the database to the sales department for use as leads (names of potential consumers who through some action or activity have indicated an interest in or ability to purchase the product) or for the purpose of conducting a mailing or similar activity. Similar relationships are necessary for providing tickets to sponsors as part of their packages, to community relations personnel for use in their efforts, and also to the promotions department.

What Do I Have to Sell?

Sales inventory refers to the products available to the sales staff to market, promote, and sell through the sales methodologies described in this chapter. Table 12.1 categorizes the types of inventory available to sellers within the sport marketing industry.

◆ **Table 12.1**   Inventories—What Do I Have to Sell?

Naming rights	Electronic inventory	Signage inventory	Print inventory	Assets related to ticket sales
Arena/stadium	Television	Dasher, score, matrix, and message boards	Game program	Court/ice/field time
Practice facility	Radio	Marquees	Media guide	Clinics
Team	Web page	Floor/field/ice	Newsletters	Fan tunnels and high-five lines
	E-newsletters	Medallions	Ticket backs	Ball boy/ball girl opportunities
		Concourse	Ticket envelopes	
		Blimps	Scorecards, roster sheets	
		Turnstiles	Faxes	
		LED signage		

Tickets and hospitality inventory	Promotions inventory	Community programs	Miscellaneous inventory
VIP parking	Premium items	School assemblies	Fantasy camps
Stadium/arena clubs	On-floor promotions	Camps, clinics	Off-season cruises, trips with players
Season tickets	Diamond Vision (or similar brand)	Awards, banquets	Road trips
Club seats, suites, PSLs		Kick-off luncheons, dinners	
Group tickets	Contests		
Parties, special events	Pre-/postgame entertainment	Golf tournaments	

Direct Data-Based Sport Marketing

Direct marketing is an interactive system of marketing that uses one or more advertising media to effect a measurable response and/or transaction at any location. All forms of direct marketing, such as direct mail and telemarketing, involve the use or creation of a database. (11) Simply stated, data-based marketing involves the collection of information about past consumers, current consumers, and potential consumers. This information can come from membership records, lists of past purchasers, credit card slips, surveys, contests, and so forth. The organization uses the information to construct a database (as discussed in chapter 5) that can be segmented according to its needs. Regardless of the sales approach or process that the sport organization is using, some type of database is necessary to generate leads. (12) Table 12.2 illustrates how a ticket-sales database can be generated and how the data could be used.

Type of ticket purchaser	Source	Use
Season-ticket holders	Ticket applications	Renewals, upgrades, additional tickets, play-off tickets, PSLs, merchandise, special events, fantasy camps, youth clinics
Co-account holders (share season tickets)	Not usually listed on the application—provided by season-ticket holders in exchange for an incentive (extra tickets, gift item, etc.)	New season tickets, partial plans, additional individual game tickets, play-off tickets, PSLs, merchandise, special events, fantasy camps, youth clinics
Corporate	Chamber of Commerce, vendor lists, Dun & Bradstreet, ticket applications	Season tickets, club seats, luxury suites, PSLs, sponsorships, groups, additional tickets, play-off tickets
Partial-plan holders (ticket plans less than a full season)	Ticket applications	Upgrades, renewals, additional tickets, play-off tickets, merchandise, special events, fantasy camps, youth clinics
Groups (usually defined as parties of 20 or more)	Group leader lists, surveys of group attendees, contest participants	Partial plans, group brochures, group leader packet, individual game tickets, merchandise, promotional schedule, special events, fantasy camps, youth clinics
Advance-ticket purchasers (tickets purchased from the team or in-house box office)	Credit card slips, ticket form	Partial plans, promotional schedule, single-game ticket brochure, play-off tickets, merchandise, special events, fantasy camps, youth clinics
Phone sales	Ticketmaster or other software phone sales list	Partial plans, promotional schedule, single-game ticket brochure, play-off tickets, merchandise, special events, fantasy camps, youth clinics
Outlet (walk-in other than the stadium/arena—department stores, grocery chains, etc.)	Point-of-sale record (voucher documenting the sale provided to the team), contest entries	Partial plans, promotional schedule, single-game ticket brochure, play-off tickets, merchandise, special events, fantasy camps, youth clinics
Day-of-game walk-up sales	No set format—many clubs use intern-run booths, kiosk computer terminals, and related formats	Partial plans, promotional schedule, single-game ticket brochure, play-off tickets, merchandise, special events, fantasy camps, youth clinics
Sweepstakes/contest entries	Entry forms	Merge/purge with other sources—promotional schedule, single-game ticket brochure, merchandise, special events
Opt-ins	Web visitors	Intro offers, welcome packages, survey info

Former NBA executive and marketing consultant Jon Spoelstra believes that the organization should attempt to secure the name, address, and phone number of everyone who purchases its products or services. According to Spoelstra, building a database qualifies as a "quick-fix silver bullet" and should be one of the first things undertaken in any sport marketing effort. (13)

Management of the database is also a key element in the process. Each group or segment in the database should be tested and its responsiveness to certain appeals measured—ticket plans, telephone solicitation, direct mail, special offers. Responses should be measured to test ROI (return on investment) and should be documented to increase the targeting and hopefully the effectiveness of future efforts.

On the negative side, ROI obviously decreases if you waste your phone calls and have your mail returned—and also if the party repeatedly fails to respond to your offers. We recommend purging (removing) a name from the database in the absence of any sales activity (tickets, merchandise, subscriptions, membership renewals) in a 36-month period.

Many organizations construct databases and use them for periodic contact (special targeted mailings, newsletters, offers, and so forth) with their consumers. The San Diego Padres and their Compadres program represent a unique use of the database—namely, monitoring attendance and encouraging the registrants to increase their attendance through an incentive program.

Don Johnson, former San Diego Padres vice president of marketing, and Brook Govan can be credited with implementing the Compadres program—one of the first and most successful frequent-attender programs in professional sport. The intent of the program was to recognize and reward fans for their attendance at the ballpark. The program is similar to frequent-flier plans in which air travelers accumulate points that they can redeem for rewards. It is designed to move fans up the escalator by rewarding them for every game they attend. The more games they attend, the more points they accumulate—which are redeemable for prizes (see the Compadres Rewards Program on page 289).

Club membership is free to any fan. To become a member, fans simply complete an application, which in actuality is a lifestyle survey (see figure 12.4). This information then becomes part of the Padres' database. Upon completing the application, the fan receives an attractive bar-coded membership card that tracks his attendance and creates a record of points earned for every game attended. Each game is worth between three and five points depending on the date.

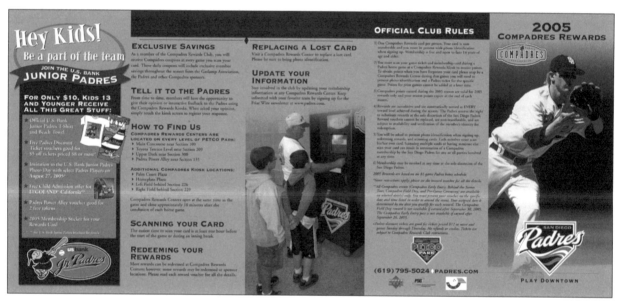

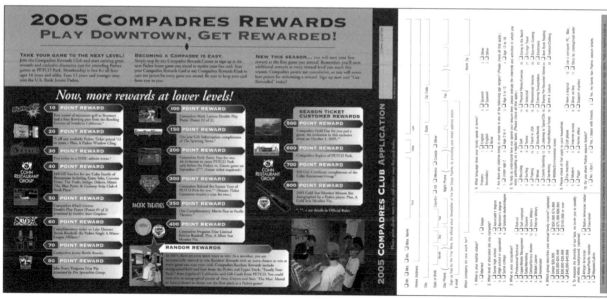

FIGURE 12.4 The Compadres Club is a highly successful direct data-based sales program that emphasizes purchasing frequency.

Courtesy of the Compadres Club

Upon arriving at the game, fans present their game tickets to enter, and once inside the gate they "swipe" their membership cards at the Compadres kiosk. Compadres members then receive a four-part coupon that has been printed inside the kiosk. The coupon contains three special offers for every game (from the Padres or from Compadres Club sponsors such as Oscar's Restaurant); the fourth part of the coupon shows the member's name and provides a cumulative point total.

According to Johnson, "The entire process of recognition and reward and creating a sense of privilege and exclusivity have allowed us to develop relationships with all of our fans—individual ticket buyers as well as ticket plan purchasers." (14)

✦ Compadres Rewards Program

Points	Reward
20-point reward	Discount ticket voucher good for Compadres Club Night on August 16, 2004. Your reward voucher is good for $3 off the purchase of available Upper Reserved or Upper Infield Reserved seating for this special game. Plus, August 16 is Compadres Double Points Night! (Reward must be earned by August 1, 2004.)
30-point reward	Hard Rock Cafe: $5 off any food purchase of $15 or more.
40-point reward	SDSU Aztecs 2-for-1 ticket voucher. Good for Aztec Baseball or Football.
50-point reward	One free ride from Mini Cab Co. in the downtown area.
60-point reward	Free ticket to a Lake Elsinore Storm baseball game. Reward must be earned by August 22, 2004. (Padres Class A affiliate)
80-point reward	Padres key chain presented by AMC Theatres.
100-point reward	PETCO Park inaugural season Frequent Friar pin presented by Pro Specialties Group.
150-point reward	Padres 2004 opening-day poster presented by Golden State Graphics.
200-point reward	PETCO Park inaugural season baseball.
300-point reward	Compadres early entry pass for one+. An invitation to enter PETCO Park early for a select Padres game. (A game ticket is required.)
400-point reward	Compadres Field Day for one+. An invitation to this exclusive event. Play catch, catch fly balls, and more on the field at PETCO Park and receive a Silver Star member pin.
500-point reward	Compadres PETCO Park tour for one+ and a PETCO Park pin.
600-point reward	One complimentary movie pass to AMC Theatres.
700-point reward	One complimentary adult admission to the San Diego Zoo (while supplies last).
800-point reward	2004 Gold Star Member Mizuno bat autographed by a Padres player. Plus a Gold Star member pin.
Win random rewards all season long	As a Compadres Rewards Member, you are automatically entered to win Compadres Random Rewards from the Padres all season long. Every game you scan your rewards card, you will have an extra chance to win. Compadres Random Rewards include a trip for two to Arizona for the last game of the season, gift cards from PETCO, an autographed Tony Gwynn batting helmet, an autographed poster of Tony Gwynn and Stan "the Man" Musial from Upper Deck, autographed baseballs, autographed bats, and much more.

Courtesy of the Compadres Club

Typical Sales Approaches Used in Sport

One of the keys to successful sales is having a product that everyone wants. Another key is to have products that people can afford. Full-menu marketing is having something for everyone. A fan of the Chicago Bulls can wear a $500 leather jacket or a $7 T-shirt. A New York Yankee fan can sit in the bleachers or in a luxury suite. The key is that the clubs or retailers recognize that demand for the product is present at different price points. Spoelstra believes that full-menu marketing is necessary not only because of price, but also because of time and the fan's level of interest and commitment. (15)

As the level of ability to pay, interest in the product or service, and availability of the product vary, so too must the approaches used to sell those products or services. A successful sport organization will employ a variety of sales approaches. And as the levels and types of products or services offered for sale within a sport organization vary, so should the sales approaches that aim to inform, persuade, and convince consumers of a product's value to them. Certain approaches are more appropriate and consequently more effective in selling types or volume of the sport product. In this section, we examine the most common sales approaches used in sport.

Unlike food, clothing, and shelter, sport is not a necessity of life; it is a want rather than a need. As such, value is more important than price. Remember, unlike the majority of purchases consumers make, sport purchases ask them to invest their time, money, and emotion. What value are they receiving in exchange for their investment? Selling then is not just about being the low-cost provider. It's about providing the best value, no matter how expensive or luxurious the product. (16)

Telemarketing

Telemarketing can be defined as a marketing approach that "utilizes telecommunications technology as part of a well-planned, organized, and managed marketing program that prominently features the use of personal selling, using non-face-to-face contacts." (17) Telemarketing via its telephone links can be used to complement, support, or substitute for a direct-sales force. Telemarketing can be one-dimensional—handling inbound calls from consumers inquiring as a response to a promotional campaign, catalog, or other source.

The other approach is two-dimensional, as an outward-oriented vehicle to prospect for customers, follow up leads, or solicit existing customers for repeat or expanded business volume. (18) A 2005 study by the Direct Marketing Association estimated that telemarketing would grow to be a $480 billion+ business by 2009. Additionally, 27.1 percent of respondents chose telemarketing as the single most important direct marketing activity for business-to-business sales leads. (19)

Telemarketing offers considerable possibilities for enhancing the productivity of the sales force by permitting more specialization by account type and better focus on high-yield accounts. Telemarketing is also valuable in terms of sales support: scheduling sales calls and deliveries, conducting surveys, checking the status of a customer, and providing customer service. The Boston Red Sox have taken such an approach in their telemarketing efforts. Using software licensed through Advantix and maintained and programmed by NEXT ticketing, the Red Sox have implemented a system that can handle up to 90,000 incoming orders in one hour, operates 24 hours per day 7 days per week, and generates a database. The system can also be used to conduct surveys. (20)

However, the most compelling reason to adopt telemarketing is the cost savings. (21) The list that follows illustrates how the average outside salesperson (a salesperson making face-to-face sales calls) spends her time by various common salesperson activities and the percentage of time spent on each. (22) Interestingly, only half of an outside salesperson's time is actually spent selling.

Selling (40 percent)

Traveling (24 percent)

Waiting (16 percent)

Paperwork and meetings (20 percent)

The Telemarketing Sales Process

Telemarketing involves training the sales personnel to "follow a script," become effective listeners, identify the objections to the sale (if any), and complete the sales process by countering the objection and selling the original offer or modifying the offer (by up-selling or down-selling) to better fit the needs of the consumer. All outbound telemarketing calls must take place after 8:00 a.m. and before 9 p.m. local time. The process looks like this:

1. Precall planning
   - Review client information
   - Plan the objective for the call
   - Psych up—get in the proper mental frame for the call
2. Approach/positioning
   - Identify who you are and where you're from
   - Identify the purpose of the call
   - Make an interest-creating statement
   - Build rapport
   - Get through the gatekeeper (secretary or receptionist) and to the decision maker
3. Data gathering
   - Gain general understanding of the client or the client's business
   - Move from general to specific types of questions
   - Identify a personal or business need
4. Solution generation
   - Tailor communication to the specific client need
   - Ask in-depth questions to test the feasibility of the solution
   - Gather data for a cost/benefit analysis
   - Prepare the client for the recommendation
5. Solution presentation
   - Get client agreement on the area of need
   - Present the recommendation clearly and concisely
   - Describe use benefits
6. Close
   - Decide on timing—when to close
   - Listen for buying signals
   - Handle objections
   - Use closing techniques
7. Wrap-up
   - Discuss implementation issues
   - Thank the client for the business
   - Confirm client commitment
   - Position the next call

Applying the Telemarketing Process

To see how this process works, let's imagine the following scenario. Jane Micelli is a telemarketer employed by the defending Stanley Cup champion, the Detroit Red Wings. Jane has been given a list of leads, derived from people who used their credit card to purchase tickets to one or more games during the past season. Jane's goal is to sell a half-season plan (20 games), but she can also sell full-season tickets (40 games) or "6 packs"—a new product just being introduced. Here are the steps Jane follows.

   1. *Precall planning.* Jane reviews the file on Mary Stuart, an attorney who purchased individual tickets to four games during the past season. Jane notices that Ms. Stuart purchased two tickets for each of the four games and attended once per month in January, February, March, and April. Jane reviews her script and places the call.

2. *Approach/positioning.* "Hello. This is Jane Micelli from the Stanley Cup champion Detroit Red Wings. May I please speak with Ms. Mary Stuart? Good evening, Ms. Stuart. As I stated, I'm calling from the Detroit Red Wings, and we want to thank you for your support of the team during the past season. I'm sure you were happy with the outcome, and I'd like to talk to you about the upcoming season. We anticipate tickets being difficult to come by next season, and we would like to provide loyal fans such as you the opportunity to purchase tickets before they go on sale to the general public. Do you have a few minutes?"

3. *Data gathering.* "According to our records, you purchased tickets to see the Avalanche, Rangers, Penguins, and Stars last season; is that correct? Did you attend any other games? How do you select the games that you will attend?"

4. *Solution generation.* "We have designed a ticket plan for people such as you who like to attend the big games against name opponents or teams with high-profile players. We also realize that these same games are great opportunities for businesswomen such as you to entertain clients. Would you be interested in a ticket plan that lets you see the best teams in the NHL yet requires a commitment of only six games?"

5. *Solution presentation.* "The Detroit Red Wings have designed a new ticket plan called the Big Game Plan. This plan lets you see the Avalanche, Stars, Penguins, Rangers, Devils, and Blackhawks. It also guarantees you the same seat for all six games and the opportunity to purchase tickets for some of the play-offs."

6. *Close.* "I'm sure that the Big Game Plan will meet your needs and be much more convenient than your current ticket-purchasing options. Can I reserve two Big Game Plans for you?"

7. *Wrap-up.* "I'm sure that you will be happy with your ticket plans. I will call you monthly in case you would like to purchase tickets to games that are not part of your plan and to make sure you are enjoying your seats."

Sport organizations are beginning to examine the benefits of expanding incoming phone-line capabilities to provide not only information, but also revenue opportunities. To better satisfy the desire of fans to stay abreast of team and player information and to increase sponsorship revenues, several teams are offering 24-hour-a-day interactive phone lines. Through this system a fan can get up-to-date team information and order a pizza all in the same phone call.

The Washington Capitals Fan Call system offers fans the following options: results and a recap of the most recent game, messages from the Coaches Corner or from a player of the caller's choosing, ticket and merchandise information and ordering procedures, news from the minor league affiliates, schedule and fan club information, and a message describing sponsor Pizza Hut's specials—including the option to order pizza directly through the Fan Call line. This latter option generated $500,000 in sales for Pizza Hut on direct-line transfers during the hockey season. (23)

Direct Mail

Like telemarketing and other forms of direct marketing, direct mail has distinct characteristics and advantages:

+ *Direct mail is targeted.* The appeal is to certain groups of consumers that are measurable, reachable, and sizable enough to ensure meaningful sales volume.

+ *It is personal.* The message can be personalized not only according to the name and other demographic characteristics, but also with regard to lifestyle interests (football fan, Panther alumnus, etc.).

+ *It is measurable.* Because each message calls for some type of action or response, the organization mailing the message is able to measure the effectiveness of the marketing effort.

- ✦ It is *testable*. Because the effectiveness is measurable, marketers can devise accurate head-to-head tests of offers, formats, prices, terms, and so forth.
- ✦ It is *flexible*. There are few constraints (other than cost) with regard to the size, color, timing, shape, and format of the mailing. Also, the marketer determines the mailing date. (24) In contrast, a face-to-face meeting takes place according to work schedules, travel commitments, family obligations, and the like.

Because direct mail does not involve any personal contact (face-to-face, as in personal selling, or ear-to-ear, as in telemarketing), there is no opportunity to explain the program or the offer, to counteract objections, or even to answer questions. Thus the sender must clearly communicate the material, including the offer itself, so that the recipient can clearly understand it.

Developing the Direct-Mail Offer

In formulating the direct-mail offer, the sport marketer should consider the following:

✦ *Differentiating the product to be offered from other products offered.* In other words, in a ticket brochure mailed to a target audience, is each ticket-plan option clearly distinguishable from the others? Can the reader easily assess the benefits of each, make a decision, and act accordingly?

✦ *Offering options or variations of the product to fit the price considerations and abilities of the marketplace.* This approach, sometimes referred to as the good, better, best scenario, was an essential part of Sears' catalog marketing for decades. The Sears approach was to list three items in the catalog with different features and at slightly increasing prices relative to the number of features. Each was then described (in ascending price order and feature order) as a good model, a better model, or the best model. The Golfsmith Store, a direct-mail merchandiser specializing in golf equipment and apparel, offers a range of options, from factory-closeout specials for the budget conscious to state-of-the-art equipment (to find out prices for the latter, the buyer calls the company). In one recent catalog, a golfer looking for a new driver could choose from 27 different drivers and pay as little as $70 or more than $400. (25)

✦ *Providing an attractive range of benefits and/or exclusivity.* In the 1990s, sport marketers appealed to consumers to "join them" in various direct-mail membership initiatives. These memberships, such as those offered by the National Baseball Hall of Fame and Museum, sometimes entailed various levels that had different fees and a set of benefits—publications, admission privileges, and premium items that acted as incentives to join a particular level.

In 1997, the PGA Tour introduced a membership club called the PGA TOUR Partners Club. Targeted to golfers, the PGA TOUR Partners Club offered the following membership benefits: (1) one free tournament pass per year, good for admission at more than 70 PGA Tour and Senior PGA Tour events, (2) the opportunity to become a golf-product tester, (3) discounts on golf schools and lessons, and (4) a database of opportunities for members to trade a round of golf at their course with another member at that member's course. (26)

Affinity-type credit cards are another sport marketing venture using direct mail and offering a set of well-targeted benefits. For example, MBNA offers a series of professional sport-related MasterCards that enable cardholders to accumulate points redeemable for merchandise from their favorite team. Citibank, targeting to the higher demographic profiles of golfers, introduced the Platinum Jack Nicklaus Visa card. This card enables golfers to earn points based on their spending. Cardholders can redeem the points for golf equipment and apparel (e.g., one dozen golf balls for 3,500 points, which equates to having spent $3,500), or they can let the points accumulate and redeem them for unique opportunities such as a golf trip to Palmilla/Cabo del Sol for two (for 187,000 points, equating to having spent $187,000). (27)

♦ *Using discounts, sales, refunds, premium items, and other incentives to enhance the perceived value of the offer.* Direct mail seeks to cause an action, and the perception that in making the purchase "I'm getting a deal" is often the catalyst in producing the action. These "deals" can take many forms. One of the most popular forms of catalog discounting allows a consumer to receive $10 off the order if the amount of the order exceeds $100. This offer is prevalent in apparel marketing, for manufacturers such as Eddie Bauer, but is also used by teams with their own catalogs or stores and by sport mass merchandisers, who may offer such deals as two New Era caps with team emblem for $25.

♦ *Offering flexible-payment or deferred-payment terms.* Some consumers may be intrigued by the opportunity to purchase merchandise now and pay for it at a more convenient time. (28) This is a common retailing practice during the Christmas holidays, but it is also gaining momentum in the sport industry—particularly with regard to higher-priced items such as season tickets. Some professional teams allow their season-ticket purchasers to agree to pay for season tickets and spread their payments over several months.

♦ *Offering a money-back guarantee.* This type of offer permits the consumer to purchase (payment in full) the product and consume at least some portion of it. Consumers who are not satisfied with the product for a specified, or in some cases an unspecified, reason may return it for a full refund of the purchase price. Tim Leiweke, president of Anschutz Entertainment, during his term as president of the Denver Nuggets, offered such a guarantee, as did Jon Spoelstra during his term as president of the New Jersey Nets. Spoelstra's direct-mail piece even specified, "You can ask for a refund if you don't like my tie or the way I comb my hair." Both guarantees were effective; they not only sold tickets and motivated consumers to try the product, but they also generated publicity.

The Appearance of the Mailing Piece

Today, when "junk mail" can fill the mailbox on a daily basis, the mailing piece must be not only unusual enough to gain attention, but also intriguing enough for the recipient to open. In the case of professional sport teams or collegiate athletics programs, the team logo on the envelope is usually enough to attract attention and motivate the addressee to open the envelope. Catalogs with the addressee's favorite team on the cover are usually effective; in other cases, it is desirable for the offer to appear on the outside of the envelope or on the cover. In any case, direct marketers must ensure that their mailing piece is sufficiently interesting to be opened, and hopefully acted on.

Accompanying the offer should be a letter from a key person associated with the product or service. If the direct-mail offer is from a team and concerns tickets, a personalized note or letter from the coaching staff or management should accompany it. The letter should express thanks for the person's past support (if appropriate), explain that purchasing the tickets is a wise business or personal entertainment decision, and also present information or an opportunity that is not available to the general public. (29) Any direct-mail marketing efforts should involve similar letters and messages. Remember, the letter should provide any and all information pertinent to the offer. As we have discussed, the major limitation of direct mail is that the sender cannot talk with the recipient. Thus the mailing piece should enable the recipient to contact the sender to clarify the information, ask questions, or solicit additional information that will help in decision making regarding the offer.

Ticket-sales materials are among the most common types of mailing materials used in sport. From our experience, these materials should be tailored to specific groups; one piece should not be used to reach all market segments. Although each piece should have its own identity in terms of appearance, all should have the same general look so it is obvious they are from the same organization. A mailing piece should be colorful and if possible should contain photos, preferably of people enjoying themselves participating or spectating; remember that the goal is to attract a crowd. Following are some of the most common mailing pieces that sport organizations use:

- *Full-season ticket brochure.* This type of brochure explains the locations of seats and the costs, levels, and benefits of being a full-season ticket holder; it includes an order form.
- *Partial ticket-plan brochure.* This is similar to the full-season brochure, but it must not confuse the reader with too many options; it includes an order form.
- *Group brochure.* The group brochure lists discounts, special promotional nights, the schedule, fund-raising options, other area attractions, and special amenities; it includes an order form. Photos are essential.
- *Pocket schedules.* These schedules of all events and promotional activities include a diagram of the venue, price listing, all phone numbers, Internet addresses, and an order form for purchasing tickets.
- *Posters.* Posters list the schedule and promotional activities and identify contact sources—how and where to order.
- *Appeal letters.* Letters of appeal, on quality letterhead, clearly state what the sender is asking for and why; they should provide support materials, photos, and brochures, and list payment options.

Direct Mail Can Be More Than an Offer

Organizations that use direct mail to do nothing more than initiate the sales process via an offer do not understand relationship marketing. As we discuss later in this chapter, the long-term goal of sales efforts is to develop relationships with the consumer. If the only time the consumer hears from the organization is at renewal time or when the aim is to sell more product, the relationship will never be expanded or strengthened. Regular communication via direct mail can also be used to enhance sales opportunities through several means:

- By providing a regular method of communication to keep the consumer informed (via letters, newsletters, and the like)
- By soliciting input and feedback via consumer questionnaires and surveys
- By showing accountability and expanding the knowledge of the consumer via an annual report
- Through thank-you letters, by acknowledging the support of the consumer over the past year and asking for continued support

A recent trend in the use of direct mail is the annual report. Much as it functions for shareholders, the annual report informs ticket holders about developments in the past year. Some teams produce an annual report in a brochure format, whereas others have used video.

As Spoelstra explained, the annual report provides all the information that interests a particular sponsor and details how the sponsor has benefited. (30) However, given that vested individuals (ticket-plan owners) also have a stake in how the organization has performed and an interest in how the organization is doing (not only on the playing surface but in the community), an annual report for these stakeholders might be in order as well.

Each organization should prepare an annual report that is distributed to all "stakeholders" at the end of every season. This annual report, described as updating the shareholders on the state of the franchise, contains the following elements:

- A letter from the ownership
- An overview of the season and of what to look forward to next season
- A synopsis of charitable activities
- Past season attendance, percentage of capacity
- An explanation (and listing) of the benefits of being a season-ticket holder
- Thank-you quotes and notes from players to the fans
- A photograph montage of last season's highlights and activities (31)

The intent of such mailings is to make the purchaser feel special and informed. The annual report can take the form of a brochure or letter; it can even be on DVD or CD-ROM so that the message has a more multidimensional feel.

Personal Selling

"Face-to-face selling is the art of convincing, the use of learnable techniques to close a transaction and the application of basic rules to show a prospect or customer that you have something he or she needs." (32) Although more costly than telemarketing, personal selling can be more precise, enabling marketers to closely target the most promising sales prospects. (33) Developing and maintaining a strong sales force can be the most expensive part of the promotional mix, and the management and motivation of this sales force require an experienced, gifted sales manager. However, the return on the investment in the sales force may be well worth the cost if one follows a few simple rules, as outlined in table 12.3.

✦ **Table 12.3** Rules for Effective Personal Selling

Rule	Rationale
Use data-based marketing.	Generate leads with a high likelihood of interest and ability to purchase.
Communicate to the consumer as you would with a friend. (34)	You have something in common—some level of interest in the product.
Follow the LIBK rule—let it be known that you are in sales and what you are selling. (35)	Be proud and enthusiastic about what you do and what you are selling.
Overcome objections and perceived barriers to the sale.	Be familiar with the most common objections or barriers to the sale, and modify the product or provide examples showing that people with the same objections have enjoyed the product.
Manage the conversation by being an effective listener as well as making your points.	Consumers want to be heard—they want a reaction to what they perceive to be concerns.
Try to develop a relationship as a consultant rather than just as a salesperson. (36)	In reality, you are consulting by proposing possible solutions to the various needs and wants of the consumer.
Match the consumer with the appropriate product.	A good sale "fits" the budget and lifestyle of the consumer.

Personal selling actually involves the integration of data-based marketing (previously discussed in chapter 5), relationship marketing, and benefit selling to effectively communicate to consumers. We will examine these individually to assess the contribution and importance of each to the personal selling process.

Relationship Marketing

Relationship marketing implies finding a way to integrate the customer into the company, to create and sustain a relationship between the company and the customer. (37) Gronroos, an expert on relationship marketing, identified three main conditions under which relationship marketing is a successful and productive marketing approach:

The customer has an ongoing desire for service.

The customer of the service controls the selection of the service supplier.

There are alternative service suppliers. (38)

These conditions are present in the sport marketplace, and they provide an excellent application forum for relationship marketing. In general, people who consume sport are highly involved consumers who have a desire for long-term association with a sport team or branded product. The sport marketplace is extremely competitive, and there are many providers for each sport product or service (not necessarily in the same sport type, but as a sport entertainment option), enabling the consumer to select his "provider" of sport entertainment. (39) Therefore, building a relationship with a customer is essential to retain that person as a repeat customer.

Benefit Selling

Benefit selling involves the creation of new benefits to offset existing perceptions or assumed negatives related to the sport product or service. (40) For example, for consumers who state that they cannot commit to a ticket plan because they don't know where they will be in August, benefit selling may be the answer. The concept of benefit selling has been responsible for the creation of new products in the sport industry such as the Flex book. The Flex book, or Fan Flex as it is sometimes called, was developed in response to the frequent objection of potential consumers that they could not commit to a certain number of games on specific dates. The Flex book contains coupons for a specified number of games, usually 11 or 13 sold for the price of 10 or 12 game tickets. The coupons have no date and can be redeemed (exchanged for a ticket) either in advance or on game day. Purchasers can use the tickets in any way they choose—all at once, in multiples of two, or one game at a time. Consumers benefit in that they are not restricted to particular dates, and in some cases they receive an extra ticket as an incentive to buy. The incentive for the organization is that the tickets are presold, so filling the seats does not depend on team performance, weather, or any other factor. The only limitation is that the coupon does not guarantee admission; redemption is based on availability. If the game is sold out when the consumer arrives, she must use the ticket for another game. Thus, for very attractive games, such as opening days or key promotions, the consumer needs to decide and redeem the coupon as soon as possible to guarantee admission. The Pittsburgh Pirates have been highly successful in selling Flex books. In addition, because of the low cost of this item, it is used in telemarketing, in direct mail, and in personal selling as a sell-down.

When these three approaches—data-based marketing, relationship marketing, and benefit selling—are integrated into the formulation of a personal selling campaign and fine-tuned into a sales style involving the personality and experiences of the salesperson, the results can be very effective.

Letting potential customers take a guided tour of the facilities and have an opportunity to work out is a great way to show that person the benefits of the facility.

When combined with concepts such as sampling, trial usage, and open houses, personal selling can be even more effective, especially in certain segments of the sport industry such as fitness clubs, sporting goods sales, and the sale of high-end professional seating options such as club seats and luxury suites. Sampling, trial usage, and open houses are designed to put the product in the hands of consumers with the intent of letting them "experience" it. Personal selling complements the "experience" by educating consumers about what they are experiencing and the benefits thereof. The fitness industry, for example, is a proponent of trial visits with professional instruction and attention. A sales presentation in the form of an interview between the salesperson and the consumer usually follows the workout. The topics of the interview usually include patterns of physical activity, fitness goals, and the benefits of the fitness club to the consumer's well-being.

Professional sport teams such as the Pittsburgh Pirates conduct open houses in conjunction with their personal selling efforts. The "open house," which occurs in the preseason, consists of stadium tours and entertainment activities—mascots, clinics, autographs—and the opportunity for potential consumers to sit in the seats available for sale. Balloons often mark these seats so potential consumers can identify the existing inventory and "check out the view." Once they are seated (indicating at least some level of interest), sales staff introduce themselves and initiate the personal selling process.

One common misperception about personal selling is that it is nothing more than verbal interaction between parties. Remember the axiom: "Actions speak louder than words." The consumer often interprets the actions taken by an organization—or, for that matter, those not taken—as evidence of what to expect in the future. Thus, hospitality management, staff interaction, and the way informational inquiries are handled are all key elements of the personal selling process. To paraphrase the Disney principle, an organization should take the approach "It's not doing one thing 100 percent better, it's doing 100 things 1 percent better." Disney's involvement in the management of the Anaheim Angels resulted in several changes: a name change, to give the consumer a feeling of ownership; a logo change, to give the consumer a sense of identity; changes in the structure of the ballpark, to provide a "parklike" atmosphere that communicated a theme-park image; and changes in service, to make the customer feel wanted, appreciated, and comfortable. Thus, Disney set the stage for personal selling efforts.

Personal selling is ideal for some types of ticket sales such as group sales, but is most commonly used in the sale of premium seating, suites, and luxury boxes. In regard to these particular products, personal selling can become "experiential selling" because a visit and trial methodology is an important aspect of the sale, and because the sales process usually begins with some type of orientation and education for the buyer. In a similar vein, sponsorships and all of their related assets are also best suited for personal selling.

Innovative Promotional Approaches for Selling Sport Products and Services

The unique nature of sport allows us to become highly imaginative in the sale of the sport product. Here we list some additional reminders.

◆ *Education can sell the fan base.* Albert G. Spalding discovered more than 100 years ago that if people understood his products (at that point, baseball equipment), they would be more likely to play the game and have a need to purchase his products. (41) Professional team sports, in particular hockey and football, have taken a similar approach and created "courses" such as Hockey 101 and Football 101 to educate the fan on the nuances and complexities of the game by simplifying and explaining the terminology. Teams such as the Dallas Mavericks have prepared printed materials to help fans become more aware—and hopefully to increase their interest in, and their consumption of, the product. Teams have also been known to offer clinics and demonstrations to help accomplish this educational process.

Innovative promotions can turn a negative into a positive, as the Pittsburgh Pirates know. During this game, fans kept dry with giveaway umbrellas.
© Associated Press

✦ *Remember your packaging.* Although we discussed promotions pertaining to sales in the previous chapter, one such promotion, tried by the New Jersey Nets, is relevant here because of its ability to attract trial users and because of its rather dramatic impact on sales. The Nets' speaker package was a three-game ticket plan targeted to New Jersey corporations and businesses as a way to enhance their companies. Lou Holtz, Tom Peters, and Harvey Mackay, packaged as motivational speakers, spoke for an hour prior to one of the three Nets games. Each speaker would appear on a particular date. The dates chosen were scheduled weeknight games against the three worst teams in the NBA, but all sold out through this package. (42) The Nets have since expanded the speaker series, and it has become part of the regular sales process.

✦ *Remember that fun is good.* The film *Field of Dreams* made famous the quote, "If you build it, they will come." This quotation now epitomizes the emphasis and dependence on building new stadiums and arenas to generate new revenue streams. However, beginning in the 1940s with Bill Veeck's giveaways and continuing in the 1990s with his son Mike, "If it's fun, they will come" has been the rally cry. The Veecks believed, and rightly so, that to attract fans you can't just sell your win–loss record. You have to sell the experience of a good time and the possibility of winning. Through their promotional flair, understanding of hospitality management (cleanliness and comfort), and their commitment to fun, they established attendance records at all levels. Veeck staples, such as giveaway days with promotional items such as bats, fireworks nights, and special theme nights, have become commonplace in baseball today. (43)

✦ *Couponing is not just for groceries and fast food.* One of the most common complaints about attending a sporting event is cost, particularly for families. The need for affordable family entertainment options is critical, and it's one that creative packaging can answer. Many sport organizations in both professional (major and minor league) and amateur sports (including those at colleges and universities) have developed and implemented one-price tickets for families. The "package" is usually based on four admissions, parking, and refreshments. Given that the traditional number of a family of four is less prevalent, many organizations prefer to offer their pricing on an individual basis, with packages beginning at

$11 per person, thus recognizing families can be smaller or larger than the traditional size of four. Some organizations elect to provide a souvenir (e.g., a cap), whereas others provide a sponsor's product. To take advantage of such offers, depending on how the redemption program is set up, the consumer redeems the coupon at the sponsor's place of business or at the team box office. As evidenced by Grant McKenzie's Blues Family Pack Initiative sidebar on this page, family nights are also a global attraction.

✦ *Remember the profitability and impact of group sales.* As discussed earlier in this book, sport consumers usually do not attend sporting events alone. Research has shown that less than 2 percent of fans attend games by themselves. We also noted that for some fans, it is the social interaction that defines their evening's enjoyment, and that for others the social component may be the sole reason for attending. For these reasons, sport organizations should make every attempt to attract and sell tickets to large groups (25 or more). Discounts (ranging from

Blues Family Pack Initiative

Grant McKenzie, marketing manager, Auckland Rugby/The Blues

Described here is a ticketing strategy designed by the Blues as part of the Rebel Sport Super 14 competition.

Tickets to the Family area are price-pointed with a discount if prepurchased (prior to match day), with an increase if purchased on game day. The family area is situated in a sideline position, albeit in uncovered seating. The capacity of this area is 3,200 seats and is sold out every game. The area is sponsored by Wizard Home Loans.

Part of the attraction of this offer is that children under 15 receive a "Footy Pack." This entertaining children's pack contains a "Bluebeard's Crew" blow-up sword, player autograph card, a pirate bandanna and eye patch, a beverage, and a delicious Nestlé product. Children redeem their tickets to receive the Footy Pack from designated distribution areas.

The Wizard Home Loans Family Area is located at the lower end of the main stand and is in close proximity to the field and the players. Although this area of the stand is uncovered and thus not as desirable in wet weather, it provides an up-close view of the game and the opportunity to meet the players following the match, as well as a chance to get autograph cards signed. This area is also used as a marketing tool to "dress up" the stadium, especially the bottom area of the main stand, which is in line with the flat camera angle during the filming of the game. The bright blue colors of the blown-up swords being waved back and fourth, as well as the popularity of this seating area, makes the stadium look full and thus provides a positive atmosphere from a television-viewing perspective and for those attending the game.

The family pack initiative also ties in with the marketing of Bluebeard, the Auckland Blues mascot, as well as the prematch entertainment of Bluebeard's pirate ship sailing around the field. As part of "Bluebeard's Crew" the children are encouraged to wave their swords like Bluebeard in support of the Blues throughout the game, once again adding to the game's atmosphere at Eden Park.

Rugby fans in Auckland, New Zealand, enjoying family night.
Courtesy of Grant McKenzie, marketing manager, Auckland Blues.

$1 to $3 per ticket depending on the size of the group), special seating sections, menus, and dining options (from catered sit-down dinners to casual buffets) are all effective means to attract groups to a sporting event. Groups can be Little League teams, scouts, employees, military units, college students—any collective that meets or exceeds the organizational minimum. The Pittsburgh Pirates are one of many sport organizations that offer birthday parties with their mascot (the Pirate Parrot) for groups of 10 or more. (44) See the "How Cool Would It Be" sidebar on page 303 for the Orlando Magic's approach to group sales.

Use Your Assets to Sell, Part I

One of the most successful sales campaigns in the history of the New Jersey Nets was the Influencer Program implemented prior to the 2005-2006 season. The signature marketing tool of Nets CEO Brett Yormark generated over $1 million in new season-ticket revenue for the Nets. (45) The program is built on connectivity, hospitality, star power, and face-to-face selling. The program begins by having a current season-ticket holder host 30 or so friends and business associates who are not season-ticket holders at his home or another setting such as a business. At this point the Nets take over, providing hospitality and catering services and entertainment—dance team and mascot. The Nets also select one or two key players from the team and a representative from the coaching staff to attend. The business side is represented, as well as Yormark or on some occasions Nets owner Bruce Ratner, and members of the marketing and sales staff are in attendance and provide a state-of-the-team overview before asking for the sale. According to star Nets player Jason Kidd, "The Nets are going out and not waiting for people to come to them. They're going out to pursue people and show them that they're going to be one of the most fan friendly franchises in the league." (46)

Use Your Assets to Sell, Part II

The goal of every sport marketer in the repeat attendance business is to provide consumers with an enjoyable experience and a lasting, positive memory that will encourage them not only to attend again but also to become customer evangelists—spreading the word to their friends and associates. One of the best ways to do that is to give them some personal connection to the event that anchors their experience. Group sales (previously discussed in this chapter) provide an ideal target for the selling of assets and creating a memorable experience for the purchaser(s). For example, the Orlando Magic offer dance clinics conducted by the Magic Dancers in the packaging of certain group tickets. The ticket price includes a clinic with the dancers during the day where participants work on a routine that they will perform with the Magic Dancers on-court during the game (see figure 12.5). Another option offered by the Magic and a number of other NBA teams (as well as teams in other sports) is the Court of Dreams. In this scenario, the group ticket provides basketball teams with an opportunity to play on the Magic Court—the actual court where NBA games are played—prior to or following the regularly scheduled NBA game. An asset such as the dance clinic is usually limited to the number of dancers the court can accommodate, whereas the Court of Dreams usually requires a minimum number of tickets (500) to be sold by the teams for the opportunity to play on the court. These are just two examples of the many assets that a sport organization can use to increase sales.

Sweepstakes   Enter to win, lucky fan promotions, specially marked packages, and the like have been part of sport sales for decades. What sport organizations have discovered is that these sweepstakes have to be highly targeted, be perceived to have high-value prizes and incentives, and have credible and convincing "pitchmen" with a high likeability index. PepsiCo's "Go Pro" and "Go Pro Al Volante" (Latino-targeted) are examples of the latest evolution of promotional sweepstakes activities. These promotions have ties with MLS, NASCAR, Major League Baseball, the And 1 Mixed Tape Tour, and the Dew Action Sports Tour and offer winners opportunities to win $100,000 and an ultimate sport pass to games or events of their choice. The "Al Volante" segment offers Univision viewers the opportunity win a new Honda Odyssey. (47) The success of a sweepstakes can usually be tied to product purchases or in this case tune-in behavior for a specified time frame.

STARZ DANCE STUDIO TO HOST **DANCE CLINIC**
WITH THE **ORLANDO MAGIC DANCERS!**
BEGINNERS THROUGH ADVANCED AGES 6-17

COMMITMENT
Fans. Team. Town

At Starz Dance Studio
1271 SR 436 #127 • Casselberry, FL 32707

SUNDAY, APRIL 23, 2006

Starbabiez, Starz I, Intermediate, Advanced: 12:30pm - 3:30pm (Check-In 11:45)
Starz II, Apprentice, Elite: 3:45pm - 6:45pm (Check-In 3:00)
Pre-registration – Lower Bowl: $75 • Upper Bowl: $50

Learn from the NBA's best...The Magic Dancers!
Ask how your school dance team or dance studio
performers can enter the **Orlando Magic State Dance
Championship** on Saturday, January 21, 2006!

Registration Includes:

★ Professional dance instruction by
  the Magic Dancers on 2 exciting
  routines in jazz and/or hip-hop!

★ 1 ticket to the Orlando Magic vs.
  Atlanta Hawks at 7pm on Monday,
  April 10th at 7pm!

★ All clinic participants will perform
  pre-game or halftime THAT NIGHT!

★ Door prizes, fun and excitement!

★ A Clinic T-Shirt

★ Team Photo Autographed by the
  Magic Dancers

magic dancers

LIMITED SPACE AVAILABLE. PRE-REGISTRATION HIGHLY RECOMMENDED.
Please turn in completed registration form and money to the front desk by Wed., Apr. 5th

LOWER BOWL SEATING OPTION

_____ x Dance Clinic registration fee (includes 1 game ticket) $75 $_____

_____ x # of Friends & Family tickets $40 (reduced ticket price) $_____

TOTAL $_____

UPPER BOWL SEATING OPTION

_____ x Dance Clinic registration fee (includes 1 game ticket) $50 $_____

_____ x # of Friends & Family tickets $20 (reduced ticket price) $_____

TOTAL $_____

DOB _____   T-SHIRT SIZE _____

❑ STARBABIEZ   ❑ STARZ I   ❑ STARZ II   ❑ APPRENTICE   ❑ INTERMEDIATE   ❑ ADVANCED   ❑ ELITE

PARTICIPANT _____ PHONE (WK) _____ PHONE (HM) _____

ADDRESS _____ CITY _____ STATE _____ ZIP _____

EMERGENCY CONTACT: _____ EMERGENCY PHONE: _____

PAYMENT TYPE: CHECK#_____ VISA__ MC__ AMEX___ DISC___ CARD#:_____ EXP. _____

SIGNATURE _____ E-MAIL _____

Please make checks payable to: **Starz Dance Studio.** Pre-
registrations must be turned in by April 5, 2006 in order to receive
the discount.

TD WATERHOUSE
CENTRE

FIGURE 12.5   Dance team clinics are one of the most popular assets for group dates.
Courtesy of Starz Dance Studio

May the Force Be With You   Being what it is, sport functions to attract people who want to do
more than just watch events: They want to identify and be identified with the sport organization. (48) Organizations have recognized this and have created some unique opportunities
for involving volunteers and charitable groups such as civic clubs in the sales process. The
Baltimore Orioles were the first to capitalize on recruiting volunteers from the community

How Cool Would It Be?
Group Sales Assets

Murray Cohn, senior director of ticket sales and service, Orlando Magic, and Shelly Driggers, assistant director of marketing

How cool would it be...just imagine playing on the same court as Dwight Howard and the Orlando Magic? Getting to high-five LeBron James? Performing on the same court as the Orlando Magic Dancers? Being recognized on the court in front of 17,000 of your closest friends?

These are a few of the opportunities made available by the Orlando Magic and the majority of NBA teams, which gives fans a once-in-a-lifetime opportunity to be a part of the game and drives group sales at the same time.

During the 2005-2006 season, the Orlando Magic led the NBA in group tickets sold involving assets, with over 46,000 tickets sold for these programs. In fact, 51 percent of all Magic group tickets sold were tied to one of these assets.

Some of the Orlando Magic's most popular assets are explained in the next few paragraphs. Please see the table for a complete list of assets and the ticket purchase required to secure an asset.

Court of Dreams

For every Magic home game, youth and adult groups have the opportunity to play where the pros play. The Magic has hosted regulation high school games, dance and basketball clinics, and corporate challenges for three hours on game days. For the past three years, the Orlando Magic has hosted the Lakeland Rotary vs. Lakeland Kiwanis Club Challenge, which benefits local community charity organizations. Bryce Philpot of the Lakeland Rotary Club stated that "the game is a chance for us to compete in athletics again in the largest arena. It may only be against another charitable group, but make no mistake, we want to win. The impact on our members does not stop when we walk off the court. The game has led to club support of several children's charities, renewed fellowship, and an increase in membership."

Kids Tunnels

Kids Tunnels give up to 25 kids, 5-16 years old, the chance to high-five the players as they are entering the court for warm-up, both pregame and at halftime. The Magic offer four of these per game, two for the Magic players and two for the visiting team. According to Deron Brown, season-ticket holder, avid Magic fan, and district manager for PCL Construction, "My son Dean, who celebrated his 10th birthday with the Magic, came home and claimed he will never wash his hand again! He said this was the best birthday party ever!"

Prime Time Court Time

Prime Time court time allows dance, cheer, karate, and gymnastics groups the opportunity to perform on the Orlando Magic court in front of thousands of fans 30 minutes before tip-off. The performances range from three to six minutes depending on the NBA team and give great visibility to the studio or gym that is performing on this stage. According to Michele Colon, owner and artistic director of Starz Dance Studio, "It is a wonderful experience for our dancers. The performance gives them a sense of pride and they really feel like they are a part of the Magic organization. We all look forward to it every year."

On-Court Recognition

The Orlando Magic offer companies, nonprofit groups, and sport teams the opportunity to be recognized for their achievements prior to tip-off or during halftime of all home games. Dillon Kalkhurst, vice president of One for the Community, and Rhett Kilmer, director of sales for Entertainment Publications, stated that "the kids involved in the check presentation said it was a thrill of a lifetime to be in front of 17,000 people and be recognized for all of their fund-raising efforts throughout the year. The kids and parents were elated. The experience is just priceless."

At the Orlando Magic, all of the assets mentioned above create Slam Dunk Moments, which people will tell their friends about. The value to the team is generating incremental revenue, creating positive goodwill in the community, and building fans for life.

✦ Group Ticket Package Assets 2005-2006

Asset	Minimum ticket purchase
Birthday parties	10
Kids Tunnel	50
NBA Kids Tunnel	50
"Prime Time" Court Time	100
Halftime*	250
Pregame/Halftime "On-Court" Recognition	100
Color guard	50
National Anthem*	50
Banquet/meeting space	30
Concourse Groups*	100
Court of Dreams	100 per hour
Group Captain of the Game	75
School Day	1,000
Read to Achieve School Assembly	300
Fund-raising	No minimum
Preferred Employer Night	Flyer Group

*Must be approved by marketing/game operations

(continued)

One of the Orlando Magic's most popular sales assets, "Prime Time court time," gives groups the opportunity to perform on court before a game.
Courtesy of the Orlando Magic

and having them function as a volunteer sales force. The Designated Hitters, as the Orioles call them, function as unpaid sales representatives of the organization, calling on their friends, relatives, and business associates to purchase tickets. The Designated Hitters do not receive a commission or wage but compete for prizes such as merchandise and trips to spring training.

On a slightly different note is the use of community groups, such as civic clubs, church groups, and Little League teams, in the sales process. These groups sell tickets and receive a percentage of the profits (via commission) to benefit their organizations. They usually buy the tickets or receive tickets on consignment at discounted prices. They then sell the tickets at face value, keeping the difference. The attraction for the organization is that these are tickets sold in some cases to benefit the charity—they would not have been sold by the team. A second benefit is the publicity and the positive public relations value of being a good citizen and assisting the community.

Web Sites   Web sites are an excellent way to sell directly or to use as a visual enhancement tool for telemarketers. Web sites can be equipped to take orders showing views of the arena. For example, to see Ballena's 3-D seats, follow these steps:

1. Go to the NBA.com Web site
2. Click on "Teams" and scroll to Memphis Grizzlies
3. Click on "visit Grizzlies.com"
4. Click on "ticket and seating"
5. Click on "seats in 3D" and follow the instructions to see virtual view of seating

Consumers can even use Web sites to chat with sales representatives. The Detroit Pistons and Intersight Technologies created a software system that allows visitors to the Pistons' Web site to chat live with ticket sales representatives. According to Michael Garrett, director of business systems for Palace Sports & Entertainment, the parent company of the Pistons: "On the phones, we have been able to up-sell ticket buyers into miniplan packages simply by discussing it with them prior to purchase. All we are doing is taking this process and merging it online giving benefits to our customers." (49) How successful is this approach? During the 2004-2005 NBA season, the Suns sold 40 percent of their single-game tickets online; five years prior, the Suns sold less than 5 percent of their tickets online. (50) The Suns' Web site permits fans not only to buy online, but also to print their tickets or forward them to someone else.

A model called the "club sandwich" is an excellent ticket-marketing strategy. It represents an attempt to create a model with a recipe for successful, balanced sales distribution. The intent of the club sandwich model is to ensure a balance and thus minimize overdependence on any one ticket-purchasing segment. The model ensures that there will always be consumers on all levels of the escalator (see chapter 10). In the club sandwich (see figure 12.6), the "meat" (our apologies to vegetarians), or main course, is the season-ticket holders.

Because the "meat" group is the one that attends the highest percentage of games, it is the most important ingredient in the club sandwich. Partial plans (entailing some level of precommitment and a large volume of games) and groups (involving a large volume of tickets) are the next most important ingredients in our sandwich. Our final stage of sandwich construction

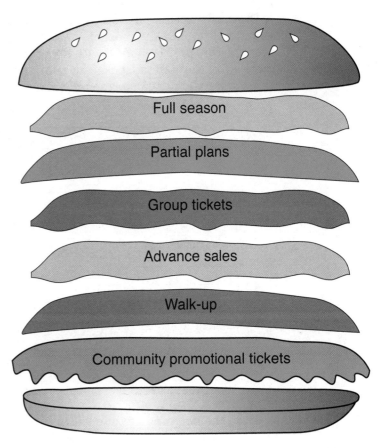

FIGURE 12.6 The "club sandwich": components of an effective ticket-sales plan.

consists of the "condiments," ingredients selected according to individual preference: a sport organization may prefer to use more than one condiment or to rely heavily on one condiment because the proverbial refrigerator is bare. Condiments include advance ticket sales (including those sold by in-house telemarketing, volunteers, and charitable groups), phone or outlet sales, walk-up and day-of-game sales, and complimentary tickets disbursed through community relations–based programs. Because the flavor of the club sandwich will change with changing ingredients or changing amounts of ingredients, so too will organizational profit margins (e.g., if there are too few season-ticket holders and too many groups or walk-ups). We recommend the following ingredients in the following proportions for a good-tasting and profitable club sandwich:

Season-ticket equivalencies (full and partial plans): 50 percent

Advance sales (telemarketing, volunteers, charitable, phone, and outlet): 25 percent

Group sales: 20 percent

Day-of-game and walk-up sales: 5 percent

Aftermarketing

The customer's lifetime value is defined as the present value of expected benefits (e.g., gross margin) minus the burdens (e.g., direct cost of servicing and communicating) associated with the customer. (51) Thus, for example, in terms of value, we should look at a season-ticket holder not as a $4,000-per-year purchaser but as someone who, depending on current age, could spend at least that amount and in addition pay for price increases, parking, and per capita items such as concessions—possibly a total of somewhere in the neighborhood of $100,000 plus—over a 20-year period.

Obviously, customers have different value levels to an organization depending on the amount of revenue they contribute, the costs of serving them, and the estimated length of time they are projected to be with the organization: The more valuable the customer is, the more effort the staff must exert to retain that customer. (52) Figure 12.7 illustrates how the value of a customer can be moderated.

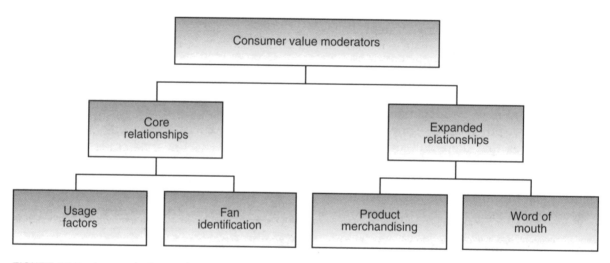

FIGURE 12.7 An organization can increase the value of a customer in a variety of ways.

Given the potential lifetime value of a customer, it becomes abundantly clear that certain activities and efforts must follow completion of the sale to ensure that the customer renews or becomes a repeat customer. The value of the fan as a customer is epitomized by San Francisco Giants' senior vice president of business affairs, Pat Gallagher, who developed an "upside-down organizational chart" (see figure 12.8) to illustrate to the Giants' staff just how important fans really are.

Gale suggested that there are four principles to ensure long-term customer relationships. These principles address the following issues:

- *Quality as conformance.* The product or service must conform to a set of standards and requirements.

- *Customer satisfaction.* The organization must get close to the customer, understand the customer's needs and expectations, and become customer driven.

- *Market-perceived quality versus that of competitors.* The organization must understand the strengths and weaknesses of the product and those of competitors through the eyes of the consumer—that is, understand why sales are won and lost.

- *Customer value management.* The organization should monitor the competition, determine its business goals, and align itself (people and processes) with the evolving needs of its targeted market. (53)

No matter how successful an organization is at servicing its clientele, there will always be some who discontinue their purchasing for one reason or another. Customers who leave an organization are often called defectors—because in effect they defect to another brand or organization. Defectors are costly to an organization, not only because the organization loses their lifetime value, but also because replacing them is very expensive (in terms of time

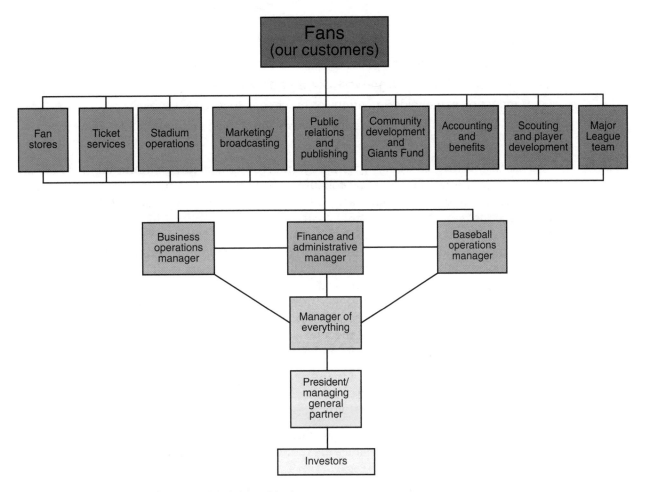

FIGURE 12.8 Upside-down organizational chart of fan importance.

Courtesy of Pat Gallagher, San Francisco Giants

and resources). According to some estimates, replacing a customer costs up to five times more than servicing an existing customer. (54) To prevent defection, the sport organization must employ activities and services collectively referred to as aftermarketing.

Aftermarketing has been defined by Vavra as "the process of providing continued satisfaction and reinforcement to individuals or organizations who are past or current customers. Customers must be identified, acknowledged, communicated with, audited for satisfaction, and responded to. The goal of aftermarketing is to build lasting relationships with all customers." (55) Or, in the words of noted authors Blanchard and Bowles, customers must become "raving fans" (56) so excited and pleased with the product that they not only remain loyal but also help attract new customers through word of mouth.

How can sport consumers become raving fans? Given the emotional nature of sport, sport consumers are already more emotional about their "product" than other consumers are about theirs. They have stronger feelings that elicit higher highs and lower lows. Because sport marketers don't control product composition or performance, they must aggressively strive to ensure customer satisfaction as it relates to product extensions, which are often service oriented. All sport organizations should develop a customer service program in the hopes of retaining customers and attracting new ones through their overall service quality and their demonstrated interest in the well-being of their customers. Sport organizations should develop customer service approaches that encompass at least the following:

+ Offering customized or personalized customer contact and treatment
+ Conducting regular customer satisfaction surveys or audits
+ Creating and sponsoring special events or activities for preferred customers

- ✦ Maintaining a database of current customers and defectors
- ✦ Publishing a proprietary magazine or newsletter for customers
- ✦ Offering an 800 telephone line, fax line, or e-mail address for customers
- ✦ Offering customers a frequency-incentive program
- ✦ Conducting stakeholder meetings or luncheons to gather feedback
- ✦ Providing shopping or purchasing services through a personal account representative (57)

Figure 12.9 illustrates a very simple way an organization can gain immediate feedback with regard to the satisfaction of its consumers—in this case, group attendees. This simple survey yields names for the database as well as a follow-up methodology through which sales personnel can contact potential customers for future offers. In terms of satisfaction and lifetime value, it can also function as an intervention vehicle—permitting staff to contact people who have indicated that they might not attend again to determine why, and also to determine whether the organization can do anything to secure their continued patronage.

The Miami Heat is known as an innovator in service and retention in the NBA. The strategy is guided by Kim Stone, the executive vice president and general manager of the Heat Group. Stone focuses on two key elements: superior service and empowerment.

To accomplish these, Stone and the staff developed the service "playbook," which spells out the department's mission, vision, and values. Following is the mission statement:

We believe every interaction is an opportunity to enhance the HEAT Experience. We will build positive relationships with our guests by addressing their needs in a timely manner and providing superior service. The ultimate goal is to create memories that last a lifetime.

The values include "Show Me the Way," which mandates that guests be personally escorted to an unfamiliar location. These values are reinforced daily during the "huddle," a 15-minute

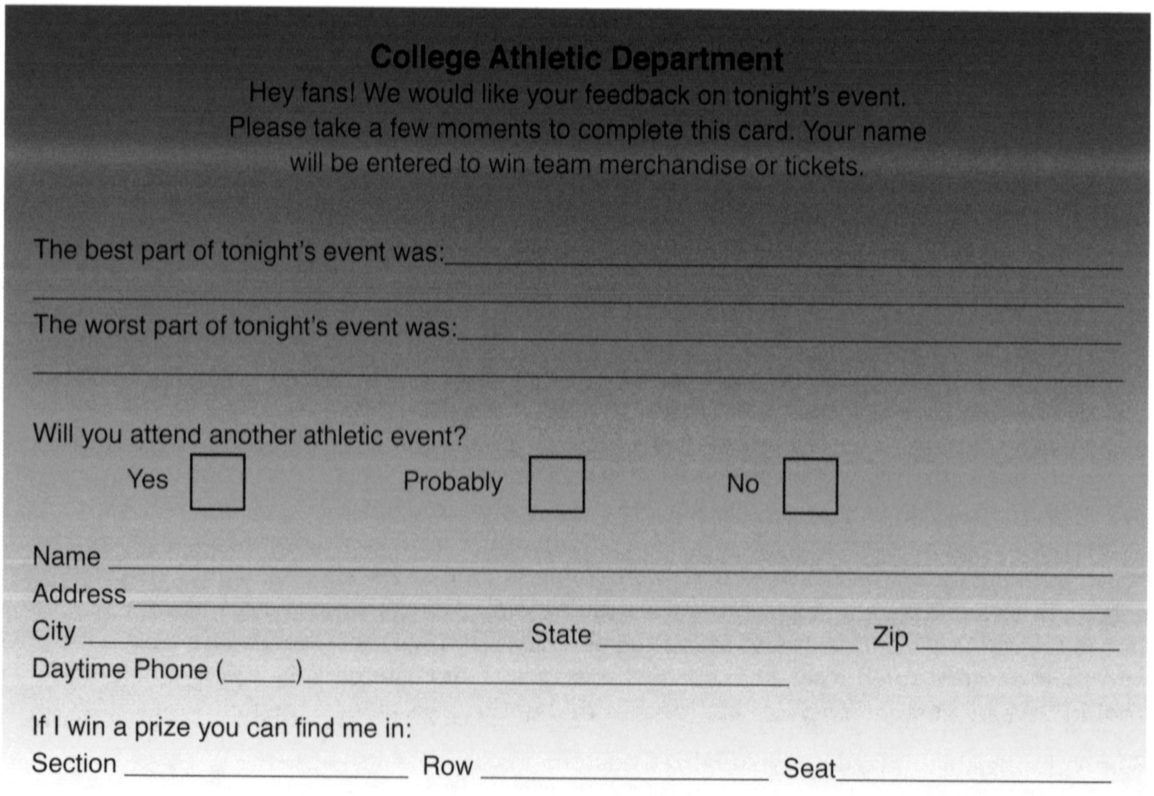

College Athletic Department
Hey fans! We would like your feedback on tonight's event.
Please take a few moments to complete this card. Your name
will be entered to win team merchandise or tickets.

The best part of tonight's event was:_____

The worst part of tonight's event was:_____

Will you attend another athletic event?

Yes ☐   Probably ☐   No ☐

Name _____

Address _____

City _____ State _____ Zip _____

Daytime Phone (_____)_____

If I win a prize you can find me in:

Section _____ Row _____ Seat_____

FIGURE 12.9 Group attendee satisfaction survey card.

refresher conducted by the staff. The playbook has empowered staff members to resolve issues without the intervention of upper management. Furthermore, each staff member is allotted a dollar amount to use at her discretion for resolving guest issues on the spot. Their decisions are never questioned, and no approval is required as long as they are guided by the playbook.

Another unique initiative is the HEAT Buddy Program. Since 2000, full-time staff members in various functional areas are given up to 20 season-ticket accounts that they are personally responsible for servicing and retaining. The accounts in this program have had retention rates above 90 percent for the last two years.

Customer Retention

In any industry, retaining current customers is the key to success for a number of reasons. Customer retention minimizes the number of new sales that must take place to be profitable and provides a stable base that can help attract new customers via referrals. It is also an indicator to the public that customers appear to be satisfied with what they have purchased. And customer retention maximizes the customer's lifetime value (LTV) to the organization.

Lifetime Value (LTV)

Customers should be viewed as an organizational asset, and like an asset their value can grow and appreciate. Usually customer retention is predicated on product use, product satisfaction, and the attitude of the consumer based on her experiences and interaction with the organization. In short, if a customer is content with what she has purchased and believes she is valued by the organization, she will not seek out another provider. That is not to say that she will not switch to another provider who contacts her with a better offer or an attractive incentive. It merely means that she won't proactively seek such a change.

Because we have focused on tickets and attendance at sporting events for much of this book, let's examine the case of a ticket-plan purchaser for a professional sport franchise. Season tickets (as few as 10 games for an NFL team and as many as 81 games for a baseball team) or partial ticket plans (anywhere from half the number of games to as a few as three in a miniplan) are the keys to successfully filling the stadium or arena. So what are the factors that affect the retention of ticket-plan purchasers?

- ✦ Satisfaction with the price/value relationship of the purchase
- ✦ Satisfaction with seat location
- ✦ Use of the benefits and amenities included in their purchase
- ✦ Enjoyment in attending the games
- ✦ Customer service and quality of information
- ✦ Performance of the team
- ✦ Convenience factors relating to attending in person
- ✦ Demand for tickets in the marketplace
- ✦ Ease of distributing or recouping investment on unused tickets
- ✦ Feeling valued and appreciated by the organization
- ✦ Problem resolution and ease of resolution

All of these factors influence the lifetime value of the season-ticket holder, which is defined as the financial return from each consumer to the organization over the course of that relationship. Thus the financial return would include not only tickets, but also any other purchases related to those tickets—parking, food and beverage, souvenirs, merchandise, game programs, and so forth. Let's assume a season-ticket account holder is spending $3,000 annually with a professional sport franchise. Over a 10-year period the value of that relationship is at least $30,000—which is not reflective of any price increases in any of the services mentioned. If 10,000 account holders are each spending the same $3,000 per year, the amount of revenue the organization could hope to collect over that 10-year period would be at least $300 million. However, that can only be realized with a retention rate of 100 percent. If, say, only 80 percent were retained over that period, the amount would decrease to $240 million More important, it would indicate that the organization would lose its entire initial base (3,000 accounts) after five years (losing 600 accounts per year for five years).

Jack Mitchell, author of *Hug Your Customers*, suggested that finding ways to "hug" your customers is the key to establishing and maintaining a satisfied client base that will remain loyal and attract others through spreading the word about their experiences. How does Mitchell do this? By finding "ways to make his customers say WOW!" (58) Organizations that go out of their way to "hug" their customers—sending anniversary cards, having the mascot wish their child a happy birthday, and the like—often have skyrocketing retention rates. Moreover, every sale becomes an incremental sale, not a replacement sale.

Tips for Effective Implementation

The sales process is one of the most vital functions of a sport organization because it ensures the organization's growth and longevity. Sales campaigns must be clearly focused and have predetermined goals and objectives. To effectively implement a productive sales campaign, a sport organization must do the following:

+ Hire and train a specialized sales force.
+ Support this sales force through a well-thought-out management and development plan.
+ Create and maintain an effective database that can be targeted in a variety of ways to reach the appropriate target market segments.
+ Use the sales techniques and methodologies most appropriate to communicate with the target market and encourage them to perform.
+ Produce and distribute sales materials that will effectively communicate the organization's offer to the target market.
+ Emphasize relations with consumers and partnerships with sponsors—and realize the long-term value of every relationship.
+ Implement a customer relations program that is proactive rather than reactive in dealing with customers.
+ Have a three-year plan: Crawl in the first year, walk in the second, and run in the third. Increase the number of sellouts every year.
+ Pick the dates that are the easiest to sell and concentrate your efforts on those dates. To create a sellout, use the power promotions approach: the best date, best opponent, and best promotions (events or giveaways).
+ Because total ticket-sales revenue is the critical factor, not just meat in the seats, don't discount season tickets.
+ Put on an exciting sport entertainment product that encourages repeat business—"sell the sizzle and the steak."
+ Develop a comprehensive ticket-sales plan and ensure that you have enough staff to implement it.
+ Advertise, promote, and preach to the choir: Use direct mail and telemarketing only to known fans and participants in your sport (from your database). Let your fans sell to nonfans through word of mouth, proclaiming the value and benefits of your sport or entertainment product.
+ Develop loyalty programs for repeat purchasers.

- Use programs and promotions to increase the attendance frequency of existing fans.
- Create a retention department that concentrates its activities on retaining current customers.
- Whenever possible, use players and coaches (past and present) to contact every season-ticket holder, during the season if possible.
- Don't be afraid to try new and creative ideas even if some innovations fail.

Wrap-Up

Sales is the revenue-producing element of the marketing process. Marketing is communication, and as such, the sales process involves a high level of two-way communication. A salesperson must listen and assess as well as talk. Depending on the organization, some sales staffs specialize in selling some of the products that we have discussed, such as group tickets or season tickets. Other sales staffs sell a variety of products but might specialize in one type of methodology such as telemarketing or personal selling. As this chapter has pointed out, there are a variety of products to sell in the sport industry and a variety of methodologies with which to sell them. Because of this variety, effective training and management of sales personnel are necessary to ensure that they understand the products they are selling, the prospective consumers to whom they are selling, and the appropriateness and benefits of each methodology they might choose to employ to complete the sale.

The sales department of a sport organization contains the largest number of job positions and is responsible for the largest percentage of revenue. Marketing leadership in the organization usually comes from people who began as members of the sales staff. Therefore, we can make a correlation and state that success in marketing usually has some basis in sales—and that successful marketers understand and can manage the sales process of an organization.

Retention has a significant impact on sales because it can dictate how much effort is necessary to replace lost customers before the resources and energies of the sales staff can be used for securing new customers and growing both the customer base and the revenue base. This is particularly true given that estimates regarding the cost of replacing a season-ticket holder with a new one can range as high as 17 to 1 ($17 dollars in cost to $1 in revenue).

Activities

1. Identify someone you recognize as a leader in the area of sport marketing. Obtain the person's bio or profile (these can usually be found on the corporate or organizational Web site). How does the person's current position or past activities reflect sales experience?

2. Visit a stadium or arena in your town to conduct a sales inventory. What items constitute the inventory that has been sold? What items have not been sold?

3. Using the inventory that you prepared, analyze the inventory items that have not been sold. Select an appropriate sales methodology for each unsold inventory item.

4. Interview someone with sport marketing responsibilities in an athletics department, fitness facility, or pro sport organization, and ask about the person's duties. Ask what percentage of the person's time is devoted to sales activities. What methodologies does he or she employ? How does he or she train the sales staff? How did the person begin in the business?

5. Visit with a small business, athletics department, or minor league team in your area. Offer to help calculate the lifetime value of a season-ticket holder based on average per capita spending and the prices associated with the various ticket plans offered by the organization.

6. Assess your career plans. Is there a sales component in the job you envision? What will it require for you to attain this position? Begin compiling a roster of people in similar positions. You can use this roster to gather information and advice as you initiate your job search.

Your Marketing Plan

In the successful implementation of a marketing plan, objectives must be identified and achieved. Sales, in terms of a revenue-production target goal, are usually accounted for in formulating the objectives leading to a goal. Sales are also viewed as strategies or tactics that are integral in achieving objectives and, ultimately, in reaching goals. In reviewing your marketing plan, how do you see sales fitting in? Do you have an objective that might be stated in sales terms relating to increasing organizational revenue? For example, an objective such as, "Increase attendance (membership, if you are interested in the fitness industry or other membership-based industry segments such as golf or tennis clubs) over last year's levels by 12 percent" implies that some sales strategies and tactics are necessary to achieve the objective. Review your objectives and select sales methodologies and approaches that will help you reach your objectives.

Chapter 13

Promotional Licensing and Sponsorship

Objectives

✦ To illustrate the relationship between the sport organization and the corporate sponsor.

✦ To provide an understanding of the scope of sponsorship and promotional licensing.

✦ To develop a comprehension of the motivations and rationale for the use of sponsorship by corporations and sport entities.

Sponsorship Fit: The Opportunity Must Make Sense for the Sponsor

A film sponsorship of a sailing race? Promoting movies through sports—once a rare occurrence—has become increasingly popular, as movies such as *Batman Begins* and *Ocean's 12* have shown with recent tie-ins to motor sports. However, Disney has taken the concept and created an opportunity that places its sponsorship position on a global platform to promote a movie on an international scale. Disney's *Pirates of the Caribbean 2: Dead Man's Chest* was released in the summer of 2006, and in an attempt to gain international exposure and a chance to attract media attention for the movie outside of the traditional entertainment press, Disney accepted a sponsorship proposal in excess of $15 million. The Volvo Ocean Race is a truly global affair that features competition between seven boats with 10-man crews who are charged with guiding their boats more than 32,700 miles between November and June. The race is considered the Mount Everest of sailing.

Let's look at how the sponsorship worked in meeting Disney's objectives:

- ✦ Disney named the boat—The Black Pearl—after the film, and the boat's number, USA 7706, refers to the scheduled release of the film on July 7, 2006.

- ✦ Disney built a brand around the boat, selling *Pirates of the Caribbean* crew caps and other clothing

- ✦ Disney developed a Web site (www.blackpearl racing.com) that mixed audio from the film with regular crew updates, photos, and a link to the movie trailer. It also had streaming video that mixed the movie's score with footage of the boat racing across the ocean.

- ✦ The event was televised weekly in more than 200 countries on weekly programs and news outlets.

- ✦ The race was shown on ESPN in a one-hour special during the week of the movie's release.

- ✦ Disney created events and generated publicity at various international stopovers during the race.

- ✦ The boat and the crew hosted sailing trips for Disney corporate partners.

- ✦ The captain, Paul Cayard, wrote a blog for the Web site on the exploits of the boat and the crew.

Based on the success of this venture, Volvo Ocean Race representatives are discussing a new event: a Pacific Ocean race that would stop in China and Japan. With the third film of the *Pirates* series set in Asia, this looks like a sponsorship match made in...Hollywood. (1)

Disney's *Pirates of the Caribbean* yacht was a unique way to promote the movie *Pirates of the Caribbean 2: Dead Man's Chest*.

© AP Photo/Lalo R. Villar

In this chapter, we examine the integrated nature of sponsorship. Sponsorship activities are more integrated than other promotional activities and contain a variety of marketing mix elements. Although a number of marketing mix elements can function as stand-alones (e.g., an open house, discounts on tickets, community relations programs), a sponsorship usually involves two or more of the elements of the marketing mix to provide sponsors with association, recognition, value, exposure, and opportunities to help them achieve their marketing objectives. In this chapter, we examine those objectives and opportunities.

Sponsorship Defined

Consider the following activities: Blockbuster Video obtaining the video rights to MLB; (2) *USA Today* sponsoring all-star ballots for MLB; Target's entitlement of the LPGA's Fan Village; and Mattel's production of Barbie dolls in the cheerleading apparel of Oklahoma State University and other collegiate athletics programs. What do all these have in common? They represent the types of promotional licensing agreements that have become commonplace in sport and lifestyle marketing. *Promotional licensing* is really an umbrella term that encompasses sponsorship, but *sponsorship* has proven to be the accepted term throughout the world. Therefore, throughout this chapter and the text, we use the term *sponsorship* to refer to the acquisition of rights to affiliate or directly associate with a product or event for the purpose of deriving benefits related to that affiliation or association. The sponsor then uses this relationship to achieve its promotional objectives or to facilitate and support its broader marketing objectives. The rights derived from this relationship may include retail opportunities, purchase of media time, entitlement (the inclusion of the sponsor name in the event or facility name, e.g., the McDonald's LPGA Championship or the RCA Dome), or hospitality. Sponsorship agreements may include, but are not necessarily limited to, the following provisions and benefits:

- The right to use a logo, a name, a trademark, and graphic representations signifying the purchaser's connection with the product or event. These rights can be used in advertising, promotion, publicity, or other communication activities employed by the purchaser.
- The right to an exclusive association within a product or service category.
- The right of entitlement to an event or facility.
- The right to use various designations or phrases in connection with the product, event, or facility such as *official sponsor, official supplier, official product,* or *presented by.*
- The right of service (use of the product or exclusive use of the product) or the right to use the purchaser's product or service in conjunction with the event or facility.
- The right to conduct certain promotional activities, such as contests, advertising campaigns, or sales-driven activities, in conjunction with the sponsorship agreement (see photo).

Sponsorship, then, includes a wide array of activities associated with a communications process that is designed to use sport and lifestyle marketing to send messages to a targeted audience. The amount of money spent on sport and special-event sponsorships, as well as the number of sponsorships, has grown dramatically (see figure 13.1).

Sponsorship's Place Within the Marketing Mix

As previously discussed, the marketing mix comprises variables that fall into five broad categories: product, price, promotions, place (distribution), and public relations. The marketer's function is to manipulate these variables to meet the target market's needs in a continually changing environment (see figure 13.2).

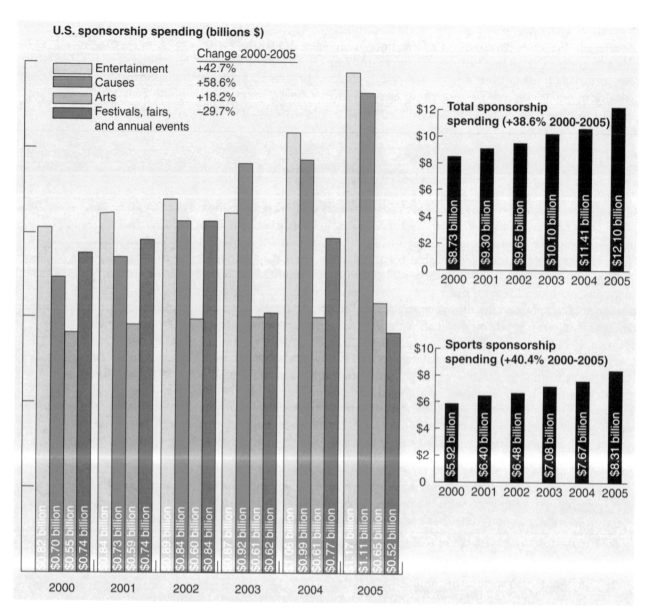

U.S. sponsorship spending (billions $)

	Change 2000-2005
Entertainment	+42.7%
Causes	+58.6%
Arts	+18.2%
Festivals, fairs, and annual events	−29.7%

Total sponsorship spending (+38.6% 2000-2005)

2000	2001	2002	2003	2004	2005
$8.73 billion	$9.30 billion	$9.65 billion	$10.10 billion	$11.41 billion	$12.10 billion

Sports sponsorship spending (+40.4% 2000-2005)

2000	2001	2002	2003	2004	2005
$5.92 billion	$6.40 billion	$6.48 billion	$7.08 billion	$7.67 billion	$8.31 billion

2000: $0.82 billion, $0.70 billion, $0.55 billion, $0.74 billion
2001: $0.84 billion, $0.73 billion, $0.59 billion, $0.74 billion
2002: $0.89 billion, $0.84 billion, $0.60 billion, $0.84 billion
2003: $0.87 billion, $0.92 billion, $0.61 billion, $0.62 billion
2004: $1.06 billion, $0.99 billion, $0.61 billion, $0.77 billion
2005: $1.17 billion, $1.11 billion, $0.65 billion, $0.52 billion

FIGURE 13.1   Growth of sponsorship.

Reprinted, by permission, from *Street & Smith's SportsBusiness Journal*, March 27, 2006, pg. 37.

As a key component of the marketing mix, promotions are often referred to by contemporary theorists as the "communications mix." (3) (See figure 13.3.) In comparison to many other promotional activities, which are often stand-alones, sponsorship activities are more integrated and are composed of a variety of marketing and promotional components.

As discussed in chapter 11, the role of promotions is to inform and persuade the customer and thus influence the consumer's purchase decision. The elements of the promotions/communications mix are traditionally considered to be advertising, personal selling, publicity, and sales promotion. Combinations of some or all of these elements are inherent in sponsorship activities (see figure 13.4).

One sponsorship activity that combines personal selling and promotion is hospitality. Hospitality opportunities are a sponsor benefit commonly associated with premier events such as the Super Bowl, Daytona 500, or the NCAA Final Four. One can define hospitality as the provision of tickets, lodging, transportation, on-site entertainment, and special events to the sponsor. The sponsor can in turn use these benefits to entertain its own clients or to reward customers for their longtime support or volume of purchases. In this guise, the sponsorship acts as a form of personal selling, because it enables the sponsor to conduct activities through face-to-face contact with key customers. This sponsorship also functions as promotion, because it is promoting the company to current and potential clients.

Sponsorship benefits and relations could also be used in a combined advertising and sales promotion campaign. For example, Quaker State might use a relationship with NASCAR to conduct a national sales promotion that could include a sweepstakes for an all-expense-paid trip to the Daytona 500 and an opportunity to meet Richard Petty. The contest could be promoted using special on-track signage, television advertising, and retail point-of-purchase displays. Thus, the sponsor has the opportunity to integrate a number of the elements of the promotional/communications mix in any sponsorship relationship.

One should realize that the costs the sponsor incurs to promote or leverage its affiliation or association with the sport organization come in addition to those costs—usually referred to as licensing or partnership fees—that grant the sponsor the relationship. For example, Sprite is a sponsor, actually a corporate partner, of the NBA. Sprite pays an annual fee to the NBA in exchange for the affiliation with the NBA and receives certain benefits that include at least the following:

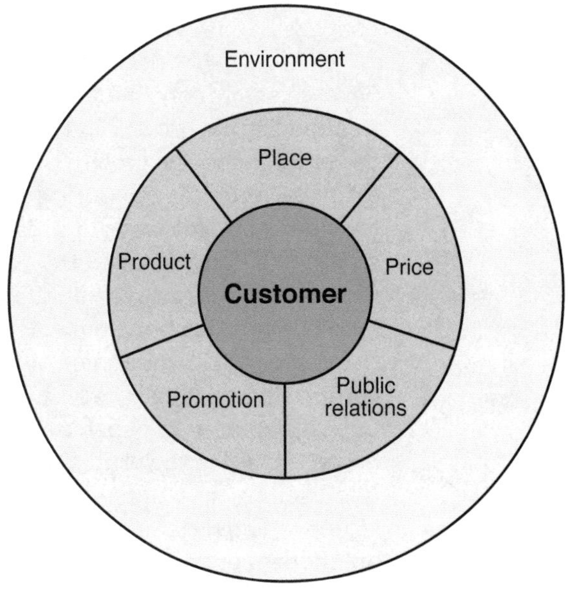

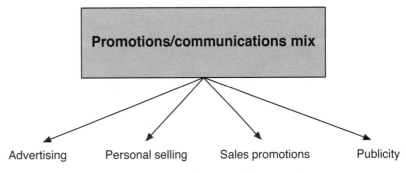

FIGURE 13.2   The marketing mix components.

✦ Category exclusivity (no direct competitors, because Sprite is a corporate partner; therefore, any soft-drink products not affiliated with the Coca-Cola family of products cannot be granted any sponsorship or promotional rights)

✦ Use of NBA registered trademarks, official product designation ("Sprite is the official soft drink of the NBA All-Star Game")

✦ Preferred ticket packages to the NBA All-Star Weekend

✦ The right to conduct in-store promotions and create point-of-purchase displays featuring NBA marks and agreed-on NBA players

✦ The right to conduct national promotional activities and contests associated with the NBA All-Star Weekend—such as NBA All-Star balloting.

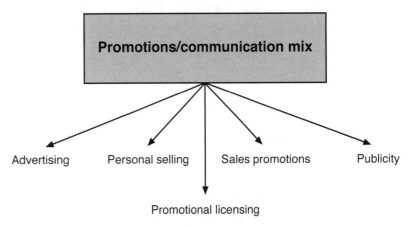

FIGURE 13.3   The traditional promotions/communications mix.

FIGURE 13.4   A broader promotions/communications mix.

Thus, when NBA corporate-partner Sprite engages in its annual NBA All-Star balloting promotion, which involves fans voting for their favorite NBA players in NBA arenas, online, and through various retail outlets, all costs associated with the promotion are assumed by Sprite and are in addition to the fee paid by Sprite to be an NBA corporate partner.

The Growth of Sponsorship

Several factors contributed to the growth of sport sponsorship in the late 1970s and continued to support this growth in the 1990s. The marketing literature shows some agreement that the emergence and growth of sponsorships coincided with the ban on tobacco and alcoholic drink advertising. (4) During that time, tobacco and alcoholic drink manufacturers were forced to look for ways of promoting their products other than through direct-advertising channels. Banning cigarette ads from the airways in 1971 was a triumph for antitobacco forces. However, as a result, these companies had to redirect their massive advertising clout (and budgets) to sport sponsorships. (5) The *IEG Sponsorship Report* noted that in 1997, tobacco firms spent $195 million on sport sponsorships—95 percent of it in the area of motor sport, comprising about 20 percent of the total sponsorship revenue for that sport segment. (6)

Companies with substantial advertising budgets gradually discovered that there was too much "noise" in the print and electronic media. The average person is exposed to more than 5,000 selling messages each day, making separation and retention of information difficult. Moreover, advertising costs, especially in television, continue to rise (see figure 13.5 for a breakdown of ad spending in 2004 and projections for 2006). For example, advertising costs for the NFL's 2004 Super Bowl amounted to $2.3 million for a 30-second ad spot, (7) almost six times more than the cost of the same sponsorship 10 years before. (8) By developing an alternative channel of communication via sport sponsorships, companies found that they could achieve new levels of exposure, in many cases at lower costs than through advertising campaigns. Figure 13.6 provides some insight into annual sponsorship spending by those corporations most vested in sponsorship activities. (9)

Promotional licensing and sponsorship agreements skyrocketed as the public and the sport governing bodies increasingly accepted the commercialization of sport. See figure 13.7 to get an idea of the use of sponsorship, advertising, and sales promotion from 1994 to 1998. The 1984 Los Angeles Olympics were the first privately organized Olympics in history, and a landmark in the evolution of corporate sponsorship and promotional licensing through

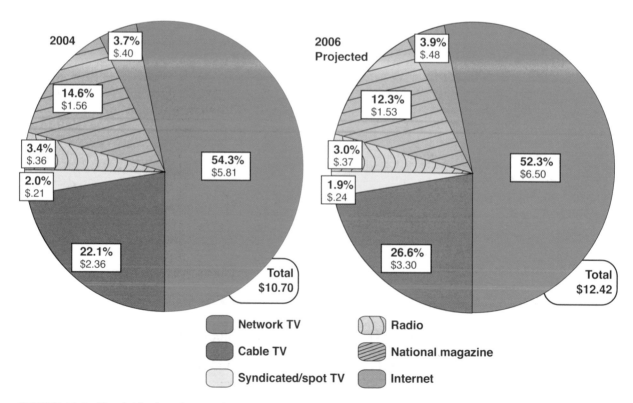

FIGURE 13.5 The distribution of sport ad spending (in millions) for 2004 and projected for 2006.

Reprinted, by permission, from *Street & Smith's SportsBusiness Journal*, March 27, 2006, pg. 37.

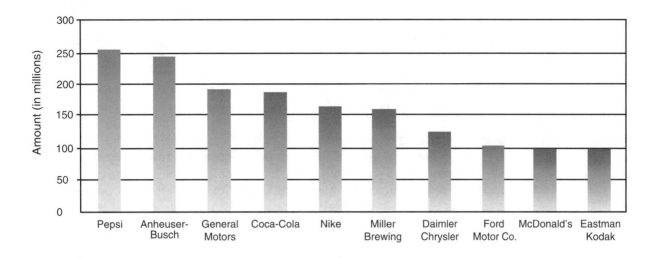

FIGURE 13.6 Top sport sponsors in the United States.

sport. The 1984 Olympic sponsors received significant media exposure and to some extent positive image building, while the games generated a profit for the Los Angeles Olympic Organizing Committee (LAOOC). Peter Ueberroth, president of the LAOOC, inaugurated his dream of a corporately subsidized Olympics by limiting the number of Olympic sponsors to 30 to avoid clutter and duplication—as well as to ensure category exclusivity. (10) Thus, Ueberroth was able to increase the value of a sponsorship in relation to the increased cost of those same sponsorships. By demonstrating that as cost increased there was a subsequent increase in value, Ueberroth demonstrated that sponsorships actually became partnerships because they were mutually beneficial for both the sport (property) and the sponsor (corporations). Experiences such as the 1984 Olympics and other mutually beneficial relationships helped give rise to the term *corporate partners,* suggesting that sponsorships could be

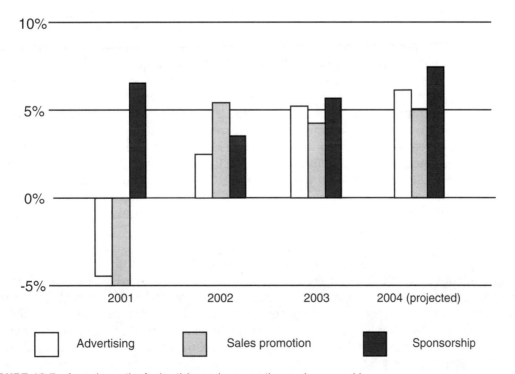

FIGURE 13.7 Annual growth of advertising, sales promotion, and sponsorship.

partnerships whereby partners who hope to achieve benefits work in harmony to create a desirable result.

Because sponsorship has been effective, sponsorship costs have risen. To combat those costs and to retain control, some deep-pocketed companies have created and own their own events. In 1997, Nike announced the launch of Nike Sports Entertainment, a division of Nike that will initiate, produce, and control its own events. According to Ian B. Campbell, the manager of Nike's Sports Entertainment division, "Asset acquisition is costing more; players and teams are more expensive than they were six months ago. I think if you are going to invest in an athlete or a team asset anywhere in the world, you've really got to justify what you're doing from an overall brand perspective and make sure it really is a total package. Why pay a third party to do that for you or interpret that for you or screw it up for you, when really you probably ought to do it for yourself." This philosophy of ownership and locus of control was a prime motivator for NBC along with Clear Channel to create and launch, with corporate partner Mountain Dew, the Dew Action Sports Tour in 2005. (11)

Another factor in the growth of sport sponsorship has been the increased media interest in sport programming, attributable mainly to the following:

+ The general public's increased leisure time and interest in sport
+ The increased commercialization of television through commercials and infomercials
+ The fact that it is less costly for television networks to broadcast sporting events than to produce shows or documentaries
+ The growth of new media sources, such as subscription services via cable or satellite transmissions and pay-per-view special events, which have increased the demand for live sport programming and provided additional channels of exposure for sport as well as sponsors

An example of a new media source is Direct TV, a satellite subscription service that offers a wide array of sport-viewing options for the sport enthusiast—and also for sponsors. Direct TV offers all its subscribers access to ESPN, ESPN2, ESPN Classic, and ESPNews, and recently launched ESPNU as a basic benefit. In addition, the basic subscriber receives the local premium sport channel at no extra charge. Thus, a subscriber in New England would receive the New England Sports Network for free as well. The next level of service gives the viewer an all-sports package, which includes all regional sport channels (including SportsChannel and Fox Sportsnet) and the Golf Channel, for a total of 29 channels for a monthly charge of $12. This is also a great opportunity for sponsors, who can select regions of the country or individual cities in which to promote their products or events. Finally, Direct TV, which has agreements with the major sport leagues, can offer subscription-based packages ranging from a low of $60 per season to a high of $169 per season. These packages include the NFL Sunday Ticket, MLB Extra Innings, NBA League Pass, NHL Center Ice, and ESPN's Game Plan packages for NCAA football and basketball and the March Madness package for complete coverage of Rounds 1 and 2 of the NCAA basketball tournament—once again, providing sponsors with a segmentation tool based on the demographics of the particular sport.

Whatever the reasons for increased sport coverage, companies were quick to capitalize on the exposure opportunities provided via sport sponsorship. At the same time, dramatic changes in consumer lifestyles offered another opportunity for sport-related sponsorship. Increased participation in fitness and sporting activities, the value placed on leisure time, and a high demand for fitness and sport opportunities all provided sport with more visibility, giving sponsors and other licensees a credible vehicle for communicating their commercial messages. In fact, it was a desire to reach Generation X through their nontraditional sport activities—skateboarding, snowboarding, and other outdoor activities with an element of risk—that led to the commercially successful X Games, developed and produced by ESPN and warmly welcomed by sponsors such as Mountain Dew and Nike, who wanted an opportunity to tap into this market.

Changes in governmental policies also contributed to the growth of sport sponsorship. Within the United States, sports have been, and continue to be, financed through the private sector. In Canada, Europe, and Asia, government funding was (and in many situations still is) the primary source. In economically difficult times, when governments reduced support for sport, corporations and industry felt pressure from the public to fill the gap. Social and environmental problems, coupled with increased awareness of corporate responsibilities to the local markets, led companies to pursue opportunities to improve perceptions of their corporate images, their activities, and their roles in society at large.

A final reason for the growth of sport sponsorship is that marketing has become increasingly global. Figure 13.8 depicts the amount of money spent on sponsorship throughout the world in 2004-2005 and how the $80 billion in total sport spending projected for this year will be divided.

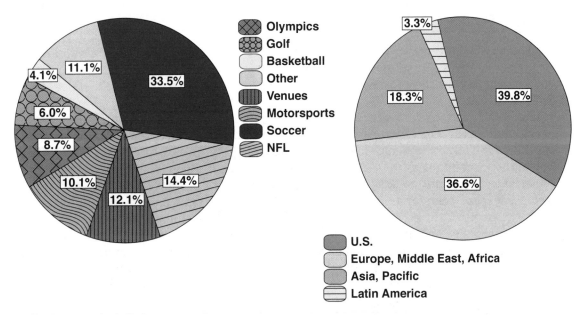

FIGURE 13.8   Global sport sponsorship spending, 2004-2005.
Reprinted, by permission, from Street & Smith's SportsBusiness Journal, March 27, 2006, pg. 44.

Multinational companies have found it increasingly difficult to communicate with their target markets in so many different languages and cultures. Sport sponsorships and licensing programs offer a unique way to bridge language and cultural barriers; this is one of the reasons the Olympics and other major international events such as the World Cup, McDonald's Challenge (basketball), and others receive such huge support from a broad range of corporate entities. In keeping with the global movement, professional teams have already begun to change their names or to incorporate the names of sponsors into their uniforms to accommodate the communication needs of companies operating in the now-unified European market.

Because of cultural, societal, and language barriers, companies that operate in Europe and throughout the world will probably use sport marketing programs increasingly to segment and effectively communicate with their target markets. Witness Nike's record 10-year, $400 million sponsorship of the Brazilian soccer team. The deal, which Nike made in hopes of growing its presence worldwide and establishing credibility in the area of soccer, grants the company not only merchandising rights, but also the rights to stage and broadcast five events per year with the team. (12) Such events may have a grassroots element that will provide exposure for Nike with emerging and developing players, as well as the opportunity to showcase and associate Nike with one of the most successful and respected soccer teams in the world.

What Does Sport Sponsorship Have to Offer?

During the 1970s, marketing through sport often served the personal interests of top executives or else served as a vehicle for charitable contributions. But beginning in the early 1980s, marketing through sport became a discipline involving serious research, large investments, and strategic planning. As the economic fortunes of companies changed, companies needed to prioritize their spending and justify the expenditures. They had to find a return on investment (ROI) and to allocate their sponsorship dollars wisely. What rationale and benefits can sport offer to its prospective corporate partners?

By marketing through sport, a company attempts to reach its target consumers through their lifestyles. According to Hanan, "life-styled" marketing is "a strategy for seizing the concept of a market according to its most meaningful recurrent patterns of attitudes and activities, and then tailoring products and their promotional strategies to fit these patterns." (13) Corporate marketing executives of both large and small companies have found that linking their messages to leisure pursuits conveys these messages immediately and credibly. The rationale is that leisure is a persuasive environment through which to relate a sales message to target consumers. The association of the company or product with the event is also important, because sporting events are well accepted by the public and have a strong fan following. By establishing a link with an event, a company shares the credibility of the event itself while delivering its message to a consumer who is apt to be relaxed and thus more receptive.

In addition, certain events enable the marketer to reach specific segments such as heavy users, shareholders, and investors, or specific groups that have been demographically, psychographically, or geographically segmented. Healthy Choice has become the official nutritional consultant to the U.S. ski team—the first sport sponsorship the company has undertaken. According to Mike Trautschold, president of ConAgra Brands, "Our goal is to create a deeper understanding of our message. Advising the team enables us to demonstrate our big strength to the consumer. Team members are young, vital people, who are not willing to compromise on nutrition or taste, so it's an exciting message for our consumers." (14) Another example is Audi, which signed sponsorship agreements with equestrian events, ski races, and sailing after research indicated that participants in and followers of these events were typical Audi buyers. Jay Houghton, marketing manager for Audi, observed, "We try to reach consumers who understand and appreciate the integration of the driver and vehicle, pilot and vessel, rider and horse." (15)

Exclusivity

Often a company will negotiate a sponsorship or licensing agreement that designates that company as the exclusive sponsor. The benefit of this type of sponsorship is a high level of exposure without the competition and clutter of traditional advertising. In other words, sponsorship can serve as a more subtle alternative to advertising; sponsorship may communicate the company's message in a "different," "new," and "less commercial" form. An example of exclusive sponsorship is the program developed by the International Olympic Committee (IOC) under the name TOP. For the first time, during the 1988 Seoul Olympics, the IOC designed worldwide exclusivity contracts that gave companies in various product categories exclusive rights to use the Olympic rings logo anywhere in the world. Exclusivity was a major factor in attracting sponsors to the WNBA. Lee Jeans, one of the four WNBA inaugural sponsors, entered into a three-year agreement with the league. Lee Jeans receives category exclusivity on all three WNBA television networks: NBC, ESPN, and Lifetime. (16)

Heightened Communication

Communications through traditional advertising channels are often hit-or-miss. The targeted reader, viewer, or listener may or may not be exposed to the message. Sponsorship

The WNBA attracted Lee Jeans as a sponsor by working out an exclusive deal.
© AP Photo/Carlos Osorio

adds dimension to the product–audience communication; this communication can create experiences that appeal to all senses, encourage fan participation and feedback, provide opportunities for sampling and merchandising, and convey some of the excitement and drama inherent in sport. Most important, these experiences can be as memorable as the event itself.

Publicity

Publicity is another integral benefit of sponsorship. The sponsored product (athlete, team, league, or event) is obligated by contract to credit the sponsor and, in entitlement agreements, to refer to the event as the "XYZ Marathon" or the "Big City Marathon presented by XYZ." In the 1970s and 1980s, this gave tobacco companies an excellent opportunity to gain visibility via the media. Good examples of this type of sponsorship are the Nextel Cup Racing Series and the Virginia Slims Tennis Tournament, commonly referred to as the Virginia Slims. Photographs as well as television coverage of the event often show boards and spots illustrating the corporate partner's name and logo. The benefit of such a sponsorship is that extensive media attention accrues to sport events and the personalities involved, and thus to their sponsors and licensees as well. Publicity via sport promotional agreements is delivered by the event or television broadcast, and this positions the company's messages more objectively in the eyes of the audience—messages that are more difficult for the audience to ignore than an advertisement is. Thus corporations, instead of paying for the news, have the chance to be the news, at a prime time and with a product for which the public has shown a strong affinity. For example, Goody's, manufacturer of a headache powder sold primarily in the South, becomes part of the national news when television broadcasts the Goody's Dash Series.

New media are another tool used by sponsors to publicize and promote themselves and their activities; they are also used by sport marketing agencies to make sponsor presentations. New media can be defined as newly created computer-based communication vehicles that allow the integration of audio, video, and animation. New media have rapidly become an integral part of the sponsorship process. Because this form of communication is often entertaining and holds an audience's attention, it is clearly more effective than traditional media that are viewed as flat, or one-dimensional.

Corporate Objectives

Not every corporation has the resources and global reach of Nike. Therefore, every approach to sponsorship or promotional licensing should take into account the fact that it is difficult to classify corporate objectives in a clear-cut way. As they develop sponsorship objectives, corporations frequently have a number of objectives that overlap and interact. For example, MCI Corporation, a telecommunications company based in Washington, D.C., invests more than $5 million annually to sponsor the Heritage Golf Classic and a number of other sporting events. The company uses the Heritage Golf Classic as a reward/entertainment vehicle for customers who spend between $1 million and $3 million per month on telecommunication services. The MCI agreement serves a number of objectives: It targets a specific market (heavy users), builds goodwill among decision makers, and facilitates prospecting (that is, finding possible sales avenues or leads) for its salespeople.

According to Meenaghan, objectives in sponsorship range from assumption of social responsibility to the commercial objectives normally proposed for advertising. (17) Our review of academic writings and empirical research, as well as practical findings on the subjects of promotional licensing and sponsorship, indicates that there is no single corporate objective in the decision-making process about whether and what to sponsor. A study by Irwin, Asimakopoulos, and Sutton showed that company image and target market fit were the most important criteria in funding a sponsorship proposal. (18) Figure 13.9 illustrates a tool that sponsors can use to screen potential sponsorship opportunities based on corporate objectives.

According to the research, the following were the objectives that most often influenced the decision to enter into sport sponsorship agreements:

- ✦ To increase public awareness of the company, the product, or both
- ✦ To alter or reinforce public perception of the company
- ✦ To identify the company with the particular market segments
- ✦ To involve the company in the community
- ✦ To build goodwill among decision makers
- ✦ To generate media benefits
- ✦ To achieve sales objectives
- ✦ To showcase unique product features, technologies, or advantages
- ✦ To create an advantage over competitors, through association or exclusivity
- ✦ To gain unique opportunities in terms of hospitality and entertainment
- ✦ To secure entitlement or naming rights

Each objective should provide the sponsor with an ROI (return on investment) that might be in monetary form, or an ROO (return on objective) that could also be measured through the media (number of impressions), the ability to exclude competitors, and so forth. In the next section, we illustrate the importance of each objective, explain what it is and why it is important, and provide examples of how each objective can be used and achieved in the context of sport sponsorship. The sponsorship paradigm depicted in figure 13.10 illustrates a simple model of what the sponsor and the sport property hope to receive as a result of their partnership. Each party has expectations to be delivered and fulfilled by the other.

Criteria	WT	-4	-3	-2	-1	0	1	2	3	4	Total
Budget Consideration											
Affordability											
Cost effectiveness											
Management Issues											
Event profile											
Organizational committee status											
Media guarantees											
Legal status											
Regulatory policy											
Athletes' cooperation											
Governing body status											
Marketing agency profile											
Positioning Image											
Product/sport image fit											
Product utility fit											
Image/target market fit											
Targeting of Market											
Immediate audience											
Demographic fit											
Size											
Fan association strength											
Extended media coverage											
National coverage											
Local coverage											
Extended Audience Profile											
Demographics fit											
Size											
Public Relations											
Hospitality accommodation											
Community leader presence											
Customers presence											
Staff sport knowledge											
Event sales/retail tie-in											
New account opportunities											
Promotional Opportunities											
Promotional licensing											
Complementary advertising											
Signage opportunities											
Competition Consideration											
Competition's interest											
Ambush market avoidance											
Sponsorship Status											
Title sponsor											
Major sponsor											
Exclusivity											
Established											
Long-term involvement											
Alternative Sponsorship											
Co-sponsor											
In-kind supplier											
Sponsorship Type											
Team											
League/championship											
Event											
Facility											
Grand Total											

FIGURE 13.9 Revised sport sponsorship proposal evaluation model.

Increasing Public Awareness

Sponsorship has sometimes been used with the sole aim of increasing the awareness, or educating the public regarding the capabilities, of a company or the benefits of its products or services. Besides Sharp Corporation's major holdings in the electronics market, the company is also the world's leading producer of solar energy (the United States is the third-largest market for solar energy in the world). To draw attention to this aspect of its business,

Situation analysis
  • What clients want

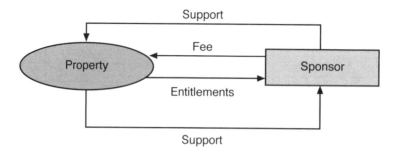

Wants:
  • Money
  • Brand-building support
  • Limited interference from sponsor

Wants:
  • Turn key program
  • Positive equity transfer
  • Marketing partnership
    with mutually beneficial goals

FIGURE 13.10 The sponsorship paradigm.

Sharp has a sign in the outfield at San Francisco's SBC Park and has installed a solar energy system on the roof—typical of the size and performance of a standard California residence. The system transfers energy directly into the ballpark's electric grid, and a multimedia kiosk located in the left-field concourse monitors its output. Using a touch-screen display, fans can access information about the system, learn how solar energy works and what its benefits are, and request additional information from Sharp. "Baseball and sunshine go hand-in-hand and when it comes to solar power, California continues to be the nation's leader," said Rhone Resch, president of Solar Energy Industries Association. "Partnerships like the Sharp-Giants initiative have the potential to turn the Golden State into the world's largest market for solar energy." (19)

Influencing Public Perception

The opportunity to capitalize on image association or image transfer makes sponsorship attractive to businesses as a marketing communications tool. The choice of a sport or event with particular attributes can help a company achieve a desired image that will reinforce or change consumers' perceptions of the company and its products. Choosing the sport or event becomes less formidable when there is an actual or logical link between the company and the sport or event. The potential for an effective sponsorship agreement is at its maximum when there is an association between the target group of the company and the target group of the sport or event, between the desired image of the company and the image of the sport or event, or between the product characteristics promoted and the credibility of the sport entity helping to promote the product.

  As the popularity of in-line skating skyrocketed in the 1990s, competition among skate manufacturers became fierce. One of the in-line skate manufacturers, Rollerblade, Inc., was looking to increase sales and also to generate publicity for a new line of hockey-specific skates. So the company entered into an agreement with the Milwaukee Admirals of the International Hockey League. Rollerblade account executive John Smid commented, "Until now we haven't had an in-line product synonymous with hockey like many of the [ice] skate manufacturers do. Our hockey program will have credibility by being connected to the Admirals." (20)

Establishing Associations With Particular Market Segments

Selecting a sponsorship agreement that matches the target has proven quite beneficial for sponsors. For example, Anheuser-Busch, the largest brewing company in the world, spends over $200 million (60 percent of its marketing budget) sponsoring a broad array of sporting events. In contrast, Coors, with a marketing budget of $20 million to $30 million, has traditionally been more selective in what it sponsors. Coors, using a demographic-lifestyle approach to sponsorship/licensing agreements, has turned down sponsorship of both tennis and golf events because fans of these sports generally prefer wine and other alcohol products to beer. Thus, Coors has decided to become involved in auto racing and motocross, noting that followers of these sports consume more beer than any other category of sport fan. (21) However in 2005, in an effort to establish itself as the clear number-two challenger to Anheuser-Busch, Coors entered into a five-year $500 million sponsorship of the NFL to continue as the official beer of the NFL. (22) As evidenced by the relations of Anheuser-Busch and the Miller Brewing Company with various NFL teams, professional football delivers a target demographic that is a great fit with the beer category.

We can see similar targeting efforts in MasterCard's sponsorship of the Alamo Bowl. In 2002, MasterCard completed an evaluation of U.S. sport properties. The results of the evaluation suggested that the company might want to add college football to its portfolio of sponsorships. According to Bob Cramer, former MasterCard vice president of global sponsorships and event marketing, "MasterCard sees college football sponsorship as a way to reach a large audience that fits the company's target demographic" (men ages 18-34 and men and women ages 25-54). (23) The fit worked out so well that MasterCard upgraded the presenting sponsorship to a title sponsorship for 2003.

With regard to identifying with a global segment, Reebok has become involved with the World Cup as a way to encourage identification with its products in South America, in particular in Colombia, Paraguay, and Chile. According to Peter Moore, senior vice president of Reebok's global soccer division, "It [the World Cup] is a message that is giving us tremendous credibility in those countries and regions—and believe me; nothing engenders more passion in South America than soccer." (24)

Becoming Involved in the Community

Sponsorship has demonstrated more potential than any other promotion tool in terms of direct impact on the community. In this context, sponsorship often takes the form of public or community relations, and its objective is usually to position the company as a concerned and interested citizen trying to put something back into the community. Companies may target community relations through sport sponsorship to specific communities, regional areas, or other geographic areas of influence as dictated by corporate objectives. Through licensing or sponsorships, the company demonstrates its awareness of local issues in an effort to influence potential customers and local social and governmental agencies. This is particularly true in cases in which the corporate partner provides financial or other support to an event that otherwise would not occur or could not continue. For example, a company could offer to help threatened local clubs or support interscholastic sport programs that cover a larger geographic area. Evidence supports the idea of using promotional programs designed to increase corporations' involvement with the community. Meenaghan cited a survey in which 72 percent of the respondents thought that business firms should sponsor more events and activities: 37 percent believed that companies should sponsor sport-related activities; 17 percent, children's activities; 11 percent, senior citizen programs; and 7 percent, charitable causes. (25)

An excellent example is the NBA's Cleveland Cavaliers' Minority Business Associates program. This is a program with two primary objectives: generating sponsorship and advertising revenue from nontraditional sources, and creating an effective way for community leaders to serve as role models for Cleveland schoolchildren. Ten African American business owners in Cleveland paid $6,500 each to join the program. They'll help support the Cavaliers' Stay in School Program—both financially and by speaking directly to kids—and provide free tickets for kids to attend games. In exchange, the business owners will receive arena signage and public service announcements during Cavaliers television broadcasts and the pregame coach's show. (26)

Building Goodwill

Sport provides an excellent environment in which to conduct or influence business on a relaxed, personal basis. In recent years, with the fast pace of market growth, the fight for increased market share among existing customers and the competition for new accounts (particularly in the international market) have been intense. Corporations that can deliver unique opportunities such as entertainment, tickets, and hospitality for key clients are also perceived to be potentially good business partners that will always overdeliver goods and service. For example, Travelers Insurance Company is a sponsor of the prestigious Masters Tournament. The firm's director of corporate advertising and promotion, Ed Faruolo, noted that "the tournament is an upscale, prestigious event that provides a fit both demographically and psychographically." Each day of the tournament, a different group of executives from around the United States is flown to the event site. As Faruolo observed, "There are many golf enthusiasts in the trade, and a lot of our agents conduct business on the golf course. When you put those two factors together, the Masters makes good sense from a business standpoint." (27)

Generating Media Benefits

Media benefits include advertising and publicity related to the promotional efforts surrounding the product or event. Media benefits are usually equated with ROI and measured in the numbers of impressions generated and the source of those impressions. Impressions are the number of viewers (television), readers (all print forms), and listeners (radio) exposed to the advertising message. The advertising message may be an actual advertisement, but it is often a logo or sign that appears during the television coverage or is evident in a newspaper photograph. In auto racing, for example, the driver often wears a cap with the name of a sponsor and sometimes changes the cap during a photo session or interview to provide exposure and impressions for the sponsor(s). The source of these impressions is also very important to the sponsor. A photograph in the *New York Times* is much more powerful in terms of impressions than a photo in the *Amherst Bulletin* (Massachusetts) because of the subscription base, the online value, and the regional editions of the paper that are sold nationally. In the following section, we examine some of the methods companies use to select events for sponsorship, some ways of evaluating media, and other benefits associated with the sponsorship opportunity.

Interest in sponsoring the World Cup is due in part to the global television audience, estimated at 3.7 billion people. Official sponsors of the World Cup receive advertising billboards at field level in every World Cup venue—and according to Marianne Fulgenzi, vice president for publicity at MasterCard, "During the World Cup we average 7-1/2 minutes per match when our logo is on camera." (28) Thus, 37 billion people are exposed to MasterCard for 7-1/2 minutes during every match. When combined with the media coverage of the product or event, media benefits may be the most important objective for a number of companies involved in sponsorship agreements. This has been particularly true for companies in the tobacco and alcoholic drink industries, although other companies with access to direct advertising channels have found the media exposure they get through sponsorship agreements to be cost effective.

For some potential sponsors, media benefits involving a variety of outlets or an association with an established entity may be the crucial element in determining whether or not to become involved with a property as a sponsor. Consider the BASS Bassmaster Classic, whose television rights are owned by ESPN/ABC. According to ESPN/ABC Sports President George Bodenheimer, BASS has its roots in rural America and is family oriented, much like NASCAR. However, NASCAR fans who want to get close to the action can buy a ticket, go to the track and watch their favorite drivers and teams. BASS fans are reliant on television to watch their favorites—and what better than television to show the types of equipment (tackle, boats, and trucks) used by the pros as well as promoting their favorite fishing locations? "Unlike most other sports, BASS can help its fans fish just like the professionals. Any bass fisherman can buy the same boat the pros use. Fish with the same tackle, drive the same truck and even drop a line into the same spot on the lake that coughed up the biggest fish in the tournament." (29) Association with ESPN and BASS along with the opportunity to show their products actually being used by the pros on television could be the "catch of the day" for a sponsor.

Unfortunately for some sponsors, the benefits of sponsorship—recognition, access to the target market, and pay—fail to materialize for one reason or another. The media benefits for sponsors of the 1998 Winter Olympics were slim because of the ambush-marketing techniques (discussed later in this chapter) of several companies. On that occasion a sponsoring company expected media benefits, but nonsponsors actually gained more exposure.

A February 1998 telephone survey conducted by the Leo Burnett Agency and its Starcom media division revealed that television viewers had a difficult time identifying Olympic sponsors when provided with a list of companies that advertise heavily on television. Of those surveyed, 73 percent incorrectly identified Nike as an official sponsor of the Olympics. Among the actual sponsors who invested a minimum of $40 million to sponsor the games, only McDonald's scored better than Nike, attaining a recognition rate of 85 percent. Visa, an Olympic sponsor, had a 70 percent recognition rate, while competitor and nonsponsor MasterCard was misidentified as a sponsor by 49 percent of the respondents. In other sponsor-versus-nonsponsor recognition (sponsor listed first), Coke had 68 percent versus Pepsi's 55 percent, and United Parcel Service had 50 percent versus 40 percent for Federal Express. Visa's Becky Saeger believed that the sponsorship was worthwhile because Visa was the only card accepted at the Olympics and is the only card that can advertise during the games on CBS. Nevertheless, Saeger went on to say that advertisers face great difficulty in determining what is worth sponsoring and also in deciding how to leverage sponsorships. According to Saeger, all sponsors must face one question: How important is it that the people know you're an official sponsor? (30)

An excellent way to measure whether your company is receiving the media benefits is to ask for the help of a business such as Joyce Julius and Associates, based in Ann Arbor, Michigan. Established in 1985, this company is an industry leader in the measurement and valuation of the benefits of sport sponsorship. Joyce Julius and Associates has two primary products—the *Sponsors Report* and the National Television Impression Value (NTIV) Analysis. The *Sponsors Report* provides complete exposure results stemming exclusively from national event broadcasts. These results assist brand and advertising managers in justifying budgetary expenditures, documenting impressions and exposure, and determining the value of the broadcast in comparison to other forms of sponsorship. For example, during the CBS coverage of the Masters Tournament, Joyce Julius and Associates found that the Nike-logoed hat and shirt worn by Tiger Woods were visible on screen for 16 minutes and 31 seconds. On the basis of an estimate of the cost of CBS's paid television ads, that loosely translates to $1,685,000 in on-air Nike exposure. (31)

The NTIV Analysis provides a comprehensive evaluation of the total sponsorship program. Thus, in addition to measuring the exposures and benefits of national television broadcasts, the NTIV examines responses generated from exposures, such as television news programming, national and event-market radio, event-site exhibits and displays, cross-corporate advertising, promotional efforts, and print media. This information is then entered into a formula and converted to a cost per impression and a corresponding value of the sponsorship. The success and acceptance of the NTIV instrument has led to the development of the NTIV Projection Analysis, which predicts the exposure return on proposed sponsorship programs. (32)

Showcasing Unique Product Features, Technologies, or Advantages

In recent years it has become increasingly common for a business to become a sponsor of a particular sport property because of an opportunity to promote unique product features or technological innovations or applications. This has always been true in technologically rich sports such as NASCAR, but the concept has also gained a foothold in more traditional

T-MOBILE LINKS BROAD MARKETING
PARTNERSHIP WITH NBA AND WNBA

NEW YORK, OCTOBER 3, 2005—T-Mobile USA, Inc., has formed a wide-reaching multi-year marketing partnership with the NBA and WNBA to become the Official Wireless Services Partner of the NBA and WNBA. T-Mobile will promote its wireless services across virtually all channels of the NBA and WNBA, appealing to the leagues' broad and avid fan bases.

From the opening tip of the NBA season to the Finals and the NBA Draft, the league will integrate T-Mobile as a marketing partner into a host of front-line events and activities throughout the year, beginning with NBA Premiere Week. T-Mobile will keep fans up-to-date on the NBA and present its users with special content offerings on their phones, including participation in NBA All-Star Balloting, voting for the MVP of the NBA All-Star Game and the Finals; and the latest NBA-related news, statistics and other fun features.

T-Mobile also will take marquee positions throughout the NBA's extensive media platforms, including the leagues' television partners, to further grow its rapidly expanding consumer base. Additionally, T-Mobile will establish promotional partnerships with various NBA teams in key local markets.

"T-Mobile and the NBA is a natural fit—both brands are youthful, dynamic and rapidly growing. This partnership is designed to further fuel the T-Mobile USA growth engine," said Mike Butler, Chief Marketing Officer, T-Mobile USA, Inc. "T-Mobile customers will 'Get More' NBA action through the innovative products, services and promotions we are developing to help power this exciting venture."

"As one of the fastest-growing wireless carriers, T-Mobile has permeated pop culture to become relevant and meaningful to the lifestyles of their young consumers," said Heidi Ueberroth, NBA Executive Vice President. "We are confident that this wide-reaching partnership will further accelerate their growth in the wireless space."

Building upon its already strong appeal to the nation's youth, T-Mobile will highlight the NBA's youngest players—the Rookies—through the NBA's Rookie program, featuring the T-Mobile Rookie Challenge, an All-Star competition between NBA rookies and second-year players, and rookie awards presentations including the T-Mobile Rookie of the Year. As part of a unique package of NBA-themed offerings, T-Mobile users will be receiving special content on NBA rookies providing insights into NBA life both on and off the court.

T-Mobile also will partner with the league on the NBA All-Star Celebrity Game, reinforcing T-Mobile's importance and appeal among celebrities and performing artists. When all of these NBA festivities are over, T-Mobile will launch into its WNBA partnership action, especially involving the WNBA All-Star Game, WNBA Playoffs and WNBA Finals.

Additionally, T-Mobile will go on the road as a major partner of numerous high-profile NBA and WNBA touring events. In particular, T-Mobile will participate in NBA Rhythm 'n Rims, the NBA's basketball and music tour; and the WNBA Be Fit Tour, which promotes healthy living and fitness among girls. (34)

sports such as golf. For example, in 2005, EDS used the Byron Nelson Championship to showcase a number of technological innovations that, although not directly related to the sport of golf, had significant applications in the hospitality areas related to golf. EDS showcased its RFID (radio frequency identification) technology in its hospitality areas and in the EDS experience—a high-tech demonstration center accessible only to corporate guests. RFID is a system that tracks certain objects, such as inventory, by means of a small sticker containing an integrated circuit. This RFID technology was used in corporate guest entry badges, and guests could monitor how they were being tracked as they moved throughout the venue. The result was a 20 percent increase in the number of guest invitations accepted. (33)

The press release on this page also emphasizes the importance of unique technology with selected demographics.

Achieving Sales Objectives

The ultimate objective of marketing is to increase sales levels or profitability. Sponsorship, along with other elements of the communications mix, is usually viewed as an element that influences the buyer to purchase. In this sense, sponsorship constitutes an important stimulus within purchasing as a multistage, multi-influence process; but it can also influence sales in a more direct manner. To address the fact that a growing number of car buyers are women, BMW paid a mid-five-figure sponsorship fee to be a presenting sponsor of the Danskin Triathlon Series. In exchange, BMW received significant media benefits that were used to promote local dealerships, because the primary goal of the event was to boost showroom traffic by suitably affluent and aware women. The program was highly successful: In one market, 25 percent of the participants in the triathlon series visited BMW dealers. (35)

Another highly illustrative case is that of John Hancock Insurance. John Hancock is an Olympic sponsor, and according to David F. D'Alessandro, senior executive vice president, the sponsorship makes sense. "One of the reasons we are investing in the Olympics is what it's doing for us in Southeast Asia, where the insurance markets are growing at a double digit rate, and they're growing here at 1 percent or negative 1 percent. They have no idea who John Hancock is, or was, in Malaysia. But by marrying it with the Olympic marks, people know us more as an Olympic sponsor than a patriotic American company." (36) John Hancock hopes that this association with the Olympics and its global image will provide familiarity and an entry point for sales efforts in Malaysia.

Sales objectives can also relate to product use as a benefit of a sponsorship or licensing agreement. A sponsorship or licensing agreement with a venue such as an amusement park or arena may require the use of a particular product at all events or functions in the facility (i.e., the Pepsi Center, which opened in Denver in 1999 as the home of the Nuggets and Avalanche). For example, when the standard of comparison is supermarket sales, Coca-Cola wins the battle for market share by only a few percentage points over Pepsi. However, when it comes to park and recreation facilities, theaters, and sporting events, Coca-Cola is the clear winner. The strategy of Coca-Cola is to sign sponsorship and licensing agreements that ensure product exclusivity and use.

Another approach to sales-driven sponsorship agreements is the one Visa employed in its five-year (1995 to 2000), $40 million sponsorship agreement with the NFL. "The bottom line reasoning at Visa is simple: Their experience with the Olympics since 1986 has shown that such activities significantly increase card use, help to retain existing cardholder accounts and generate significant numbers of new cardholder accounts. Visa saw a 28 percent jump in payment service to a total of $290.7 billion. Visa credits its sport marketing, particularly the Olympics, as well as non-sport promotions, as having a significant influence on those results. Visa believes the Olympic experience suggests that the NFL will also achieve these goals for them." (37)

Creating Exclusivity

In some cases, particularly when the sponsorship fee is high or the commitment is long term, an area integral to licensing agreements is product or category exclusivity. This ensures, for example, that a particular soft drink will be the only soft drink or (in many cases) the only refreshment associated with the event or product or used at the venue. As stated previously, the great benefit is that this provides an opportunity for sales-driven use of the sponsorship agreement and at the same time prohibits competitors from using the event, venue, product, or activity to transmit a message to the audience. This limitation of communication avenues can improve the ability of the marketing message to increase sales, and may affect the profitability of both the sponsor and the competitor. The exclusivity, in light of the strong emotional attachment and following that sport inspires, allows the marketer to position brands or products as supporting an event or the efforts of a particular team (while implying that the competitor's product does not), thereby encouraging consumer support where it counts most—at the cash register.

In its corporate-partner agreement with the NCAA, Gillette is guaranteed category exclusivity. As Gillette delineates it, the category consists of grooming/personal care, which includes the following products: blades and razors, shaving preparation, aftershave, cologne, deodorants, shampoo, conditioners, styling gel, mousse, hair spray, home permanents, styling aids, ethnic hair care products, and skin care products (hand and body lotion); toothbrushes, toothpaste, oral rinse, and dental floss; and electric shavers and electric hair care appliances.

Gillette's two divisions, PaperMate and Braun, are also granted exclusivity for their respective products: stationery, pens, markers, highlighters, and correction fluid; coffee makers, clocks, toasters, and food processors. Thus, Gillette can promote any or all of these items as it chooses while preventing any of its competitors from doing so via a relationship with the NCAA.

Gaining Opportunities in Hospitality and Entertainment

Although hospitality and entertainment relate to a number of the other concepts, this function is worthy of examination on its own. Hospitality and entertainment play a critical role in the packaging of sponsorship and promotional licensing programs. These concepts enable the sponsor to construct certain benefits and opportunities that are often unique and unavailable in the marketplace. Such opportunities may include trips to the Super Bowl or the NCAA Final Four and on-site hospitality and special events. According to William Pate, vice president of advertising for BellSouth (which sponsors a NASCAR Nextel Cup team, the Atlantic Coast Conference, and the Atlanta Braves), "Business people are more open to messages when they are at leisure than when they are working." (38)

Hospitality opportunities have become an integral part of sponsorship agreements for college athletics programs, which package hard-to-obtain tickets in prime locations along with tents, catering, and other amenities. There are similar hospitality programs on the professional golf tours and throughout professional football; such programs often form the basis for the sale of luxury suites and boxes in sporting venues throughout the world. The key to successful use of hospitality is to ensure that the hospitality is not available except as part of a comprehensive sponsorship or promotional licensing agreement.

Corporate partners use hospitality benefits to reward their own personnel, or, in the majority of cases, to induce their own clients to increase product use or consumption, renew agreements, or sign new ones. This is done through entertaining. For example, "IBM ponied up $2,500 each for twenty $20 passes to the 1997 Masters Tournament, and used them as a centerpiece for a week of entertainment for its top golf-nut clients to reward them for their continuous business."(39) Hospitality has long been an integral part of European sponsorship programs and accounts for as much as 25 percent of corporate-partner expenditures. Hospitality packaging is receiving more attention and has higher priority in the United States than ever before.

Securing Entitlement or Naming Rights

Corporations interested in purchasing naming rights to venues or events such as concert tours, auto racing events, and bowl games have an agenda in mind when they consider such sponsorship possibilities. This agenda consists of the following elements and their value to the company in terms of cost and organizational priority:

- ✦ Number of impressions or exposures
- ✦ Sponsorship and cross-promotional activities
- ✦ Tax-deductible expenses
- ✦ Brand exclusivity
- ✦ Public relations and community image
- ✦ Related amenities (hospitality) (40)

Red Bull, an Austria-based sport energy drink maker, purchased the MSL NY/NJ Metro Stars for $30 million, which includes the naming rights so the team will be known as the "Red Bulls."(41) According to one national sport marketing expert, Alan Friedman of *Street & Smith's SportsBusiness Journal* and founder of *Team Marketing Report*, "Naming rights are the most expensive sport marketing investment in the current marketplace, the best dollar-for-impression sponsorship bargain, and one of the most underutilized promotional assets in a company's marketing arsenal." (42) Corporations that elect to become involved in securing naming rights or entitlements must have a strategic plan in place to leverage the opportunity and the additional financial resources to support it. One industry that has capitalized on sponsorship deals with naming rights is banking. Banks have led the way in the naming rights revival of the past three years because naming a sports venue conveys the concept of permanence, giving the impression that the bank is part of the community for the long term. (43)

Entitlement and naming rights have a very high profile in NASCAR. In stock car racing, the corporate role, by tradition, has great prominence. If a company sponsors a racing event, the company's name is incorporated into the event name. For example, Mountain Dew, one of PepsiCo's many soft drinks, sponsors Darlington's Southern 500. Hence, the race itself is known as the Mountain Dew Southern 500. If a company becomes a racing team sponsor, the corporate name or brand is used in conjunction with the team name. Rick Hendrick owns a car sponsored by Kellogg's and Chevrolet and driven by Terry Labonte. In alluding to the team and its race car, commentators and fans refer to the car as Labonte's Kellogg's Chevrolet Monte Carlo (44), an excellent opportunity for both Kellogg's and Chevrolet to leverage their sponsorship.

Evaluating and Ensuring Sponsorship Effectiveness

The last decade of the twentieth century saw an increase in research measuring the impact of sponsorship programs. A demand for fiscal accountability was the driving force behind these research efforts—an attempt to insist that corporate decision makers be held accountable for budget allocations and related spending. The majority of research throughout the 1980s and the mid-1990s centered on calculating the number of impressions generated or counting the number of coupons redeemed. A significant number of organizations either conduct their own proprietary research or engage a marketing research firm to do so for them.

In an era where "return on investment" (or ROI) and "activation" are buzzwords heard in every conversation, it's no surprise that companies with long-term million-dollar (sponsorship) contracts want quantifiable data to justify their partnership with a team (45) or other sport organizations. According to Gordon Kane of Victory Sports Marketing, "The biggest reason for this move toward justification is quite simply an increased sophistication among buyers. Even if a property makes strategic sense, the sponsor may still need to ask, could my money be better used in another medium or with another association that provides a better ROI." (46) A large portion of this ROI that defines sponsorship effectiveness is expected in the form of a sales "lift." (47)

The NBA's Toronto Raptors have developed a rather innovative approach to determine how effectively their sponsorships are working: They formed a research partnership with their sponsors to find out. The team offered all of its sponsors the opportunity to share the cost of a $50,000 survey to track consumer recall of, and reaction to, Raptors sponsorship programs every year. According to Michael Downey, Raptors vice president of sales and marketing, 11 of the team's major partners are participating. Mike Scarlett, communications manager for Ford Motor Company of Canada, has said that the company is "getting a lot of good feedback about the results of our sponsorship. . . . We very rarely track the performance [of a sponsorship] versus our objectives." Also according to Scarlett, in-stadium research indicated that a significant portion of Raptors attendees are potential buyers of sport utility vehicles and full-size pickup trucks. Despite Ford's good feedback, initial survey results have returned some less-than-flattering statistics regarding fans' recognition of the Raptors' sponsors. "We got some numbers back that weren't all rosy and we expected that and some of our partners expected that," said Downey. "Now we'll try and find out what's working and fix what's not." (48)

Research and evaluation of the deliverables and the results of the sponsorships will be the key to measuring effectiveness. According to Mike Lynch, senior vice president of event and sponsorship marketing for Visa USA, "Properties will be challenged to show more and more deliverables on their end because we are all changing the way we look at deals. At the end of the day, it's all about usage and sometimes you have to put the properties on the hook in order for them to fully understand our position after the deal has been signed." (49)

Why Sponsorships Work—Affinity Marketing

Affinity marketing refers to an "individual's level of cohesiveness, social bonding, identification and conformity to the norms and standards of a particular reference group." (50) Affinity marketing comprises certain specific components and tactics such as frequency marketing, loyalty marketing, relationship marketing, and data-based marketing. The reference group, depending on its size and characteristics, can be an attractive market for sponsors. MBNA, a major player in the field of sport sponsorship using affinity marketing, explains their interpretation of affinity marketing as follows:

> We identify organizations made up of people with a common interest, obtain their endorsements of our company and its products, and market to their members under the endorsement. We have been doing this for a long time, and we dominate the field with more than 5,000 affinity organizations including professional associations, colleges and universities, sports teams, financial institutions and many other groups throughout the world.

> MBNA's unique position in the consumer lending business rests on partnering with affinity organizations that people care about—organizations inspiring pride and passion among their members. We provide products and services that express loyalty and help organizations strengthen relationships with their members. (51)

In sport marketing, bank credit cards with the team logo, university identification, or special-purpose cards such as the Jack Nicklaus Platinum card are the most recognizable and common forms of affinity marketing. These types of programs usually offer an attractive introductory interest rate and allow the cardholder to earn points for each purchase—thus appealing to their loyalty and identification with the group to capture their spending. Points are redeemable for team merchandise, golfing fees, donations to the athletic department, and so forth.

Perhaps the best example of consumer loyalty and support of a sport product is illustrated in the relationship between NASCAR and its fans. According to a study conducted by Performance Research, NASCAR fans have a higher level of trust toward sponsors' products than other fan groups do—approximately 60 percent of NASCAR fans surveyed compared to only 30 percent of football fans. More important, over 40 percent of NASCAR fans purposely switched brands when a manufacturer became a NASCAR sponsor. (52)

The key to the successful use of sponsorship in sport is activation. Activation describes how the sponsorship is used—how the rights to the sport property that have been purchased are leveraged and used by the purchaser. According to Raymond Bednar, activation brings a sponsorship to life, or in some cases fails to bring it to life (poor activation or complete lack of activation is one reason sponsorships agreements fail and are not renewed). (53)

Why Sponsorships Don't Always Work—Ambush Marketing

Sandler and Shani defined ambush marketing as "a planned effort (campaign) by an organization to associate themselves indirectly with an event in order to gain at least some of the recognition and benefits that are associated with being an official sponsor." (54) This definition related directly to the issue of sponsors paying for an association with the product or event and "ambushers" not paying. Several years later, Meenaghan added to the definition, to include within ambush activities "a whole variety of wholly legitimate and morally correct methods of intruding upon public consciousness surrounding an event." (55) Including this broader scope of activities underscores the harm to the sponsor; namely, confusion in the mind of the consumer that denies the sponsor clear recognition of its role and support, resulting in less benefit than originally planned when the sponsorship agreement was enacted.

Most ambush marketing aims at major events (such as the Olympics, World Cup, Super Bowl or NCAA Final Four) and other events with high sponsorship price tags or limited partnership and sponsorship opportunities. One of the more noteworthy examples of ambush marketing occurred at the 1992 Barcelona Olympic Games. Reebok was the official Olympic sponsor, and Nike was the ambusher. Throughout the games, Nike conducted a highly visible advertising campaign featuring Olympic athletes who happened to be under Nike endorsement or personal-services contracts—without paying a penny in (Olympic) sponsorship fees. A common ambush tactic is to pass out spirit signs (see the photo for an example). Nike also held press conferences for Olympic athletes under contract with Nike and additionally displayed large murals of U.S. basketball team members (a.k.a. the Dream Team) on the sides of Barcelona buildings. As Nike explained its position, "We feel like in any major sporting event we have the right to come in and give our message as long as we don't interfere with the official proceedings." (56) It is also interesting to note that the biggest controversy regarding this ambush occurred when Michael Jordan, Charles Barkley, and other athletes under contract with Nike initially refused to take part in the medal ceremony because participation required them to wear a warm-up suit with the Reebok vector. The amount of free publicity surrounding this event was of great benefit and value to Nike.

Learning their lessons from 1992, the IOC aggressively responded to Nike ambush marketing attempts prior to and associated with the 1996 games in Atlanta. Nike had created an ambush campaign aimed once again at upstaging Reebok, the official Olympic sponsor. An ad campaign in *Sports Illustrated* rammed their message home: "If you can't stand the heat —get out of Atlanta" and "If you're not here to win you're a tourist." The ads proved controversial and attention-generating, as Nike intended them to be. However, as an unintended consequence, they also upset the athletes, causing Olympic swimmer Amy White to say, "The ads are basically ridiculing us [the athletes]." The IOC responded by promising to hurt Nike where it mattered most—by threatening a ban of Nike branding from all sports equipment at the Games and immediately withdrawing all accreditation for any Nike service personnel, making it impossible for them to move through the venue to attend to their athletes. Nike responded by ceasing to circulate advertising signs for spectators to take into the venues, and by reining in its advertising and public relations campaigns and stunts. The result was a more controllable and enjoyable experience for the IOC and their corporate partners. (57)

Even though Checkers/Rallys was not a sponsor for this event, ambush marketing provided the company with an opportunity to receive brand exposure at a college football game.

Courtesy of Tim Ahn

Is It the Number of Impressions Generated or the Impression Created?

Speaking at the World Congress of Sports, Julie Roehm, director of marketing communications for Chrysler, Dodge, and Jeep, when asked about impressions, responded by saying, "Tell me what the *impression of Dodge* is, not how many impressions." (58)

Ms. Roehm raised an interesting point. Perhaps we have been focused on counting eyeballs for too long rather than trying to understand what the eyeballs are actually conveying to the consumer. The following list offers some thoughts when planning how to make a lasting, impactful impression rather than just creating something to see.

✦ Is the sponsorship a fit between the product and the sponsor and targeted to an appropriate market segment? (Think Mountain Dew and Action Sports.)

✦ Does it create an impression with multiple anchors and touch points—heart, mind, and intellect—such as MasterCard's "priceless" campaign with Major League Baseball?

✦ Is it "fresh," unique, and able to stand out? (Think of Burger King and the NFL.)

✦ Is the association between the image of the sponsor's product or service and the image of the property mutually enhancing and beneficial, such as with Toyota and the NBA?

✦ Is the property on the upswing, such as poker and NASCAR?

✦ What other corporate partner brands are you joining in this new venture?

Selling the Sponsorship

Before beginning the sales process to locate a sponsor for your team or event, develop a strategic planning process for how to conduct the sales campaign. Strategic planning steps should include the following:

✦ Make a comprehensive list of all assets in your inventory.

✦ Establish a list price for each item based on cost per impression (usually 5 to 50 cents), demand, and the prestige of each item.

✦ Establish packaging discount policies.

✦ Total all inventories at list price; then set a sales goal based on these discount policies.

✦ Remember, you must determine the real cost of the sponsorship, which may include any or all of the following elements: tickets (full face value), promotions (premium items, shipping, fulfillment, and labor costs), print and point-of-sale pieces, staffing costs, dasher boards and program ads (production, design, and layout costs), and developmental costs.

✦ Establish your sales strategy. Which, if any, categories are exclusive? What sales do you expect from each category? In which order will you proceed?

✦ Initiate the six-step sales process (see the next section) with the top three product and service categories, then the next three, and so on. Sell your best inventory first.

✦ The order in which you present categories and potential sponsors is critical: large categories first, major national sponsors first, easy closures first. Gain momentum; use the recognition of "name sponsors" to attract lesser sponsors, and leverage the relationships to gain other relationships.

✦ Talk to competitors (Coke-Pepsi, Bud-Miller, Visa-MasterCard-American Express) simultaneously to ensure a decision at the same time.

✦ Remember—All sponsor decision makers know each other; don't exaggerate and don't make special deals.

The Six-Step Sponsorship Sales Process

Once your organization has agreed on and implemented the strategic planning process, you can initiate the sales process. The success of the sales process depends on adherence to the principles of the strategic planning process.

1. Schedule a meeting with the sponsorship decision maker. Meet only if the decision maker is present: Remember, don't accept no from someone who is not empowered to say yes.

2. At the first meeting, listen 80 percent of the time and sell only when you have to. You are there to observe and learn. Where does the potential sponsor spend its marketing dollars right now? What is working? What isn't working? What other sport organizations or events does the company sponsor or support? What does the company like or dislike about these relationships?

3. Arrange a follow-up meeting for the presentation of your proposal before leaving this initial meeting. Try to schedule it within one week of this first meeting.

4. Create a marketing partnership proposal. Give the potential sponsor something unique (creative handles, program elements, or ownership). Act more like a marketing partner or an agency than a salesperson.

5. Present the proposal as a "draft" that you will gladly modify to meet the organization's needs. Custom-tailored proposals are much more likely to succeed than generic proposals.

6. Negotiate the final deal and get a signed agreement. Close the deal when you have the opportunity; ensure that the final signed deal has agreed-on deliverables, payment terms, and a mutually agreed-on timetable.

Creating New Inventory: The Advantages of E-Marketing Opportunities for Sponsorships

Some of the biggest advantages of e-marketing is that it is not dependent on existing traditional inventory, does not have to take place during a game, does not to happen at the venue, does not take inventory away from radio and television, and finally, is limited only by the creativity of the content. One excellent example of creating new inventory through Web sites and other forms of e-marketing is when the Cleveland Cavaliers, along with corporate partner K. Hovnanian Homes, created a Design and Win Home Giveaway on the Cavaliers' Web site. Fans logged on to the Web site to enter the contest and voted each week, as elements of the home developed and changed, on how they wanted the home to look. An actual home worth $200,000 was given away to one registered fan on Fan Appreciation Day (April 19, 2005). (59)

Co-Op Sponsorship Opportunities

A co-op sponsorship agreement is the joining together of two or more entities to capitalize on a sponsorship or licensing opportunity. Co-op sponsorships are viable in today's marketplace for a number of reasons. Such agreements

+ allow companies to share the total cost of the sponsorship;
+ allow the promotion of several product lines (with distinct organizational budgetary lines) within the same corporate structure (e.g., Budweiser and Eagle Snacks);
+ enable corporations to use existing business relationships that make sense (e.g., Coca-Cola and McDonald's);
+ enable a weaker corporation with something to offer to leverage the strength and position of another corporation to gain the sponsorship and a position of advantage over its competitors;
+ allow testing of a relationship when future opportunities are under consideration; and

◆ create a pass-through opportunity, typically involving grocery chains that agree to a sponsorship and pass some or all of the costs (and benefits) to product vendors in their stores (e.g., Stop & Shop could agree to a sponsorship with the University of Connecticut and pass costs on to Pepsi, Frito-Lay, and Wonder Bread).

Let Me Tell You a Story....

As a society, we are bombarded with thousands of messages and pieces of information every day. Some of these messages are ignored, others are examined and then discarded, and others are digested and acted on. Most of the time what happens is dictated by the relevancy of the message to the recipient, at other times it is the timing, and sometimes it is the way the information is presented—perhaps in a fun and engaging way.

In any case, the most effective way for a sponsor to send a message that a potential consumer will receive and act on is to have a story or an activation platform that makes an impression. Sponsors must be more conscious about making a memorable impression on their audience than on counting the number of impressions viewers and readers see. It's no longer just about the quantity of impressions; it is about the quality and the impact of the impression. Thus, sponsors must have a story and find a way to bring the story to life in a meaningful way.

Having a story is the foundation for companies such as Nike. According to Adam Helfant, Nike VP of global sports marketing, "[At Nike] we focus on . . . creating meaning . . . and we create meaning through the stories we tell." (60)

Why do we need stories? Because stories do the following:

◆ Entertain us

◆ Inspire us

◆ Inform us

◆ Persuade us

◆ Motivate us

◆ Engage us

Sport, because of its universal appeal, emotional connections, and associations, and because of its unscripted nature, is a uniquely effective marketing platform for sponsors to use to creatively position their products and services to create impressions and memories that become stories. The "Priceless Campaign" by MasterCard created vignettes that resonated with consumers because they used the emotional connections to sport and sport experiences that resonated with viewers who may or may not have been athletes but nevertheless were connected to sport in some way and could relate to the feelings, memories, and experiences that the stories (actually, commercials) conveyed.

Do you have a story for your product or services? Do you have customer testimonials? Do you have an athlete (for example, Lance Armstrong) talking about endurance and overcoming obstacles, someone who has meaning for your brand?

There are essentially five steps in creating a story that can become a compelling message.

1. *Determine your objectives.* What are the essential tasks that you must accomplish this year? What is it you want to say to your customers?

2. *Identify your appropriate assets.* What potential sport property assets can you use to achieve your objectives? The game? A player? A broadcast or television program? A grassroots initiative?

3. *Consider a variety of platforms to achieve the desired objectives.* What communication forums can you use to convey your message?

4. *Design an engaging activation program.* How will you bring your message to life?

5. *Create a delivery system that capitalizes on the opportunity for storytelling.* Upon review of all of the possible activation platforms and communication mediums, which one has the best likelihood of creating a story that can be told and retold by everyone who comes in contact with it?

The late Bill Veeck, one of the pioneers of sport marketing in the United States, was a master of creating promotional activities that were fun, innovative, and engaging. One of the key considerations for Veeck was to have an activation platform so unique that people would tell and retell their experiences to their friends and relatives; he called this primitive viral marketing. It's no surprise that Veeck established attendance records in every market in which he owned a team.

Let's translate Veeck's principles into practice. Let's say that after winning the 2006 NBA Championship, the Miami Heat want to thank their fans and sponsors for their support. The organization could send out a letter thanking them, stage an event thanking them, or work with a sponsor and create replicas of the championship trophy or rings (done for less than $20 per item) and have an event in which the players thank the fans and sponsors for their support and present them each with a ring or trophy replica. They could even have photos taken of the presentation to each recipient. All three gestures have meaning, but the last one creates a story. The photo of the event hanging in an office or home creates memories and opportunities to retell the story to others. Clearly an objective can be achieved in many ways, but they do not all provide the opportunity for an enduring story.

Sponsors and organizations have difficulty making sure that their messages are heard over the abundance of "noise" in the marketplace today. How marketing rights are activated is often the determining factor between success and failure. Marketers must differentiate—stand out and be heard and seen. Selecting an innovative activation platform that creates the opportunity to tell an engaging story is an effective way to be seen, heard, and most important, remembered. According to Seth Godin, successful marketers are just the providers of stories that consumers choose to believe. (61)

Ethical Issues in Sponsorship

As sponsorship has grown in scope and impact, sport organizations have become highly reliant on sponsorship income to make a profit, or in some cases to secure new facilities or balance their bottom line. This dependence on sponsorship revenue has in certain instances caused the sport organization to make decisions that the affected parties have viewed unfavorably. For example, an exclusive contract between Reebok and the University of Wisconsin brought the university millions of dollars along with a great deal of criticism and protest. The contract, valued at $9.1 million over five years, provides shoes, uniforms, and other apparel for all 22 varsity sport teams. In addition, the contract provides $2.3 million in cash for scholarships, payments to coaches, recreational sport programs, and community service projects. (62) The contract engendered protests and campus debate about affiliating the university with Reebok, which was accused of "sweatshop" practices in the plants in the Far East that produce its athletic shoes. People felt that given the strong spirit of trade and unionism in the state of Wisconsin, there should have been input from a variety of sources and possibly public hearings before the university entered into the agreement.

Currently institutions are debating the issue of sponsorship by brewing companies of intercollegiate athletics programs or events. In the light of several well-publicized deaths of college students in alcohol-related incidents during the past decade, current sponsorship agreements are being scrutinized and new proposals carefully studied and debated. Alcohol-related companies are currently involved in intercollegiate athletics through advertising in game programs, commercials during game broadcasts, and in some cases, sponsorship deals with individual institutions. Coors sponsored a Nebraska football commemorative

When to Say When: Alcohol Sponsorships and College Athletics

Beer companies spend more than $50 million annually just on advertising during NCAA football and basketball telecasts. (63) This does not include other spending related to radio broadcasts, venue signage, ticket and suite purchases, and other promotional activities, which account for millions more dollars. Representatives of the three leading beer companies (Anheuser-Busch, Coors, and Miller Brewing Company) say that their focus is not marketing on campus, even though many students on campus are of age. Instead, they say, their interest is in reaching the audiences that follow and watch college sports. (64) From other perspectives, college athletics directors state that partnering with beer companies is another way to both search for new revenue streams and balance the budget, with agreements that can be as high as $450,000 annually. (65) The Ohio State University and the University of North Carolina, two of the NCAA's most financially sound athletics programs, do not endorse beer-related sponsorships but are unique in that their fiscal position allows them to decline such associations and their related revenue.

On the flip side of this controversial issue, the Center for Science in the Public Interest has launched the Campaign for Alcohol-Free Sports, which seeks to ban alcohol advertising in all sports, while currently focusing its efforts on college sports. This group is supported by more than 210 universities across Divisions I, II, and III, but only a handful are Division IA schools. Coincidentally, 70 percent of these Division IA schools receive some type of revenue from beer companies.

In an era of both general budget cuts and cuts in sport programs, it is difficult to say when and even harder to say no.

championship can, has a sponsorship and contest with the Heisman Trophy committee, and provided a silver inflatable tunnel (resembling a Coors Light can) for the Fresno State basketball team's entrance onto and exit from the court. (66) Does the need for the money outweigh the requirement to be a good citizen and to refrain from promoting products that might harm the very students one seeks to assist? What about sponsorships from lotteries? Do they inadvertently promote gambling? These are some of the ethical issues that sport marketers face every day in their struggle to fund their organizations and remain competitive.

Wrap-Up

Sponsorships and licensing agreements should be positioned as partnerships. Partnerships imply a win–win situation for both parties. This is a progressive way of thinking, rooted in the principles of relationship marketing (as defined in chapter 12). Partnerships imply mutual interest, consideration, negotiation, and benefits. (67) For example, Nike, a noted ambush marketer, is very protective of its own agreements and relationships and never uses the word *sponsor* but always *partner,* believing that the term *sponsor* doesn't take into account the importance of partners working together to meet the needs and goals of each partner.

For sponsors to justify the ever-increasing cost of sponsorships, there must be a multifaceted ROI or ROO (return on objective). The ROI should contain multiple benefits; that is, more than one of the following: media/exposures, sales opportunities, image enhancement, effective communication with the target market, hospitality opportunities, and brand positioning.

The rationale for entering a sponsorship agreement varies according to the size, mission, vision, geographic scope, target market, and resources of an organization. Regardless of the particulars of the organization, all sponsorship decisions should be based on the suitability and fit of the opportunity with the organization and its priorities, as well as on how the sponsorship opportunity helps achieve organizational objectives.

Activities

1. Select a prominent company involved in sport marketing sponsorship activities. Review the activities and events that the company sponsors and determine, based on the criteria listed in this chapter, whether that sponsorship is meeting its objectives. Why or why not?

2. Sponsorships are often referred to as partnerships. Do you believe this is an appropriate term? Provide one sponsorship example to support your answer.

3. Nike is referred to as a company involved in ambush marketing. Explain ambush marketing and provide an example, other than Nike, of a company involved in such activities.

4. What is meant by the term *exclusivity* as it relates to sponsorship?

5. Imagine that you are employed by a marketing agency to provide hospitality for the clients of a large international courier service at an international sporting event viewed as very prestigious (e.g., the Super Bowl, the World Cup). What factors would you consider when planning your schedule of activities?

6. Why is sponsorship viewed as more beneficial than advertising?

Your Marketing Plan

In developing your marketing plan, you have generated a list of objectives, strategies, and tactics. Sponsorship can be instrumental in helping you achieve these elements of a marketing plan by providing the resources (not necessarily just financial) needed to be successful. Integrate one or more of the concepts of sponsorship discussed in this chapter into your marketing plan.

Chapter 14

Place or Product Distribution

A Real "Racket" in Grand Central Station

On an early June day, many New York City train commuters contended with more than the usual urban "racket." The Professional Squash Association held one of its premier events—the New York Sports Clubs Tournament of Champions—in the middle of Grand Central Station. Sound bizarre? Not really. Construction crews had set up a portable, one-way glass squash court, in which the world's best 64 softball squash pros would compete for $65,000 in cash prizes. The six-day event sold a total of 3,500 tickets, for seats around the "Fish Bowl." More important, however, an estimated 20,000 commuters caught a glimpse of the action, which included the reigning champ, Jansher Khan of Pakistan. *Sports Illustrated* claimed that this one train stop had "exposed the sport to more people than had ever before seen it live." (1)

Just think; in one week, the squash industry had exposed its product to over 20,000 customers, most of whom had never seen the game played at a high level of skill, if at all. Further, the commuters in Grand Central Station were likely to fit the perfect demographics for growing squash as a popular sport —urban professionals with discretionary time and income, who might be persuaded to pursue a game that combined skill, exercise, and a limited time commitment. It was a simple matter of "taking the game to the people," because the people were unlikely to stumble across squash on their own.

In this chapter, we discuss a number of facets related to the effective distribution of the sport product—both the core event and its extensions. We begin with a look at the facility, its location, its layout, and its image. Next we consider other types of distribution channels related to sport, including retail distribution of sporting goods. Finally, after outlining some features of effective ticket distribution, we discuss some creative approaches to product distribution in sport. Chapter 15 addresses the related topics of print, broadcast, and Internet distribution.

Placing Core Products and Their Extensions

In many respects, "place," or distribution, decisions may be the most important ones a marketer makes, because they have long-range implications and are sometimes harder to change than product, price, promotion, and public relations decisions. Think just briefly about the range of product elements that require distribution by a typical sport team:

+ The live event itself
+ Tickets to the live event
+ Concessions
+ The image of the live event, via media
+ Players and coaches via personal appearances
+ Merchandise and memorabilia

These elements require an integrated strategy with long-term commitments of assets. Take the game form itself. In a competitive marketplace, most sport governing bodies are looking to "grow their game" by introducing it into new markets. The Professional Squash Association had a good idea, and it was not a costly risk. Major leagues like the NFL, the NHL, and the NBA have likewise recognized their stake in "growing" their sports worldwide. But such strategies are not limited to big-time leagues and big-time budgets. High schools, small colleges, and clubs can also use any of the following tactics:

+ *Scheduling competitions in new markets.* NASCAR has enjoyed tremendous expansion within the United States, but the sport had been insular since running an event in Toronto in 1958. In 2005, NASCAR chairman Brian France set his sights on the international market, specifically

Mexico, where nearly 100,000 fans jammed a venue near Mexico City, paying upward of 1,800 pesos ($160) for seats. Better yet, nine of the drivers were from Mexico. NASCAR is a latecomer to such international placements. Major League Baseball, the NFL, and the NBA have scheduled international exhibitions and tours for years. In the late 1990s, the NHL looked globally when the Anaheim Mighty Ducks and the Vancouver Canucks played two games in Tokyo's Yoyogi national gymnasium. Capacity crowds of over 10,000 paid up to $400 for a ticket, $50 for hats and T-shirts, and $25 for a program. Outside the rink, the NHL's interactive "Hockey Fest" exhibit was free to the public. Players made appearances around the city. By all accounts the visit succeeded. Said NHL Executive Vice President Brian Burke: "We came to pour a big load of fertilizer on the sport in a great market. . . . It's not just about selling T-shirts. This is a huge broadcast market with a professional hockey league already here. This is a market where we want to be active and popular from a marketing standpoint and a broadcasting standpoint." Many U.S. college teams play annual or biennial "home" games in outlying areas—sometimes known as "outer rim" markets. In the 1880s, Yale and Princeton began playing some big football games in Manhattan to attract a bigger paying crowd and expand the fan base. The tradition has continued in college sports. University of New Hampshire men's hockey, for instance, plays one or two "home" games in Manchester's new Verizon Center, some 30 miles (48 kilometers) from its campus arena—all in an effort to develop and satisfy a broader consumer market. (2)

✦ *Reaching out and touching somebody.* In an age of instant global images and datasets, there is little sports action or information that can't be consumed just about anywhere there is a television and a telephone or cable line. But nothing sells like a real human being. This is why tours of star players have spurred fan frenzy for at least 150 years. In the 19th century, boxers, cricket clubs, and baseball teams made well-publicized circuits on rail and steamer, bringing their skills to far distant markets. But what sets apart the market-making tour is the extra touch of special appearances, clinics, or autograph sessions, where heroes can mingle with their audience. It is one thing to watch a star; it is another to shake his hand or go home with her personalized autograph. Even the most star-studded clubs, however, must be careful to protect themselves from promising more than they deliver. In the summer of 2005, for instance, Real Madrid made a four-day stop in China as part of a world tour. Although the club made over $7 million in appearance fees and gate receipts, its lackluster effort (both on and off the pitch) and a no-show (due to injury) by David Beckham led to sour feelings. Ninety-six percent of Chinese respondents to one Internet survey believed that "Real had come to China with the sole goal of making money." Sixty-two percent said they would "not support Real if the team returned to China." (3)

✦ *Supporting the growth of grassroots activity.* An occasional visit by star athletes can spur interest, but it seldom sustains real development of a consumer base. That requires building enthusiasm and participation at the grassroots level. Hockey is a good example. Both the NHL and USA Hockey have realized that ice hockey might develop on a base of interest in street hockey played on in-line roller skates. To this end, the NHL began a traveling street hockey tournament called NHL Breakout in 1995. By 1998, the tour had expanded to 22 cities, including Anaheim, Nashville, and Tampa. NHL Breakout was a clear success at grassroots development. In early 2005, however, the NHL announced that it was suspending the operation of NHL Breakout, embracing instead a partnership with the North American Roller Hockey Championships (NARCh). For a good look at grassroots placement, see the sidebar on Nike Bauer Hockey. (4)

✦ *All sports require specialized space for practice and competition.* These can appear too costly (or too exotic) for some markets. Although football is clearly the number-one team sport spectacle in the United States, the NFL has not taken its grass roots for granted. The NFL Youth Fund, for instance, has supported multiple initiatives including the NFL Grassroots Field Grant Program, which "provides non-profit, neighborhood-based organizations with financing and technical assistance to improve the quality and safety of local football fields in schools and parks." The program has helped build over 100 fields in some four dozen cities, at a cost of nearly $15 million. (5)

♦ *Recognizing and respecting national, regional, and local culture.* The phrase "think globally, act locally" has special meaning for marketers. Although some brands—Coca-Cola, Toyota, or Nokia, for example—enjoy international recognition, they must still adapt their marketing campaigns to reflect cultural differences around the globe. The same is particularly true with sport products. As powerful a brand as the NFL may be in the United States, it has had only mixed success selling its product in Europe. Since the founding of the World League of American Football in 1991, the NFL has looked to "grow" its game in Europe, especially in Britain and Germany. Franchises and leagues have come and gone, with clear success only in Germany. Some of the NFL's failure has stemmed from a certain arrogance that led NFL marketers to think they could sell their game anywhere. One executive finally admitted in 2003 that "Europe has a number of indigenous sports, and American football is not one of them." Whereas the histories of soccer, hockey, and basketball are rich with examples of national cultures embracing a "foreign" game and making it their own (think Brazilian soccer or Russian hockey), American football has been marketed as a set product. Until American football is allowed to adapt to different cultures (i.e., with control at local levels), its international growth will be limited. (6)

Any sound marketing plan considers the careful distribution of all critical components of the sport product, from basic game knowledge to specialized team merchandise.

Nike Bauer Brings Hockey to the Grass Roots

Ed Saunders, marketing manager, U.S., Nike Bauer Hockey

The ice hockey equipment industry is relatively small compared to other major sporting goods categories such as basketball, baseball, etc. At under $500 million globally, the limited market is further hampered by little to no growth in participation.

Ice hockey as a whole receives little major media coverage, and most of that is strictly regional in nature. The challenge this presents to hockey equipment manufacturers is quite simply one of broad-based communication with the core consumer, who are generally adolescent males, although an increasing number of females are taking up the sport. All consumer packaged goods companies struggle to vie for the attention of teens, but without a significant media platform relevant to its market, Nike Bauer Hockey has developed a new strategy for establishing mindshare with the 15-year-old "hockey crazy kid" (HCK).

Nike Bauer's marketing team has developed an integrated approach to brand marketing that gets its message to places that are culturally relevant to its consumers, allowing the brand to live where the players live. With teens spending increasing amounts of time on the Internet, it should be no surprise that digital marketing has become a major factor in the mix. Traditional methods (such as regional vertical print advertising, in-store merchandising, and direct mail) continue to play a significant role as well. But a new method of direct, face-to-face interaction via grassroots events has become the most powerful means for effective, quantifiable connection.

From regionally significant events around the globe such as the Minnesota state high school championships, to the internationally recognized Quebec Peewee tournament, Nike Bauer engages consumers on the ground with a fresh-faced staff and a firm grasp of pop cultural influences that resonate with teens. The marketing staff routinely builds out grand presentations, complete with hip-hop DJs, elaborate sound and light systems, and precisely merchandised displays that feature all the latest gear. As if the music isn't enough to entice the HCKs, large-format video displays and high-definition screens aglow with video games certainly close the deal. Bubble hockey and other forms of activity keep the audience on hand long enough to hear a pitch or two. The objective is to achieve near overstimulation and trigger a strong sense of euphoria around the brand.

Hosting these brand celebrations is an eager group of staff members in their mid-20s. Hardly much older than the target consumer, but old enough to deliver the brand message in an effective way, this team is well versed in both product and brand knowledge and ready to share as much as they can in a short period of time.

Once captivated, consumers are treated to first looks at the latest gear, some of which has yet to hit retail shelves. They are urged to join the Nike Bauer Nation on live digital kiosks featuring the company's Web site, nikebauer.com. In return for joining the Nation, patrons are rewarded with promotional items and a guarantee to receive follow-up communication through large-scale e-mail blasts and regular mail drops. Much of the follow-up revolves around contests and promotions that keep kids coming back to nikebauer.com on a regular basis.

Nike Bauer Hockey engages consumers directly at large-scale grassroots events such as the Minnesota State High School League hockey championships.
Courtesy of Nike Bauer Hockey

Theory of Sport and "Place"

One could argue that sports are no different from fast foods—it's all location, location, location. Because the core sport product is a game form, simultaneously produced and consumed, it makes sense that the venue of that game form should maximize exposure. For the New York Sports Clubs Tournament of Champions, that meant setting up a "Fish Bowl" in Grand Central Station. Many sports, however, require less controllable topographic or geographic factors, such as a mountain, beach, or white-water river, where it is impossible to guarantee high levels of exposure. McDonald's or Safeway does not operate under such constraints. As we discussed in chapter 7, however, the "core experience" of the game or the event can be extended in many creative ways, through media distribution, videotapes, merchandise, and apparel—which is exactly the approach the NHL is taking to "grow" its game.

Location is critical to the experience of every sport consumer, whether participant or spectator. At the University of Massachusetts, the lacrosse field is located near the middle of campus. The men's lacrosse team has enjoyed tremendous student support with crowds in the thousands for big games. By contrast, the baseball team plays "America's game" in an out-of-the-way location where crowds have rarely exceeded a few hundred, even for teams stocked with future Cy Young Award winners! But the difference goes beyond sheer proximity to the campus center. The lacrosse field is bounded in part by a long bank of grass that is perfectly sloped for students seeking a spot in the warm spring sun, where they can relax, kibitz, root for the home team, and maybe even crack open a book. The grassy

The Minnesota Wild have filled the Xcel Energy Center with wonderful historical exhibits that connect old hockey memories to a brand new place.

Courtesy of Roger Godin

embankment is part of an ensemble of elements that make this lacrosse field a special "place" in the campus life.

The notion of the ensemble—developed by geographers—is important for sport marketers who work with core events. They must recognize the elements that enhance or diminish the attractiveness of their venue and surroundings. Take Boston's historic Fenway Park, one of the few North American sport venues that are truly cherished. Fenway's ensemble includes the following elements:

+ *Landscapes*. Fenway Park's surrounding landscapes include both the urban rhythms of Kenmore Square and the rural serenity of the nearby Back Bay Fens, the first park in Frederick Law Olmsted's "Emerald Necklace."

+ *Artifacts*. Fenway Park enjoys two noteworthy artifacts: the "Green Monster" (the left-field wall) inside the park and the giant neon "CITGO" sign outside.

+ *History and memories*. Although Fenway Park is full of memories, none stands out more than Carlton Fisk's game-winning home run in the 1975 World Series.

+ *Ideologies*. Fenway Park may not conjure up serious political or social ideologies, but it does evoke notions (true or not) that baseball was somehow a better game when ballparks were simple and quaint, like Fenway.

+ *Experiences*. As baseball's premier writer, Peter Gammons, put it, "Fans know the soul of baseball is its atmosphere—the sights, smells, sounds, the very feel of the game."

+ *Aesthetics*. Besides the Green Monster, Fenway Park has irregular dimensions around the outfield, with various nooks and crannies that not only look interesting but also create havoc for visiting fielders and delight the home fans.

+ *Problems*. Fenway has plenty of problems, including traffic jams, limited and outrageously expensive parking, and all too many seats with views obstructed by support columns.

The ballpark's capacity—36,108 as of 2006—is the smallest in Major League Baseball. Although this may add to its charm, it is a serious liability in the highly competitive—and salary-cap-less—world of Major League Baseball, especially when the "Evil Empire" can fill Yankee stadium with over 57,000 fans. As noted in chapter 7, the new Red Sox owners—who paid $660 million in 2001—either needed to squeeze more revenues from Fenway or build a new park (something the prior owners had announced their intention to do). To date, they have chosen the path of renovation, and they have done so with care and imagination, under the leadership of Janet Marie Smith, vice president for planning and development. Smith has built carefully on the core "place" elements described previously. This has included a statue of Ted Williams near one of the gates and new seats atop the Green Monster and above right field, the latter including a concourse and concession area. Smith has also announced plans to build restaurants, office and party facilities, and a museum in adjacent buildings. The Red Sox also plan much more than baseball on the park's sacred turf, including a regular stream of rock concerts, youth activities, and even winter skating, with an occasional ice hockey game. All of this will alter Fenway's ensemble of "place" elements, but the Red Sox and their neighbors are cautiously optimistic that Fenway's future will be even brighter than its past. (7)

The Facility

The facility is the central element of any sport "place" ensemble. An essential part of the marketing mix, it includes a number of ingredients that influence the attractiveness of the events held within—from accessibility and other transportation-related issues, to design and layout, amenities, and personnel.

External Accessibility

Most sport marketers and consultants believe in the "location, location, location" school of thought. Placement is paramount in retail sport products and services such as sporting goods stores, as well as in single-purpose health and fitness facilities. Where high levels of impulse business are to be expected, a high-traffic location is crucial. For the majority of sport products, the high level of visibility gained through media coverage can often overcome a less exposed site as long as the product is in demand and is getting good media coverage. Nonetheless, remember that up to 90 percent of a sport facility's customers (court or health club, retail sporting goods store, etc.) can be expected to live within 20 minutes' traveling time. Placement on the periphery of a market area leaves the door open for competition and results in inconvenience for the consumer.

The facility should be readily accessible by major highways and mass transit. The latter is especially important when the facility aims to attract senior citizens, youth, or lower economic groups. Baseball magnates very early recognized the importance of access, and they linked their early "modern ballparks" (Comiskey Park, Fenway Park, Ebbets Field) to the paths of new trolley lines. The last five decades have demanded access by automobile. This caused problems in the 1980s for urban stadiums, situated as they were amid decaying infrastructures in need of repair. For example, the White Sox had long benefited from Comiskey Park's proximity to the Dan Ryan Expressway, which Mayor Richard Daley had allegedly routed near his beloved ballpark. Necessary repairs in 1988, however, had shut down the highway, adding to the White Sox' attendance woes. (8)

The Trade Area or "Drawing Radius"

Accessibility influences the size of a facility's "drawing radius." Good highways and mass transit allow more people to travel farther in less time, and time is the critical cost factor in the consumer's mind. People will endure more or less traveling or "drive time" depending on the nature of their destination. For instance, most people expect to travel only 10 minutes to their local shopping center or strip mall. They will, however, drive 30 minutes to a "super" center that houses a few mass merchandisers, and it appears they will happily drive an hour or more to a new "megamall" that features many "big-box" discounters such as Best Buy or Circuit City. Bostonians make regular two-and-a-half-hour trips to Freeport, Maine—a manufacturer's outlet mecca and the home of L.L. Bean.

As introduced in chapter 5, facility directors used to simply draw concentric circles around a facility, usually at five-mile (eight-kilometer) intervals, as if mileage alone dictated a market. Figure 14.1 illustrates the modern methodology of drawing radii based on drive or traveling time. At multipurpose facilities, the drawing radii change markedly for various events. The traveling-time drawing radii are much better predictors as each radius becomes elongated along major arterial and transit systems, providing a more accurate reflection of equal traveling-time segments.

Although the specific dynamics of the sport drawing radius demands much more rigorous consumer research, it appears that the following factors are critical:

♦ *Demographics.* Discretionary time varies with income, occupation, and stage in the life cycle.

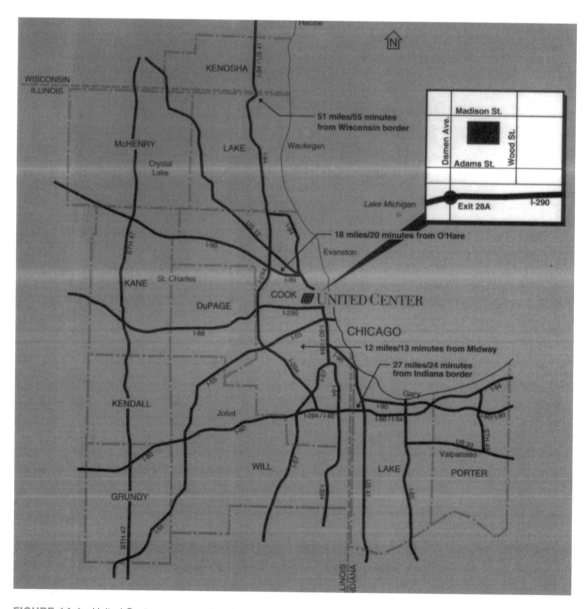

FIGURE 14.1 United Center area map showing drive time as well as mileage.
Courtesy of United Center

◆ *Duration and frequency of the event.* Most people will travel much longer for an infrequent event (a concert by a favorite artist) than they will for a twice-weekly activity (a game of tennis).

◆ *Emotional commitment.* Parents will travel hours to watch their children play; casual high school fans may never leave town.

◆ *Perception of quality.* The "big" game or the "big" star will typically expand the drawing radius.

The drive-time methodology has several applications: (9)

◆ When locating a new facility and performing market feasibility studies, organizations sometimes make accurate market assessments of facility drawing power in the various market segments. Vision regarding drive time has been the key to opening southern markets. For instance, Max Muhleman sold the NBA on a Charlotte, North Carolina, franchise by demonstrating that 5 million people lived within a two-hour drive of a proposed facility—two hours being a perceived maximum for events of NBA quality and frequency. Likewise, "Big Bill" France expanded NASCAR by building facilities with expansive drive-time markets. Jim Foster, France's longtime assistant, recalled the trips to Alabama, when France was negotiating to build a track in Talladega: "Alabama might seem in the middle of nowhere, but if you draw a 300-mile [480-kilometer] circle around Talladega—that is the distance race fans come from—they can drive down, see the race, and drive home in one day. There were 28 million people inside the circle." By overlaying radii for competing facilities, it is also possible to determine areas of competition and even probabilities of facility success. (10)

◆ By analyzing how drawing radii change for various events offered at a multipurpose facility, marketers can make adjustments in the event mix to satisfy all market segments. They can also segment the promotional media in direct response to the drawing radii. At the Springfield Civic Center in Springfield, Massachusetts, the analysis of drawing radii revealed a totally different drawing pattern for the Ice Capades than for professional wrestling, yet remarkably similar media had been used to promote both events.

◆ Analyzing drawing radii will change due to scheduling of events at different times and on different days. Many sport marketers have scheduled their events at the same time every day. (Most baseball games start at 7:30 p.m. Monday through Saturday.) However, the New York Yankees, having long recognized that their market is different, have started their weekday games later, and have varied the starting time on Friday evenings. When setting starting times, a facility manager should account for "traveling lead time." Is the market primarily suburbanites who work in the city and stay in town up to the starting time? Or do these people attempt to commute home, and then return to the event? Is the market primarily city dwellers? Or is it a mix of the two?

Parking

The facility should offer ample parking spaces. For sport facilities such as court and health clubs, resorts, YMCAs, or recreation programs, four parking spots for every court is an industry guide. A rule of thumb for stadiums and arenas is one parking space for every four seats in environments where mass transit is available (see photo on page 350). In 1998, for instance, the San Francisco Giants decided to schedule only 13 weekday games at what was then the new Pac Bell Park (now AT&T Park), largely because of limited parking. The Giants estimated that they needed 12,000 to 13,000 parking spaces for each game at the 42,000-seat facility. This corresponded to about a 1 to 3.3 space-to-seat ratio. With only 5,000 off-street spaces, the Giants will have a greater-than-normal dependence on mass transit. (11)

From a financial, security, and service perspective, the facility operator should also own or at least operate the parking facilities. Parking revenues from a 50,000-seat stadium may average over $100,000 per game for football or baseball games with over 70 percent of seats

A rule of thumb for stadiums and arenas is one parking space for every four seats where mass transit is available.
© AP Photo/ Robert E. Klein

filled. Control of the parking also permits control of pricing and hence reduces gouging and "patron defection" due to high cost of product extensions. Finally, it permits control of parking personnel, who are a crucial part of the overall facility image-building process.

Surrounding Area

As noted in our discussion of the place ensemble, a facility is—and must be—linked to its surroundings in several ways:

✦ *Design*. New or renovated facilities must fit with the local landscape aesthetics. As concluded in one recent study of urban ballpark design, "Ballparks must build upon the character of surrounding structures. Otherwise, they appear as intrusions in the urban fabric." New ballparks in Baltimore, Dayton, Cleveland, and Louisville have integrated seamlessly with each city's overall development plans. Whether or not the facilities yield the economic impact that boosters anticipate, they will contribute to the aesthetics of their communities—no mean accomplishment and nothing to take for granted. Baltimore's Oriole Park at Camden Yards blends ultramodern features inside the park with old buildings and alleys outside. Pittsburgh's is also built with an eye on blending with nearby bridges and buildings. (12)

✦ *Politics*. Sport facilities have never been welcomed by everyone, especially nearby residents, who care less about their own easy access to games than they do about the regular infusion of hordes of fans, their cars, and their often unruly behavior. No sport organization is wise to develop its venue without clear "neighborly" dialogue. In the early 1990s, Boston College ran into a maelstrom of protest when it announced plans for expanding the football stadium. Local residents claimed that the school had broken a promised moratorium on facilities expansion. In little time, BC faced new legislative and regulatory hurdles, as well as enormous ill will that might have been avoided with clearer, early dialogue. (13)

✦ *Sense of safety*. The immediate environment surrounding a sport facility is an extremely important factor in determining attendance frequency. When a facility is located in an area that customers believe is "unsafe," sales will suffer. The environment can also determine the pattern of attendance. A court club or health club located in an industrial park will draw well during the day; but after 5 p.m., few people will venture into an industrial park, so evening and weekend attendance levels will be extremely low. Contrasting with this situation is the court or health club located in the suburbs, where the heaviest demand occurs on weekday evenings and during the day on weekends.

Design and Layout

Design and layout are crucial to consumer satisfaction. These are some of the key aspects of facility design:

◆ *Ease of access and exit to minimize length of lines.* Few things upset today's consumers more than waiting in long lines, especially if their intent had been to "get away from it all."

◆ *Access and sight lines for consumers with physical disabilities.* Providing access to those with physical disabilities entail much more than simply conforming to legal requirements such as the Americans With Disabilities Act (ADA). Some of the key applications of the ADA in stadium design include the fact that 1 percent of total seating must be for wheelchairs; accessible seating must be integrated and not isolated; companion seats must be provided; 1 percent of wheelchair seats must be aisle seats; and "lines of sight" must be "comparable" to those of surrounding seats. Accessibility is more than an ethical issue, although that should be a central consideration. With an aging population, and with technologies that facilitate a more active lifestyle for all people with physical disabilities, facility designs should incorporate the needs of this growing and important market.

◆ *Location and design of food services, bars, concession stands, and bathrooms, with a sufficient number of these amenities to reduce lines.* Given the rising tide of female fans, sport venues will have to provide additional facilities for women. A recent study used by the designers of Seattle's new Safeco Field found that women spend an average of three minutes in a rest room; men spend about 82 seconds. These facilities should also be clean and well maintained and should be as close as possible to where the consumer participates or watches. The location of any concourse is critical to this equation. As noted by one authority, "Today, architects, team owners, and vendors think the concourse is as vital to any venue as the circulatory system is to the human body." (14)

◆ *Provisions for crowd management, crowd flow, and control.* Crowd management provisions should allow ample screening on entrance and minimum use of stairways for exiting the facility. Ramps are a much safer form of access and exit. In court and health clubs and YMCAs, the location of the control desk is a major factor in the success or failure of the

A centralized check-in desk lets health clubs control who enters their facility.

© Human Kinetics

operation. The control desk needs to become a control center from which the management of the facility can completely regulate access and oversee all amenities. In all venues, a key objective is to minimize bottlenecks and maximize crowd flow. The best designs consider consumer "flow" from the point they arrive (and even their travel to the venue) to the point they depart and head safely home. (15)

♦ *Flexible versus dedicated usage.* In the last decade, professional sport teams have moved away from multipurpose venues toward single-use facilities. A main reason has been to maximize sight lines and intimacy for fans. Baseball simply doesn't "play" well in a cavernous stadium meant for 70,000 football fans. Likewise for soccer—America's Major League Soccer has averaged fewer than 20,000 fans per game, which has prompted the development of new dedicated soccer facilities in Columbus and other franchise cities. On the other hand, few schools or colleges can afford specialized venues; flexibility is dictated by budgets and often by space. Further, such facilities must anticipate changes in consumer interest. The last two decades have seen volatile swings of interest in racquetball, soccer, and aerobics. Recent trends have turned court and health clubs into holistic health centers, complete with seminar rooms for stress management and educational classes, swimming pools, and basketball courts. What consumer interests will the 21st century bring?

♦ *Aesthetics.* As with any piece of architecture, the sport facility design requires an appealing blend of form, scale, color, and light. The media focus attention on the multimillion-dollar venues such as Memphis's new FedEx Forum, which is a masterpiece of design (for images, see www.fedexforum.com). In many cases, sponsors are pouring millions into the creation of attractive and interactive "entitlement zones." But even small-budget venues can enhance their attractiveness with concepts used at the big-time. For instance, a number of schools and colleges have been imaginative with the use of new colorful logos and marks in

The University of New Hampshire used posters, a gallery of team pictures, and a good paint job to dress up its old Field House.

Courtesy of Stephen Hardy

otherwise drab entrances, concourses, and gymnasiums. The University of New Hampshire revitalized the atmosphere in its gym, its football field, and its field house with a lot of paint, signs, posters, and images, as well as gallery of team pictures along all the hallway walls. Collectively, a small investment has drastically changed the aesthetic experience not only for fans but, more important, also for the athletes and coaches who call the place home. Marketers should keep abreast of the facility design literature, at all levels, by tracking the Architectural Showcase Awards presented annually by *Athletic Business,* one of the industry's most widely read trade magazines (www.athleticbusiness.com). (16)

Game, Spectacle, and Festival: Framing the Steak and the Sizzle

For as far back as historical sources take us, humans have tended to "frame" sporting contests with layers of spectacle and festival (see figure 14.2). Like today, history was filled with people motivated to watch sporting contests. In boxing, they formed a "ring" around the combatants—hence the term *boxing ring.* Formal venues simply defined in wood, stone, or concrete the threshold that separated the game from the spectacle. But there was always more than just watching. A "festival" frame developed outside the layer of spectators. At ancient venues such as Olympia, people mingled, ate, enjoyed musical performances, and listened to poets—all outside the spectacle frame. Modern venues reflect these very ancient practices in the forms of special tailgating areas, large concourses, and atriums where vendors hawk their wares. In some arenas, the concourse-festival frame lies outside the frame of seats. In Boston's TD Banknorth Garden, fans who have milled around between periods, buying concessions and mingling in groups, must reenter the spectacle through tunnels. In other venues, concourses offer direct sight lines to the action. Camden Yards is a case in point. Similarly, Hadlock Field in Portland, Maine, offers a group picnic area along the right-field line. Here festival and spectacle are combined inside the park. (17)

American football has a long tradition of fusing the three frames into a single experience. As early as the 1890s, Manhattan hosted "big games" between Yale and Princeton, closely covered in national magazines by feature writers like Richard Harding Davis. Manhattan Field would be packed with 30,000 spectators singing songs and chanting cheers in ways now largely lost in North America (but alive in the world's great soccer venues). The bigger show, however, was before the game, outside the field, in the long parades of partisans marching and riding down Fifth Avenue hours before game time, in what Davis called a

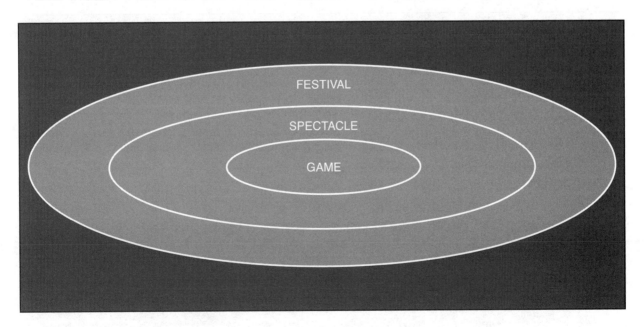

FIGURE 14.2 The standard frames of sport.

"circus procession many miles long," coaches festooned in yellow or blue, filled with young men and women "smothered in furs; and the flags, as they jerk them about, fill the air with color," cheered on by crowds four deep along the sidewalks. As Davis concluded, "Today the sporting character of the event has been overwhelmed by the social interest." (18)

Davis captured a phenomenon that is now an essential part of marketing—managing the three frames, balancing the sizzle with the steak, the festival and spectacle, with the game itself. It is not always easy. People want food and drink—festival elements—in the spectacle frame. But they don't want vendors blocking their view. And they don't want drunks dowsing them in beer. Leagues want to enhance spectacle, but they don't want players running into the stands, and they limit celebrations that detract from the game.

Sometimes, however, it makes sense to scramble the frames. In the NHL, the Columbus Blue Jackets placed a game in the lobby. Called "Big Hockey," it is the old "push and pull" table game, in which tiny plastic players are controlled by levers. Except this game is huge; so big that each fan controls one only lever. Even during games, fans line up for a chance to play. And when they are waiting to play, the Blue Jackets hope they're paying attention to the real hockey game on television monitors. It's always a gamble to pull fans away from the live action, but this scrambling of the frames makes sense. "They're connecting with young people," said Phoenix Coyotes' president Shawn Hunter. "In that arena, fans are going wild about Big Hockey. And fan development is on the top of everyone's list." There are many other examples of effective "frame management." Giant scoreboards now provide separate spectacles (e.g., league or team highlights) during breaks in live game action. Or they create "games within games," such as the interactive, on-screen tug of war developed by Flying Spot, Inc. In this game, fan sections "tug" with their cheering, and the screen moves accordingly. (19)

Some high school and college administrators worry that fans—especially those familiar with all the promotions and giveaways at professional events—will expect the same at the grassroots level. Diedre Jones, sports information director at Jackson State, put it this way: "When people come to the game, they expect to get something for free. If we don't do something, I hear about it. . . . It is eclipsing the game somewhat for a smaller school . . . I think people are going to get so caught up in the entertainment that they're going to overlook the actual talent of the athletes." Ohio State's Dave Brown, past president of the National Association of Collegiate Marketing Administrators, played on an old hockey joke to capture the conundrum: "I went to a concert and a baseball game happened." There is no easy answer to this problem, but grassroots programs can be creative in managing venue frames. Ultimately, the answer involves a return to core mission and strategy (as discussed in chapter 2). (20)

Amenities: Convergence Toward the "Sports Mall"

Today's sport consumers, who pay hundreds of dollars to attend one event with their family, expect a range of amenities that enhance their spectacle and festival experience. Bench seats, boiled hot dogs, a mimeographed program, and a scoreboard that displays only the score—none of this will do. So the "big-time" venues have responded with a range of amenities. Many of them are designed to provide what is called "technological WOW." Following are some examples:

♦ *Ever more expensive big screens and electronic message centers and sound systems.* When arena managers think about fan comfort these days, their concerns go well beyond the older notions of sight lines, seat backs, and warm fannies. St. Paul's Xcel Energy Center seats 18,064 for National Hockey League games, with four seating levels, four separate concourses, and a press level. As described on the arena's Web site, the center scoreboard is 35 feet (10.7 meters) high and 36 feet (11 meters) in diameter. It is animated by "full-color LED (light emitting diode) large-screen video displays and seven levels of display equipment." But some of the zanier displays are on the "ribbon board signage" that wraps around both the suite level and the two upper levels. These provide continuous "animation, graphics and cropped video in 16.7 million shades of color." At times it must be hard to focus on the actual game action! (21)

◆ *Connectivity.* In the late 1990s, the "next rage" was going to be "smart seats" wired with small computer screens from which fans (for a premium price) could request replays from various camera angles, check a rule, call up stats, and order food or merchandise. But the costs were very high, so relatively few smart seats were developed. More important, today's and tomorrow's fans want wireless connections. As the Charlotte Bobcats built their new arena in 2005, their VP for arena development promised that "we're not going to have 80 hot spots or 111 hot spots (for wireless connectivity). We're having one. It's called the whole arena." But there have been problems with the concept. Providing connectivity is easy. The problems have been in finding a way to provide and control (and profit from) access to data that drives fans up an escalator of commitment. After all, who wants to provide wireless connections so that fans browse for another game, a rock concert, or shop in an online fashion catalog? Cell phones can already do that. As Jeffrey Pollack, NASCAR's former guru for digital entertainment, put it: "The key to success for products like this is enhancing the event, not competing with it. It's critical that these devices are bringing fans closer to the competition, not detracting from the live action." To that end, Purdue University is experimenting with a system in which fans will lease wireless PDAs (personal digital assistants) that would give them controlled access to in-game replays, stats, menus, and other bits of data. Says Purdue's Jay Cooperider: "We have what amounts to a hand-held JumboTron." (22)

◆ *Upscale food and drink.* Luxury-suite patrons have been munching on shrimp and caviar for years. Suite patron pay on average over four times what the "average" fan pays per game on food and beverages. But if the highbrows demand their Alsatian noodles with kangaroo fillets, that doesn't mean the hoi polloi will settle for the same old stale hot dogs. Around the American market, stadiums and arenas are typically expanding their offerings at stands, kiosks, and food courts to include items unheard of less than a generation ago—Philly cheesesteak, jalapeño "poppers," pierogis, chef's salads, chicken fajitas, North Carolina–style barbecue, low-calorie wraps, microbrews, sweet tea, Bacardi Breezers, Krispy Kreme donuts, homemade sopapillas, and hand-dipped ice cream. (Of course, after paying the bill, some parents might prefer to go back to the old days!)

◆ *Special zones for networking and interactivity.* College football programs have for years developed and used special fan, kid, and family zones, often using end zone space that was in light demand. This was an example of managing spectacle and festival frames (see the club seat sidebar on page 356). Washington State University added a twist for basketball with a "Hot Spot" hot tub for use by the first eight WSU basketball fans to reach its corner location in the Beasley Performing Arts Coliseum. In the last decade, sport venues have given new meaning to the term *zoning.* Phoenix's Chase Field offers much more than its well-publicized outfield hot tub. It also has included a Walk of Fame Museum, an interactive play area called Diamondtown, and a miniversion of baseball's Hall of Fame in Cooperstown. The newest arenas, such as the Philips Arena and the FedEx Forum, provide sponsors the opportunity to connect with everyday fans in "entitlement zones" that sponsors control and fill with fun, interactive games and "experiences" that blend sports with high-tech entertainment and commercial messages. The Tampa Bay Lightning have turned a section of their arena into a special "B to B" networking zone called the X/O Club. The club plan allows businesses to purchase individual club seats that are tied to membership in an adjoining suite of dining areas, lounges, even a cigar room—all with perfect lines of sight on the action. The club's Web site invites prospects to "be a part of the only membership club in the entertainment industry offering an all-inclusive buffet, beer, wine and VIP parking." Why limit the corporate experience to 20 people in a single suite? The X/O Club expands the networking to hundreds of other people. It has been a sellout since its inception. (23)

The quest for amenities drives more than ballparks and arenas. In some respects, athletic clubs led the way in the 1980s with the "full-concept club" offering a complete line of courts, supervised health programs, a social bar or lounge area, pro shop, pool, day care, sauna, whirlpool, and the like. Some of today's clubs even offer videotaping services so members can save (and learn from) their performances in lessons or in competition. As noted in chapter 6, the bowling industry has also transformed some of its venues in an effort to attract a younger generation.

It would be easy to get cynical about the merger of sport and a "mall mentality"—that is, providing every conceivable outlet to induce a consumer to part with hard-earned money. On the other hand, no one requires a patron to buy more than a ticket, a court rental fee, or a membership. It appears that in the court club or the hometown arena, consumers want more than sport. Brad Clark, a senior designer at Ellerbe Becket, summed up these attitudes nicely to *Street & Smith's SportsBusiness Journal*: "Yes, they want to see the Michael Jordans and the Troy Aikmans, but they also want to be able to get a microbrew, buy some designer clothes, and maybe play an interactive game or two. It's not just a sports arena anymore. It's a sports and entertainment center." The more serious issue may be that grassroots sport organizations, such as high school programs and town recreation facilities, simply can't afford to provide the amenities many fans welcome or demand. (24)

Personnel

The people who work in a facility may be the major force in projecting a facility's image and in its ultimate success. The attitudes of "operations" personnel directly affect consumer satisfaction because these workers are the primary (and in many cases, the only) personnel that consumers contact. Yet such nonmanagement personnel are often the least trained among a facility's staff. A stark example of this phenomenon can be seen in athletic and racquet clubs, where desk personnel are usually college or high school students employed part-time. The same is true in stadiums and arenas, whose events staff are almost all part-

The Club Seat

Club seats have become a standard component in today's sport venues. The club seat concept was clearly designed to offer the upscale consumer something between the luxury suite and the best box or loge season seat. Like the suites, club seats are clearly segregated from the crowd; they also offer exclusive amenities. On the other hand, like the loge or box seat, the club seat can stand alone. For a higher price, the club seat patron gets special treatment, as the United Center's Club Seating Handbook makes clear:

✦ Special parking—"reserved parking in fenced, well-lit and clearly marked parking lots adjacent to the United Center for all Blackhawks or Bulls preseason, regular season and play-off games."

✦ Membership in the Chicago Stadium Club—a "spectacular 'members only' 260-seat restaurant."

✦ Controlled seat access through gates reserved for club seat ticket holders.

✦ Waiter/waitress service during the event.

✦ Concierge service from "special attendants located in the Club seating level."

✦ "Coat check and parcel services."

✦ "Fully furnished, hotel-style lounge areas complete with full bar service."

✦ "Private telephone booths."

✦ Delayed postgame departure—up to one hour in lounge areas, "while traffic clears . . . Of course, guests in the general seating areas of the United Center must depart the building immediately following the conclusion of the event."

✦ Priority access to purchase tickets to special events (e.g., concerts, ice shows).

Most of all, as the handbook states clearly in the introduction, club seats offer the "privileges that are so often only associated with suite ownership—spectacular seats in the lap of luxury—at a fraction of the cost." Clearly not for the working-class family, clubs seats have been a "deep well" for teams and venues precisely because they slake a thirst for more amenities, including the desire to be segregated. Although some teams and venues have experienced weakening demand for club seats, they remain a staple in the lineup of consumer options. (25)

timers. How often do patrons face an uncaring or even a surly usher? Too often. All of this is unnecessary, especially when professional trade associations such as the International Health, Racquet and Sportsclub Association (IHRSA) and the International Association of Assembly Managers (IAAM) offer training manuals and videos. The IAAM's list of video training programs includes the following titles:

Managing the Crowd

Service Excellence: Dealing With Guests

Service Excellence: Patrons With Disabilities

Clubs, schools, colleges, and youth programs all run events in venues. Some of the events draw tens of thousands patrons. Staff training for such events is no longer a luxury; it is a necessity. Stanford University now conducts extensive staff training, beginning each August with a four-hour program for all full- and part-time "guest services" employees, who are paid to attend the program. Equally important, Stanford has developed an extensive guest services manual that helps to ensure consistency in the way staff members interact with consumers. (26)

Sense of Security

The IAAM training videos include a healthy emphasis on safety and security, with good reason. Nothing drives consumers away faster than a fear for their safety. The terrorist attacks of September 11, 2001, prompted elevated security provisions at sport venues as much as at airports. By early 2003 the vice president of the Stadium Managers Association estimated that the industry had already spent "around $100 million on capital improvements for security." But terrorists are not the only menace. Rowdy, unruly, drunken fans can quickly ruin a rare, long-planned outing for a family with young children. That may be four or five consumers lost for a long time, and with the word-of-mouth multiplier, the effect could reach into the dozens. The Philadelphia Eagles had a growing concern about rowdy fans that finally reached crisis proportions at a Monday night game that was punctuated by dozens of fights in the stands and a flare that a drunken fan rocketed across the field into the stands (luckily into an empty seat). The Eagles' answer to the crisis was to work with the city to increase security and run an on-site municipal court, which in the next few games heard 20 cases ranging from disorderly conduct to violating the city's open-container law. Seventeen rowdies pleaded guilty and accepted fines up to $300. The Eagles promised to punish offending season-ticket holders by revoking their tickets. (27)

Evaluating Consumer Opinion

The facility is the initial "place" of most sport experiences. Other sport products are generally derivative. As such, the facility needs to do its own evaluation by asking consumers key questions, such as, How do you perceive the facility, its physical layout, crowd flow, cleanliness, parking, amenities, surrounding area, personnel? and, What amenities might increase your attendance or participation? Research suggests that stadium satisfaction rivals team loyalty in determining fan intensions to attend events. Marketers should ask the previous questions regularly as part of the comprehensive data-based marketing system (DBM). The answers form basic data components for effective facility layout, design, and customer service. (28)

Marketing Channels

Although the facility is the primary element in distributing the core sport product, there are other aspects to the concept of "place" in the sport marketing mix. These involve the various channels by which marketers can deliver the product, in this case beyond the facility.

"Channels" are simply various sets or configurations of organizations linked together to deliver a product to consumers. Channel systems often vary by product line or sales territory within a company's distribution network. Channel systems can be complex; they may shift and share functions, as is often the case in sport marketing. Standard channel elements have included the following:

Manufacturers (M)

Wholesalers (W) and jobbers (J)

Retailers (R)

A traditional channel for hard goods would look like this:

$$M \rightarrow W \rightarrow J \rightarrow R \rightarrow C$$

This made sense for much of the sporting goods industry. A manufacturer such as Spalding made balls, sold them to wholesalers, who worked with "jobbers" to sell to local stores, where consumers (C) would buy the balls.

On the other hand, a family ski outing would look more like this:

$$M \leftarrow C$$

Here the consumers actually work backward in the standard channel by traveling to the place of production, and then taking part in the production and consumption of the product simultaneously. The Internet and direct mail have reconstructed traditional channels of equipment and apparel to look similar to the ski outing. Consumers can surf the Web to find manufacturers' sites, check the online catalog, and order by direct mail, all without using wholesalers or retailers.

In the increasingly complex world of sport marketing channels, it is more typical to find the two types of systems operating in parallel, sometimes to reach the same consumer. Take a professional sport team. It has a traditional channel of on-site box offices and kiosks for event tickets:

$$M \leftrightarrow C$$

But it also may televise the event and distribute it via television to a wider audience, so that the channel looks like this:

$$M \leftrightarrow C = Event \rightarrow Media \rightarrow C$$

If the on-site consumer taped the game on a home TiVo, he would be part of both the beginning and the end of the channel! As teams use Web sites for the redistribution of broadcast highlights and for direct sale of team merchandise, the channel loops become more complicated.

As any sport organization considers channels for product distribution, it must weigh at least four factors in tandem:

Expertise

Cost

Control

Adaptability

The NHL, for instance, wants a name presence in grassroots roller hockey, but it is comfortable ceding product control to the North American Roller Hockey Championships. On the other hand, Nike's move into Niketown stores signaled a desire for more direct control of product presentation at the retail level. Finally, the great consumer embrace of the Internet is a double-edged sword. Although Internet sales certainly offer consumers more access and control, retailers are realizing that cost savings are not always as high as expected. Although the Internet may reduce the payroll for a sales force, it also forces a retailer to expand distribution warehouses (with all the associated labor costs). In summary, there is no simple formula for determining the best marketing channels. It is a constant balancing act.

Retail Sport Operations

Despite the rise of the Internet, traditional retail outlets remain important elements for sport marketing channels. Specialized outlets for sport products grew rapidly in the 19th century, as entrepreneurs recognized—and promoted—an interest in fishing, cricket, baseball, hunting, and other activities among urban populations that could support their businesses. Today's big-box firms such as the Sports Authority have a long list of ancestors that include hardware stores and retail chains such as Sears and Montgomery Ward. But today's sport marketplace has seen some new twists as well, especially the channel movement by teams, clubs, and governing bodies forward into the retail business. (29)

To some degree, college programs led the way. The University of Michigan was one of the first to realize the value of merchandising. Offering a wide array of novelties, Michigan developed a range of retail outlets in the 1970s, including souvenir stands at Michigan Stadium, Crisler Arena, Yost Ice Arena, the tennis/track building, the golf course, and the ticket office. These were not all the outlets. Michigan had partnerships with high school booster clubs and cheerleader organizations, which sold Michigan novelties as part of their own fund-raising efforts. Finally, Michigan effectively used direct-mail sales to season-ticket holders and other targeted customers on mailing lists that the athletic department purchased. These practices are now fairly standard. (30)

Professional teams had long operated "pro shops" in arena lobbies, but the presence of these outlets was generally not part of a branding/distribution strategy. By contrast, the NBA opened a retail store in Manhattan that is more than a place to buy NBA goods. As described on its Web site, the NBA Store is a "two-level basketball extravaganza that provides a unique backdrop for corporate functions, cocktail receptions, sit-down dinner parties, and more." The NBA Store was clearly part of a broad distribution strategy that included branded television shows, branded merchandise, and branded fan experiences. In the last decade, dozens of professional teams have opened off-site retail outlets, although there have been as many failures as successes. Internet stores are the current outlet of choice (see the sidebar on the New Jersey Devils' store on page 360).

The central concept behind the new sport retail outlets is a fusion of branded and licensed goods with the fan experience one would ordinarily associate with a big game. When all goes well, the consumer does not simply buy a shirt, a cap, or a pair of shoes. The consumer learns more about the team or the league, picks up a playing or coaching tip, and walks out of the store holding or wearing not a hat, but a touchstone of greater commitment and involvement. There is no reason a high school athletics director or a soccer club manager could not develop similar marketing opportunities on a smaller scale. Network and cable television have not eliminated the need for grassroots education and grassroots heroes.

The Ticket Distribution System

Ticket distribution is a good example of the fast-changing environment of sport marketing channels. The trend is clearly away from buying tickets at the gate, at least for the big-league teams with high demand on the part of suburban fans. Within the last decade, many clubs have seen huge swings away from box office sales toward Internet sales—with some box-office-to-Internet-sales ratios going from 90:10 to 25:75. New electronic technologies expanded the possibilities of ticket distribution, largely because computerized ticketing eliminated the problems of duplicate tickets, excess stock, and limited choice—all of which had plagued earlier efforts to go beyond the single box office. As with any decision on marketing channels, however, there is a balance to be struck among the aforementioned factors of expertise, cost, control, and adaptability. The last decade has seen a few new standard distribution programs beyond the box office. We will take a brief look at these.

♦ *Partnerships with ticket firms.* A decision to move ticket sales beyond a simple box office typically means a partnership with a ticketing company. In 1968, Ticketron used computer networking to open new worlds of ticket distribution for all kinds of events. Today's sport

Team Merchandise: It Takes a Team to Have a Sellout

Dave Perricone, director of merchandise, New Jersey Devils

Working for an organization that has won two Stanley Cups in the last decade doesn't solve all merchandise sales problems. But it does teach one thing: To have a successful department in any organization, you need to function as team. Here are some aspects that help make us a successful merchandise department.

Products

Everyone has different opinions of what products are good and what are bad. In the end, the only opinions that matter are the consumers'. We keep our personal opinions out and order what our research and our data tell us will sell. Some of our research techniques include:

- Reviewing what our league teams as well as other leagues are selling.
- Contacting all approved licensees that sell products in our league.
- Visiting local shopping malls and seeing what the stores are selling and what the shoppers are buying.

Vendors

These are the people we depend on for high-quality products that we can sell to our consumers. We look for quality rather than quantity; that is, we would rather deal with a few vendors who we know will consistently ship the product on time than many vendors who are always delayed in shipping their product. Having the merchandise in hand is crucial, because we must ship to our customers in a timely fashion, if we expect them to place any reorders. We use a few key tactics in developing and maintaining our vendor/client relationship:

- We communicate with vendors even after the order is placed.
- We don't take orders for granted.
- We demand honesty about the product, its shipping date, etc.

Employees

Our employees are the key to our success. While our team on the ice has wingers and centermen, we break down our staff by customer service and pickers/packers. The customer service duties include taking phone orders and inputting the orders into the computers. The pickers/pack-

Dave Perricone runs a business, but he is also a fan.
Courtesy of Dave Perricone

ers are the ones who pick the merchandise off the shelves, pack the orders, and input the shipping information into our shipping computers.

The customer service employees must have knowledge of our products and must be familiar with our computer software program. We do not want someone taking an order who keeps putting the customers on hold to figure out how to use the program. The way the employee talks to a customer can determine whether that customer will place an order. We don't want our employees to rush the customer off the phone or to be rude in any way to the customer. This may lead to the customer not placing an order, but more important, word of mouth will suggest that our operation was not professional. As with all aspects of Devils marketing, we don't want to make promises that the company can't keep. For example, if our normal time frame is two weeks for shipping, we don't want our customer service people promising three-day delivery, just because they think that is what the customer wants to hear.

The other employees in the department are the ones who pick and pack the merchandise. We make sure that these people know where every item is on the self. Each product is labeled with a number. When we print out a picking slip, it has the part number along with the shelf number where the product is located. Each picker checks the size of the actual item in case it was put in the wrong bin. After they check the size, they sign the picking slip. The packer then double checks the item and also signs their name on the picking slips. By doing this, there are two employees that check each package before it goes out to the customer. The last thing we want is a customer receiving wrong merchandise.

Inventory

Once we have decided what products to purchase, we always ask ourselves the question, How much should we order? This process is like being a general manager of a sports team. We want to get the best output of our products (players) for the money we are spending. In this case, we want to turn inventory over (sell the same item—shirt, hat, doll) as many times as possible. The less inventory we have, the better job we did in purchasing and managing the products.

Following are some keys to controlling purchases while increasing sales:

- *Use drop-ship items.* This is when vendors will send the products out only when you send the customer's order. This means that you have no inventory to stock. You are taking less risk with this kind of purchase.
- *Work with vendors who will allow you to order low minimum quantities.* By doing this, the inventory will remain low. If something doesn't sell, you will not be stuck with a lot of inventory.
- *Find a local vendor who will produce the product.* Importers often keep their own inventories lean, which may prevent you from getting timely reorders for hot products.

If you end up with a high inventory, consider the following:

- Were your products correct for your target market?
- Was your price too high? How much were other retailers selling the same product for?
- Did only a few sizes sell of a certain product? This may lead you to adjust your ordering scale in the future.
- Is your inventory easy to access so the people who are picking the merchandise for shipping can find it without a problem? You don't want them spending valuable time because they don't know where the product is located. We provide picking slips that will show the person the bin and shelf number of the product and where it is located on the shelf.

In conclusion, managing a merchandise store effectively requires tight teamwork, among people both inside and outside our organization. When customers are happy and we turn our inventory well, for us it's like winning the Stanley Cup.

ticket market is dominated by Ticketmaster (which bought Ticketron in 1991 and absorbed ETM in 2000), Tickets.com (which absorbed BASS Tickets), Paciolan, CyberSeats, Choice Ticketing Systems, and a few others. Firms vary in the scope of their services, the degree to which their systems are integrated into those of the client team or venue, and the associated costs. Some of the issues to be addressed in any partnership include consumers' ability to print tickets on their own computers or at a kiosk or automated teller and ticket machine (ATTM), transaction fees, and consumers' ability to return or resell tickets. (31)

- *Partnerships with other consumer retail outlets.* Ticket distribution often goes hand in hand with new sponsors and new promotions. In the late 1990s, for instance, MLB's San Francisco Giants created a 10-year partnership with Chevron, whose corporate headquarters are local. Part of the estimated $15 to $20 million deal included the prospect of Chevron gas stations selling Giants tickets. A few years earlier, the Cleveland Lumberjacks had worked out a deal with northeastern Ohio Burger King stores in which BK purchased 15,000 tickets for each of two "Burger King Buyout Nights." Fans who wanted tickets to either game had to get them at a Burger King outlet, which enabled BK to create a number of promotional packages to drive store traffic. Many of these deals include ticket kiosks at targeted retail outlets such as grocery stores, which can provide leverage for other forms of sponsorship. In 1998, for example, the Texas Rangers established electronic kiosks—provided by ETM Entertainment Network—at 60 Kroger supermarkets in north Texas. Ranger fans could use a credit card to buy the best tickets available for the games of their choice, with hard tickets printed on the spot. In 2004, the New Orleans Saints worked a ticket distribution deal with minor league baseball teams in Jackson, Tennessee, and Mobile, Alabama. This is one avenue that high school and small college programs can use, especially if most or all of their tickets are general admission. Partnering with local or "outer market" retailers—especially in sporting goods or clothing—is a good way to drive sales. Such programs may be particularly effective ways to help promote holiday or postseason tournament sales. (32)
- *Television telethons.* In the 1980s, a number of teams began buying television time and running telethons to sell tickets. The Pittsburgh Penguins had an annual summer telethon, built around the movie *Slap Shot.* The NBA's Cleveland Cavs transformed the concept into an infomercial, aired before Cleveland Indians games. The Cavs bought the time for a season preview show and used breaks to offer a television-only package of 16 games for the price of 15. Colleges and high school programs might use the same concept by using local cable access channels or by developing sponsor packages with local cable operators who might donate some of the local advertising time they retain on national networks such as ESPN. (33)
- *Payroll deductions with selected companies.* Colleges have for some time offered direct payroll deductions for employees who were also season-ticket holders, maximizing ease of access and payment. With the expansion of electronic banking systems, this possibility

has extended to employees of any company that uses electronic payrolls. In the early 1990s, the Hamilton Canucks of the American Hockey League worked with the City of Hamilton to offer the city's 6,000 public employees season tickets via payroll deduction. The city had an interest because the Canucks played in a city-owned rink, and a portion of ticket and concession revenues returned to the city. (34)

✦ *Telephone systems.* In the late 1990s, the Boston Red Sox began using the NEXT ticketing system, which is an automated, credit card, phone order system designed as an alternative to Ticketmaster. Unlike Ticketmaster, the NEXT system did not brand its own tickets. In the case of the Red Sox, for example, the consumer appeared to be dealing directly with a Red Sox operation (even though it was all automated), and the tickets were issued on Red Sox stock. Better yet, there was no $6 surcharge. The NEXT system (still used by the Red Sox) handles 400 calls at a time and can sell 75,000 tickets in an hour—a task that would be impossible for humans. (35)

✦ *Home delivery.* Sometimes computers can't solve a problem. In the fall of 2004, Ball State University football faced serious pressure to sell tickets. An NCAA rule (since loosened) required all Division IA programs to average 15,000 fans in home game attendance. To reach this goal for the home opener, Associate Athletics Director Matt Wolfert came up with a novel ticket distribution system to faculty and staff. On "Terrific Ticket Tuesday," he hand-delivered tickets, within 30 minutes of any telephone order, or the tickets would be free. As Wolfert chased around campus in his SUV—what he called a "traveling ticket window"—he felt energized: "If I can't be excited about it and I'm in charge of selling it, how can I expect anyone else to be excited about it?" His "home delivery" program paid off in additional sales of over 250 tickets. (36)

Creative Distribution

As the previous examples suggest, the marketer must use creativity in planning and implementing new channels of distribution. Keeping abreast of the latest technologies and keeping an open mind are critical to success. The following are some simple questions marketers need to ponder continually:

✦ Who are my consumers and what are their needs?
✦ Where are my consumers?
✦ What are my products and their extensions?
✦ What vehicles—especially using new technologies—are available for distribution?

New Internet technologies, for instance, have helped some organizations solve the long-vexing problem of ticket returns. Although every team or event hopes to get all tickets in the hands (virtual or real) of its consumers well ahead of competition day, what happens if a fan wants to return the ticket? Getting to a ticket outlet to exchange or return a ticket has never been an easy task. And a short-sighted marketer might say, "Too bad, no returns." This may boost the "paid attendance" figure for that event, but it can also push good fans right off the escalator. The Internet has changed the prospects.

In 2000, the San Francisco Giants were among the first teams to unveil an electronic ticket exchange for season-ticket holders. By using the Giants' "Double Play Ticket Window" (at www.sfgiants.com), season-ticket holders can sell tickets "at any price above the face value of the ticket." The price is determined by the season-ticket holder. A "convenience fee" of 10 percent is added to the ticket price. Fans buy the tickets via credit cards and receive them either by mail or at the park. The system works because the Giants use electronic turnstiles. When a season-ticket holder gives up a ticket, the original bar code is invalidated, with a new one allotted to the new ticket.

In a way, this is legalized scalping, but the system allows the Giants to control transactions. It puts more tickets online to the public well in advance of games. And more than anything, it keeps season-ticket holders happy. Giants COO Larry Baer was optimistic about the new system: "We think we'll be looking at something like a 90 percent renewal next year because of this program." (37)

The University of Maryland uses ticket distribution to drive student commitment to its football and basketball teams. Any fully enrolled (and athletic-fee-paying) student may request and print tickets for football and men's basketball via a secure Web site (at www.tickets.umd.edu). In both sports there are often not enough tickets to meet student demand, so tickets are distributed via lotteries weighted by several variables, including "loyalty points" gained from past attendance (determined by a gate-based scanning system). The students' secure personal accounts allow them to do several tasks online, including the following:

Track their attendance history

View their loyalty point total

Print tickets that become available

Cancel a previously claimed ticket

The last function is crucial, because if students do not cancel tickets at least a day ahead of a game, they lose loyalty points. But a late cancellation is still better than a no-show. More than two no-shows in a football season (or five in a career), or three in a basketball season (or eight in a career) means no tickets at all, ever! (38)

The wireless age means that data of all kinds can be distributed to consumers almost anywhere at any time. By the fall of 2004, an estimated 160 million Americans carried cell phones. Businesses of all stripes looked for ways to tap into the expanding market. Major League Baseball cut a deal with m-Qube Inc. that would give subscribing fans ($4 per month) game updates, recaps, trade and injury news, special ringtones, and "wallpaper," as well as access to special contests.

Advertisers salivated at the prospect of interactive, personalized ads sent to this haunch of consumers, who almost by definition were prone to react and click. Young people with cell phones, PDAs, and iPods were the kinds of consumers who might push a new product (or maybe an old team) over the "tipping point" (see sidebar on page 364). As Tom Burgess, CEO of Third Screen Media, put it: "There's a generation coming of age that will never have known a landline telephone. Marketers are going to have to go there." Dunkin' Donuts joined other pioneers in reaching out to this audience through the "third screen"—after television and personal computers. And in a wireless age, with handheld phones that could also connect to the Internet, the "third screen" was the crucial new venue. Dunkin' Donuts planted a pop-up banner coupon on 10 weather and entertainment sites popular with wireless users. Clicking on the ad created a text message with a unique numeric code that the user could show at a Dunkin' Donut counter for a discount. Not only could Dunkin' Donuts reach a mobile audience less prone to reading newspapers, but it could also get instant feedback on the coupon's effectiveness.

It would only be a matter of time before sport franchises—at least those with available seats—would jump on this bandwagon. There were two hurdles. The first was technological—dealing with the quickly shifting landscape of wireless Web sites and carrier networks. The second was ethical, political, and (if abused) legal. Reading and clicking on a "coupon" placed on a Web site was an entirely voluntary experience. In this sense it was different from opening a personal e-mail account and feeling overwhelmed with spam. But would consumers see it that way? As Jay Emmert, an industry rep, put it, "Network operators are very concerned about the lessons they've learned from e-mail. What we don't want is to turn short messaging into one more thing that people turn off because they can't stand it." Would irate consumers push their political representatives to regulate such cell phone ads? Only time would tell. (39)

Finding Mavens, Salesmen, and Connectors

Sport marketers seeking to distribute their products in new markets would do well to read Malcolm Gladwell's best-selling book, *The Tipping Point: How Little Things Can Make a Big Difference*. In Gladwell's words, "ideas and products and messages and behaviors spread just like viruses do." But just as a few people can spread a deadly virus, so too with ideas and products. As Gladwell argued, "Change often occurs not through some mass frontal assault of ideas or ads or directives from above. The tipping point comes through the human connections of an influential few in everyday circles. They may be connectors—people who just know people; or mavens—people who are recognized as having knowledge; or salesmen—people who are persuasive." But how to find or identify these influential people?

Ted Leonis, owner of the Washington Capitals, understands that little things can matter, that a few people can push something over the tipping point. For Leonis, the objective was to show fans that his organization cared. That meant providing fans with his e-mail address, and answering his mail. But he found that fans appreciated the personal touch from an owner. When Leonis promised one disgruntled fan that he would look into his complaint, the fan responded with a very positive note that was also copied to 11 other people. As Leonis recognized, "Now, I know those 11 people probably sent this correspondence to another two or three people. So I did this one little thing, but I'll bet you 100 people ended up seeing that we really care."

This is why Ted Leonis was so insistent on answering e-mails. Although most people would be content with one exchange, Leonis was looking for some mavens, some salesmen, or some connectors who might interact with him about his team plans, and then begin viral support of the idea that the Caps cared! (40)

The Product-Place Matrix

Ultimately, the marketer wants to ensure an effective and efficient use of all available distribution channels. The Boston Red Sox, for instance, recognized a need to extend the "communal" baseball experience beyond the ever-sold-out Fenway Park. Television and radio were doing an excellent job for most fans, but many others wanted to share the game with others in a large venue. In 2004, the Red Sox answered the need by partnering with selected area movie theaters for live, high-definition video screenings of several games. At some theaters, vendors hawked beer and hot dogs, some fans sang "Take Me Out to the Ballgame" during the seventh-inning stretch, and others did the "wave." Tickets cost between $5 and $10. Said one fan: "If you want to take your family you have to take out a mini-mortgage to go to Fenway Park. But this gives you a chance to feel as close as you can to being in the ball park." (41)

Of course, not many teams have the draw and power of the Red Sox. But anyone can be thoughtful and imaginative. A valuable analytical tool is the product-place matrix (see table 14.1), which helps to conceptualize both the array of products and the distribution channels.

✦ **Table 14.1** Product-Place Matrix

Product	Place				
	Field house, fields	Media	Retail outlets	Greeks, civic groups	Outer markets
Events	Games	Releases, TV, radiocasts, Internet	Game highlights on video kiosks in mall	Highlight films, pep rallies	Schedule a home game in a remote city
Players, coaches	Autograph sessions	Coach's Corner on radio, TV, Internet	Clinics, autographs	Speeches on substance-free living	Clinics, press meetings
Tickets	Box office	Trade-outs with media, Internet	Schedule cards, posters, electronic kiosks	Group sales	Group sales
Merchandise	Concourse	Local cable, direct mail, Internet	Licensed outlets	Fund-raisers	Licensed outlets

A simple start to a matrix for a collegiate sport program might look like this. Each row represents a product element (event, players, coach), and each column represents a distribution outlet (venues, media).

The matrix simply provides a graphic representation of current or planned product distribution. In this example, the players and coaches are "distributed" in many ways beyond the game itself. They have autograph sessions after games; they offer clinics and talks to Greek houses and civic groups nearby or in "outer" markets. The coaches also are "distributed" via "Coach's Corner" shows on radio and television, or even in Internet chat rooms. Marketers can consider how best to fill each part of such a grid, using their imagination and creativity.

Wrap-Up

Although the place function in sport marketing bears remote resemblance to the distribution function in consumer product marketing, its importance among the five Ps of sport marketing should not be minimized. The "place" in sport begins with the ensemble of elements comprising the venue or facility and its surroundings. The facility location is critical to the success of most sport businesses. Of equal importance are the facility image and operation, which are influenced by physical design, amenities, and the attitudes of facility personnel. The core event and its extensions must then be distributed by way of marketing channels that include retail outlets and the media (which we examine in detail in the next chapter). The marketing channels for sport products are limited only by budgets and imaginations, but the possibilities can be graphically illustrated by the use of a product-place matrix.

Activities

1. Apply the "theory of place" to your favorite sport venue, the way we did to Fenway Park. What are the most important elements of the ensemble? What elements of the "place" ensemble could be accentuated in the design or in promotions?

2. Analyze a local facility in terms of its accessibility, flow, drawing radius, parking, aesthetics, staffing, security, surroundings, design and layout, and amenities. How would you improve these areas?

Your Marketing Plan

1. Outline a ticket distribution plan for your organization that makes use of some new technologies mentioned in this chapter.

2. Create a product-place grid for your organization. Think carefully about alternative channels for distributing your various products.

Chapter 15

Electronic Media

Tim Ashwell

University of New Hampshire

Objectives

- To gain an overview of today's electronic media.
- To become familiar with the technological basics and terminology of electronic media.
- To examine how the sport industry can use electronic media to market and promote products.
- To gain an understanding of how sporting events are produced and distributed through the electronic media.

Nobody Knows Anything

Sport marketing, we know, relies on solid research. If your marketing plan isn't based on accurate information, you can wind up promoting the wrong product to the wrong audience with the wrong strategies.

The importance of the electronic media to the sport business is self-evident. And media gurus have over the years generated exquisitely detailed research studies on every aspect of the media, the sport audience, and how best to combine our national love of sport with new technology.

If the truth is out there, the experts must have discovered it by now, right? Perhaps, but if you were to pore over all those years of reports, white papers, statistical abstracts, and texts of forward-looking speeches by industry leaders, you'd come to one inescapable conclusion: If these guys are so smart, how come they're wrong so often?

Sports and the electronic media have been partners since the beginning of radio broadcasting in the 1920s. Broadcasters have used sports to attract audiences and introduce new technologies. Sport producers have used the media to attract fans and build their images and revenues. It's just that neither partner has ever been quite sure how to do it.

In the earliest days of radio, both sides agreed there would never be any real money involved in broadcasting. Broadcasters knew that the listening public would never tolerate advertisements in the middle of a ball game, and sport promoters routinely let anyone who showed up with a microphone produce a broadcast. As a result, well into the 1930s, fans could tune up and down the dial and listen to the World Series, the Olympic Games, or the big college football game of the week on three or four different stations.

When television came on the scene at the end of the 1930s and created a sensation by showing a baseball game live, John Reed Kilpatrick, the president of Madison Square Garden, confidently predicted that no one would ever want to watch televised sports at home. No, he said, we would pay for tickets and watch the games in theaters, because being part of an enthusiastic crowd is a vital part of enjoying sporting events.

A decade later, after it became obvious that people would in fact watch sports at home, the same John Reed Kilpatrick proudly announced an agreement with a local television station to broadcast every Madison Square Garden event, from horse shows to hockey games, live for six months, because these free samples would surely inspire ticket sales.

At the same time, in Chicago, the athletics directors of the Big Ten universities, reacting to growing interest in college football telecasts, voted to bar live television of all Big Ten football games because television would certainly cause fans to stay home and depress ticket sales.

The history of sports and the electronic media is replete with examples of mistakes and miscalculations. Most industry experts agreed in the late 1970s that few television viewers would agree to pay for cable television to access, let alone actually want to watch, a 24-hour all-sports channel. The experts were wrong.

A dozen years later, emboldened by the success of ESPN and cable sports, NBC was positive that millions of fans would pay $125 to watch the hundreds of hours of Olympic preliminaries that couldn't be fit into the network's wall-to-wall coverage of the 1992 Barcelona Games. NBC was wrong.

Each new technology offers dazzling possibilities. Radio and television, the Internet, and digitized data streams, each in turn offered unseen possibilities for a glorious future.

But, as Yogi Berra might have said, the problem with unseen possibilities is, you can't see 'em.

Radio used to be called wireless, because its inventors saw it as a way for people to communicate privately over distance without the necessity of telephone or telegraph wires. The problem was, if someone in New York sent a wireless message to someone in Philadelphia, millions of people could listen in. When Owen Young, the chairman of General Electric and one of the most respected businessmen in the United States, testified before Congress on radio regulation at the end of radio's first decade, he admitted somewhat sheepishly that radio's backers, distracted by the privacy issue, had not foreseen the model of radio broadcasting, the possibility that it might be a good thing that millions could hear that message.

When asked how the movie industry regularly manages to mix box office hits with films you couldn't pay people to attend, Academy Award–winning screenwriter William Goldman famously said, "Nobody knows anything." Sports and the electronic media, like Hollywood studios, seek to entertain and make money in the process.

It sounds simple, but it turns out that figuring out how to entertain us and how to use emerging media technology is harder than it looks.

This chapter offers an overview of today's competitive and rapidly changing electronic media environment. Television, radio, the Internet, and emerging digital technologies are powerful tools for marketing, promotion, and publicity, but sport marketers must remember that they are only tools that must be properly used to achieve maximum results. This chapter explains how the media are organized and addresses several ways sport organizations partner with the electronic media to get their games on the air.

The Electronic Media Landscape

The long-anticipated age of media convergence is at hand. No longer can we make meaningful distinctions among radio, television, and the digital devices that bring our sports to us. In a technical sense, convergence was inevitable. Although there are obvious differences among the electronic media, all follow the same simple model: Information (the sounds of a contest, pictures of an event, or textual accounts) is encoded as digital bits and bytes and sent via satellite, wire, or over-the-air transmission to a receiving device that decodes the impulses and reproduces the information in usable form. These elegant machines produce streams of digitized pictures, sounds, and words and offer 21st-century sport fans locker room access and front row seats to events around the world. Fans can watch their favorites play, check out an upcoming event, or discuss their sport passion at home, at work, or as they travel on wall-sized screens or pocket-sized devices. These infinite choices offer limitless marketing opportunities and more information than anyone can absorb.

As the century began, the experts who have so often been mistaken peered toward the horizon and tried to discern the next big thing. For the time being, traditional television remained the dominant electronic medium in terms of both market penetration and audience impact. Radio, often overlooked, continued to reach local and regional sport audiences efficiently. The Internet and its digital offspring offered immediate, international reach and the ability to pinpoint specific consumers, but have yet to approach either television or radio in terms of mass audience numbers or response. Broadcasters continue to pay billions of dollars each year for rights to deliver games to loyal audiences of sport fans. Loyal fans pay billions more to access games, up-to-the-second information, and behind-the-scenes details about their favorites. In addition, the electronic media help motivate millions of consumers to purchase such items as tickets, team merchandise, and memorabilia worth billions of dollars more. Sport, in turn, makes billions for broadcasters in advertising revenue and subscription fees while also allowing broadcasters to gain identity with consumers and burnish their images.

The media have also shared a common business plan: Television, radio, and the Web sites that populate the Internet rely on the audience to survive. Sport attracts audiences to Web sites and radio and television stations—audiences advertisers pay to address or who pay to subscribe to the service.

Media Platforms: TV, Radio, Digital Media

The electronic media are our windows on the world. The Television Bureau of Advertising, an industry trade association, estimates that 110 million of the approximately 112 million U.S. households own at least one television, and nearly four out of five homes own two or more sets. In the typical household, the television is tuned into one of the nation's 1,600 TV stations or hundreds of cable channels for eight hours every day. Women, on average, watch for five hours a day; men, a half hour a day less. Advertisers paid an estimated $68 billion for commercials to reach those viewers in 2004. (1)

Radio is no longer the dominant medium it once was, but it remains a potent force, reaching 94 percent of the population every week. Traditional terrestrial broadcast stations have been joined by satellite radio services to offer listeners nearly limitless options. The listening audience is fragmented as stations seek to be heard amid the noise by fine-tuning their formats to capture carefully defined demographics. With some 10,000 commercial stations and 2,500 noncommercial stations on the air in the United States, and rival satellite services offering hundreds of channels of personalized programming, many stations struggle to survive financially despite the fact that advertisers spent nearly $21.5 billion on radio in 2005.

The Internet, conceived as a research tool in the 1960s, became a mass medium by the 1990s. In 2005, more than two thirds of all Americans had Internet access at home, school, or work, and about a third of all users enjoyed high-speed broadband connections that allowed them to download audio and video effortlessly. No longer do you need a radio to listen to "radio programs" or a television set to watch "TV broadcasts." Computers and portable digital devices make it possible to watch games in progress, get the latest sports news, and retrieve past performances and feature material from vast digital archives any time and any place, creating an immense—and extraordinarily valuable—inventory of new products for consumers. Advertisers followed consumers into cyberspace, spending nearly $10 billion on Internet advertising in the United States in 2005.

Although the financial pie is huge, the competition to capture desirable slices of the audience is becoming more intense as viewers' choices expand. ESPN capitalized on such niche programming with its debut on September 7, 1979. It marked the beginning of a new era in sport broadcasting by offering nothing but sports 24 hours a day. ESPN's success quickly spawned imitators. Today, fans can choose among dozens of regional and national sport channels, hundreds of sport-oriented radio stations, and tens of thousands of sport Web sites, each seeking to find a loyal and quantifiable audience.

Choice is good for fans, but the fragmentation of the audience into ever-smaller pieces has made life much more exciting and perilous for broadcasters. As the number of viewing options has increased, the audience for each individual program has dwindled. In an industry based on the belief that advertisers will pay to present their messages to mass audiences, that is big news.

Knowing the Market

Because television, radio, and the Internet are fundamentally advertising media, success or failure in the field is largely judged by audience size and composition. Just as the scoreboard tells us who won or lost on the playing field, audience measurements tell us who won or lost on the air and online. To play the media game effectively, sport marketers must be able to place their product in the right medium at the right time to reach the right audience. This requires that they understand the audience they are trying to reach and how best to reach it. Astute sport marketers carry out research to define their audience. Media research organizations conduct the same kind of research to define and quantify the broadcast audience. Sport marketers who want to use the electronic media should be as familiar with the substance and terminology of the media as they are with their own games.

Television audiences are scientifically measured and researched by both broadcasters and advertisers in hopes of discovering exactly who is watching what. Nielsen Media Research, since 1942 the leading audience analyst, judges audience size from data collected by electronic devices attached to televisions in a representative sample of more than 9,000 homes across the country. (2) Audience numbers are commonly expressed in terms of *ratings* and *shares*.

A program's rating represents the percentage of homes in the survey universe that are tuned to the program. For a nationally broadcast program available in every television home, one rating point represents 1 percent of the national total, 1.1 million households in 2006. Ratings are also calculated locally. Nielsen divides the country into 210 designated market areas (DMAs). In 2006, there were nearly 7.4 million television homes in the New York DMA, the nation's largest, spanning the metropolitan area covering portions of New York, New Jersey, Connecticut, and Pennsylvania, so a single local rating point represents about 74,000 homes, 1 percent of the total. In the smallest DMA, Glendive, Montana, with just over 5,000 homes, a rating point equals 500 homes.

A program's share represents the percentage of those homes using television at the time that are tuned to the program. Research—and common sense—tells us that not every television set is on all the time. The viewing audience climbs gradually throughout the day and peaks during the evening hours before declining again. More people typically watch television on weeknights than on weekends. Accordingly, although ratings remain a constant measurement, shares fluctuate depending on the size of the total viewing audience.

Nielsen estimated that the 2006 Super Bowl earned a 41.6 rating and 62 share. That means that televisions in nearly 46 million homes—41.6 percent of the nation's TV households—were tuned into the game, and those homes represented 62 percent of the homes where folks were watching television that Sunday night. (3) Although the Super Bowl annually attracts television's largest audience (over 144 million people tuned in for at least part of the 2006 game), most programs, and nearly all sporting events, draw far smaller audiences. Hit network shows commonly earn ratings in the teens, and ratings in the single digits are common for sporting events. One audience study determined that regular-season big-league baseball games garnered 3.0 to 3.6 ratings, NBA games registered in the 2s, and NHL contests typically received ratings between 1.0 and 1.5. (4)

When it comes to audiences, size matters, because broadcasters and advertisers calculate the cost and value of commercials by the number of people in the audience. The standard yardsticks are cost per thousand, often abbreviated CPM (because M represents one thousand in Roman numerals), or cost per point (CPP), which refers to the cost of reaching 1 percent of the audience, or one rating point. In addition to the size of the audience at any given time, broadcasters and advertisers look at the total number of households and viewers that a series of programs reaches over time. A single baseball broadcast, for example, may reach a relatively small audience; but over the course of a 162-game season, the total number of viewers will be much larger. The number of different viewers who tune in over time, usually termed the reach or cume, measures the true audience for sport broadcasts and is used to convince sponsors to sign on for season-long advertising contracts.

Similar survey techniques measure radio and Internet audiences. Critics carp about the accuracy of audience ratings, complaining that away-from-home television audiences in sports bars and college dormitories are constantly understated, that survey samples do not properly represent minority communities, or that Internet usage statistics don't adequately measure how surfers consume the new medium. Audience measurement firms, advertisers, and programmers continue to massage their methods to make the numbers more accurate while emphasizing data that go beyond raw size.

Although the number of people in the audience is vital, the composition of the audience may be even more important to the savvy sport marketer. Although women typically make up the majority of the television audience, sport programs traditionally attract a high percentage of male viewers. Compared to the typical prime-time television audience, sport viewers are older, better educated, wealthier, and overwhelmingly male—often two thirds are men. Studies show a similar skew among radio listeners. Sport stations attract overwhelmingly male audiences, making them an attractive option for advertisers seeking an efficient means of targeting male consumers. Although sport audiences are typically older on average, they also contain a higher-than-usual concentration of younger male viewers and minority groups, target audiences that advertisers find notoriously hard to reach through traditional mass media. The sport audience is also intensely loyal. At a time when viewing options are expanding, sport fans will seek out, watch, or listen to broadcasts featuring their favorite teams and sports.

Sport and the Electronic Media: A Symbiotic Relationship

The sport audience is attractive to advertisers. Broadcasters therefore are willing to pay for rights to broadcast games that produce audiences that can be sold to advertisers. Sport has also played an important role in driving new technology. Millions of fans bought radios in the 1920s and televisions in the 1950s to listen to and watch sporting events in their living rooms. The growth of both cable television in the 1980s and home satellite systems in the 1990s was also driven in large part by the lure of additional sport programming. The same trends are evident in the growth of portable digital devices. Among the key selling points are immediate access to sport scores, up-to-the-second statistics, and game highlights. Just as fans in the 1920s bought radios to hear live accounts of the World Series as it happened, enthusiasts in the early 21st century subscribe to services that promise to alert them to the latest score and allow them to see the game-winning homer on their desktop computers or handheld digital devices.

The growth of today's sport industry has been driven by media exposure, and television, the most successful medium, leads the way. Televised games create new fans, increase

State-of-the-art production trucks are television studios on wheels. Fully loaded with the best equipment, a production truck can easily cost $5 million or more.

interest among existing fans, and serve as powerful promotional and marketing tools. The explosive growth of the NFL can be credited in large part to the league's television policies in the 1960s, which rationed game broadcasts and emphasized the league as an entity rather than individual franchises. The NFL continues to blaze the media trail with branded digital services that offer football fans ever-greater access to their favorite teams and players at a price payable to the NFL. Following the NFL's lead, dozens of teams and leagues have used the electronic media to raise the profile of their products in the marketplace.

Sports also create instant credibility and ultimately profits for broadcasters. When the fledgling Fox television network in 1993 paid the NFL a then-astonishing $1.58 billion for rights to National Football Conference games, the network immediately joined ABC, CBS, and NBC as a major player in the broadcasting business. The games attracted new viewers, new advertisers, and new affiliates to the network. Although Fox's accountants admitted the network lost money on the deal, most media analysts agree that it would have taken Fox years to gain parity with the older television networks if it hadn't taken its football gamble. Prime-time profits and higher values for Fox stations across the country helped offset the red ink generated by the NFL contract. ABC used a similar sport strategy to climb out of the television basement in the 1960s and 1970s, and today ABC and ESPN, both owned by Disney, have used sport to promote cross-viewership on the company's cable, satellite, and Internet outlets. General Electric, corporate owner of the NBC family of broadcast and cable networks, purchased exclusive U.S. rights to the Summer and Winter Olympic Games beginning in 2000 with the same long-range strategy in mind. The Olympics had a proven television audience that would attract viewers to NBC's cable and Internet outlets, including some who had not previously discovered those services. Once tuned in, those new viewers were exposed to promotional announcements and would, NBC believed, return for non-Olympic programming.

Building Broadcast Partnerships

Sport and the electronic media, then, rely on one another and enjoy a truly symbiotic relationship that benefits both sides. Broadcasters want sport to attract a proven audience, to create advertising and subscriber revenue streams, to take advantage of the public relations opportunities afforded by sport relationships, and to establish credibility within the industry. Teams, leagues, and events covet broadcast coverage because it expands their audience and revenue and helps establish them as significant "big-time" entities in the minds of fans. Cash forms the strongest bond between the industries; but, as Dick Ebersol, president of NBC Sports, observed, "Not far away is the marketing and promotion of those sports, and the people in the future who understand that best are the people who are going to succeed." (5)

Spectator sports are valuable commodities, and the organizations that stage the games have the legal right to control media access to their stadiums. Well-established legal precedents give the home team, the tournament organizer, or the event promoter the exclusive right to determine who can and cannot broadcast the events. Sport managers should understand how the broadcasting industry works so they can determine how their particular product fits in. Established teams, leagues, and events usually auction their broadcast rights to the highest bidder. In exchange for a guaranteed payment, the winning bidder receives exclusive rights; pays production, distribution, and promotional expenses; and sells advertising time to cover its costs.

Proven commodities such as the NFL can demand huge payments from national networks because they have a track record of attracting huge national audiences. Some industry analysts blanched when the NFL completed a $3.7 billion multinetwork deal in 2005. How, they asked, could broadcasters commit to the fixed costs of rights payments with virtually no hope that advertising revenue offset the cost? George Bodenheimer, the chairman of ESPN who signed off on the plan to switch Monday night NFL games to his cable network, made it clear that ESPN had little choice. "You can't be the leading sports network without televising the leading sport," he said. "It was never a question of whether we would renew the NFL, but on what terms. You can't just look at this and add up the CPMs and the ratings and declare 'good deal' or 'bad deal.' It's deals like this that fuel the growth of the entire company." (6)

The NFL-ESPN partnership on the national scene is replicated on a smaller scale across the country. Regional broadcasters battle for the rights to broadcast the state college's football or basketball games. Local radio stations line up to become the radio voice of the local high school athletics program. The revenues may be smaller, but the concept remains the same: Sport partnerships matter!

Sport managers must understand, however, that as they move down the media hierarchy, the rights fees that broadcasters are willing to pay dwindle rapidly. Many sport organizations will discover few broadcasters knocking at their door in search of permission to broadcast their games or events. Either the product is unproven or the broadcasters fear they will not be able to recoup the cost of production, let alone any rights payment, through advertising revenue. Often, inertia is an issue: A television or radio station has a successful program in place and sees no advantage in disrupting what works. In that case, sport managers must become even more aggressive and more involved in broadcast production. If a manager's goal is to get his team on the air, he can achieve it by putting together a financial package that works for both the team and the broadcaster.

As audiences fragment, many teams find that they must accept lower guaranteed rights fees and share advertising revenue with their broadcast outlet. Indeed, it is not unusual for a station or cable programmer to agree to broadcast a team's games only if the team agrees to subsidize the cost, either through cash payments, production assistance, marketing opportunities, or some combination of these. Known in the broadcast business as "syndication," this is a tried-and-true formula for program distribution. The simplest arrangement, "cash syndication," requires the sport organization to purchase airtime from a station or stations for a negotiated fee. The broadcasters are guaranteed income, and the team gains positive exposure and retains all revenue from advertising sales. This is how those myriad infomercials for products and services find their way onto the air. Many television stations and cable services are only too glad to sell blocks of time for a guaranteed price rather than go through the trouble and risk of producing or purchasing programming and selling advertising.

Depending on the demand for an organization's events and the state of the television market, syndication can take several other forms, all involving an exchange of advertising time and sometimes cash. "Barter syndication" means that the producer of the program and the broadcaster are trading advertising time for the right to carry the program. The producer retains a portion of the advertising time to sell while making the rest available to the local station to sell. Each side keeps the revenue it receives from selling its allotment of time. "Cash-barter" is a hybrid arrangement that includes both an exchange of advertising and a cash payment, either from the producer to the broadcaster or from the broadcaster to the producer.

In lieu of guaranteed fees or contractual syndication agreements, a growing number of broadcasters and sport organizations have agreed to base rights payments on a percentage of advertising revenue generated by the broadcasts. Revenue-sharing agreements protect broadcasters from fluctuations in the volatile advertising market and, by lessening the broadcaster's risk, can make a team's games a more attractive package. If the games turn into hit programming, revenue sharing also allows the broadcaster to cash in on the success. Revenue sharing can also ultimately produce a higher return for the sport organization, because it allows the team or event to bundle media advertising availabilities with its sponsorship agreements. The NBA was the first major sport league to sign a revenue-sharing contract with its primary network partners, but this type of arrangement has become increasingly common in broadcast agreements.

Another proven strategy is for a team to retain its broadcast rights, produce its own game broadcasts, line up sponsors, and offer broadcasters a complete package. Some sport organizations go even further and create their own delivery systems by establishing cable channels based on their product. Professionally producing a broadcast of a football game or a tennis tournament sounds like a daunting task—and it is. Fortunately, sport managers can hire independent production firms to provide the equipment, personnel, and expertise needed to handle the technical details.

For television broadcasts, production trucks stocked with an array of cameras, tape machines, and graphic design generators and equipped with portable satellite dishes or microwave transmitters to send the game back to the station are commonly used. Technicians arrive at the game site the morning of the contest to run cables and set up cameras, lights, and sound equipment. As the game unfolds, directors and producers choose from a wall of monitors inside the truck what they want the audience to see. The cost of producing a game depends on numerous variables: transmission and travel costs, the amount and quality of equipment used, talent fees for popular announcers whose names will lend prestige to the broadcast, and the like.

Television broadcasts require dozens of technicians and truckloads of expensive equipment, but a radio broadcaster needs only a modest remote kit and a telephone line or low-power transmitter to get the signal back to the station. Whereas the cost of producing and transmitting a single football game, on a local station or regional cable channel using four or five cameras, two or three tape machines, and a well-known local announcer might be $25,000 or more, for example, that sum could easily pay for the equipment, transmission, and production costs of an entire season of radio broadcasts.

A growing number of major sport organizations have taken the next logical step and created their own distribution systems, bypassing existing broadcast organizations entirely. The NFL, NBA, and NHL have all launched cable and satellite channels devoted to their leagues. The Boston Red Sox and Boston Bruins co-own NESN, the New England Sports Network, the regional sport cable and satellite service featuring Red Sox and Bruins broadcasts. When the Red Sox franchise was purchased in 2001 for $700 million by an ownership group including television executive Tom Werner, it was clear that the Sox' majority stake in NESN was a vital part of the package. As Werner explained when the new owners held their first postpurchase press conference, "Obviously part of what made the price so high was the ability the Sox have to control not just the distribution of their product but to control both the content and the distribution." Fans pay a monthly fee through their cable company to watch NESN, and NESN sells commercial time to advertisers who want to sell products to the fans. It was, Werner said, "very important to the health of the Red Sox to have the dual revenue streams to allow the team to be as competitive as possible." (7) The New York Yankees and New York Mets launched similar sport cable channels, and the trend is growing in major markets.

As broadband Internet access becomes standard, sport producers have begun to supplement broadcast coverage by offering game broadcasts to fans around the world on the Internet. Some bypass traditional broadcasters entirely and rely on the Internet as their primary medium for game coverage. Major sports with lucrative distribution agreements with broadcast or cable outlets have been reluctant to offer unlimited access to their games over the Internet for fear of devaluing their existing contracts. Sport organizations and events with smaller audiences, on the other hand, have embraced Internet webcasts as a means of delivering their games to an audience that is too small or geographically diverse to be served by traditional mass media.

Ideally, advertising sales and sponsorships will offset the costs associated with producing and distributing the games; but, should revenues fall short, sport managers should consider the return on that investment from a marketing and promotion perspective. A college football game broadcast or live coverage of a golf tournament attracts viewers because it provides an "up close and personal" account of the event as it happens. Astute sport managers understand that the broadcast is much more than that. Media exposure allows a college to showcase its team, of course, but it is also an opportunity to display the beauty of the campus and generate interest and raise morale among potential fans, students, faculty, staff, and alumni. A golf tournament broadcast allows fans to follow their favorites, but it also showcases the sport itself and perhaps inspires lapsed golfers to pick up their clubs once more or attend a future event. By making sure that the broadcast includes frequent announcements promoting upcoming events, giving ticket information, and noting the availability of licensed merchandise and the like, sport marketers can generate future revenue. A positive broadcast of an intercollegiate event can energize alumni to contribute to the annual fund, encourage high school students and their parents to consider the school at application time, and build school spirit and public awareness.

Regardless of the financial arrangements, sport managers can and should insist that their games be broadcast so as to maximize interest and present their team or institution in a positive light. Standard broadcast agreements between sport organizations and broadcasters often include specific clauses reserving airtime for promotional announcements. Parties may also negotiate contracts that give the team power to approve announcers or grant advertising time to the organization's corporate partners, or that bar or limit broadcasters from selling advertising time to businesses such as gaming casinos or breweries that might reflect unfavorably on the institution. Colleges and athletic conferences have negotiated contracts allowing coverage of popular sports such as basketball and football only if the broadcaster also agrees to broadcast emerging sports such as women's volleyball.

When the NCAA sold CBS the exclusive broadcast rights to the men's Division I basketball tournament in 1989, the contract limited beer advertising to one minute per hour and banned any advertisement featuring professional basketball players. The NCAA also required CBS to set aside 90 seconds of airtime during each game for promotional announcements, produced by the NCAA, touting the organization's student-athlete and community services. Additionally, CBS agreed "to consult annually" with the NCAA before hiring announcers for the games and stipulated that it would not hire current NBA players, coaches, or team officials to broadcast the tournament. The NCAA also required CBS to telecast portions of a dozen other NCAA championships in sports ranging from wrestling to track and field. For its part, the NCAA agreed to several conditions aimed at maximizing CBS's audience by staggering starting times of first- and second-round games and consulting with network programmers to ensure that attractive early-round match-ups were scheduled in prime time when they would attract the largest possible audience. (8)

Contract negotiations, of course, require give-and-take on both sides. Sport managers must realize, for instance, that limiting potential advertisers or holding back salable airtime for promotional use may reduce the amount of revenue that the broadcaster can generate and subsequently may mean a reduction in rights payments. The "cost" of lost revenue, however, can be offset by the benefits of positive exposure and future income. The NCAA's insistence in 1989 that CBS broadcast the Division I women's basketball Final Four made it possible for millions of new fans to see the sport, and helped pave the way for a 1995 agreement with ESPN that significantly expanded coverage of—and revenue from—the women's tournament.

If sport managers view broadcast partnerships as promotional opportunities and as part of a well-designed marketing plan, rather than exclusively as sources of immediate revenue, the finances of broadcasting games can change. A bottom-line deficit may well be offset by the promotional value of several hours of positive exposure.

It's Not Just Play-by-Play

Although play-by-play game broadcasts are important marketing tools, sport managers should not ignore other opportunities to promote their products through the electronic media. To reinforce their identity as "the official station" of a team, broadcasters are often eager to air additional programming: interviews with coaches and players, daily reports from the training camp or the practice facility, pregame broadcasts from the stadium parking lot, profiles of players, and the like. Programs such as these, as well as pregame and postgame interviews and scoreboard shows, are sometimes referred to in the media business as "spot-hangers"—programming designed for the express purpose of creating additional advertising time to sell. The additional income from such advertising helps defray the cost of buying rights, or makes the idea of devoting blocks of airtime to game broadcasts more financially attractive.

Game Broadcast Basics

So you want your fans to be able to follow your team when they can't get to the game? Well, you'll need to make sure a television or radio station, network, digital service, or Web site carries the games. Determining the most efficient transmission method and how your sport products fit into the media food chain is the hard part.

Live From the Press Box

A radio broadcast, whether transmitted by AM, FM, satellite, or via the Internet, is much like a telephone call. The sounds of the game and the announcer's description are transmitted to a central distribution studio by landline, cellular telephone, or satellite. Portable, digital codec (encode/decode) mixers allow audio signals to be transmitted with studio quality. Television broadcasts follow the same transmission model but require far more equipment and people. Three or four cameras are enough for an indoor event in a confined space such as a boxing match; a major outdoor event such as an auto race or a football bowl game may demand two dozen or more cameras with replay capabilities and sophisticated computer graphics systems. Instead of a portable mixer, television usually requires broadcasters to bring a truck full of equipment and skilled personnel to the game site to serve as an on-site studio to combine the visual and aural elements into a coherent whole.

Meanwhile, Back at the Studio

Before the game broadcast reaches its audience, it must make one or more additional stops. The game broadcast is transmitted to a central studio that serves as the hub of a hub-and-spoke distribution center. Producers, announcers, and technicians in the studio insert advertising and promo-tional announcements that were not inserted at the game site. They may also produce pregame, intermission, and postgame programming to complement the play-by-play broadcast. The finished broadcast is then transmitted by satellite or landline to affiliated radio or television stations, local cable TV systems or satellite service providers. If the broadcast is to be streamed on the Web, the game will be transmitted to an Internet service provider. These local distributors will often add still more material to the broadcast such as local advertising and promotional announcements relevant to their audience. Some distributors will transmit the finished broadcast live; others will record the broadcast for later distribution. Only after the total broadcast package travels out through the spokes of this hub-and-spoke system will it be sent on to the fans who will tune in on their radio or television or log on to their computer to catch the game.

Fitting Your Product to the Model

Every sport broadcast follows a similar path from the playing field to the fans. The challenge is finding the right path for your game. Distributors battle for the rights to the established heavyweights of the sport broadcasting business, proven audience magnets such as the major professional sport leagues. Pro football fans can follow their team on television, radio, and the Internet worldwide. A midlevel college athletics program may have an avid regional fan base sufficient to support a network of radio stations or justify a place on a regional cable sport service. A high school sport team might find a home on the local radio station, the community cable television station, or the high school's Web site.

Sport managers should remember that every media exposure, whether it is a live game broadcast or a two-minute preview of an upcoming event, provides a marketing and promotional opportunity. A live "stand up" from the arena by the local sportscaster on a television station's evening news program or a radio station broadcast from the stadium parking lot on football game day may be designed by the broadcasters to promote the station and connect the station in the listeners' minds with the local team; but it also serves to remind listeners that there is a home game today and that the stadium is an exciting place to be. Many sport organizations routinely distribute free game tickets to local broadcasters as prizes to be given away over the air. The local disk jockey gives the tickets to listeners who call in, creating excitement and a sense of value for the station. In the process of gifting the tickets, however, the DJ also reminds the audience that there is a game coming up that would be fun and exciting to attend—so much fun, in fact, that the station wants to give a loyal listener a chance to go for free!

Cross-promotional opportunities between sport organizations and broadcasters abound, and creative financing arrangements are plentiful. In the world of the electronic media, time and money are fungible. This is especially true in smaller markets in which broadcasters are struggling to make ends meet. Tickets, arena signage, and advertising space in game programs can be, and often are, exchanged for advertising time to promote ticket sales or licensed merchandise. Local television and especially radio stations, because of the relative flexibility of their daily broadcast schedule, are often willing to accept programming from outside producers. If the team's media relations staff is willing to prepare three- to five-minute game previews, postgame summaries, or daily features in a radio-friendly format that allow the station to sell a local commercial or two, a local broadcaster will likely find airtime to carry the programs. Because of radio's lower production costs and typically smaller audiences, the medium may provide a lower-cost alternative than television. Radio is also the ideal medium for last-minute marketing efforts. If a block of tickets suddenly becomes available, if the weather forces a change in schedule, or if one last promotional effort seems needed, new advertising copy can be written and hand delivered or faxed to a radio station and be on the air immediately.

The Digital Future

The rapidly evolving digital environment presents sport marketers and broadcasters with remarkable challenges and opportunities. Soon we will no longer differentiate among radio, television, and computer technology. The game coverage, highlights, statistics, player biographies, and sport news will all be electronically delivered to devices that will allow us to see, hear, and read what we want, when we want.

Technology is racing ahead. We can watch games on crystal-clear, wall-sized, high-definition television screens and hear the bands play and coaches shout in stereo sound. We can log on to the Internet and ride along with our favorite race car drivers via in-car cameras, and listen in as the crew chiefs and drivers plot pit strategy. Fans can choose what camera angles they prefer, summon instant replays on demand, check the archives to see what the coach said about his game plan before the contest started, and switch from game to game around the country to see how their teams' rivals are doing. Need the latest statistical update for your fantasy league team? Want to purchase a replica game uniform just like the one on the player you are watching? Just click a button and connect to the press box computer or the team's licensed-merchandise cyberstore! Instantaneous, interactive communication on demand, experts say, is what we, the fans, want. Many of the nation's largest media corporations are betting billions of dollars that consumers want more information and entertainment and want it now. Television networks, cable services, telephone companies, and computer hardware and software providers have launched new television and Internet services that—they hope—will attract consumers willing to pay for the latest information, or at least enough consumers to make the new media attractive advertising buys.

Unfortunately, once the experts describe the latest technological bells and whistles, they begin to disagree. As we have seen, media experts have a decidedly poor track record when it comes to predicting the future. The vital question is whether the services made available by this new technology will survive in the marketplace. As one knowledgeable industry analyst observed, no one yet knows what consumers want and, more important, what they are willing to pay for—and "there is no way to find out except to 'build it and hope they will come.'" (9)

One thing does, however, seem likely: Sport will continue to play an important role in the digital marketplace. Loyal fans will seek out their favorite sports, teams, and players; recognizable sport brands will attract an audience. Just as sport drove sales of radios, televisions, and cable and satellite services, it will play a role in introducing, promoting, and selling tomorrow's digital hardware and software.

A well-designed, interactive Web site has become a basic marketing and public relations tool for sport organizations. A colorful home page with links to up-to-date news releases, player biographies, statistics, and results has become a vital promotional tool. Recorded video and audio clips allow fans to witness key plays or hear from a star player. As consumers

Building a Winning Web Site

Every sport organization should have a presence on the Web. Here are some ideas to keep in mind as you develop your organization's Web site:

✦ *Content is king.* Don't let the technology divert your attention from the basic fact: Visitors will return to your Web site only if you provide information, activities, and services that meet their needs. Glitzy animation, dynamic effects, and the latest streaming audio and video are wonderful—and incorporate as much as you can in your site—but remember that your Web site should be a marketing and public relations tool that cultivates your fan base and introduces your sport product to new consumers.

✦ *Promote, promote, promote!* Even the best Web site won't help you if no one knows it's there, and with billions of Web sites out there, the odds of surfers stumbling across yours by chance are slim. When you launch your site, publicize the uniform resource locator (URL) widely. Make sure your Web address appears prominently in your media releases, advertisements, publications, letterhead, tickets, and posters. See if you can include your site as a recommended link on related sites.

✦ *Make it interactive.* The Internet is a two-way medium, so take advantage of the technology! Get the visitors to your Web site involved and collect contact and demographic information you can use to market your projects. Standard software allows you to keep track of visitors to your site, but you'll have to be creative to gather the personalized information you need. Many surfers are reluctant to register for a site or sign up for newsletters, but you can harvest much of the same data by creating a trivia contest or sweepstake giveaways for event tickets, game-used memorabilia, or similar keepsakes. Be sure to include e-mail contact forms on the site so visitors can write to the organization, comment on last night's game, or send fan mail to their favorite players.

✦ *Use quick-hitting eye and ear appeal.* Web surfers are impatient. If your home page doesn't grab their attention, they'll move on. If they can't find the information they're looking for right away, they'll look to someone else's site. Strive for a clean, colorful home page featuring eye-catching images. Put that award-winning action shot or the portrait of the star player up front. As broadband penetration grows, streaming video will become a standard Web site feature. Even a homegrown Web site can include downloadable digital video files offering a glimpse of the athletic facilities or a greeting from the coach. Make sure your visitors can move around the site easily. Include clear and easily understood icons and a navigation bar on each screen to allow browsers to access information. Arrange the navigation tools to guide visitors to where you want them to go.

✦ *Keep it current.* The Internet means instant information, so don't let your site get old! By all means, include game-by-game results, updated standings, and news of upcoming events on your site, but make sure the information is refreshed quickly and accurately, so when fans log on to find out what happened in yesterday's contest, they'll get the results. If your organization doesn't have the personnel to keep its site up-to-date on a daily basis, it's better to include background information that won't turn into yesterday's news.

✦ *Don't get lost in the links.* Be careful not to lose surfers in a maze of pages. Every screen on your site should have a clearly marked Home Page button to get visitors back to the beginning. Avoid links to your conference Web site, other teams in the league, and the like, that take your visitor to another site with no way to return to yours. Make sure those links open in a new window. Try to avoid internal links that take visitors several levels past your home page. When in doubt, keep it simple.

✦ *Remember, not everyone is state of the art.* Avoid pages that take too long to load or require special software downloads to function properly. High-speed broadband Internet access reached about one third of U.S. homes in 2006 and is becoming the standard for computers at workplaces and schools, but it isn't universal. Test your site on an older computer linked to the Internet by the local telephone company and see how it looks. Make sure visitors who don't yet have broadband can access the information they're looking for. Surfers want information now and won't wait patiently if it takes several minutes for your home page to appear.

✦ *Don't be afraid to borrow ideas.* Keep your Web site current by visiting the busiest Internet sites and see what they're up to. How does your site stack up? Is it looking a little dated when compared to the industry leaders? Are there design elements, layouts, or other features that might improve your site? Even if your local soccer team isn't ready to take on the pros, there's no reason the team's Web site can't look professional. There's an old saying in the broadcasting business: An exciting new idea is something that's worked successfully in 25 other markets.

Computer technology and the Internet offer sport managers an unparalleled opportunity to identify, build, and communicate with their audience. Print, radio, and television are one-way media that talk to the audience. The Internet is a two-way communication medium that allows you to talk to the audience and the audience to talk back. A well-designed Web site can be used to market future events and target products to fans with a demonstrated interest in the team or event.

have grown more comfortable with encryption technology and secure servers, links to ticket offices and team stores or similar providers of licensed merchandise have become standard as well. Computer graphics allow marketers to use color, sound, and movement to sell products. Interactivity allows the consumer to play an active role in the transaction. A feature of many Web sites that demonstrates the marketing power of digital technology is a program allowing a potential ticket buyer to see the view from the seats she has chosen.

Wrap-Up

Broadcasters spend billions for the rights to bring sporting events to fans at home. That revenue has helped turn sport into a major industry. What has generated those billions, however, is advertising sales. New technology means more choices for fans, but it could mean trouble for advertisers. If audiences for individual sporting events decline, advertisers may no longer be willing to pay ever-higher prices for commercials. If broadcasters can no longer generate revenues, rights fees to sport organizations will inevitably decline. Will fans be willing to make up the difference through pay-per-view or subscription fees? There is no way to know, but some optimists predict that the marketing value of sporting events will climb as consumers embrace new technologies. Why? Because major sporting events are time sensitive and lend themselves to real-time viewing. Perhaps in the on-demand future, the only way to ensure that consumers see your message when you want them to see it is to attach it to an event such as the Super Bowl or the Daytona 500 that fans will watch as it happens, rather than record and view days later. Although the financial future of the electronic media may be uncertain, new technology forges ahead. Digital technology makes it possible for fans to see more games, and allows sport managers to tailor and target their products to specific groups of consumers.

What remains constant is the loyalty of sport fans and their willingness to use both new and old technology to find out about their favorites.

Sport managers should be familiar with the broad spectrum of electronic media options and should understand how each can reach potential consumers. They should also recognize the importance of taking an active role in using the electronic media. Organizations should investigate the relative cost and benefits of producing their own media products. Sport managers should also realize that they control valuable assets in today's hypercompetitive media environment and should exercise their bargaining power to make sure that their products are presented in a positive and creative manner.

Activities

1. To get a sense of today's "media-saturated" environment, examine your local media market. How many television stations are on the air? Radio stations? What cable or satellite services are available? How about Internet access? Broadband or dial-up? Try to get a sense of how many information sources are competing for our attention.

2. Broadcasters are concerned about audience fragmentation. Analyze your local television schedule on a given day and see how many different genres are represented. Can you predict the audience demographic each type of program will likely attract? How do sport programs fit into the overall television schedule?

3. Suppose you are a college athletics director, and you're negotiating a new broadcast package for your teams. What are some of the nonmonetary benefits you hope to receive from media exposure? How can you ensure a positive presentation of your athletics program and institution?

4. Explore the Internet and critique the Web sites of several sport organizations. Are there certain features common to interesting, easy-to-use sites? How do the organizations use the Web to market their products? What Web elements could you use on your site?

Your Marketing Plan

How will you use radio, television, and the Internet to market your product or organization? Create a radio or television network, design a Web site, or strategize an advertising campaign that takes advantage of the electronic media.

Chapter 16

Public Relations

Shaping and Influencing Opinion: The Role of Blogging

A blog is an online opinion, and it can take any or all of the following forms:

✦ Collection of thoughts

✦ Series of random comments

✦ Reviews or critiques

✦ Recommendations or things to avoid

Blogs have become an essential component of sports and entertainment—two areas where their consumers have no shortage of opinions—because they enable the sport organization, athlete, entertainer, or whomever to establish a connection with their stakeholders or fans. According to Corey Miller, executive story editor and blogger for *CSI: Miami*, "It's nice for shows to have connections with the fans. It makes you closer and more involved in the product you're watching." (1)

Mark Cuban, owner of the Dallas Mavericks, is one of sport and entertainment's most prolific bloggers. On his site, www.blogmaverick.com, Cuban offers his opinion on the possibility of NBA teams not playing to win because it might not be in their best interest to do so. While this is only an opinion, it is interesting to note that the opinion Cuban stated in his blog—see excerpt that follows—resulted in this issue (and the possibility of the scenario playing out) being addressed by the NBA in a news release and also in their subsequent Board of Governors meeting (as reported by ESPN on April 14, 2006).

NBA Playoff Seeding…what if?

Right now the Grizzlies and the Clippers are battling it out for the 5th playoff spot. The Nuggets pretty much have their division locked up, locking in the 3rd seed.

The 5th seed plays the 4th seed. The 3rd seed plays the 6th seed. The interesting tidbit, however, is that between the 3rd and 6th seed, the team with the better record gets home court advantage.

So riddle me this, NBA fans.

What happens if both the Grizz and Clips clinch home court advantage over the Nuggets? Put another way, it's possible that (and I'm just picking numbers here) the Grizz and Clips are tied with 4 games to play, and both teams know that the team that loses more of those 4 games gets home court advantage against the Nuggets. The team that wins more of those four games gets the Mavs or Spurs starting on the road.

Isn't the goal of the whole season to gain home court advantage for as many play-off series as possible?

How much fun would it be to see the teams trying to lose games? Or more to the point, lying about trying to win games, but "resting" their players.

Remember, home court isn't just about having a better chance to win with your fans behind you. It's an opportunity for teams to make more money.

If this isn't a reason to change the play-off series seeding right now, I don't know what is. (2)

Courtesy of Mark Cuban

The power of positive public relations to amplify a good marketing communications plan should never be underestimated. In today's instant information society, the media and public opinion continue to dominate how we perceive the world around us. The term *spin*—the ability to present an argument in several ways, sometimes minimizing negative aspects and overstating positive ones—was coined to describe the process of combating a poor image. Blogging, an opinion-based Internet tool designed to create opinions or influence them, is an excellent example of spin. The power of personality also is evident in the spin process. In April 2006, ESPN produced *Bonds on Bonds*—billed as a reality show that provides the only real and honest information about Barry Bonds (that coming from Bonds himself). Although the term *spin* evolved primarily in a political context, sport has seen similar efforts as they related to player behavior, franchise movement, the manufacture of athletic shoes, personnel problems such as coaching changes, and a variety of other situations. Thus, it has become critical in the sport setting to have effective public relations efforts and personnel that can function in times of crisis. However, it is just as important to use public relations to promote local initiatives and positive actions occurring as a result of day-to-day operational activities and strategic planning.

Throughout this text we have discussed a variety of ways the sport marketer can use advertising and promotions to position the organization and its sport product(s) effectively in the marketplace. Unfortunately, these efforts can be undermined and rendered ineffective if the organization does not also have a good public relations program. In this chapter, we examine the role of public relations in the sport context, where it consists primarily of community relations and media relations. We also discuss and provide examples of three distinct forms of community relations—those initiated by players, those initiated by teams or institutions, and those initiated by leagues or governing bodies—and consider how they contribute to overall organizational marketing efforts.

Public Relations Defined

Probably the most widely accepted definition of public relations, or PR as it is commonly called, is a practical definition developed by the *Public Relations News:* "Public Relations is the management function which evaluates public attitudes, identifies the policies and proce-dures of an individual or an organization with the public interest and executes a program of action to earn public understanding and acceptance." (3)

According to a more corporate definition, offered by Clarke L. Caywood, public relations is "the profitable integration of an organization's new and continuing relationship with stakeholders, including customers, by managing all communications contacts with the organization that create and protect the reputation of the organization." (4)

Finally, Govoni, Eng, and Galper emphasized the relationship between the sender and the audience in terms of the credibility of the message. They define public relations as "a multifaceted form of communication, with the intent to foster a positive company or prod-uct image in a non-sponsored framework." A key aspect of this definition is its emphasis on nonsponsorship. The authors believe that nonsponsorship "enhances the credibility of the message and cloaks the company with the respectability of the source, which may be viewed by the audience as either the spokesperson or the medium." (5)

For the purposes of sport marketing, we will define public relations as

an interactive marketing communications strategy that seeks to create a variety of media designed to convey the organizational philosophies, goals, and objectives to an identified group of publics for the purpose of establishing a relationship built on comprehension, interest, and support.

This communication strategy, which may take the form of activities as well as formal com-munication, may also involve players, media personnel, staff, mascots, and other product extensions, sponsors, and other key components of the organization.

Public relations is a management function in that it reflects policies and programs devel-oped at the top levels of management. Public relations systematically evaluates attitudes toward the organization and its products and hence depends on an effective and current marketing information system. Public relations identifies the impact of the public interest; this consumer or marketing perspective differentiates public relations from press agentry, a propitiatory agenda, and advertising. What can be inferred from this impact? What conse-quences flow from a given course of action or inaction? How can the entity best disseminate messages or action to respond to this identified impact?

These and other questions, once identified and answered, form another function of public relations, namely that of executing a program of action. In this regard, public relations usually involves implementing specific marketing plans and tactics designed to alter or reinforce con-sumer perceptions, attitudes, or levels of awareness. The goal of this function is to earn public understanding and acceptance. Finally, the source, or more accurately the "perceived source," will in many cases lend credibility to the message or course of action. The use of consultants, market research firms, and other third-party sources lends the message an air of objectivity that in many cases might otherwise not be perceived. Kathy Connors, director of strategic com-munications for Octagon, a multipurpose sport marketing agency, presents a very functional view of the role and functions of PR in a sport marketing agency in the sidebar.

In sport, public relations (PR) is often perceived to be synonymous with publicity or media relations (MR). Many people have developed this perception because public relations directors (especially those functioning as sport information directors) often deal largely with developing statistics and providing information to the media to gain increased media exposure for the sport organization. Effective public relations programs (both media relations and community relations) usually create publicity—news stories, articles, interviews, and other activities. However, because this publicity is not paid media, it is not controllable. Thus, activities can create both good and bad publicity.

Media relations is just one half of the public relations function. In the short term, media relations is probably the more important function. But in the long term, community relations (CR) can often be more or at least equally significant in affecting sales, generating positive public sentiment, and building a long-term relationship (and base) with the community.

Public relations, then, has two components, both of which must be developed and pursued if the public relations function is to reach its full potential and impact. In short, public relations can be expressed in the form of an equation:

$$PR = MR + CR$$

An examination of these components will illustrate their importance individually and collectively.

The Role of a PR Professional

Kathy Connors, Octagon

Public relations is the function of communicating an organization's message to the press, and the public relations professional is the liaison between those two parties. In the modern 24-hour/7-day-a-week omnipresent media world we live in, there is an ever-growing need for competent public and media relations specialists who understand the art of effectively communicating with the press on behalf of their organization or client. The chief role of the public relations department is to serve as the company's spokesperson to the media and external constituents. The spokesperson in interviews can also be an appropriately deemed individual—an executive, coach, or athlete.

The public relations department plans campaigns; facilitates interviews; and disseminates press releases, statistical information, and other helpful promotion information. The department also hosts press conferences or events for more formal announcements. The ultimate goal for the public relations department is to cultivate the most positive image of the company as possible by proactively seeking and accommodating as many favorable opportunities in the press as possible.

Most organizations integrate their public relations efforts with advertising, marketing, and community relations so that the messages are all reflecting the same theme. The synergy among these areas of the company is vital in order to present a unified company image through all of its external communication.

Good public relations specialists should adopt the following skills in their practice:

✦ *Building relationships.* Public relations professionals should possess the following attributes: credibility and integrity, a commitment to serving the press in a timely manner, excellent communication skills both written and spoken, and an ability to work on and with deadlines. The cornerstone of having a successful career in public/media relations is possessing the ability to forge and maintain good working relationships with the press. Even if a reporter has written a negative story or is difficult to deal with, you should still seek to manage a working relationship with that reporter—always trying to keep the lines of communication open. The need for relationship building should also be important in serving internal constituents as well. It is really important that the internal subjects understand the value of the publicity and are willing participants in the process. Trust is probably the most important skill in building effective working relationships in life, and public relations is no exception. A skilled public relations person needs to be a trusted and valued member of the company and a trusted resource for the press.

✦ *Communication.* It may seem obvious, but one of the most important skills in public relations is effective communication. Direct all of your communication both internally and externally in the most clear, concise, and efficient way. Produce materials that contain the necessary information, and make sure that it is presented in the best possible way. As mentioned earlier, building good interpersonal working relationships is important, but when routine information is being exchanged, use technology to its advantage. For example, to exchange basic information, use e-mail instead of trading voicemails.

✦ *Creating the public relations plan.* When working on a large-scale public relations project, a comprehensive plan should be designed detailing the strategy to promote that message. The plan should detail a chronological outline of how you plan to achieve the objective of the campaign. When crafting the plan, consider the time lines and deadlines of the publications that you are targeting. Pick outlets that make sense for your message, and make sure you leave adequate time to meet deadlines and achieve all of the objectives and reach the targeted outlets. For instance, if the goal is to increase exposure for the company in a certain segment of the population, build a plan around outlets that demographic group reads, watches, and so on. It is also critical to manage multiple tasks at once and maximize on both the major outlets as well as the smaller ones; they all play a role in the overall strategy.

◆ *Making the pitch.* After creating the plan, you need to start pitching the story. It is really important to always know who you are pitching to—that you are pitching the right reporters and that the pitch is catered to the specific publication or outlet. Be aware of deadlines, and be considerate of the time that will be required to cover the story. Don't pitch a reporter a story idea that makes no sense for either their outlet or the subject matter they cover.

◆ *Managing the story.* One of the most important skills in media relations is the ability to manage a story while it is being written. The routine story does not necessarily require more than basic follow-up skills. The art of managing a story is a practice generally reserved for more in-depth pieces or pieces in major publications. Always make sure at the beginning of the process that the tone or spirit of the piece is established. By keeping a dialogue going with the reporter as they conduct their interviews (a process that the public relations professional should be involved in) and collect their facts, you can get an idea of the general direction of the piece. By being actively involved in the process, you can correct inaccuracies, make appropriate suggestions, and emphasize key points.

◆ *Talking points.* A talking points document is a helpful resource to use in the public relations practice to help subjects speaking to the press stay on the desired message. The document should include a carefully crafted response to every conceivable question that could be asked on that particular subject. It is especially recommended when dealing with a difficult or complicated matter. The talking points will help the spokesperson stay "on message."

◆ *Crisis management.* Not all public relations is positive, and unfortunately, there is an increasing trend of negative press. Managing the bad press is a special skill in itself and obviously the response required depends on just the nature and scope of the story. The first step in this type of reactive situation is formulating the plan for the response. A quick, effective response will help to minimize the damage, and generally decreases the shelf life of the story—the goal in all crisis or damage situations.

Media Relations

Public opinion is one of the most powerful forces in our society, and media relations is designed to formulate and shape favorable opinion via the mass media. Media relations—communicating with the news media verbally or through other vehicles—must also balance public opinion with business strategy. Depending on its role within the organization, media relations takes one or more of the following approaches: reactive, proactive, or interactive. (6)

Those involved in reactive media relations field and respond to inquiries. They respond to questions, queries, and requests from the media and other interested parties. In a sport setting, such requests may concern player interviews, appearances, autographs, photos, biographies, or profiles. In addition to these simple requests, the reactive function might also relate to requests for statements about or reactions to situations involving organizational policy.

In proactive media relations, the point of initiation is the organization rather than some external entity. For example, sport organizations could choose to contact media outlets with possible stories, distribute packages of player bios and media guides, or highlight films to a preselected audience without having been requested to do so. We see an excellent example of a proactive approach in a 1907 correspondence between R.J. Hellawell of Spalding & Bros. to James E. Sullivan, the Amateur Athletic Union driving force, whose real job was president of the American Sports Publishing Co., a firm owned by Spalding. In his letter, Hellawell wrote:

> We should have articles in the newspapers praising and telling of the decrease in accidents [in football]. We could have these in the shape of interviews with head Coaches, Trainers and others prominent in Foot Ball. Of course, it would add weight to them. You no doubt will see some way to work out this matter and perhaps you have something in mind that will be better than this suggestion, but I really think that we should do all we could to turn sentiment in favor of Foot Ball. (7)

Although media relations will always have reactive functions, the primary mode will be proactive—to take the initiative in providing information and creating publicity as a marketing function. The sidebar on this page, featuring a proactive approach by the Boston Celtics, is an excellent illustration of this approach.

Interactive media relations involves developing mutually beneficial relationships with the media and assisting the media on a variety of issues. This function relates closely to relationship marketing and focuses on building lasting long-term relationships rather than

The Value of Internal Public Relations

Internal PR is an effective way to inform, educate, and build relationships with stakeholders. Sponsors and ticket holders are key stakeholders for every sport franchise. The emotional nature of sport dictates that these stakeholders have a strong connection to the organization that can be weakened when they do not support a decision made by the franchise because they do not have the information or they are influenced by the media or other third parties in their interpretations of those decisions. The Boston Celtics have tried to minimize the risk of such occurrences by treating their stakeholders as "insiders"—first to know and straight from the organization. The following e-mail was sent to all Celtics e-news subscribers on December 16, 2003, following a trade that was pending at the time. (8)

From: Danny Ainge [dainge@enews.celtics.com]
Sent: 12/16/2003 04:47 PM
To:
Subject: Celtics Beat: Trade Alert

Dear Lou,

As you know, we made a trade yesterday with Cleveland for Ricky Davis, Chris Mihm, Michael Stewart, and a second round draft pick for Eric Williams, Tony Battie, and Kedrick Brown. We hope to have the trade finalized later today pending the completion of physicals.

I think this trade helps us in both the short and the long term. In the short term, it gives us better immediate scoring and rebounding. In the long term, we just got a lot younger and more athletic. Red has always told me you make deals when you are winning. These are two players I tried to get this summer and in the early part of the season, but they were unavailable. I believe the way Tony and Eric have played to start the season made this deal available.

I picked Ricky up at the airport last night and we spent about an hour together. He is thrilled to be a Boston Celtic. We spoke about Celtic tradition, Jim O'Brien's work ethic and expectations, and how things are different here in Boston than they are in most cities. Ricky is a very talented young man. He averaged 20 points, 5 rebounds, and nearly 5 assists per game last season. Even though he is an effective player right now, at only 24 years old I believe he is just starting to come into his prime as a player with all-star caliber upside. I spoke with Paul yesterday regarding the deal. Paul knows Ricky well as they work out together in the summer in Los Angeles and he is very excited to have Ricky as a teammate. He will complement Paul when they are on the court together because he will defend the other team's best offensive wing player.

Chris Mihm is a 24-year-old kid who had some health issues and is now healthy for the first time and playing well. He's 7-feet, 265-pounds, athletic, and he can shoot. He is a better rebounder than anyone we have on our team right now and ranks fifth in the NBA in rebounds on a per minute basis. I believe Chris's future price tag will be much higher than what we had to give up yesterday in the trade to obtain him. I think both Davis and Mihm are at a very good time in their careers where their "stock values" so to speak are at a good purchase price.

Michael Stewart has kind of been the odd man out in a couple of organizations. He is a Mark Blount type of player with great character. He is not offensive minded but can really rebound and block shots.

As I said, the players involved will be going through physicals today, and we hope to get the deal finalized, get them on the court, and begin the process of getting them acclimated to our system. Thank you for your continued interest and support of the Boston Celtics.

Sincerely,
Danny Ainge
Executive Director of Basketball Operations

Courtesy of Danny Ainge

accomplishing short-term public relations objectives. Although these short-term public relations objectives might be part of the "mix," they are just a component of a larger mission designed to facilitate relationships and the essentials of a media relations program. In interactive media relations, either party can initiate the action or activity knowing that the other will cooperate fully because doing so is in the best interests of both.

Community Relations

Once viewed as an afterthought or as a "as-funding-permits" budget item, community relations has become an integral part of the marketing efforts of sport organizations. Community relations programs have emerged as a strategy that sport organizations (particularly those at the professional level) use to deliver outreach-type programs. The aim of such programs is to achieve corporate public relations objectives related to enhancing public understanding and gaining public approval and acceptance, and hopefully leading to public support. (9)

Community relations programs usually are implemented in one of three ways. These efforts can be player initiated, team initiated, or league initiated. Within recent years, sport organizations have acknowledged the importance of community relations programs and have added staff to execute these programs, or have added community relations responsibilities to the job descriptions of existing staff. These community relations staff help to implement leaguewide initiatives (e.g., the NBA's Stay in School program or the NCAA's clinics), team-based initiatives (e.g., the Cleveland Cavs' Read to Succeed program or the Pittsburgh Pirates' Major League Math program), and on occasion, player-based programs (e.g., Shaquille O'Neal's Shaqsgiving program).

Assets like fan tunnels let fans get up close and personal with their heroes, like the Orlando Magic's Dwight Howard.
Courtesy of the Orlando Magic

Players are an integral part of all three types of community relations initiatives. Almost all community relations programs have some element of player involvement because it is the presence of the players and their involvement that attract funding to the program via sponsorship, that garner media interest and coverage, and that finally attract an audience of participants and observers to the programs. Ray Allen of the Seattle Supersonics understands the importance of building relationships between the players and fans as evidenced in the sidebar on page 390.

Community relations programs complement media relations programs and their goal of raising awareness levels among consumers and the general public. In addition to raising awareness by being visible in the community, community relations programs attempt to create goodwill. Although the intent of both efforts is to generate publicity for the organization, media relations yields greater immediate results; community relations programs, on the other hand, often have objectives—such as fan development—that are very long term. However, although the long-term value and effectiveness of community relations programs can be measured in the goodwill and publicity generated, they should also be measured

Using PR to Build a Bridge Between Players and Fans: Ray Allen

Early in 2003, but following the completion of the 2002-2003 season, Ray Allen, who had been traded to the Seattle Supersonics from the Milwaukee Bucks, reached out to his new fans in Seattle. Following is Ray's attempt (hugely successful) to thank the fans for their acceptance of him in what was a somewhat controversial trade because it sent the "face of the Supersonics," Gary Payton, to Milwaukee. The trade was not embraced by a significant portion of the Seattle stakeholders. Allen's gesture—combined with his playing performance on the court and his persona off the court—helped to turn public opinion back in favor of the trade and the franchise in general. (10)

April 18, 2003

Dear Sonics fans,

By now you've probably heard a good many things about me in the media and by way of the rumor mill: from the most trivial detail (my favorite meal is steak and a loaded baked potato); to the factual (my favorite movie is *Schindler's List*); to the completely untrue (no, I did not buy a ten million dollar house in Woodinville!). Although all of these things are fun to talk about, I would love the opportunity to tell you something I've wanted to say for the past two months: THANK YOU! Thank you, Sonics fans, for your generous hearts, welcoming me with open arms, making me feel like I belong and for adopting me as one of your own.

Growing up as a military child, I was privileged to live in many different places, but I've never been able to establish real roots. It is my hope that I have found the ground in which to lay down these roots here in the lush land that supports your Emerald City. Words cannot adequately describe the overwhelming sense of welcome and encouragement that I have felt since arriving in this area. It is my sincere wish that I can return your warm display of support by giving all that I have on the basketball court and through donating my time and passion to benefit this community.

I have been endowed with many blessings in my life and feel it is my honor and duty to devote all my available resources to enrich the lives of children and those in need. Through the years I have been fortunate to meet and share experiences with many people through my non-profit organization, The Ray of Hope Foundation. With your support, I would like to continue those efforts in my new home here!

Please know how excited I am to be a part of your thriving community and the Sonics. I cannot tell you how great it feels to be excited about playing basketball again. To be a member of such a world-class organization, a dynamic and driven team with an inspiring coaching staff feels unbelievable. They've all claimed me as their own and it's like being part of a family. This has been a thrilling two months and it's only the beginning. I would be lying if I said I wasn't nervous that first night in The Key, but you came out and supported us and made me feel wanted. I could not have done it without you. I will never forget that moment and will always be grateful for your generosity. Thanks, Sonics fans! I hope you share my great anticipation for next season.

With sincere thanks and best wishes,
Ray Allen #34

Courtesy of Ray Allen

in terms of fan building. Fan building leads to not only ticket sales, but also broadcast ratings, merchandise sales, and sponsor interest and value. Fan building through community relations programs is a key ingredient in creating fan identification—the emotional involvement customers have with a sport organization and the basis for creating relationships with long-term value (11) (e.g., ticket sales, broadcast ratings, merchandise sales, positive word-of-mouth advertising) that we have previously discussed.

In terms of professional sport organizations, community relations may involve designating certain games as community nights so that marketing efforts are directed specifically at a geographic target market. In fact, this concept has been so successful that certain professional sport teams, most notably the New York Yankees and Pittsburgh Pirates, have defined community as ethnic groups and have set aside certain themed days for ethnic celebrations with special food, music, and player appearances (when players from that particular ethnic background are team members).

Community relations can also take the form of corporate philanthropy. Like sales promotion, advertising, event marketing, and sponsorship activities, corporate philanthropy is intended to position the company in the mind of the stakeholder. However, unlike these activities, which are budget-line items in an operating budget, corporate philanthropy activities come from a company's profits. (12) Corporations such as Yankee Candle Company (Deerfield, Massachusetts), McDonald's, and Coca-Cola use philanthropy not only to position themselves as good neighbors, but also to challenge their employees and other businesses to match their efforts and provide contributions to the selected beneficiaries.

Shortly before the beginning of the 2005-2006 NBA season, Commissioner David Stern announced a new and far-reaching community outreach platform for the NBA called NBA CARES. The new initiative positions NBA CARES as the umbrella name for all NBA community efforts including the following:

Read to Achieve

Jr.NBA/Jr.WNBA program

Basketball without Borders

In addition, the NBA CARES program will continue working with a myriad of internationally recognized youth-serving organizations including UNICEF, Reading Is Fundamental (RIF), Boys and Girls Clubs of America, American/International Red Cross, Feed the Children, Global Business Coalition on HIV/AIDS, KaBOOM!, Habitat for Humanity International, the Make-A-Wish foundation, and many others. (13) According to Commissioner Stern, "NBA CARES will be the platform through which players and teams will raise and contribute $100 million dollars for charity, donate more than one million hours of volunteer service to communities worldwide, and build more than 100 educational and athletic facilities where children can learn and play, all over the next five years." (14) The program will also serve as a platform for NBA corporate sponsorship partners and broadcast partners to join with the NBA in these initiatives.

What are the possible outcomes of such a commitment? According to Marc Pollick, president and founder of the Giving Back Fund, a national nonprofit organization that helps athletes and entertainers create and manage high-impact philanthropy, there is much to be gained. According to Pollick, "Sports possess a loyal and devoted fan base, virtually unlimited access to the media and substantial persuasion with its corporate sponsors. And perhaps the most powerful tool of all: The opportunity, and maybe even the responsibility to *role model* socially conscious behavior in ways that have transformative staying power, in ways that reach across all social strata and boundaries. What other industry in our society has the power in the palm of its hand to make giving back cool? If the NBA says giving is cool, it becomes a self-fulfilling prophecy. Once its fan base is convinced of that notion, imagine the possibilities." (15)

Numerous activities can generate goodwill and revenue for an organization. The key is that both long- and short-term benefits derive from the development of a balanced, strategically designed community relations program. The three examples that follow, the Orlando Magic Youth Foundation, the Cleveland Cavaliers' programs, and the sidebar on Amare Stoudemire's generous giving on page 392, all possess distinct elements that can be part of any effective community relations programming. The Orlando Magic Youth Foundation illustrates a bigger, more inclusive approach designed to help the community help itself.

The Cleveland Cavaliers' efforts illustrate that these programs, if effective, can generate self-sustaining support from local businesses and corporations. Finally, Amare Stoudemire illustrates how an individual player, through commitment and involvement, can make a difference in the community.

The Orlando Magic Youth Foundation

The Orlando Magic have taken a foundation approach to community relations. The Orlando Magic Youth Foundation was founded in 1988 to raise funds and community awareness to help combat the many physical, emotional, and social challenges facing the children of central Florida. OMYF is part of RDV Sports Team Charities, the nonprofit, private foundations representing the company's three professional sports teams.

In over 17 years of giving, the OMYF has had a positive effect on more than 1 million kids. Through private donations, fund-raising events, and contributions, more than $10 million has been raised and distributed to nonprofit organizations that support the mission statement of OMYF. It is truly a team effort by Magic players, coaches, staff, and the DeVos Family, in partnership with season-ticket holders, corporate sponsors, fans, and the community.

In addition to receiving a 60-cent match from its funding partner, the Robert R. McCormick Tribune Foundation, 100 percent of every donation to OMYF goes back into the community with an even greater impact. It's a winning combination for everyone.

OMYF fund-raising events and programs include Outback Steakhouse/Orlando Magic Down Under Gold Scramble, Black Tie & Tennies Charity Gala, state Magic license plate program, SunTrust Magic checks, Games Autographed Auction, the Outback Steakhouse 25 Point Program, and the Game 50/50 Raffle. (16)

The Cleveland Cavaliers

Umbrella programs, such as the NBA Cares Program, encourage teams to develop programs and opportunities that are indicative of local needs. The Cleveland Cavaliers have also developed a program called Minority Business Associates (referred to in chapter 13) that was designed to accomplish two primary objectives: generating sponsorship and advertising revenue from nontraditional sources and creating an effective way for community leaders to serve as role models for Cleveland schoolchildren. The program involves 10 African American businessmen who have each paid $6,500 to participate. These businessmen are in actuality helping support the Cavaliers' Stay in School initiative, both financially and by speaking directly to kids, and providing tickets for kids to attend games. In exchange, the business owners receive arena signage, public service announcements during Cavaliers broadcasts, and ads during the pregame coach's show. In addition, each participant is the subject of two features during the Cavaliers' "Fast Break Show" (which airs before televised games) and travels with the team to a game in Chicago. (17) It's a win–win situation for all concerned.

One Player's Approach to Giving Back: Amare Stoudemire (Phoenix Suns) and Toyota

The efforts and activities of one person can make a significant impact, particularly if those efforts are joined by a corporate partner with a social conscience. Amare Stoudemire of the NBA's Phoenix Suns, and Toyota, an NBA sponsor, teamed up in 2006 to help victims of Hurricane Katrina–rav- aged New Orleans by donating 10 Toyota Prius hybrids to residents of Louisiana affected by the disaster. The efforts and activities of Stoudemire and Toyota are detailed in the following press release. (18)

Amare Stoudemire Donates 10 Toyota Vehicles to New Orleans Residents in NBA TV's Toyota's Moving Forward Moments

Phoenix Suns Star Presents Toyota Prius Hybrids to Residents Impacted by Hurricane Katrina

NEW YORK, March 21, 2006—NBA TV's news series *Toyota's Moving Forward Moments* follows Amare Stoudemire of the Phoenix Suns as he teams up with Toyota to travel to Hurricane Katrina–ravaged New Orleans and donate 10 Toyota Prius Hybrids to residents of Louisiana impacted by the disaster, in its upcoming episode on Tuesday, March 28, at 6 p.m. ET.

"It leaves you speechless," says Stoudemire as he drives past devastated homes and overturned cars destroyed by the August storm. "Once you see it up close and personal, it is pretty rough to take. It just isn't a certain area. The whole city and just about the whole state have been wiped out."

Hosted by Andre Aldridge, this half-hour series follows an NBA player as he returns to his hometown to surprise his mentor and to reminisce about the powerful influence that person had on his life. In this special edition, Stoudemire visits 10 women, who have served as mentors in their communities as 4-H volunteer leaders, but lost almost everything as a result of the hurricane. He takes viewers through parts of Louisiana and visits some of the victims' homes on his way to meet the women, whom he surprises with the gift to help get their lives back on track.

Viewers will witness Stoudemire present a Toyota not just to one of the women, as they were told that he was going to do, but to all 10 of them. Stoudemire and Toyota teamed up for the special presentation of the free cars and covered all taxes and registration fees.

4-H is the youth development and outreach program of the nation's land-grant university system. The organization provides young people with a variety of educational projects and activities designed to help them develop knowledge and skills that will benefit them throughout their lives. Volunteer leaders play vital roles in helping to reach young people across the country.

Continuing a tradition of basketball and service to the community, the NBA and its players have been helping with the rebuilding efforts throughout the Gulf Region through *NBA Cares*. The league's global community outreach initiative, *NBA Cares* builds on the league's long tradition of addressing important social issues with an emphasis on programs that support education, youth and family development, and health-related causes.

NBA TV's *Toyota's Moving Forward Moments* presents a unique opportunity for NBA players to share their stories, experiences, and ideals while touring a community that has impacted their lives in a new Toyota. In a surprising conclusion to each episode, NBA stars display their appreciation for the community that supported them and the mentor that helped drive them towards their goals. Each mentor is presented with a gift of the Toyota vehicle showcased during the tour as a sign of appreciation for the vital role that person played in the NBA player's life.

Past episodes in this series have included the New Jersey Nets Richard Jefferson's journey to his hometown of Phoenix, Arizona; the L.A. Clippers Elton Brand's return to Peekskill, N.Y.; the Milwaukee Bucks T.J. Ford's Houston homecoming; and New Orleans/Oklahoma City Hornets Chris Paul's emotional return to Winston Salem, N.C., where he presented a Toyota to the foundation he created in memory of his mentor, his beloved grandfather who was tragically murdered while Chris was in high school.

Toyota's Moving Forward Moments also are featured in the form of one-minute vignettes during select NBA halftime programming on ESPN. In addition, a dedicated page devoted to the series is located on NBA.com.

Courtesy of NBA

Public Relations Functions

This section covers public relations functions and outlines a sport application for each, with the aim of clarifying the variety of roles public relations can play and the value of the various roles. To illustrate these roles and their value, we will consider the following list of functions:

- ✦ Provision of information and general communication (to consumers, shareholders, suppliers, competitors, government agencies, and the general public)
- ✦ Image shaping or enhancement via organizational publicity

- Community relations (previously discussed)
- Employee relations
- Educational efforts for the purpose of gaining political or popular support for the organizational agenda
- Recruiting and business development
- Launching new products or innovations
- Obtaining feedback and reaction
- Coping with crisis (19)

Informing and Communicating

This function of a public relations program serves to maintain contact with the grassroots support of the organization. Sport organizations are acutely aware that a good community relations program can result in positive perceptions and, ultimately, financial or other benefits. For example, in intercollegiate athletics, community relations often take the form of stories about "hometown heroes" that are written by sport information staffers at the university and disseminated to local papers. According to a former sport information director and award winner, Howard Davis, the "hometown" feature is one of the most important functions of a sport information office. (20) This information is important for several reasons: (1) It provides a "common denominator" for residents of the athlete's hometown and the university; (2) it may prompt residents of the area to attend an athletic contest at the university or to apply for admission; and (3) it may assist the athletics department in recruiting future athletes from that town or region.

Public relations departments communicate with consumers, shareholders, suppliers, competitors, government agencies, and the general public. Clearly, this is the aspect of a public relations program that is best understood (by the general public) and most used. This function involves the compilation, presentation, and dissemination of product or organizational information to the general public and/or to special segments of the population (alumni, sportswriters, newspapers, electronic media, web browsers, and so on). The process may be as simple as compiling statistics from basketball games; and it may be as complex as providing statisticians, spotters, and other personnel for national broadcasts of games and events in order to give the broadcast "breadth, depth, and color" and make it informative and entertaining.

The communications function also involves publishing programs, brochures, sales support materials, and manuals; working with special-interest groups to ensure the accuracy of information (e.g., the Baseball Writers' Association); maintaining and regularly updating a Web site and the appropriate linkages; and answering mail and other inquiries from the general public. Although informing and communicating constitute only one of the functions essential to developing and managing an effective public relations program, organizations often allocate resources and energies almost exclusively to this function at the expense of a strategically sound holistic program. Figure 16.1 illustrates the variety of publics with which a collegiate sport information director or media relations director must correspond and interact.

Shaping and Enhancing Image

Image shaping and enhancement constitute a complex function through which the organization attempts to demonstrate to the public that its products are well made, that its services are first-rate and vital to the industry, and that the organization itself is a responsible citizen and contributor to the community. Corporations, institutions, teams, leagues, and individuals may engage in this function.

In a corporate context, McDonald's represents an excellent example of how to shape and enhance one's image. McDonald's, a pioneer in cause marketing, has long been a leader in

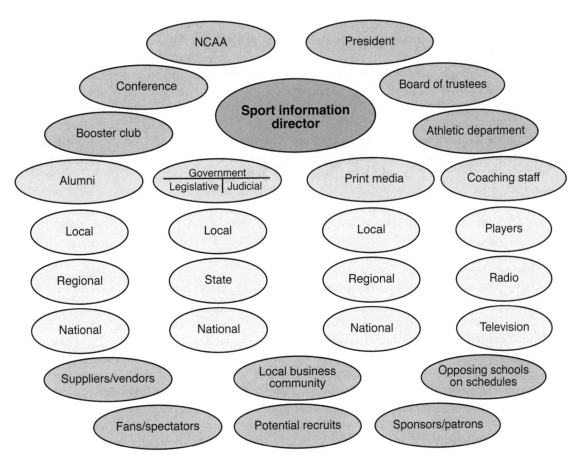

FIGURE 16.1 An effective sport information director works with a variety of publics.

this image-building, enhancement, and protection approach to business. McDonald's has advertised the value of its meals, the friendliness and warmth of its staff, and the idea of taking a "break" from routine by visiting its restaurants. However, McDonald's has complemented these advertising efforts with charitable activities that have enhanced the image of the corporation, portraying it as a vital member of the community. These efforts have been mostly local, taking such forms as donations to high schools to purchase band uniforms and involvement with local charities, particularly those sponsored by newspapers. Supporting a visible charity was not just an inexpensive form of advertising for the company; it was better, because it provided a visible association with an important element of community life.

For a drive-in restaurant chain looking to appeal to a family market and seeking respectability in an industry burdened with a questionable reputation, community involvement on the part of local operators produced the type of image boosting that McDonald's needed. This sponsorship of community programs became widespread, and it was logical that some type of national effort would evolve as the corporation grew. The Ronald McDonald House movement, long an integral part of NFL Charities' fiscal allocations, began in Philadelphia in 1974 and now includes over 100 houses nationwide. Located adjacent to children's hospitals, these houses provide free or low-cost room and board for families with children who require extended hospital care. (21)

McDonald's has also proven to be very nimble in not only shaping its image, but also in reshaping that image when societal issues cause the company's mission to be questioned. The fast-food industry has been under attack for more than a decade for providing unhealthy food choices and contributing to the national problem with obesity. During that same period, McDonald's has made adjustments and added healthy menu choices. McDonald's began looking at sports for the most fundamental reasons: the affinity that athletes and their associated lifestyles could add to a brand so intent on attracting families. According to longtime

McDonald's marketing executive Paul Schrage, "We didn't want to turn McDonald's into a health food store, but the feeling was that if you eat right and take care of yourself and be active, you'll be healthy." (22)

Similar to the growth of McDonald's charity involvement and image building was the development and growth of NFL Charities, the official leaguewide charitable effort that disburses profits generated by NFL Properties. This endeavor began simply enough. At the time of the merger agreement (with the American Football League), NFL Properties was the league's independent marketing and promotional company; and as a condition of the agreement, all member teams were required to grant it control of NFL copyright privileges. The organization also printed all of the league's game programs and developed other self-liquidating premium items, which it worked out with advertisers and sponsors, that were designed to promote the league. This included the NFL's fledgling licensing program, which is now one of the largest in sport. At that time (around 1970), NFL Properties generated a relatively small income, and NFL Charities was designed to distribute those revenues. It was, one NFL executive commented, a good public relations gesture. (23)

Although NFL Properties and its licensing and sponsorship agreements have been under attack recently by some owners (particularly Jerry Jones of the Dallas Cowboys), NFL Charities has established itself as an excellent image-enhancement tool for the NFL. This organization provides funds for community centers, minority scholarships, and educational assistance and also contributes to medical research and social service agencies.

Image shaping and enhancement make up a function closely associated with marketing, because public relations personnel work jointly with marketing personnel to introduce new programs, themes, campaigns, sales approaches, and promotional efforts. For example, the public relations staff might assist the marketing department in developing and implementing a new theme for season-ticket sales, a tennis tournament, or a campaign for a new stadium. The Orlando Magic, plagued by questions about the future of the team as plans for a new arena were put on hold and a Kansas City Magic Internet site appeared, decided to go with the theme "Commitment" for their 2005-2006 season (they extended the theme for the 2006-2007 season) because of the number of inquiries and concerns about their future in Orlando, which began to affect ticket sales. The Commitment campaign (see sidebar, "Seats for Soldiers Night") was an attempt to show that the Magic were committed to playing in Orlando and ask the community to make the same type of commitment by supporting the team.

Seats for Soldiers Night

Chris D'Orso, vice president of marketing, Orlando Magic

On March 31, 2006, the Orlando Magic held its first "Seats for Soldiers" theme night during their home game versus the Dallas Mavericks. The vice president of marketing along with the community and government relations manager spearheaded this program. The goal was to host over 3,000 military members and their families. "Seats for Soldiers" night was created to recognize and honor the men and women of the United States armed forces for their continued support of our country.

The creation of this night was part of the Orlando Magic's 2006-2007 season branding campaign: "Commitment. Fans. Team. Town." The success of this program was accomplished through the collaboration of multiple departments within the Orlando Magic, including marketing, community relations, communications, retail, broadcasting, fan relations,

corporate partnerships and ticket sales. More than 50 Magic employees took part in the planning of this program along with the representatives of the local military bases.

The goal was successfully achieved through ticket donations from the Orlando Magic owners, players, staff, season-ticket holders, and corporate partners. These groups donated more than 3,000 seats for this game. Tickets were then distributed to Patrick Air Force Base, MacDill Air Force Base, Jacksonville NAS, and Orlando Area Army National Guard.

The "Seats for Soldiers" theme was evident to all fans attending the game. The usual external activities were enhanced by the presence of two military Humvees, a military mascot, and camouflage face painting. All military members and their guests were presented with "Commit-

Nights honoring hometown heroes have become prevalent among American professional sports teams.
Courtesy of Orlando Magic

ment to our Country" T-shirts with a red, white and blue Magic logo.

Each military base participated in various special in-game events, which included the following:

✦ Kids Tunnel—Select children of military personnel from each base had the opportunity to line up pregame and high-five the Magic players as they entered the court for pregame warm-ups.

✦ Ball Kids—two children of soldiers were selected to be honorary ball kids for the game. They sat on the basket and helped with all duties related to being a ball kid.

✦ Color Guard and Anthem—The Florida National Guard acted as the color guard for the game during the anthem, which was sung by the fans as a salute to honor the military guests.

✦ High-Five Line—Servicemen and -women were able to line up and high-five the Magic players during the on-court introductions.

The night aimed to communicate the Orlando Magic's commitment and gratitude to members of the armed forces through:

✦ A pregame presentation honoring two personnel from each base was conducted on court with the mayor of Orange County and Magic owner and president Bob

Vander Weide. Each person was recognized and given an autographed team ball.

✦ Surprise Message—During the game one family was surprised with a live video call to their loved one in Iraq. The message was viewed by all in attendance on the Jumbo Tron. The moment was truly moving. Additionally, taped messages of Magic players and dancers thanking the soldiers and their families for all they do for our country were played throughout the evening.

✦ Dance Performances—The Magic Dancers performed themed dance routines to Decorated and 7 Nation Army. They also wore military gear in honor of those in service.

Additionally, the Orlando Magic players participated in a postgame meet-and-greet to show their support of our troops. The reception included food and beverages for more than 100 guests and their families. The Magic players posed for photos and signed autographs. Dwight Howard, Grant Hill, Bo Outlaw, and Carlos Arroyo spent valuable time with the troops and their families at this reception.

The Orlando Magic was extremely proud of the "Seats for Soldiers" night. We received many letters of gratitude from the servicemen and -women along with their families. Because of the tremendous success of this program, we are looking forward to continuing the tradition.

Generating publicity about new programs or products, affiliating with "cause" programs or organizations, and reaching the public are essential public relations functions for sport organizations. For example, in 1997, the LPGA announced a partnership with the United States Golf Association (USGA) and the Girl Scouts of America in hopes of expanding its LPGA Junior Girls Golf Club. The goal of the program is to provide a network through which girls learn to play golf, build friendships, and sample competition in a fun and nonthreatening environment. (24) The partnership made it possible to promote and publicize this program through three organizations; additionally, it allowed the LPGA to associate with the values and traditions of the USGA and the Girl Scouts of America to attain its organizational and, in particular, its public relations and publicity goals.

Effective sport organizations such as the LPGA are able to integrate the marketing function (or other functions such as membership or development) with the public relations or media relations function to reach the target markets more effectively and efficiently.

One of the most intriguing examples of cause marketing that was not only an enormous fund-generating concept ($30 million+) but also became a fashion statement was the yellow LIVE STRONG plastic wristband popularized by Lance Armstrong. A veritable case study in cause marketing, the Lance Armstrong Foundation and Nike partnered to launch the Wear Yellow Live Strong campaign in May 2004 as a tribute to Armstrong's fight against cancer and his attempt to win a record sixth consecutive Tour de France. Wristbands are priced at $1 each, and all proceeds benefit the foundation. Several factors contributed to the campaign's success. First, cancer does not discriminate: It has affected or will affect most people (directly or indirectly) at some point. Second, the price point is low: "It is an easy, affordable purchase that is personal, yet very expressive and has the ability to make purchasers feel good about what they are doing via the purchase." (25) Finally, the bracelet demonstrated visible support for one of America's greatest athletes in a struggle to complete a remarkable achievement.

Promoting Employee Relations

Most corporations recognize that an open flow between management and employees is essential—not only for purposes of morale, but also so that employees, who are often the public's first line of contact and communication with the organization, are capable of positive and favorable interaction. Because of the widespread public interest and involvement in sport, which has been documented by the Miller Lite Report on American Attitudes Toward Sport, the Sports Illustrated Sports Poll '86, (26) and regular polling and measurement by services such as the ESPN/Chilton Sports Poll, all employees of a sport organization should understand management's position on a variety of issues and be able to convey this position to the public and especially the media. Players fall into this category of employees, and a number of universities and professional organizations provide formal training for these "player/employees" in the areas of public speaking and dealing with the media.

For "nonplayer employees," organizations can use a number of effective vehicles to disseminate information from management to employees and vice versa. These include employee newsletters, brochures, and documents explaining organizational policies; an effective ongoing employee-orientation program; in-service training programs and seminars; and regularly scheduled staff meetings and special-topic luncheons that work like the "town meeting" in political election campaigns. Pat Williams, senior executive vice president of the Orlando Magic and a talented author and motivational speaker, is part of an Orlando Magic initiative called Magic University. This ongoing program is designed to educate and inform all employees with regard to the goals, objectives, and functioning of the Orlando Magic. According to Williams, "Sharing and openness erase barriers and distinctions within the team so that there is no perception of an inner circle or an outer circle. Nobody's in, nobody's out, everyone's together. If people feel that they are in the outer circle, that they are benchwarmers, they soon begin feeling expendable and powerless—and you lose valuable contributors to the team effort." (27) Lack of information can turn players into benchwarmers; thus, the sport organization must ensure that everyone is informed and feeling part of the "team."

Gaining Political or Popular Support

Clearly, a critical function of public relations is to educate as well as inform. Providing information is not necessarily the same as educating. Education, as defined in public relations, includes developing comprehension, understanding information, and applying information in the appropriate context. Publications such as the *IEG Sponsorship Report* and the *NCAA News* provide information on industry trends, educating their readerships on the implications of legislation and tax laws and promoting conferences and meetings that will increase understanding and promote growth.

Because of a failure to understand, the 1990s were a decade of "franchise free agency" in professional sport. For the most part, this movement of professional sport teams, which essentially began when the Brooklyn Dodgers left after the 1957 season to become the Los Angeles Dodgers, (28) has been the product of consumer perception with regard to the value and costs of providing a "home" for a professional sport franchise. When we looked at consumers as voters, we saw that some consumers believed that a sport franchise was a vital part of the community at any cost (Indianapolis, Nashville, and Baltimore), whereas others initially believed that it was not the community's responsibility to pay the costs (of stadiums, practice facilities, and revenue subsidies) (Baltimore, Houston, and Cleveland) only to change their minds and build new venues and pay significant new franchise fees to attract an expansion fee or to woo an existing team. As this edition goes to press, two cities who built downtown arenas with the hopes and expectations of attracting a professional sport franchise are reviewing their options: Oklahoma City's Ford Center will continue to be the temporary home of the Hurricane Katrina–displaced New Orleans Hornets while also a suitor for baseball's Florida Marlins. Kansas City's new arena, with the naming rights purchased by Sprint, is the likely destination for an NHL team (Pittsburgh's Penguins are often mentioned) or possibly an NBA team from another city (Seattle and Orlando at the current time) unwilling or unable to build a new venue—at least for now.

Recruiting and Developing Business

Because of their need to continuously recruit new athletes, intercollegiate athletics programs—particularly high-profile Division IA programs—have provided some of the most fertile opportunities for public relations personnel to apply their skills. Public relations in this context essentially involves image construction (and reconstruction) and refinement. College life must be effectively portrayed to a variety of potential "recruits" who are looking to ensure that their visions of college, in terms of the educational and athletic experience, are compatible with the image of college presented during the recruiting visit. The function of public relations then is to ensure that questions are answered; that facilities are portrayed in their best light; that coaches and faculty are prepared to respond properly to questions and provide needed information; that the image presented is within conference and NCAA rules and regulations; that well-meaning alums and boosters comprehend what they can and cannot do; and that the recruit becomes aware of the entertainment, cultural, and growth opportunities as well as the educational benefits and athletic promises.

The public relations staff (media relations personnel, recruiting coordinator, institutional public relations officer) can accomplish all this by using a variety of media that we discuss in chapters 12, 13, 14, and 18. The primary medium is personal selling (chapter 12), which involves one-to-one discussions between the recruit and the recruiter that take place at the recruit's home and high school and later on the campus itself.

Prior to this visit to campus, and in many cases again during or after the visit, the recruit may receive a variety of brochures and printed material describing the college, the athletics program, and the opportunities available. This printed material is often augmented by video, CD-ROM, and other multimedia presentations designed to help the recruit "picture" the realities and also the possibilities. Since the mid-1970s, these multimedia presentations have sometimes taken a fantasy or "what if" approach and are often highly emotionally charged. For example, the recruit may sit in the field house or stadium and watch or listen to a scripted hypothetical broadcast of her future exploits and contributions at State University. Another approach is to use films depicting the tradition and stature of the university and its storied athletics program. These films usually feature famous alumni and past athletes endorsing the program and urging the recruit to make the right decision.

The term *recruiting,* not limited to intercollegiate athletics, can refer to any or all of the following:

- ✦ At the professional level, convincing draft choices and free agents to sign with a team, promoting the community, and offering various incentives in addition to the financial package. In a similar professional sport context, recruiting would entail describing the activities of agents seeking to enter into representation agreements with future and current professional athletes.
- ✦ The efforts by cities and sport commissions to attract professional franchises, amateur sporting events, and special events.
- ✦ The efforts of sport marketing agencies to secure sponsorship and corporate involvement for products, concepts, athletes, and events.

In terms of soliciting business opportunities, public relations programs help the organization attract corporate sponsorships by informing the potential corporate partner of the history and tradition of the product, event, or athlete and by helping to build a case to justify the pending financial agreement. One can determine what information is most influential by means of a little research. This may involve generating a basis of comparison with other teams by examining demographic factors or calculating numbers of impressions and the value of those impressions.

Launching New Products or Innovations

If new products (or services) or product innovations are going to attract interest and gain market share, an effective public relations campaign is necessary to ensure that the people in the target market are aware of the product, understand the benefits of the product, and most important, understand why the product is important to them and how it can become part of their lifestyle. The public relations campaign to introduce and launch the WNBA is an excellent example.

According to marketing consultants Al Ries and Jack Trout, the easiest way to get into a person's mind is to be first, and if you can't be first, you must find some way to position yourself against the product that did get there first. (29) The now-defunct American Basketball League preceded the WNBA into women's professional basketball by one full season and signed significantly more "star" players than the WNBA did during that first year. The WNBA was not first, so why was it perceived to be the more successful of the two leagues and generally considered more likely to endure (a belief that proved to be correct)? Simple. The NBA preceded the American Basketball League, and the WNBA was able to capitalize on the recognition and brand equity of the NBA to introduce itself and launch its marketing initiatives. The NBA brand provided an entree to television and print sources to publicize and promote the league, and owners and sponsors to help sell it. "Even before it had signed up all 80 players to do the passing and shooting, the WNBA brought in a host of ringers—three television networks (NBC, ESPN, and Lifetime) and a mighty roster of corporate sponsors, to do the selling. No other league in the history of American sport has made its debut with huge, glossy advertising spreads in *Glamour* and *Self* magazines." The goal of the launch? "Developing the players into household names," according to then NBA marketing chief Rick Welts. (30)

The WNBA launch and ultimate success provide a case study in using existing platforms (arenas, teams, owners, contracts [television], sponsorships, and broadcasts) to launch a new product; the case also illustrates how to use media and public relations to capture the imagination of the public even if you didn't introduce the product first.

The war in Iraq has magnified North America's dependence on energy resources and the fragility of acquiring those resources consistently and affordably and illustrates another example of an organization successfully launching new products. Sharp Electronics has a mission to develop a true domestic solar energy industry to educate consumers on the value of such a source, but more important, to assist consumers in thinking about the possibilities of energy from solar power. Sharp, in conjunction with a sponsor agreement with the San Francisco Giants and SBC Park, has equipped the stadium to generate solar energy for the power grid and has signage and informational kiosks to demonstrate the amount of energy being produced and the benefits of that energy. According to Rhone Resch, president of Solar Energy Industries Association, "Baseball and sunshine go hand in hand and when it comes to solar power, California continues to be the nation's leader in helping grow and transform our business." (31)

This positioning can be effective in getting consumers to think about products and services in a different way. Take, for instance, the case of a municipal parks and recreation department wanting to justify current levels of funding or perhaps seek a budget increase. Some type of media and community relations program is essential, but what is the best approach? An open house? An annual report? Both might be effective, but the Needham (Massachusetts) Park and Recreation Department came up with a rather innovative way to create attention and stand out. The department created a campaign that featured the following information:

It costs $30,000 to incarcerate a juvenile offender for one year. If that money were available to the Park and Recreation Department, we could:

- Train him to be an American Red Cross-certified lifeguard in six weeks and
- Give him 36 weeks of archery lessons and
- Give him six weeks of lacrosse lessons and
- Give him 8 weeks of tennis lessons and
- Take him on two ski trips and
- Take him swimming every day for 11 weeks and
- Give him 8 weeks of skating lessons and
- Provide him with 22 weeks of after school activities and
- Let him play volleyball every week for 21 weeks and
- Let him learn the value of volunteering for a whole summer and
- Let him visit the Town Forest whenever he wanted, and
- Give him space to grow his own fruits and vegetables

After which, we would return to you $28,582 and one exhausted, but much happier kid. (32)

Generating and Collecting Feedback

Feedback is essential in the strategic planning process and critical to determining the acceptance and effectiveness of organizational policies and procedures. Public relations personnel play an integral role in monitoring the pulse of the public with regard to their interest in and acceptance and rejection of organizational products, concepts, and practices. Public relations people gather data on public attitudes, economic indicators, consumer preferences and behavior, and political and societal events with which the organization is involved. Feedback may be generated by request (survey or poll) or simply as a result of past action or inaction, without an official request (unsolicited and uninitiated letters or phone calls).

For example, consider developments with regard to the NCAA. In recent years, the NCAA has solicited feedback on recruitment, retention, academic performance, and graduation rates of athletes; on issues relating to Title IX and gender equity; and on a variety of other issues. For the most part, the NCAA has used this feedback to monitor progress and assess public perception, and in some cases to initiate reforms or modify regulations. Although the majority of feedback has been positive, there have also been negative feedback and criticism. As a result, the NCAA began to alter the structure of intercollegiate athletics. The most notable changes have included the formation of a presidents' council and a shift of power to these presidents; higher standards for student-athletes' academic performance; fewer scholarships; increased opportunities for women; fewer coaches (full- and part-time) in particular sports; a football national championship; equipment redesign (baseball); and the right of student-athletes to be employed during the academic year. Some of the changes have elicited a positive response, some have aroused criticism, and still others have resulted in litigation. Although some of this feedback was solicited, a portion was generated as a result of a lack of attentiveness and control in practices within the system. When the outcry and interest became great enough, the feedback, both solicited and unsolicited, spurred reform.

Based on NCAA feedback, more sporting opportunities now exist for women.
© Human Kinetics

Coping With Crisis

One of the most visible roles that a public relations professional performs is coping with crisis. Because the majority of these cases elicit media interest, the words and actions of the public relations department and its professionals are often in the news and engender as much interest as the incident that precipitated the crisis. The annals of sport are rife with the results of both crisis and "spin"—attempts to change the way people are interpreting the actions and words of the principals involved in the crisis. The following are some notable examples:

◆ *The steroid scandals in baseball in 2005-2006.* Primarily related to the sanctity of baseball's records and the issue of fair competition, the steroids issue has been examined by the electronic and print media, which has spent countless hours and resources covering congressional hearings, debating new negotiated penalties including a lifetime ban for repeat offenders, and examining the personas of certain suspected violators—most notably, Jose Canseco (who also authored *Juiced*), Barry Bonds, Mark McGwire, Sammy Sosa, and Rafael Palmeiro. A tradition-rich sport such as baseball that is in large part measured in terms of historical accomplishment and records can be heavily damaged if the records are viewed as suspect.

◆ *Reebok International Limited and the resultant furor in 1997 surrounding a women's running shoe named the "Incubus."* In doing its due diligence, the marketing team concentrated on a name that did not exist in the marketplace and did not infringe on any existing trademarks. Thus the shoe was named Incubus, which according to the dictionary is an "evil spirit that has sexual intercourse with women while they are sleeping." Damage control became essential for obvious reasons, and also because the mistake was large enough to merit coverage on the front page of the *Boston Globe* as well as a mention in *USA Today* and numerous newspapers throughout the country. Reebok Vice President of Public Relations Dave Fogelson acknowledged that a mistake had been made and that steps had been implemented to ensure that such a gaffe didn't happen again. (33)

✦ *In 1995, remarks about women golfers by CBS golf commentator Ben Wright at the McDonald's LPGA Championship.* Wright commented that "lesbians in the sport hurt women's golf" and that "women golfers are handicapped by having breasts because their boobs get in the way of their swing." (34) Not only the quotes, but also attempts by Wright and others to attack the credibility and integrity of the reporter, Valerie Helmbreck, kept this story in the news for an extended period of time. Ultimately, Wright, admitting that he had made the remarks, received a suspension, and underwent counseling. The Wright incident was even more infamous because it was not the first time that callous and flip opinions and remarks had damaged a segment of society and also hurt the reputations and careers of notable sport personages, such as Al Campanis and Jimmy "the Greek" Snyder.

✦ *The 1997 sex scandals in Canadian hockey.* The scandals involved a noted junior hockey league coach, Graham James, as well as separate incidents pertaining to workers at Toronto's Maple Leaf Gardens, in which young men were promised tickets and autographs in exchange for participation in group sex. These scandals served to tarnish the image of Canada's beloved national sport.

✦ *The NFL's New England Patriots and their drafting and termination of Christian Peter.* Peter, who had a checkered past at the University of Nebraska (with eight arrests for charges ranging from trespassing and disturbing the peace to third-degree sexual assault), was drafted by the Patriots in the fifth round of the 1996 NFL draft. After criticism in the media and through phone calls from fans protesting his presence on the Patriots' roster, Peter was dumped by the Patriots, who claimed that they had not investigated his background thoroughly—a contention that Peter disputed. (35)

Situations such as these have caused certain organizations to demonstrate that they can be proactive by implementing procedures to be followed in the event of a crisis. The NFL has developed an internal 10-point crisis-control plan for addressing volatile situations. As presented and discussed on ESPN's *Outside the Lines,* components of the plan included the following:

✦ First response should be "no comment."
✦ Convene an immediate meeting of the crisis team.
✦ Formulate a statement that can be distributed to the media.
✦ Develop talking points and send them to allies who will be speaking to the media. (36)

Media Impact on Sport Public Relations

The media's impact on the daily lives of people throughout the world cannot be underestimated. The death and funeral of Princess Diana, the Clinton-Lewinsky "Interngate" fiasco, the Oklahoma City bombing, the acts of 9/11, and coverage of the Gulf War and the war in Iraq have illustrated the "magnifying glass" that media coverage can become. Daily, if not hourly, the media provides not only coverage of the events taking place, but also global reactions and interpretations of those events.

Sport is not immune to this magnifying-glass effect, as we can saw in the coverage of the 1998 pursuit of the baseball one-season home run record by Mark McGwire and Sammy Sosa, since broken by Barry Bonds and now under scrutiny. ESPN provided live coverage of every potential record-breaking at bat as well as reactions from past baseball heroes such as Hank Aaron and the family of the late Roger Maris. In fact, because of our levels of interest and involvement, sport has become one of the most interesting specimens for examination by the media. The late James Michener stated that "sport, and in particular baseball (during its professional infancy), prospered, because it received, at no cost, reams of publicity in daily and Sunday papers." (37) Michener explained that this coverage, which any other business would have had to pay for, was given freely because of its entertainment value and because a newspaper that contained information about sport would sell more copies, creating both higher circulation and higher advertising rates. In his classic *Sportsworld: An American Dreamland*, Robert Lipsyte echoed this sentiment: "Without the aid and abetment of sportswriters, Judge Kenesaw Mountain Landis would never have been able to revirginize baseball after the 1919 Black Sox scandal, Tex Rickard would never have been able to introduce the million-dollar boxing gate, and college football would never have been able to grow into America's grandest monument to hypocrisy." (38)

In addition to the contribution of the print media to the growth of sport, the electronic media—initially radio, later television, and now the Internet—have also publicized sports heavily, particularly golf and football, and created the mechanism responsible for their popularity today.

Three factors, namely the publication of Jim Bouton's *Ball Four*, (39) the creation and success of *Monday Night Football*, and the founding and emergence of ESPN, changed the way sports were presented and accepted in American households, subsequently altering the role of public relations in sport from reactive to proactive. In other words, whereas the role had once been to maintain a protected image, free from the restraints and constraints of society, the new aim was to create an image of sport as a segment of American life, mirroring the larger context in which it operates. This image, reflecting all that is good and bad in society, placed sport in the "daily mix" of our lives—off the pedestal it had previously occupied. Public relations personnel were quick to capitalize on this new image, and community relations personnel began to plan how to rebuild and reshape it.

Athletes Get Real

For decades, the press (as an unofficial public relations area of sport), as well as public relations directors of sport teams or organizations, had taken great pains to ensure that the only sport stories were about athletes' on-field performances, or about athletes visiting children in hospitals and otherwise functioning as ideal role models and pillars of the community. With *Ball Four* (followed by *I'm Glad You Didn't Take It Personally*—the satirical title referred to the reaction to *Ball Four*), Bouton changed the face of sport reporting in terms of the scope of material covered and the way it would be covered. This change in sport reporting directly changed the role of public relations in sport.

After the publication of *Ball Four* in 1970, sport and its collective heroes were "set on their collective ear." Bouton had shown that many activities and behaviors that are part of the lives of ordinary people are an integral part of the lives of professional athletes as well. In other words, he explained that "role models" and superstars were, for the most part, like everyone else and that they had the same likes, dislikes, problems, and dreams. Interestingly enough, one person Bouton discussed in his book was the late Mickey Mantle, his contemporary and teammate. Bouton wrote about Mantle's "problem" with alcohol—a subject that was responsible for much of the negative reaction to the book. Before his death, and more than 25 years after the publication of Bouton's book, Mantle acknowledged his "problem," became a spokesperson for organ donations, and in a sense justified and recaptured his identity and value as a role model—because of his humanity and personal situation, apart from his baseball immortality.

Ball Four was the first book to deal with the off-field exploits of athletes; if Bouton set out to illustrate that sport is truly a microcosm of society, he could not have selected better subject material. But as the mystery and glamour were removed from our sport heroes and some of the luster was dulled, public perception of sport was altered. We were no longer interested solely in box scores and heroic exploits; we were also interested in the problems and pitfalls encountered along the way. We wanted, perhaps needed, to know the behind-the-scenes stories about Mike Tyson, Tonya Harding, the Dallas Cowboys, the O.J. Simpson trial, the exploits of Dennis Rodman, Allen Iverson, the decline of the Portland Trailblazers, the destruction of Maurice Clarett, Tony Parker's romance with actress Eva Longoria, and most recently, Vince Young's Wonderlik test at the 2006 NFL Combine. Sport organizations now had to determine how much of this new information, in the best interests of the sport (including financial interests), they could present to the public and how they should present it. This is among the many problems that the public relations professional has had to face in the continuing "glass house" that sport has become.

Focus on Entertainment

The positioning of ABC's *Monday Night Football,* now in its fourth decade and beginning its first season as ESPN's *Monday Night Football* in 2006—as not just sport but as entertainment—marked a change in the public perception regarding sport that greatly aided the work of public relations professionals. These professionals no longer treated sport as though it existed in a cathedral; they could now use techniques common in business and the entertainment industry to promote and publicize sport. Bill Gunther and Marc Carter chronicled the development of *Monday Night Football* through the vision of its executive producer, Roone Arledge, and his belief that "Monday Night Football would be as much entertainment as football. It would be a spectacle that people would watch whether or not they cared about the game, and would appeal to women as well as men." (40) *Monday Night Football* and future sport television such as ESPN's *SportsCenter* would provide intriguing opportunities for the public to see athletes in a variety of roles from performer to entertainer to spokesperson to humanitarian.

The two-decade-plus history of ESPN as the ultimate sport broadcasting network began in 1979. The success of ESPN (the first station to broadcast 24 hours a day, seven days a week, 365 days a year), besides giving birth to ESPN2 ("the deuce") and ESPNews, has given rise to Fox Sportsnet, a satellite of regional sport networks located throughout the country, and several similar ventures. In addition to live programming, ESPN has initiated a series of programs called *Outside the Lines* that probe issues in sport such as homosexuality, gambling, and violence. These and similar issues and related situations may attract positive or negative attention, requiring a reactive response on the part of public relations or perhaps proactive planning to alleviate adverse effects. In addition to *Outside the Lines,* ESPN offers a program called *Up Close* that presents interviews with players and leaders in sport. In terms of public relations, *Up Close,* in a one-on-one format, gives the public an opportunity to learn more about the sport figure in a pleasant, conversational format.

The kind of information covered on ESPN sometimes necessitates a great deal of attention from public relations professionals. For instance, in "Outside the Lines: Sports Under Arrest" on September 2, 1997, ESPN examined athletes in trouble with the law. In his introduction, ESPN's Bob Ley said, "You can point to all the money, all the media or simply society, but there has never been such a time when so much of the sports news is right here in a court of law."

In a segment on managing a sport crisis, Ley explained how teams, leagues, agents, and corporate sponsors plan for and respond to arrests of players. After 76er Allen Iverson's recent arrest on weapons and marijuana charges, the response of his sponsor, Reebok, was quick and positive. Reebok Director of Public Relations Dave Fogelson stated, "Our first reaction is certainly going to be that we're going to support the athlete. And this is not a knee jerk reaction...In the short term if there's some negativity, that's for the short term." Ley, who also interviewed executives at Advantage International, noted that crisis management by a player's agent is perhaps most critical immediately after an incident. According to Advantage International Senior Vice President Tom George, "They're looking for us to make things right.

That's part of our job—to make those things go away so that they can concentrate on what they do best." Ley reported that in the wake of Warren Moon's arrest two years earlier for domestic violence (Moon was later acquitted), Moon and his agents took the public relations offensive by holding two press conferences. (41)

Our interest in athletes has shifted because sport fills an entertainment role in our culture. On television, in particular on *Monday Night Football* and ESPN's *SportsCenter,* the entertainment has to be first-rate because it airs in and around prime time, affects network ratings, and influences advertising revenues. Howard Cosell and Chris Berman became premier sport broadcasters and personalities because they, like Bouton, shared information that was more than play-by-plays or game summaries; they offered information regardless of the consequences.

Strategic Planning and Public Relations

"Strategic planning is a philosophy of management based on identifying purpose, objectives, and desired results, establishing a realistic program for obtaining these results, and evaluating the performance." (42) Too often, public relations personnel are not in the planning loop, and their role has been to react to the plan and create vehicles to support the objectives that others have identified for them. In truth, public relations personnel should help create the corporate mission and objectives. As discussed earlier in this chapter, publics and their individual and collective relationships dictate how successful an organization or corporation will be. A key function of public relations departments is to monitor, understand, and develop communication platforms with these publics. Establishing and maintaining this communication system is integral to defining objectives and projecting outcomes. For example, in the public relations office of a professional sport franchise or athletics department, community relations is an integral function. Such community relations efforts (as we have previously discussed) usually encompass the following functions:

Speaker's bureau

Clinics and player appearances

Mascot, cheerleaders, and band appearances

Correspondence (e.g., fan mail, photo requests)

By implementing and maintaining these functions, the public relations department can monitor the "pulse" of the community with regard to the organization. Monitoring provides significant feedback relating to program element performance; budgetary needs; the selection of programs to be renewed, redefined, or terminated; and so forth. The public relations department should use this information in strategic planning as it formulates its short- and long-term objectives. This should result in a more focused and targeted strategic plan that serves the constituency adequately and that can play a key role in developing long-term relationships and growth.

Integrating Sales, Promotion, Sponsorship, Media, and Community Relations

The former International Hockey League Denver Grizzlies (now the Utah Grizzlies) give us an excellent example of successful integration of the concepts discussed in this chapter. The Grizzlies set out to create a community relations program with multiple interrelated goals:

- ✦ To generate high awareness, visibility, and publicity for the Grizzlies in the community
- ✦ To generate goodwill and positive feelings about the Grizzlies throughout the community

- To develop new programs and support existing programs that encourage youth participation in hockey (ice and street)
- To identify quality organizations and provide them with Grizzlies tickets

To accomplish these goals, the Grizzlies created a variety of activities and approaches that not only complemented each other but were fully integrated to capitalize on existing resources and generate income to pay for the programming. These activities and approaches included the following:

- *The Grizzlies Speaker's Bureau.* Bureau representatives speak once the group has contracted to purchase a group outing at a Grizzlies game. All honorariums and speakers' fees (if any) were payable to the Grizzlies Youth Foundation and used to purchase tickets for the Plus/Plus Club.

- *The Plus/Plus Club.* The name of the club was based on the idea that it was a win–win proposition. The Plus/Plus Club was an umbrella program that provided an opportunity for economically disadvantaged youth or at-risk youth to attend Grizzlies games. Tickets were complimentary but were funded by donations to the Grizzlies Youth Foundation or provided via corporate sponsors, player charitable efforts, and donations of unused tickets by Grizzlies ticket holders. The organization hoped the program was building fans for the future.

- *Preseason caravan.* Before training camp began, the Grizzlies hosted a preseason caravan consisting of players, coaches, and announcers. The caravan made stops at all the major towns and cities in the Grizzlies' market area (Colorado, Wyoming, Utah, and New Mexico). Clinics, shopping mall appearances, on-air interviews, and civic club appearances were integral because of the opportunity to sell tickets and merchandise as well as to maintain interest for radio and television broadcasts.

- *The school assembly program.* Hockey is a great lesson for life. This was a program of 50-minute presentations via school assemblies at area schools for children in kindergarten through fifth grade. Presentations included player and mascot appearances, skills demonstrations, video highlights, sponsor-provided gifts, and coupons for two youth tickets for that school district's night. Parents could buy tickets, and all tickets were upgradable (the upgrades alone paid for the cost of this program). Sponsors could, as part of their contracts and fees, provide free products to be distributed at the assemblies. Figure 16.2 illustrates the relationships that can be used in conducting this program.

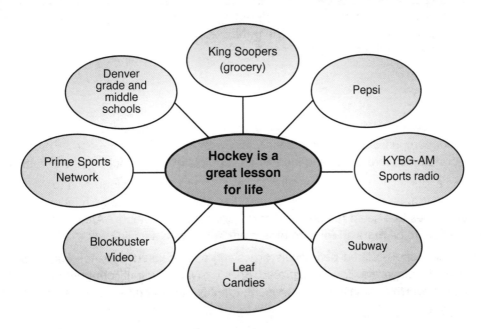

FIGURE 16.2 An example of a community outreach program.

◆ *"Bear Foot in the Park."* A cooperative effort among the City of Denver Parks and Recreation Department, the YMCA of Denver, the Grizzlies, and their sponsors, this street hockey and roller hockey program was designed to increase interest in the sport of hockey and build long-term fans through these grassroots efforts.

◆ *Charitable involvement.* The Grizzlies selected three youth-related local organizations for charitable involvement: Children's Hospital, the Make-A-Wish Foundation, and the YMCA of Denver. Although there were no cash contributions, the Grizzlies were active in serving on boards and committees; assisting in their respective fund-raising efforts; providing memorabilia items and donated tickets for the charity to use in its own fund-raising efforts; and targeting one special event (season Face-Off Luncheon, annual golf tourney, and annual awards banquet) to generate funds for each charity.

Wrap-Up

For public relations to be effective, the public relations specialist must not only react and respond to requests and situations, but also actively initiate and develop media relations and community relations efforts in an integrated, proactive methodology. This methodology should focus on both short- and long-term objectives with attention to building and fostering relationships. These activities, and the public relations functions in general, must play an integral role in both the strategic planning process for the organization and the implementation and management of the strategic plan.

Public relations programs fulfill a variety of roles, including image shaping and enhancement, educational efforts, business development, recruiting, coping with crisis, and community relations. Community relations efforts can take many forms; they can be initiated by players, can be related to teams or institutions, and can be initiated by leagues or governing bodies. These programs must have reasonable organizational resources or receive corporate or philanthropic support to ensure their longevity and the credibility of the sponsoring organization.

In the sport setting, players have an integral role in the success of such programs, because they can attract media interest and coverage, corporate or philanthropic support, and participants and beneficiaries.

Finally, because media are their own muse, they may be influenced but are never controlled by the public relations department. Thus, public relations professionals must build relationships with the various publics related to their particular sport industry segment. Again, these publics are best served if the public relations program is not only reactive, but also proactive and well integrated.

Activities

1. Set up an informational interview and visit the sport information or media relations entity on your campus. During your interview, discuss the concepts of reactive, proactive, and integrated media relations and identify an example of each function in that setting.

2. Begin a journal that you will keep for 30 days. The focus of the journal is to identify crises in sport (drugs, gambling, moral issues) that have required public relations efforts. Are there issues that seem to come up more frequently than others? Are there organizations that seem to be more adept than others at dealing with a crisis?

3. In reading sport-related periodicals or visiting sport-related websites (e.g., *USA Today, ESPN: The Magazine, Sports Illustrated, Sporting News*), identify controversial incidents or issues in which a "spin" factor is present. Identify the strengths and weaknesses of each argument.

4. Among the roles of a public relations professional in sport, what role and functions are the most common (present almost every day)? Which activities are only occasional?

5. Assume that you are a community relations director for the WNBA's Phoenix Mercury. Identify the various publics with whom you should communicate on a regular basis.

Your Marketing Plan

In any market plan (even those developed primarily for an internal audience), public relations is a critical function. Effective public relations can garner support for your concepts. A solid media relations component can ensure awareness and comprehension of your ideas and intent, and attention to community relations may generate acceptance of your ideas and programs. Review your marketing plan to determine how each of these elements should be addressed to achieve acceptance and support of your objectives internally, externally, or both.

Chapter 17

Coordinating and Controlling the Marketing Mix

Objectives

- ✦ To be able to compare and contrast the interaction and impact of the five Ps on one another.

- ✦ To understand how organizational structure, job descriptions, and staff training affect organizational control of the marketing function.

- ✦ To understand the need for control in achieving marketing effectiveness and to recognize some standard benchmarks of marketing performance in sport.

Beer Promos Brew Trouble for Some Colleges

The Fresno State men's basketball team entered the court to the thundering applause of their ardent fans. They came through an inflated silver tunnel, provided by a local sponsor for free. You can imagine the scene—it happens all over the country, at all levels. The crowd is whipped into a frenzy of anticipation by an announcer, until the home team makes its triumphant entrance though the tunnel, accompanied by smoke, lasers, and loud rock music. The same Fresno sponsor helped juice up the crowd by providing small, parachuted objects that fans could toss at a target for prizes. Neither was an unusual promotional gimmick; all were standard parts of the carefully staged sport/entertainment event of the last decade.

There was, however, one major difference. The sponsor was a local Coors Light distributor. With the Coors name and the Coors colors, it was easy for most fans to perceive the tunnel as a giant beer can. What an image. A collegiate team vomited out of a giant beer can for every home game! That is not what Fresno had in mind. The beer promotion ran headlong against a rising awareness of alcohol abuse on the nation's campuses. A Harvard University survey had just found that 44 percent of responding college students had engaged in binge drinking in the two weeks prior to the survey. And here was Fresno projecting its players out of a beer can. A Fresno administrator, John Zelezny, said the tunnel was not designed to look like a beer can, but in the face of withering criticism he concluded: "If that was how people were perceiving it, then that was not appropriate." Fresno pulled the tunnel and stepped back to assess its engagement with the promotion of alcoholic beverages. "We need to find the line for our university," said Zelezny, "and decide what is acceptable and what is not." (1)

As of the fall 2004, Fresno still reported beer sponsorships in a survey by *Street & Smith's SportsBusiness Journal.* They were not alone. Fifty-five NCAA Division I programs acknowledged some kind of beer sponsorship—dollars for signage, radio and TV ads, promotions (such as the Fresno tunnel), and sometimes tickets. Such deals work at some institutions and not at others, largely because alcohol abuse is such a contentious issue. Even if Anheuser-Busch, Miller, and Coors also pay for ads promoting responsible drinking, that message is often lost. Ohio State, for instance, prohibited beer and alcohol ads on its local radio broadcasts and coaches shows, in large part because the institution still reels from images of drunken student riots after the 2002 Michigan game. (2)

As Fresno and Ohio State recognized, tying beer sponsorships to college sports can lead to backlash from an unanticipated and negative *cross-impact* of promotion and public relations. The potential synergies among and between the five Ps of sport marketing require constant evaluation. The San Jose Sharks might never feel such pressure against a beer promotion because professional sports—right or wrong—have been so historically entwined with beer sales that the public expects such promotions. Not so at the college level. Along similar lines, some college coaches have taken heat for their endorsement deals with dietary supplements, some of which have been linked to dangerous and deadly side effects. (3)

In this chapter, we examine the range of cross-impacts among the five Ps—the sport marketing mix. We also consider some principles necessary for the effective control of these elements and their related functions in the sport organization. As we noted in chapter 2, the marketing strategy, with its integration of product, price, place, promotion, and public relations, must be managed in a way that moves the organization toward its overall objectives.

Cross-Impacts Among the Five Ps

So far we have treated each element of the marketing mix in a somewhat isolated fashion, yet clearly these elements have a simultaneous cross-impact on the consumer. A potential buyer of a sport product does not view the price of a product in isolation from the promotional mix, the place function, or the nature of the product and product extensions. This impact can be assessed using a cross-impact matrix (see figure 17.1). The figure summarizes the

	Product	Price	Place	Promotion	Public relations
Product		Price = value	Images interact	Product position	Consumer receptivity
Price			Images interact	Choice of media	Sincerity of public relations
Place				Images interact	Images interact
Promotion					Completely interdependent
Public relations					

FIGURE 17.1 Cross-impact matrix for the five Ps of sport marketing.

degree to which each element interacts with the others. In this section, we provide a more complete assessment of these interactions.

The Impact of Product and Price

The impact of product and price is more truly the impact of price on product. Price, as we have discussed previously, is the most visible and most readily communicable variable of the marketing mix. Price influences perceptions of quality and value, and thereby directly affects the product image. More often than not, consumers are balancing product and price in their minds as they consider purchasing a sport product. For instance, one ESPN/Chilton poll surveyed 800 people aged 12 to 44 who had purchased logoed sport merchandise within the past three months. The results (see tables 17.1 and 17.2), broken down by age groups, suggest that all the age cohorts viewed quality and price as important purchase criteria, but that consumers under age 25 viewed product quality (in this case, brand name) as slightly more important (than did their elders), whereas consumers aged 25 to 44 viewed price as slightly more important than did their juniors.

Consumers often view low-priced products as being low-quality products and high-priced products as being high-quality or prestigious products. Price–product strategies based on such perceptions depend on supply, demand, and market elasticity. They can also be tricky business. Nike was burned badly in the late 1990s when it misread the market for its new Tiger Woods line of apparel. The style and the

✦ **Table 17.1** Results of ESPN/Chilton Poll Asking, How Important Is the Brand Name on the Item When Purchasing Sports Logo Clothing?

	Age			
Importance	**12–17**	**18–24**	**25–34**	**35–44**
Not at all/not so important	19.4%	25%	36.%	29.9%
Somewhat/very important	80.5%	75%	63.9%	70.1%

Reprinted, by permission, from "ESPN Chilton sports poll: Are purchasing discussions based on brand?" *Sports Business Daily*, July 24, 1998, pg. 16.

✦ **Table 17.2** Results of ESPN/Chilton Poll Asking, How Important Is the Price of the Item When Purchasing Sports Logo Clothing?

	Age			
Importance	12–17	18–24	25–34	35–44
Not at all/not so important	17.3%	24.4%	16.3%	12%
Somewhat/very important	82.7%	75.6%	83.8%	88%

Reprinted, by permission, from "ESPN Chilton sports poll: Are purchasing discussion based on brand?" *Sports Business Daily*, July 24, 1998, pg. 16.

supporting ads had Nike's usual hard-edge, "in-your-face," antiestablishment look and feel. As *Sports Illustrated* reported, however, such products did not appeal to the core of golf's consumers. They appealed to kids, who could not afford the $75 shirts or the $225 shoes. Said one Oregon golf shop operator: "Young kids like it, but young kids don't have the money to buy it." Or, as another golf executive put it, "Nike tries to use the different-is-cool theme that works well in sports. But in golf that formula doesn't work."

Parents might part with $120 for a pair of Air Jordans, but a golf shirt or golf shoes? (4)

Marketers of women's athletics have faced the related conundrum of increasing the cost of their products at the same time that they seek increased attendance. They have hoped that fans perceive higher value in higher prices. For instance, in the late 1980s, as women's basketball began to draw a larger fan base, the Ohio State women's program recognized the need to charge admission to a "free" event but knew that the move would be a gamble. Their answer was to develop a promotion with local Big Bear supermarkets that focused on key games. Television, radio, and newspaper ads detailed the availability of coupons with any Big Bear purchase—coupons were redeemable, with a dollar, for a ticket with a face value of $2 or $3. This created a sense of value for the product and helped raise the team's average attendance by 1,500. (5)

The Impact of Product and Place

Consumers develop a product image based on their perceptions of the product's attributes. Similarly, sport consumers develop perceptions of the place in which an event occurs, namely, a facility image. These two images are interactive. When the New York Stars of the old Women's Professional Basketball League (WBL) played their home games in the Iona College gymnasium in White Plains, New York, the small, remote college gym hurt the image of the product. It was almost impossible for the Stars to convince fans that their sport was big time when it was played in a minor facility. A move to Madison Square Garden helped; however, the increased overhead could not be borne by the severely underfinanced team. The Stars, who had been champions in 1980, folded, and a year later, so did the WBL. Consumers are convinced of one thing in sport: Big-league products demand big-league places—a sentiment played out again in the WNBA's more recent "victory" over the American Basketball League. As we noted in chapters 7 and 14, the sport venue is part and parcel of the product. That immutable law helps drive the move to "techtainment" venues and sports malls with multiple screens and speakers and games that assault all senses simultaneously.

The smartest marketers, however, recognize that sport consumers seek multiple places for their product consumption. Michael Eisner once described Disney's strategy as "operating on two tracks . . . yin and yang, the paradoxical pull of the opposites." "We're convinced," he said, "that people will seek more diverse entertainment in their homes, but also that they'll take advantage of familiar outdoor gathering spots and seek out new ones." In retrospect, Eisner's plan was clear—the careful placing of Disney's branded products in multiple strategic locations. Take ESPN. The ESPN consumer can stay home to watch *SportsCenter*, read ESPN's magazine, or surf through ESPN.com. When she tires of home, she can travel to the nearest ESPN Zone restaurant to mingle with like-minded ESPNies, trading "Boomer" Berman imitations with a well-schooled waitstaff. (6)

The Impact of Product and Promotion

Products define appropriate formats and media for promotions. For instance, Nike is unlikely to promote its Tiger Woods line via classified ads in the local paper; that is not the place to advertise high-priced golf apparel. Full-color ads in a golf magazine would make more sense. Similarly, the promotional mix defines the product position. As we saw earlier, Nike appeared to miss the mark in its first attempt to position the Woods line. The ad campaign influenced consumers who were not in a position to buy the product. We can see a more successful blend of promotion and position in the Utah Jazz's efforts to attract families. One winter, the Jazz ran a promotion with Continental Baking Co., the makers of Hostess Sno Balls. Continental distributed special packages of Sno Balls throughout the Jazz's market, in purple and green "Jazz" colors, complete with a special wraparound label that offered a family discount package for any of five designated games. What better way to project a product of family entertainment than through the family's favorite snack food? (7)

Sometimes, efforts to "enhance the fan experience" do just the opposite. Although fan songs and chants have defined many venues (and still do in the world of soccer), the art form has waned in North America. Cleverness has given way to vulgarity and cheap taunting, as we noted in chapter 7. Too many teams have abdicated responsibility to control fan behavior, and instead they have simply cranked up contemporary rock music. Rick Church, president of the Information Display and Entertainment Association (a trade group for big-screen producers), wondered if louder was better: "If it's 150 decibels, are you really having fun?" More teams should take a cue from the Cincinnati Reds and encourage local bands (or fan groups) to create special songs that celebrate the team and its community. Some teams just don't seem to get the linkage of promos and product position. In 2000, for instance, Arena Football's Albany Firebirds announced that they would put microphones on four or five players, who fans could hear "close up and personal" by renting a headset for $12. The headsets included a warning about profanity, a point recognized by the Firebirds' own running back, Eddie Brown. "I wouldn't wear it because of the language I use," he said. Although Brown worried about young fans picking up bad language, the Firebirds seemed oblivious. (8)

The Impact of Product and Public Relations

Public relations, a special part of promotions in sport, has an obvious effect on product image and position. But public relations efforts rely on the goodwill of the media to a much greater extent than do promotional efforts such as advertising, which the marketer controls. This is tricky business. Although marketers hope to cultivate the media, they cannot expect a reporter to become a shill. When franchises exercise contractual rights to fire radio or television announcers they handpicked, the press and the public are usually outraged. Consumers expect spin control, but they have a sense of limits.

At a national level, leagues and corporations play the game with greater stakes on the table. For instance, Nike earned a well-deserved reputation in the late 1980s and early 1990s for its innovative advertisements and promotions, which created such high brand equity that most people didn't need a name to know what a "Swoosh" stood for. But the very same aggressive, cocksure, antiestablishment image may have fueled a backlash in public relations. As Nike became the 500-pound gorilla of sport, the media focused on troubling aspects of Nike's labor practices in the Asian factories where its products were made. No matter what data Nike offered about the relative value of its wage scale, no matter how many celebrities returned satisfied from inspection tours, Nike could not seem to win on its own turf of media images. To make matters worse, Nike was further burned by distribution of a new "Nike Air" model that outraged Muslims, who saw a resemblance between the flame-shaped image on the shoe and the Arabic word for Allah. In 1999, Nike joined the World Bank, the Gap, the International Youth Foundation (IYF), and other organizations to form the Global Alliance for Workers and Communities. The Alliance interviewed thousands of workers in an effort to improve labor conditions. As one might expect, Nike was aggressive in its PR about the Alliance's work. But the controversy continues, as a quick Google search of "Nike and labor" will reveal. (9)

If it is difficult to prevent public relations gaffes in developing athletic shoes, it is nearly impossible to develop a foolproof player who conforms to a sport's chosen image both in the venue and out. For most consumers, players are the game. When they misbehave in their personal lives, the whole product suffers. For every Michael Jordan, it seems there are two Terrell Owenses. Rafael Palmeiro can be a hero one day and a bum the next. NBA Commissioner David Stern admitted that "we have to consider, in an honest way, what impact we have on society. We have to let our players know that we like their contributions but also that they have to behave themselves on and off the court." Amid the seamless components of the sport product, including players, venues, equipment, apparel, rules, and so on, any little action may have massive implications for public relations. As we outlined in chapter 16, a "crisis" plan is critical for handling the fires that continually erupt. (10)

The Impact of Price and Place

There are two major impacts of price and place. First, sport consumers expect to pay higher prices for better facilities. Witness the growth in racquetball and fitness clubs in the 1970s. The YMCAs and YWCAs had offered such programs for years, yet the newer clubs with their sleek decor and sophisticated facilities charged higher prices and still captured the bigger share of the market. During the 1980s, Ys responded by building upscale facilities to capture the "yuppie" market; the private clubs then attacked the tax-exempt status of the Ys. The controversy focused on the interaction of price and place, because both sides recognized that in sophisticated markets the consumer will pay a higher price for a more prestigious facility. The same principle applies to spectators who line up to pay higher prices for the benefits of club seats, personal or permanent seat licenses, and luxury suites. The converse is also true, as the Boston Bruins discovered when their overpriced "upper-bowl" seats did not sell. Lower prices were a prerequisite to ticket sales in those remote locations. (11)

Another place–price principle is that consumers tend to pay more for convenience (which is a benefit). Most people still expect to pay a surcharge for tickets they purchase at a Ticketmaster outlet or a kiosk in a mall. They save time (another important benefit) if they don't have to drive to a central box office, and for the most part they accept the additional convenience fee. Attitudes are changing on this, however, as more and more people are online and expect instant, downloadable service anyway. Similarly, consumers have traditionally paid more for sporting goods that they purchase at local sporting goods stores. Although the larger discount houses may stock the same product, the local store's convenience (and more personal service) often compensates for the additional cost. In summary, sport consumers will pay more to view a sport in a more attractive or convenient location, to play a sport at a more attractive (or more challenging, as in golf) facility, or to purchase sporting goods in a local store. The concept of place includes manifold benefits (or costs) that influence the consumer's perception of a fair price.

The Impact of Price and Promotion

In the majority of cases, the price of a product dictates the media for advertising the product, for several reasons. First, the price determines the profit margin on the product, hence the promotional budget and in turn the media choice. Second, the price of a product reflects not only its nature and cost, but also the market to which the product is targeted. In both cost-plus and market-based pricing, the price reflects the target market's demographics and its media choices. Even a casual look at newspapers or television reveals this pattern. Whereas the maker of a new "foolproof" fishing lure might run a 30-second spot during a cable television fishing show (whose viewers match the product's target audience), a large chain like MVP or Dick's sporting goods will prefer a multipage, multicolor insert for regional newspapers whose readers cross a wide range of demographics.

The last example suggests that size and scope influence price and promotion. With so much consolidation in ownership of "big-time" sports, we can expect to see interesting twists in strategies addressing price and promotion. For instance, in the late 1990s, the Texas Rangers (MLB) and the Dallas Stars (NHL), both owned by Tom Hicks, offered a special ticket package of 13 Rangers games and 6 Stars games, with play-off option guarantees for both teams. In the first hour and a half, 100 combo plans were sold, and after one week, 200 had been sold. Cross-ownership of teams and venues may lead to more interesting ticket packages that cross sports and entertainment categories. (12)

The Impact of Price and Public Relations

Any superticket is promoted on the basis of value. Sport consumers keep value front and center when they make purchase decisions. In that respect, pricing strategies can have a strong effect on public relations, for better or worse. College and university athletics programs learned this lesson, sometimes the hard way, as they moved in the last two decades to required "donations" for the right to buy football or basketball tickets in preferred locations. This was the forerunner of the personal or permanent seat license, and some schools didn't handle things well. Alabama, for instance, could not keep ahead of one maelstrom of criticism, as word spread about a surcharge. One administrator admitted, in words that have since echoed across the industry, "We didn't handle it right. We should have called a press conference and explained everything in great detail."

University of Northern Colorado Athletics was likewise under media attack in the fall of 2005 when Director Jay Hinrichs announced a first-ever parking fee for home football games. UNC was moving up from Division II to Division IAA, so revenue was a greater issue. Hinrichs further argued that the $5 fee would support additional "customer service." This didn't sit well with Matt Schuman of the *Greeley Tribune,* who responded that most of the 4,500 or so regular fans cared little about "customer service." The team was coming off a 2-9 season. The program needed a way to attract more fans to the newly expanded 8,500-seat Nottingham Field. In Schuman's opinion, "An additional $5 may give them just another reason to stay away." (13)

As we mentioned in chapter 10, the Pittsburgh Penguins earned lots of positive PR in 1987 with their "Playoff or Payoff" ticket campaign. The idea was alive and well in 2003, when the Nashville Predators, the Atlanta Hawks, and the Florida Panthers ran similar promotions for season-ticket sales. But the Predators knew there was a payoff for their own coffers even if the had to give money back to their fans. A survey indicated that without a "playoff or payoff" pledge, season-ticket renewals would have been 70 percent. With the pledge, renewals were 83 percent, close to the year before, despite a price hike. Although these teams gambled with revenues, they had a sure bet on positive PR. (14)

In the late 1990s, Coca-Cola walked away from its long-term sponsor relationship with the NFL, in part because it feared negative publicity from the "deep-well" pricing of concessions at NFL stadiums. Coke correctly felt that it did not need high-priced stadium signage to gain brand recognition. More important, exclusive "pouring rights" were backfiring. Consumer research showed Coke that 4 out of 10 people blamed Coke, at least partially, for the overpriced, watered-down stadium beverages. The question was simple for Coke executive Steve Koonin: "I'm going to pay for the privilege to upset people?" (15)

Some player agents—to many the epitome of venality—have recently shown similar concern about image. In this case, the issue was high-priced autographs. Autograph-show promoters, recognizing the players' myopic greed, started contacting players directly rather than working through their agents, who might suggest to their clients that gouging an owner is one thing, but gouging a young fan is another. Wade Arnot, whose firm represented several Detroit Red Wings players, was blunt about autograph shows: "It's not something we support." (16)

The Impact of Place and Promotion

The ability to promote an old, dilapidated facility's interior design or layout parallels a tailor's ability to make "silk purses out of sows' ears." In other words, it is almost impossible. The sport facility image is a strong one, and it directly influences the product image, as we discussed in chapter 14. Take San Francisco's Candlestick Park. The cold, windy, wet environment may not have affected 49er ticket sales where season-ticket holders make only a 10-game commitment for a sport filled with legends of "ice bowls" and "mud bowls." And to be sure, a great record didn't hurt either. Not so with Giants fans, whose sport (baseball) evokes images of lazy, sunny summer days. The Giants tried valiantly to overcome their location's liabilities, with clever promotions such as "glow glove" night and "ski cap" night, but the final answer was a new facility that promised more shelter from the chilly Bay elements. (17)

Some organizations have promoted special components of their venues. Take, for instance, ice hockey's penalty box—a place that conjures up images of tough guys cooling off in the "sin bin" (see photo). The San Antonio Dragons (International Hockey League, 1996-1999) developed a clever promotion playing off this special "place." Once per period, the Dragons' mascot, Freddy the Fanatic, would move into the stands and haul an unsuspecting attendee (for being too quiet, for wearing the opponent's colors, whatever Freddy thought inappropriate) off to a "fan penalty box" (sponsored by Miller Brewing) behind one of the goals. Besides a close-up view, the fan got a small prize as part of the sentence. Fans seemed to love the promotion, cheering wildly whenever Freddy neared their sections. The Dragons even planned to make an inflatable version of the box for outside events. (18)

Specific to hockey, the concept of the penalty box can be used as a promotional device.
Scott Cunningham, Atlanta Thrashers Team Photographer

The Impact of Place and Public Relations

A new facility has implications for all the other Ps. For instance, a new seat configuration requires a rescaling of ticket prices, which must be done with care for the overall franchise image.

Excessive jumps in price usually backfire into images of gouging and greed, which can take years to overcome. Likewise with other new policies, as the New England Patriots discovered when they moved to Gillette Stadium in 2002 on the heels of their first Super Bowl championship. Hoping to open more tickets to the thousands of fans on their season-ticket waiting list, the Patriots invoked a new policy that prohibited existing ticket holders from transferring their seats to anyone else—by deed, contract, will, or any other means. Many longtime holders were upset, like Tom Maguire when he learned that he and his brothers could not "inherit" their father's tickets: "It felt like a slap in the face." The *Boston Globe* ran a bold headline: "Pass Interference: The Patriots Prohibition on the Transfer of Season Tickets Has Some Fans Crying Foul." But the Patriots argued that they built Gillette Stadium without the use of seat licenses. In their opinion, allowing the transfer of tickets would amount to recognizing de facto licenses, which would unfairly deny others access to tickets. Fans on the waiting list agreed, but the Patriots had learned a hard lesson. (19)

To maximize the positives in their move to the new PNC Park, the Pittsburgh Pirates commissioned the local PR firm of Burson-Marsteller to manage a 14-month campaign leading to the grand opening in April 2001. The campaign included direct mail, a series of press conferences, special events, news releases, newspaper inserts, and a Web site. The campaign paid off in very positive images, a two-month sellout of luxury boxes, and record-breaking season-ticket sales. With a small market and a small revenue base, the Pirates knew they had one chance for a "place-based" spike in image and sales. They made the most of it. (20)

The Impact of Promotion and Public Relations

Publicity is one of the four elements of promotion; therefore, the two are interdependent. As stated previously, the impact of a favorable or unfavorable public relations image cannot be underestimated. It is conceivable that the public relations image can totally negate immense promotional efforts. The source credibility and high level of exposure from media coverage cannot be duplicated by promotional efforts. By the same token, a promotional "bomb" can return savage mockery from press and public alike. Arena Football's Orlando Predators found their franchise the subject of unflattering attention in *Sports Illustrated* when the league fined them $10,000 for scheduling a promotion that would have awarded a keg of beer and $500 to the fan who brought the "best" inflatable doll. Apparently, the Predators were slow learners. A year before they had paid for billboard that "featured scantily clad women bent over to snap a football with the catchphrase 'Get Behind Your Team.'" (21)

Controlling the Marketing Function

We have seen that each element of the marketing mix is interdependent, some to a larger extent than others. Because each has the ability to influence the others, the only way to ensure marketing effectiveness is to control all parts of the marketing effort. In this section, we outline a comprehensive marketing control plan that has as its ultimate goal ensuring the creation and delivery of products that satisfy consumer wants and needs.

A sound control system can nurture and preserve the credibility of the image that consumers hold of both the product and the organization. The notion of "control" spans all levels of the industry—from the NFL's dictating specifications on player uniforms (shirts tucked in, socks pulled up and taped) to a local YMCA's training its staff to react courteously to member complaints; control is a central feature in successful marketing. Even the smallest item can create negative images that seriously undermine the overall organizational image. A small flaw may not affect all consumers or publics that interact with an organization, its personnel, products, services, or facilities; but it can affect enough people to cause damage. The athletic club that has cigarette machines in the lobby communicates inconsistency, insincerity, and a stronger adherence to the profit motive than to the health motive. Coaches who violate NCAA recruiting rules send a subtle but powerful message that their other promises cannot be believed. Maintaining consistency is important in a marketer's ability to communicate a clear and precise position. Inconsistencies blur images and project incoherent product positions.

The key to controlling the marketing mix lies in the ability to set a clear direction for all units and personnel. Employees need a road map to tell them where to go and how to get there. They need to know how they will be evaluated and how their efforts relate to those of others in the organization. An effective marketing control system, then, must be part of an ongoing planning system that has at least four components:

+ Mission statements and objectives that have been established in light of current market position vis-à-vis desired position
+ An organizational structure that marshals resources to meet objectives
+ Employee performance standards and criteria that logically link performance to objectives
+ Methods to adjust strategy, structure, and personnel in light of performance

In short, marketing control must be incorporated into an overall strategic plan. (22)

Mission Statements and Objectives

Mission statements and objectives link strategic planning (which forces the organization to assess its relationship to its wider environment) with operational planning (which moves the organization toward its goals). One type of planning cannot succeed without the other. In other words, every piece of the marketing mix should be framed within a broader strategic vision. A good example of a broad strategic mission statement comes from Middlebury College, a highly competitive Division III program in Vermont:

> Athletics are an essential part of the overall educational experience at Middlebury College. The College endeavors to provide athletic programs that are comprehensive and varied, offering athletic opportunities to all students. The Athletic Department is committed to the following:
>
> * A physical education/wellness program that stresses good health, physical fitness and lifetime activities.
> * A vigorous intercollegiate sports program that strives for achievement and excellence.
> * An intramural program that encourages students of varied abilities and skills to participate in a wide range of recreational athletic activities.
> * A club sports program that offers opportunity for intercollegiate competition in a less structured environment.

This statement makes it clear that, unlike its counterpart at Ohio State (see chapter 2), Middlebury's Athletic Department must support a broad base of activities, not just intercollegiate competition. This is rather typical in Division III. Middlebury's coaches and athletes want to win as much as anyone, but the department stands for something more, which will influence decisions on budgets, staffing, facilities, and marketing. The same principles apply to the high school, the multinational equipment company, or the local racquet and fitness club: The mission statement is the touchstone for all strategy and tactics. (23)

Clear, realistic, measurable objectives are the next step in setting the marketing course. Later in the chapter, we will consider some standard indexes of performance (e.g., attendance levels) that are often used in setting objectives. Leaders, however, should not wait until after the fact to consider objectives. Objectives must always be viewed as part of a continuous chain of ends and means, targets along the road to success. Vague or unrealistic objectives can be problematic, as Major League Soccer (MLS) has found. In the league's second season, the commissioner set a public attendance objective of 20,000 fans per game—a target that would bring owners close to the break-even point, but a good 30 percent increase over attendance averages the year before. Unfortunately for MLS, the final attendance average was 14,616 per game, almost a 10 percent decrease from the first season. Did this mean that MLS was in serious trouble? Not necessarily. But it required a reassessment and realignment of goals and strategies from short-term to long-term outlooks. As the commissioner put it, "A lot of people want to instantly assess you as a breakthrough or as a lack of a breakthrough." It was clear to him and the league owners that MLS could no longer think in those terms. (24)

Linking Organizational Structure to Strategy

In many organizations, marketing functions are not centralized, and this has caused problems. For instance, in professional and collegiate sport there is often minimal linkage between the public relations or sport information director (who is usually a journalist) and the director of promotions. At times, the units are antagonistic, vying for scarce resources or the ear of a higher executive. Such organizational conflict—usually the result of historical development—is illogical, given that public relations and promotion should be part of an integrated marketing plan. A comprehensive marketing structure is needed to direct the efforts of marketing personnel and to ensure that these efforts are consistent with organizational goals and policies—and that they complement and do not duplicate one another.

As we noted in chapter 2, structure should evolve from organizational strategy. When the Atlanta Braves realized the need to juice the "fan experience" in 2004, they reorganized their marketing department to include a "stadium" group that focused on the "in-game presentation." Likewise, in the late 1990s, the Dallas Burn of MLS realized that their objective of building a stronger base of Hispanic fans required a change in their marketing structure. At the time they had only one person working on this objective—a Hispanic media liaison who also worked in community relations. The Burn made him director of the new Department of Hispanic Marketing and Community Development, with a staff of two account executives and a community liaison. From a single person trying to do several jobs, the Burn now had four people with a single mission. The Burn had reconfigured structure to follow strategy. On the other hand, the Women's United Soccer Association failed to see that structure must align with strategy. A start-up league that required strong ticket sales to survive, the WUSA was top-heavy with senior executives and hollow at the level of sales staff. No wonder the league folded so quickly. (25)

We offer a sample design for a sport marketing function in figure 17.2. Although the sample is geared to high-performance spectator sports, the framework can be adjusted to the needs, resources, and products of other sport organizations. After outlining the basic positions, we provide indexes and measures for evaluating performance.

✦ *Director of marketing.* Responsible for all marketing efforts, reporting directly to the organization's chief executive. Oversees all other directors. Responsible for planning marketing activities and controlling their effectiveness. Determines budgets and resource allocations.

✦ *Director of advertising.* Responsible for the design, layout, and media selection of all advertising materials. The advertising director is also responsible for all creative copy and illustrations in all print media published by the organization. (In small organizations, this

FIGURE 17.2 An optimal organizational chart for the sport marketing function.

function is contracted out to an advertising agency. The coordination with the agency is the responsibility of the director of marketing.)

✦ *Director of sales.* Coordinates all personal selling functions and is responsible for directing, training, and evaluating sales staff, who represent the following functions:

Advertising sales. The sale of all advertising space in programs, on the broadcast network, over the public address system, and on the electronic scoreboard, as well as all signage space in the venue that the organization controls.

Corporate sales. The sale of private boxes and group-rate plans or individual "company nights" to corporations, private businesses, and public institutions.

Premium seats. Sales of club or premium seats that combine box amenities with the lower cost of a single-season ticket.

Group sales. Efforts (closely allied to corporate sales) to attract groups to events. Differs from corporate sales in that group-sales personnel target social groups, volunteer organizations, and clubs.

Season-ticket/full-membership sales. Sales to "heavy users" who have purchased season tickets or full memberships in the past or who are probable heavy users.

Game or event ticket sales. Function that falls under joint control with the ticket manager, who directs day-of-game sales by ticket salespeople.

✦ *Ticket manager.* Directs the efforts of the ticket-office staff (and sales staff on day of game). Responsibilities include allocation of tickets to ticket outlets (distribution network); allocation of press or guest passes and media credentials; control of and accounting for tickets; and management of sales records broken down by location, ticket plan, game, or event day.

✦ *Director of market research and development.* Provides primary and secondary market data, develops and maintains the marketing information system, identifies new markets, and creates preliminary penetration plans for new markets. Provides service support to sales and public relations staff in terms of market research and intelligence. The person in this position is the logical person to oversee development and management of a Web site, because the Web serves and supports many interests (e.g., public relations, sales, promotions).

✦ *Director of promotions.* Responsible for generating, planning, and implementing sales promotions. Role is coordinated with those of director of advertising, director of public relations, and director of community relations.

✦ *Director of merchandising.* Responsible for marketing and merchandising the team logo and name and for any licensing activities. Controls and establishes the production of souvenirs and programs that bear team name or logo. Responsible for marketing the athletes of the team and for endorsement contracts bearing the team name or logo. Controls the concessions and souvenir stands and pro shops.

✦ *Director of public relations.* Directs the media relations and community relations functions. In small organizations, the public relations director may be responsible for one of these two functions:

Media relations director. Responsible for all relations with the media. Disseminates information, distributes press releases, creates media guides, manages Web site, and organizes press conferences. Coordinates with the ticket manager on press credentials and the assignment of media to the press box. Controls the press box and develops game-day statistics.

Community relations director. Develops, coordinates, and executes all community relations activities. Responsible for activity development in the community and at the facility, including sport camps or clinics, community nights, athlete and personnel appearances, and relationships with general consumers other than the media. Also responds to fan mail.

Each of these functions is essential to an effective marketing effort. The failure to perform one of these functions substantially reduces marketing efficiency. Small organizations might subcontract these functions to sport marketing firms or advertising agencies. Organizations with limited resources or light workloads can combine some of the functions. When necessary, the directors of various functions can carry out the operational activities as well as maintain their primary responsibilities for planning and control. However, a small organizational structure can have a "collapsing effect," and combining roles can have the following counterproductive results:

✦ Lack of specialization results in lack of expertise. A manager hires either a person who is expert in one task and not good in the other, or someone who has general ability but no expertise in either task. This often happens in colleges that hire one person to direct both sport information and sport marketing.

✦ The emphasis becomes an operational emphasis (getting the job done), rather than a planning or control emphasis. Accomplishing the operational tasks precludes planning or reflecting on performance or strategies. The ability to effectively analyze staff performance and provide training rapidly diminishes.

This latter effect can be visualized from figure 17.2. In small structures, the higher levels of management activity are lost and the degree of specialization is severely reduced; planning and control cease. Some might claim that the structure in figure 17.2 is unwieldy and too expensive. Obviously, size and scope will vary with the organization's objectives and resources.

Performance Measures for the Marketing Units

As noted earlier, the entire marketing unit needs clear objectives that move it closer to the organization's overall goals. A large college athletics department, for instance, may have marketing goals that include (1) improving the program image, (2) increasing ticket revenues, and (3) obtaining a larger share of the entertainment market.

Such organizational goals can be translated into specific marketing objectives that clarify, for instance,

✦ the number of favorable stories the public relations staff should nurture in print or electronic media;

✦ improved results in consumer satisfaction surveys;

✦ the amount of revenue to be generated through various ticket packages, licensing agreements, or television contracts; or

✦ relative increases in television or radio ratings vis-à-vis those of competitors (e.g., regional professional teams).

Marketers must recognize and employ standard units of measurement to determine whether their goals are being reached. In the club industry, trade associations like the International Health, Racquet & Sportsclub Association (IHRSA) have prepared standard industry data reports that provide club averages on such items as revenue per member, revenue per square foot, and membership turnover.

Historically, the spectator sport industry lacked regular, rigorous surveys that established such benchmarks of performance. Leagues commissioned occasional surveys, but these did little to grab the attention of managers and marketers. In the last decade, however, trade publications such as *Team Marketing Report, Sports Business Daily,* and *Street & Smith's SportsBusiness Journal* have created indexes of performance, such as TMR's "fan cost index" (discussed in chapter 10). Following are some other recent attempts to develop performance ratios and indexes: (26)

✦ Alan Friedman (*Team Marketing Report* founder) and Paul Much also created a "penetration index" to analyze the performance of professional sport teams. The penetration index simply took a team's "total attendance for the most recent season divided by the total population of the team's Metropolitan Statistical Area." Of course the penetration index must be analyzed with other data such as the number of competing franchises in other sports (given the spillover of seasons), but it offers a starting place for analysis.

✦ The rise of Internet commerce has resulted in greater efforts to measure success. The industry no longer accepts "hits" as an index of popularity, because "hits" is a technical measure of the number of files served. The industry standard is "unique visitors" as well as the average time a visitor spends at a given site (typically per month).

✦ *Street & Smith's SportsBusiness Journal* offer regular features that analyze marketing performance. These include attendance variations as a function of special promotions such as bobblehead giveaways, mascot birthday parties, or fireworks; Internet popularity; television ratings; and radio penetration.

✦ Likewise, academic journals such as the *Sport Marketing Quarterly* and the *Journal of Sport Management* have fostered public dialogue on the strengths and weaknesses of measurements such as signage exposure, consumer recall and recognition, and economic impact studies.

✦ Consulting firms such as J.D. Power and Associates have provided teams with customer service assessments.

As we discussed in chapter 3, indexes are always subject to debate. But they must be developed in order to be debated and tested in the marketplace, so the trends noted earlier are all to the good, for the industry, its marketers, and its consumers.

Screening Promotions Against Objectives

Minor league baseball is known for its constant stream of promotions. It seems that every inning of every game is filled with some attraction beyond the game itself. As reported by Dan Migala in the *Migala Report,* the Brevard County (Florida) Manatees, a Single A ballclub, developed a set of criteria against which to screen all proposed promotions. With good reason, because the Manatees saw families, especially moms, as their principal targets for promotions. They wanted to move casual fans up the escalator. Some of the promotions might flop, but there was no room for negative press or word of mouth because of an offensive program. Here is the Brevard County Manatees Promotional Idea Checklist: (27)

✦ Is it fun?
✦ Is it feasible?
✦ Is it affordable?

✦ Will it add to the fan experience?
✦ Will it be a $2 bill? (i.e., unwanted/avoided)
✦ Is the timing right?
✦ Is it suffering from the "8-ball syndrome"? (dead in the corner)
✦ Has the remainder of the staff approved?
✦ Is it marketable?
✦ Will we have to apologize tomorrow?
✦ Will it promote the team/sponsor positively?
✦ Will it pass the "family test"? (What if your immediate family came to the game? Would Mom be proud or ashamed?)
✦ What will happen if we don't seize the moment?
✦ And last of all, when in doubt, WWVD (What Would Veeck Do?)

As the Manatees example suggests, general objectives must be refined for the people working in each unit. The Manatees built their checklist on the basis of a general objective—to attract more casual customers and families and move them up the escalator. The following are some sample measures that can be adjusted for any overall plan.

Sales

✦ Sales dollar volume measured by actual sales
✦ Market share or increase in sales volume measured from year to year
✦ Number of prospects contacted from salesperson's "contact" records
✦ New business developed, measured from actual sales records

Public Relations (each component of the public relations function can be monitored using appropriate criteria):

Media Relations

- Amount of media coverage (e.g., column inches, airtime) as evidenced by records such as clippings files
- Quality of coverage and media receptivity to the sport organization
- Quantity of legitimate media complaints received
- Number of unique visitors to the organization's Web site

Community Relations

- Number of community groups contacted
- Number of community projects held in the community or at the facility
- Sales revenues (e.g., merchandising) that result from the community relations effort
- Number of positive and negative letters received from the general public
- Number of children who participate in special programs (summer reading, student achievers)
- Measurable outcomes of community projects (e.g. reading level improvement among children who participated in a team-sponsored reading program; total square footage of new fields built for a community)

Ticket Manager

- Accuracy of financial records
- Minimization of errors, losses, or "unaccountables"
- Development of ticket distribution network and innovations in distribution policies

Promotions

- The number of promotions generated
- Sales response to promotions
- Overall image developed from promotional activities

Sponsorships

- Media exposure of sponsor images (e.g., minutes of television time)
- Sponsor renewal rate

Pro Shop or Team Store

- Revenue per square foot
- Stock turn

Market Research and Development

- Timeliness and accuracy of data collected (primary)
- Recentness of secondary data supplied
- Ability of data-based marketing system to stimulate sales and marketing effectiveness
- Number of new markets developed and direct sales from these leads

This last function is perhaps one of the hardest to control because the output is the least subject to quantitative performance appraisal. However, some relationships can be computed as shown.

Research and development is surely a creative process; a good data-based marketing system processes and analyzes consumer complaints as carefully as it does ticket sales.

Nike Bauer Hockey Event Metrics

Ed Saunders, marketing manager, USA, Nike Bauer Hockey

When I develop grassroots marketing events for Nike Bauer Hockey (see the sidebar in chapter 14), here are some of the ratios or "metrics" that I use in determining feasibility and postevent success:

+ Show fee per square foot of booth space. Some shows charge $500 for a standard 10-foot-by-10-foot (3-meter-by-3-meter) booth; others charge $5,000. Marketers must quantify value in the following ways:

+ Show fee per attendee: Is it worth the cost per head to invest?

+ Total cost per square foot of booth space (including show fee, production, shipping, drayage, travel, staff, etc.).

+ Cost per attendee (including show fee, production, shipping, drayage, travel, staff, etc.). Generally, we try to stay within a budget per anticipated patron.

This varies based on the magnitude of a show and whether it is a trade or consumer show.

+ Staff per attendee. We usually allow for 1 per 500. It will vary based on the complexity of the presentation and setup.

+ On-site drayage. This one always nails people. Building, freight handling, and storage fees can get out of hand fast and should be evaluated as a percentage of total cost. More than 10 percent of total expense and you've wasted too much money on moving stuff around in crates, not on display.

+ Travel expenses. This one can get out of hand quickly too. Set a meal per diem, room rate cap, and travel allowance based on destination. Try to keep the hotel in walking distance of event to keep cab fares and car rentals down. I shoot for 15 percent of the total budget; keep it to 10 percent, and that's a big win.

Likewise, the chief operating officer for the marketing functions must be creative in fashioning a system of appraisal criteria that is both fair and challenging. The effective manager is aware of all industry standards—from concession "per caps" to sponsor recognition rates, unique visitors, and attendance as a percentage of venue capacity. The manager is limited only by imagination and data availability.

Linking Personnel Performance to Strategy

The marketing effort may be conceptualized as a series of goals and objectives, but nothing happens without a dedicated and competent staff. Someone or some group, then, must also lead and manage. We discussed sales staff training in chapter 12, but we reiterate here some simple steps to follow to enhance staff performance across the marketing functions.

+ *Step 1.* The manager or director sits down with the staff, using a participative approach to setting performance goals and objectives. The manager or director clearly communicates expectations, performance goals, methods of evaluation, probable rewards for success, and negative reinforcements for failure.

+ *Step 2.* Performance is evaluated, initially at monthly intervals (with intervals lengthening over time). Once satisfactory performance occurs, staff members are evaluated only once every 12 months.

+ *Step 3.* Where there are areas of weakness or areas showing room for improvement, the director or manager should outline the course for training, development, or corrective action.

+ *Step 4.* At each annual review, a new "contract" is developed that builds on the experience of the previous evaluation period.

Dr. Roland Smith, who has consulted with major league teams on their human resources strategies, has a series of useful questions to ask about any performance evaluation system:

- Does it encourage the "behavior" you are looking for resulting in higher levels of performance?
- Is it fair?
- Does it reward top performers for their efforts?
- Does it clearly represent a roadmap to success for average performers?
- Does it identify poor performers in a real-time manner (for corrective action)?
- Is it easily administered?
- Are the performance metrics clearly identified and easily understood?

Through a systematic approach to managing the marketing function, the director can directly influence the organization's success. Each function is crucial to the marketing effort, whether performed by specialists or by individuals who generalize in two or more activities. To make a simple sport analogy, the marketing staff are the athletes out on the field, in the trenches, day after day. To ensure a coordinated, successful effort, they need intelligent, hands-on, face-to-face, constructive coaching. (28)

Numbers Versus Core Values

Jack Welch, the longtime CEO of General Electric, told the authors of *Built to Last* that GE boiled its personnel evaluation to two sets of items: core values and "numbers." Although one could argue that "numbers" should always reflect core values, Welch understood that too often the most easily measurable "numbers" crowded out equally important but sometimes unquantifiable criteria. Welch's description conjures the image of a small table that provides a simple, preliminary screening tool (see table 17.3).

The table reinforces the firm's belief that core values count more

✦ **Table 17.3** Core Values and Numbers

		Embodies Core Values	
		Yes	No
Numbers Performance	Yes	Promote onward and upward	Take a hard, long look
	No	Give another chance	Fire them

than numbers. Someone who advances core values always gets another chance; someone who makes the numbers but does not embody values gets a "hard, long look." As Welch put it: "The problem is with those who make the numbers but don't share the values...We try to persuade them; we wrestle with them; we agonize over these people." Welch's attitude is an important one for sport managers to remember. Numbers should never trump values in personnel evaluation. (29)

Wrap-Up

The notion of control moves the sport marketer from a land of wishful thinking to a realm of meaningful management. We have emphasized the need to control the marketing function, from research on potential consumers and their needs, to market segmentation, to product position, to the marketing mix, to sponsorships, and finally to an evaluation of success. In today's sport marketplace, marketers must be managers and managers must be marketers.

As we have illustrated with countless examples throughout this textbook, the sport industry is evolving rapidly. In this new century, the pressures will only increase for effective, innovative, and creative sport marketing techniques. The simple "selling-of-sport" approach—a giveaway here, some fireworks there—will not suffice. The market is more crowded and consumers are more complex than was the case in 1928, when sport promoter Tex Rickard told a reporter, "By merely reading the newspapers, most anybody can tell what the public wants to see." The future Tex Rickard will be part scientist, armed with the latest techniques for research and development, and part artist, reshaping the product with creative inspiration that evokes passion and inspires colleagues and consumers alike. Whatever the game, the technique will be the same. A comprehensive and controlled marketing effort, coupled with creative ideas, will be the winning formula.

Activities

1. As a simple review, find at least two examples of each cross-impact among the five Ps, either in this book or in some other resource.

2. Using an example from a current sport organization, illustrate the effects of price on the remaining four Ps. Describe scenarios that demonstrate both positive and negative effects.

3. In your estimation, does one of the five Ps have greater cross-impact than the others? Price perhaps? Find examples to defend your position.

Your Marketing Plan

Lay out a clear diagram of the marketing structure for your organization. Be sure that the structure logically follows the direction and requirements of your overall strategy and its related plans. Include job descriptions and performance criteria for each position. Outline a process for evaluating each staff member, each unit, and the marketing unit as a whole.

Chapter 18

The Legal Aspects of Sport Marketing

Steve McKelvey and Lisa Pike Masteralexis

University of Massachusetts, Isenberg School of Management

Objectives

- To introduce the key legal concepts and issues that affect the marketing of the sport product.

- To inform sport marketers about the need, and the methods, to protect intellectual property associated with the creation of a sport product or event, or with ideas developed out of sport sponsorship and licensing programs.

- To examine the legal limits of sport marketing and promotion so sport marketers can avoid legal liability.

Competition Begets Ambushing

Given the tremendous publicity and consumer audiences generated by major sporting events, it is not surprising that companies seek to associate themselves with these events—often without securing the official rights from the event organizer or owner. While such activity, commonly referred to as "ambush marketing," is usually not illegal, the practice does raise ethical issues. It also poses challenges for sport organizers who seek to protect the integrity and financial viability of their event, as well as to fulfill contractual obligations to their official sponsors. For instance, during the 2006 Major League Baseball All-Star Game in Pittsburgh, nonsponsor Consol Energy attached two 100-foot lighted signs on a barge traveling up and down Pittsburgh's rivers; the signs carried the message, "This coal creates enough energy to cook every hot dog ever served at baseball's big game." (1)

During the 2006 Olympic Winter Games in Turin, Italy, nonsponsor Target negotiated a deal with Trenitalia, the Italian train system, to have its red-and-white bull's-eye logo, along with pictures of models in red and white winter ice-skating costumes and luge suits, prominently featured on its trains taking spectators to various events (called "Target Express" trains). Target employees greeted spectators as they boarded trains and distributed logoed noisemakers and large red and white foam gloves in the shape of hands with the index finger pointed to the sky. By teaming with Trenitalia, "Target skirted the federal law here that makes it a crime to affiliate a non-sponsor with the Olympics." (2)

Competition is paramount to the proper functioning of our capitalist market. Viewed in its simplest terms, competition provides consumers with the best-quality products at the lowest prices. In a capitalist market, companies use sport marketing techniques to compete for consumers. As with competition in sport, market competition is not always fair. In a competitive market, a sport marketer may decide to engage in aggressive marketing tactics, such as ambush marketing (as in the examples provided above) or deceptive advertising, to get ahead. As with all competition, there is a fine line between marketing behavior that is viewed as good, healthy competition and marketing behavior that is unethical and illegal. To rid the market of unethical and illegal conduct, state and federal governments have enacted laws to regulate anticompetitive business practices and unfair trade practices.

This chapter addresses the issues that arise at the intersection of sport marketing and the law. Without attention to the legal aspects of sport marketing, those who market sport or market their products and services through sport risk losing their intellectual property and jeopardizing their investment and financial return on their ideas. Without an understanding of this area of the law, sport marketers also risk potential liability from the misuse of, or infringement on, the intellectual property and publicity rights of others. At the outset, we must recognize that many of these legal issues are complex and often require assistance from an attorney specializing in intellectual property and right-of-publicity law. The issues are presented here to alert readers to the general concepts and practical issues surrounding intellectual property and right-of-publicity law, so that they understand the rights, and the potential risks, associated with the protection and use of intellectual property and publicity rights.

What Is Intellectual Property?

After many decades, Jill B. Fan's favorite hometown team, the Aces, has finally reached the World Series. As both a die-hard fan and an entrepreneur, Jill is anxious to put to use all of the marketing ideas that she has been dreaming up to take advantage of this momentous event. For instance, she has come up with a catchy slogan that she plans to place on T-shirts, above a logo that is remarkably similar to that of the Aces, and sell outside the stadium. She's also developed her own special logo to commemorate the event: two interlocking baseballs that prominently feature the colors of her hometown team, with the words *World Champs* superimposed across the baseballs. She plans to create and manage a new Web site called www.WorldChampAces.com, where she will promote her love of her hometown team and sell her wares. She can't wait to begin cashing in.

The law of "intellectual property" comprises three areas: trademarks, copyrights, and patents. The primary goal of intellectual property law is to reward invention, ingenuity, and creativity, in an effort to maintain an open and competitive marketplace. To encourage this type of progress in science and the arts, the framers of the U.S. Constitution delegated to Congress the power to protect the intellectual property rights of artists, authors, and inventors by granting them "the exclusive right to their writings and discoveries." (3) In other words, property rights are granted to protect the products of one's intellect. If Jill B. Fan has a unique idea, she should be entitled to capitalize on it . . . as long as she is not infringing on the prior rights of others. Although people often see the symbols identifying intellectual property rights (© [copyright], ™ [trademark], and ® [patent]), most do not realize the exact nature of the legal protection provided to a trademark, copyright, or patent owner. This first section of this chapter examines each of these three areas that sport marketers need to be familiar with to protect themselves and to ensure that they do not infringe on the intellectual property rights of others. The chapter focuses primary attention on the area of trademark law, the area of greatest relevance to sport marketers. The law of copyrights and patents, and their relevance to sport marketers, are also discussed briefly.

To decide the type of legal protection one should use to protect new ideas or products, one must first examine the character of the intellectual property. For example, trademarks protect unique words, names, symbols, and slogans; copyrights protect original works of authorship; and patents protect inventions (new designs and processes). Ownership rights to trademarks may last forever, whereas rights to copyrights and patents have time limits. A trademark, copyright, or patent owner may grant permission for its use to others for a fee, an arrangement known as *licensing*. When another does not have permission or licensed rights to use the copyright, trademark, or patent, that person is said to be "infringing" on the intellectual property owner's rights.

A single product can conceivably receive intellectual property protection across all three intellectual property categories. Take, for instance, the latest in popular in-stadium giveaway items, the CelebriDuck. The manufacturer of this product could receive a patent for the product's design; a copyright on the information on the product's label; trade dress protection for the product's unique packaging; and a trademark for the actual name of the product ("CelebriDuck").

Rubber ducks depicting the likenesses of athletes, called CelebriDucks, have become a popular collectible among sports fans.
Courtesy of Jezali Ratliff

Overview of Trademark Law

Trademarks serve five important purposes. A consumer's decision to purchase a T-shirt featuring the logo of his or her favorite team, the Blue Sox (a fictional sports team) provides a good illustration of these purposes. First, trademarks serve to *identify the source or origin* of the product (or service) and to distinguish it from others. Based on the logo on the T-shirt, the consumer knows that the Blue Sox team is the source of this product. Second, trademarks *protect consumers* from confusion and deception. In other words, the law allows the Blue Sox to sue any other person (individual or company) who seeks to confuse or deceive the consumer into believing that the Blue Sox were the source of the product purchased, when they weren't. Third, a trademark is used to designate a *consistent level of quality* of a product (or service). Thus, the consumer knows when he or she buys a T-shirt with the Blue Sox logo that it has been thoroughly checked for quality and won't fall apart in the washer. Fourth, a trademark represents the *goodwill* of the owner's products (or services). In other words, the consumer has chosen to buy a Blue Sox T-shirt because he or she has "good feelings" about the Blue Sox. Fifth, trademarks signify a *substantial advertising investment*. The Blue Sox have invested tremendous time and financial resources in building the value and goodwill of their name and trademarks, and the law is designed to discourage other companies who seek to trade off this goodwill or diminish this value by using similar marks on their competitive products (or services).

Trademarks are protected on the national level by the Federal Trademark Act of 1946, commonly referred to as the Lanham Act. (4) The Lanham Act, which has become increasingly important for sport marketers involved in the marketing of sport products, teams, and events, protects three primary types of marks: trademarks, service marks, and collective marks.

A *trademark* is a word, name, symbol, or device used by a person, generally a manufacturer or merchant, to identify and distinguish its goods from those manufactured and sold by others, and to indicate the source of the goods. (5) This section also covers trade dress, a particular type of trademark that protects the distinctiveness of the appearance and image of a product. It involves the product's size, shape, color or color scheme, texture, graphics, and particular sales techniques. (6) Trade dress provides protection for the packaging of a product. Because sport marketers are often involved in the development of names and logos and the creative packaging of sport products, trademark and trade dress protection become important tools for protecting their ideas. The logos of sport organizations such as Adidas or the Red Sox are protected through trademark law.

One example of a collective mark is that of the National Collegiate Athletic Association.
© NCAA

A *service* mark is a word, name, symbol, or device used to identify and distinguish a company's services, including a unique service, from those of another service provider. (7) Service marks are typically used in the sale or advertising of an intangible service, such as the entertainment value of a sport event. For example, the "World Series" and the "NCAA Final Four" are service marks, in that they are events (services provided to fans), as opposed to tangible products (you can't go out and buy a "World Series," although some fans would argue otherwise!).

A *collective* mark is defined in the Lanham Act as a trade or service mark used by the members of a cooperative, an association, or other group or organization, and serves to indicate membership in a union, an association, or other organization. (8) A good example of a collective mark is the mark used by each of the players associations in the professional sport industry.

To gain national trademark protection under the Lanham Act, the trademark must be registered with the United States Patent and Trademark Office (USPTO), which also resolves any disputes related to trademark registration.

For the trademarks of local, community-based sport events and properties, in which federal trademark protection may be deemed not necessary, protection is still afforded under various state statutes that provide their own protections similar to those provided by the Lanham Act, but which typically fall under the theory of unfair competition (discussed later). Although federal registration of a mark is not required to establish ownership rights in a mark, it does provide several important benefits, including the following:

- The ability of the trademark owner to invoke the jurisdiction of the federal court system for any future legal action
- The use as a basis for obtaining mark registration in foreign countries
- The opportunity to file the trademark with the U.S. Customs Service to prevent the importation of infringing foreign goods
- The ability to limit others from deceiving consumers by selling goods or offering services as the goods and services of the original source, thus enabling the consumer to distinguish between different producers of products or services

- The acknowledgment and protection of the goodwill of the trademark holder
- The provision of public notice throughout the nation of an owner's claim, evidence of trademark ownership, which thus creates an easier burden of proof of ownership (9)

Ownership of a trademark generally requires the holder to appropriate the mark and to use it for commercial purposes. (10) Since 1988, however, the Lanham Act has allowed an individual to apply for registration to the USPTO if the applicant can establish "a bona fide intention" to use a trademark in commerce within a reasonable time period. (11) Unlike copyrights and patents, which have expirations, trademarks can last indefinitely. Trademark registrations granted prior to November 16, 1989, have a 20-year term and may be renewed at 20-year intervals, whereas those granted after November 16, 1989, have 10-year terms and 10-year renewals. (12)

What Marks Can Be Protected?

In one of the early trademark infringement cases involving a sport organization, the University of Georgia sued a local beer manufacturer for marketing a product called Battlin' Bulldog Beer in red and black cans. The beer can featured an English bulldog wearing a red sweater decorated with a black G, which the University of Georgia claimed was very similar to its well-known bulldog mascot. (13) The beer manufacturer also included a disclaimer on the cans ("Not associated with the University of Georgia"), after having sought but being denied permission from the university to use an exact reproduction of the University of Georgia Bulldog mascot. This case, the outcome of which we will explain shortly, serves to illustrate the factors that determine whether a mark can be protected at all.

The value and effectiveness (strength) of a trademark or service mark relates to the distinctiveness of the mark and the level of protection afforded the mark under the federal trademark laws. Marks are classified into various levels based on their distinctiveness. Simply put, the more distinctive the mark, the more likely it will be considered for registration by the USPTO and thus afforded protection under the Lanham Act. The issue of distinctiveness will typically come up during the registration process, raised either by the USPTO or by a competitor seeking to challenge the registration of a proposed mark (legal counsel for sport properties regularly review trademark application lists to ensure that a person is not seeking to register a mark that the sport property would find objectionable).

Trademarks that are inherently distinctive and completely distinguishable are characterized as *fanciful* or *arbitrary*. (14) Sport marketers challenged with creating a trademark (for instance, the name of a team, an event, or product) want to create a mark that is fanciful or arbitrary. Such marks are invented for the sole purpose of functioning as a trademark. In the past several years, minor league baseball teams have led the way in creating fanciful names, such as the Wisconsin Timber Rattlers, the Cedar Rapids Kernels, and the West Tennessee Diamond Jaxx (such fanciful names and corresponding logos have also proven a boon to merchandise sales). Other common examples of fanciful trade names are Pepsi, Polaroid and Speedo; and event names such as MotoX and Hoop-D-Do (outdoor three-on-three basketball tournaments).

Arbitrary marks, although not as distinctive as fanciful marks, are words, names, symbols, or devices that are commonly known words, but through the advertising and marketing efforts of the owner have become associated with a particular product or service. Examples in the sport world include the Gravity Games, Field Turf, and Arena Football League.

The last category of inherently distinctive marks is *suggestive* marks. Although weaker than fanciful or arbitrary marks, a suggestive mark subtly connotes something about the product or service but does not actually describe any specific ingredient, quality, or characteristic of the product or service. With suggestive marks, the consumer must use her imagination to draw an association. The more suggestive the mark, the more consumer imagination is required to make the association. Examples include PowerAde, a word that suggests certain characteristics that the isotonic beverage provides to sweating consumers, and Nike (a Greek goddess who was the personification of victory).

On the opposite end of the spectrum are trademarks that, on their face, do not distinguish one product or service from another, and typically use common words in their ordinary spelling and meanings. Such marks are referred to in trademark law as being either *descriptive* (which is very difficult, although not impossible, to protect) and *generic* (which is never entitled to trademark protection). Thus, sport marketers are advised to refrain from creating marks that would be deemed either descriptive or generic.

The Meaning of "Secondary Meaning"

Secondary meaning is defined as "a mental recognition in buyers' and potential buyers' minds that products connected with the symbol or device emanate from or are associated with the same source." (15) For example, the Baltimore Orioles logo (a black and orange bird) is distinct and widely associated with the Major League Baseball club, even though neither the word *Baltimore* nor the word *Orioles* appears anywhere in the logo design. However, because of its widely recognized association with the baseball club, the Lanham Act would prevent the unauthorized commercial use of an identical or similar image to promote the sale of a product or service because the mark has acquired secondary meaning. A 2003 court case involving the phrase "March Madness" (does this phrase conjure up any specific event in your mind?) further illustrates how common words, although used in their ordinary meaning, can over time gain trademark protection through advertising and public exposure. In *March Madness Athletic Ass'n, LLC v. Netfire, Inc.*, a court determined that the phrase "March Madness" was a protectable trademark (in the context of basketball competitions) because it had acquired secondary meaning. (16)

Given this, how did the court hold in the Georgia Bulldog case? The court, in ruling for the University of Georgia, held that the "University of Georgia Bulldog" was not a descriptive mark, stating that "the portrayal of an English bulldog chosen by the university as a symbol for its athletic teams is, at best, 'suggestive,' if not downright 'arbitrary.'" (17) Thus, because the mark was deemed to be stronger than merely descriptive, the university was not required to prove secondary meaning. The court also held that there was ample evidence that the "Battlin' Bulldog" beer would likely cause consumers to be confused or deceived into believing that the beer product was associated with the university. (18)

In addition to a mark's being deemed descriptive, there are several other grounds on which the USPTO will refuse to grant trademark registrations. These include instances in which the proposed trademark possesses immoral, deceptive, or scandalous matter; disparages or falsely suggests a connection with persons (dead or alive), beliefs, institutions, or national symbols; possesses any insignia of the United States, any state or municipality, or a foreign nation; consists of a name, portrait, or signature of any living individual without the person's consent, or consists of the name, portrait, or signature of a deceased president during the life of his widow without her consent; or is merely a surname. (19)

The issue of disparaging or slanderous trademarks arose in the 1990s when a group of Native Americans applied to the Trial and Trademark Appeal Board to cancel the trademarks of the Washington Redskins. (20) Although the Native American group initially won the case, the Redskins appealed and ultimately prevailed, based in part of the court's determination that there was a lack of evidence that the trademarks were disparaging to a substantial group of Native Americans. (21) The loss of trademark protection would not have meant that the Redskins could not have continued to use the team name and logo. However, the loss of its registration would have made enforcing its rights in the unregistered marks, either under federal or state law, much more difficult and might have allowed others to make and sell products bearing the previously registered logos. (22)

When creating a new trademark, sport marketers would be wise to hire intellectual property counsel to initially conduct a trademark search to determine whether any conflicting marks exist (this can typically be done for several hundred dollars). Although it is not required, it is highly advisable given that the USPTO registration application fee of $335 (for each class of goods and/or services) is not refundable if a conflicting mark exists. The USPTO does not conduct searches for the public, but it does provide a public library of marks as well as an electronic searchable database (available at www.uspto.gov/).

Trademark Infringement

In 2003, the licensed apparel business accounted for sales of over $4 billion in North America alone. (23) Additionally, the 2004 spending on sport sponsorship in North America was projected to exceed $7 billion. (24) To preserve these revenue streams, sport marketers must be increasingly vigilant to protect against trademark infringement. The Lanham Act provides a variety of claims designed to cure different harms. The first is *traditional trademark infringement*, which protects against uses of a trademark that are likely to cause confusion or mistake, or to deceive. (25) The second potential claim under the Lanham Act is *false designation of origin*, which is designed to prevent uses of another's trademark that cause confusion as to affiliation or sponsorship. (26) Finally, the Lanham Act authorizes suit to prevent *dilution* of a famous mark's distinctive quality. (27)

Traditional Trademark Infringement

The Lanham Act defines infringement as "any reproduction, counterfeit, copy, or colorable imitation of a registered mark in connection with the sale, offering for sale, distribution, or advertising of any goods or services on or in connection with which such use is likely to cause confusion, or to cause mistake, or to deceive" without the consent of the trademark holder. (28) The owner of the mark has the burden to prove this his mark is being infringed on. If a mark is registered, then the owner can demonstrate that he is the only authorized user, and a valid registration is evidence of a protectable property right. If the trademark is inherently distinctive, there is no need for a plaintiff to establish the existence of secondary meaning, as was seen in the *University of Georgia v. Laite* case. If the trademark is descriptive, the plaintiff must show that it possesses secondary meaning, as was shown in the "March Madness" case discussed earlier.

The linchpin of a trademark infringement case is the likelihood of confusion, which plaintiffs typically prove through the use of consumer surveys. The factors used by the courts in determining likelihood of confusion were first developed in the seminal case of *Polaroid Corp. v. Polarad, Inc.* (known as "the Polaroid Test"). (29) Although other federal district courts have added to or modified the factors over the years, they all generally adhere to the same eight factors.

Assume the Aces sue Jill B. Fan, alleging that creating and selling her T-shirts (sporting her catchy slogan above a logo remarkably similar to that of the Aces) constitutes trademark infringement. The Aces' ability to prove likelihood of confusion will be based on the court's evaluation of the following eight factors, or a combination of these factors:

- The *strength of the Aces' trademark* (Is the Aces' trademark fanciful? Arbitrary? Suggestive? Descriptive with secondary meaning? Nondistinctive?)
- The *degree of similarity* between the Aces' trademark and Jill B. Fans' alleged infringing trademark
- The *similarity of the products* involved
- The *market channels involved* (Do the Aces offer their product to a group of consumers that is similar to that which Jill B. Fan seeks to target?)
- The *distribution channels involved* (Do the Aces sell their product in the same places as Jill B Fan is offering her product?)

- The *intent of the defendant* in adopting the trademark (Is there evidence that Jill B Fan is actually trying to confuse consumers into believing that her product is somehow sponsored by or affiliated with the Aces?)
- The *sophistication of the potential consumers* (Are buying consumers sophisticated enough to understand that the Aces are not the source of Jill B Fan's product?)
- The *evidence of actual confusion* (Can the Aces provide evidence, typically through consumer surveys, that consumers are actually confused as to the source of Jill B. Fan's product?)

Based on the limited facts of this hypothetical case, which party do you think is more likely to prevail in court? If you were making the ruling on the likelihood of confusion in this case, what additional information might you need?

Occasionally, trademark infringement cases involving a likelihood-of-confusion analysis hinge on a theory called *reverse confusion*, in which the plaintiff filing a trademark infringement action is the original, although less recognizable, party. One well-publicized sport case was *Harlem Wizards Entertainment Basketball, Inc. v. NBA Properties, Inc.* (30) This case arose when the Washington Bullets changed their name to the Washington Wizards. The plaintiff, the Harlem Wizards, was a barnstorming theatrical basketball team founded in 1962 that operated in much the same way as the Harlem Globetrotters. The Harlem Wizards claimed that the infringement by the Washington NBA team would diminish the recognition consumers have with them and with the name *Wizards*, thereby diminishing their goodwill by giving people the impression that they had stolen the name *Wizards* from the dominant NBA team. The court disagreed, stating that the two organizations were not competing in the same market and thus the two names could coexist without causing consumer confusion. Although the Harlem Wizards argued that both plaintiff and defendant were in the business of basketball, the court narrowed the scope in which to compare the two organizations.

False Designation of Origin

A second claim under which a trademark owner may sue is termed *false designation of origin.* Section 43(a)(1) of the Lanham Act protects trademark owners by prohibiting a competitor's false designation of origin when it "is likely to cause confusion … or to deceive as to the affiliation, connection, or association of such person with another person, or as to the origin, sponsorship, or approval of his or her goods, services, or commercial activities by another person." (31) Under this theory, the owner of the trademark must establish that the public recognizes that the trademark identifies the owner's goods and services and distinguishes its goods or services from others. Once such public recognition is established, the plaintiff must then prove that the defendant's use of the trademark is likely to confuse or deceive the public into thinking that the plaintiff was the origin of the use.

One of the leading sport-related cases is *Dallas Cowboys Cheerleaders, Inc. v. Pussycat Cinema, Ltd.* (1979). (32) In this case, the defendant owned and operated an X-rated cinema in which it showed a pornographic film titled "Debbie Does Dallas." In the film, an actor was shown wearing a uniform strikingly similar to that of the Dallas Cowboys Cheerleaders. The marquee posters advertising the film depicted Debbie in a Dallas Cowboys Cheerleader uniform and made references to Dallas and the Dallas Cowboys Cheerleaders. The appellate court affirmed the preliminary injunction granted to bar the defendant from distributing the film. The plaintiff, the Dallas Cowboys Cheerleaders, established that they had a trademark in their uniform's white boots, white shorts, blue blouse, and star-studded white vest and belt. They also established a likelihood of proving that the public would associate them with the movie and would be confused into believing that the plaintiffs had sponsored the movie, had provided some of the actors, and had licensed the uniform to the defendants. (33) Although the defendants argued that no reasonable person would ever believe that the Dallas Cowboys Cheerleaders would be involved with such a film, the court challenged such a reading of consumer confusion as too narrow. Instead the court stated that to evoke consumer confusion, the uniform depicted in the film need only bring to mind the Dallas Cowboys Cheerleaders, which the court stated it unquestionably did. (34)

Dilution

A third potential claim is for dilution of a famous trademark through what is known as "blurring" or "tarnishment." The underlying purpose of bringing a claim for dilution, under the Federal Trademark Dilution Act of 1996, (35) is to protect the value of the trademark to the trademark holder. Although similar to trademark infringement, dilution occurs when the defendant is not a direct competitor, but the defendant's use of a similar mark either blurs ("blurring") the ability of the plaintiff's trademark to distinguish the plaintiff's goods and services from those of the defendant, or tarnishes ("tarnishment") the reputation of the plaintiff's marks by linking the plaintiff's products to products of shoddy quality, or that portray the plaintiff in an unwholesome or unsavory context. A key ingredient of a famous mark is its value or selling power, and a showing of likelihood of consumer confusion is not required. However, the Supreme Court recently held that a plaintiff must prove actual dilution or actual economic loss to prevail on a trademark dilution claim. (36)

Taking Action Against Alleged Infringers

What should a sport property or manufacturer do when it discovers a case of alleged trademark infringement? The property owner (or his attorney) typically drafts a letter to the alleged infringer asking the person to "cease and desist" (i.e., stop) the alleged infringing use of the protected intellectual property. If the alleged infringer refuses to cooperate, the Lanham Act (as well as applicable state laws) entitles the trademark owner to bring suit for injunctive relief. An injunction is a court order to stop the infringing activities prior to and during the trial for a copyright, trademark, or patent infringement case. To be granted an injunction against an alleged infringer, the intellectual property owner has to prove three elements to the court: (1) that he will be irreparably harmed by the infringing activities; (2) that the owner will be more harmed if the injunction is not granted than the defendant will be harmed if the injunction is granted; and (3) that the owner can demonstrate a strong likelihood of success on the merits of the case (in other words, a strong chance of winning the infringement case). Once the injunction is received, the owner seeks a trial on the merits of the case to receive a financial remedy for the infringement.

Defenses to Trademark Infringement

When a trademark infringement claim is brought, the defendant may raise a number of defenses, including abandonment, fair use, that the trademark is or has become generic, or that the trademark is merely functional (the functionality test).

Abandonment

Unlike copyrights and patents, which expire, trademarks can last indefinitely, provided the holder continues to renew the registration. However, under the Lanham Act, a trademark can be deemed to be abandoned when the trademark owner discontinues its use *and* does not intend to resume using the mark within a reasonable amount of time. (37) Thus, even when a sport property changes its name or logo, if it wishes to retain ownership of previous marks, it must take precautionary steps to prevent abandonment of these marks. Typically, these steps include maintaining the marks' registration at the appropriate renewal periods and periodically using the old marks in some manner. Sport marketers should note that marks can also be deemed to be abandoned as a result of excessive licensing, lack of supervision over other parties' licensed use of the marks, or both. Because trademarks are valuable, courts do require substantial proof of abandonment.

One of the leading sport-related cases on alleged abandonment involved the Indianapolis Colts, who brought suit for trademark infringement against what was then the new Baltimore team of the Canadian Football League (CFL), which sought to be called the "Baltimore CFL Colts." (38) The defendants claimed that the Baltimore Colts had abandoned the name *Colts* when it moved to Indianapolis. However, the plaintiffs were successful in obtaining an injunction to stop the defendants from using the name *Colts*, or *Baltimore Colts*, or *Baltimore CFL Colts* in connection with the playing of professional football, the broadcast of football games, or the sale of merchandise to football fans. In this case, the former owner of the alleged abandoned mark continued to market the same product or service under a similar name. It was clear that the Indianapolis Colts were the NFL team that had previously been the NFL's Baltimore Colts. The court determined that a team named the Baltimore CFL Colts would be confusingly similar to the Indianapolis Colts by virtue of the history of the Indianapolis team and the overlapping product and geographical markets served by the Indianapolis Colts and by the new Baltimore CFL Colts. The Indianapolis Colts' abandonment of a trademark confusingly similar to their new trademark did not break the continuity of the team. The court declared that it was the same team, despite the fact that the team was now in a different home city and as a result had adopted a different geographical designation. Therefore, the CFL was not entitled to acquire and use the name, which would realistically confuse NFL Colts fans and other actual or potential consumers of products and services marketed by the Colts or by the NFL, with regard to the identity, sponsorship, or league affiliation of the new Baltimore team. The court agreed that the Indianapolis Colts owned the goodwill associated with the name *Baltimore Colts* and that the new Baltimore team was trying to acquire it from them.

Another case, *Abdul-Jabbar v. General Motors Corp.*, (39) raised the issue of abandonment of a birth name. During the time leading up to the 1993 NCAA men's Final Four, General Motors ran an advertisement for its Olds 88 that used trivia regarding Kareem Abdul-Jabbar's University of California at Los Angeles and NCAA records. When Abdul-Jabbar had set the records, his name was Lew Alcindor. Besides citing the trivia question, Abdul-Jabbar alleged that the advertisement compared the car to him. General Motors responded that when he had converted to Islam he had abandoned the name Lew Alcindor and thus, there was no infringement. In finding for Abdul-Jabbar, the judge stated, "One's birth name is an integral part of one's identity . . . it is not "kept alive" through commercial use. . . An individual's decision to use a name other than the birth name . . . does not therefore, imply intent to set aside the birth name, or the identity associated with that name." (40)

Fair Use Defense

Trademark rights are not absolute, and the law allows the use of another's trademarks on or in connection with the sale of one's own goods as services as long as the use is not deceptive. (41) Thus, a fair use defense allows, for instance, a company such as Adidas to use the Nike trademark in its ads to compare the two products. The fair use defense has also been successfully used by a company that sold refurbished discounted golf balls manufactured by another company. (42) The fair use defense has also been found applicable under the constitutional protections of commercial speech. In a recent case involving the United States Olympic Committee, a court found that a publisher who produced a magazine titled *OLYMPICS USA* did not infringe on the USOC's rights to the word *Olympics*. (43) The court held that to restrict a publisher's use of the word *Olympics* would raise serious issues regarding the First Amendment protection afforded news media organizations. Finally, although it has not yet been tested in the courts, the fair use doctrine arguably applies when trademarks are used merely to describe a sweepstakes prize (i.e., win two tickets to the World Series) or in a similarly nominal fashion (e.g., a radio commercial that invites consumers to "come to the All-Star Café to watch all the action of the NFL, NASCAR, and March Madness").

Genericness

As discussed earlier, one cannot obtain trademark protection for generic terms, even through the acquisition of secondary meaning. Thus, an alleged infringer can argue that the trademark in question is generic. Because of this, leagues cannot claim to own phrases such as "championships," or "the big game." It is also possible for what was a well-known trademark to become generic over time, if not aggressively protected by the trademark holder. Well-known examples include aspirin, cellophane, and trampoline, all of which were at one time registered trademarks and have fallen into the public domain. The possibility of a trademark becoming generic points out the need for companies to aggressively protect and promote their trademarks.

Functionality

A final defense involves marks that do not describe or distinguish the product or service, but are necessary for the product to exist. The functionality defense was unsuccessfully raised in the Dallas Cowboys Cheerleaders case discussed previously, whereby the defendant claimed that its depiction of an actress in a cheerleading uniform similar to those worn by the Dallas Cowboys Cheerleaders was not trademark infringement because the uniform design was not a trademark but rather a functionality of performing. The court disagreed, holding that the uniform was not just a function of performing as a cheerleader. Thus, the fact that the item serves or performs a function does not mean that it may not at the same time be capable of indicating sponsorship or origin.

Trademarks and the Internet

Legal issues for sport marketers continue to emerge from the use of the Internet for commerce, communication, public relations, and advertising. The advent of the Internet led to a wild, wild west of trademark issues, most notably cybersquatting, whereby individuals registered domain names solely for the purposes of trying to sell the name back to the rightful trademark owner. Both the courts and the legislature have addressed this earliest form of trademark infringement on the Internet. Numerous cases have held that use of another's trademark in a domain name can constitute trademark infringement in violation of the Lanham Act. (44) Prior to 1999, a trademark owner's sole remedy for the use of its trademark in a Web address was limited under the Lanham Act to infringement or dilution claims. However, in 1999 Congress passed the Anticybersquatting Consumer Protection Act (ACPA). (45) Under the ACPA, a person is liable if that person "has a bad faith intent to profit from that mark" and registers, traffics in, or uses a domain name that "in the case of a mark that is distinctive at the time of registration of the domain name, is identical or confusingly similar to that mark" or "in the case of a famous mark that is famous at the time of registration of the domain name, is identical or confusingly similar to or dilutive of that mark." (46) Under the ACPA, several remedies are available, including forfeiture or cancellation of the domain name, transfer of the domain name, and recovery of monetary damages. For example, in the March Madness case, discussed earlier, the court found the defendants to be in violation of the ACPA, concluding that the defendants had acted with bad faith intent in creating the website www.marchmadness.com. (47)

Ambush Marketing

One of the largest sources of revenue for sport properties comes from the sale of "official sponsor" rights. Corporations often invest significant amounts of money to secure the rights, typically exclusive within its product or service category, to utilize the sport property's trademarks in their advertising and promotional campaigns as a means of associating with the sport property's positive goodwill. However, marketers working on the properties side of the sport industry face challenges that result from a method of marketing called ambush marketing. Ambush marketing occurs when a company capitalizes on the goodwill of a sports event by using a variety of advertising and promotional tactics to *imply* an official association with that sport event. The ambusher's tactics weaken a competitor's official association with the event acquired through the payment of sponsorship monies. (48)

The larger and more popular the event, the more often ambush marketing arises. Hence, one of the most fertile grounds for ambush marketing has historically been the Olympic Games. The most recent Olympics hosted by the United States was the 2002 Winter Olympic Games in Salt Lake City, Utah. This event serves to illustrate the legal challenges along a spectrum ranging from blatant trademark infringement to ambush marketing activity. Generally, the Olympics, when confronted with alleged ambush marketing activity, have been successful in negotiating business settlements with infringers who, more often than not, are simply unaware that their activities are in violation of the Olympics' broad trademark rights secured through the Olympic and Amateur Sports Act of 1998 (OASA). (49) Of the nearly 700 cases of alleged intellectual property infringement that were investigated between 1999 and 2001, more than half of the cases were "successfully resolved" by the end of 2001. (50) Thirty percent of the infringement cases were related to advertising and promotions; 20 percent were related to counterfeiting; 3 percent were related to names; and 11 percent were designated as "other." The remaining 36 percent of the cases involved cybersquatting, (51) a clear indication that tech-savvy marketers are moving their ambush tactics to cyberspace to reach consumers online. The Olympics brought an action for cybersquatting against the registered owners of over 1,800 domain names that were alleged to include registered Olympic marks, making it the single largest cybersquatting suit. (52) The case resulted in the transfer of ownership of dozens of domain names, including those using words and phrases such as *Salt Lake 2002, Olympic, Olympic Winter Games,* and *SLC 2002.* (53)

The SLOC was, however, only marginally successful in negotiating a halt to an ambush marketing campaign by a local brewery, Schirf Brewing, the makers of Wasatch Beer. Anheuser-Busch, maker of Budweiser beer and originator of the slogan "Whassup," paid $50 million for the rights to use the word *Olympic* and the five-ring logo. (54) The Olympics, as well as Anheuser-Busch, were ambushed by a microbrewery that painted its trucks with the words "Wasatch Beers. The Unofficial Beer of the 2002 Winter Games." (55) The USOC, under threat of litigation, was successful in getting Schirf Brewing to remove the reference to the trademarked phrase *2002 Winter Games,* although the company continued to engage in other blatant ambush marketing activities. (56)

However, when alleged ambush marketers are not amenable to settlement, the Olympics have been vigilant in resorting to the courts. Several high-profile ambush marketing efforts in Salt Lake City resulted in lawsuits. In one such case, the USOC filed a claim against Discount Tire Company alleging that the tire company knowingly violated the OASA through the unauthorized use of Olympic imagery in an advertising campaign that implied a sponsor relationship with the USOC and the Olympic Games. (57) At issue was a billboard advertising campaign that depicted tires in the form of the Olympic rings. (58) In addition, the billboard welcomed visitors to the Games in several languages, which the USOC alleged "shows an intent to use Olympic terminology and Olympic Games imagery to inaccurately suggest a commercial affiliation with the Olympic Games and the Olympic Movement." (59) The complaint was filed after Discount Tire failed to remove the billboards as they had promised. (60)

In a second case, the USOC brought suit against Brighton Ski Resort, located near Salt Lake City. (61) The ski resort created a logo with five linked snowflakes resembling the five Olympic rings and, in addition, used the word *games* in an advertising campaign and in the resort's Web site address, www.Brightonupthegames.com. (62) The USOC sought an injunction in federal court to stop Brighton Ski Resort from using the word *games* as part of its Internet domain name. (63) The USOC also demanded that the ski resort remove billboard advertising at the Salt Lake City airport that showed five overlapping snowflakes logo, similar to the Olympic's trademarked use of the five interlocking rings. (64) In a letter to Brighton Ski Resort, USOC legal counsel Scott Blackmun requested that the resort cease its "humorous" ads, including one saying, "Proud Host of Zero Olympic events." (65) Blackmun suggested that "without stopping even 'humorous' ads, other unauthorized ads might pop up and Olympic symbols could lose 'distinctiveness' and even 'all commercial value.'" (66) The ski resort eventually agreed to comply with all of the USOC's requests. (67) A third significant case involved Nabisco's attempt to ambush PowerBar, an official Olympic sponsor. (68) PowerBar notified the USOC of Nabisco's attempt at ambush marketing in advertisements for Nabisco's Fig Newton cookies. (69) The advertisements depicted an ancient Olympic athlete throwing a discus and contained the following text: "The ancient Olympians worshipped the fig and used it for energy during training." (70) The USOC filed suit alleging that Nabisco unlawfully used the USOC's trademarks in an attempt to create an association in consumers' minds between the Fig Newton cookies and the Olympic Movement. (71) Nabisco eventually settled the case for a confidential amount and ceased its advertising campaign. (72)

The Olympics decided against pursuing several alleged ambush marketing campaigns, illustrating some of the loopholes and legal limitations of the OASA and other potentially applicable laws such as the Lanham Act and state unfair competition statutes. One common loophole is for a company to secure and aggressively leverage an association with an Olympic athlete. For instance, although AT&T and Qwest had official sponsorship relationships with the USOC and SLOC, Sprint PCS, in an attempt to promote its wireless services, signed high-profile Olympic athletes such as Jimmy Shea and Jonny Moseley a year in advance of the 2002 Games, and featured them in Olympic-themed ads before and after the actual Games. (73) Furthermore, because Olympic rules ban athletes from appearing in nonsponsors' ads during the Games, ads for those two weeks were shot with actors in snowy settings using "a catchy—and ambiguous—tag line, 'Sprint: Proud sponsor of everything fast, new and really quite amazing.'" (74)

Numerous other companies engaged in thematic advertising that did not rise to the level of trademark infringement, but arguably traded off the goodwill of the Olympics and was designed to create an impression of an association. For instance, Post-It Notes brand ran newspaper advertising that featured the letters U, S, and A, on gold-colored Post-It Notes, followed by the tag line, "Go for the Gold, America." (75) Nonsponsor RCA, a division of Thomson, Inc., also capitalized on the Olympics with a promotion, advertised nationally, offering consumers a free USA jacket with the purchase of selected RCA television sets. (76) Given that the letters USA are not trademarked, this activity was within RCA's rights, again illustrating the challenges facing the Olympics to thwart companies that are clever and determined to conduct promotional activity during the time of the Olympic Games.

First Amendment free speech rights also presented challenges for the USOC and SLOC. For instance, a religious organization published and distributed a pamphlet that included five colored fish in the format of the Olympic rings, with the phrase, "Sowing the Seed in Salt Lake City—The New Testament Souvenir—Winter Games Salt Lake City, Utah." Given First Amendment freedoms, the USOC and SLOC opted not to pursue a legal challenge against this religious organization. (77)

Although ambush marketing is difficult to combat, there are a few ways to help limit it. For instance, to prevent nonsponsors from purchasing advertising within the broadcast of an event, the sport property can negotiate a clause in its agreement that requires its broadcast rights holders to provide official sponsors the right of first refusal to purchase advertising within the broadcasts, as well as a clause requiring the rights holders to monitor for potential trademark infringements by nonsponsors.

The sport property can also negotiate with the host city and the event site to ban marketing activity that directly competes with official sponsors. For instance, the NFL requires that the host city create a "clean zone" for its annual Super Bowl, imposing a ban on advertising in the area surrounding the facility hosting the event. Furthermore, to effectively block sponsorship conflicts or ambushing, good communication and cooperation must exist between the two levels of governance. For example, during the 1994 World Cup, a conflict arose after MasterCard obtained the exclusive right to use World Cup '94 trademarks on all card-based payment and account-access devices. A few months later, the local organizing committee entered into a sponsorship agreement with Sprint to become an official partner of the 1994 World Cup. MasterCard sought and was granted an injunction to stop Sprint from using the World Cup trademark on any card issued by Sprint, despite Sprint's argument that its phone cards were distinguishable from the card-based payment and account-access devices intended in the MasterCard-World Cup '94 agreement. (78)

A sport property seeking to protect itself against ambush marketers must be proactive. The property should use advertising to explain the negatives of ambush marketing to consumers and to the media. When faced with ambush marketing activity, the property should also consider launching a public relations campaign accusing the ambusher of unfair business tactics. In the past, the Olympics have even threatened to run print advertisements featuring the photograph of the ambush marketing company's CEO, under the headline "THIEF"! Even the threat of such action is often enough to get potential ambush marketers to reconsider their plans.

To date, sport properties have been reticent to bring lawsuits on ambush marketing grounds, in part for fear of an adverse decision. Also, there is very little settled law. In the only decided case that specifically addresses ambush marketing, a Canadian court upheld Pepsi-Cola Canada's ambush marketing activities, much to the chagrin of the NHL. (79)

Unfair Competition and Unfair Trade Practices

In addition to trademark infringement claims, plaintiffs also bring claims of unfair competition and unfair trade practices, which encompass a large number of illegal actions and are bad business etiquette. The legal theories of unfair competition and unfair trade practices apply generally to fraudulent activity in trade or commerce, but they are specifically applied to the practice of "passing off" the goods or services of one party as those of another with a better-established reputation. (80) For example, in *NCAA v. Coors* (see sidebar), in addition to its breach of contract theory, the NCAA also accused Coors of violating the common law of unfair competition in Indiana, premised on Coors' allegedly wrongful attempt to associate itself with the NCAA and the Final Four and to confuse the general public into believing that Coors was somehow associated with, sponsored by, or endorsed by the NCAA (81)

Unfair competition and unfair trade practices may also give rise to lawsuits based in such torts as fraud, deceit, misrepresentation, and violations of rights of privacy and publicity, as well as violations of state consumer protection laws.

Copyright Law and Sport Marketing

In her excitement over the Aces' pending World Series victory, Jill B. Fan has also written a clever song, titled "The Aces Clear the Bases," that she intends to market. Using her entrepreneurial spirit, she also plans to tape the World Series games, edit it herself, and sell copies of the video, called "The Road to the Title," over the Internet. She can't wait to begin cashing in.

An understanding of copyright law is also important for sport marketers. Copyrights, for instance, protect the music that is played during games, and require sport marketers to seek approval through ASCAP, which protects musicians' copyrights of their works. Sport marketers who are responsible for creating advertising or promotional campaigns that use music, pictures or graphic designs, and/or audiovisual works need to also be aware of copyright laws. They may also need to consider copyright permission when contemplating the use of clips of athletic events that are protected.

At the outset, it is important to understand that, in the context of copyright law, one cannot "copyright" a mere *idea*. This concept was illustrated in the case of *Hoopla Sports and Entertainment, Inc. v. Nike, Inc.*, (82) in which the plaintiff unsuccessfully sued Nike for allegedly stealing its idea for a high school basketball all-star game. Although the plaintiff alleged copyright infringement, the court, in granting Nike's motion to dismiss, held that the idea for the game was not copyrightable.

Copyright law is primarily governed by the Copyright Act of 1976, (83) which protects original works of authorship appearing in any tangible medium of expression. In addition, the Digital Millennium Copyright Act provides copyright laws regarding digital creations and the Internet. (84)

A copyright can be for something currently in existence or something to be developed later; but the work must be something that can be perceived, reproduced, or otherwise communicated. Works of authorship include the following:

- ◆ Literary works, such as books and stories
- ◆ Musical works, including any accompanying words
- ◆ Dramatic works, including any accompanying music
- ◆ Pantomimes and choreographic works
- ◆ Pictorial, graphic, and sculptural works

Jury's Still Out on Ticket Promotions

Steve McKelvey

Unless specifically authorized in advance, this ticket may not be used in a commercial promotion or as a prize in a sweepstakes.

Every sport event ticket-back bears a warning of this type. But that prompts an age-old question for sport properties seeking to protect the value of their sponsorship programs, and for promotion agencies and nonsponsors seeking to use tickets in ambush marketing: Is this language enforceable in a court of law?

To date, this issue has never been contested in court, but thanks to the vigilance of the NCAA, we almost had an answer. [In 2002,] the NCAA sued Coors Brewing Co. in Indiana state court, thus becoming the first sport property to specifically challenge the unauthorized use of its tickets as a prize in a consumer sweepstakes. The lawsuit derived from Coors' 2001 college basketball championships-themed promotion (titled "Tourney Time") that offered "two tickets to the final three games of the tournament run annually in March and April." The lawsuit was settled in April 2003, and, although it establishes a strong anti-ambush platform for the NCAA—use our Final Four tickets in the future and we'll see you in court!—the settlement left no legal precedent. . .

Why did Coors blink? It's likely that Coors' $75,000 settlement, which the company agreed to while denying any wrongdoing, was a lot less than the legal fees that would be incurred in trying the case. Coors also would have had a hard time arguing its legal right to use NCAA tickets in unauthorized sweepstakes, while at the same time telling the NFL it is not acceptable for Anheuser-Busch, Miller, and other breweries to engage in the same tactics to ambush Coors' newly minted multimillion-dollar NFL sponsorship.

Despite a "victory" for the NCAA, the settlement leaves the burning question unanswered: Can companies use special event tickets, typically secured through ticket brokers, as a prize in consumer sweepstakes promotions?

The arguments presented in *NCAA vs. Coors* briefs are instructive for future claimants. In pretrial motions, both parties agreed to the well-settled proposition that tickets are revocable licenses. The NCAA charged Coors with "breach of a revocable license" and sought to apply contract law principles to its case. The NCAA relied on a 1907 Supreme Court decision in a railroad case and a series of 1990s decisions involving airlines, cases that upheld ticket-back restrictions on the resale in a secondary market of railroad

(continued)

Jury's Still Out on Ticket Promotions *(continued)*

tickets and frequent flier tickets. The obvious dilemma the state court would have faced, in trying to compare these cases to unauthorized promotional use of tickets, is that Coors is neither a ticker broker nor in the business of reselling tickets.

Coors argued that the NCAA's only remedy would be to enforce the terms of the ticket-back language solely against the holder of the ticket (the sweepstakes winner attending the Final Four). The NCAA claimed that this "remedy" would put it in a no-win situation of having somehow to identify the holders of the tickets from among its 45,000 spectators, and then bear the brunt of the negative publicity for refusing to admit these unsuspecting fans. Had the court had the opportunity to rule on this point, it would again have had wide-ranging ramifications for sport properties seeking to enforce their ticket-back language.

The NCAA also claimed that Coors violated Indiana's unfair competition statute, which, like the federal Lanham Act, protects trademark owners against companies who employ identical or similar marks likely to cause consumer confusion or to deceive consumers as to the origin, sponsorship, or approval of the alleged infringer's goods, services, or commercial activities.

Had this case gone to trial, it could have set new guide-

lines with respect to the "likelihood of confusion" question: Would a point-of-sale promotion featuring basketballs, titled "Tourney Time" and offering "two tickets to the final three games of the tournament" be likely to confuse consumers as to Coors' affiliation with the NCAA Final Four? Proving "likelihood of confusion" is an issue of fact that the NCAA would have been entitled to demonstrate.

U.S. courts have had no experience with sport-related ambush marketing cases based on trademark infringement and unfair competition claims that involve only the creative reference to a sporting event, as opposed to the alleged use of identical or similar marks. Hence, Coors, which did not use any NCAA trademarks in its promotion, argued that to deny it the right to engage in college basketball-themed promotions would, in effect, be granting the NCAA a monopoly on college basketball promotions.

Give credit to the NCAA for being the first sport organization to push the envelope on this issue. Both parties faced a tremendous risk in placing these nuanced ambush-marketing issues in the hands of a judge and jury. A decision favoring Coors could have opened the floodgates for ambush marketers; a ruling in favor of the NCAA would have sent ambush marketers back to square one. With [the] settlement, we just don't know—for now.

Reprinted, by permission, from S. McKelvey, 2003, "Jury's still out on ticket promotions," *Street & Smith's SportsBusiness Journal* May 19-25, pg. 27.

+ Motion pictures and other audiovisual works
+ Sound recordings
+ Architectural works (85)

Because of the large number of advances in technology, these protected works are defined in very broad terms. Copyright protection for an original work of authorship does not, however, extend to any idea, procedure, process, system, method of operation, concept, principle, or discovery, regardless of the form in which it is described, explained, or illustrated. (86)

The Copyright Act grants a copyright owner the right to do the following:

+ Reproduce and/or distribute copies or sound recordings of the copyrighted work to the public by sale, rental, lease, or lending
+ Prepare derivative works based on the copyrighted work
+ Perform the copyrighted work publicly (literary, musical, dramatic, and choreographic works; pantomimes; motion pictures, and the like)
+ Display the copyrighted work publicly (literary, musical, dramatic, and choreographic works; pantomimes; and pictorial, graphic, or sculptural works, including individual images of a motion picture or other audiovisual work)
+ Perform the copyrighted work publicly by means of a digital audio transmission (sound recordings) (87)

Under common law, copyright protection begins at the time the idea originates and is "fixed" in a tangible form. However, registering a copyright with the U.S. Copyright Office, like registering a trademark, provides several benefits to the copyright owner in the event of its unauthorized use. For instance, registering a copyright allows the copyright owner to immediately sue for infringement (otherwise, if the copyright is infringed, the owner must first register the copyright). Also, if a copyright is not registered prior to alleged infringement, there are limits to the amount of recoverable damages. In the event that a person does not choose to register her work with the U.S. Copyright Office, she should be sure to at least keep excellent records of her work as she is creating it; and place a copyright symbol, or write out the word *copyright,* along with the origination date and the copyright owner's name, on the work. It is also a good idea to notarize the ideas expressed to prove that the date listed on the copyrighted work has been accurately reported.

The U.S. Copyright Office also accepts registration for online works. The key factor in determining whether the online site is copyrightable is whether it possesses original authorship. (88) Garrote and Maher (1998) suggested that the trade dress of a Web site may be protected. They warn, though, that trade dress requires that the "packaging" create a distinctiveness that the public associates with that site. This may happen quickly if the site makes a swift, strong impact; but it is more likely to take time for the trade dress and site to create an association in the public's mind. (89)

Copyright protection for works created on or after January 1, 1978, exists for a term consisting of the life of the author and 70 years after the author's death, after which time the work of authorship falls into the public domain. (90) If the work was created by more than one person, the protection endures for the term consisting of the life of the last surviving author and another 70 years after the last surviving author's death. An employer holds the copyright on works created for an employer. For works made for an employer, the duration of the employer's copyright protection is 75 years from the time of publication or 100 years from the time of creation, whichever expires first. (91)

Copyright Infringement

Copyright infringement occurs when someone makes an unauthorized use of a copyrighted work. Courts consider four factors when determining whether copyright infringement has occurred:

- ✦ The purpose of the use, including whether such use is of a commercial nature or is for nonprofit educational purposes
- ✦ The nature (character) of the copyrighted work
- ✦ The amount and substantiality of the portion used in relation to the copyrighted work as a whole
- ✦ The effect of the use on the potential market for, or value of, the copyrighted work (92)

Defenses to Copyright Infringement

In a copyright infringement case, a defendant may challenge the authenticity of the copyright. However, as is more commonly the case, a defendant may claim the defense of the fair use doctrine, which was originally created by the courts as a means of ensuring that creativity was not stifled through a rigid enforcement of copyright law. The fair use doctrine, as first enunciated by the courts, has since been incorporated into the Copyright Act. (93) As such, it allows for the fair use of a copyrighted work when the use is "for purposes such as criticism, comment, news reporting, teaching (including multiple copies for classroom use), scholarship, or research." (94) The courts use the four factors stated earlier to determine whether the use made of the work falls within the fair use defense.

In a leading sport-related case, film clips of Muhammad Ali fights appeared in the documentary *When They Were Kings* despite an attempted preliminary injunction by the copyright owner of the clips to bar their use. (95) The court found that the defendant was likely to succeed on the fair use defense, thus allowing the film clips (between 9 and 14 clips, amounting to a total duration of 41 seconds to two minutes) to be used. (96) The key factors appeared to be that the work was a documentary and, although clearly commercial, it was also a combination of comment, criticism, scholarship, and research. In addition, public interest favored the production of Ali's biography, the use was quantitatively small, the clips were not the focus of the work, and use of the clips would have little or no impact on the market for the plaintiff's copyrighted fights. (97)

Copyrights and Sporting Events

You hear it every game and no doubt know it by heart: "This telecast is a copyright of the National Football League. Any rebroadcast, retransmission or any other use or description or accounts of this telecast without the express written consent of the National Football League is prohibited." But what does it really mean?

The question of whether sport events are copyrightable has yet to be fully answered. Currently, only broadcast or cable transmissions of sport events are copyrightable. (98) In 1976, Congress amended the Copyright Act to expressly ensure that simultaneously recorded broadcasts of live performances and sport events would be protected by copyright law. (99) Congress found authorship in the creative labor of the camera operators, director, and producer. On the other hand, it would appear that the actual sporting events are not copyrightable because no authorship exists. In an event-related case, *Prod. Contractors, Inc. v. WGN Continental Broad. Co.*, the District Court for the Northern District of Illinois determined that a Christmas parade was not a work of authorship entitled to copyright protection. (100)

As technology has progressed, the issue of who owns what intellectual property has expanded. A seminal case in determining who owns the statistics and scores of games while in progress arose in 1996 when the NBA sued Motorola and STATS, Inc. for copyright infringement. (101) Motorola's SportsTrax pager system displayed the following information on NBA games in progress: the teams playing, the core changes, the team in possession of the ball, whether the team was in the free-throw bonus, the quarter of the game, and the time remaining in the quarter. The information was updated every two to three minutes, with more frequent updates near the end of the first half and the end of the game. There was a lag of approximately two to three minutes between events in the game and the information's appearance on the pager screen. SportsTrax's operation relied on a "data feed" supplied by STATS reporters, who watched games on television or listened to them on the radio. Using a personal computer, the reporters keyed in changes in the score and other information such as successful and missed shots, fouls, and clock updates. The information was then relayed by modem to STATS's host computer, which compiled, analyzed, and formatted the data for retransmission. The information was then sent via satellite to various FM radio networks that in turn emitted a signal received by the individual SportsTrax pagers. On its America Online Web site, STATS also provided slightly more comprehensive and detailed real-time game information. There, game scores were updated at 15-second to 1-minute intervals, and the player and team statistics were updated each minute.

The Second Circuit Court of Appeals was asked to determine whether the NBA owned the statistics and scores of its games while they were in progress. The court determined that Congress intended to protect the league's interest only in the recorded broadcasts of games, not in the real-time data (scores, key plays, etc.) acquired by Motorola's employees and then broadcast on Motorola pagers. Thus, the court found that Motorola and STATS did not unlawfully misappropriate NBA's property by transmitting "real-time" NBA game scores and statistics taken from television and radio broadcasts of games in progress.

Although the competition itself may not be copyrightable, event organizers can take steps to protect their proprietary interest in an event. Wall analyzed some of the steps taken by EPSN to protect its interest in its Extreme Games (now most popularly known as the X Games). (102) ESPN used a trademark symbol for the name *Extreme Games* and for the X symbol, indicating that it had applied for trademark registration. A copyright notice was also affixed on all of ESPN's Extreme Games promotional materials. Publicity waivers were required from all athletes. Although these steps cannot protect ESPN from another organization's holding an event similar to the Extreme Games (witness the subsequent emergence of the Gravity Games), it will protect ESPN from another's use of the name *Extreme Games* and the X symbol. (103) Reed suggested that additional steps, such as choosing a distinctive trademark, establishing long-term contracts with participants, and prohibiting sponsors from creating or sponsoring similar competitive events, can further protect event ideas. (104)

Patents

Jill B. Fan is also exploring, through an overseas manufacturer, the production of what she believes is a novel contraption—a plastic baseball that, with the push of a button, releases a banner that says "World Series Champs" and plays "Take Me Out to the Ballgame" (Jill has, to her credit, researched and determined that the copyright to this song has expired). She has been advised to procure a patent on this product, which she intends to sell on the Internet. Once again, she can't wait to cash in.

Sport marketers will typically have the least involvement with the area of patent law. However, for those involved in the manufacturer's side of the sport industry, an understanding of patent law is especially important. Companies invest tremendous amounts of money in developing new technologies for everything from shoes to scoring apparatus, and the ability to profit from this ingenuity is found in the protections under patent law. One recent case illustrating patent law in the sport industry arose in 2003 when an inventor from Canada sued Nike for $200 million in a Canadian court, claiming that Nike unlawfully used his Z-shaped, spring-loaded, tube-designed soles on its successful line of athletic shoes, the Nike Shox. (105)

A patent may be granted to anyone who invents or discovers any new and useful process, machine, manufacture, or composition of matter, or any new and useful improvement. (106) A patent cannot be granted for a mere idea, only for the actual invention or complete description of it. Like a copyright, a patent has a limited duration. Currently, its duration is 20 years from the date on which the application was filed with the Patent and Trademark Office. (107) During those 20 years, a patent owner must not violate antitrust laws by virtue of having a patent, such as by unreasonably limiting the licensing of the patent or by using the patent to fix prices or restrain trade. Once the 20 years expires, anyone may make, use, sell, or import the invention without the permission of the patent owner.

Patent law is the most complex of the three areas of intellectual property. As a result, it is the area in which one will most likely need legal guidance for the patent registration process and patent protection.

In the sport context, inventors of sport equipment seek patents to protect their inventions. The invention of sport products is driven by consumer need. Sport equipment is invented and updated regularly in an effort to keep participants ahead of their competition and to keep them safe in sports of high contact or risk. As new materials are developed, new types of sport equipment and improvements on current equipment are also developed. These range from new types of bicycles, golf clubs, tennis rackets, and baseball bats to new protective gear, such as helmets and padding.

New methods or processes for playing sport have also been deemed to be patentable. For example, the Arena Football League (AFL) and its parent company, Gridiron Enterprises, Inc., have been issued patents in the United States and Mexico for Arena Football's game system and method of play. (108) Debate, primarily academic in nature, has also arisen as to whether athletes can patent their moves (as processes). (109) For instance, could Jim Fosbury, noted inventor of the Fosbury flop, have secured a patent on his revolutionary way of clearing the high bar (bended, back-first), thus preventing his competitors from using this technique?

Could Michelle Kwan create and subsequently patent a revolutionary figure skating jump that would stifle her competitors? Although some have argued, persuasively, that such athletic moves fall squarely within the definitions of what is patentable, courts and commentators have suggested that from a practical standpoint, the enforcement of such patent rights, as well as the chilling effect it would have on competition, makes this a moot point. But perhaps it's only a matter of time.

Right of Publicity and Invasion of Privacy

J.B. Fan has decided that, during the World Series games, she is going to stand outside the stadium and sell a poster bearing illustrations of a few Aces players. She has asked a friend of hers in art school to provide artist renderings of the players. The poster is going to read "Good Luck Aces Stars." She has secured a local hardware store to underwrite the printing costs of the posters, in exchange for the store logo being displayed on the posters.

Whether you are employed as a marketer for a sport team, a sporting goods manufacturer, or an individual athletes, the intersection of right of publicity and invasion of privacy are critical areas to be aware of. It is important to understand that, although these claims fall within the area of tort law, versus intellectual property law, these are extremely important areas at the intersection of sport marketing and the law.

The right of publicity was originally intertwined with invasion of privacy, but courts have since separated the right to be left alone from the commercial right to control the use of one's likeness or identity. (110) Invasion of privacy arises out of the common law of torts or state statutes. Among other things, the right of privacy protects against intrusion on one's seclusion, the misappropriation of one's name or likeness, unreasonable publicity, and placing one in a false light. One of the landmark sport-related cases dealing with invasion of privacy was *Spahn v. Julian Messner, Inc.*, (111) in which Hall of Fame pitcher Warren Spahn sued the publishers of an unauthorized fictional biography, *The Warren Spahn Story*. The book, the whole tenor of which projected a false intimacy with Spahn, was fraught with inaccuracies and fabricated events dealing with Spahn's marriage, family life, and relationship with his father, among other things. Although the book was quite laudatory of Spahn, the court held that "the offending characteristics of the book comprehend a non-factual novelization of plaintiff's alleged life story and an unauthorized intrusion into the private realms of the baseball pitcher's life—all to Spahn's humiliation and mental anguish." (112)

The right of publicity, on the other hand, prevents the unauthorized commercial use of a person's name, likeness, or other recognizable aspects of his or her persona. It gives individuals the exclusive right to license the use of their identity for commercial purposes. More than half of all jurisdictions in the United States recognize the right of privacy, but nine states, including New York and Illinois, have rejected the right of publicity after death. In a legal action arising from the misappropriation of one's name or likeness for a product, an advertisement, or any other commercial use, a plaintiff may choose to sue under invasion of privacy, the right of publicity, or both.

Cases often arise on both of these legal theories in the sport setting when a sport celebrity attempts to stop the misappropriation of his or her name and likeness. Athletes have discovered the commercial value in their names and likenesses, and thus enforcing the right of publicity is crucial in this age of the "branding" of athletes. The first such case in sport, *Haelan Laboratories v. Topps Chewing Gum*, involved a dispute over the right to market trading cards of professional baseball players. (113) In that case, the court established a property right in a person's identity, naming it the right of publicity. (114) The court recognized the right of the players to grant a license (or exclusive privilege) to merchandisers to use their likenesses for the manufacture and sale of the cards. This case opened the door for athletes and celebrities to enforce a right of publicity against those misappropriating their names and likenesses. In a similar case, *Uhlaender v. Henricksen*, a court enjoined the maker of a table game from using MLB players' names without their consent because the players had a proprietary interest in their names, likenesses, and accomplishments. (115)

Because of the strength of the First Amendment protection of free speech or expression, permission is not needed to use a celebrity's name or likeness in a book, newspaper, magazine, television news show or documentary, or other news media outlet. Courts have also found allowable the use of the name or likeness of an athlete or entertainer to advertise or promote media publications in which the athlete or entertainer once appeared. In both *Namath v. Sports Illustrated* (116) and *Montana v. San Jose Mercury News, Inc.*, (117) courts allowed the defendants to use the plaintiffs' photos from prior editions of their publications in advertisements to sell their publications. The court stated that the photographs represented newsworthy events and that a newspaper had a constitutional right to promote itself by reproducing its news stories. These cases differ from the previously discussed *Abdul-Jabbar v. General Motors*, in which Alcindor's name and likeness were misappropriated in an advertisement for the Olds 88 automobile. Although Alcindor's record is in fact newsworthy, its use was to advertise an Oldsmobile and thus was not protected by the First Amendment. (118)

The First Amendment may also play a role in the appropriation of a person's name or likeness in parodies. In a lead case on this issue, *Cardtoons, L.C. v. Major League Baseball Players Association*, (119) the Court of Appeals for the Tenth Circuit granted full protection to the parody cards created by the plaintiff on the basis of its First Amendment rights. The court determined that the parody cards provided social commentary on public figures, MLB players, who were involved in a significant commercial enterprise, Major League Baseball. The court stated that the cards were no less protected because they provided humorous rather than serious commentary. Thus, the plaintiff's First Amendment right to create the parody trading cards outweighed the MLB Players Association's right of publicity in their members' names and likenesses. (120)

Courts have also recognized a right of publicity and trademark protection for nicknames. In *Hirsch v. S.C. Johnson & Son, Inc.*, (121) the plaintiff, Elroy "Crazylegs" Hirsch, alleged that the nickname belonged to him, that it had commercial value, and that knowing this, the defendants marketed a shaving gel for women called Crazylegs. In an action against S.C. Johnson & Son, Inc., Hirsch sought a remedy under two legal theories. Hirsch argued that the defendant violated his right to privacy by misappropriating his name and likeness for commercial use and infringed on his trademark rights to the nickname *Crazylegs*. The court determined that a celebrity's nickname had value and that Johnson could not use the name *Crazylegs* without permission from or payment to Hirsch for its use. The court found that all that is required to protect a nickname is that the nickname clearly identifies the wronged person. (122)

Debate continues as to where to draw the lines between athletes' right of publicity and media and marketers' First Amendment freedoms. (123) A recent case on this issue, *ETW Corp. v. Jireh Publishing*, involved Tiger Woods. (124) Noted sport artist Rich Rush created and distributed prints titled "The Masters of Augusta" that prominently featured Tiger Woods. Notwithstanding the fact that Rush profited from his artwork by selling lithographs of his artwork, the U.S. Court of Appeals held in favor of the artist, suggesting that such creative works of art are protected under the First Amendment and thus can trump an athlete's right of publicity. Interestingly, the court reasoned, among other things, that Woods earns more than enough money from his tournament winnings and other commercial endorsement deals. The Woods case, as well as the more recent Missouri Supreme Court decision awarding former NHL player Tony Twist a $15 million judgment for the unauthorized use of his name and likeness in a comic book series, (125) has served to further blur the legal lines in the evolving debate between the right of publicity and the First Amendment.

Emerging Issues

In this section, which in no way is intended to be inclusive, we consider several emerging issues at the intersection of the law and sport marketing.

Global Protection of Intellectual Property

As we move toward a global economy in which more and more companies seek to do business abroad, and more and more information is carried and commerce transacted through the World Wide Web, it has become increasingly important for owners of intellectual property to consider registering copyrights, trademarks, and patents in foreign countries. To better protect trademark owners operating in international commerce, the Madrid Protocol went into effect on November 2, 2003. Under the Protocol, a U.S. trademark applicant is now able to file a single application with the USPTO to obtain protection in all Protocol member countries. To date, over 60 countries are signatories to the Protocol. Thus, U.S. trademark applicants no longer need to endure the costly and time-consuming process of filing separate registrations in each country in which they seek protection. Once an application is filed in the United States, the USPTO forwards it to the International Register of the World Intellectual Property Organization (WIPO) for processing. Fees, which depend on the number of countries in which registration is sought, can be paid entirely to the USPTO in one currency.

Another intellectual property system that has become significant recently is the European Community Trademark System, which processes applications for European Community trademark registrations. European Community registrations are accepted and protected in all European Community member countries (currently 25 countries). The trademarks are effective for 10 years and allow 10-year renewals.

The sale of licensed products and the staging of sporting events in foreign countries has become an increasingly important revenue stream for U.S.-based sport properties. Furthermore, there continues to be tremendous growth in sport industries abroad such as China, Korea, and the nations of Europe, particularly for sports such as baseball, basketball, American football, and extreme sports. U.S.-based sport marketers need to be cognizant of the importance of ensuring that the trademarks that identify their products, services, and events are protected in these foreign countries.

Ownership of "Real-Time" Information and Player Statistics

Technological advancements in "broadcasting" over the Internet continue to raise challenging intellectual property issues for sport events and properties. The distribution of "real-time" scores to pager subscribers, as seen in the *NBA v. Motorola* case, has been replaced by webcasts that show instantaneous game information, in much more detail, on sport property Web sites. For instance, MLB fans can "watch" the progress of any MLB game, pitch by pitch, with details that even include pitch location. Given the ever-closing time gap between actual game event and its "description" on a webcast, can a sport property such as MLB claim a copyright interest in its webcast? Could a competitor reproduce or repackage the game information and offer it to consumers?

This issue arose in the recent case of *Morris Communication Corp v. PGA Tour, Inc.,* (126) in which the 11th U.S. Circuit Court of Appeals affirmed a lower court's ruling that the PGA Tour was justified in denying Morris Communication, a Georgia publisher of print and electronic newspapers, the right to sell real-time tournament data collected and produced by the PGA Tour through a system called ShotLink. Morris compiled golfers' scores and syndicated its service to other media outlets; its scores would sometimes even appear before those on the PGA Tour's Web site. Although the case was brought and decided strictly on antitrust grounds (and not a copyright claim), the court's decision was swayed by its reasoning that compiling scores in golf is more difficult than in other sports because of the simultaneous action of numerous players, and that the PGA Tour had spent millions of dollars building the only system that does it. The court stated that the PGA Tour's real-time golf scores compiled by ShotLink "are not a product that Morris has a right to sell because they are a derivative product of ShotLink, which the PGA Tour owns exclusively." (127) The court added that the PGA Tour "has the right to sell or license its product, championship golf, and its derivative product, [compiled] golf scores, on the Internet in the same way the [PGA] currently sells its rights to television broadcasting stations." (128) Morris contemplated an appeal to the U.S. Supreme Court, on the belief the scores are in the public domain once they occur.

Despite this court ruling upholding the PGA Tour's right to limit how media companies use real-time data, several key questions regarding sport properties' commercial control over information emanating from its competitions remained open. (129) The ruling in *Morris* was limited to whether Morris was engaging in unfair competition by selling a product that the tour produces. Within this interpretation, the court ruled that because the tour owns and operates its real-time scoring system, it has valid business reasons for protecting its investment by insisting that news organizations not sell the product. However, the court "opted not to address . . . the broader issues of copyright law, or who owns the rights to real-time data from sporting events, and freedom of the press, or to what extent a league can legally limit the media's access to such information." (130)

In the fall of 2003, MLB Advanced Media (MLBAM) announced plans to ask that sport Internet sites concede MLB's proprietary rights to game data. In fact, SportsTicker, ESPN's wholly owned statistics subsidiary, agreed to purchase content from MLBAM to deliver real-time data on games. (131) Several others, however, including STATS, Inc., refused to comply. Numerous legal experts believe that were MLB to wage a legal battle, its case would be different enough that the Copyright Act that protected STATS, Inc., in the 1996 case with the NBA would not be as helpful today. One way that leagues such as MLB could resolve the issue is by making and enforcing more restrictive media credential guidelines that prohibit the real-time transmission of game data. As one commentator suggested, "If leagues decide to take further steps to regulate data transmitters such as STATS, legal experts say the leagues would likely be successful, considering common-law landowner rights permit the owner of private property to exclude people who do not comply with the requirements imposed for entry." (132) This would not, however, stop companies from, for instance, watching games on television, compiling the data, and than transmitting it. At this point, no sport property appears ready to test such legal ground, but it will likely occur at some point in the future as sport properties continue to derive an increasing percentage of their revenues from Web site activities, including the transmission of real-time data.

A similar legal debate is currently being waged over who owns player statistics and the corresponding player names in the context of online fantasy games. (133) In August of 2006, a U.S. District Court judge granted a declaratory judgment motion filed by St. Louis-based CDM Fantasy Sports against Major League Baseball Advanced Media (MLBAM). The decision gave CDM legal backing for the unlicensed use of player names and statistics in commercial fantasy games. MLBAM, joined by the Major League Baseball Players Association (MLBPA), plans to appeal the ruling on the grounds that CDM's use of player names and statistics violates the players' publicity rights. The eventual outcome of this case will have far-reaching ramifications for the sports fantasy league industry. (134)

Wrap-Up

Copyrights, trademarks, and patents are property rights granted to protect the intangible products created by people's intellect. Intellectual property law is complex. As sport marketers seek to protect their own creativity and to avoid infringing on the creativity of others, they would do well to have a basic understanding of copyright, trademark, and patent law, as well as the torts of invasion of privacy and the right of publicity. When complex legal issues confront sport marketers, a good rule of thumb is to rely on legal counsel with expertise in this field to handle the situation.

Activities

1. Discuss how you would advise Jill B. Fan on each of her ideas as she prepares to capitalize on her team's trip to the World Series.

2. Describe the differences among the three forms of intellectual property. Give at least one sport example of each form.

3. Watch or attend a major sporting event and identify all the activities that you believe constitute ambush marketing.

Your Marketing Plan

Assume you are the head of marketing for Koka-Kola, a national soft drink company. Your leading competitor is the official sponsor of the upcoming World Series. Devise a marketing plan that outlines the tactics that you will recommend your company use to capitalize on the excitement of this upcoming event—without violating trademark laws.

Chapter 19

The Shape of Things to Come

Objectives

✦ To provide insight with regard to the challenges and opportunities facing sport marketers in the next five years.

✦ To share opinions from leaders in the sport marketing industry about the next five years.

✦ To consider projections concerning future developments in the sport industry and the ramifications of those developments for sport marketers.

Technology and Leadership

Adam Silver, deputy commissioner and president, National Basketball Association Entertainment

Rapid advances in technology have changed our approach to virtually every aspect of the sport business. Therefore, in figuring out how to plan for the future, the core question would seem to center on forecasting the next 10 years in technology, predicting what impact changes in technology will have on what we do and making anticipatory adjustments to our operations.

Not so.

Truly revolutionary technologies are not easily anticipated, and even if they were, there's no way to know exactly how consumers and society will respond to them. This isn't to say that the opportunities and challenges that technology enables aren't potentially game changing; they are. But the fundamental challenge is one of leadership and management in a time of accelerating change—how to embrace radical change quickly to protect, grow, and evolve all aspects of your business.

Technology has already been a catalyst for change in many areas of our business from new ticketing models to nontraditional media platforms, digital marketing, and virtual signage to extraordinarily sophisticated coaching analytics using statistical and video databases. With so many facets of our business in play, leading a team or a company in a period of rapid change can be exhilarating, intellectually challenging, and creatively rewarding; it can also be exhausting, overwhelming, and seemingly never-ending. To best position your property and yourself for success, here are a few tips for how to decide when to jump and when to wait and see as you explore new opportunities:

- *Sometimes the emperor really doesn't have any clothes.* Technology demos on laptops can look awesome, but not every technology that gets pitched or written up in the trades is worth your time. Whether or not you have a background in technology, ask the same kinds of questions you would ask of any new business prospect. Ask simple questions about how it works, who has invested in the company, who their competitors are in the marketplace, whether they own any patents, what deals they have signed, and what their (and your) business model is. Don't worry about trying to look smart. Just make sure you understand the concept and the business. And feel free to tell them to come back to you once their product is more developed. It's nice to pick some areas to be out front on, but you don't always have to be the first mover.

- *Track trends and develop opinions about what ideas work.* You don't have to be right 100 percent of the time—if you are, spend your days day trading instead of running a sport business! Look to global markets for adoption curves of technologies that are just being rolled out domestically. Developing opinions, staying current with companies and products in the industry, and talking to your colleagues about what's working and not and why will help you build and hone a strategy based on the technologies that will have the greatest impact for your business. If you get stuck in information-gathering mode and don't form opinions, you'll lose the edge of testing and comparing competing ideas that can lead to new products and original thinking. And don't worry about changing your opinion down the road as your thinking changes and the marketplace develops. Flexibility is a hallmark of good leadership.

- *Don't take the pitch too literally.* Many of the most innovative technologies are developed by tech-savvy but not necessarily business-, media-, or sport-savvy companies. Make sure you understand what the technology can do and how it works and think about whether that product, service, or function fits other areas of your business. Also, business models in the digital space frequently take some time to evolve, so don't be shy about suggesting or proposing other consumer models or business structures. Everything is fair game as long as it makes sense for both parties.

- *Think about what you wish you were being pitched.* Technology is a toolbox. It can make new stuff, it can fix old stuff, and it can help connect seemingly disparate parts of your business. If there's something you wish you could do, from automating a sales function to streamlining content distribution, there's probably a way to make that happen. If you suggest what you wish the sales software or video technology could also do, you may find that it's already on the company's list for a next release—or they're willing to add the feature to the list or move it up in priority. Real-world feedback can help inform the pitches and ensure that you get a better product than you would have otherwise.

+ *Give it a try.* Protect your fans, protect your intellectual property, and protect your partners. Other than that, don't be afraid to experiment. Do short-term deals, run trials, get fan feedback, and decide on your longer-term strategy after you have more information. You don't need to have everything figured out up front for the next five years—in fact, if you do, you're probably wrong. In the meantime, make sure you get reports on what's working and what's not, own any interaction with your fans and clients, and make sure you personally use the products and services so that you have a consumer's perspective on what works and what could be better. None of these approaches is fundamentally technological in nature. Each is about some facet of leadership, including asking questions, analyzing opportunities, making decisions, and taking some calculated risks. The ability to manage change itself is the essence of leadership, and that is much more important than any one trend in technology. Listen to consumers who embrace anything that enhances their experience of sport media, and find ways for your business to meet those desires. Be true to your brand. And don't be afraid to make changes on the fly.

In developing this chapter, we jokingly referred to it as the "Nostradamus Chapter." Our intent was to provide our thoughts on what the future—the next five years or so—might hold for sport marketing. We presented our thoughts, but then we believed it might be more effective to also include the thoughts of some of the leading experts in sport marketing who have helped shape the past 10 years. In Shakespeare's *Hamlet*, Ophelia sums it up best when she says, "We know what we are, but know not what we might be." What follows, then, is our humble attempt to look "beyond the veil" and see what *may* be. We gratefully acknowledge the contributions of our contributing visionaries. We do ask you to remember only the things we predicted correctly and to please forget those we did not.

Looking Ahead to 2011: A Sports Business Odyssey

Abraham Madkour, executive editor of both *SportsBusiness Journal* and *SportsBusiness Daily*

The first thing I did when was I was asked to write about where the sports business will be in five years was to think back to where we were five years ago . . . in the spring of 2001. Even though it wasn't very long ago, memory fades, and I couldn't recall the pressing issues facing the industry at that time. So, as I do every day, I tapped into the trusty archives of *SportsBusiness Daily* and *SportsBusiness Journal* to find out what was in the news and generating buzz. Here were the headlines:

+ The launch of a new licensing partnership between Reebok and the NFL
+ The nexus of sport and entertainment—Aerosmith promoting its new release with a sponsorship of a race car
+ A debate over the television ratings during the NBA and NHL play-offs
+ Fellow agents suing each other

All sounded strikingly familiar to today's news. The point being—the more things change, the more they stay the same. So, following that premise, I don't expect a great deal of dramatic change in our business in terms of leagues forming or shutting down or significant shifts in consumer feelings or the behavior of sport fans. And we won't hear echoes of the Doors singing, "This is the end, my only friend, the end," when it comes to the sports business.

This is what I do see:

✦ *New media.* Yes, it's the subject all the properties and agencies and sponsors are talking about. It has already changed the way we think about and access sports. Consumer adoption is the wild card. I'm still not convinced that in five years we will know the answer of how much users will adopt—and use—these new technologies. Many of the young people I talk with are still using their cell phones for traditional means. That will change once ease-of-use and picture quality improves. Video on demand also can't be overlooked. The possibilities of all of these platforms are so powerful. Patriots fan, displaced or even in New England, can have 24/7 access to information and special programming about their team throughout the day. This access may include special conferences with coach Bill Belichick; the ability to purchase the new hooded sweatshirt that Belichick wore the previous Sunday in the team's win over the Jets; daily video updates from team vice chair Jonathan Kraft sent directly to their e-mail, in which he talks about plans for a new premium club; an edited look at game film of the next opponent; exclusive recaps of that day's practice from Tom Brady—oh, and yes, it's all brought to you by Dunkin' Donuts, which is paying a premium to be the exclusive sponsor. This is where we will see the biggest advancements and where properties will see the greatest revenue growth. Keep an eye on the NFL Network, which is emerging as a significant sport media presence.

✦ *Sponsorship and marketing.* We will continue to see more product immersion and branded content in sports. One property will likely take the step of selling major advertising and corporate branding on their uniforms. Leagues will consider divvying up on-field, on-court, or on-ice areas for sponsorship and branding. The revenue streams are narrowing, so teams will have to create more branded sections of facilities—each with its own unique experiences. We are seeing that now, and it will only increase over the next five years as teams develop more premium areas that sponsors can "own," thereby controlling the experience of the consumer.

✦ Sports will become more entwined with the entertainment industry. I often find the courtship between sports and Hollywood forced (that is, that the sport industry is trying too hard to be "liked" by Hollywood). Sometimes it smacks of desperation. But this will only increase. What NASCAR has done in Hollywood will be mirrored; every sport property and brand will build out its entertainment division and have specific staff develop brand and product immersion in movies, television shows, music, theater, videos, and all forms of downloadable content.

✦ *Leagues and governing bodies.* I see stability in this area; I don't see the development of many new leagues or properties. I imagine that 2011 will largely feature the same set of properties we have today, with variations in one form or another. We should see the growth and development of action sports and the emergence of new leagues for a niche sports such as lacrosse or cycling or some other outdoor sport that is strong at the grassroots level. I don't see any properties shuttering, save for consolidation in the world of motorsports (i.e., possible reunification in open wheel racing). Some would ask, What about the WBNA? It's safe as long as David Stern and his lieutenants are there. MLS? It's secure as long as new soccer-specific facilities are developed and Philip Anschutz remains interested in the growth of soccer.

✦ *Facility/stadium experiences.* At sport events, there will be a growing bifurcation between the haves and the have-nots; and the experiences of the haves will become more exclusive. We've already seen the development of all-inclusive ticketing packages that offer premium services at premium prices. These packages will continue to offer more powerful experiences and incorporate special access points during the competition. The views from the cheap seats won't change; rather, teams will have to offer more value to premium and luxury suite holders just to be able to afford to offer a more economical section.

✦ *The leaders.* The sports business—like entertainment and politics—is driven by personalities, not just on the field but also in the boardroom. In the late 1980s and early 1990s, there was a growing emphasis on the general managers who picked the talent and crafted the teams, and the early 1990s saw an explosion of young people beginning to develop their careers in sports business. Fueled by business publications such as *SportsBusiness Daily* and *SportsBusiness Journal*, these people slowly became celebrities and garnered national attention. This focus on our young leaders will only grow more intense. Like any maturing business segment, the industry will see a new generation of leaders emerge who will shape the messages, tactics, and themes for a generation. Over the next five years, we will likely see new commissioners for the major sport properties, ushering in a new era of sports business agenda setters. To me, that will be one of the most exciting developments in our industry.

Now, when you see me in 2011, I hope you'll mock me and tell me just how bad a prognosticator I am. Until then, let's sit back and enjoy the ride.

Abraham Madkour is executive editor of both *SportsBusiness Journal* and *SportsBusiness Daily.* He can be reached at amadkour@sportsbusinessjournal.com.

Looking Back for Inspiration but Looking Forward for Disruption

Matt Levine, CEO and managing director, SourceUSA

What will be commonplace sport management practices by 2015 that are merely seedling ideas today?

Consider what can be learned from relatively recent sport management history:

+ It has been 30 years since systematic, self-administered fan surveys were first conducted and put to immediate marketing and ticket sales use by the NBA's Golden State Warriors.

+ In 1977 *Sports Management Review*, a quarterly journal published for six years, surfaced as the first periodical of original content targeted at sport industry executives.

+ In 1979 *Sports Illustrated* shed popular media light on the business of sport in a seven-part series that further paved the way for sport marketing (a concept broader than its current focus on advertising, sponsorships, and partnerships) to become a pivotal aspect of the sport industry.

+ Between 20 and 25 years ago, Major League Baseball's Oakland A's, Chicago White Sox, New York Yankees, and Houston Astros first embraced integrated, real-time, technology-facilitated access to pitch-by- pitch performance information for general managers, scouts, managers, and play-by-play broadcasters.

+ In the early 1980s the Major Indoor Soccer League's Baltimore Blast and league counterparts went against the arena sports grain and reinvented game presentation.

+ In 1995, MLB's Seattle Mariners and the NHL's San Jose Sharks launched the professional sport world's first franchise Web sites, beating their respective leagues to the Internet and foreshadowing a revolution in franchise–fan communications and sport industry commerce.

Within these innovations and milestones are the seeds of what lies ahead.

These earlier breakthroughs are characterized by three driving forces that will help build revenue streams and marketing effectiveness in the decade ahead, namely (1) the application of new technologies to increase entertainment values, tighten ties with fans, and improve decision-making effectiveness; (2) a hunger among more customer-conscious, higher-profile, and competitively paid marketing executives (who are increasingly schooled outside the sport industry) for faster, more comprehensive, and usefully segmented fan information; and (3) profit economics and innovation-motivated courage to make testing of unprecedented practices an integral part of every league and franchise marketing plan.

Looking forward, with varying probabilities, the following five developments appear highly likely:

◆ *Sponsored players.* Contracts will continue between players and teams, but they will be supplemented by corporate and wealthy people's patronage of individual players. These links will be prominent, brought to the attention of fans in a tasteful manner, and include recognition in programs and on Web sites. A version of this practice, with different tax consequences, occurs in the world of ballet.

◆ *Microsegmentation.* Probing business, marketing, and sales managements, no longer satisfied with insights that stem from the massaging of traditional demographic and high-level socioeconomic profiles, will demand and secure more behavioral and experiential detail about their fans' lives, interests, preferences, values, childhood drivers, networks, and affinities. This will help them identify new and infrequently attending prospects more efficiently and characterize regular customers more thoroughly—speaking their language, addressing their distinct motivations, and offering them an avenue for purchase action suited to their respective comfort zones.

◆ *Speckled computing.* This emerging technology will revolutionize the way we gather, exchange, and communicate information. It will also increase computational capability, including peer-to-peer networking (including an application that affects fans' communications with one another, teams' relationships with fans, and fans' relationships with players), building on a "smartdust" concept (one cubic millimeter) that can sense, compute, and communicate wirelessly (each being an autonomous "speck"). This technology is under development at Intel and UC Berkeley and through the Speckled Computing Research Consortium.

◆ *Smartpaper.* Imagine being able to convert collateral sponsorship and ticket sales materials, game magazines and programs, media guides, merchandise catalogs, yearbooks, direct mail, and printed schedules into digital media highways. Smartpaper Networks Corporation has developed and patented the first technology to transform ordinary paper into a wireless control device, bringing printed pages to life by activating the power of video, audio, and/or the Internet with the touch of a finger. Users will now be able to navigate all forms of digital media directly from the printed page.

◆ *Segment relationship management.* With the advent of new technologies, such as Speckled Computing and Smartpaper, and an increasingly intense urgency to understand fan behavior and motivations as cited earlier, there will be a need for staff specialists or experts who are immersed in the most important microsegments, who are capable of designing and implementing targeted programs to convert the knowledge into action and revenue, and who will be held accountable for the results.

Other technologies include VoIP and wireless telecom for airplane passengers, as well as iPods, which are now being used as data storage tools, not just music players. The question of how sport industry marketing executives will leverage these new technologies will make the decade ahead more dynamic than the previous three.

My Fearless Predictions for the Next Five Years in Sport Sponsorship

Bob Cramer, president, Genesco Sports Enterprises

One cannot predict the future without analyzing the present. Although this is difficult to do in a brief essay, one thing has clearly defined the sport industry in the last 15 years: Sport is big business, and the marketers that engage in sport sponsorship spend big money.

Sport sponsorship as a marketing vehicle has definitely arrived. Traditional marketers look at sponsorship as a measurable medium by which to connect with consumers in our increasingly fragmented society. I believe the maturation of sport sponsorship over the next five years will follow four main trends.

Media Content Consumption Patterns

Content will continue to dominate, but the way that content is consumed will drastically change. New technologies and devices that affect consumer attention are everywhere. Cell phones, PDAs, iPods, TiVo, Broadband, HDTV, satellite radio, and video games are expanding our consumption patterns, while at the same time fragmenting audiences.

Sport is benefiting from this massive consumption shift because it has relevant and engaging content that appeals to a large and passionate consumer base: sport fans. Sport leagues are capitalizing on this fact and are starting to retain (or regain) greater control of their digital media rights. One recent development that reinforces this trend is the NFL bringing NFL.com back "in-house," substantially altering its relationship with CBS SportsLine. Back in 2001 Major League Baseball centralized its digital media rights through the formation of MLB Advanced Media, a progressive move for a historically stodgy enterprise. The next era of media rights negotiations with leagues will move beyond a narrowly defined network negotiation for game broadcasts, and instead will involve all media platforms from television to wireless to others. This new media platform will in turn introduce new content distributors to the negotiating table (think Verizon, Comcast, Microsoft, and others that have not yet been born).

Sponsors will need to respond to this change accordingly. Marketers must develop efficient and effective ways to embrace new media and marketing strategies to reach their fragmented audiences. To ensure that their message reaches consumers, media planners and buyers will have to adjust their media plans significantly to reflect a 360-degree marketplace.

Technology Defining the Fan Experience

Over the next five years, new technology will continue to affect the sport landscape. LED and other signage technology, once cost-prohibitive for most venues, will take on a more important role. Teams and venues will have to be careful not to overload their fans with too many intrusive commercial messages. The winners will be the sponsors that can use the technology to engage with fans through storytelling and compelling content.

Ticketing technology will continue to develop. Teams will regain control of the secondary market through enhanced Web-based ticketing technology. This will allow teams to further monetize their ticket inventory and allow fans to buy, trade, sell, and upgrade their offerings through team-controlled means.

The introduction of RFID payment technology will enhance the consumer buying experience and will increase *per caps* with concessionaires, as well as increase the speed of throughput of fans at the concession lines. This technology will provide increased data mining, which will enable teams to track and reward purchase behavior, while also providing critical data that can drive more profitable and effective decision making.

Broadcast technology will continue to evolve and enhance the viewing experience. The last five years have introduced the "first and ten yard-line" marker, digitally inserted signage, and other broadcast enhancements that viewers have not only accepted, but even come to expect. In the next five years, pay-per-view content will mature and consumer choices of the total viewing experience will arrive: Fans will choose their viewing angles, replays, screen setups, and other options (for an extra fee, of course).

Fans are being put in charge of their own experience, and the sponsor's task is to intrinsically link itself to this experience in a brand-relevant manner.

A Launching Point for China

Most sport marketers believe that Beijing 2008 will be the climax of China as a sport business powerhouse. However, I believe it will simply act as a launching pad; the Olympics will provide China with the media stage and physical infrastructure it needs to create a truly commercialized sport marketplace.

Brands and leagues that are not prepared to capitalize on this enormous increase in consumers will be left behind. The NBA and PGA Tour have currently made the most progress to date in China, and the NFL is quickly following suit. In five years these entities will continue to flourish with organized leagues and events, grassroots efforts, and internationally recognized global stars.

Additionally, sponsors must remain cognizant of other emerging countries such as Korea, India, and Brazil. Otherwise, they will meet the same fate as that of the companies who miss the opportunities in China.

Segmenting Profitability

Sponsorships will continue to be a key means of reaching consumers and will be a surefire way to reach passionate segments of the marketplace. However, mainstream sports will not be the most effective way to reach everyone. Smart marketers will exploit new sport and sponsorship opportunities to reach each segment of their target market (not just men or the mass market).

The segmenting trend will see emerging properties such as action sports and soccer rise to the top as they reach the youth and Latino segments. Nontraditional properties that cater to women will also realize substantial gains. Many of the new sponsorship platforms will be different from the traditional "stick-and-ball" offerings. Without major broadcast components or 50,000-seat stadiums, the new sponsorship packages will encompass new elements: new media, grassroots opportunities, targeted cable programming, and licensing opportunities. Sponsors that incorporate nontraditional properties will be ahead of the curve in leveraging these platforms to reach their desired audiences.

It is an exciting time to be involved in the business of sport. Instead of marketers perceiving sport sponsorships as "nice to have" or as hobbies for CEOs, the next five years will further prove the value of sport platforms and the audiences they deliver.

The Future of the Team Sport Business

Scott M. O'Neil, senior vice president of marketing and team business operations, National Basketball Association

There has never been a more exciting time to be in the team business. As I travel around the country visiting the 53 cities playing home to the 56 teams in the NBA, WNBA, and NBA Development League, I see more cheering fans, the highest-quality fan experience, and corporate partners leveraging sports to a level and sophistication we have never seen before. Tickets, sponsorship, and media will continue to be the largest buckets of team revenue over the next several years, but the landscape of each is likely to change.

Tickets

The pricing, selling, and delivery of tickets will change over the next five years.

◆ *Pricing tickets.* Teams will be under tremendous pressure to understand the changing nature of the buying pattern of fans. To help make smarter decisions faster, teams will be using more sophisticated and analytical pricing models. As dynamic and real-time pricing emerges, teams will continue to better understand the variable demand by fans for various opponents, days of the week, time of year, weather, and so on. The risk, however, is that there will be an increase in the gap between the haves and the have-nots because teams with high demand will be able to better capitalize on the demand, raise prices, and drive more revenue. Prices for seats in arenas will be much more segmented by location, and in some cases, aisle seats may cost more than middle seats. Ticket prices will continue to increase at a much more rapid rate in the higher-demand locations as additional premium seating amenities such as all-inclusive food and beverage, VIP parking, and experiential events are added to close the price and value gap.

✦ *Selling tickets.* Ticket departments will be structured the way they are today, with account executives, the more experienced sales team, inside sales, an entry-level telemarketing room, and dedicated group sales. Likely to emerge, however, will be a separate group focusing on selling through wireless and online platforms. This will be the base until the worlds collide and all reps are comfortable selling across all platforms. Although the structure will stay relatively the same, staff sizes of each of these segments will likely double in the next three years. Moving forward, teams will continue to develop their databases and become much more skilled at understanding the characteristics of existing buyers, identifying potential buyers, and developing programs and plans these fans want to buy. Additionally, the ticket sales staffs will become much more efficient at delivering the right offer to the right person at the right time. If used effectively, this increased information will drive more effective up-sell and cross-sell programs.

Even though the Chicago Cubs didn't win the 2006 World Series, their success during the season will make it easier to sell tickets, even as ticket prices increase.
© Associated Press

✦ *Delivering tickets.* Tickets are already being forwarded online and scanned at the arena gates. The result is that the paper ticket will slowly be replaced with a paperless one. The next wave of technology will allow us to send tickets back and forth via our cell phones, which will carry a bar code that will be scanned at the arena entrances. As more tickets are bought and sold through phones and online channels, the cost of selling tickets will begin to decrease.

Sponsorships

The sponsorship business will experience tremendous change as well over the next five years.

✦ *Rate card reconstruction.* Teams are continuing to sell more deals across more categories. This is pushing sponsorship sales executives to walk their buildings with "fresh eyes" in an attempt to be more aggressive in developing new inventory. They will also become more comfortable pricing, packaging, and selling online and wireless technologies as they begin to play a larger role in sponsors' objectives.

✦ *Inventory management.* The continued emphasis on creating and selling integrated packages will create the need for more effective inventory management. Inventory management systems, such as that developed by StoneTimberRiver, will gain prominence as team executives are challenged to carve out areas of dominance for the increasingly cluttered categories of consumers and sponsors.

✦ *Category yield.* More deals will be done in categories as both sponsors and salespeople understand the need to meet the sponsor's objectives and as teams are more pressured to increase revenue. Will we see Pepsi and Coke in the same arena? Or Miller, Bud, and Coors? It will be more likely in the coming years. Those that have a plan and manage this well will thrive in this new environment.

✦ *Presentations.* Teams will build on their already dynamic presentations. The sport operations side (e.g., basketball, hockey, football, baseball, soccer, etc.) will be playing a larger role in raising the level and impact of the presentations. As the business gets bigger and pressure continues to increase, coaches, legends, and players will all be part of the bigger pitches as will locker room tours, visits to watch practice, and even locker room visits prior to the games.

Media

As the last of the TiVo-proof programming, sport television rights fees will continue to increase, as will the rights fees for teams. Local game broadcast will become anchors in local markets. Additionally, product placement and integration within these broadcasts will help teams garner additional revenue.

As the revenue teams generate continues to increase, so will the complexity of this business. This complexity will bring change, and with change will come tremendous opportunity.

Sport Industry Jobs in the Next Five Years

Buffy Filippell, president, Teamwork Consulting

If I had a crystal ball and could predict the future, I can assure you I would not be in the sport industry. But because I'm only an executive recruiter and, like most, use past history to predict future performance, I will give you my vision of where I see the biggest areas of growth in sport jobs in the future. The industry, you must realize, is very dependent on a healthy U.S. economy for attracting wealthy owners to purchase and maintain sport teams, and on healthy corporations to support them.

Not many businesses can survive without sales, and the sport industry is no different. It will continue to need sales executives. The most necessary job, whether it is with a minor league team, major league team, or special event, will continue to be in ticket sales. Ticket sales are the lifeblood of live events because without people watching, no corporation would advertise. Young people wanting to be in the sport industry will have plenty of opportunities to secure one of these jobs if they are recent college graduates, have had at least one internship with a sport or live event organization, have sales experience, and preferably have been involved in sports in high school or college. Niche sports such as soccer and Olympic sports such as rugby, speedskating, and water skiing are going to need passionate athletes, preferably from those disciplines, to market to those sport fan bases. All live events will continue to need ticket sales executives to market to corporations, groups, and individuals. This is one-on-one marketing (the buzzword for marketing today), and no one does it better than the sport industry.

Because technology is the tool through which we communicate to a new generation, I believe that the biggest area of growth in new jobs will be in technology-based marketing and communications. The sport industry needs to develop better technologies and hire people dedicated to developing fans or live event customers through more high-tech ways, rather than through the usual telephone and face-to-face selling. The industry still relies on its "bricks-and-mortar" communication platforms. Although there have been fits and starts in new technologies such as ticketing systems for purchasing tickets online, an even bigger business was developed around the industry in the creating and servicing of secondary ticket offerings. One such company was sold to eBay for a sizable sum. The teams and leagues themselves need to develop these kinds of entrepreneurial companies within and be the vehicle to develop and grow these technological enhancements in the industry much the way ESPN introduced the first sport television station.

I envision that at both the league and team levels, marketing and sales departments looking to sell tickets and merchandise and interact with fans will be split into competing areas: traditional face-to-face and online. Teams and leagues will need to have strategies to gain and build customers both ways. They will need ticket schemes for those who want to be "called" through the Internet or on their cell phones. Thus, those with online marketing backgrounds from other successful dot-com disciplines will be recruited to the teams and leagues, but will not eliminate the traditional techniques. Touchpoint measurements (measurements of the number of times a team successfully interacts with a fan—both personally and virtually) will become a necessary daily statistic.

Leagues will need to develop better strategies for reaching consumers via the Internet or cell phone video space. As leagues and teams not only take their rights in-house, but also create television networks, they will need to develop more partners to help bring customers to their dedicated media sites. People with technological solutions for moving people from one site to another will be in demand. What used to be the need to put "butts in seats" will be a need for "online eyeballs" or "clicks" that move people from one site to another. Technological marketing gurus will be needed to provide their teams with tools to enhance their Web sites. Leagues may also start taking more control of teams' sites the way Major League Baseball Advanced Media took control of MLB teams' Web sites.

Outside companies or agencies that can provide these technologies to teams, leagues, and events will have viable job opportunities—that is, until the teams or events can bring that talent in-house.

Agencies will be called on to attract a generation of people who have become accustomed to communicating via the Internet and enjoying quick bursts of entertainment experiences. Adults today grew up on television shows such as *Sesame Street*, which changed topics, characters, and songs in seconds. Will this change the live event? Consider the fact that the U.S. Army hired an agency to create its own online game to provide young people the video experience of serving our nation at war. The army has also contracted with an agency to create virtual army experiences at NASCAR events. Banks and other businesses are devising online games to teach us about products through interactive games. Soon iPods and cell phones will broadcast our sport events (iPods already air our favorite television shows, and even college professors' speeches). The challenge—and this is for any product out there—will be to market and deliver sport and live events across all generations through both high-tech and low-tech means.

Given that sport management programs have evolved from exclusive graduate programs to undergraduate programs, I envision that the high school level will be the next frontier. Additionally, high schools beset with continual financial problems will open more opportunities for corporations to be involved in high school athletics. Junior Achievement Clubs will be transformed into "sport internships," and the more aggressive, focused future sport executive will participate in these internships at the high school level. These high schoolers will generate additional revenue for their high school teams by selling groups of tickets and interactive corporate sponsorship at their schools' events. Those students will be the most sought after students for college sport management degree programs and in turn will have easier access to jobs with professional and Olympic teams when they graduate.

We're at the beginning of a convergence of technologies vying to be our communication platforms of broadcast, audio, and visual media. Consumers want to touch, feel, and participate in the product in person, online, and through other "virtual" technologies yet to be developed. Those who have the technological wherewithal, broad-based marketing ingenuity, creativity, an ability to communicate across all generations, and a strong ability to analyze and synthesize these platforms to engage fans and their dollars, in my crystal ball, will be the new leaders in sport business.

Nevertheless, the person who develops the first human jet propulsion system enabling us to fly might alter all of this.

From Our Crystal Ball

Before looking forward, let's review what we said in 2000.

✦ *Growth of international exhibitions will continue.* We were dead on predicting a sanctioned international competition in baseball. The 2006 World Baseball Classic was very successful and will continue. We were a little ahead of the curve when we predicted a more formalized international dimension for the NBA. Although there is no regular-season competition between NBA teams and teams from other countries, in 2006 the Phoenix Suns and San

Antonio Spurs conducted their training camps in both Italy and Germany, and also played an exhibition schedule against top European clubs.

✦ *Women's professional team sports will continue to develop.* Although the WNBA and LPGA are healthy and growing, the WUSA folded, as have several attempts at professional softball. At this writing there are plans to try to revive the WUSA in some format or another, but sadly, women's professional sport has not shown much growth since 2000.

✦ *There will be a true national championship play-off format for NCAA football.* We're not sure whether we agree that the Bowl Championship Series (BCS) represents a true national championship (we don't think it does), but it represents movement from where we were six years ago. There is still a lot of work to do in this area—stay tuned to 2011.

✦ *College athletes will receive compensation.* OK, we missed on this one—but the furor and debate continues. The amount of money being generated by NCAA athletes for their respective schools, and by the NCAA in general, borders on the obscene. A class action lawsuit on behalf of these athletes to share the revenue they are producing has to be the dream of some law firm.

✦ *There will be more mergers among sport marketing agencies and corporations involved in producing sport apparel and other merchandise.* We were right on with this one—particularly given the Reebok–Adidas merger of 2006. The sport agency mergers have been too numerous to mention, and will continue.

✦ *Multiple ownership of sport teams in various leagues will continue—as will corporate ownership of those teams.* We not only missed, but the trend is exactly the opposite, with TBS and Disney both divesting themselves of their sport ownership positions. There is, however, a trend for major league team to own their own minor league teams; in 2006 the Los Angeles Lakers took ownership of a team in the NBA Development League.

✦ *Player salaries will continue to escalate.* We really didn't go out on a limb on this one, but the numbers, buoyed in part by large increases in television money (except for the NHL), continue to keep the spiral headed upward.

✦ *The unfolding soap opera of the haves and have-nots will continue and will become more pronounced.* We were speaking primarily of baseball because football, basketball, and hockey (because of the lockout) have avoided such a precarious situation. If you don't believe us, check the postseason records for the past six years. The New York Yankees, Boston Red Sox, Atlanta Braves, and St. Louis Cardinals are represented every year and could be joined in 2006 by the New York Mets, Los Angeles Angels, and Chicago White Sox. There seems to be little hope for the Pittsburgh Pirates, Kansas City Royals, and several others to compete.

✦ *Facilities will continue to become complete entertainment palaces.* The growth and development of technological applications, the importance of entertainment for guests of all ages, and the need to continually find more sources of non-sport-related revenue (that does not need to be shared with the players) have been the drivers in this area. New NBA basketball arenas in Houston, Charlotte, and Memphis; new NFL venues in Houston, Phoenix, and Washington; and new baseball venues in Houston, Pittsburgh, Atlanta, Detroit, and Cincinnati have played a key role in attracting fans and providing multifaceted entertainment experiences.

✦ *Sports and activities with an increasing element of risk, challenge, and inherent danger will continue to be developed.* The popularity of the X Games and the inclusion of X Game–type sports in the Olympics have given birth to a variety of exhibitions and tours—most notably the Dew Action Sports Tour.

✦ *Enter the age of choice or on-demand television.* We were speaking primarily of satellite television, but TiVo and premium cable services have made this offering much more available to the public.

Looking back on what we said, and based on what has happened, we feel safe in rewarding ourselves a grade of B+. But let's forget about the past and once again peer into the future.

From Our Crystal Ball Redux: By the Year 2012

✦ *The portability of sport viewership will provide true connectivity and on-demand information.* Podcasting, video clip downloading, real-time broadcasts, and special features will continue to drive consumers to upgrade cell phones and PDAs to achieve higher levels of connectivity with their sport broadcasts and sport news regardless of where they are.

✦ *Sport facilities in Europe and Asia will take on a decidedly American look as American interest, the potential of media dollars, affiliation opportunities with American professional leagues, as well as investment have a major influence.* Opportunities to create global sport events on a regular basis and the possibility of revenue from televising these events will result in the design and construction of arenas and stadiums that have the technological setups and broadcast capabilities necessary to accommodate television broadcasts. Two such facilities are under construction in Europe under the auspices of the Los Angeles–based Anschutz Entertainment Group (AEG). As opportunities for expansion or affiliation by the NBA and other United States–based professional leagues become a reality, more facilities will follow in both Europe and Asia.

✦ *Small-market baseball owners will pressure MLB to find a solution to the lack of competitiveness that plagues the league.* As previously mentioned, with few exceptions (one or two teams each year), the same teams (New York Yankees, Boston Red Sox, St. Louis Cardinals, Atlanta Braves) are competing for postseason opportunities year in and year out. In 2006 it looked as though other large-market teams such as the New York Mets and the Chicago White Sox (the previous year's champions) would also be in the midst of the competition. Unfortunately, the message to the other markets (20+ teams) is that they are irrelevant and have little opportunity other than to develop talent that will later need to be sold to large-market teams who can afford players' contracts as they approach free agency. This lack of relevance will not be lost on the ticket-buying and viewing public who—unless they can once again become convinced that every team has an equal chance to win—will begin to find other outlets for their interest and entertainment dollars. Although a revenue sharing program is in place, the financial gap between the Yankees and other teams is more like a chasm.

✦ *Corporate sponsors' names, logos, or both, will appear on the uniform of at least one professional league in the United States.* As spiraling player contracts and demands spur professional leagues to continue to search for new revenue streams with high net yields, this seems to be one of the most lucrative assets to sell. Commonplace everywhere else in the world—and also in U.S. recreational club sports and youth leagues—these assets seem likely to be sold at some point. One concern would be the huge variance in the amount of revenue teams could generate. Will the New York Yankees, for instance, distance themselves even further from other MLB teams in terms of revenue generation? And could the allure of huge financial rewards be significant enough to cause a team such as the Dallas Cowboys to disrupt that equitable partnership in the NFL that has evolved from a league-think (league-first) mentality? It is also interesting to ponder whether the NCAA might consider such a relationship because it could help schools meet Title IX considerations without cutting sports. At the high school level, it could mean the elimination of pay-for-play requirements and provide a source of funds that could be used to further enhance educational programs and opportunities.

✦ *Collegiate athletics programs will figure out that they are also in the sport entertainment business and need to sell tickets. Ticket sales departments in major universities will become more prevalent.* Why this has not already occurred is mystifying to the authors. Like their professional counterparts, collegiate athletics programs are the proud owners of large football stadiums and basketball arenas that are in some cases larger than those of professional sport teams. But like professional teams, athletics departments must generate revenue from those seats. Whereas the Notre Dames, Ohio States, Alabamas, and Floridas of the world have the luxury of doing little marketing or selling of their premier athletics programs, the Oregons, Oklahoma States, Pittsburghs, and North Carolina States need to undertake an immense amount of aggressive and proactive marketing and selling. Failure to generate revenue from ticket sales forces institutions to cut athletics programs or become dependent on other funding sources to provide a cash bailout. This unacceptable outcome can be prevented by creating a sales force that can be counted on to generate an ROI of at least 3 or 4 to 1. Arizona State, Louisville, and UCF (University of Central Florida) have begun such programs; their success should lead the way for others to follow.

◆ *Women's professional sport leagues will show little "real" growth.* We feel terrible making this prediction, but there are few indicators that the types of changes necessary for growth in women's professional sports will occur: significant interest and ticket demand, being perceived by corporate potential partners as a solid medium to reach a desired target market, and a significant national television contract (which will only come about if the first two factors occur). The WNBA, entering its 10th season, should be applauded for its resiliency and visibility as well as for surviving and continuing to compete for recognition and acceptance. The LPGA is ushering in a new era that promises to be competitive with a battle of personalities among its newest group of young stars. If any of these new stars can capture the imagination of the media and corporate America, the tide could turn quickly. At the same time, if Michelle Wie and other female stars continue to seek opportunities in the PGA, then the LPGA could experience declining interest, just as the Negro Leagues did when Jackie Robinson left to play in Major League Baseball.

◆ *Cell phones and PDAs will becomes the ticket and credit cards accepted at all major worldwide sport venues, while continuing to be a valued source of interactive marketing and participation opportunities.* PDAs will be our wallets, credit cards, debit cards, tickets, and cash. We will transfer tickets and cash for food and beverage electronically to our business clients, staff, family members, and associates via cell phones and PDAs. Customers will swipe their phones at the entry gates, get the requisite number of printed seating passes, and proceed to their seats. They will get their merchandise and concessions the same way. While in the arena, they will receive all kinds of offers that they will be able to accept with a click, and that will promptly be delivered to their seats. Arena guests will be able to answer polls that include questions such as which play should be called or which players should be on the power play. Or they'll play giant electronic video games on the Jumbotron with other fan to win prizes.

◆ *At least one more major U.S. sport league will follow the lead of the NFL and hold its championship game at a neutral site. In addition, more All-Star Games will be located in major entertainment and tourism destinations both in the United States and abroad.* The NFL has been the standard in this area for many years, playing the Super Bowl at a neutral site since its inception in 1967, and playing its All-Star Game, the Pro Bowl, in Hawaii. In February of 2007, the NBA will play its All-Star Game in Las Vegas, which is a significant departure from the past practice of rotating the game from city to city among the members of the league. The guarantees and accommodations from this game (along with the lesser-known benefit of not inflicting hardships on the host team and their season-ticket holders who are often displaced and in some cases excluded) will bear watching. Given the global nature of the game, is an All-Star Game in Paris, Rome, or Berlin in the realm of possibility? In terms of a championship game, could an MLS (or other sport) championship be moved to a more lucrative site because it is a better market for the sport or offers a national platform? We believe that in a marketing context—particularly one with a history of rewarding the highest bidder—sadly, everything is for sale, at the right price.

◆ *The availability of national media outlets (i.e., regional sport television channels) and the lure of quick cash infusions will begin having a noticeable effect on top-tier high school athletics programs, which will schedule athletics contests on a national scale and "rent" athletes for one- or two- year terms to become attractions.* Who would have thought six years ago, when the second edition of this text was published, that we could tune into ESPN and watch high school basketball games being televised to a national audience? Well, we all followed the exploits of then–high school student Lebron James (now a member of the Cleveland Cavaliers) as his team, St. Vincent-St. Mary, played a national schedule against high-profile schools and other highly recruited high school players, receiving financial contributions that not only covered expenses, but also provided revenue for the school. The school since entered into a merchandising agreement related to the sales of replica Lebron high school jerseys. Given the revenue opportunities at the professional and collegiate levels and the business practices at those levels, how long will it take for these practices to become rooted in premier high school programs? Because high school athletes plan to attend college for one or two years before attempting to turn professional, will it become more common (it already occurs) for high school students to leave their regional high school their senior year and opt for a school affording opportunities to better showcase their talents nationally to potential collegiate suitors? What will be the role of booster clubs? Will the phenomenon then trickle down to middle schools? These are all very unsettling possibilities that, unfortunately, could become probabilities.

Wrap-up

While no one can truly predict the future, the trends, particularly those involving technology, are very evident. As on-demand connectivity and real-time access continue to move past the buzz word stage and become reality, it means a decline in the role and impact of newspapers, magazines and other traditional forms of the printed word. Not only will they no longer be timely, they will also become inefficient due to cost and ROI for sponsors and advertisers alike. Why wait for the six o'clock news when instant news can be downloaded to your cell or PDA whenever you want it? Why construct permanent signs in sport venues when LED or virtual signs can be changed on demand and offer better ways to tell your story?

Sport marketing will continue to evolve and will continue to receive more than its fair share of attention and coverage. It will always be a story generating attention and coverage because it will continue to be what it always has been: much more than just a game but an essential part of the global social fabric.

Appendix A

Sport Industry Organizations

This appendix has been created to provide the reader with a representative sample of organizations and contacts within the sport industry. It should serve as a "quick and dirty" directory to help the reader understand the breadth of the industry while providing some pertinent contact information along the way.

Please note that this directory is not meant to be a full listing of all sporting groups within the industry.

The items in this appendix are first grouped by category and then sorted alphabetically within each category. The categories are listed below. Each entry contains the name and address of the organization.

The categories listed are as follows:

✦ Single Sport Organizations and Publications
✦ Amateur Leagues and Teams
  High School
  College
  Olympic
✦ Multisport Media
  Electronic
  Multisport Magazines, Journals, Newsletters
  Newspapers
  Sport Business Directories
✦ Sport Sponsors
✦ Sport Sponsorship/Marketing/Event Agencies
✦ Professional Services
  Sports Agents
  Executive Search Services
  Market Research Services
✦ Sporting Goods (Equipment, Apparel, and footwear)

Single-Sport Organizations and Publications

Auto Sports

National Association for Stock Car Auto Racing (NASCAR)
1801 W. International Speed Blvd.
Daytona Beach, FL 32114
386-253-0611
For more information, visit www.nascar.com.

Baseball

Major League Baseball Properties
245 Park Ave
New York, NY 10167
212-931-7800
For more information on individual league teams, visit www.majorleaguebaseball.com.

Basketball

National Basketball Association
645 Fifth Ave.
New York, NY 10022
212-826-0579
For more information on individual league teams, visit www.nba.com.

Soccer

Major League Soccer
110 E. 42nd St., 10th Fl.
New York, NY 10017
212-450-1200
For more information on individual league teams, visit www.mlsnet.com.

Field Hockey

U.S. Field Hockey Association
One Olympic Plaza
Colorado Springs, CO 80909
719-866-4567
For more information, visit www.usfieldhockey.com.

Football

National Football League
410 Park Ave.
New York, NY 10022
212-758-1742
For more information on individual league teams, visit www.nfl.com.

Golf

Ladies' Professional Golf Association
100 International Golf Drive
Daytona Beach, FL 32124-1092
386-274-6200
For more information on the association, visit www.lpga.com.

Professional Golfers' Association of America/PGA of America
100 Avenue of Champions
P.O. Box 109601
Palm Beach Gardens, FL 33418
561-624-8400
For more information on the association, visit www.pga.com.

Ice Hockey
National Hockey League
1251 Avenue of the Americas
New York, NY 10020-1198
212-789-2000
For more information on each particular league team, visit www.nhl.com.

Tennis
U.S. Tennis Association (USTA)
70 W. Red Oak Ln.
White Plains, NY 10604
914-696-7000
For more information on the association, visit www.usta.com.

Track and Field
USA Track & Field
One RCA Dome, Ste. 140
Indianapolis, IN 46225
317-261-0500
For more information on the organization, visit www.usatf.org.

Amateur Leagues and Teams (High School, College, and Olympic)

High School Leagues and Teams
National Federation of State High School Associations
P.O. Box 690
Indianapolis, IN 46206
317-972-6900
For information on a particular state association, visit www.nfhs.org.

National Interscholastic Athletic Administrators Association (NIAAA)
11724 N.W. Plaza Cir.
Kansas City, MO 64195
816-464-5400
For more information on the association, visit www.niaaa.org.

National High School Sports Hall of Fame
P.O. Box 690
Indianapolis, IN 46206
317-972-6900

College Leagues and Teams
National Collegiate Athletic Association (NCAA)
P.O. Box 6222
700 W. Washington St.
Indianapolis, IN 46206-6222
317-917-6222
For more information on a particular team or conference, visit www.ncaa.org.

National Junior College Athletic Association (NJCAA)
1755 Telstar Dr. Suite 103
Colorado Springs, CO 80920
719-590-9788
For more information on a particular team or conference, visit www.njcaa.org.

Olympic Organizations and Teams

ARCO Olympic Training Center
c/o San Diego National Sports Training Foundation
1650 Hotel Cir. N., Ste. 125
San Diego, CA 92108-2817

U.S. Olympic Committee
One Olympic Plaza
Colorado Springs, CO 80909
719-632-5551
For more information on the committee, visit www.usoc.org.

Multisport Media

Electronic

ABC Sports, Inc.
Subsidiary of Capital Cities/ABC Inc.
47 W. 66th St.
New York, NY 10023
212-456-7777

CBS Sports
51 W. 52nd St., 25th Fl.
New York, NY 10019
212-975-5230
For more information, visit http://cbs.sportsline.com.

ESPN—Entertainment & Sports Programming Network
Subsidiary of Capital Cities/ABC Inc.
ESPN Plaza
Bristol, CT 06010
860-585-2000
For more information, visit www.espn.com.

NBC Sports Division
Subsidiary of General Electric Company
30 Rockefeller Plaza
New York, NY 10112
212-664-4444
For more information, visit www.nbcsports.com.

Multisport Magazines, Journals, Newsletters

Athletic Business Magazine
4130 Lion Rd.
Madison, WI 53704
608-249-0186
For more information, visit www.athleticbusiness.com.

NCAA News
P.O. Box 6222
700 W. Washington St.
Indianapolis, IN 46206-6222
317-917-6222
For more information, visit www.ncaa.org.

Sport Marketing Quarterly

P.O. Box 4425
Morgantown, WV 26504
304-599-3482

Sporting Goods Business

One Penn Plaza
New York, NY 10119-1198
646-654-5446
For more information, visit www.sportinggoodsbusiness.com.

Sports Illustrated

1271 Avenue of the Americas
New York, NY 10020
212-522-1212
For more information, visit www.si.com.

Newspapers

New York Daily News

450 W. 33rd St.
New York, NY 10001
212-210-2100
For more information, visit www.nydailynews.com.

USA Today

7950 Jones Branch Dr.
McLean, VA 22108-0605
703-276-3400
For more information, visit www.usatoday.com.

Sport Business Directories

IEG Sponsorship Sourcebook

640 N. La Salle Suite 450
Chicago, IL 60610-3777
312-944-1727
For more information, visit www.sponsorship.com.

Sports Market Place

P.O. Box 860
185 Millerton Rd.
Millerton, NY 12546
518-789-8700

Sports Sponsor FactBook

660 W. Grand Ave., Ste. 100E
Chicago, IL 60610
312-829-7060
For more information, please visit www.teammarketing.com.

Western Sports Guide

3984 Doniphan Dr.
El Paso, TX 79922
915-584-7791

Sport Sponsors

American Express Company
American Express Tower
C 3 World Financial Center
New York, NY 10285
212-640-1494
For more information, please visit www.americanexpress.com.

Anheuser-Busch Companies, Inc.
Sports Marketing Group/Bud Sports
One Soccer Park Rd.
Fenton, MO 63026
636-343-5347
For more information, please visit www.abconference.com.

Arthur Andersen LLP
33 W. Monroe
Chicago, IL 60603
312-580-0033
For more information, visit www.andersen.com.

BellSouth Corporation
1155 Peachtree St. N.E.
Atlanta, GA 30309-3610
404-249-2000
For more information, please visit www.bellsouth.com.

Benetton Sportsystem Active
997 Lenox Dr., Bldg. 3, Ste. 105
Lawrenceville, NJ 08648
609-896-3800

Blockbuster Entertainment Corp.
1 Blockbuster Plaza
Fort Lauderdale, FL 33301-1860
954-524-8200
For more information, visit www.blockbuster.com.

Carquest Auto Parts
2635 E. Millbrook Rd.
Raleigh, NC 27604
1-800-492-PART
For more information, please visit www.carquest.com.

Chase Manhattan Bank
One Chase Manhattan Plaza, 56th Fl.
New York, NY 10081
212-552-2818
For more information, please visit www.chase.com.

Coca-Cola Company, The
One Coca-Cola Plaza
Atlanta, GA 30313
404-676-2121
For more information, please visit www.cocacola.com.

Frito-Lay, Inc.
Subsidiary of PepsiCo, Inc.
7701 Legacy Dr.
Plano, TX 75024
972-334-7000
For more information, please visit www.fritolay.com.

Gillette Company
Prudential Tower Building
Boston, MA 02199
617-421-7000
For more information, visit www.gillette.com.

Goodyear Tire & Rubber Company, The
1144 E. Market St.
Akron, OH 44316-0001
330-796-2121
For more information, please visit www.goodyear.com.

Home Depot, Inc., The
2455 Paces Ferry Rd.
Atlanta, GA 30339
770-433-8211
For more information, please visit www.homedepot.com.

John Hancock Mutual Life Insurance Co.
1 John Hancock Way Suite 1000
Boston, MA 02217-1000
617-572-6000
For more information, visit www.jhfunds.com.

Kellogg Company
One Kellogg Square
Battle Creek, MI 49016
269-961-2000
For more information, please visit www.kelloggcompany.com.

Kraft USA/Oscar Mayer
3 Lakes Dr.
Northfield, IL 60093
847-646-2000
For more information, please visit www.kraft.com.

Lipton, Inc., Thomas J.
Subsidiary of Unilever United States, Inc.
800 Sylvan Ave.
Englewood Cliffs, NJ 07632
201-871-8217
For more information, visit www.lipton.com.

M&M/Mars
6865 Elm St.
McLean, VA 22101
703-821-4900
For more information, visit www.mars.com.

MasterCard International, Inc.
2000 Purchase St.
Purchase, NY 10577
914-249-2000
For more information, please visit www.mastercard.com.

Mercedes-Benz of North America, Inc.
One Mercedes Dr.
Montvale, NJ 07645
201-573-0600
For more information, visit www.mbusa.com.

Miller Brewing Company
Subsidiary of Philip Morris Cos., Inc.
3939 W. Highland Blvd.
Milwaukee, WI 53208
414-931-2000
For more information, please visit www.millerbrewing.com.

Motorola, Inc.
Corporate Advertising
1303 E. Algonquin Rd.
Schaumburg, IL 60196
847-576-5000
For more information, please visit www.motorola.com.

Ocean Spray Cranberries, Inc.
One Ocean Spray Dr.
Lakeville-Middleborough, MA 02349
508-946-1000
For more information, please visit www.ocean-spray.com.

Pennzoil Company
P.O. Box 2967
Houston, TX 77052-2967
713-546-4000
For more information, please visit www.penzoil.com.

Gatorade Brand
555 W Monroe St
P.O. Box 9004, Ste. 17-9
Chicago, IL 606661-3605
312-222-7111
For more information, please visit www.gatorade.com.

R.J. Reynolds Tobacco Company
Subsidiary of RJR/Nabisco, Inc.
401 N Main St
Winston-Salem, NC 27102
336-741-2000
For more information, visit www.reynoldsamerican.com.

Sara Lee Corporation
3 First National Plaza
Chicago, IL 60602-4260
312 726-2600
For more information, please visit www.saralee.com.

Shoprite
Subsidiary of Wakefern Food Corp.
Somers Manor, Ste. 202
599 Shore Rd.
Somers Point, NJ 08244
609-927-7888

3M Company
3M Center
St. Paul, MN 55144-1000
612-733-1110
For more information, visit www.mmm.com.

Time Warner Inc./Sports Illustrated
1271 Avenue of the Americas
New York, NY 10020
212-522-0684
For more information, please visit www.pathfinder.com.

Walt Disney World Company
1950 W. Magnolia Palm Dr.
Lake Buena Vista, FL 32830
407-824-2250
For more information, please visit www.disney.com.

Xerox Corporation
800 Long Ridge Rd.
Stamford, CT 06904
203-968-3000
For more information, please visit www.xerox.com.

Sport Sponsorship/Marketing/Event Agencies

Advantage Marketing Group
10030 N. McArthur Blvd 19
Irving, TX 75063-5001
972-869-2244

American Sports Marketing, Inc.
636 Meadowview Rd.
Bristol, TN 37620-9510
423-844-0232

Championship Group Inc.
1954 Airport Rd. St. 2000
Atlanta, GA 30341
770-457-5777
For more information, visit www.championshipgroup.com.

CMG Worldwide
10500 Crosspoint Blvd.
Indianapolis, IN 46256
317-570-5000
For more information, visit www.cmgworldwide.com.

Event Marketing & Management Intl.
1102 N. Mills Ave.
Orlando, FL 32803
407-896-1160

Executive Sports Management
1720 Mars Hill Rd. Suite 8 #321
Acworth, GA 30101
770-792-6676
For more information, visit www.executivesports.com.

Host Communications Inc.
546 E. Main St.
Lexington, KY 40508
859-226-4678
For more information, visit www.hostcommunications.com.

International Management Group/IMG
1360 E. 9th St. Suite 100
Cleveland, OH 44114
216-522-1200
For more information, visit www.imgworld.com.

PSP Sports Marketing
519 8th Ave. 25th Floor
New York, NY 10018
212-697-1460

Russ Cline and Associates
2310 W. 75th St.
Prairie Village, KS 66208
913-384-8920

Sports Entertainment Group
25 E. Willow St.
Millburn, NJ 07041
201-467-1001

Triple Crown Sports
3930 Automation Way
Fort Collins, CO 80525
970-223-6644

Professional Services

Sport Agents

Arthur Andersen & Co./Athlete Advisory Services
633 W. 5th St., 32nd Fl.
Los Angeles, CA 90071
213-614-6552

Falk Associates Management Enterprises/FAME
5335 Wisconsin Ave. NW, Ste. 850
Washington, DC 20015
202-686-2000

Golden Bear International
11780 U.S. Highway One
Palm Beach, FL 33408
561-227-0300

R.L.R. Associates, Ltd.
7 W. 51st St.
New York, NY 10019
212-541-8641

Executive Search Services

Sports Careers
Division of Stratford American Sports Corp.
2400 E. Arizona Biltmore Cir., Ste. 1270
Phoenix, AZ 85016
602-956-7809

TeamWork Consulting, Inc.
22550 McCauley Rd.
Shaker Heights, OH 44122
216-360-1790
For more information, visit www.teamworkconsulting.com.

Market Research Services

ESPN/CHILTON Sports Poll
Subsidiary of Capital Cities/ABC Inc.
201 King of Prussia Rd.
Radhor, PA 19089-0193
610-964-4285

Nielsen Co., A.C.
Subsidiary of Dun & Bradstreet
770 Broadway
New York, NY 10003
646-654-8300

Sponsorship Research International USA
Subsidiary of Sponsorship Research International UK
1281 E. Main St.
Stamford, CT 06902
203-975-4450

Sports Information Resource Centre
180 Elgin Street Suite 1400
Ottawa, Ontario
Canada
613-231-7472

Sporting Goods (Equipment, Apparel, and Footwear)

Adidas America
5055 N Greeley Ave.
Portland, OR 97217
503-230-2920
For more information, please visit www.adidas.com.

Brine, Inc.
47 Summer St.
Milford, MA 01757
508-478-3250
For more information, visit www.brine.com.

Callaway Golf
2180 Rutherford Rd.
Carlsbad, CA 92008
760-931-1771
For more information, visit www.callawaygolf.com.

Champion Products, Inc.
P.O. Box 1550
Winston-Salem, NC 27102
910-519-6500
For more information, visit www.championusa.com.

Danskin, Inc.
530 Seventh Ave.
New York, NY 10018
212-764-4630
For more information, visit www.danskin.com.

Fila USA, Inc.
1 Fila Way
Sparks, MD 21152
410-584-8196
For more information, visit www.fila.com.

New Balance Athletic Shoe, Inc.
61 N. Beacon St.
Boston, MA 02134
617-783-4000
For more information, please visit www.newbalance.com.

Nike, Inc.
One Bowerman Dr.
Beaverton, OR 97005
503-671-6453
For more information, please visit www.nike.com.

Precor, Inc.
20031 142nd Ave. NE
Woodinville, WA 98072-4002
425-486-9292
For more information, visit www.precor.com.

Rawlings Sporting Goods Co., Inc.
510 Maryville University Dr. Suite 110
St. Louis, MO 63141
314-349-2800
For more information, visit www.rawlings.com.

Reebok International Ltd.
1895 J.W. Foster Blvd.
Canton, MA 02021
781-401-5000
For more information, please visit www.reebok.com.

Russell Athletic
3330 Cumberland Blvd. Suite 800
Atlanta, GA 30339
678-742-8000
For more information, visit www.russellcorp.com.

Spalding Sports Worldwide
1500 Brookdale Dr.
Springfield, MA 01104
1-800-SPALDING
For more information, please visit www.spalding.com.

Titleist and Foot-Joy Worldwide
333 Bridge Street
Fair Haven, MA 02719
508-979-2000
For more information, visit www.titleist.com.

Houston Rockets Premium Items Survey

1. Please rank the following Rockets premium items on a scale of 1 to 11, 1 being the item you would most like to receive at a Rockets game and 11 being the item you would least like to receive at a Rockets game.

   _____Yao Ming Growth Chart

   _____Moochie Norris CelebriDuck with life-like hair

   _____Rudy T. Taling Bobblehead Doll

   _____Yao Ming CelebriDuck

   _____Hardwood Classic Rockets green and gold T-shirt

   _____"Be Part of Something Big" Rockets commemorative T-shirt

   _____Eddie Griffin water bottle with headband

   _____Rockets Power Dancer Calendar

   _____Calvin Murphy Bobblehead Doll with changeable clothes

   _____Rockets Trading Card Set

   _____Commemorative Ticket Key Chain

2. Which Rockets player/staff member would you like to see on future premium items? (Select all that apply)

_____Cuttino Mobley	_____Glen Rice	___ Rudy Tomjanivich
_____Moochie Norris	_____Jason Collier	___ Bill Worrell
_____Steve Francis	_____Tito Maddox	___ Calvin Murphy
_____Yao Ming	_____Bostjan Nachbar	___ Clutch
_____Eddie Griffin	_____Terence Morris	___ Turbo
_____James Posey	_____Maurice Taylor	___ Big Bank Drummers
_____Kelvin Cato	_____Juaquin Hawkins	___ Other (please specify): _____

3. Which of the following is the most important factor in determining how much you like a particular premium item? (select only ONE answer)

   _____Player/staff member featured on item (e.g., Francis, Rudy T., Yao, etc.)

   _____Type of premium item (e.g., bobblehead dolls, CelebriDucks, water bottles, etc.)

   _____Special features associated with the item (e.g., life-like hair, headband, exchangeable clothes, etc.)

   _____Other (please specify):_____

4. Please give us any suggestions for premium items you would like to see the Rockets give away in the future.

   _____

   _____

   _____

5. Which of the following describes your level of affiliation with the Rockets?

_____Rockets full-season ticket holder	___ Rockets mini-package holder
_____Rockets half-season ticket holder	___ Individual game ticket purchaser

6. What area of the Compaq Center do you *usually* sit in when attending Rockets games? (select only ONE answer)

_____Upper level corners/behind basket	___ Lower level corners/behind basket
_____Upper level facing the court	___ Lower level facing the court

FOR CLASSIFICATION PURPOSES ONLY–will NOT be resold or distributed

7. **Gender:** _____ Male _____Female

8. **Age:**

   _____17 and under   _____35-44

   _____18-24   _____45-54

   _____25-34   _____55+

9. **To measure the diversity of our attendees, please identify your ethnic background.**

   _____Hispanic   _____African American   ____ Native American

   _____Caucasian   _____Asian/Pacific Islander ____ Other _____

10. **Marital Status:**

    _____Married   _____Divorced/Separated

    _____Single   _____Widowed

11. **How many children under the age of 18 (including yourself if you are under 18 years of age) live in your household?**

    _____0   _____3   _____ more than 5 (please specify: _____)

    _____1   _____4

    _____2   _____5

12. **What is your annual household income (before taxes)?**

    _____Less than $25,000   _____$75,000-$99,999

    _____$25,000-$49,999   _____$100,000-$149,999

    _____$50,000-$74,999   _____$150,000 or more

THANK YOU FOR YOUR TIME AND PARTICIPATION!

Win a Rockets Team Autographed Basketball!

As a token of our appreciation for taking the time to fill out this survey, we would like to offer you a chance to win a basketball autographed by the entire 2002-2003 Houston Rockets team. Simply fill out the entry form below and hand it back along with the completed survey to the designated Rockets survey distributors.

First Name: _____   Last Name: _____

Address: _____

City: _____   State: _____   Zip: _____

Phone: (_____) _____   Date of Birth: _____

Email Address: _____

❏ Please email exclusive Rockets offers and promotions

❏ Please email me selected offers and promotions from Rockets partners

Preferred email format: _____Text _____ HTML

For complete rules, please refer to the Official Rules at the survey table

Courtesy of the Houston Rockets

Houston Rockets Rocket.com Internet Survey

The Houston Rockets want to know what you think about Rockets.com. Please take a few moments to complete the following survey. Read every question carefully and answer honestly. Your feedback and suggestions are important to us and will be used to improve rockets.com.

By completely filling out the survey *and* the sweepstakes entry form at the end of the survey, you will be registered for a chance to win a **basketball autographed by the 2002-2003 Houston Rockets team including Yao Ming, Steve Francis, Rudy T, and the rest of this year's squad.**

Please note: The Rockets organization holds your privacy with the utmost respect and the information you provide us within the following survey will **NOT** be resold or distributed outside of the organization.

Thank you for your time and participation!

1. **How often do you visit Rockets.com?**

   _____More than once a day   _____A few times a month
   _____Daily   _____This is your first time on the site
   _____More than once a week

2. **Which one of the following is the main reason you visit Rockets.com?**

   _____Best source of Rockets information
   _____Exclusive Rockets features
   _____Visually appealing and easy to navigate
   _____Information about Rockets promotions and events
   _____Rockets ticket information

3. **Please rank your interest in the following features offered by Rockets.com. (1 being not at all interested, 5 being very interested and 0 if you are not aware of the feature).** [buttons corresponding with each of the numbers given below]

Not Aware	Not at all Interested				Very Interested
0	1	2	3	4	5

   _____ a. Current News
   _____ b. Feature Stories
   _____ c. Game Reports
   _____ d. Video Highlights/Interviews
   _____ e. Entertainers Sections (Power Dancers/Clutch/Turbo)
   _____ f. Rockets Fan Poll
   _____ g. Photo Galleries
   _____ h. Rockets History
   _____ i. Online Contests (i.e., Rockets Three Point Play)
   _____ j. Wallpaper

4. **When looking for specific information on Rockets.com, do you find what you are looking for?**

   _____Always
   _____Almost always
   _____Sometimes
   _____Rarely
   _____Never

5. When visiting Rockets.com, do you typically:

_____Always find something interesting with little or no trouble

_____Have to look around the web site for something interesting before finding it

_____Have a difficult time finding something interesting

_____Cannot find anything interesting

6. What additional features would you like to see on rockets.com?

_____

_____

_____

7. How often do you utilize Rockets.com video features?

_____Everytime I log on   _____Rarely when I log on

_____Most of the time I log on   _____I never use Rockets.com video features

_____Some of the time I log on

8. If you do not use any video features, which of the following reasons best represents why you don't utilize the video features?

_____Unaware of them   _____ Computer system won't allow me to view them

_____Don't like the content   _____ Get the same information from other sources

_____Modem connection is too slow   _____ Does not apply—I use all of the video applications

9. Please rate the quality of the video features you use on Rockets.com.

_____Excellent   _____ Poor

_____Good   _____ Do not use video features on Rockets.com

_____Fair

10. How would you rate Rockets.com compared to other sports sites that you visit?

_____Better   _____ A little worse

_____A little better   _____ Worse

_____About the same

11. How many Rockets games did you watch on TV this season?

_____0   _____ 6-10   _____ 16-20

_____1-5   _____ 10-15   _____20 or more

12. How many Rockets games did you attend this season?

_____0   _____ 4-6   _____ 10-20

_____1-3   _____ 7-9   _____ 21 or more

FOR CLASSIFICATION PURPOSES ONLY—will NOT be resold or distributed

13. Gender: _____ Male   _____Female

14. Age:

_____17 and under   _____35-44

_____18-24   _____45-54

_____25-34   _____55+

15. **To measure the diversity of our attendees, please identify your ethnic background.**

_____Hispanic   _____African American   _____ Native American

_____Caucasian   _____Asian/Pacific Islander   _____ Other _____

16. **Marital Status:**

_____Married   _____Divorced/Separated

_____Single   _____Widowed

17. **How many children under the age of 18 (including yourself if you are under 18 years of age) live in your household?**

_____0   _____3   _____ more than 5 (please specify:_____)

_____1   _____4

_____2   _____5

18. **What is the highest level of education you have completed?**

_____Some high school   _____Some college

_____High school or equivalent   _____Bachelor's degree

_____Associate's degree   _____Postgraduate degree

19. **What is your annual household income (before taxes)?**

_____Less than $25,000   _____$75,000-$99,999

_____$25,000-$49,999   _____$100,000-$149,999

_____$50,000-$74,999   _____$150,000 or more

20. **Please give us any comments or suggestions you might have about how we can improve Rockets.com.**

_____

_____

_____

THANK YOU FOR YOUR TIME AND PARTICIPATION!

Win a Rockets Team Autographed Basketball!

As a token of our appreciation for taking the time to fill out this survey, we would like to offer you a chance to win a basketball autographed by the entire 2002-2003 Houston Rockets team. Simply fill out the entry form below and hand it back along with the completed survey to the designated Rockets survey distributors.

First Name: _____   Last Name: _____

Address: _____

City: _____   State: _____   Zip: _____

Phone: (_____) _____   Date of Birth:_____

Email Address: _____

❏ Please email exclusive Rockets offers and promotions

❏ Please email me selected offers and promotions from Rockets partners

Preferred email format: _____Text _____ HTML

For complete rules, please refer to the enclosed Official rules

Houston Rockets Rocket.com Internet Survey

The Houston Rockets want to know what you think about our current in-arena food and beverage services as well as get your feedback on potential offerings for the new arena. Please take a few moments to complete the following survey. Read every question carefully and answer honestly. Your feedback and suggestions are important to us and will be used as we plan our concession services for the new arena.

As a bit of background information regarding the new facility, we are planning a high-end restaurant and wine bar that will be open to the public on a suite level in the new arena. This restaurant will feature gourmet-style food and have a vast selection of wines and liquors. We are also considering adding a restaurant/bar that will be open to the public and will overlook the court on the upper level of the new arena. Your feedback in this survey will help us work out the details as to what kind of amenities a restaurant/bar on the upper level would feature should we choose to construct one in the new arena.

As a token of our appreciation for taking a few moments to fill out this survey, we are giving you a chance to win a Compaq Center luxury suite for yourself and fourteen of your friends for a 2002-2003 Rockets home game. After completing the survey, fill out the entry form and send it, as well as the completed survey, back to us in the provided self addressed envelope.

Thank you for your time and participation!

Please note: The Rockets organization holds your privacy with the utmost respect and the information you provide us within the following survey will **NOT** be resold or distributed outside of the organization.

1. **What area of the Compaq Center do you typically sit in when you attend Rockets games?**
   _____Upper bowl
   _____Lower bowl behind the baskets
   _____Lower bowl between the endlines

2. **How many Rockets games did you attend last season?**

_____1-4	_____15-19
_____5-9	_____20+
_____10-14	

3. **When you attended Rockets games last season, which of the following best describes your food and beverage purchasing behavior?**
   _____I purchased food/drinks at every Rockets game I attended
   _____I purchased food/drinks at most of the Rockets games I attended
   _____I purchased food/drinks at a few of the Rockets games I attended
   _____I did not purchase food/drinks at any Rockets games I attended **(skip to Question14)**

4. **Which of the following items did you purchase at Rockets games last season? (select all that apply)**

_____Soft Drinks	_____ French Fries	_____ Nachos	_____ BBQ
_____Beer	_____ Hamburgers	_____ Mexican Food	_____ Sausages
_____Wine	_____ Chicken Products	_____ Baked Potato	_____ Italian
_____Cocktails	_____ Seafood	_____ Sandwich	
_____Candy	_____ Popcorn	_____ Ice Cream/Yogurt	
_____Pizza	_____ Hot Dog	_____ Pretzel	

5. **Compared to other entertainment venues (i.e., other sporting events, concerts, amusement parks, etc.) that you have attended, would you say the prices for food and drinks at the Compaq Center are:**

_____More expensive	_____ Less expensive
_____About the same price	_____ Don't know

Please rank your satisfaction with the food and drink offerings at Rockets games (7 beng very satisfied, 1 being not satisfied, and 0 if the question does not pertain to you)

	Not Satisfied						Very Satisfied	Not Applicable
6. Selection of food	1	2	3	4	5	6	7	0
7. Quality of food	1	2	3	4	5	6	7	0
8. Portion of food	1	2	3	4	5	6	7	0
9. Price of food	1	2	3	4	5	6	7	0
10. Selection of alcoholic beverages	1	2	3	4	5	6	7	0
11. Price of alcoholic beverages	1	2	3	4	5	6	7	0
12. Amount of time waiting in line	1	2	3	4	5	6	7	0
13. Service of concession staff	1	2	3	4	5	6	7	0

14. Which of the following best describes your usual activity *before* Rockets games?

_____I come to Rockets games directly from work

_____I go out to a restaurant/bar before Rockets games

_____I come to Rockets games from home

_____Other (Please specify): _____

15. Which of the following best describes your usual activity *after* Rockets games?

_____I go out to bars after Rockets games

_____I go to restaurants and eat after Rockets games

_____I go home after Rockets games

_____Other (Please specify): _____

16. Which of the following alcoholic beverages would you most likely purchase at the new arena? (Select all that apply)

_____Wine   _____ Import Beer

_____Mixed Drinks   _____ Would not purchase alcoholic beverages

_____Domestic Beer

17. How interested would you be in visiting a bar/restaurant that overlooks the basketball court in the upper bowl of the new arena *before* a Rockets game?

_____Very interested   _____ Somewhat uninterested

_____Somewhat interested   _____ Not at all interested

18. How interested would you be in visiting a bar/restaurant that overlooks the basketball court in the upper bowl of the new arena *during* a Rockets game?

_____Very interested   _____ Somewhat uninterested

_____Somewhat interested   _____ Not at all interested

19. How interested would you be in visiting a bar/restaurant that overlooks the basketball court in the upper bowl of the new arena *after* a Rockets game?

_____Very interested   _____ Somewhat uninterested

_____Somewhat interested   _____ Not at all interested

20. When would you be most likely to visit a bar/restaurant that overlooks the court in the upper bowl of the new arena?

_____Before a Rockets game   _____ After a Rockets game
_____During a Rockets game   _____ Not likely to visit at all

21. Which of the following foods would you most likely purchase at a bar/restaurant that overlooks the court in the new arena?

_____Gourmet/Specialty Foods
_____Brewpub-Type Food (burgers, chicken sandwiches, wings)
_____Deli Food (sandwiches, salads, sides)
_____Italian Food (pastas, pizzas)
_____Mexican Food (burritos, tacos)
_____Chinese Food (egg rolls, orange chicken, beef and broccoli)
_____Would not purchase any food items

22. Which of the following best describes a bar/restaurant in the upper bowl that you would be most likely to visit?

_____A lounge with chairs and couches, dim lighting
_____A sports bar with interactive sports games
_____A wine bar with a vast selection of wines/liquors
_____Other (Please specify): _____

FOR CLASSIFICATION PURPOSES ONLY—will NOT be resold or distributed

23. Gender: _____ Male   _____Female

24. Age:

_____17 and under   _____35-44
_____18-24   _____45-54
_____25-34   _____55+

25. To measure the diversity of our attendees, please identify your ethnic background.

_____Hispanic   _____African American   _____ Native American
_____Caucasian   _____Asian/Pacific Islander _____ Other _____

26. Marital Status:

_____Married   _____Divorced/Separated
_____Single   _____Widowed

27. How many children under the age of 18 (including yourself if you are under 18 years of age) live in your household?

_____0   _____3   _____ more than 5 (please specify: _____)
_____1   _____4
_____2   _____5

28. What is the highest level of education you have completed?

_____Some high school   _____Some college
_____High school or equivalent _____Bachelor's degree
_____Associate's degree   _____Postgraduate degree

29. **What is your annual household income (before taxes)?**

    ____Less than $25,000   ____$75,000-$99,999

    ____$25,000-$49,999   ____$100,000-$149,999

    ____$50,000-$74,999   ____$150,000 or more

30. **Please give us one suggestion on how you would improve the current food and beverage service at the Compaq Center.**

31. **If you were the owner of the new arena, what is the one thing you would do with the food and beverage services?**

THANK YOU FOR YOUR TIME AND PARTICIPATION!

Win a Luxury Suite for a Rockets Home Game!

As a token of our appreciation for taking the time to fill out this survey, we would like to offer you a chance to win a Compaq Center luxury suite for a 2002-2003 Rockets home game. Simply fill out the entry form below and send it back in the enclosed prepaid addressed envelope with the completed survey. This is what's included:

- ◆ The use of one luxury suite for a 2002-2003 Rocket home game
- ◆ Fifteen (15) luxury suite tickets
- ◆ Food and beverages provided in the suite

First Name: _____ Last Name: _____

Address: _____

City: _____ State: _____ Zip: _____

Phone: (_____) _____ Date of Birth: _____

Email Address: _____

❏ Please email exclusive Rockets offers and promotions

❏ Please email me selected offers and promotions from Rockets partners

Preferred email format: _____Text _____ HTML

For complete rules, please refer to the enclosed Official rules

Courtesy of the Houston Rockets

2002-2003 Houston Rockets Group Leader Survey

How many groups did you organize this Rockets Season?

_____1   _____3

_____2   _____ 4 or more

How many people were in the group(s) that you organize? (If you organize more than one group this season, please give the number of people for each group)

_____

Which of the following best describes your history as a Rockets group leader?

_____This is my first year organizing groups

_____I've organized groups to Rockets games for the last two seasons

_____I've organized groups to Rockets games for the last three seasons

_____I've organized groups to Rockets games for five or more seasons

Which of the following areas of the arena does your group(s) typically sit in at Rockets games? (If you organize more than one group this season, select the **ONE** area that best fits with most of your groups that you organized)

_____Lower bowl behind the baskets

_____Upper bowl behind the baskets

_____Upper bowl facing the court (behind/in front of the players benches)

Were you aware that it is possible to set up an online ordering page for your group?

_____Yes   _____No (skip to question _____)

If you purchased your group tickets online, how would you rate your online ticket-purchasing experience?

_____Excellent   _____Fair

_____Very Good   _____Poor

_____Average   _____Did not purchase any group tickets online

Please rate the following items pertaining to your group leader experience this season. Using a 1 to 10 scale, where 1 is *Unacceptable*, 10 is *Outstanding*, and 5 is *Average*, please rate the following: (circle one number for each line)

	Unacceptable				Average				Outstanding	
Customer service received from group account representative	1	2	3	4	5	6	7	8	9	10
Group recognition (i.e., PA announcement, floor recognition, scoreboard recognition)	1	2	3	4	5	6	7	8	9	10
Group discount ticket pricing	1	2	3	4	5	6	7	8	9	10
Group seating	1	2	3	4	5	6	7	8	9	10

Please rate your **OVERALL** experience this season as a Rockets group leader. Using a 1 to 10 scale, where 1 is *Unacceptable*, 10 is *Outstanding*, and 5 is *Average*.

Unacceptable				Average				Outstanding	
1	2	3	4	5	6	7	8	9	10

Given your experience this year as a Rockets group leader, how likely are you to organize a group next season?

_____ I definitely will organize another group

_____ I probably will organize another group

_____ I am not sure whether I will organize another group

_____ I probably will *not* organize another group

_____ I definitely will *not* organize another group

Please rate your interest in having the option to add on additional items (such as food and/or merchandise packages) for an additional cost with the purchase of your group tickets.

_____ Very interested   _____ Somewhat uninterested

_____ Somewhat interested   _____ Not at all interested

FOR CLASSIFICATION PURPOSES ONLY—will NOT be resold or distributed

Gender: _____ Male   _____ Female

Age:

_____ 17 and under   _____ 35-44

_____ 18-24   _____ 45-54

_____ 25-34   _____ 55+

To measure the diversity of our attendees, please identify your ethnic background.

_____ Hispanic   _____ African American   _____ Native American

_____ Caucasian   _____ Asian/Pacific Islander   _____ Other _____

Marital Status:

_____ Married   _____ Partner/Unmarried couple living together

_____ Single   _____ Divorced/Separated/Widowed

How many children under the age of 18 (including yourself if you are under 18 years of age) live in your household?

_____ 0   _____ 3   _____ more than 5 (please specify: _____)

_____ 1   _____ 4

_____ 2   _____ 5

What is the highest level of education you have completed?

_____ Some high school   _____ Some college

_____ High school or equivalent   _____ Bachelor's degree

_____ Associate's degree   _____ Postgraduate degree

What is your annual household income (before taxes)?

_____ Less than $25,000   _____ $75,000-$99,999

_____ $25,000-$49,999   _____ $100,000-$149,999

_____ $50,000-$74,999   _____ $150,000 or more

Please give us any suggestions you have on how we can improve your group leader experience in the future.

_____

_____

_____

_____

Houston Rockets In-Game Experience Survey

The Houston Rockets want to know what you think about our current game entertainment features. Please take a few moments to complete the following survey. Read every question carefully and answer honestly. Your feedback and suggestions are important to us and will be used as we plan our future in-game entertainment.

As a token of our appreciation for taking a few moments to fill out this survey, we are giving you a chance to win a 2002-2003 Rockets team autographed basketball and one of ten Rockets T-shirts. After completing the survey, fill out the entry form and hand them back to a designated Rockets survey distributor.

Thank you for your time and participation!

Please note: The Rockets organization holds your privacy with the utmost respect and the information you provide us within the following survey will **NOT** be resold or distributed outside of the organization.

1. How many Rockets games have you attended so far this season?

   _____1-4   _____ 13-16
   _____5-8   _____ 17-20
   _____9-12   _____ 20+

2. How many total Rockets games do you plan on attending this season?

   _____1-4   _____ 13-16
   _____5-8   _____ 17-20
   _____9-12   _____ 20+

3. Which of the following describes your level of affiliation with the Rockets?

   _____Rockets full-season ticket holder   _____Rockets mini-package holder
   _____Rockets half-season ticket holder   _____Individual game ticket purchaser

4. How would you describe the volume of music in the area?

   _____Too loud—turn it down
   _____Just the right volume
   _____Too soft—can't hear anything

Please tell us about your entertainment experience at today's game. Using a 1 to 7 scale where 1 is *Unacceptable*, 7 is *Outstanding*, and 4 is *Average*, please rate the following: (Select *one* number for each item)

	Unacceptable			Average			Outstanding
5. Pregame player introductions	1	2	3	4	5	6	7
6. Halftime entertainment	1	2	3	4	5	6	7
7. Big Bang Drummers	1	2	3	4	5	6	7
8. Clutch	1	2	3	4	5	6	7
9. Air Clutch	1	2	3	4	5	6	7
10. Turbo	1	2	3	4	5	6	7
11. Rockets Power Dancers	1	2	3	4	5	6	7
12. Game Announcer	1	2	3	4	5	6	7
13. Game Sound Effects	1	2	3	4	5	6	7

14. How would you describe the content of videos played on the video board (i.e., game clips, replays, etc.)?

    _____Excellent   _____ Fair
    _____Good   _____ Poor
    _____Average

15. Please select your favorite element of our in-game entertainment features. (Select only *one*)

_____ Big Bang Drummers   _____ Turbo
_____ Clutch   _____ Air Clutch
_____ Rockets Power Dancers

16. Without taking the game itself into consideration, how would you rate your OVERALL in-arena experience at today's game? (Select *one* number)

Unacceptable				Average			Outstanding
0	1	2	3	4	5	6	7

17. Please select the kind of music that you would most like to hear played at Rockets games. (Select only *one*)

_____ Rap   _____ Classic Rock   _____ Oldies
_____ Rock   _____ Pop   _____ R&B
_____ Alternative _____ Country

18. Which of the following best describes your usual activity before Rockets games?

_____ I come to Rockets games directly from work
_____ I go out to a restaurant/bar before Rockets games
_____ I come to Rockets games from home
_____ Other (Please specify): _____

19. Given your activities before Rockets games, which one of the following night game tip-off times works best with your schedule?

_____ 7:00 p.m.   _____ 7:30 p.m.

FOR CLASSIFICATION PURPOSES ONLY—will NOT be resold or distributed

20. Gender: _____ Male   _____ Female

21. Age:

_____ 17 and under   _____ 35-44
_____ 18-24   _____ 45-54
_____ 25-34   _____ 55+

22. To measure the diversity of our attendees, please identify your ethnic background.

_____ Hispanic   _____ African American   _____ Native American
_____ Caucasian   _____ Asian/Pacific Islander   _____ Other _____

23. Marital Status:

_____ Married   _____ Divorced/Separated
_____ Single   _____ Widowed

24. How many children under the age of 18 (including yourself if you are under 18 years of age) live in your household?

_____ 0   _____ 3   _____ more than 5 (please specify: _____)
_____ 1   _____ 4
_____ 2   _____ 5

25. **What is the highest level of education you have completed?**

    _____Some high school   _____Some college

    _____High school or equivalent   _____Bachelor's degree

    _____Associate's degree   _____Postgraduate degree

26. **What is your annual household income (before taxes)?**

    _____Less than $25,000   _____$75,000-$99,999

    _____$25,000-$49,999   _____$100,000-$149,999

    _____$50,000-$74,999   _____$150,000 or more

27. **Please give us any suggestions you have that would help us improve our in-game entertainment features.**

THANK YOU FOR YOUR TIME AND PARTICIPATION!

Win a Rockets Team Autographed Basketball!

As a token of our appreciation for taking the time to fill out this survey, we would like to offer you a chance to win a basketball autographed by the entire 2002-2003 Houston Rockets team and one of ten Houston Rockets T-shirts. Simply fill out the entry form below and hand it back along with the completed survey to the designated Rockets survey distributors.

First Name: _____ Last Name: _____

Address: _____

City: _____ State: _____ Zip: _____

Phone: (_____) _____ Date of Birth: _____

Email Address: _____

❏ Please email exclusive Rockets offers and promotions

❏ Please email me selected offers and promotions from Rockets partners

Preferred email format: _____Text _____ HTML

For complete rules, please refer to the Official rules at the survey table

2002-2003 Houston Rockets Season-Ticket Holder Survey

As a Rockets season-ticket holder, your support and opinions are very important to us. In a continuous effort to improve the quality of customer service you receive, we want to hear your ideas about how we can better serve you.

Please take a few minutes to complete the following customer service questionnaire and return it in the postage-paid envelope provided. If you like, you may also return it via fax at 713-513-8396 Attn: Aaron Bryan.

As a token of our appreciation for taking a few moments to fill out this survey, we are offering you a chance to win an **autographed Yao Ming Rockets jersey**. After completing the survey, fill out the entry form and send it, as well as the completed survey, back to us in the provided self-addressed envelope (Houston Rockets Season-Ticket Holder Survey, Two Greenway Plaza, Suite 400, Houston, TX 77046). *Envelopes must be postmarked by May 16, 2003, in order to be entered into the drawing.*

Thank you for your time and participation!

Please note: The Rockets organization holds your privacy with the utmost respect and the information you provide us within the following survey will **NOT** be resold or distributed outside of the organization.

1. **In what section are your season tickets located?** _____

2. **How many Rockets games did you attend this season?** _____ home games

3. **Who do you most often attend Rockets games with?** (Select ALL that apply)

   _____ Spouse/partner   _____ My son(s) age(s) _____

   _____ Friends   _____ My daughter(s) age(s) _____

   _____ Clients/Coworkers   _____ Alone

4. **From where do you most often travel when you attend Rockets games?** (Select ONE per line)

	Work	Home	Restaurant/Bar
On weeknights?	_____	_____	_____
On weekends?	_____	_____	_____

5. **How are your season tickets purchased?**

   _____ By a business/company/organization   _____ By a family member

   _____ By me personally   _____ I split my ticket package (with friends or family)

6. **Do you or your company own season tickets or ticket plans for any of the following?** (Select ALL that apply)

   _____ Houston Texans   _____ UH Football   _____ Cynthia Woods Mitchell Pavilion

   _____ Houston Astros   _____ UH Basketball   _____ Houston Symphony

   _____ Houston Aeros   _____ Rice Football   _____ Other _____

   _____ Houston Comets   _____ Rice Basketball

7. **How many of the 81 televised Rockets games do you typically watch in a season?**

   _____ games

8. Please tell us about your game experience this season. Using a 1 to 10 scale, where 1 is *Unacceptable*, 10 is *Outstanding*, and 5 is *Average*, please rate the following: (Circle one number for each line)

	Unacceptable				Average					Outstanding
a. Cleanliness of arena in general	1	2	3	4	5	6	7	8	9	10
b. Availability of ushers to assist you	1	2	3	4	5	6	7	8	9	10
c. Helpfulness of ushers	1	2	3	4	5	6	7	8	9	10
d. Safe and family friendly environment	1	2	3	4	5	6	7	8	9	10
e. Cleanliness of restrooms	1	2	3	4	5	6	7	8	9	10
f. Attitude/Behavior of fans around you	1	2	3	4	5	6	7	8	9	10
g. Quality/Variety of music	1	2	3	4	5	6	7	8	9	10
h. Quality/Variety of video board content	1	2	3	4	5	6	7	8	9	10
i. On-court contests	1	2	3	4	5	6	7	8	9	10
j. Halftime entertainment	1	2	3	4	5	6	7	8	9	10
k. Game announcer	1	2	3	4	5	6	7	8	9	10
l. Clutch Rockets Mascot	1	2	3	4	5	6	7	8	9	10
m. Rockets Power Dancers	1	2	3	4	5	6	7	8	9	10
n. Big Bang Drummers	1	2	3	4	5	6	7	8	9	10

9. Please rate your OVERALL game experience this season. Using a 1 to 10 scale, where 1 is *Unacceptable*, 10 is *Outstanding*, and 5 is *Average*

Unacceptable				Average				Outstanding	
1	2	3	4	5	6	7	8	9	10

10. Please rate your overall VALUE received based on price paid for tickets this season. Using a 1 to 10 scale, where 1 is *Unacceptable*, 10 is *Outstanding*, and 5 is *Average*

Unacceptable				Average				Outstanding	
1	2	3	4	5	6	7	8	9	10

11. How likely are you to renew your Rockets season tickets?

_____Definitely will   _____ Probably will not
_____Probably will   _____ Definitely will not
_____Do not know yet

12. If you marked anything except "Definitely will," what do we need to do to earn your business in 2003-2004?

_____

_____

_____

_____

13. **From where do you most often travel when you attend Rockets games?** (Select ONE per line)

	1:00 p.m.	3:00 p.m.	7:00 p.m.	7:30 p.m.
On weeknights?	____	____	____	____
On Saturdays?	____	____	____	____
On Sundays?	____	____	____	____

14. **The Houston Rockets have sponsorship relationships with various companies. From the following list, which companies do you recognize as sponsors of the Rockets?** (Select ALL that apply)

____Administaff   ____Chevrolet   ____HP   ____Reliant

____AIM   ____Cingular Wireless   ____Jiffy Lube   ____Southwest Airlines

____Allstate   ____Compass Bank   ____Kim Son   ____State Farm

____American Express   ____Continental Airlines   ____MBNA   ____24 Hour Fitness

____Anheuser-Busch   ____Ford   ____Miller Lite   ____Visa

____Bally Fitness   ____Gallery Furniture   ____P.F. Chang's   ____Yanjing

____Brake Check   ____Gatorade   ____PowerAde

FOR CLASSIFICATION PURPOSES ONLY—will NOT be resold or distributed

15. **Gender:**   ____ Male   ____Female

16. **Age:**

____17 and under   ____35-44

____18-24   ____45-54

____25-34   ____55+

17. **To measure the diversity of our attendees, please identify your ethnic background.**

____Hispanic   ____African American   ____ Native American

____Caucasian   ____Asian/Pacific Islander   ____ Other _____

18. **Marital Status:**

____Married   ____Partner/Unmarried couple living together

____Single   ____Divorced/Separated/Widowed

19. **How many children under the age of 18 (including yourself if you are under 18 years of age) live in your household?**

____0   ____3   ____more than 5 (please specify:____)

____1   ____4

____2   ____5

20. **What is the highest level of education you have completed?**

____Some high school   ____Some college

____High school or equivalent   ____Bachelor's degree

____Associate's degree   ____Postgraduate degree

21. **What is your annual household income (before taxes)?**

____Less than $25,000   ____$75,000-$99,999

____$25,000-$49,999   ____$100,000-$149,999

____$50,000-$74,999   ____$150,000 or more

22. Please give us any comments or suggestions on how we can improve your experience as a Rockets full season ticket holder.

_____

_____

_____

_____

THANK YOU FOR YOUR TIME AND PARTICIPATION!

Win an Autographed Yao Ming Rockets Jersey!

As a token of our appreciation for taking the time to fill out this survey, we would like to offer you a chance to win an autographed Yao Ming Rockets Jersey. Simply fill out the entry form below and send it back in the postage-paid envelope, along with the completed survey.

First Name: _____ Last Name: _____

Address: _____

City: _____ State: _____ Zip: _____

Phone: (_____) _____ Date of Birth: _____

Email Address: _____

❏ Please email exclusive Rockets offers and promotions

❏ Please email me selected offers and promotions from Rockets partners

Preferred email format: _____ Text _____ HTML

For complete rules, please refer to the enclosed Official Rules

Courtesy of the Houston Rockets

Endnotes

Chapter 1

1. Dream team quotes in www.nba.com/history/dreamT_moments.html. For the NBA's golden decade, see David Higdon, "Basketball Goes Global," *US Air Magazine*, May 1996, 48-51, 68, 70; Marc Gunther, "They All Want to Be Like Mike," *Fortune*, 21 July 1997, 51-53; Steve Rushin, "World Domination," *Sports Illustrated* (hereafter cited as *SI*), 27 October 1997, 68-71. For an outstanding monograph on this expansion, see Walter LaFeber, *Michael Jordan and the New Global Capitalism* (New York: Norton, 1999).

2. Jack McCallum, "Third World," *SI*, 6 September 2004, 47.

3. Len Elmore, "Dream Team Yields a Sporting Nightmare," *Street & Smith's SportsBusiness Journal* (hereafter cited as *SSSBJ*), 6-12 September, 2004, 49; Oscar Robertson, "NBA Markets Style at Expense of Substance, *New York Times Sunday*, 15 February 2004, S-9.

4. M. Swift, "From Corned Beef to Caviar," *SI*, 3 June 1991, 75-89, quote on 80.

5. Ibid., 83.

6. Jeff Coplon, "The People's Game," *NY Times Magazine*, 23 November 2003, 73-77.

7. L. Jon Wertheim, "The Whole World Is Watching," *SI*, 14 June 2004, 72-85; John Lombardo, "Game Plan Calls for Growth Overseas," *SSSBJ*, 27 October-2 November 2003, 25; John Lombardo, "Stellar Rookies Help Lead NBA to Heights It Hasn't Reached Since Jordan Left," *SSSBJ*, 19-25 April 2004, 36; John Lombardo, "Global Trade: NBA Imports Talent and Exports the Game," *SSSBJ*, 25-31 October 2004, 21-25; Jack McCallum, "Wake-Up Call," *SI*, 27 June 2005; Johnny Ludden, "Argentina in Love With Its Hoop Star," *Globe and Mail*, 7 July 2005.

8. "World Cup Viewed by 1.5 Billion," NYTimes.com, 30 July 2002; Associated Press, "World Cup Boosts Soccer Market in U.S.," NYTimes.com, 19 August 2004.

9. "Globalisation Shakes Up Japanese Baseball," *The Economist*, 11 September 2004, 58; "Passion, Pride, and Profit: A Survey of Football," *The Economist*, 1 June 2002, 6, 9, 12.

10. "The Gauntlet of Global Competition," AFP, 31 August 2004, www.channelnewsasia.com/stories/afp_sports/view/104044/1/.html.

11. Daniel Kaplan, "Is Sports Business Recession-Proof?" *SSSBJ*, 19-25 October 1998, 37; LaFeber, *Michael Jordan and the New Global Capitalism*, 22; Marcy Lamm, "Sports' Grip on Public Slips in Poll," *SSSBJ*, 31 January-6 February 2000, 47.

12. Bill King, "Passion That Can't Be Counted Puts Billions of Dollars in Play," *SSSBJ*, 11-17 March 2002, 32.

13. Bill King and Noah Liberman, "Dot.Com Busts Executives Left With Only Memories, Not Millions," *SSSBJ*, 26 July-1 August 2004, 15-19.

14. Daniel Kaplan, "ISL Slams Its ATP Deal Into Reverse," *SSSBJ*, 19-25 February 2001, 1, 44.

15. "Sponsorships on the Decline in Current Economic Slowdown," *Sports Business Daily* (hereafter cited as *SBD*), 14 August 2001, 5.

16. Dan Bickley, "Pro Sports May Be Pricing Fans Out of Stadiums," *Arizona Republic*, 24 June 2001; Gil Fried, "Blood Sport: The Boom Turns Into a Glut," *SSSBJ*, 24-30 December 2001, 29.

17. David Sweet, "Post-Attacks Poll Backs Sports," *SSSBJ*, 8-14 October 2004, 8.

18. Alfie Meek, "An Estimate of the Size and Supporting Economic Activity of the Sports Industry in the United States," *Sport Marketing Quarterly* (hereafter cited as *SMQ*), 6 December 1997, 15-22; King, "Passion," 25-39.

19. Scott Thomas, "Norfolk Primed to the Pros," *SSSBJ*, 11-17 January 1999, 1, 18-21. See an update in G. Scott Thomas, "Tinseltown Streaming With Extra Cash for Sports, Study Says," *SSSBJ*, 6-12 January 2003, 1, 26-29.

20. Jayson Blair, "Attendance Requirement Leaves Colleges Sweating," NYTimes.com, 23 November 2002.

21. Tony Case, "Sports Heaven or Niche Hell?" Media Week.com, 2 December 2002, http://mediaweek.com/mediaweek/headlines/article_display.jsp?vnu_content_id=1771609; LaFeber, *Michael Jordan and the New Global Capitalism*, 17.

22. Andy Bernstein, "Among Dropping Ratings, Fox Touts NASCAR's Lack of Decline for Spring," *SSSBJ*, 30 June-6 July 2003, 4.

23. The International Hockey Industry Association, press release, 20 October 2004, IHIA7 Melbourne Ave., Mont-Royal, QC Canada H3P 1E9.

24. Michael Popke, "Survival Tactics," *Athletic Business*, November 2003, 36-40; Bobby Caina Calvan, "Budget Ax Falls on School Sports," *Boston Globe*, 14 March 2004, A-17; Michael Kurtz, "Paying to Play," Boston Globe, 14 July 2003; participation data available at www.nfhs.org.

25. L. Kesler, "Man Created Ads in Sport's Own Image," *Advertising Age*, 27 August 1979, 5-10.

26. The classic work on marketing is Philip Kotler, *Marketing Management*, 11th ed. (Upper Saddle River, NJ: Prentice Hall, 2002).

27. T. Levitt, "Marketing Myopia," *Harvard Business Review* (July-August 1960): 45-56; William Weilbacher, "Yesterday's Realities Are Today's Myths," *Advertising Age*, 7 June 1993, 7.

28. D. Cooke, "Packaging for Prestige: The Tennis Advantage," *IRSA Club Business*, July 1987, 62.

29. *SBD*, 22 August 1997, 11; Andy Bernstein, "Despite Stanley Cup Win, Devils Play to Few Fans," *SSSBJ*, 11-17 December 2000, 1, 58; Andy Bernstein, "Hot Teams' Leader on Hot Seat?" *SSSBJ*, 9-15 June 2003, 45.

30. Laura Bollig, "Professional Marketing Finds Its Way Into College Basketball," *NCAA News*, 6 December 1993, 12.

31. Marcy Lamm, "Teams Take Their Pitch to the Big Screen," *SSSBJ*, 21-27 February 2000, 13.

32. Dan Shaughnessy, "Eyes of Many Are Trained on Workouts," *Boston Sunday Globe*, 8 August 2004, C-1, 4.

33. "Profile/Interview With Matt Levine," *SMQ* 5 (2) (September 1996): 5-12.

34. *SBD*, 16 October 1997, 10.

35. Kenny Berkowitz, "Selling Your Sports," *Athletic Management*, August/September 2004, 52, 56.

36. Bozeman Bulger, "Twenty-Five Years in Sports," *Saturday Evening Post*, 26 May 1928.

37. Frank Deford, "No Death for a Salesman," *SI*, 28 July 1975, 56-65.

38. Robert Steven et al., "Sport Marketing Among Colleges and Universities," *SMQ* 4 (1) (March 1995): 41-47.

39. Darryl Lehnus and Glenn Miller, "The Status of Athletic Marketing in Division IA Universities," *SMQ* 5 (3) (1996): 38-39.

40. Carol Barr, Mark McDonald, and William Sutton, "Collegiate Sport Marketers: Job Responsibilities and Compensation Structure," *International Sports Journal* 4 (2) (Summer 2000): 64-77; W. Sutton, M. McDonald, and D. Covell, "Collegiate Marketing Directors Survey," *Athletics Administration*, October 1995, 38-42. For broader coverage of industry trends, see "2002 SBJ Salary Survey," *SSSBJ*, 27 May-2 June 2002, 22-41.

41. Hall of Fame bio at www.baseballhalloffame.org/hofers_and_honorees/plaques/veeck_bill.htm. Hustler definition in Bill Veeck with Ed Linn, *The Hustler's Handbook* (New York: Fireside Books, 1989), 12; 12 commandments in Pat Williams, *Marketing Your Dreams: Business and Life Lessons From Bill Veeck Baseball's Marketing Genius* (Champaign, IL: Sports Publishing, 2000), xiv.

42. B. Enis and K. Roering, "Services Marketing: Different Products, Similar Strategy," in *Marketing of Services*, ed. J.H. Donnelly and W.R. George (Chicago: American Marketing Association, 1981), 1. The classic definition of sport comes from John Loy, "The Nature of Sport," *Quest* 10 (May 1968), 1-15.

43. The human interaction renders sport more of a "service," in business terms. For the growing literature on marketing services, see Scott Edgett and Stephen Parkinson, "Marketing for Service Industries," *Service Industries Journal* 13 (3) (July 1993): 19-39.

44. B. Stavro, "It's a Classic Turnaround Situation," *Forbes*, 1 July 1985, 70.

45. R. Poe, "The MBAs of Summer," *Across the Board*, October 1985, 18-25.

46. Tom Moroney, "Hopkinton Finds Itself in the Winner's Circle," *Boston Globe*, 3 April 1996, 1, 24.

47. Research and Forecasts, Miller Lite Report on American Attitudes Toward Sports (Milwaukee, WI: Miller Brewing Co., 1985), 131-136.

48. Franklin Foer, *How Soccer Explains the World: An Unlikely Theory of Globalization* (New York: HarperCollins, 2004).

49. Charles Sennott, "Glee Over Soccer Signals a Larger Shift Within Iran," *Boston Globe*, 12 August 1997, A-1, A-10; Kevin Cullen, "Score One for Belfast," *Boston Globe*, 9 January 2001, A-1, A-12.

50. Jeff McGregor, "The New Electoral Sex Symbol: NASCAR Dad," *New York Sunday Times*, 18 January 2003, A-1; Wayne Washington, "Bush Cruises for Votes on NASCAR Circuit," *Boston Globe*, 16 February 2004, A-10; Jorge Rueda, "In Hustle for Votes, Chavez Airs NBA," *Boston Globe*, 26 May 2004, A-26; "Bush Olympic Gambit in Scorecard," *SI*, 30 August 2004, 30.

51. "NCAA 2005-06 Budgeted Expenses," www1.ncaa.org/finance/pie_charts.

52. "NBA News and Notes," *SBD*, 20 February 1998, 5; "Marketplace Roundup," 20 March 1998, 4.

53. "Who Owns What?" *Columbia Journalism Review*, www.cjr.org/tools/owners/.

54. NSGA, "Sporting Goods Store Sales Increase 25%," November 2004, www.nsga.org; Tom Doyle, "Changes and Trends in the Retail Segment of the Sporting Goods Industry," NSGA Report, 1998.

55. National Ski Areas Association, "Number of Ski Areas Reports," 2005, www.nsaa.org/nsaa/press/industryStats.asp; Steve Cohen, "It's Not Your Father's Ski Business Anymore," *Hemisphere*, January 1998, 62-66; "Let's Hit the Slopes" *SBD*, 24 April 1998, 11.

56. Andy Bernstein, "Sportlight on SFX: Triumph or Tragedy?" *SSSBJ*, 2-8 December 2002, 1, 41-43.

57. "Family Ties," *SBD*, 3 April 1998, 9.

Chapter 2

1. Bill King, "Sports-Showbiz Marriage No Runaway Hit," *SSSBJ*, 10-16 March 2003, 36.

2. The most comprehensive account of the NFL–MTV debacle is Lawrence Wenner, "Recovering (From) Janet Jackson's Breast: Ethics and the Nexus of Media, Sport, and Management," *Journal of Sport Management* 18 (2004): 315-334. See also Michael Miller, "Say It Ain't So, Joe: NFL Cans Ad Over Lyrics," *SSSBJ*, 15-21 November 1999, 6.

3. For an excellent discussion of strategy in sport organizations, see Trevor Slack, *Understanding Sport Organizations* (Champaign, IL: Human Kinetics, 1997; 2nd ed. with Milena Parent, 2006).

4. Andrew Cohen, "Can the Game Return," *Athletic Business*, March 1996, 40; Joe Burris, "Repairing the Damage," *Boston Globe*, 24 June 1997, C-1, C-7; www.TennisWelcomeCenter.com; Dan Kaplan "Tennis Courting Irrelevance," *SSSBJ*, 26 August-1 September 2002, 22; Ross Nethery, "Watching and Waiting," *SSSBJ*, 23-29 August 2004; Michael Popke, "Serving Up an Ace," *Athletic Business*, March 2000, 43-52.

5. "Golf's Biggest Supporters," *SBD*, 14 November 1998, 4; Uihlein and Luker quotes in Noah Liberman, "Luring More Players to the Links," *SSSBJ*, 14-20 June 2004, 20-21; golf data in "GOLF 20/20 Vision for the Future: Industry Report for 2002," available at www.golf2020.com/frip/resources/2003frip.pdf; Summary 2003 National Golf Foundation Rounds Played in the United States Report 2004, 2, www.golf2020.com/wgf/; SBRnet, "Golf Participation: Total vs. Frequent Participation," www.sbrnet.com/Research/Research.cfm?subRID=199. On the issue of overbuilding, see E.M. Swift, "If You Build It, They Won't Necessarily Come," *SI*, 15 November 2004, np.

6. "Grow Hockey Summit," press release from Bill Hattem, executive director of the IHIA, 7 Melbourne Ave., Mont-Royal, QC, Canada H3P 1E9.

7. David Hoch, "Signs of the Times," *Athletic Management*, August/September 2001, 47-48.

8. Philip Kotler, *Marketing Management*, 9th ed. (Upper Saddle River, NJ: Prentice Hall, 1997); William A. Sutton, "Developing an Initial Marketing Plan for Intercollegiate Athletic Programs," *Journal of Sport Management* 1 (1987): 146-158; Shelly Reese, "The Very Model of a Modern Marketing Plan," *Marketing Tools*, January/February 1996, 56-65. For a very detailed checklist for marketing planning, see the 50-page appendix

in David M. Carter, *Keeping Score: An Inside Look at Sports Marketing* (Grant's Pass, OR: Oasis Press, 1996), 262-310.

9. James C. Collins and Jerry I. Porras, *Built to Last: Successful Habits of Visionary Companies* (New York: HarperCollins, 1999), 220.

10. Personal communication from Andy Geiger, 6 June 2003; Jennifer Lee, "Geiger Blends On-Field Success With Overall Mission," *SSSBJ*, 9-15 June 2003, 17.

11. Peter Drucker, "The Theory of the Business," *Harvard Business Review* 72 (September-October 1994): 95-104; Carole Hedden, "Build a Better Image," *Marketing Tools*, May 1996, 68-72.

12. Stephen Hardy, "Profile/Interview With Dick Lipsey," *SMQ* 7 (September 1998): 5-9; Alberto Disla, "Market-Driven Programming," *Fitness Management*, September 1994, 36-38; "Burton Rides Philosophy of Focus on Pros to Top of Market," *SBD*, 5 December 2000, 4; Steve Cameron, "Customers-for-Hire Help Venue Sharpen Their Service," *SSSBJ*, 22-28 April 2002, 16.

13. John Mahaffie, "Why Forecasts Fail," *American Demographics*, March 1995, 34-40; John Kelly and Rod Warnick, *Recreation Trends and Markets: The 21st Century* (Champaign, IL: Sagamore, 2000).

14. Erik Brady and MaryJo Sylwester, "More and More Girls Got Game," *USA Today*, 1 July 2003, 1-2C; Grant Wahl, "Rebound Attempt," *Sports Illustrated*, 29 March 2004, 34. For an excellent postmortem on the WUSA, see Richard Southall, Mark Nagel, and Deborah LeGrande, "Build It and They Will Come? The Women's United Soccer Association: Collision of Exchange Theory and Strategic Philanthropy," *SMQ* 14 (3) (2005): 158-167.

15. www.ncaa.org/stats/; www.usahockey.com; "Women Love the NHL," *SBD*, 7 May 1998, 9; "Can Men's Hockey Ride on Coattails?" *SBD*, 21 April 1998, 15; Paula Hunt, "Gear," *SI Womensport*, Fall 1997, 166-167.

16. Jeff Ostrowski, "Corporate America Making Pitchmen of Pariahs," *SSSBJ*, 12-18 August 2002, 19, 26; Russell Adams, "Sports No Longer Going to Extreme for Identity," *SSSBJ*, 12-18 August 2002, 21; Russell Adams, "League, Players Team to Expand Youth Football, *SSSBJ*, 2-8 September 2002, 20; www.usafootball.com.

17. "Turnkey Sports Poll" at SBJ-online, 26 July-1 August 2004; http://www.sportsbusinessjournal.com/index.cfm?fuseaction=search.show_article&articleId=39990&keyword=turnkey,%20sports,%20poll; Pew Research Center for the People and the Press, "Biennial News Consumption Survey," 2004, 5, 17, 21; "Special Report, the Future of Tech," *BusinessWeek*, 20 June 2005, 73-82; Hiawatha Bray, "Race Fans' View Goes Wireless," *Boston Globe*, 26 July 2006, C-1, C-7. For a cautionary note, see Eric Fisher and John Durand, "Analysts Put Mobile ESPN on the Defensive," *SSSBJ*, 31 July-6 August 2006, 4.

18. Suzanne Smalley, "New Advertising Ploy Runs Afoul of Marathon," *Boston Globe*, 20 April 2005, B-5; "Ambushing 101: Socog, Sponsors to Face Educated Guerrillas," *SBD*, 9 June 2000, 4; Peter Graham, "Ambush Marketing," *SMQ* 6 (March 1997): 10-12; "Well, Who Does," *SBD*, 12 February 1998, 15; Terry Lefton, "Ambush Tactics Evil, Effective," *SSSBJ*, 3-9 November 2003, 9; Alycen McAuley and William Sutton, "In Search of a New Defender: The Threat of Ambush Marketing in the Global Sports Arena," *International Journal of Sports Marketing and Sponsorship* 1 (1) (1998): 64-86.

19. Martin Letscher, "How to Tell Fads From Trends," *American Demographics*, December 1994, 38-44; Martin Letscher, "Sports Fads and Trends," *American Demographics*, June 1997, 53-56; L. Jon Wertheim, "Trout May Jump for Joy," *SI*, 23 March 1998, 22.

20. Collins and Porras, *Built to Last*, 238. For a view of Nike at its height of power, see Donald Katz, *Just Do It: The Nike Spirit in the Corporate World* (Holbrook, MA: Adams, 1994).

21. "Post No Billboards," Stanford Magazine, 2000, online edition, www.stanfordalumni.org/news/magazine/2000/sepoct/farm_report/billboards.html.

22. Drucker, "Theory of Business"; Carole Hedden, "Build a Better Image," *Marketing Tools*, May 1996, 68-72. List of bullets adapted from Edward Pitts, "Imagination Is Better Than Knowledge," *Fitness Management*, March 1995, 33-35.

23. Collins and Porras, *Built to Last*, 111-112; Denver Grizzlies Hockey Club, Draft Community Relations Plan, 1994-1995 Season.

24. David Hoch, "Signs of the Times," *Athletic Management*, August-September 2001, 47-48.

25. David Shani, "A Framework for Implementing Relationship Marketing in the Sport Industry," *SMQ* 6 (June 1997): 9-15.

26. Hardy, "Dick Lipsey," 6. For a closer look at the fan escalator, see William Sutton et al., "Escalating Your Fan Base," *Athletic Management*, February-March 1997, 4-5.

27. Terry Lefton, "Hockey Tips From the Stars," *SSSBJ*, 6-12 October 2003, 5.

28. Al Ries and Jack Trout, *Positioning: The Battle for Your Mind* (New York: Warner Books, 1982).

29. Peter May, "Zooming Into Prominence," *Boston Globe*, 17 September 2004, E-1, E-16; Michael Smith "NASCAR Tracks Roll Out Upscale Seating Options," *SSSBJ*, 17-23 July 2006, 6.

30. "MLS Faces Tests," *SBD*, 24 March 1998, 12.

31. D. Cooke, "Packaging for Prestige," *IRSA Club Business*, July 1987, 65.

32. Rachel Sherman, "Softball City," *Athletic Business*, July 1997, 28-29; www.big8softball.com, 2 February 2005.

33. Marianne Bhonslay, "Selling the 'Less Than Best,'" *SSSBJ*, 8-14 March 1999, 25.

34. Terry Lefton, "Guarascio: Research Will Help NFL Understand Its Fans," *SSSBJ*, November 8-14, 2004, 6.

35. Alfred Chandler, *Strategy and Structure: Chapters in the History of Industrial Enterprise* (Cambridge, MA: MIT Press, 1962); Alan Friedman, "Coke Agreement May Leave NFL Teams Scrambling," *SSSBJ*, 8-14 June 1998, 6.

36. "Is There a Spell Over the MLS Wizards' Marketing Efforts?" *SBD*, 25 July 1998, 12; Bruce Schoenfeld, "Pro Team Takes a Hit in Lacrosse's Stronghold," *SSSBJ*, 18-24 March 2002, 38.

37. Sergio Zyman, *The End of Marketing As We Know It* (New York: Harper Business, 1999), 51.

38. "Oregonian Editorial Calls Harrington Promo a Good PR Move," *SBD*, 13 August 2001, 24.

39. Laura Nash, "Ethics Without the Sermon," *Harvard Business Review* (November 1981): 79-90; G.B. Laczniak and Patrick Murphy, "Sports Marketing Ethics in Today's Marketplace," *SMQ* 8 (December 1999): 43-53; C. Spindel, *Dancing at Halftime: Sport and the Controversy Over American Indian Mascots* (New York: New York University Press, 2000); Ellen Staurowsky, "Privilege at Play: On the Legal and Social Fictions That Sustain American Indian Sport Imagery," *Journal of Sport and Social Issues* 28 (February 2004): 11-29; Amalie Benjamin, "Sense and Sensitivity," *Boston Globe*, 21 June 2005, F-1, F-7; Sean Smith, "NCAA: Mascot Ruling," *Boston Globe*, 6 August 2005, D-1-D-2; Gary Brown, "Policy Applies Core Principles to Mascot Issue," *NCAA News*, 15 August 2005, 1, 19.

40. "Univ. of Memphis Gambles on Sponsorship," *SBD*, 23 April 1998, 3.

Chapter 3

1. "GOLF 20/20 Vision for the Future: Industry Report for 2002," available at www.golf2020.com/frip/resources/2003frip.pdf, 15. For an assault on GOLF 20/20's numbers, see James Koppenhaver, "My Shot," *SI*, 14 March 2005, G-34.

2. All quotes and data from B. King, "NASCAR: It Ain't Just Racin'," *SSSBJ*, 18-24 May 1998, 1, 48; "Panels Dig Into Changes in Motorsports Landscape," *SSSBJ*, 6-12 December 2004, 12-13.

3. "NCAA Launches Marketing Campaign to Promote College Basketball," *NCAA News*, 22 February 1999; Michelle Brudag Hosick, "What's in a Brand: Core Attributes Set Marketing Guideposts," *NCAA News*, 23 May 2005, A2. Yale University's School of Organization and Management and National Demographics and Lifestyles, Inc., "Economic Impact Study and Demographic Profile of the 1991 Volvo International," in authors' possession; Frank B. Ashley et al., "Professional Wrestling Fans: Your Next-Door Neighbors? *SMQ* 9 (3): 140-148.

4. Perrier Great Waters of France, Inc., *The Perrier Study: Fitness in America* (New York: Perrier, 1979).

5. Many sponsor research firms are listed in K.J. Myers, ed., *Sports Market Place* (Phoenix: Franklin Covey, 1999); William Sutton, "Profile/Interview With Joyce Julius Cotman," *SMQ* 7 (June 1998): 6-7; Theresa Howard, "Where Have Baseball Players' Endorsements Gone?" *USA Today*, 28 September 2003, www.usatoday.com/money/advertising/adtrack/2003-09-28-visa_x.htm.

6. S. Hardy, "Profile/Interview With Richard Lipsey," *SMQ* 7 (September 1998): 5-9.

7. Excerpts from Scarborough may also be found in the weekly issues of *SSSBJ*. See www.sportsbusinessjournal.com.

8. J. Steinbreder, "Golf's Boom Figures to Stay in Bounds," *SSSBJ*, 4-10 May 1998, 1, 31.

9. For a valuable analysis of the U.S. soccer market, see "Special Report: Soccer," *SSSBJ*, June 1-7, 1998, 19-33.

10. "The Fans," *SBD*, 19 August 1997, 8. For an example of clarifying participants, see J. Larson, "The Bicycle Market," *American Demographics*, March 1995, 42-50.

11. "GOLF 20/20 Vision for the Future: Industry Report for 2002," www.golf2020.com/frip/resources/2003frip.pdf.

12. For a discussion of Web usage measurement, see www.computerworld.com/managementtopics/ebusiness/story/0,10801,71989,00.html.

13. R. Thav, "Changes in Magazine Research," *American Demographics*, February 1995, 12-13; *1982-2003 NCAA Sports Sponsorship and Participation Report* (Indianapolis: NCAA, 2004), www.ncaa.org/library/research/participation_rates/1982-2003/2003ParticipationReport.pdf, 10; see the valuable caveats in M. Chubb and H. Chubb, *One Third of Our Time? An Introduction to Recreation Behavior and Resources* (New York: Wiley, 1981), 261-263.

14. "ASD Launches Study on Sporting Goods Industry," *Sport Business* 7 (June 1984): 3.

15. Darren K. Carlson, "Although Fewer Americans Watch Baseball, Half Say They Are Fans," Gallup News Service, July 10, 2001; for information on Gallup Poll subscriptions, see www.gallup.com; "Stats at George Mason University," www.stats.org/index.jsp; "Statistics Home Page," www.statsoftinc.com/textbook/stathome.html.

16. G. Scott Thomas, "Cleveland Roots Its Way to the Top," *SSSBJ*, 24-30 January 2000, 1, 47-48. For a good discussion of college rankings, see www.library.uiuc.edu/edx/rankoversy.htm. For an excellent review of various problems associated with data analysis, see Mark H. Maier with Todd Easton, *The Data Game: Controversies in Social Science Statistics*, 3rd ed. (Armonk, NY: M.E. Sharpe, 1999).

Chapter 4

1. C.F. Springwood, *Cooperstown to Dyersville: A Geography of Baseball Nostalgia* (Boulder, CO: Westview Press, 1996).

2. Our general list of topics follows that found in most texts on marketing and consumer behavior. See, for instance, H. Berkman and C. Gilson, *Consumer Behavior: Concepts and Strategies*, 3rd ed. (Boston: Kent, 1986); Michael Solomon, *Consumer Behavior*, 6th ed. (Upper Saddle River, NJ: Prentice Hall, 2004); Leon G. Schiffman and Leslie Lazar Kanuk, *Consumer Behavior*, 8th ed. (Upper Saddle River, NJ: Prentice Hall, 2004). We have tried to link the material on general consumers with that on sport consumers.

3. Bill King, "What Makes Fans Tick?" *SSSBJ*, 1-7 March 2004, 26.

4. On sport socialization, involvement, and commitment, see J. Loy, B. McPherson, and G. Kenyon, *Sport and Social Systems* (Reading, MA: Addison-Wesley, 1978), 16-23, 215-248; R. Brustad, "Integrating Socialization Influences Into the Study of Children's Motivation in Sport," *Journal of Sport and Exercise Psychology* 14 (1992): 59-77. For an interesting study of sport consumers, with implications about socialization, see A. Shohlan and L. Kahle, "Spectators, Viewers, Readers: Communication and Consumption Communities in Sport Marketing," *SMQ* 5 (March 1996): 11-20.

5. Bill King, "The 24/7 Fan," *SSSBJ*, 7-13 March 2005, 25.

6. P. Graham, "A Study of the Demographic and Economic Characteristics of Spectators Attending the U.S. Men's Clay Court Championships," *SMQ* 1 (1) (March 1992): 25-30.

7. Daniel Funk, Daniel Mahony, and Mark Havitz, "Sport Consumer Behavior: Assessment and Direction," *SMQ* 12 (4) (2003): 200-205; D. Wann et al., *Sports Fans: The Psychology and Social Impact of Spectators* (New York: Routledge, 2001), 2-3; Bob Stewart, Aaron Smith, and Matthew Nicholson, "Sport Consumer Typologies: A Critical Review," *SMQ* 12 (4) (2003): 206-216; Hyungil Harry Kwon and Ketra Armstrong, "An Exploration of the Construct of Psychological Attachments to a Sports Team Among College Students: A Multidimensional Approach," *SMQ* 13 (2) (2004): 94-103; H. Kwon and G. Trail, "The Feasibility of Single-Item Measures in Sport Loyalty Research," *Sport Management Review* 8 (2005): 69-89.

8. Michael Farber, "Wild Times," *SI* 19 May 2003, 42-45; D.L. Wann and N.R. Brascombe, "Sports Fans: Measuring Degree of Identification With the Team," *International Journal of Sport Psychology* 24 (1993): 1-17.

9. Research and Forecasts, Inc., *Miller Lite Report on American Attitudes Toward Sports* (Milwaukee: Miller Brewing Co., 1983); Frank B. Ashley et al., "Professional Wrestling Fans: Your Next-Door Neighbors?" *SMQ* 9 (3): 140-148.

10. Game Plan, Inc., *Why People Join: A Market Research Study for Racquet and Fitness Clubs* (Boston: International Racquet Sports Association, 1985), 41-43; "The Power of Pals," *Marketing Tools*, March 1997, 39; C. Walker, "Word of Mouth," *American Demographics*, July 1995, 38-44.

11. K.L. Wakefield, "The Pervasive Effects of Social Influence on Sporting Event Attendance," *Journal of Sport and Social Issues* 19 (1995): 335-351.

12. On the national "sports creed," see H. Edwards, *Sociology of Sport* (Homewood, IL: Dorsey Press, 1983), 334. For an excellent history on the creed, see S.W. Pope, *Patriotic Games: Sporting Traditions in the American Imagination, 1876-1926* (New York: Oxford University Press, 1997); M. Dyreson, *Inventing the Sporting Republic: American Sport, Political Culture, and the Olympic Experience, 1877-1919* (Urbana: University of Illinois Press, 1997).

13. P. May, "Entertaining Idea," *Boston Globe*, 26 May 1996, 49, 56; K. Kennedy, "Spice on the Ice," *SI*, 1 April 1996, 3-4; Terry Lifton, "Octagon's Passion Drivers Research Look for Keys to Reaching Chinese Sports Fans," *SSSBJ*, 26 September-2 October 2005, 54. Contemporary "sports regions" are described in J. Rooney and R. Pillsbury, *Atlas of American Sport* (New York: Maxwell Macmillan, 1992). For a good article on southern culture and sport, see Ted Ownby, "Manhood, Memory, and White Men's Sports in the Recent American South," *International Journal of History of Sport* 15 (2) (August 1998): 103-118.

14. R.P. Coleman, "The Continuing Significance of Social Class to Marketing," *Journal of Consumer Research* 10 (December 1983): 265-280.

15. D. Booth and J. Loy, "Sport, Status, and Style," *Sport History Review* 30 (1999): 1-26; T. Veblen, *Theory of the Leisure Class* (New York: New American Library, 1899); concerning "prole sports," see D.S. Eitzen and G. Sage, *Sociology of North American Sport*, 3rd ed. (Dubuque, IA: Brown, 1986), 244-245; G. Lipsitz, *Class and Culture in Cold War America* (South Hadley, MA: Bergin, 1982), 173-194; R. Gruneau, *Class, Sports, and Social Development* (Amherst: University of Massachusetts Press, 1984).

16. James F. Crow, "Unequal by Nature: A Geneticist's Perspective on Human Differences," *Daedalus*, Winter 2002, 84. For a fine review of the historical literature, see J.T. Sammons, "'Race' and Sport: A Critical, Historical Explanation," *Journal of Sport History* 21 (Fall 1994): 203-278; D. Wiggins, "'Great Speed but Little Stamina': The Historical Debate Over Black Athletic Superiority," *Journal of Sport History* 16 (Summer 1989): 158-185.

17. R. Brown and R.T. Jewell, "Is There Customer Discrimination in College Basketball?" *Social Science Quarterly* 75 (2) (June 1994): 401-413; "Do NBA Ratings Increase With White Athletes' Playing Time?" *SBD*, 20 April 1998, 4.

18. Ketra L. Armstrong and Terese Peretto Stratta, "Market Analyses of Race and Sport Consumption," *SMQ* 13 (1) (2004): 7-16.

19. S. Hardy, "Profile/Interview With Donna Lopiano," *SMQ* 5 (4) (December 1996): 5-8; S. Greendorfer, "Socialization Into Sport," in *Women and Sport: From Myth to Reality*, ed. C. Oglesby (Philadelphia: Lea & Febiger, 1982), 115-142; Vivian Acosta and Linda Carpenter, "Women in Sport," http://webpages.charter.net/womeninsport/2006.

20. D. Branch, "Tapping New Markets: Women as Sport Consumers," *SMQ* 4 (4) (December 1995): 9-12; S. Hofacre, "The Women's Audience in Professional Indoor Soccer," *SMQ* 3 (2) (June 1994): 25-27.

21. W. Gantz and L. Wenner, "Men, Women, and Sports: Audience Experience and Effects," *Journal of Broadcasting and Electronic Media* 35 (2) (Spring 1991): 233-243.

22. The literature on sport and gender is vast. For an introduction, see S. Cahn, *Coming on Strong: Gender and Sexuality in Twentieth Century Women's Sport* (Cambridge, MA: Harvard University Press, 1995); M.B. Nelson, *The Stronger Women Get, the More Men Love Football* (New York: Avon, 1994).

23. For a solid review, see Vikki Crane and Heather Barber, "Lesbian Experiences in Sport: A Social Identity Perspective," *Quest* 55 (2003): 328-346. See also Dan Woog, *Jocks: True Stories of America's Gay Male Athletes* (New York: Alyson Books, 1998).

24. M. Rossman, *Multicultural Marketing* (New York: AMACOM Books, 1994), 33.

25. "GOLF 20/20 Vision for the Future: Industry Report for 2002," www.golf2020.com/frip/resources/2003frip.pdf. 2003. Contemporary sports regions are described in Rooney and Pillsbury, *Atlas of American Sport*; B. Hunnicutt, "Sports," in *Encyclopedia of Southern Culture*, eds. C.R. Wilson and W. Ferris (Chapel Hill: University of North Carolina Press, 1989), 1239. On the South and baseball, see K. Greenburg, *Honor and Slavery* (Princeton, NJ: Princeton University Press, 1996). For a more expansive analysis of southern styles, see T. Ownby, *Subduing Satan: Religion, Recreation, and Manhood in the Rural South, 1865-1920* (Chapel Hill: University of North Carolina Press, 1990).

26. John Betts, "The Technological Revolution and the Rise of Sport," *Mississippi Valley Historical Review* 40 (September 1953): 231-256; Terry Lefton, "Survey Results Push NFL.com to Increase Fantasy Content," *SSSBJ*, 9-12 September, 2002, 4; Bill King, "Reaching Today's Sports Fans," *SSSBJ*, 14-20 March 2005, 17-21; Tracy Mayor, "What Are Video Games Turning Us Into?" *Boston Globe Magazine*, 20 February 2005, 18-37.

27. T. Chamberlain, "A Clash of Cultures," *Boston Globe*, 23 December 1993, 61-63. Research on the impact of competitors is limited; see James J. Zhang et al., "Negative Influence of Market Competitors on the Attendance of Professional Sport Games: The Case of a Minor League Hockey Team," *SMQ* 6 (3) (1997): 31-39.

28. Berkman and Gilson, *Consumer Behavior*, 101-102; M.J. Sirgy, "Self Concept in Consumer Behavior: A Critical Review," *Journal of Consumer Behavior* 1 (December 1982): 287-300.

29. "Why Teenagers Participate in Sports," *Fitness Management*, March 1991, 15-16.

30. R. Burton, "Profile/Interview With Sara Levinson," *SMQ* 6 (4) (December 1997): 5-8; J.R. Kelly, *Leisure* (Upper Saddle River, NJ: Prentice Hall, 1982), 133-156.

31. W. Gantz et al., "Televised Sports and Marital Relationships," *Sociology of Sport Journal* 12 (1995): 306-323; D. Wann et al., *Sports Fans: The Psychology and Social Impact of Spectators* (New York: Routledge, 2001), 46.

32. Berkman and Gilson, *Consumer Behavior*, 273.

33. ESPN and ESPN2, "Guide to the X Games," insert in *Rolling Stone*, 25 June 1998.

34. J.J. Zhang et al., "Spectator Knowledge of Hockey as a Significant Predictor of Game Attendance," *SMQ* 5 (September 1996): 41-48; S. Nottingham, "Juggling the Learning Curve," *Fitness Management*, August 1994, 40-43.

35. R.F. Young, "The Advertising of Consumer Services and the Hierarchy of Effects," in *The Marketing of Services*, eds. J.H. Donnelly and W. George (Chicago: American Marketing Association, 1981), 196-199; "Basketball According to Me," insert in *Sports Illustrated*, 10 November 1997.

36. "Rollerblading Looks to Put the Brakes on the Competition," *SBD*, 5 June 1997, 6; William Sutton, "Educate Your Buyer," *SSSBJ*, 23-29 February 2004, 29.

37. B. Berelson and G. Steiner, *Human Behavior: An Inventory of Scientific Findings* (New York: Harcourt Brace, 1964), 88; P. Kotler, *Marketing Management*, 5th ed. (Upper Saddle River, NJ: Prentice Hall, 1984), 140.

38. D. Wann, C. Bayens, and A. Driver, "Likelihood of Attending a Sporting Event as a Function of Ticket Scarcity and Team Identification," *SMQ* 13 (4) (2004): 209-215; B. Enis and K. Roering, "Services Marketing: Different Products, Similar Strategy," in *The Marketing of Services*, 1-4; B. Veeck, *Veeck as in Wreck* (New York: Signet, 1986); D. Kerstatter and G. Kovich, "An Involvement Profile of Division I Women's Basketball Spectators," *Journal of Sport Management* 11 (1997): 234-249; A. Rohm, "The Creation of Consumer Bonds Within Reebok Running," *SMQ* 6 (2) (June 1997): 18.

39. Bill King, "What Makes Fans Tick?" *SSSBJ*, 1-7 March 2004, 26, 32; Robert Cialdini et al., "Basking in Reflected Glory: Three (Football) Field Studies," *Journal of Personality and Social Psychology* 34 (1976): 366-375; Lynn Kahle and Chris Riley, eds., *Sport Marketing and the Psychology of Marketing Communication* (Mahwah, NJ: Erlbaum, 2004), 67-79; G. Trail et al., "Motives and Points of Attachment: Fans Versus Spectators in Intercollegiate Athletics," *SMQ* 12 (4) (2003): 217-227; S. Hardy, "Sport," in *Encyclopedia of Social History*, ed. P. Stearns (New York: Garland, 1994), 713-714; Wann et al., *Sports Fans*; L. Kahle, K. Kambara, and G. Rose, "A Functional Model of Fan Attendance Motivations for College Football," *SMQ* 5 (December 1996): 51-60; H. Hansen and R. Gauthier, "The Professional Golf Product: Spectators' Views," *SMQ* 3 (4) (December 1994): 9-16; M. Grunwald, "Taking Funny Business Seriously," *Boston Globe*, 5 January 1998, A-1, A-12; A. Guttmann, *The Erotic in Sports* (New York: Columbia University Press, 1996); "Gator Bait" ["Scorecard"], *SI*, 19 May 1997, 29-30; "Oh Oscar," *SBD*, 9 September 1997, 5; J. James and S. Ross, "Comparing Sport Consumer Motivations Across Multiple Sports," *SMQ* 13 (1) (2004): 17-25.

40. Kotler, *Marketing Management*, 9th ed., 188; D. Zillman, J. Bryant, and B. Sapolsky, "Enjoyment of Watching Sport Contests," in *Sport, Games, and Play: Social and Psychological Viewpoints*, ed. J. Goldstein (Hillsdale, NJ: Erlbaum, 1979), 279-335; C. Lupton, N. Ostrove, and R. Bozzo, "Participation in Leisure-Time Physical Activity," *Journal of Physical Education, Recreation and Dance* 55 (November 1984): 20.

41. "Why Not Try Playing a Game That Starts Out Love-Love," press release from Brouillard Communications to authors, 4 May 1993.

42. For basic models, see Berkman and Gilson, *Consumer Behavior*, 472-511; Kotler, *Marketing Management*, 9th ed., 192-198; J. O'Shaughnessy, *Why People Buy* (New York: Oxford, 1987), 92-97; M. Chubb and H. Chubb, *One Third of Our Time? An Introduction to Recreation Behavior and Resources* (New York: Wiley, 1981), 230-250. See also Galen Trial, Janet Fink, and Dean Anderson, "Sport Spectator Consumer Behavior," *SMQ* 12 (1) (2003): 8-17.

43. D. Wann et al., *Sports Fans*; Funk et al., "Sport Consumer Behavior"; R.J. Fisher and K. Wakefield, "Factors Leading to Group Identification: A Field Study of Winners and Losers," *Psychology and Marketing*, 15, 23-40; Sutton et al., "Creating and Fostering Fan Identification."

44. T. Crossett, "Toward an Understanding of On-Site Fan-Athlete Relations: A Case Study of the LPGA," *SMQ* 4 (June 1995): 31-38; W. Sutton, "Profile/Interview With Don Johnson," *SMQ* 6 (June 1997): 5-8; "Adoption Program Breeds Early-Season Ticket Sales," *Team Marketing Report* 8 (July 1996): 9; W. Sutton et al., "Creating and Fostering Fan Identification," *SMQ* 6 (1): 15-22; D. McGraw, "Big League Troubles," *U.S. News and World Report*, 13 July 1998, 40-46.

45. Game Plan, Inc., *Why People Join*, 42-44; D. Smith and N. Theberge, *Why People Recreate* (Champaign, IL: Human Kinetics, 1987), 111-118.

46. Kotler, *Marketing Management*, 464; J. Faircloth et al., "An Analysis of Choice Intentions of Public Golf Courses," *SMQ* 4 (March 1995): 13-21. For a good introduction to factors influencing spectator choice, see J. Zhang et al., "Factors Affecting the Decision Making of Spectators to Attend Minor League Hockey Games," *International Sports Journal* 1 (Summer 1997): 39-53.

47. Funk et al., "Sport Consumer Behavior."

48. Chubb and Chubb, *One Third of Our Time?* 231-234.

49. Christine Brooks, "Sport/Exercise Identity Theory and Participation Marketing," *SMQ* 7 (1) (March 1998): 38-47; Sutton et al., "Creating and Fostering Fan Identification."

50. Craig Hyatt, "An Interpretive Analysis of Hartford Whalers Fans' Stories" (unpublished doctoral dissertation, University of Massachusetts, Amherst, 2003); Funk et al., "Sport Consumer Behavior." For an interesting look at alienated Scottish football fans, see Richard Giulianotti, "Sport Spectators and the Social Consequences of Commodification," *Journal of Sport and Social Issues* 29 (November 2005): 386-410.

51. Malcom Gladwell, "Annals of Style: The Coolhunt," *New Yorker*, 17 March 1997, www.look-look.com/looklook/html/Test_Drive_Press_Yorker.html.

Chapter 5

1. Frederick Reichfeld, "The One Number You Need to Grow," *Harvard Business Review* (December 2003): 50.

2. Ibid., 52.

3. A.R. Andreasen, "Cost-Conscious Market Research," *Harvard Business Review* (July-August 1983): 74-77.

4. We base the format of figure 5.1 on that in P.D. Boughton, "Marketing Research and Small Business: Pitfalls and Potentials," *Journal of Small Business Management* (July 1983): 37. See also the questions in M. Levine, "Making Market Research Hustle: The Essential Sweat of Attendance Building and Fund Raising" (paper presented at Athletic Business Conference, Las Vegas, NV, December 8, 1987).

5. Forrestor Online Marketing Research, 15 March 2006.

6. NBA Team Marketing Survey, 2005.

7. Andy Stevens, "Standing Out for the Crowd," *SportBusiness International*, February 2006, 8-14.

8. E. Spanberg. "Good research starts with knowing what to ask." *SSSBJ*, 11-17 August 11-17 2003, 21.

9. For an approach to such data collecting, see J. Naisbitt, *Megatrends: Ten New Directions for Transforming Our Lives* (New York: Warner, 1982). For an analysis on how trends affect business and how to best prepare, see F. Popcorn, *The Popcorn Report* (New York: Doubleday, 1991).

10. S. Godin, *Permission Marketing* (New York: Simon and Schuster, 1999), 131.

11. One short reference study of secondary material is the United States Small Business Administration (SBA) pamphlet entitled "Marketing for Small Businesses," part of the small business bibliography available from SBA, P.O. Box 15434, Fort Worth, TX 76119.

12. G.R. Milne, W.A. Sutton, and M.A. McDonald, "Success With Surveys," *Athletic Management* 9 (4) (1997): 12.

13. One short reference study of secondary material is the United States Small Business Administration (SBA) pamphlet "Marketing for Small Businesses," part of the small business bibliography available from the SBA, P.O. Box 15434, Fort Worth, TX 76119.

14. J. Johansson and I. Nonaka, "Market Research the Japanese Way," *Harvard Business Review* 65 (May-June 1967): 16-22.

15. W.A. Sutton, R.L. Irwin, and J.M. Gladden, "Tools of the Trade: Practical Research Methods for Events, Teams and Venues," *SMQ* 7 (2) (1998): 45-49.

16. R.P. Heath, "Seeing Is Believing," *Marketing Tools,* March 1997, 4-10.

17. For an actual example of how the results of such research can be used to increase marketing effectiveness and strategic planning, see "76ers Community Intercept Surveys Suggest New Marketing Tactics," *Team Marketing Report* 8 (9) (June 1996): 7.

18. J. O'Shaughnessey, *Why People Buy* (New York: Oxford, 1987), 54; K. Ericsson and H. Simon, "Verbal Report as Data," *Psychological Review* 87 (May 1987): 215-251. The authors seem to call for protocol analysis in L. Fishwick and S. Greendorfer, "Socialization Revisited: A Critique of the Sport-Related Research," *Quest* 39 (April 1987): 1-8.

19. G. Moeller and E. Shafer, "Use and Misuse of Delphi Forecasting," in *Recreation Planning and Management,* eds. S. Lieber and D. Fesenmaier (State College, PA: Venture, 1983), 96-104. See the use of "experts" in the marketing research of the NHL in H.C. Mitchener, "The Influence of Selected Changes, Developments, and Events on the Promotion and Marketing of National Hockey League Teams" (master's thesis, University of Ottawa, 1983).

20. W. Sutton and R. Warnick, "LPGA Panel Survey on Merchandising and Attitudes Related to Golf" (consulting report, 1995). A study using 417 consumers to solicit opinions and feedback regarding golf apparel purchasing behavior documented the relationship between age and purchasing and the ways golf fashion is affected by age and apparel worn by LPGA golfers.

21. Internet World Stats, www.internetworldstats.com/stats.html.

22. Pew Internet and American Life Project, www.pewinternet.org/pdfs/PIP_Generations_Memo.pdf.

23. M.A. Wylde, "How to Read an Open Letter," *American Demographics,* September 1994, 48-52.

24. J. Spoelstra, *Ice to the Eskimos* (New York: Harper Business, 1997).

25. P. Kephart, "The Spy in Aisle 3," *Marketing Tools,* May 1996, 16-21.

26. B. Veeck and E. Linn, *Veeck as in Wreck* (New York: Putnam's, 1962); B. Veeck and E. Linn, *The Hustler's Handbook* (New York: Putnam's, 1965).

27. Sutton, Irwin, and Gladden, "Tools of the Trade," 45-49.

28. Game Plan, Inc., *Why People Play: A Report on the Sport of Tennis* (Lexington, MA: Game Plan).

29. L. Rea and R. Parker, *Designing and Conducting Survey Research: A Comprehensive Guide* (San Francisco: Jossey-Bass, 1992), 107.

30. Rea and Parker, *Designing and Conducting Survey Research.*

31. For a useful guide for designing quantitative surveys, see Rea and Parker, *Designing and Conducting Survey Research;* for assistance in developing a more qualitative instrument, see C. Marshall and G. Rossman, *Designing Qualitative Research* (Newbury Park, CA: Sage, 1989).

32. Rea and Parker, *Designing and Survey Conducting Research,* 101.

Chapter 6

1. For more on the LPGA clinics, see www.jbcgolf.com/welcome.htm; K. McCabe, "Lowering a Gender Handicap," *Boston Sunday Globe,* 27 July 1997, C-1, C-4; "Women Golfers: By the Numbers," *Golf Market Today,* September-October 1998, 4; Jolee Edmondson, "Queen of Clubs," *Sky,* March 1999, 59. The authors thank Melanie Bedrosian of the Jane Blalock Company for research assistance on this vignette.

2. On the notion of global marketing, see T. Levitt, *The Marketing Imagination* (New York: Free Press, 1984).

3. For a general discussion, see P. Kotler and K. Keller, *Marketing Management,* 12th ed. (Upper Saddle River, NJ: Prentice Hall, 2005), chapter 8: "Identifying Market Segments and Targets."

4. P. Kotler, *Marketing Management,* 9th ed. (Upper Saddle River, NJ: Prentice Hall, 1997), 251; S. Ruibal, "Horwath Seeks Niche for Snow Skating," *USA Today,* 31 January 1997, 2C; G. Milne, W. Sutton, and M. McDonald, "Niche Analysis: A Strategic Measurement Tool for Sport Managers," *SMQ* 5 (3) (29 September 1996): 15-22; Martin Kaufmann, "Small Sports Dream Big Despite Woes," *SSSBJ,* 18-24 March 2002, 19, 24.

5. www.burton.com/company; Marvin Bynum, "Target Audience," *Athletic Business,* September 2004, 40.

6. See www.claritas.com.

7. Langdon Brockinton, "Miami May Look to Lure Far-Off Fans," *SSSBJ,* 22-28 October 2001, 9; L. Mullen, "Chargers' New Campaign Will Test Drawing Power in LA," *SSSBJ,* 6-12 July 1998, 13; M. Levine, "Making Marketing Research Hustle: The Essential Sweat of Attendance Building and Fund Raising" (paper presented at the annual Athletic Business Conference, Las Vegas, NV, December 1987).

8. Ross Kerber, "Sox, Yanks Fight for Conn. Viewers," *Boston Globe,* 6 August 2003, A-1, B-8.

9. Andrew Grossman, "Where Have All the Young Viewers Gone?" *SSSBJ,* 22-28 November 2004, 8; Bill King, "Where The Teens Are," *SSSBJ,* 20-26 February 2006, 17-24; Bill King, "Reaching the 18-34 Demo," *SSSBJ,* 17-24 April 2006, 1, 19-26.

10. Sean Brenner, "Reaching Tomorrow's Fans," *SSSBJ,* 13-19 September 2004, 19-23.

11. "NASCAR Targets Kids, but Must Dance Around RJR's Sponsorship," *SBD,* 22 May 1998, 7.

12. C. Cox, "Rock 'n' Bowl," *Boston Herald,* 20 August 1997, 37; www.generationjets.com; www.newyorkjets.com/community.

13. Tim Mask, "Gen Y a Gold Mine for Marketers Who Dig It," *SSSBJ,* 12-18 August 2002, 29; Gregg Bennet, Robin Henson, and James Zhang, "Generation Y's Perceptions of the Action Sports Industry Segment," *Journal of Sport Management* 17 (2003): 95-115; D. Turco, "The X Factor: Marketing to Generation X," *SMQ* 5 (1) (March 1996): 21-26; Christopher Palmeri and David Kiley, "In Hot Pursuit of Yoga Mama," *BusinessWeek,* 7 November 2005, 128-130.

14. J. Rude, "Making the Mature Decision," *Athletic Business,* January 1998, 31-37.

15. Ross Nethery, "Watching and Waiting," *SSSBJ,* 23-29 August 2004, 22; "Who the Fans Are," *SSSBJ,* 9-15 December 2002, 26.

16. Harry Hurt, III, "Sure, It's Not Bowling, but Polo Is Catching On," *New York Times Sunday,* 22 August 2004, BU-9; M. Babineck, "Ralph Lauren's Firm Sues Magazine to Drop Polo Name," *Boston Globe,* 27 May 1998, C-3.

17. "Fan Breakdowns," *SSSBJ,* 16-22 June 2003, 24.

18. Andy Bernstein, "Do Sports Market to the Right Sex?" *SSSBJ,* 2-8 November 1998, 44; T. Cassidy, "Football 101," *Boston Sunday Globe,* 26 October 1997, C-1, C-11; N. Kapsambelis, "Football 101," *Foster's Sunday Citizen,* 16 November 1997, 9B.

19. S. Hardy, "Profile/Interview With Donna Lopiano," *SMQ* 5 (4) (December 1996): 5-8; Galen Trail, Dean Anderson, and Janet Fink, "Examination of Gender Differences in Importance of and Satisfaction With Venue Factors at Intercollegiate Basketball Games," *International Sports Journal* 6 (Winter 2002): 51-64.

20. Grant Wahl, "Rebound Attempt," *SI*, 29 March 2004, 34.

21. "Gay in Sports: A Poll," *SI*, 18 April 2005, 64; "Dodgers Apologize," *SBD*, 24 August 2000, 10; "Debate Over Marketing to Alternative Lifestyles Continues," *SBD*, 15 May 2001, 18; "Sparks' Alterative Marketing Effort," *SBD*, 15 June 2001, 18; "WNBA Teams' marketing Toward Lesbians Continues to Draw Reax," *SBD*, 2 August 2001, 17; Tom Weir, "WNBA Sells Diversity Marketing, Recognizes Lesbian Fans," *USA Today*, 24 July 2001, 1-C ; H. Kahan and D. Mulryan, "Out of the Closet," *American Demographics*, May 1995, 40-47.

22. Daniel Kaplan, "Tennis Courting Irrelevance," *SSSBJ*, 26 August-1 September 2002, 22; "NBA Fan Demographics," *SSSBJ*, "By the Numbers," 29 December 2004, 41. Ketra Armstrong is the leading researcher on African American sport consumers. See, for example, "An Examination of the Social Psychology of Blacks' Consumption of Sport," *Journal of Sport Management* 16 (2000): 267-288.

23. Cindy Rodriguez, "At Fenway, It's Fiesta Time," *Boston Globe*, 6 June 2001, A-1, A-11; Scott Warfield, "MLS' Grassroots Tournament Grows by 58%," *SSSBJ*, 27 September-2 October 2004, 6.

24. K. Armstrong, "Ten Strategies to Employ When Marketing Sport to Black Consumers," *SMQ* 7 (3) (September 1998): 11-19; L. McCarthy, "Marketing Sport to Hispanic Consumers," *SMQ* 7 (4) (December 1998): 19-24.

25. R. Desloge, "Cards Make Pitch for Blacks," *SSSBJ*, 18-24 May 1998, 9; Tom Cordova, "Building a Diverse Network of Suppliers Can Pay Big Dividends," *SSSBJ*, 12-18 September 2005, 29.

26. "USA Today Looks at MLS' Target Marketing of Ethnic Groups," *SBD*, 3 March 1998, 9; Sean Brenner, "A World of Opportunity," *SSSBJ*, 31 May-6 June 2004, 16.

27. Announcement in *SSSBJ*, 6-12 July 1998, 15.

28. Information on VALS may be found at www.sric-bi.com/VALS/. For information on discovery segmentation, see R. Piirto, "Cable TV," *American Demographics*, June 1995, 40-47.

29. Galen Trail et al., "Motives and Points of Attachment: Fans Versus Spectators in Intercollegiate Athletics," *SMQ* 12 (4) (2003): 217-230; Daniel Mahoney, Robert Madrigal, and Dennis Howard, "Using the Psychological Commitment to Team (PCT) Scale to Segment Sport Consumers Based on Loyalty," *SMQ* 9 (1) (2000): 15-25.

30. A. Bernstein, "MLS Narrows Its Aim to Game's Core Fans," *SSSBJ*, 15-21 November 1999, 4.

31. J. Seabrook, "Tackling the Competition," *New Yorker* 18 (August 1997): 42-51.

32. WNBA fan data at http://aol.wnba.com/about_us/historyof_wnba.html; John Lombardo, "WNBA Looks for Answers to Attendance Dip," *SSSBJ*, 5-11 September 2005, 7; NCAA data from "NCAA Study Shows Extent of Basketball's Popularity," *NCAA News*, 30 March 1998, 1, 17. For information on women's team fans, see D. Antonelli, "Marketing Intercollegiate Women's Basketball," *SMQ* 3 (2) (June 1994): 29-33; S. Hardy, "Profile/Interview With Donna Lopiano."

33. André Richelieu and Frank Pons, "Reconciling Managers' Strategic Vision With Fans' Expectations," *International Journal of Sports Marketing and Sponsorship* 6 (3) (April, 2005): 150-163.

34. M. Nowell, "The Women's Golf Market," *SMQ* 4 (2) (June 1995): 40. See also the excellent usage segmentation analysis in D. Howard, "Participation Rates in Selected Sport and Fitness Activities," *Journal of Sport Management* 6 (September 1992): 191-205.

35. Joanna Weiss, "TV Marketers Seek Audience With You," *Boston Globe*, 10 June 2005, D-1, D-4. For a valuable review of research on consumer categories, see Bob Stewart, Aaron Smith, and Matthew Nicholson, "Sport Consumer Typologies: A Critical Review," *SMQ* 12 (4) (2003): 206-216.

36. John Lombardo, "A Whole New Ball Game in South Florida," *SSSBJ*, 28 March-3 April 2005, 1, 38-39.

37. James Zhang et al., "Understanding Women's Professional Basketball Game Spectators: Sociodemographics, Game Consumption, and Entertainment Options," *SMQ* 12 (4) (2003): 228-243. For a valuable orientation to "nested" segments, see Mick Jackowski and Dianna Gray, "SportNEST: A Nested Approach to Segmenting the Sport Consumer Market," in *Sport Marketing and the Psychology of Marketing Communication*, eds. Lynn Kahle and Chris Riley (Mahwah, NJ: Erlbaum, 2004), 271-292.

Chapter 7

1. John Lombardo, "AFL: Overnight Success After 16 Years? *SSSBJ*, 17-23 February 2003, 19; John Lombardo, "AFL Counts Gains at Gate, in Sponsorships," *SSSBJ*, 7-13 June 2004, 7; Jeramie McPeek, "Football in a Box," *Sport*, September 1998, 99-101; Daniel Kaplan, "This Time Around, NFL Loves AFL," *SSSBJ*, 3-9 August 1998, 16; "Arena Football Hasn't Reached Its Ceiling Yet," *Boston Globe*, 25 April 1999, D-2.

2. Theodore Levitt, "Marketing Intangible Products and Product Intangibles," *Harvard Business Review* (May-June 1981): 94-102.

3. "Adios Sportschannel, Hola Fox Sports Net," *SBD*, 29 January 1998, 6; Rick Jones, "Sponsorship as Experiences," *Team Marketing Report*, March 2001, 8.

4. "Names in the News," *SBD*, 9 June 1998, 16.

5. "The Real Deal," *The Economist*, 3 July 2004, 53. Classic articles on the importance of product extensions are: Frank Deford, "No Death for a Salesman," *SI*, 28 July 1975, 56-65; Ray Kennedy, "More Victories Equals More Fans Equals More Profits, Right? Wrong, Wrong, Wrong!" *SI*, 28 April 1980, 34-45.

6. For information on event management, see Jerry Solomon, *An Insider's Guide to Managing Sports Events* (Champaign, IL: Human Kinetics, 2002); Guy Masterman, *Strategic Sports Event Management: An International Approach* (Oxford: Elsevier, Butterworth, Heinemann, 2004). Mascot information can be found in "Acme Mascots Inc.," *Sport's Pages* 1 (1) (Winter 1994).

7. Laura Nash, "Ethics Without the Sermon," *Harvard Business Review* (November 1981): 79-90.

8. For material on fan behavior, see Kay Hawes, "Sportsmanship: Why Should Anybody Care? *NCAA News*, 1 June 1998, 1, 18; "Strides in Sportsmanship Require First Step From All," *NCAA News*, 15 June 1998, 1, 6, 7; Mark Hyman, "Maryland Concocting a Code to Kick the !@#$% Out of Its Arena," *SSSBJ*, 10-16 May, 2004, 13; Laurie Smith, "Cheer Pressure," *Athletic Management*, June-July 2004, 43-49; "Football Hooligans," *The Economist*, 12 June 2004, 54; Jack McCallum, "The Ugliest Game," *SI*, 29 November 2004, 44-51.

9. Aaron Conklin, "Opening-Round Upset," *Athletic Business*, August 1998, 28-32.

10. James Trecker, "The Freddy Factor," *SSSBJ*, 10-16 May 2004, 10; Scott Warfield, "Adu Mania Spurs MLS Attendance," *SSSBJ*, 8-14 November 2004, 1, 38-39.

11. "A New Meaning to Patented Move," *Boston Globe*, 16 June 1996, 74.

12. "She's Venus, She's on Fire," *SBD*, 4 September 1997, 7; Mark Beech, "Star-Powered," *SI*, 11 June 2005, 30; "Lack of Star Power Seen as Major Detriment to CART and IRL," *SBD*, 15 May 1998, 9.

13. Terry Lefton, "Retired Players Still Scoring in the Latest Sports QScores," *SSSBJ*, 23-29 May 2005.

14. "Tuna Helps Boost Ad Sales," *SBD*, 1 August 1997; Laura Cohn and Stanley Holmes, "Can Glazer Put This Ball in the Net?" *BusinessWeek*, 30 May 2005, 40.

15. "Hats Off," *SBD*, 4 September 1998, 4; Lefton, "Retired Players Still Scoring," 11.

16. National Scouting Report products may be found at: www.nsr-inc.com. For an attempt to analyze the NBA's management of "race," see Glyn Hughes, "Managing Black Guys: Representation, Corporate Culture, and the NBA," *Sociology of Sport Journal* 21 (2004): 163-184.

17. Bill King, "Passion That Can't Be Counted Puts Billions of Dollars in Play," *SSSBJ*, 11 March 2002, 25-39; Tracy Grant, "Cold Team, Hot Jersey," *Boston Globe*, 7 February 1995, 61.

18. "Ski Federation Spins Web Control on Itsy, Bitsy Spyder Suits," *SBD*, 10 October 1997, 4. For a discussion of the importance of sporting goods in the development of the industry, see Stephen Hardy, "Adopted by All the Leading Clubs: Sporting Goods and the Shaping of Leisure, 1800-1900," in *For Fun and Profit, The Transformation of Leisure Into Consumption*, ed. Richard Butsch (Philadelphia: Temple University Press, 1990), 71-101.

19. "Babe Ruth Bat Hits Auction Record," *Boston Globe*, 3 December 2004, A-2; Dan Shaughnessy, "For Now, He's Having a Ball," *Boston Globe*, 7 January 2004, E-1, E-3.

20. "Five Cities Compete to Host NASCAR Hall of Fame," *USA Today*, 27 May 2005, 2B; Alexander Wolff, "Rockin' the Retros," *SI*, 22 December 2003, 46-54; Liz Mullen, "Tracks Ride 'Seabiscuit' to Attendance Gains," *SSSBJ*, 18-24 August 2003, 1, 46; Terry Lefton, "NHL Turns Silver Icon Into Promotional Gold," *SSSBJ*, 19-25 April 2004 6; Penn State Memento: A Game of Recollection (Lemont, PA: Knuetes, 1998).

21. Bill King, "Finding the Pop for Kids, Teens," *SSSBJ*, 16-22 July 2005, 1, 28-29; Andy Bernstein, "Sports Leagues Get Serious About Toys, *SSSBJ*, 10-16 August 1998, 9; "One Man Gathers What Another Man Spills," *SBD*, 4 December 1997, 4.

22. Bill King, "Cubs Try Topps Twist on Traditional Promotion," *SSSBJ*, 11-17 June 2001, 3; Terry Lefton, "Extra, Extra! Sports Pins and Coin Programs Hot With Newspapers," *SSSBJ*, 20-26 September 2004, 14.

23. Chris Ballard, "Fantasy World," *SI*, 21 June 2004, 83; Bill King, "The 24/7 Fan," *SSSBJ*, 7-13 March 2005, 34.

24. "Fielding Football Fantasies," *Athletic Management*, August-September 2004, 10; LPGA news release, 8 January 1997; Peter Mandel, "A Week Playing With the Big Boys," *Boston Globe*, 2 April 2004, M-10, M-11.

25. Bruce Kuklick, *To Everything a Season: Shibe Park and Urban Philadelphia, 1909-1976* (Princeton, NJ: Princeton University Press, 1991), 191, 193.

26. Naomi Aoki, "Red Sox Owners Fielding More Nongame Revenue," *Boston Globe*, 16 October 2004, D-1, D-3.

27. "Islanders Ticket Request: Look Out Below," *SI*, 14 September 1998, 23.

28. A.J. Magrath, "When Marketing Services, 4 Ps Are Not Enough," *Business Horizons*, May-June 1986, 44-50.

29. Charles L. Martin, "The Customer Relations Dimension of the Employee-Customer Interface: An Empirical Investigation of Employee Behaviors and Customer Perceptions," *Journal of Sport Management*, 4 (January 1990): 1-20; Bernard Mullin, "Applying Disney Techniques to Sport Organizations," unpublished manuscript; Randal Ross, "Creating the Service Experience," *Fitness Management*, September 1993, 32-33; Delpy Goldman, *The Ultimate Guide to Sports Events* (Burr Ridge, IL: Irwin, 1996), 92. The notion of customer service lies at the heart of Thomas Peters and Robert Waterman, *In Search of Excellence* (New York: Warner Books, 1982), one of the best-selling business books of all time.

30. Larry McCarthy and Richard Irwin, "Permanent Seat Licenses as an Emerging Source of Revenue Production," *SMQ* 7 (September 1998): 41-46; *SBD*, 18 August 1997, 10.

31. Richard Irwin and Brian Fleger, "Reading Between the Lines," *Athletic Management*, May 1992, 15-18; Stuart Miller, "ESPN Creates a Rumble at the Newstand," *SSSBJ*, 12-18 October 1998, 12.

32. Gregg Krupa, "Patriots Keep on Clicking," *Boston Globe*, 19 September 1998, F-2, F-3; "Trade a Clapton For a Piazza: New CD Baseball Cards," *SBD*, 9 July 1998, 1.

33. "NASCAR: Moving to the Music" insert, *SI*, 3 August 1998; "Marquee Group's New Team Service," *SBD*, 24 June 1998, 3; "Alphabet City," *SBD*, 5 September 1997, 4.

34. Russell Adams, "Red Sox DVD Already a Record Breaker," *SSSBJ*, 15-21 November 2004, 4.

35. Lisa Altobelli, "Scorecard," *SI*, 27 September 2004, 44.

36. Hiawatha Bray, "Sega Blitzes EA's Madden With NFL Hit," *Boston Globe*, 1 November 2004, B-1, B-8.

37. Nash, "Ethics," 79-80; "Selling Violence With Vulgarity," *SI*, 17 August 1998, 129-130.

38. D. Cooke, "Packaging for Prestige: The Tennis Advantage," *IRSA Club Business*, July 1987, 62-67.

39. Geraldine Willigan, "High-Performance Marketing: An Interview With Nike's Phil Knight," *Harvard Business Review*, July-August 1992, 92, 99; "Nike's Knight Announces Reforms," *SBD*, 13 May 1998, 3.

40. Michael Hiestand, "NBA Puts Clout to Test," *USA Today*, 5 February 1997, 3C.

41. Philip Kotler, *Marketing Management*, 9th ed., (Upper Saddle River, NJ: Prentice Hall, 1997), 282.

42. Stephen Hardy, "Profile/Interview With Matt Levine," *SMQ* 5 (September 1996): 5-12; Douglas Robson, "Sharks Sink in Sales Rankings," *SSSBJ*, 2-8 November 1998, 40.

43. Susan Higgins and James Martin, "Managing Sport Innovations: A Diffusion Theory Perspective," *SMQ* 5 (March 1996): 43-48; E.M. Rogers, *Diffusion of Innovation*, 3rd ed. (New York: Free Press, 1983).

44. Paul Hemp, "In Hockey, the Goal Is Image," *Boston Globe*, 6 January 1993, 53, 55; Kostya Kennedy, "Twilight of the Goons," *SI*, 8 March 1999, 29; "No Competition," *SBD*, 30 July 1997, 12; "Are the Islanders' Preseason Ads Too Much for NHL Office?" *SBD*, 4 September 1998, 5.

45. NTRA advertising supplement to *USA Today*, June 1999.

46. Lawrence Fielding, Lori Miller, and James Brown, "Harlem Globetrotters, Inc." *Journal of Sport Management* 13 (1999): 45-77.

47. Gary Brown, "A Balanced Brand," *NCAA News*, 31 March 2003, A-1-4.

48. Brett Mendel, "Up Against the Pros: Converting the Community," *Athletic Management,* September 1993, 13.

49. Sergio Zyman, *The End of Marketing as We Know It* (New York: Harper Business, 1999), 80-82.

50. Vanessa Abell, "What's in a Name?" *NCAA News,* 28 September 1998, 9.

51. Malcolm Gladwell, *The Tipping Point: How Little Things Can Make a Big Difference* (New York: Back Bay–Little, Brown, 2002), 131-132.

52. For suggestions on the use of perceptual maps, see James Martin, "Using a Perceptual Map of the Consumer's Sport Schema to Help Make Sponsorship Decisions," *SMQ* 3 (3) (September 1994): 27-33.

53. Zyman, *End of Marketing,* 35-36.

54. Geraldine E. Milligan, "High Performance Marketing: An Interview With Nike's Phil Knight," *Harvard Business Review* (July-August 1992): 91-101.

55. "ESPN's Full-Court Press," *Men's Journal* (March 1998): 30; Kotler, *Marketing Management,* 442-460; Jay Gladden, G. Milne, and W.A. Sutton, "A Conceptual Framework for Assessing Brand Equity in Division I College Athletics," *Journal of Sport Management* 12 (1) (1998): 1-19; L.E. Boone, C.M. Kochunny, and D. Wilkins, "Applying the Brand Equity Concept to Major League Baseball," *SMQ* 4 (September 1995): 33-42; D.A. Aaker, *Building Strong Brands* (New York: Free Press, 1996); Terry Lifton, "Study Helps NFL Unify Branding Efforts," *SSSBJ,* 5-11 September 2005, 34.

56. Nariman Dhalla and Sonia Yuspeh, "Forget the Product Life Cycle Concept!" *Harvard Business Review* (January-February 1976): 102-112.

Chapter 8

1. J. Stuart, "Man U Popularity Yields Booming Sales, Profit," *SSSBJ,* 14 October 2002, 17.

2. Ibid.

3. S. Warfield, "Revenue Up, Attendance Down for Champions World," *SSSBJ,* 9 August 2004, 43.

4. "Turnstile Tracker," *SSSBJ,* 1 November 2004, 32.

5. D.A. Aaker, *Managing Brand Equity* (New York: Free Press, 1991), 7.

6. P. Williams, "Franchise Rebranding: Out With the Old...In With the New," *SSSBJ,* 23 February 2004, 17.

7. D. Travis, *Emotional Branding: How Successful Brands Gain the Irrational Edge* (Roseville, CA: Prima Venture, 2000), 15.

8. M. Gobé, *Emotional Branding: The New Paradigm for Connecting Brands to People* (New York: Allworth Press, 2001), xiv.

9. D. Bolger, speech delivered to the University of Massachusetts Sport Management Program, Amherst, MA, 10 September 2004.

10. Aaker, *Managing Brand Equity,* 15.

11. James M. Gladden and Daniel C. Funk, "Understanding Brand Loyalty in Professional Sport: Examining the Link Between Brand Associations and Brand Loyalty," *International Journal of Sports Marketing and Sponsorship* 3 (1) (2001): 45-69.

12. For examples of studies that have shown that winning is not the only important factor to realizing brand loyalty and positive marketplace outcomes, see James M. Gladden and George R. Milne, "Examining the Importance of Brand Equity in Professional Sport," *SMQ* 8 (1) (1999): 21-29; and Gladden and Funk, "Understanding Brand Loyalty."

13. Information gathered 24 September 2004 from http://sports.espn.go.com/mlb/attendance and www.kenn.com/sports/baseball/mlb/mlb_chc_attendance.html.

14. Aaker, *Managing Brand Equity,* 22.

15. T. Lefton, "NASCAR Deal Fuels Gains, Survey Shows," *SSSBJ,* 20 September 2004, 1.

16. Aaker, *Managing Brand Equity,* 208.

17. K.L. Keller, *Strategic Brand Management: Building, Measuring and Managing Brand Equity* (Upper Saddle River, NJ: Prentice Hall, 1998), 50-51.

18. Aaker, *Managing Brand Equity,* 19.

19. Keller, *Strategic Brand Management,* 93.

20. "Duncan Named Rotary Club's Outstanding Young San Antonian," San Antonio Spurs Web site, 4 November 2004, www.nba.com/spurs/community/duncan_rotary_041025.html.

21. "An Inside Look: Guido D'Elia PSU's New Director of Brand Communications," 5 November 2004, www.psuplaybook.org/modules.php?name=News&file=article&sid=987&mode=&order=0&thold=0.

22. D. Katz, *Just Do It: The Nike Spirit in the Corporate World* (Holbrook, MA: Adams Publishing, 1994), 7.

23. G.W. Prince, "Give Them Their Dew: Credit Pepsi for Marketing a Mountain of a Brand," *Beverage World* 54 (January 1998): 54-60.

24. For more on this topic, see James M. Gladden and Richard Wolfe, "Sponsorship and Image Matching: The Case of Intercollegiate Athletics," *International Journal of Sports Marketing and Sponsorship* 3 (1) (2001): 71-98.

25. Retrieved 9 November 2004 from www.1800bepetty.com/index2.html.

26. Retrieved 9 November 2004 from www.wnba.com/playerfile/rebecca_lobo/bio.html.

27. Bernd Schmitt, *Experiential Marketing: How to Get Customers to Sense, Feel, Think, Act, and Relate to Your Company and Brands* (New York: Free Press, 1999).

28. Ibid., 22.

29. Joe Mandese, "On the Road to Hollywood, MPG Makes Stop on 'Madison & Vine,'" *Mediapost,* 31 August 2004, www.mediapost.com/dtls_dsp_news.cfm?cb=051123A&newsID=266777&newsDate=08/31/2004; Kathleen Joyce, "Show Me the Money," *Promo Magazine,* 1 May 2004, 6.

30. "Chrysler Million Dollar Film Festival," 17 October 2004, www.chryslermdff.com.

31. "Hypnotic Case Study Portfolio," 17 October 2004, www.hypnotic.com/portfolio.aspx.

32. Lee Watters, "No Doubt About It," *iMedia Connection,* 12 April 2004, www.imediaconnection.com/content/3200.asp.

33. Anderson, M., "Dissecting 'Subservient Chicken,'" 7 March 2005. Retrieved 31 July 2006 from http://www.adweek.com/aw/national/article_display.jsp?vnu_content_id=1000828049.

34. "Airborne and 49ers Tackle Wireless Initiative," *Business Wire,* 12 October 2004.

Chapter 9

1. D. Century, "In Hip-Hop, Unitas and Chamberlain Live Again," *New York Times,* 5 January 2003, 9-1, 9-2.

2. S. Rushin, "Throwback Hip-Hop Style Points," *SI,* 4 November 2002, 15; M. Hiestand, "Sports Gear So out of Style It's in Style," *USA Today,* 19 August 2002, 3C; A. Wolff, "Rockin' the Retros," *SI,* 22 December 2003, 46-54.

3. Wolff, "Rockin' the Retros," 2003; J. Lee, "Firms Give Retro Jerseys the Old College Try," *SSSBJ*, 15 March 2004, 3.

4. M. Gladwell, *The Tipping Point: How Little Things Can Make a Big Difference* (Boston: Back Bay Books, 2002); S.H. Higgins and J.H. Martin, "Managing Sport Innovations: A Diffusion Theory Perspective," *SMQ* 5 (1) (1996): 43-48.

5. Hiestand, "Sports Gear So out of Style"; M. McCarthy, "'Old Stuff' Scores With Fashionistas," *USA Today*, 16 June 2003, 3B; B. Simmons, "The Sports Guy," *ESPN Magazine*, 20 December 2004, 12.

6. R. Adams, "Licensing Issue Could Shake Up Fantasy Market," *SSSBJ*, 5-12 August 2003, 26.

7. N. Aoki, "Profitable in Pink," *Boston Globe*, 28 January 2005, D-1, D-8; C. Ballard, "Fantasy World," *SI*, 21 June 2004, 80-89; H. Bray, "Game On!" *Boston Globe*, 31 May 2004, D-1, D-4; M. Chambers, "Colleges' Jersey Sales Raise Ethics Concerns," *New York Times*, 31 March 2004, C15, C16; "High School Delays Merchandise Deal," *USA Today*, 2 September 2004, 7C; G. Rivlin, "The Chrome-Shiny, Lights-Flashing, Wheel-Spinning, Touch-Screened, Drew-Carey-Wisecracking, Video-Playing, 'Sound Events'-Packed, Pulse-Quickening Bandits," *New York Times Magazine*, 9 May 2004, 42-47, 74, 80-81; T. Rozhon, "Clothing Retailers Struggle to Size Up Teenagers," *New York Times*, 3 December 2003, C1, C6; R. Walker, "Go Team, Go Figure," *New York Times Sunday Magazine*, 18 April 2004, 24; L. Weisman, "Super Teams Raiders, Bucs Reign at Cash Register, Too," *USA Today*, 23 July 2003, 3C; L. Weisman, "Raiders Merchandise Is NFL's Silver-and-Black Lining," *USA Today*, 22 July 2004, 1C; "Keeping Track of Sports Apparel…in the U.S.," Sporting Goods Manufacturers Association, 2002, www.sgma.com/press/2002/press1021663331-29354.html; "Scorecard: Of a Certain Age," *SI*, 9 June 2003, 23; "Sports Apparel Spending Declines as Buyers Hunt Bargains," Sporting Goods Manufacturers Association, 2002, www.sgma.com/press/2002/press1012917846-298.html.

8. W. Goldstein, *Playing for Keeps: A History of Early Baseball* (Ithaca, NY: Cornell University Press, 1989); M. MacCambridge, *America's Game: The Epic Story of How Pro Football Captured a Nation* (New York: Random House, 2004).

9. A. Murphy, "Make Way for Ducks," *SI*, 29 September 2003, 53-59; P. Taylor, "Wild Ducks," *SI*, 8 September 2003, 54; P. Taylor, "Phil Taylor's Sidelines," *SI*, 27 October 2003, 157.

10. F. Davis, *Fashion, Culture, and Identity* (Chicago: University of Chicago Press, 1992); MacCambridge, *America's Game*; Simmons, "The Sports Guy," 12.

11. M. Bowden, "A Beautiful Mind," *The Atlantic Monthly*, January-February 2004, 195-204; L. Dave, "Fan Fashion: Ball Gowns," *ESPN Magazine*, 2 February 2004, 36; M. Hiestand, "Here's Something to Chew On: NBA Enters Dog Apparel Market," *USA Today*, 9 January 2004, 9C; S. Sennot, "Rubber Made," *Boston Magazine*, August 2003, 50; W. St. John, *Rammer Hammer Yellow Hammer: A Journey Into the Heart of Fan Mania* (New York: Crown, 2004).

12. M. Sperber, *Shake Down the Thunder: The Creation of Notre Dame Football* (New York: Henry Holt, 1993); Hiestand, "Here's Something to Chew On"; M.A. Nichols, "A Look at Some of the Issues Affecting Collegiate Licensing," *Team Licensing Business* 7 (4) (April 1995): 18; C. Plata, "Ducks and Dollars," *Team Licensing Business* 8 (6) (September-October 1996): 38.

13. Lanham Act, 15 U.S.C. § 1051–1127 (1946); R.A. Peterson, K.J. Smith, & P.C. Zerillo, "Trademark Dilution and the Practice of Marketing," *Journal of the Academy of Marketing Science* (Spring 1999): 255-258.

14. "Basic Facts About Registering a Trademark" (Washington, DC: U.S. Government Printing Office, 1994).

15. R. Adams, "Leagues Favor Fewer Deals, Higher Quality," *SSSBJ*, 7-13 July 2003, 21-22.

16. B. Werde, "Photographers and NFL Collide Over Licensing Plan for Archives," *New York Times*, 14 June 2004, C2.

17. E. Sylvers, "Are Origins of Italian Star Found in the Hills of Kentucky?" *New York Times*, 27 February 2004, W1, W7; "W. Kentucky Mascot in Italian Imbroglio," *USA Today*, 2 March 2004, 1C.

18. T. O'Toole, "Copyright Case Over 'Buzz' Costly to Georgia Tech," *USA Today*, 3 October 2001, 1C; J. Carey, "Long Beach State Gets Money's Worth From Baseball Nickname," *USA Today*, 17 August 2004, 3C.

19. J. Feinstein, *Open: Inside the Ropes at Bethpage Black* (Boston: Little, Brown, 2003).

20. D. Kaplan, "Divide on Revenue Sharing Persists in NFL Trust Debate," *SSSBJ*, 23-29 February 2004, 1, 36.

21. MacCambridge; "Sports Merchandising Industry Loses Its Creator, David Warsaw," *Team Licensing Business* 8 (5) (July-August 1996): 18.

22. MacCambridge, "Sports Merchandising Industry."

23. J. Helyar, *Lords of the Realm* (New York: Random House, 1994); R. Lipsey, ed., *Sports Market Place* (Princeton, NJ: Sportsguide, 1996).

24. T. Lefton, "Reebok Adds Rights for MLB to Its Deals With NFL and NBA," *SSSBJ*, 23-29 February 2004, 36.

25. M. Smith, "No Longer a Ty That Binds," *Boston Sunday Globe*, 29 February 2004, E-11.

26. Adams, "Licensing Issue"; Ballard, "Fantasy World," 87; Helyar, "Lords of the Realm."

27. R. Sandomir, "Bonds to Try Going It Alone in Marketing of His Image," *New York Times*, 18 November 2003, C20.

28. The Collegiate Licensing Company, 2003, http://clc.com/Pages/home2.html.

29. S. Brenner, "Rivals Stand Guard Against Ambush Tactics. *SSSBJ*, 22-28 September 2003, 21, 26; S. Brenner, "Texas-Sized Effort Aims to Please Nike," *SSSBJ*, 22-28 September 2003, 21; J. Lee, "College Deals Build Brand and Relationships," *SSSBJ*, 22-28 September 2003, 25.

30. W.C. Rhoden, "Clothier Fears St. Joseph's University May Outgrow Him," *New York Times*, 24 March 2004, C15, C17.

31. A. Bernstein, "Eye on Licensing," *Sporting Goods Business*, 10 February 1997, 22.

32. A. Bernstein, "Maker of U.S. Team Uniforms Boosts Sales Estimate 400%," *SSSBJ*, 18-24 February 2002, 1, 30.

33. S. Woodward, "Red, White and Who? Roots Designing Subdued Gear for Athens Games," *SSSBJ*, 15-21 December 2003, 1, 32; S. Woodward, "Beret of Hope: Will 'Unisex Poorboy' Be Roots' Follow-Up to '02 Hit?" *SSSBJ*, 24-30 May 2004, 10.

34. R.D. Putnam, *Bowling Alone: The Collapse and Revival of American Community* (New York: Touchstone, 2001).

35. M. Bose, *Manchester Unlimited* (New York: Texere Publishing, 2000); D. Kaplan, "Manchester's Red Tide," *SSSBJ*, 6-12 August 2001, 1, 30-31; S.L. Price, "A Yank in Manchester," *SI*, 22 March 2004, 90-94.

36. Kaplan, "Manchester's Red Tide," 31.

37. Bose, *Manchester Unlimited*.

38. Bose, *Manchester Unlimited*; F. Dell'Apa, "Promotion Unites Manchester, Yankees," *Boston Globe*, 13 February 2001, F-2; D. Kaplan, "Yanks–Man U Team Leaves U.S. Soccer on Bench," *SSSBJ*, 12-18 February 2001, 4; D. Kaplan, "Club's Financial Rise Dates to Market Debut. *SSSBJ*, 6-12 August 2001, 30.

39. Bose, *Manchester Unlimited*, 188, 192.

40. R.H. Hagstrom, *The NASCAR Way: The Business That Drives the Sport* (New York: John Wiley and Sons, 1998); A. Rosewater, "Keepsakes Keep Fans Sold on Racing," *USA Today*, 29 August 2003, 9E; T. Weir, "Earnhardt's Image Alive and Collectible," *USA Today*, 22-24 June 2001, 1A-2A.

41. N. Liberman, "Tricks of the Trade," *SSSBJ*, 12-18 July 2004, 21, 28.

42. N. Aoki, "Retailers Ride a Wave," *Boston Globe*, 28 August 2003, C-1, C-8; T. Rozhon, "Hot on the Charts? Then How About the Racks?" *New York Times*, 13 May 2004, C1-C6.

43. H. Lindgren, "Tearing Up the Runway in $400 Cleats," *New York Times*, 8 February 2004, BU4.

44. T. Gray, "The Bounce Is Back for Sneaker Makers," *New York Times*, 23 May 2004, BU8; K.J. O'Brien, "Focusing on Armchair Athletes, Puma Becomes a Leader," *New York Times*, 12 March 2004, W1, W7; S. Stevenson, "How to Beat Nike," *New York Times Magazine*, 5 January 2003, 29-33.

45. F. Lidz, "Rebuilt to Last," *SI*, 2 August 2004, 38.

46. Rozhon, "Hot on the Charts? Then How About the Racks?"

47. S. Langehough, "Symbol, Status, and Shoes: The Graphics of the World at Our Feet," in *Design for Sports: The Cult of Performance*, ed. A. Busch (New York: Princeton Architectural Press, 1998), 20-45; J.D. Toma, *Football U.: Spectator Sports in the Life of an American University* (Ann Arbor: University of Michigan Press, 2003).

48. S.S. Holt, "Notes on an Infinity of Sports Cultures," in *Design for Sports: The Cult of Performance*, ed. A. Busch (New York: Princeton Architectural Press, 1998), 1-19.

49. P. Williams, "Out With the Old…In With the New," *SSSBJ*, 23-29 February 2004, 17-22.

50. Helyar, *Lords of the Realm*.

51. P. Williams, "Phoenix Designs an Updated Logo That's Not Coyote Ugly," *SSSBJ*, 23-29 February 2004, 20; Williams, "Out With the Old."

52. S. DeSimon, "Bird Bath," *ESPN Magazine*, 9 June 2003, 20; Williams, "Out With the Old," 22.

53. M. Hiestand, "Red Sox's Coined Phrase Has Wyoming Company Tall in the Saddle," *USA Today*, 16 October 2003, 7C.

54. Bray, "Game On!" D-4; T. Lefton, "EA Set to Pay Players Inc. $1 Billion," *SSSBJ*, 3-9 May 2004, 1, 34.

55. E. Medina, "With XSNSports and NFL Fever 2004, Xbox Brings Fantasy to Life," *Boston Globe*, 7 September 2003, N-18; E.A. Taub, "No Longer a Solitary Pursuit, Video Games Move Online," *New York Times*, 5 July 2004, C4.

56. D. Wetzel and D. Yaeger, *Sole Influence: Basketball, Corporate Greed, and the Corruption of America's Youth* (New York: Warner Books, 2000).

57. Chambers, "Colleges' Jersey Sales," C16.

58. S. Greenhouse, "Hip-Hop Star's Fashion Line Tagged With Sweatshop Label," *New York Times*, 28 October 2003, C16; "NBA Pulls Sweatshirts Made in Myanmar," *USA Today*, 22 January 2004, 1C.

59. J. Naughton, "Exclusive Deal With Reebok Brings U. of Wisconsin Millions of Dollars and Unexpected Criticism," *Chronicle of Higher Education* 43 (2) (6 September 1996): A65.

60. Code of Conduct for University of Notre Dame Licensees. (Notre Dame, IN: University of Notre Dame, 1997).

61. C. Spindel, *Dancing at Halftime: Sports and the Controversy Over American Indian Mascots* (New York: New York University Press, 2000).

62. Spindel, *Dancing at Halftime*; C.D. Leonnig, "Redskins Can Keep Trademark, Judge Rules," *Washington Post* online, 2 October 2003, www.washingtonpost.com/ac2/wp-dyn/A28449-2003Oct1; MacCambridge, *America's Game*, 165.

63. B.C. Boyd and F.C. Harris, *The Great American Baseball Card Flipping, Trading and Bubble Gum Book* (New York: Ticknor & Fields, 1991).

64. Boyd and Harris, *Baseball Card Flipping*; Helyar, "Lords of the Realm"; S. Rushin, "Sweet Smell of Innocence," *SI*, 13 May 2002, 17.

65. R. Forman, "New Basketball Cards Go for $500 a Pack," *USA Today*, 8 June 2004, 3C; "Scorecard: Go Figure," *SI*, 5 July 2004, 20.

66. M. Chass, "On Baseball," *New York Times*, 4 July 2004, SP5; N. Cobb, "Tribute Is in the Cards for Jewish Ballplayers," *Boston Globe*, 13 October 2003, D-1, D-5; P. Keating, "Played Out," *ESPN Magazine*, 15 March 2004, 104.

67. Aoki, "Profitable in Pink," 2005, D-1; L. Ogunnaike, "Hottest Thing on Wheels, No Wheels Required," *New York Times*, 7 September 2003, ST13.

68. R. Adams, "Fo' Shizzle, MLB Properties to Outfit Snoop," *SSSBJ*, 7-13 June 2004, 36; S. Brenner, "Reebok Sees Rappers as "Must-Have" Pitchmen," *SSSBJ*, 19-25 January 2004, 20; H. Lindgren, "Sampling Bob Griese," *New York Times Magazine*, 14 December 2003, 90.

69. Wolff, "Rockin' the Retros," 54.

70. Lee, "Firms Give Retro Jerseys," 3; Wolff, "Rockin' the Retros," 54.

71. Wolff, "Rockin' the Retros," 15.

72. Simmons, "The Sports Guy."

Chapter 10

1. Kevin Paul Dupont, "Bruins' Price Reduction Is Just the Ticket to Fans," *Boston Globe*, 23 April 1998, C-1, C-8; "The B's Are Back in Business in the Hub," *SBD*, 23 July 1998, 12; Andy Bernstein, "NHL Clubs Try Lower Prices in Higher Seats," *SSSBJ*, 17-23 July 2000, 1, 55; Kevin Paul Dupont, "Front-Row Special for Bruins," *Boston Globe*, 19 June 2003, C-1, C-7; Kevin Paul Dupont, "Touching Base With Fans," *Boston Globe*, 24 July 2005, C-6.

2. Mary Nowell, "The Women's Golf Market," *SMQ* 4 (2) (June 1995): 40; James Faircloth, Michael Richard, and Victoria Richard, "An Analysis of Choice Intentions of Public Course Golfers," *SMQ* 4 (March 1995): 13-21. For a good review of pricing basics, see Allan MaGrath, "Ten Timeless Truths About Pricing," *Journal of Consumer Marketing* 8 (1) (Winter 1991): 5-13.

3. "Getting to the First Tee," *SSSBJ*, 4-10 May 1998, 20; "Early Snow Boosts Chances for Strong Winter Sports Season," *SBD*, 24 November 1997, 16.

4. FCI data may be found at www.teammarketing.com.

5. Gordon Edes, "Club Rebuts Report on Costs at Fenway," *Boston Globe*, 17 July 1997, D-5; Lisa Wangsness, "House Bill Targets Fenway Parking Fees," *Boston Globe*, 16 June 2005, B-2.

6. Suzanne Lainson, "Sports News You Can Use," e-mail newsletter, 6 (1996).

7. MCI club tickets explained in "Yeah, That's the Ticket," *SI*, 6 October 1997, 18-19. List of objectives adapted from Dennis

R. Howard and John L. Crompton, *Financing, Managing and Marketing Recreation and Park Resources* (Dubuque, IA: Brown, 1980); Philip Kotler, *Marketing Management,* 9th ed. (Upper Saddle River, NJ: Prentice Hall, 1997), 494-497.

8. For helpful overviews on standard practices, see Roger Kerin et al., *Marketing,* 7th ed. (New York: McGraw-Hill Irwin, 2003), 340-387; Dan Toxin, "The Membership Pricing Game," *Club Industry,* October 1990, 32-43; Melissa Campanelli, "The Price to Pay," *Sales and Marketing Management* (September 1994): 96-102; Allan Magrath, "Ten Timeless Truths About Pricing," *Journal of Consumer Marketing* 8 (Winter 1991): 5-13. For empirical data on professional team pricing, see P. Riche and M. Mondello, "Ticket Price Determination in the National Football League: A Quantitative Approach," SMQ 12 (2) (2003): 72-79; P. Riche and M. Mondello, "Ticket Price Determination in Professional Sports: An Empirical Analysis of the NBA, NFL, NHL, and Major League Baseball," SMQ 13 (2) (2004): 104-112.

9. We would like to thank Eric Krupa for help in developing this section.

10. Camp example adapted from Howard and Crompton, *Financing, Managing and Marketing,* 435-437.

11. For more applications, see Jeffrey Newkirk, "Break Into Profit," *Fitness Management,* March 1998, 36-38; Thomas Sattler and Julie Mullen, "The Particulars of Pricing Your Product," *Fitness Management,* May 1996, 44-46.

12. Charley Swayne, "Pricing Memberships: What Are You Worth?" *Club Industry,* November 1986, 27-32; "Sports Marketing: The Elusive Event Pricing Formula," *Athletic Business,* May 1989, 18.

13. Suzanne Hildreth, "The New Corporate Market," *CBI—Club Business International,* August 1995, 38. Our thanks also to Lee Seidel, professor of health management and policy at the University of New Hampshire, for explaining the general use of capitation in the health care industry.

14. Eric Mitchell, "PSLs Leap From Curiosity to Necessity," *SSSBJ,* 4-10 January 1999, 12-13; Larry McCarthy and Richard Irwin, "Permanent Seat Licenses (PSLs) as an Emerging Source of Revenue Production," SMQ 7 (September 1997): 41-46; *Wall Street Journal* story outlined in "PSL Concept Gets Ink in WSJ," *SSSBJ,* 20 July 1998, 13.

15. "Not Out of the Woods Yet, Nike Revamps Tiger Line," *SBD,* 3 September 1998, 6; M. Sharon Baker, "Publicist Hired to Sell Seahawks," *SSSBJ,* 6-12 July 1998, 13.

16. Milton H. Spencer, *Contemporary Economics,* 6th ed. (New York: Worth, 1986), 346-347.

17. Kerin et al., *Marketing,* 351-352; Kotler, *Marketing Management,* 499.

18. Charles Stein, "Like It or Not, Scalping Is a Force in the Free Market," *Boston Globe,* 1 May 2005, E-1, 5; Bruce Mohl, "Pro Teams Find a Hot Ticket in Secondary Market," *Boston Globe,* 27 February 2005, E-1, E-5; Steve Bailey, "Red Sox Crack Down on Scalping," *Boston Globe,* 22 September 2005, D-1, D-16; Tim Layden, "The Hustle," *SI,* 4 July 1997, 103-120; Jonah Keri and Mike Sunnucks, "D.C's Ticket Pros Getting Skinned," *SSSBJ,* 30 November-6 December 1998, 13; Eric Fisher, "Secondary Ticketing," *SSSBJ,* 31 October-6 November 2005, 17-21.

19. "MPG: Octane for Management," *Sports Management Review,* Fall 1979, 20.

20. "College Football Ticket Prices," *SSSBJ,* 23-29 September 2002, 42; Howard and Crompton, *Financing, Managing and Marketing,* 429.

21. Toxin, "Membership Pricing Game"; Jill Wagner, "Pricing to Demand," *Fitness Management,* March 1996, 38, 40.

22. John Rofe, "Six Tix Deal Is Hot Seller for San Francisco" *SSSBJ,* 18-24 May 1998, 6.

23. Thomas C. Boyd and Timothy C. Krehbiel, "Promotion Timing in Major League Baseball and the Stacking Effects of Factors That Increase Attendance," SMQ 12 (1) (2003): 173-183, quote at 182.

24. Knicks ticket prices at www.nba.com/knicks/tickets/arena.html#seatingchart; Kevin Paul Dupont, "A Glut of Tickets at Fleet Center," *Boston Globe,* 24 September 1996, A-1, E-7.

25. "Dasherboard Pricing Strategy Helps Avalanche Shatter Revenue Goals," *Team Marketing Report,* July 1996, 4-5.

26. John Morell, "How Much for Tickets?" *New York Times,* 8 June 2003, 4BU; Paul Steinbach, "Value Judgments," *Athletic Business,* December 2002, 22-26; Steve Cameron, "Bruins to Set Prices Hourly," *SSSBJ,* 27 May-2 June 2002, 1, 50.

27. "Slow Back-to-School Sneaker Sales Has Venator Cutting Prices," *SBD,* 1 September 1998, 5.

28. Kotler, *Marketing Management,* 521-22; Kerin et al., *Marketing,* 377.

29. David Scott and John Roach, "Here Comes the Pitch," *Sport,* June 2000, 43.

30. E.M. Swift, "Hey Fans: Sit on It!" *SI,* 15 May 2000, 70-76.

31. *Boston Globe* article quoted in "Does PGA's Fee for Ryder Cup Tickets Fall Under 'Gray Area'?" *SBD,* 28 July 1998, 9.

32. *Orange County Register* article quoted in "Ducks Not Laying Golden Eggs: Team to Raise Ticket Prices," *SBD,* 17 April 1998, 11.

33. Bruce Mohl, "Cable Rates Could Take a Big Jump," *Boston Globe,* 22 June 1998, A-1, A-7; "Are ESPN Execs Ready to Hear an Earful From Cable Operators?" *SBD,* 1 May 1998, 5.

34. Michael Popke, "Up in the Air," *Athletic Business,* January 2005, 28, 30.

35. Chuck Finder, "Penguin Ticket Prices Up Again," *Pittsburgh Post-Gazette,* 6 May 1987.

36. Lou Ann Gorsuch, "Pricing Theory and AD Strategy: How Retailers Compete," *Sporting Goods Dealer,* June 1982, 27-31; Tom Sitek, "Consumers Speak Out," *Sporting Goods Dealer,* February 1987, 99-104.

37. "Hurricanes Admit Mistake in Pricing and Cut Most Ducats," *SBD,* 1 April 1998, 12.

Chapter 11

Portions of this chapter are copyright © 1985 The Michie Company. Material adapted from *Successful Sport Management,* edited by Guy Lewis and Herb Appenzeller, with permission of the Michie Company, Charlottesville, VA. All rights reserved.

1. D. Raley, "New Ichiro Mania: Bobbleheads," *Seattle Post-Intelligencer Reporter,* 27 July 2001.

2. For general overviews, see P. Kotler, *Marketing Management: Analysis, Planning, and Control,* 5th ed. (Upper Saddle River, NJ: Prentice Hall, 1984), 636-715. For an outstanding compilation of promotional activities used by sport organizations, see D. Wilkerson, *The Sport Marketing Encyclopedia* (Champaign, IL: Human Kinetics, 1986). The Chicago-based *Team Marketing Report* is the most current source of promotional ideas used in professional and collegiate sport. The *NACMA Resource Book* is another worthy source of promotional concepts.

3. Mike Veeck, address at the National Basketball Association Game Presentation Workshop, Secaucus, NJ, 23 September 2003.

4. N. Sylvester, "Marketing Fitness: Sell the Imagery Not the Agony," *Athletic Business,* July 1984, 8-16; "Producing a Winning

Ad: Industry Leaders Reveal What Counts," *IRSA Club Business*, May 1986, 28-31.

5. R. Batra, J.G. Myers, and D.A. Aaker, *Advertising Management*, 5th ed. (Upper Saddle River, NJ: Prentice Hall, 1996), 47.

6. D.E. Schultz, S.I. Tannenbaum, and A. Allison, *Essentials of Advertising Strategy*, 3rd ed. (Lincolnwood, IL: NTC Business Books, 1996), 49.

7. D. Stotler and D. Johnson, "Assessing the Impact and Effectiveness of Stadium Advertising on Sports Spectators at Division Institutions," *Journal of Sport Management* 3 (July 1989): 90-102.

8. Batra, Myers, and Aaker, *Advertising Management*, 12.

9. R.F. Gerson, "What to Expect From Your Ad Agency," *Fitness Management*, January 1994, 22-23.

10. Batra, Myers, and Aaker, *Advertising Management*, 45.

11. Audience Analysts conducted proprietary research studies for MLB Properties and the Pittsburgh Pirates during the period of 30 June-7 July 1998. The research for the Pirates was conducted by videotaping interviews with respondents prior to entering Three Rivers Stadium. The research regarding MLB's FanFest was conducted in Denver using an exit survey format with a self-administered survey.

12. A. Bernstein, "High-Tech a (Virtual) Sign of the Times," *Sports Business Journal* 1 (9) (22-28 June 1998): 24, 36.

13. Stotler and Johnson, "Assessing the Impact," 14-20.

14. N.K. Pope and K.E. Voges, "Sponsorship Evaluation: Does It Match the Motive and the Mechanism?" *SMQ* 3 (4) (1994): 37-45.

15. D.M. Turco, "The Effects of Courtside Advertising on Product Recognition and Attitude Change," *SMQ* 5 (4) (1996): 11-15.

16. J. Lombardo, "Toyota Making Most of Unusual Combination," *SSSBJ* 8 (35) (9-15 January 2006): 5

17. "MLB Initiative Helps Cardinals Land New Sponsor; Shell Dealers Sign on for Scorekeeping Promotions," *Team Marketing Report* 9 (6) (March 1997): 1-2.

18. C. Brooks and K. Harris, "Celebrity Athlete Endorsement: An Overview of the Key Theoretical Issues," *SMQ* 7 (2) (1998): 34-44. See also H. Friedman and L. Friedman, "Endorser Effectiveness by Product Type," *Journal of Advertising Research* 19 (5) (1979): 63-71; and G. McCracken, "Who Is the Celebrity Endorser? Cultural Foundations of the Endorsement Process," *Journal of Consumer Research* 19 (December 1989): 310-321.

19. McCracken, "Who Is the Celebrity Endorser?"

20. B. Sugar, *Hit the Sign and Win a Free Suit of Clothes From Harry Finklestein* (Chicago: Contemporary Books, 1978), 327-329.

21. D.K. Stotler, F.R. Veltri, and R. Viswanathan, "Recognition of Athlete-Endorsed Sport Products," *SMQ* 7 (1) (1998): 48-56.

22. J. Sivulka, *Soap, Sex and Cigarettes: A Cultural History of American Advertising* (Belmont, CA: Wadsworth, 1998), 397.

23. T. Lefton, "Old Pros Rule SportsQ Scores, Starting With Jordan," *SSSBJ*, 10-16 May 2004, 11.

24. "Rayovac Taps Michael Jordan to Recharge Battery Brand," *Sports Marketing Letter* 7 (4) (April 1995): 1, 3.

25. T. Lefton, "Nike deal was talk of the shoes forum," *SSSBJ*, 6-12 October 2003, 12.

26. G. Strauss, "The Ultimate Success Story: From Drug Dealer to Rapper to Movie Star," *USA Today*, 11 February 2004, 1A-2A.

27. G. Johnson, "Shoe Makers Sizing Up Performance of Celebrity Endorsements," *Los Angeles Times*, 11 September 1997, D5.

28. L. Mullen, "Morals Clauses Give Companies an Out," *SSSBJ*, 11-17 August 2003, 5.

29. "Experts Weigh Bryant Team's Response to Crisis," *SSSBJ*, 28 July-3 August 2003, 6.

30. T. Howard, "Advertisers Get in the Game," *USA Today*, 10 September 2004, 4B.

31. M. Hiestand, "Ads Muscling Into Live TV Events," *USA Today*, 28 October 2004, 11C.

32. M. Poole, "Image Is Everything but What Do These Brands Want?" *SSSBJ* 8 (33) (19-25 December 2005): 13.

33. M. Phillips, "Taking Stock: Top Sports Pros Find a New Way to Score: Getting Equity Stakes," *Wall Street Journal*, 18 April 1997, A1-A3.

34. B. King, "Retired but Still in the Game," *SSSBJ* 3 (25) (9-15 October 2000): 27.

35. Ibid.

36. D. Gellene, "Outlived by Fame and Fortunes," *Los Angeles Times*, 11 September 1997, D4.

37. S. Wollenberg, "Jackie Robinson a Celebrity Endorser Again," *Marketing News* 31 (9) (28 April 1997): 1.

38. "Advertising Practices," *Sporting Goods Dealer*, November 1982, 24-29.

39. Batra, Myers, and Aaker, *Advertising Management*, 94-95.

40. "Ad Spotlight," *Team Marketing Report* 16 (11) (August 2004): 3.

41. For some interesting approaches by the University of Virginia, see "Virginia's Marketing Plans Increase Sales," *Team Marketing Report* (November 1989): 8.

42. Batra, Myers, and Aaker, *Advertising Management*, 425.

43. M.J. Houston, T.L. Childers, and S.E. Heckler, "Picture-Word Consistency and the Elaborative Processing of Advertisements," *Journal of Marketing Research* 24 (December 1987): 359-369.

44. These systems are also used to recognize individuals for birthdays, anniversaries, and so forth; the actual practice varies from venue to venue.

45. "Advertising Rates on 1998 MLB Radio Broadcasts," *Team Marketing Report* 10 (5) (February 1998): 7.

46. "Knicks and Padres Use Television to Tune Into Hispanic Population," *Team Marketing Report* 10 (6) (March 1998): 3.

47. "Regional Marketing Effort Drives Ford to Multi-University Radio Deal," *Team Marketing Report* 9 (9) (June 1997): 6.

48. "Phillies Radio Network Tunes in to Kids With Hopes to Attract Listeners for Life," *Team Marketing Report* 10 (6) (March 1998): 9.

49. Batra, Myers, and Aaker, *Advertising Management*, 438.

50. B. King, "Sonics' Home Movies Are a Hit," *SSSBJ* 1 (5) (25-31 May 1998): 8.

51. R. Alridge, "This Movie's the Real Thing," *Chicago Tribune*, 16 October 1981, 6-16.

52. K. Kranhold, "Golf's High Profile Drives Firms to Take Whack at Big Campaigns," *Wall Street Journal*, 28 July 1997, B6.

53. D. Enrico, "Heart-Warming Ad Impresses Consumer Panel," *USA Today*, 5 August 1996, 1B-2B.

54. Material for this sidebar compiled from B. Sugar, *Hit the Sign*, 369-374.

55. This material derived from M. Wells, "Ads Featuring Athletes: They Shoot, They Score," *USA Today*, 13 July 1998, 5B.

56. J.R.B. Ritchie, "Assessing the Impact of Hallmark Events: Conceptual and Research Issues," *Journal of Travel Research* 3 (1) (1984): 2-11.

57. P. Kotler, D.H. Haider, and I. Rein, *Marketing Places* (New York: Free Press, 1993), 173.

58. W.A. Sutton, M.A. McDonald, G.R. Milne, and J. Cimperman, "Creating and Fostering Fan Identification in Professional Sports," *SMQ* 6 (1) (1997): 15-22.

59. For an example of such a linkage, see www.nba.com.

60. For an example, see www.nba.com/sonics.

61. D. Migala, "If Your Web Site Doesn't Have These Features, You're Losing Business," *SSSBJ* 7 (19) (13-19 September 2004): 15.

62. A. Bernstein, "Blogger Puts Readers Inside NHL Labor Talks," *SSSBJ* 8 (5) (23-29 May 2005): 1, 26.

63. "Smoking Out Ticket Sales," *Team Marketing Report* 15 (9) (June 2003): 4.

64. "Sun Drop On-Can Promotion Could Pop Top for Future Sponsorships," *Team Marketing Report* 10 (5) (February 1998): 4.

65. D. Ziccardi, *Masterminding the Store* (New York: Wiley, 1997), 214.

66. B. Veeck and E. Linn, *Veeck as in Wreck* (New York: Putnam's, 1962), 104-118.

67. G. Collier, "Drunken Fans Can Turn on a Dime," *Pittsburgh Post-Gazette*, 4 June 1994, D1.

68. Ziccardi, *Masterminding the Store*, 215-235.

69. Phoenix Coyotes 1997 ticket brochure.

70. Cleveland Cavs sales brochure, Gund Arena, 1 Center Court, Cleveland, OH.

71. B. King, "Theme Nights, Events Boost Lagging Giveaway Promotions," *SSSBJ* 6 (26) (20-26 October 2004): 43.

72. Ibid.

73. L. Berling-Manual, "Family Fun Comes to the Forefront," *Ad Age*, 2 August 1984, 11.

74. K. Higgins, "Play Ball," *Marketing News*, 26 April 1985, 8.

75. J. Lopiano-Misdom and J. DeLuca, *Street Trends* (New York: Harper Business Books, 1997), xi-xii.

76. N. Martinez and R. Van Kleeck, "Neophytes Making a Name on Madison Avenue," *USA Today*, 30 March 1998, 3B.

77. Lopiano-Misdom and DeLuca, *Street Trends*, 147.

78. Ibid., 142.

79. B. Giles, "Special Efforts Needed to Attract New Fans," *Athletic Purchasing and Facilities*, October 1980, 16-19.

80. C. Rees, "Does Sports Marketing Need a New Offense?" *Marketing and Media Decisions*, February 1981, 66-67, 126-132.

81. W.A. Sutton, R.L. Irwin, and J.M. Gladden, "Tools of the Trade: Practical Research Methods for Events, Teams and Venues," *SMQ* 7 (2) (1998): 45-49.

82. S. Brenner, "76ers Community Intercept Survey Suggests New Marketing Tactics," *Team Marketing Report* 8 (June 1996): 9.

Chapter 12

1. Material compiled from G. Groeller, "Royal Marketing," *Orlando Sentinel* 25 April 2004, H1, H7, and J. Vitale, *There's a Customer Born Every Minute* (New York: AMACOM Books, 1998), 47.

2. R. Burton and R.Y. Cornilles, "Emerging Theory in Team Sport Sales: Selling Tickets in a More Competitive Arena," *SMQ* 7 (1) (1998): 33.

3. www.mlb.com, March 2005.

4. Y. Berra, *The Yogi Book* (New York: Workman, 1998), 16.

5. T. Hopkins, *Selling for Dummies* (Foster City, CA: IDG Books Worldwide, 1995), 9.

6. M. McCormack, *On Selling* (West Hollywood, CA: Dove Books, 1996), 7.

7. P. Honebein, *Strategies for Effective Customer Education* (Lincolnwood, IL: NTC Business Books, 1997), 25.

8. N.J. Stephens, *Streetwise Customer-Focused Selling* (Holbrook, MA: Adams Media, 1998), 4.

9. McCormack, *On Selling*, 9-10.

10. J. Mielke, "Specialization Through Departmentalization," *That's the Ticket* 1 (1) (May 1997): 5.

11. S.K. Jones, *Creative Strategy in Direct Marketing* (Lincolnwood, IL: NTC Business Books, 1990), 4-5.

12. For an excellent discussion of the importance of building a database and clear-cut examples of how this has been done in professional sport, see J. Spoelstra, *How to Sell the Last Seat in the House* (Portland, OR: SRO Partners, 1991), 72-94.

13. J. Spoelstra, *Ice to the Eskimos: How to Sell a Product Nobody Wants* (New York: Harper Business, 1997), 32-38.

14. W.A. Sutton, "SMQ Profile/Interview: Don Johnson," *SMQ* 6 (2) (1997): 5-8.

15. Spoelstra, *Ice to the Eskimos*, 40-42.

16. J. Lehman, *The Sales Manager's Mentor*, 2nd ed. (Seattle, WA: Mentor Press, 2006), 225.

17. B. Stone and J. Wyman, *Successful Telemarketing: Opportunities and Techniques for Increasing Sales and Profits* (Lincolnwood, IL: NTC Business Books, 1986), 6.

18. G.S. Day, *Market Driven Strategy: Processes for Creating Value* (New York: Free Press, 1990), 234.

19. Statistics compiled from a study by the Direct Marketing Association, April 2005.

20. "Red Sox Telephone Ticket System Dials Up Immediate Sales Results," *Team Marketing Report* 10 (5) (February 1998): 3.

21. R.T. Moriarity, G.S. Swartz, and C.A. Khuen, *Managing Hybrid Marketing Channels With Automation* (Cambridge, MA: Marketing Science Institute, 1988).

22. Stone and Wyman, *Successful Telemarketing*, 102.

23. "Teams, Sponsors Use Phone System to Ring Up Results," *Team Marketing Report* 6 (8) (May 1994): 4-5.

24. Jones, *Creative Strategy*, 7-9.

25. Golfsmith International, L.P., Golfsmith Store catalog, Austin, TX, August 1998.

26. PGA TOUR Partners Club, PGA TOUR Partners Club brochure, Minnetonka, MN, 1998, 4-10.

27. Jack Nicklaus rewards brochure, Citibank, 1997-1998.

28. Jones, *Creative Strategy*, 101.

29. W.T. Knudsen, Kiro Direct sales and marketing materials, Seattle, WA, 1997.

30. Spoelstra, *Ice to the Eskimos*, 173.

31. Phoenix Coyotes, 1996-1997 annual report, Phoenix, AZ, 1997.

32. B. Breighner, *Face-to-Face Selling* (Indianapolis, IN: Park Avenue, 1995), x.

33. D. Ziccardi, *Masterminding the Store* (New York: Wiley, 1997), 238.

34. Spoelstra, *Ice to the Eskimos*, 146-151.

35. Breighner, *Face-to-Face Selling*, 84-85.

36. Stephens, *Streetwise Customer-Focused Selling*, 25.

37. R. McKenna, *Relationship Marketing: Successful Strategies for the Age of the Consumer* (Reading, MA: Addison-Wesley, 1991), 4.

38. C. Gronroos, *Service Management and Marketing: Managing Moments of Truth in Service Competition* (New York: Lexington Books, 1990).

39. D. Shani, "A Framework for Implementing Relationship Marketing in the Sport Industry," SMQ 6 (2) (1997): 9-15.

40. Burton and Cornilles, "Emerging Ticket Theory," 29-37.

41. For an excellent study of how to create a market, see P. Levine, *A.G. Spalding and the Rise of Baseball* (New York: Oxford Press, 1985).

42. Spoelstra, *Ice to the Eskimos*, 91-93.

43. For a truly enjoyable read and examples of how to sell, see B. Veeck and E. Linn, *Veeck as in Wreck* (New York: Putnam's, 1962). Mike Veeck's successful exploits with the independent Northern League St. Paul Saints is chronicled in S. Perlstein, *Rebel Baseball: The Summer the Game Was Returned to the Fans* (New York: Holt, 1994).

44. Pittsburgh Pirates group sales brochure G, 1998.

45. G. Boeck, "Winning Friends and Influencing Ticket Buyers," *USA Today*, 13 September 2005, 3C.

46. Ibid.

47. S. Warfield, "Pepsi Promotion Targets Latinos," SSSJ 8 (8) (13-19 June 2005): 12.

48. For an explanation of this need, see W.A. Sutton, M.A. McDonald, G.R. Milne, and J. Cimperman, "Creating and Fostering Fan Identification in Team Sports," SMQ 6 (1) (1997): 15-22.

49. D. Migala, "New Software Lets Pistons' Ticketing Staff Chat Live With Web Visitors," SSSBJ 7 (31) (6-12 December 2004): 16.

50. C. Harris, "Suns Tickets Get Wired," 23 December 2004, www.nba.com/suns/news/azcentral_harris_041223.html.

51. F.R. Dwyer, "Customer Lifetime Valuation to Support Marketing Decision Making," *Journal of Direct Marketing* 3 (Autumn 1989): 8-15.

52. M.A. McDonald and G.R. Milne, "A Conceptual Framework for Evaluating Marketing Relationships in Professional Sport Franchises," SMQ 6 (2) (1997): 27-32.

53. B.T. Gale, *Managing Customer Value* (New York: Free Press, 1994), 3-23.

54. Forum Consulting, Boston MA; Customer Service Institute, Silver Spring, MD.

55. T.G. Vavra, *Aftermarketing: How to Keep Customers for Life Through Relationship Marketing* (New York: Irwin, 1992), 22.

56. K. Blanchard and S. Bowles, *Raving Fans* (New York: Morrow, 1993).

57. Created on the basis of materials from Vavra, *Aftermarketing*, 25.

58. J. Mitchell, *Hug Your Customers* (New York: Hyperion, 2003), 7.

Chapter 13

1. Compiled from T. Mickle, "How Disney Put Its 'Pirates' in Thick of Volvo Ocean Race," SSSBJ 9 (2) (1-7 May 2006): 1, 28.

2. "Chain-Specific Promotions Yielding New Alliances Among Licensors, Retailers, Fast-Food Chains," *Entertainment Marketing Letter*, October 1990, 1.

3. J. Meenaghan, *Commercial Sponsorship* (West Yorkshire, England: MCB University Press, 1984).

4. Meenaghan, *Commercial Sponsorship*.

5. S.A. Wichmann and D.R. Martin, "Sport and Tobacco—the Smoke Has Yet to Clear," *Physician and Sports Medicine* 19 (11) (1991): 125-131.

6. N. Meyers and L. Clarke, "No Trouble Foreseen in Finding Sponsors," *USA Today*, 23 June 1997, 3B.

7. B. Horovitz, "Viewer's Favorite Ads Crude, Rude and Furry," *USA Today*, 2 February 2004, 7B.

8. N. Lieberman, "Putting the Pieces Together," SSSBJ 8 (3) (9-15 May 2005): 19-23.

9. R.G. Hagstrom, *The NASCAR Way: The Business That Drives the Sport* (New York: Wiley, 1998), 50.

10. P. Ueberroth, *Made in America* (New York: Morrow, 1985), 61.

11. W. D'Orio, "Just Doing It," *Promo* 10 (4) (March 1997): 38.

12. L. Ukman, notes from Sponsorship Trends Workshop, Chicago, IL, 2000.

13. M. Hanan, *Life-Styled Marketing* (New York: AMACOM Books, 1980), 2-3.

14. "Healthy Choice Creates Integrated Promotions Around Ski Team Deal," *IEG Sponsorship Report* 16 (16) (18 August 1997): 1-3.

15. D. Wilber, "Linking Sports and Sponsors," *Journal of Business Strategy* (July-August 1998): 8-10.

16. M. Littman, "Sponsors Take to the Court With the New Women's NBA." *Marketing News* 31 (5) (1997): 1, 6.

17. Meenaghan, *Commercial Sponsorship*.

18. R.L. Irwin, M. Asimakopoulos, and W.A. Sutton, "A Model for Screening Sponsorship Opportunities," *Journal of Promotional Management* 2 (3-4) (1994): 53-69.

19. "New Juice for Giants: Solar Energy Powering Up Portion of SBC Park Through Partnership With Sharp," *Team Marketing Report* 17 (7) (April 2005): 1-3.

20. "In-Line Manufacturer Gets Hockey Marketing Strategy Rolling With IHL Milwaukee Admirals," *Team Marketing Report* 8 (3) (December 1995): 1-2.

21. S.C. Schafer, "How Coors Picks Its Winners in Sports," *BusinessWeek*, 26 August 1985, 56-61.

22. D. Kaplan and T. Lefton, "Molson, Coors Renewing With NFL," SSSBJ 8 (18) (5-11 September 2005): 1, 59.

23. J. Lee, "MasterCard Finds an Opportunity Deep in the Heart of Texas," SSSBJ 6 (31) (24-30 November 2003), 22.

24. G. Krupa, "Cup Runneth Over," *Boston Sunday Globe*, 7 June 1998, F-1, F-7.

25. Meenaghan, *Commercial Sponsorship*.

26. "Cavalier's New Community Relations Program Draws New Advertisers From Local Minority-Owned Businesses," *Team Marketing Report* 8 (2) (November 1995): 1-2.

27. J. Carlucci, "Linking Sports Sponsorship to the Trade," *Marketing Communications*, November-December 1995, 1-2.

28. F. Coleman, "Major Sponsors Love World Cup's Marketing Power," *USA Today*, 9 June 1998, 7B.

29. R. Nethery, "Holy Mackerel! Pro Bass Fishing Snags a Major Fan Following," SSSBJ 7 (15) (16-22 August 2004), 17-18.

30. S.G. Beatty, "Public Is Confused on Olympic Sponsors," *Wall Street Journal,* 18 February 1998, B8.

31. M. Heistand, "Woods Gets Nike Logo Maximum Exposure," *USA Today,* 17 April 1997, 9C.

32. W.A. Sutton, "SMQ Profile/Interview With Joyce Julius Cotman," *SMQ* 7 (2) (1998): 6-7.

33. N. Lieberman, "EDS to Use Tourney as Launch Pad," *SSSBJ* 8 (2) (2-8 May 2005): 8.

34. "T-Mobile Links Broad Marketing Partnership with WNBA and NBA," National Basketball Association press release, 3 October 2005.

35. A.L. Schreiber, *Lifestyle and Event Marketing* (New York: McGraw-Hill, 1994), 140.

36. D.M. Halbfinger, "D'Alessandro: To Market, to Market," *Boston Globe,* 10 April 1996, 55-56.

37. "Visa signs NFL Sponsor Pact for $40 Million+," *Sports Marketing Newsletter* 7 (4) (April 1995): 1-2.

38. S. Lainson, "Client Entertainment," Sports News You Can Use (1997), 12, 1-3, slainson@sportstrust.com.

39. C. Sampson, *The Masters: Golf, Money and Power in Augusta, Georgia* (New York: Villard, 1998), xxiv.

40. A. Friedman, ed., *Naming Rights Deals* (Chicago: Team Marketing Report, 1997), 8.

41. S. Warfield, "Red Bull Energizes MLS With Team Purchase," *SSSBJ* 44 (13-19 March 2006), 3.

42. A. Friedman, "Naming Rights May Be Bargain for Companies Going National," *SSSBJ* 1 (3) (1998): 8.

43. N. Lieberman, "Banking on Sports: Industry Aims to Score Big With the Consumers," *SSSBJ* 7 (29) (22-28 November 2004), 19-21.

44. Hagstrom, *The NASCAR Way,* 52.

45. "The Price of Pricing: Breakdown of Sponsorship Analysis Companies and Why or Why Not to Hire One," *Team Marketing Report* 16 (9) (June 2004) 1-2.

46. G. Kane, "Sharp Sponsors Demand a Sharp ROI," *SSSBJ* 6 (31) (24-30 November 2003), 24.

47. "Moving Target: Survey Reveals Sponsorships Shift from advertising to Integrated Marketing Strategies," *Team Marketing Report* 16 (7) (April 2004): 1-2.

48. "Raptors Arrange Consumer Research to Show Partners How Their Sponsorships Are—or Aren't Working," *Team Marketing Report* 9 (9) (June 1997): 1-2.

49. "Commissioned Work: Incentive-laden Sponsorship Packages Becoming More Prominent Formula," *Team Marketing Report* 15 (6) (March 2003): 1-2.

50. B. Macchiette and R. Abhijit, "Affinity Marketing: What Is It and How Does It Work?" *Journal of Services Marketing* 6 (3) (1992): 47-57.

51. "What Is Affinity Marketing?" http://mbna.com/canada/about_company_affinity.html.

52. Hagstrom, *The NASCAR Way,* 59-60.

53. R. Bednar, *Sponsorship's Holy Grail* (Lincoln, NE: iUniverse), 9.

54. D.M. Sandler and D. Shani, "Olympic Sponsorship vs. 'Ambush' Marketing: Who Gets the Gold?" *Journal of Advertising Research* 29 (4) (1989): 9-14.

55. T. Meenaghan, "Point of View: Ambush Marketing: Immoral or Imaginative Practice?" *Journal of Advertising Research* 34 (5) (1994): 77-88.

56. R.N. Davis, "Ambushing the Olympic Games," *Villanova Sports Law and Entertainment Journal* 3 (1996): 423-442.

57. B. Payne, "Facing an Ambush: How the IOC Took on Nike in Atlanta," *SSSBJ* 8 (11) (11-17 July 2005), 20.

58. N. Lieberman, "Cultivating an Organic Approach," *SSSBJ* 7 (44) (14-20 March 2005), 8.

59. "Homing Device: Cavaliers Draw Fans to Web Site With Personalized Giveaway," *Team Marketing Report* 17 (7) (April 2005): 9.

60. Phone interview with Adam Helfant, Nike Olympic Sport Marketing, 15 September 2005.

61. Seth Godin, *All Marketers Are Liars* (New York: Portfolio, 2005), 35.

62. J. Naughton, "Exclusive Deal With Reebok Brings U. of Wisconsin Millions of Dollars and Unexpected Criticism," *Chronicle of Higher Education,* 6 September 1996, A65-A66.

63. J. Lee, "Alcohol on Campus: When to Say When," *SSSBJ* 7 (17) (30 August-5 September, 2004): 1, 32-35.

64. Ibid, 32.

65. Ibid, 32.

66. K. Hawes, "A Brewing Dilemma on Campus," *NCAA News* 35 (14) (1998): 1, 6, 7, 20.

67. W.A. Sutton and M.A. McDonald, "Building a Partnership," *Athletic Management* 10 (4) (1998): 16-19.

Chapter 14

1. J. Fraiberg, "A Racket at Rush Hour," *SI,* 9 October 1995, 16.

2. Lars Anderson, "Going Global," *SI,* 14 March 2005, 20; "NHL's Two-Game Stint in Japan Concludes With All Sides Happy," *SBD,* 6 October 1997, 6.

3. "Real Madrid's Tour of China Leaves Fans Wet and Disappointed," the *Star* Online, 26 July 2005, www.thestar.com; Yu Yilei, "Clubs Should Be Serious About Trips to China," *China Daily,* 28 July 2005, www.chinadaily.com.cn/english/doc/2005-07/28/.

4. "NHL Breaks Out Another Three-Year Deal With Streetball," *SBD,* 7 May 1998, 4; www.nhl.com/laceemup/breakout/index.html, 2006.

5. NFL Youth Football, www.nflyouthfootball.com, 2006.

6. Daniel Kaplan, "World of Uncertainty for NFL Europe," *SSSBJ,* 9-15 June 2003, 1, 4; Maarten van Bottenburg, "Thrown for a Loss? (American) Football and the European Sport Space," *American Behavioral Scientist* 46 (11) (July 2003), 1550-1562; J. Maguire, "More Than a Sporting Touchdown: The Making of American Football in England, 1982-1990," *Sociology of Sport Journal* 7 (1990): 213-237.

7. P. Gammons, "The Place Is the Thing," *Boston Globe,* 25 April 1995, 76, in special section, "No Replacement for Fenway." The notion of ensemble is developed in J. Bale, *Sport, Space and the City* (London: Routledge, 1993); J. Bale, *Landscapes of Modern Sport* (Leicester, UK: University of Leicester, 1994); J. Raitz, ed., *The Theater of Sport* (Baltimore: Johns Hopkins University Press, 1995); Megan Tench, "Making Fenway Bright," *Boston Globe,* 24 November 2004, B-1, B-6; Thomas Palmer, "Sox Make Off-Season Pitch," *Boston Globe,* 16 December 2004, E-1, E-4; Sasha Talcott, "Hockey Games, Skating Proposed for Fenway Park," *Boston Globe,* 26 March 2005, A-1, A-5.

8. R. Sandomir, "Sox Detour Time," *Sports Inc.,* 28 March 1988, 32-33. For an excellent historical analysis of ballpark placement, see S.A. Riess, *Touching Base: Professional Baseball and American*

Culture in the Progressive Era (Westport, CT: Greenwood Press, 1980). Two valuable guides to stadium design—including most of the topics in this section—are Geraint John and Rod Sheard, *Stadia: A Design and Development Guide,* 2nd ed. (Oxford: Architectural Press, 1997), and Rod Sheard, *Sports Architecture* (London and New York: Spon Press, 2001).

9. E. Cohen, "Miles, Minutes, and Custom Markets," *Marketing Tools,* July-August 1996, 18-21; M. Levine, "Know Your Facility's Drawing Radius," *Sport Marketing Review,* Spring 1977, 1.

10. P. Gollenback, *American Zoom* (New York: Macmillan, 1993), 87. On Charlotte, see E. Hinton, "Long Way to Go," *SI,* 18 December 1995, 59-62.

11. "Will There Be a Giant Parking Problem at Pac Bell Ballpark?" *SBD,* 20 August 1998, 13. See also the parking ratio issue related to the L.A. Coliseum in L. Mullen, "Coliseum Parking Could Add $100M to Cost," *SSSBJ,* 26 April-2 May 1999, 5.

12. M. DiNitto, "Fields of Vision," *Athletic Business,* January 1999, 38-45.

13. Z. Dowdy, "BC Told to Redo Plan for Parking," *Boston Globe,* 2 September 1993, 25, 30.

14. "Head Count," *SBD,* 22 June 1999, 15; A. Goldfisher, "Concourses Designed to Serve Up Profits," *SSSBJ,* 24-30 August 1998, 22.

15. For a classic account of changes in "flow" made at Stanford Stadium in anticipation of the 1985 Super Bowl, see J. Anderson, "Management by Design," *Athletic Business,* August 1985, 28-34; Steve Cameron, "Traffic Flow Inside Venue as Important as Outside," *SSSBJ,* 30 July-5 August 2001, 22.

16. Paul Steinbach, "Venue Visuals," *Athletic Business,* August 2005, 63-70.

17. The seminal work on framing in sport is John MacAloon, "Olympic Games and the Theory of Spectacle in Modern Societies," in *Rite, Drama, Festival, Spectacle: Rehearsals Toward a Theory of Cultural Performance,* ed. John J. MacAloon (Philadelphia: Institute for the Study of Human Issues, 1984), 241-280.

18. Richard Harding Davis, "The Thanksgiving Day Game," *Harper's Weekly* 37 (December 1893, 1170-1171) in *Major Problems in American Sport History,* ed. Steven Riess (Boston: Houghton Mifflin, 1997), 116-118.

19. Dan Bickley, "Pro Sports May Be Pricing Fans Out of Stadiums," *Arizona Republic,* 24 June 2001.

20. Michelle Brutlag Hosick, "More Than a Game," *NCAA News,* 27 September 2004, A1-4.

21. "Arena Features," www.xcelenergycenter.com, 2006.

22. Bill King, "Keeping Fans Connected," *SSSBJ,* 1-7 November 2004, 15-17. See also Cade Metz, "The NFL's Wireless Game Plan," *PC Magazine,* 23 August 2005, 74.

23. www.tampabaylightning.com; www.philipsarena.com, 2006.

24. D. Schwartz, "Good Food, Shops Are Open for Business," *SSSBJ,* 24-30 August 1998, 26.

25. United Center, Club Seating Handbook, available at www.unitedcenter.com/pdfs/cshandbook.pdf; Don Muret, "Once-Hot Club Seats Have Fewer Fans," *SSSBJ,* 23-29 February 2004, 1, 34-35.

26. See the IAAM Web site at www.iaam.org. The Stanford training program is described in Roy Purpur and Betsy Alden, "The Guests Are Here," *Athletic Management* 13 (2) (February-March 2001): 6-11.

27. "Courtside at the Eagles' game" ["Scorecard"], *SI,* 1 December 1997, 24; Steve Cameron, "Response to Terrorist Attacks Uniquely American," *SSSBJ,* 3-9 February 2003, 17.

28. Kirk Wakefield and Hugh Sloan, "The Effects of Team Loyalty and Selected Stadium Factors on Spectator Attendance," *Journal of Sport Management* 9 (2) (May 1995): 153-165.

29. S. Hardy, "Adopted by All the Leading Clubs: Sporting Goods and the Shaping of Leisure," in *For Fun and Profit,* ed. R. Butsch (Philadelphia: Temple University Press, 1990), 71-101.

30. M. Palmisano, "Merchandising Can Mean Added Revenue for You," *Athletic Purchasing and Facilities,* October 1980, 22-24.

31. For issues related to electronic ticket distribution, see L. Miller and L. Fielding, "Ticket Distribution Agencies and Professional Sports Franchises: The Successful Partnership," *SMQ* 6 (March 1997): 47-55; Andrew Cohen, "Ticket to the Future," *Athletic Business,* September 2001, 55-61.

32. "Chevron Inks Reported $15-20M Pact With MLB Grants," *SBD,* 4 December 1997, 3; "Burger King Sells Tickets Their Way—Lots of Them," *Team Marketing Report* (January 1994): 4, 7; "ETM Remote Locations and Kiosks," *SBD,* 9 February 1998, 10; *The Migala Report,* 1 July 2004, www.migalareport.com.

33. "What Are This Year's Tickets to Success for NBA Team Marketers?" *Team Marketing Report* (December 1997): 8.

34. "Payroll Deductions Add Up to Hamilton Season Tickets," *Team Marketing Report* (October 1992): 5.

35. W. Suggs, "Sox Ticket System Target Ticketmaster," *SSSBJ,* 18-24 May 1998, 7.

36. Kevin O'Connor, "Football Tickets Delivered in 30 Minutes, or Less," *NewsLink Indiana,* 31 August 2004, www.newslinkindiana.com.

37. "Giants Offer Web Ticket Exchange for Season-Ticket Holders," *SBD,* 14 June 2000, 15.

38. "2005-06 Maryland Student Ticket Distribution Policy for Football and Men's Basketball Home Games," 2005, https://ticketreturn.solidspace.com/umd/.

39. Peter Howe, "Cellphone Ads Bring Wariness All Around," *Boston Globe,* 20 October 2004, A-1, A-6; Peter Howe, "Major League Baseball Pitches Cellphone Content," *Boston Globe,* 14 March 2005, C-5; Terry Lefton, "NFL's Newest Content Deal Targets Fans' iPods," *SSSBJ,* 17-23 January 2005, 1, 16.

40. Malcolm Gladwell, *The Tipping Point: How Little Things Can Make a Big Difference* (New York: Back Bay-Little, Brown, 2002), 131-132; "Leonsis Uses Viral Marketing to Win Fans," *SBD,* 30 January 2001.

41. Jenn Abelson, "High-Definition Heroes," *Boston Globe,* 9 June 2004, B-1, B-7; Jenn Abelson, "New Season for 'Game Night' Screenings, *Boston Globe,* 8 April 2005, C-1, C-3.

Chapter 15

1. Good sources for up-to-date statistics on the media industry include trade organizations such as the Television Bureau of Advertising (www.tbvb.org), the Radio Advertising Bureau (www.rab.com), the Interactive Advertising Bureau (www.iab.net), and the Federal Communications Commission (www.fcc.gov).

2. Nielsen Media Research maintains a public Web site at www.nielsenmedia.com.

3. Associated Press, "Super Bowl 2nd-Most Watched Show Ever," 7 February 2006.

4. S. Miller, "With NHL Frozen Out, Baseball, Basketball Score Big," *Broadcasting & Cable,* 7 March 2005, 36.

5. "TV's Battle Royal," *Broadcasting & Cable,* 13 May 1996, 35.

6. J. Higgins, "TV Touchdown," *Broadcasting & Cable,* 25 April 2005, 18.

7. B. Griffith, "Red Sox Sale, Cable Picture," *Boston Globe,* 21 December 2001, G-8.

8. "National Collegiate Basketball Championship Agreement" between the NCAA and CBS Sports, dated 21 November 1989.

9. K. Auletta, "The Magic Box," *New Yorker,* 11 April 1994, 45.

Chapter 16

1. A. Oldenburg, "TV Goes to Blogs," *USA Today* (5 April 2006), 1D.

2. M. Cuban, "NBA Playoff Seeding...What If?" www.blog maverick.com (3 April 2006).

3. R.T. Bronzan, *Public Relations, Promotions and Fund Raising for Athletic and Physical Education Programs* (New York: Wiley, 1977), 4.

4. C.L. Caywood, "Twenty-First Century Public Relations," in *The Handbook of Strategic Public Relations and Integrated Communications,* ed. C.L. Caywood (New York: McGraw-Hill, 1997), ix.

5. M. Govoni, R. Eng, and M. Galper, *Promotional Management* (Upper Saddle River, NJ: Prentice Hall, 1986), 15-16.

6. M.P. Gonring, "Global and Local Media Relations," in Caywood, *The Handbook of Strategic Public Relations,* 63.

7. R.J. Hellawell, letter to J.E. Sullivan, 14 February 1907, c/o American Sports Publishing.

8. D. Ainge, "Celtics Beat: Trade Alert," 23 December 2003, dainge@enews.celtics.com.

9. R.L. Irwin and W.A. Sutton, "Roles, Responsibilities and Effectiveness of Urban Community Relations Programs Within Professional Sport Franchises," presented at "Sport in the City: An International Symposium on Cultural, Economic, and Political Considerations," Memphis, TN, 10 November 1996.

10. Ray Allen, 18 April 2003, nba@exclusives.nba.com.

11. W.A. Sutton, M.A. McDonald, G.R. Milne, and J. Cimperman, "Creating and Fostering Fan Identification in Professional Sports," SMQ 6 (1) (1997): 15.

12. J.A. Koten, "The Strategic Uses of Corporate Philanthropy," in Caywood, *The Handbook of Strategic Public Relations,* 150.

13. 2005-2006 NBA Community Report, 2006, New York, 2.

14. Ibid.

15. M. Pollick, "Stern, NBA Make Doing Well by Doing Good Contagious," SSSBJ 8 (43) (6-12 March 2006): 29.

16. "The Magic Touch," Orlando Magic Youth Foundation brochure, Orlando Magic, 1997.

17. "Cavaliers' New Community Relations Program Draws New Advertisers From Local Minority-Owned Businesses," *Team Marketing Report* 8 (2) (April 1995): 1-2.

18. F. Winiker, "Amare Stoudemire Donates 10 Toyota Vehicles to New Orleans Residents in NBA TV's Toyota's Moving Forward Moments," NBA press release, 21 March 2006.

19. Compiled from D. Ziccardi, *Masterminding the Store* (New York: Wiley, 1997), 254-259; and D. Wilcox, P. Ault, and W. Agee, *Public Relations: Strategies and Tactics* (Philadelphia: Random House, 1986).

20. H.M. Davis, *Basic Concepts of Sports Information,* 2nd ed. (East Longmeadow, MA: Jeste, 1996), 15.

21. J.F. Love, *McDonald's: Behind the Arches* (New York: Bantam, 1986), 213-214.

22. T. Lefton, "The Meal Deal," SSSBJ 8 (6) (30 May-5 June 2005): 16.

23. D. Harris, *The League: The Rise and Decline of the NFL* (New York: Bantam, 1986), 67-68.

24. "LPGA Girls Golf Club Announces Additional Expansion: Partnership With USGA and Girl Scouts of the U.S.A. Fosters Growth," LPGA press release, Daytona Beach, FL, 29 July 1997.

25. J. Oliver, "Surprise Fashion Hit of '04 Tied to Cause," SSSBJ 7 (4) (27 December-2 January 2005): 10.

26. For an examination of America's interest in terms of both participation and spectatorship, see the following: Research and Forecasts, Inc., "Miller Lite Report on American Attitudes Toward Sport" (New York: Miller Brewing Co., 1983); and Lieberman Research Inc., *"Sports Illustrated* Sports Poll '86" (New York: Sports Illustrated, 1986). There are also proprietary studies such as those published by American Sports Demographics of Dallas, TX, that can be obtained for a fee.

27. P. Williams, *The Magic of Teamwork* (Nashville, TN: Thomas Nelson, 1997), 159.

28. Although the St. Louis Browns moved to Baltimore and the Boston Braves moved to Milwaukee prior to the Dodgers' leaving Brooklyn for L.A., each of these teams was the least successful team in a two-team market. When they left, the Cardinals were still in St. Louis and the Red Sox remained in Boston. When the Dodgers left Brooklyn, there was no other franchise competing in that unique market. For a unique and compelling analysis of that move, see N. Sullivan, *The Dodgers Move West* (New York: Oxford University Press, 1987).

29. A. Ries and J. Trout, *Positioning: The Battle for Your Mind* (New York: McGraw-Hill, 1986), 19-27.

30. R. Thurow, "Full Court Press: Women's NBA Pins Hopes on Clean Play and Hard Marketing," *Wall Street Journal,* 12 June 1997, A1, A8.

31. "New Juice for Giants: Solar Energy Powering Up Portion of SBC Park Through Partnership With Sharp," *Team Marketing Report* 17 (7) (April 2005): 1-3.

32. Needham Parks and Recreation Department brochure, Needham, MA, 1998.

33. C. Reidy, "Reebok Kicks Itself Over Name With Bad Fit," *Boston Globe,* 20 February 1997, A-1, A-16.

34. R. Martzke, "Wright: 'Lesbians Hurt Women's Golf,'" *USA Today,* 12 May 1995, C1.

35. P. King, "Patriot Games: New England Fumbled When It Drafted Christian Peter and Tried to Recover by Cutting Him Loose," *Sports Illustrated,* 6 May 1996, 32-33.

36. ESPN broadcast, "Outside the Lines—Athletes in Trouble," produced/moderated by Bob Ley, 2 September 1997.

37. J.A. Michener, *Sports in America* (New York: Random House, 1976), 355.

38. R. Lipsyte, *Sportsworld: An American Dreamland* (New York: Quadrangle, 1975), 170.

39. J. Bouton, *Ball Four* (New York: Stein and Day, 1970).

40. M. Gunther and M. Carter, *Monday Night Mayhem* (New York: Morrow, 1988), 34.

41. "ESPN's Outside the Lines Examines Athletes in Trouble," SBD, 3 September 1997, 15.

42. W. Sutton and R.H. Migliore, "Strategic Long-Range Planning for Intercollegiate Athletic Programs," *Journal of Applied Research in Coaching and Athletics* 3 (4) (1988): 233-261.

Chapter 17

1. Kay Hawes, "A Brewing Dilemma on Campus," *NCAA News*, 6 April 1998, 1, 6, 7; L. Kinney and S. McDaniel, "Public Says 'Yes' to Corporate Role in Sports," *SSSBJ*, 1-7 March 1999, 33.

2. Jennifer Lee, "Alcohol on Campus: When to Say When?" *SSSBJ*, 30 August-5 September 2004, 1, 32-35.

3. L. Jon Wertheim, "Jolt of Reality," *SI*, 7 April 2003, 69-79.

4. "SI Says NIKE Made 'Vast Miscalculation' on Tiger Woods Line," *SBD*, 19 August 1997, 3.

5. L. Zepp, "Supermarket Promo Lifts Attendance for Ohio State Lady Buckeyes Games," *Amusement Business*, 6 February 1988, 13, 15.

6. Michael Eisner with Tony Schwartz, "Running the Mouse House," *Newsweek*, 28 September 1998, 58.

7. "Jazz and Hostess Offer Fans a Colorful Snackfood," *Team Marketing Report* (March 1994): 6.

8. Stuart Miller, "New Technology Is Transforming Games Into Multimedia Events," *SSSBJ*, 10-16 March 2003, 33; Russell Adams, "Before Game and After, Razzle-Dazzle Reigns," *SSSBJ*, 10-16 March 2003, 32; "Full Immersion: AFL Offers Fans a Wired Experience," *SBD*, 19 April 2000.

9. For scholarly assaults on Nike, see Steven Jackson and David Andrews, *Sport, Culture and Advertising: Identities, Commodities, and the Politics of Representation* (New York: Routledge, 2005); "Nike Pulls Shoe Offensive to Muslims," *Boston Globe*, 25 June 1997, C-2.

10. "Stern Says League Needs to Address Player Behavior Issues," *SBD*, 2 June 1997, 13.

11. P. Amend and W. Tobin, "Tax Exempts: A Snake in the Grass?" *Club Business*, November 1988, 34-38, 64-67.

12. "New Texas Twister: Rangers/Stars Combine Ticket Packages," *SBD*, 6 March 1998, 17; D. Kaplan, "Tom Hicks Eyes Profits—and Wins—in His Sports Ventures," *SSSBJ*, 8-14 February 1999, 1, 46.

13. Matt Schuman, "Paying the Price: Parking Fees Will Hurt UNC Fans," *Greeley Tribune*, 8 September 2005, www.greeleytrib.com; B. Lumpkin and P. Finebaum, "Alabama Weathers Storm Over Priority Ticket Plan," *NCAA News*, 10 June 1987, 9.

14. Tom Weir, "Promise of Refund Paying Off in PR," *USA Today*, 19 March 2003, 3C.

15. A. Bernstein, "NFL's Soft-Drink, Fast-Food Deals Slow in Coming," *SSSBJ*, 15-21 June 1998, 9.

16. "Are Autograph and Collectible Shows Worth It for Athletes?" *SBD*, 1 September 1998, 5.

17. L. Berling-Manuel, "Giants Weathering Bay City Blues," *Advertising Age*, 2 August 1984, 10-11.

18. "IHL Dragons Increase in-Arena Interaction by Putting Partisans in Penalty Box," *Team Marketing Report* 9 (January 1997): 9.

19. Bruce Mohl, "Pass Interference," *Boston Sunday Globe*, 3 October 2004, E-1, E-8.

20. Wayne Henninger, "Road to New Home Smoother With Fine-Tuned Campaign, Pirates Find," *SSSBJ*, 11-17 June 2001, 12.

21. "For the Record," *SI*, 26 April 2004, 24.

22. For excellent insight into strategy and control in sport organizations, see T. Slack, *Understanding Sport Organizations: The Application of Organizational Theory* (Champaign, IL: Human Kinetics, 1997); D. Howard and J. Crompton, *Financing Sport*, 2nd ed. (Morgantown, WV: Fitness Information Technology, 2003).

23. Middlebury College Athletics Web Site, http://web.middlebury.edu/athletics/about/mission.htm, 2005.

24. A. Bernstein, "Without a Breakaway Threat, MLS Aims for Steady, Long-Term Growth," *SSSBJ*, 13-19 July 1998, 14.

25. Russell Adams, "Braves New World: Gains at Tate, on TV," *SSSBJ*, 10-16 May 2004, 6; *SBD*, 27 November 1997, 8. On the WUSA, see Richard Southall, Mark Nagel, and Deborah LeGrande, "Build It and They Will Come? The Women's United Soccer Association: Collision of Exchange Theory and Strategic Philanthropy," *SMQ*14 (3) (2005): 158-167.

26. A. Friedman and P. Much, *Inside the Ownership of Professional Team Sports* (Chicago: Team Marketing Report, 1997); "Top Sports Radio Stations," *SSSBJ*, 14-20 August 2000, 30; "Web World: NBA Scores With Playoffs," *SSSBJ*, 28 June-4 July 2004, 14; Langdon Borckington, "Texans Bring in J.D. Power to Gauge Service," *SSSBJ*, 29 July-4 August 2002, 8; "Giveaways That Paid Off at the Gate," *SSSBJ*, 18-24 October 2004, 18; Mark McDonald and Daniel Rascher, "Does Bat Day Make Cents? The Effect of Promotions on the Demand for Major League Baseball," *Journal of Sport Management* 14 (2000): 8-27. For a different look at community relations, see Stephen Hardy et al., "Image Isn't Everything," *Athletic Business*, May 2006, 50-56.

27. The Migala Report, 1 August 2004, www.migalareport.com; Official Web site of Brevard County Manatees, www.manateesbaseball.com, 2005.

28. Roland Smith questions in the *Migala Report* 1, 1 March 2004, www.migalareport.com.

29. James C. Collins and Jerry I. Porras, *Built to Last: Successful Habits of Visionary Companies* (New York: HarperCollins, 1999), 72.

Chapter 18

1. Terea F. Lindeman and Anya Sostek, "Consol Tests Ad Waters," *Pittsburgh Post-Gazette Online*. 8 July 2006. retrieved July 11, 2006, from http://www.post-gazette.com/pg/06189/704254-28.stm.

2. Michelle Hiskey, "Target Able to Infiltrate Trains to Venues With Bull's-Eye Logo," Ajc.com (*Atlanta Journal-Constitution*). 14 February 2006. Retrieved June 2006, from http://www.ajc.com/tuesday/content/epaper/editions/tuesday/business_341ff59a0526d03e000d.html.

3. U.S. Constitution, art. 1, § 8, states, "Congress shall have the power to promote the progress of science and useful arts, by securing for limited times to authors and inventors the exclusive right to their own writings and discoveries."

4. 15 U.S.C. §§ 1051-1127 (2004).

5. 15 U.S.C. § 1127 (2004).

6. *Two Pesos Inc. v. Taco Cabana, Inc.* 505 U.S. 763, 765 (1992), citing *John H. Harland Co. v. Clarke Checks, Inc.* 711 F. 2d 966 (11th Cir. 1983).

7. 15 U.S.C. § 1127 (2004).

8. 15 U.S.C. § 1127 (2004).

9. U.S. Patent and Trademark Office, "Basic Facts About Registering a Trademark." Retrieved June 23, 2004, from www.uspto.gov/web/offices/tac/doc/basic/basic_facts.html.

10. *Blue Bell, Inc. v. Farah Manufacturing Co. Inc.*, 508 F. 2d 1260 (5th Cir. 1975), citing *United Drug Co. v. Theodore Rectanus Co.*, 248 U.S. 90 (1918).

11. 15 U.S.C. § 1051 (b) (1) (2004).

12. F. Foster and R. Shook, *Patents, Copyrights, and Trademarks: The Total Guide to Protecting the Rights to Your Invention, Product or Trademark...Now Better Than Ever*, 2nd ed. (New York: John Wiley & Sons, 1993), 185.

13. *University of Georgia Athletic Association v. Laite,* 756 F. 2d 1535 (11th Cir. 1985).

14. *AMF, Inc. v. Sleekcraft Boats,* 599 F. 2d 341, 349 (9th Cir. 1979).

15. *National Football League Properties, Inc. v. Wichita Falls Sportswear, Inc.,* 532 F. Supp. 651, 658 (1982), citing *Levi Strauss & Co. v. Blue Bell, Inc.* 632 F. 2d 817 (9th Cir. 1980).

16. U.S. Dist. LEXIS 14941 (N.D. Tex. 2003).

17. *University of Georgia Athletic Association v. Laite,* 756 F. 2d 1535, 1541 (11th Cir. 1985).

18. Ibid., 1546.

19. 15 U.S.C. § 1052 (2004).

20. *Harjo v. Pro-Football, Inc.,* 50 U.S.P.Q. 2d 1705 (T.T.A.B. 1999).

21. *Pro-Football, Inc. v. Harjo,* 284 F. Supp. 2d 96 (D.D.C. 2003).

22. "Redskins Win Appeal Over Cancellation of Trademark Protection," *Sports Lawyers Association* 3 (10) (November 2003). Retrieved June 20, 2004, from www.sportslaw.org/members/news/novnl2003.htm.

23. "Meteoric Sports-Licensed Apparel Growth Obscures Solid Giants in Other Categories," *The Licensing Letter* 28 (7) (5 April 2004): 1.

24. "Sponsorship Spending to Increase 8.7 Percent in 2004," *IEG Sponsorship Report* 22 (24) (22 December 2003): 1.

25. 15 U.S.C. § 1114 (1) (a) (2004).

26. 15 U.S.C. § 1125 (2004).

27. Trademark Dilution Act of 1995, 15 U.S.C. § 1125 (c) (2004).

28. 15 U.S.C. § 1114 (1) (2004).

29. 319 F. 2d 830 (7th Cir. 1963).

30. 952 F. Supp. 1084 (D.N.J. 1997).

31. 15 U.S.C. 1125 (1999).

32. 604 F. Supp. 2d 200 (2d Cir. 1979).

33. Ibid., 205.

34. Ibid.

35. 15 U.S.C. § 1125 (c) (2004).

36. *Moseley v. V Secret Catalogue, Inc.,* 123 S. Ct. 1115 (2003).

37. 15 U.S.C. § 1127 (2004).

38. *Indianapolis Colts, Inc. v. Metropolitan Baltimore Football Club, L.P.,* 34 F. 3d 410 (7th Cir. 1994).

39. 85 F. 3d 407 (9th Cir. 1996).

40. Ibid., 410.

41. 15 U.S.C. § 1127 (2004).

42. *Nitro Leisure Products, L.L.C. v. Acushnet Co.,* 341 F.3d 1356; 2003 U.S. App. LEXIS 17822 (2003).

43. *United States Olympic Committee v. American Media, Inc.* 156 F. Supp. 2d 1200 (D. Colo. 2001).

44. See "Protecting Your Trademark on the Internet: Courts Limit Free Riding on the Information Superhighway," Newsletter, Intellectual Property Law section of the ABA 2 (3): 1-12.

45. 15 U.S.C. § 1125 (d) (2003).

46. 15 U.S.C. § 1125 (d) (1) (A) (2003).

47. Steve McKelvey, "MMAA v. Netfire: 'March Madness' Protection Strengthened for NCAA," SMQ 13 (2) (2004): 117-119.

48. Steve McKelvey, "Atlanta '96: Olympic Countdown to Ambush Armageddon?" *Seton Hall Journal of Sport Law* 4 (2): 397-445, at 401.

49. 36 U.S.C. § 220501 et. seq. (2000).

50. Noelle K. Nish, "How Far Have We Come? A Look at the Olympic and Amateur Sports Act of 1998, the United States Olympic Committee, and the Winter Olympic Games of 2002, 13," *Seton Hall Journal of Sport Law* 53 (2003), 68.

51. Anne M. Wall, "The Games Behind the Games," 12 *Marquette Sports Law Review* 557 (2002), 574, citing *United States Olympic Comm. v. 2000 Olympic.com,* No. CV-00.1018.A (E.D. Va. 2000).

52. Ibid.

53. Ibid., 574-575.

54. Emiko Terazano, "Ambush Marketing Tactics to Be Kicked Into Touch," *Financial Times Limited,* 2 September 2003, at 9.

55. Ibid.

56. Telephone interview with Kelly Maynard, assistant general counsel, USOC (8 June 2004). The USOC, however, was unable to stop Schirf Brewing from engaging in other ambush marketing activity, including the distribution of T-shirts with a red circle with a line through it superimposed over the word *2002* and the words *Unofficial Beer* above it. Such brash activity illustrates that with ambush marketers seeking to generate publicity, where there is a will, there is a way.

57. *U.S. Olympic Committee v. Discount Tire,* No. 2:02cv17 (D. Utah, filed Jan. 7, 2002).

58. Jeff Howard, *USOC Files Complaint Against Discount Tire Co. for Olympic Marks Infringement,* 8 January 2002, www.usocpressbox.org (Retrieved 25 May 2004).

59. Ibid.

60. Ibid. Discount Tire eventually agreed to remove the billboards. Telephone interview with Kelly Maynard, assistant general counsel, USOC (7 March 2004).

61. John Manasso, "USOC Puts the Heat on Utah Resort," *Atlanta Journal and Constitution,* 22 November 2000, 2C.

62. Ibid.

63. Curt Baltzley, "Copyright Disputed," *Houston Chronicle,* 1 November 2000, 12.

64. Ibid.

65. Michael Hiestand, "USOC Not Laughing Off Ads," *USA Today,* 15 December 1999, 1C.

66. Ibid.

67. Ibid.

68. Wall, "The Games Behind the Games," 557, 574.

69. Ibid.

70. Ibid.

71. Ibid., citing *United States Olympic Committee v. Nabisco, Inc.,* Case No. C 00 3086 (N.D. Cal. 2000).

72. Ibid.

73. Theresa Howard, "Sprint Ads Capture Olympic Feel," *USA Today,* 18 March 2002, 6B.

74. Ibid.

75. Advertisement in *Newark Star-Ledger,* 7 February 2002, 43.

76. Advertisement in *USA Today,* 22 February 2002, 8D.

77. Dan Perini, assistant general counsel, USOC. "Protecting Olympic Intellectual Property," Presentation at National Sports Law Institute Conference, Marquette University Law School (25 October 2002).

78. *Mastercard International, Inc. v. Sprint Communications Company,* 23 F. 3d 397 (2d Cir. 1994).

79. 42 C.P.R. 3d 390 (B.C. 1992).

80. H.C. Black, J.R. Nolan, and M.J. Connolly, *Black's Law Dictionary*, 5th ed. (St. Paul, MN: West, 1979), 1371.

81. Steve McKelvey, "Unauthorized Use of Event Tickets in Promotional Campaign May Create New Legal Strategies to Combat Ambush Marketing: NCAA v. Coors," *SMQ* 12 (2) (2003): 117-119.

82. 947 F. Supp. 347 (N.D. Ill. 1996).

83. 17 U.S.C. §§ 101 et. seq. (2004).

84. 17 U.S.C. §1201-1205 (2004).

85. 17 U.S.C. § 102 (2004).

86. 17 U.S.C. § 102 (2004).

87. 17 U.S.C. § 106 (2004).

88. N.E. Garrote and K.C. Maher, "Protecting Website's Look and Feel via Copyright and Trademark Law," *New York Law Journal*, 9 June 1998, www.nylj.com.

89. Garrote and Maher, "Protecting Website's Look."

90. 17 U.S.C. § 301 (2004) (Sonny Bono Copyright Term Extension Act).

91. Foster and Shook, *Patents, Copyrights, and Trademarks*, 154.

92. 17 U.S.C. § 107 (2004)

93. 17 U.S.C. § 107 (2004).

94. 17 U.S.C. § 107 (2004).

95. *Monster Communications, Inc. v. Turner Broadcasting System, Inc.*, 935 F. Supp. 490 (S.D.N.Y. 1996).

96. Ibid., 495.

97. Ibid., 496.

98. *N.B.A. v. Motorola, Inc.*, 105 F.3d 841 (1997).

99. 17 U.S.C. § 101 et. seq. (2004).

100. 622 F. Supp. 1500 (N.D. Ill. 1985).

101. *N.B.A. v. Motorola, Inc.*, 105 F.3d 841 (1997).

102. Anne M. Wall, "Sports Marketing and the Law: Protecting Proprietary Interests in Sports Entertainment Events," *Marquette Sports Law Journal* 7 (1996): 77.

103. Wall, "Sports Marketing and the Law," 77.

104. M.H. Reed, *IEG Legal Guide to Sponsorship* (Chicago: International Events Group, 1989), 180-182.

105. "Nike Shox Quebec Inventor: Patent Suit Filed," *Sports Lawyers Association* 4 (1) (January 2004): 1.

106. 35 U.S.C. § 101 (2004).

107. 35 U.S.C. § 154 (a) (2) (2004).

108. Liz Mullen, "Arena Football Asks Court to Crack Back on Rival," *SSSBJ* 1(7) (June 1998): 13.

109. See Jeffrey A. Smith, "It's Your Move—No It's Not! The Application of Patent Law to Sports Moves," 70 *University of Colorado Law Review* (1999): 1051-1065.

110. *Cardtoons v. Major League Baseball Players Association*, 95 F.3d 959, 967 (10th Cir. 1996), citing Vol. 1, J. Thomas McCarthy, *The Rights of Publicity and Privacy*, § 1.1[A] [1] (1996).

111. 43 Misc. 2d 219, 250 N.Y.S. 2d 529 (1964).

112. Ibid., 232.

113. 202 F.2d 866 (2d Cir. 1953), cert. denied, 346 U.S. 816 (1953).

114. Ibid.

115. 316 F. Supp 1277 (D. Minn. 1970).

116. 363 N.Y.S. 2d 276 (1975).

117. 34 Cal. App. 4th 790, 40 Cal. Rptr.2d 639 (1995).

118. 85 F. 3d 407 (9th Cir. 1996).

119. 95 F. 3d 959 (10th Cir. 1996).

120. Ibid.

121. 280 N.W. 2d 129 (1979).

122. Ibid.

123. See D.E. Wanat, "Entertainment Law: An Analysis of Judicial Decision-Making in Case Where a Celebrity's Publicity Right Is in Conflict With a User's First Amendment Right," *Albany Law Review* 67 (1) (2003): 251-277.

124. 99 F. Supp. 2d 829; 2000 U.S. Dist. LEXIS 4816 (20 April 2000), aff'd, 2003 U.S. App. LEXIS 12488 (6th Cir. 2003). Woods also claimed a violation of his trademark rights, which the court rejected, reasoning that a person's likeness was not a valid subject of trademark protection.

125. *John Doe, a/k/a Tony Twist v. TCI Communications et al.*, 110 S.W. 3d 363 (2003). See S. McKelvey, "Sport Celebrities and the Right of Publicity Take a New 'Twist,'" *SMQ* 14 (3): 188-190.

126. 364 F. 3d 1288 (2004).

127. Ibid., 1296.

128. Ibid.

129. Russell Adams, "Real-Time Uncertainties Remain," *SSSBJ* 6 (50) (12 April 2004): 8.

130. Ibid., 8.

131. Ibid.

132. Ibid.

133. See Tresa Baldas, "Pro Sports: Technology Changes Rules of the Game." Retrieved 7 December 2005, from www.law.com/jsp/article.jsp?id=1109128216973.

134. Eric Fisher, "MLBAM Risks Alienating Fans with Fantasy-League Fight," *SSSBJ*, 6 December 2006.

Index

Note: The letters *f* and *t* after page numbers indicate figures and tables, respectively.

Jaworski, R. 193
Jay-Z 203, 211
Jefferson, R. 393
Jeter, D. 15, 247
Jewish ballplayers 210-211
jobs, sport industry
    future of 462-463
    public relations professionals 386-387
    salaries of sport marketing executives 14, 15t
Johnson, C. 211
Johnson, D. 208
Johnson, D. 87, 250, 288, 289
Johnson, J. 14, 139, 176
Johnson, M. 2, 3
Johnson, M. 253t
Johnson, R.C. 50
Jones, B. 153
Jones, D. 254
Jones, D. 354
Jones, J. 13, 196
Jones, R. 149
Jordan, B. 140
Jordan, M. 2, 9, 22, 25, 74, 178, 180, 183, 184, 186, 198, 201, 210,
    211, 246, 247, 248t, 253t, 256, 261, 335, 416
Journal of Sport Management 116, 424
journals and magazines 15, 116, 423, 424
Joyner-Kersee, J. 246, 248t
junk mail 294

K
Kalkhurst, D. 303
Kane, G. 333
Kaplan, D. 5
Kariya, P. 165
Karl, G. 252
Karmanos, P. 232
Kemppinen, R. 5
Kennedy, J. 20
Kenyon, P. 200
Khan, J. 342
Kidd, J. 253t, 301
Kilmer, R. 303
Kilpatrick, J.R. 368
King, B.J. 137
King, D. 255
Knievel, E. 255
Knight, P. 162, 168, 192
Kollar-Kotelly, C. 209
Koonin, S. 417
Kotler, P. 31, 85, 87, 163
Koufax, S. 210
Kraft, J. 456
Kraft, R. 12
Kroenke, S. 148
Krzyzewski, M. 154
Kukon, B. 203
Kwan, M. 448

L
Labonte, T. 333
Lance Armstrong Foundation 398
Landis, F. 184, 247
Landis, K. 404
Lanham Act 194, 432, 433, 434, 435, 436, 437, 439, 441
Lansing, D. 68
Latino Sports Marketing LLC 15
Lauer, H. 64
Layne, S. 228
leadership and technology 454-455
lead time 226
league data sources 99

learning and consumer behavior 81-82
LED signage 245, 256
Lee, J. 198, 199
Lefton, T. 154
legal aspects of sport marketing
    ambush marketing 38, 334-335, 430, 439-442
    copyright law 442-447
    emerging issues 450-451
    intellectual property 430-431, 450
    patents 447-448
    right of publicity and invasion of privacy 448-449
    secondary meaning 434-435
    summary on 451
    ticket promotions 443-444
    trademark infringement 435-439
    trademark law 431-433
    unfair competition and unfair trade practices 442
Leiweke, T. 294
Leland, T. 40
Leonsis, T. 179, 364
Leslie, L. 2, 163
Letscher, M. 39
letters, appeal 295
letters, open 122
Levine, M. 13, 17, 164, 226, 457
Levitt, T. 12
Ley, B. 405, 406
licensed products
    defined 191-193
    history of 193-194
    statistics on 191-192
    throwbacks 190-191, 211
licensing and brand equity 177
licensing industry structure
    branded merchandise 202-203
    collegiate licensing 198-199
    international licensing 200-201
    licensed merchandise 194-196
    licensing in professional and individual and tour sports
      201-202
    licensing programs of other sport organizations 199-200
    players association licensing 197-198
    professional league licensing 196-197
licensing trends and issues
    brand identity 204-206
    cross-licensing 206
    electronics and technology 206-207
    licensee, licensor, and manufacturer conduct 207-209
    list of 203
    product innovation 209-212
life cycles, product 169-170
life stage and sport involvement 79t-80t
lifetime value (LTV) 309-310
light users 271f, 273
Lindow, C.J. 229
Lipsey, D. 17, 34, 42, 58, 59
Little, G. 206
Lobo, R. 163, 184
Logan, D. 44
logos 204-206
Long, J. 39
Longoria, E. 405
Lopez, J. 203
Lopiano, D. 138
Louganis, G. 76
Louis, J. 153, 203
loyalty cards 93
loyalty programs 102, 105
Loyalty Rules! 92
Luker, R. 6, 30
Lynch, M. 333

About the Authors

Courtesy of Bernard Mullin

Bernard J. Mullin, PhD, is currently president and chief executive officer of Atlanta Spirit, LLC. In this role he is in charge of guiding all facets of the Spirit's operations, including overseeing all team and business operations for the NBA's Hawks and NHL's Thrashers and management of the world-class Philips Arena.

Mullin has nearly 30 years of experience in the sport management industry, involving executive positions with professional teams and leagues where he specializes in start-ups and turnarounds, breaking numerous all-time league ticket sales and attendance records. Before coming to Atlanta, Mullin served as the NBA's senior vice president of marketing and team business operations. Mullin has also served as president and general manager of a minor league hockey team, the IHL's Denver Grizzlies; senior vice president of business operations for the Colorado Rockies; and senior vice president of business for the Pittsburgh Pirates. He has also acted as the owner's representative on major design and construction projects, including Coors Field and University of Denver's award-winning athletic facilities.

Before and during his career in professional sports, Mullin spent several years in intercollegiate athletics and higher education. He served as vice chancellor of athletics for the University of Denver and as professor of sport management at the University of Massachusetts.

Mullin holds a PhD in business, an MBA, and an MS in marketing from the University of Kansas, where he coached the varsity soccer program, and a BA business studies from Coventry University in England, where he played soccer semiprofessionally for the Oxford City Football Club.

Courtesy of Stephen Hardy

Stephen Hardy, PhD, is professor of kinesiology and coordinator of the sport studies program at the University of New Hampshire, where he is also an affiliate professor of history. At UNH since 1988, he serves as faculty representative to the NCAA and chairs the president's Athletics Advisory Committee. In 2003-2004, he served as interim vice provost for undergraduate studies.

Hardy has also taught at the University of Massachusetts (where he earned his PhD), the University of Washington, Robert Morris College, and Carnegie Mellon University. Over three decades, he has taught courses in sport marketing, athletic administration, and sport history, as well as a popular introduction to the sport industry. Besides *Sport Marketing,* his publications include *How Boston Played* (1982, 2003) and numerous articles, book chapters, and reviews in academic presses. His reviews and opinions have also appeared in popular outlets such as the *Boston Globe,* the *New York Times,* and the *Sports Business Journal.* From 1995 to 1999, he was coeditor of the *Sport Marketing Quarterly.* In 1997, he was elected a fellow of the American Academy of Kinesiology and Physical Education. In May 2001, he won the Lifetime Research Award from UNH's School of Health and Human Services.

Hardy has extensive experience in college athletics. He played hockey for Bowdoin in the late 1960s and cocaptained the 1969-1970 team with his twin brother, Earl. After coaching stints at Vermont Academy and Amherst College, he joined the Eastern College Athletic Conference in 1976, where he served as assistant commissioner and hockey supervisor until 1979. During this time, he supervised collegiate championships in venues such as the Boston Garden and Madison Square Garden, and he worked closely with the NCAA Ice Hockey Committee and its affiliated championships. He served on the board of directors of the America East Athletic Conference from 2000 to 2002. In 2003, he was selected by the Hockey East Association as one of 20 special friends to celebrate the league's 20th anniversary.

William A. Sutton, EdD, currently serves as a professor and associate department head for the DeVos Sport Business Management graduate program at the University of Central Florida. In addition to his duties at UCF, Dr. Sutton is the founder and principal of Bill Sutton & Associates, a consulting firm specializing in strategic marketing and revenue enhancement. Before assuming his current positions, Dr. Sutton served as vice president of team marketing and business operations for the National Basketball Association and has held academic appointments at Robert Morris University, Ohio State University, and the University of Massachusetts at Amherst.

Courtesy of William Sutton

In addition to *Sport Marketing*, Dr. Sutton is a coauthor of *Sport Promotion and Sales Management*. He has also authored more than 100 articles and has made more than 100 national and international presentations. Dr. Sutton is a past president of NASSM and a founding member of the Sport Marketing Association (SMA) and *Sport Marketing Quarterly*, where he has also served as coeditor. Dr. Sutton is a featured author for *Street & Smith's SportsBusiness Journal* (SBJ) and for the basketball strategy and business magazines *Basketball Gigante* and *FIBA Assist* published in Italy.

Dr. Sutton's professional experience includes service as a special events coordinator for the City of Pittsburgh, a YMCA director, vice president of information services for an international sport marketing firm, commissioner of the Mid-Ohio Conference, and cofounder and principal of the consulting firm Audience Analysts. Dr. Sutton received his BA, MS, and EdD from Oklahoma State University, where he was inducted into the College of Education Hall of Fame in 2003. Dr. Sutton is also an inaugural member of the Robert Morris University Sport Management Hall of Fame (2006).

You'll fir
other outstandir.
sport management resources

www.HumanKinetics.com

In the U.S. call

1-800-747-4457

Australia..08 8372 09
Canada 1-800-465-73
Europe..+44 (0) 113 255 56
New Zealand......................................0064 9 448 12